regards
Steve Talley

Chinese Architecture

Chinese Architecture

LAURENCE G. LIU

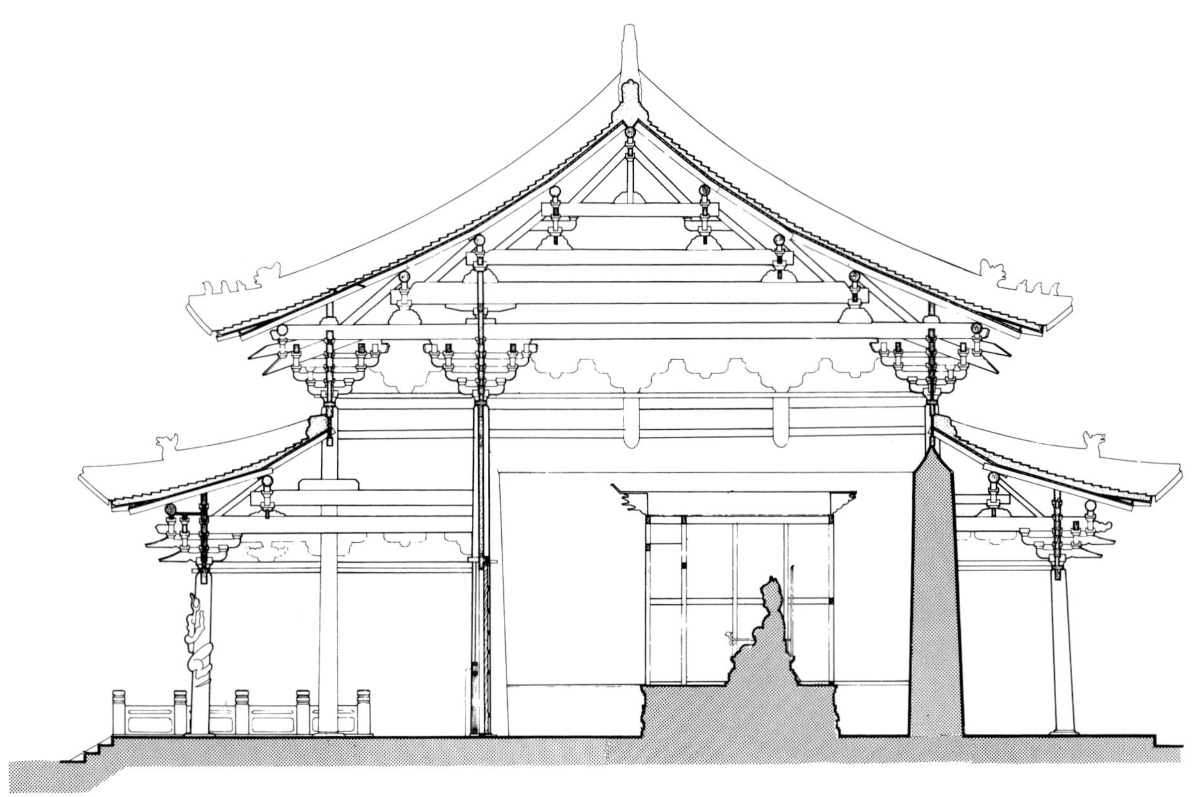

ACADEMY EDITIONS · LONDON

To My Parents

Research for this book was supported by a grant from the Graham Foundation for Advanced Studies in the Fine Arts.

Published in Great Britain in 1989 by
ACADEMY EDITIONS
an imprint of the Academy Group Ltd,
7 Holland Street, London W8 4NA

ISBN 0-85670-980-8

Printed and bound in Hong Kong

page 2:
Huhehot, Inner Mongolia, Cideng Si Pagoda, Qing Dynasty, 1727-32

page 3:
Kaifeng, Henan, Youguo Si Pagoda (the Iron Pagoda), Song Dynasty, 982

page 4:
Zhending, Hebei, Longxing Si, Song Dynasty, 971, Zhuang Lun Zhang

page 5:
Datong, Shanxi, Yungang Caves, Northern Wei, 460, niches and Buddha images

page 6:
Wutai Shan, Shanxi, Nanchan Si, Tang Dynasty, 782

page 7:
Taiyuan, Shanxi, Jinci, Song Dynasty, 1023-32, Hall of the Sacred Mother, section

CONTENTS

FOREWORD

◁ Beijing, Tianan Men Gate, Ming and Qing Dynasties, Huabiao Pillar, detail

ARCHITECTURE IS A PRODUCT OF HUMAN ACTIVITIES, A mirror of human life. People inhabiting different areas of the world are influenced by their political, social and cultural environments, as well as historical and geographical backgrounds of each specific region or nation. These influences gradually form their particular life and culture, which are then translated into specific spatial forms of buildings and cities. Thus, different nations produced characteristically unique national architectural forms.

Architecture is also art, and every work of art comes from numerous sources. In the past 3000 years or so, China has developed its own unique architecture. It is not as many thought. The architecture did not develop independently, but had many differing influences. To study Chinese architecture, be it of the past or the present, it is necessary to study its interdependence with other cultures of the world. Cultures of other countries were, in their turn, mutually fed, nourished, and strengthened through contact with the architecture of China.

The artistic characteristics of classical Chinese architecture include the harmonious relationship between the parts and the whole, with emphasis on the feel of the materials and the unity between materials and structure. The effort to create a place for the coexistence of people also exerts sympathy with nature and conveys symbolic meanings. Since past principles are faithfully followed, the environment is organized to be attuned to nature and achieve a harmony among people. This humanistic philosophy and approach of Chinese architecture and environmental design can be an inspiration to contemporary practice and a resource for the creation of a new architecture. This book will identify the principles and explore their adaptations to contemporary world practice.

Since China was separated geographically from other countries for so many years, its architecture was largely unknown, particularly in the West. As modern architecture progressed between the two great wars, the attempts to create a special environment failed to succeed. The humanistic approach of Chinese architecture might be an inspiration to contemporary architecture. Our experience proves that whenever China had cultural relations with other cultures, its culture was enriched and the country flourished. I firmly believe that the study of classical Chinese architecture at this critical time will be both beneficial to Chinese and Western architecture for the creation of a humane architecture and environment.

At present, there have not been sufficient studies on Chinese town planning, city spaces and buildings, and the basic principles and rules that can contribute to today's thinking. Although many Chinese architectural history books were written, most dealt only with types of buildings. Their documentary style paid more attention to structure and style, and less to the basic principles. Architectural history thus becomes dry, futile and lifeless, disrupting continuity between the past and the present. These tendencies mistakenly lead one to believe that the great buildings and towns of the past have no meaning or use for the creation of a new architecure today. My aim is to fill this gap.

In this book the meaning and symbolism of the art of Chinese architecture is examined, focussing on the cultural, philosophical, and religious influences and life-style of the people. Special attention is paid to the cultural communications between China and foreign countries. I hope this book will provide the reader with a view of architecture rich in tradition and meaning. I believe that when architects, artists, even tourists who happen to be fascinated by the unique art of China, discover its meaning through the forms and spaces, their spirits will be lifted.

While working on the manuscript, there was one thing that always occupied my mind – my gratitude to all who assisted me with my work. I owe a number of acknowledgements to those who love Chinese culture and supported me in the making of this book. Without their aid and advice it would almost certainly never have been completed. Inadequate though this may be, I want to express my thanks to a few of those who have helped.

Firstly, to my father K.S. Liu. From his unpublished essay, 'The Prolegomena to a Study of The Development of Chinese Thought', I understood the essence of Chinese philosophy and the Chinese cultural impact on human thinking. To my sister Beatrice and her husband S.P. Tao, who believed in this book from the start. They time and again provided invaluable help in the writing and publication of this book. To the Department of Architecture of Ball State University and Marvin E. Rosenman for their understanding kindness in allowing me the use of equipment and facilities. To the Graham Foundation for Advanced Studies in the

Fine Arts who granted me funds for the writing. To Janice and John Fisher, and the Ball Brothers Foundation, who voluntarily sponsored the publication of this book. To Charles Jencks and Andreas Papadakis who brought this book into being.

During the preparation period I was helped by Zhu Jiabao and Benny Tao in taking architectural photographs. They accompanied my wife Xiyu and I, trudging mountainous areas in a hot summer for nearly two months and took many precious pictures. To my daughter Si and her husband Tungxiu Wu, architects trained in China to interpret, in line drawings, the spirit of Chinese architecture. To the Department of Architecture of Southeast University, where I was kindly permitted the use of their documents and drawings.To all who allowed me to photograph and measure the buildings they administered, I wish to express my gratitude. To many friends who constantly showed solicitude to the progress of the book, and rendered unselfish assistance and advice. I sincerely hope this book be worthy of their expectations.

But last and not least I must thank my wife, Xiyu. It was during a most difficult time in my life that I made plans for the writing of this book. My wife participated in the work directly, went to the wilderness to collect necessary literature and photographs with me, and subsequently edited and criticised my work and gave constructive advice. Her enthusiasm, her patience and competence have greatly inspired me. Without her help, the completion of this book would be inconceivable. To her, I am very grateful.

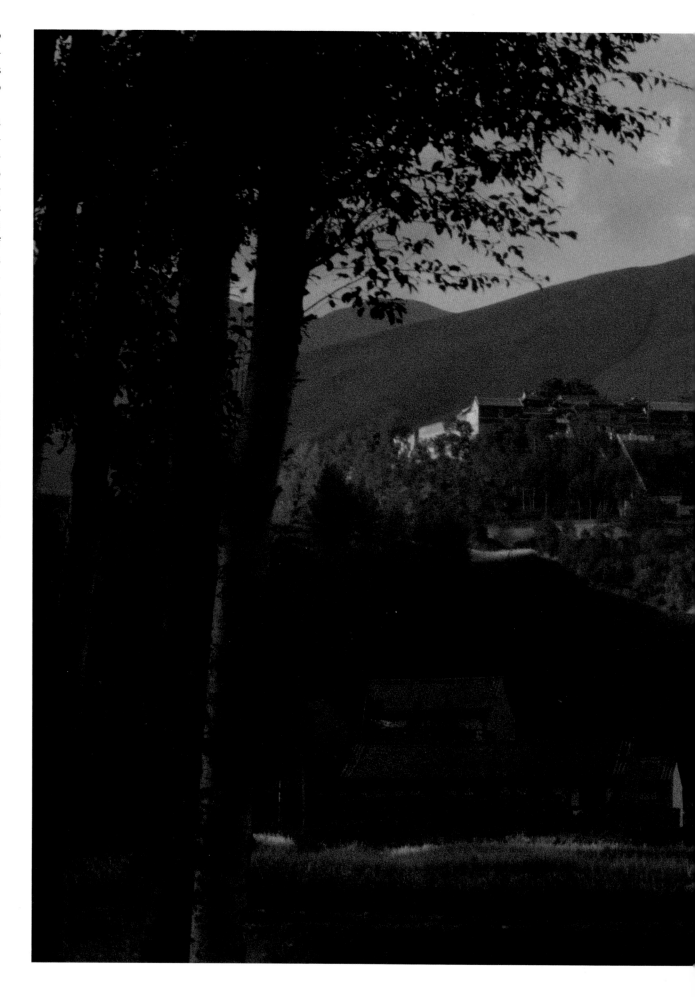

▷ Wutai Shan, Shanxi, The Great Stupa and Buddha's Peak

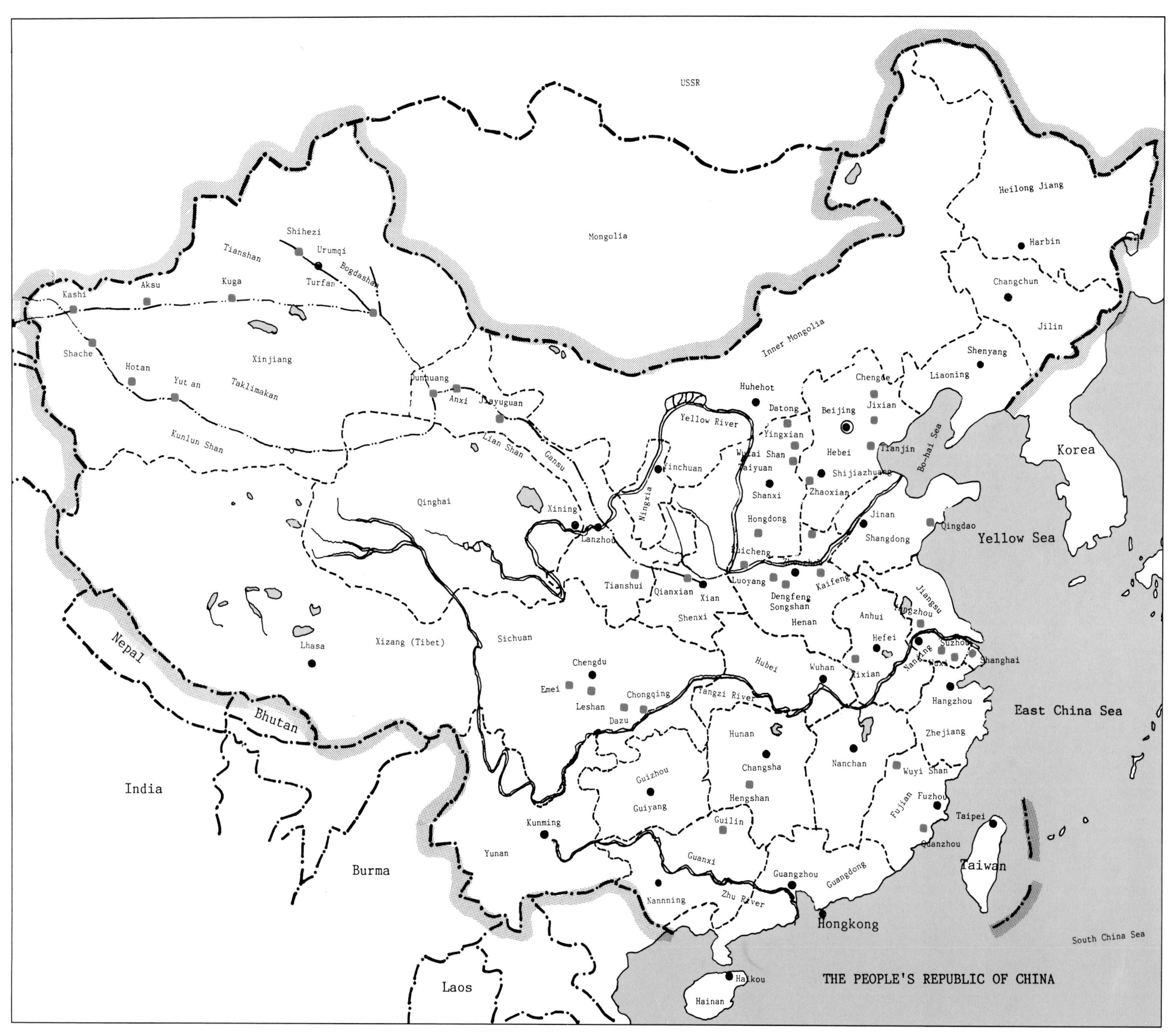
USSR
Mongolia
Heilong Jiang
Harbin
Changchun
Jilin
Shenyang
Liaoning
Korea
Inner Mongolia
Shihezi
Urumqi
Tianshan
Bogdashan
Turfan
Kuga
Aksu
Kashi
Shache
Hotan
Xinjiang
Yut an
Taklimakan
Kunlun Shan
Anxi
Lian Shan
Gansu
Qinghai
Xining
Lanzhou
Ningxia
Yellow River
Huhehot
Datong
Yingxian
Beijing
Chengde
Jixian
Tianjin
Bo-hai Sea
Hebei
Shijiazhuang
Zhaoxian
Shanxi
Hongdong
Jinan
Shangdong
Qingdao
Yellow Sea
Tianshui
Qianxian
Xian
Luoyang
Dengfeng
Songshan
Kaifeng
Henan
Shenxi
Jiangsu
Anhui
Hefei
Shanghai
Hubei
Wuhan
Hangzhou
Zhejiang
East China Sea
Nepal
Lhasa
Xizang (Tibet)
Sichuan
Chengdu
Emei
Leshan
Chongqing
Dazu
Yangzi River
Hunan
Changsha
Hengshan
Nanchan
Wuyi Shan
Fujian
Fuzhou
Taipei
Taiwan
Guizhou
Guiyang
Kunming
Yunan
Guilin
Guanxi
Guangzhou
Guangdong
Zhu River
Nannning
Hongkong
South China Sea
Bhutan
India
Burma
Laos
Hainan
THE PEOPLE'S REPUBLIC OF CHINA

CHAPTER I

HISTORICAL BACKGROUND

◁ Map of China

THE CREATION AND DEVELOPMENT OF A NATIONAL architecture has its roots in the cultural background of any nation. China is a country with a long history of over 5000 years, a land expanse of over three million square miles and a population of more than one thousand million. A large country, with such a long history, inevitably produces many myths, mystical figures, politicians, philosophers and schools of philosophy. For thousands of years, Chinese philosophical concepts, firmly rooted in the minds of the people, continually grew and developed, influencing thinking and governing behaviour. Here, in ancient China, religion and myth, philosophy and politics, science and superstition, humanity and ritual were constantly confronting and complementing each other. These phenomena eventually formed a unique architecture which was, and is, both imposing and humane, fully expressing the thoughts of the people. However, in China, as well as in other parts of the world, building activity initially was concerned with providing for the basic physical needs of the people, satisfying spiritual needs only as culture developed.

Classical Chinese architecture was a true reflection of the life and culture of the Chinese people, fulfilling physical need while simultaneously expressing meaning through its unique symbolic vocabulary. This marriage of the physical and the symbolic are the rudimentary elements of all great architecture, and become the metaphysical resource for each advancing stage of development.

BEFORE THE DAWN OF CIVILIZATION

According to historical documents, fossil bones were first found at Zhou Kou Dian in the northwestern area of Beijing (Peking), where Swedish geologist, J. Gunner Anderson, and a Chinese geologist, Pei Wen-Zhong, picked up a number of flint tools in a cave. During subsequent excavation, Pei discovered fossils of human bones which, with the exception of late Java man, were the oldest human remains yet discovered. The bones were those of an ancient man named *Sinanthropus Pekinensis* (now called Peking Man), who lived about 500,000 years ago during the Pleistocene Period. In 1964, in a deposit on an open hillside at Lantian, Xian, Shenxi Province, a human skull was discovered that geologists believed to be at least 100,000 years older than Peking Man, and roughly the same age as, or older than, Java Man. Later, additional significant remains were found in Inner Mongolia and northeastern China. From these discoveries, we are certain that from 500,000 to 600,000 years ago ancient men were living in the northwestern and northeastern areas of China, forming the beginnings of distinct cultures.

In 1921, Anderson and Pei discovered at Yang-shao, Mian-chi in Henan Province, an extensive deposit of polished tools and red pottery painted with black geometrical designs. This was the first confirmed evidence of a late neolithic culture in China and was named the Yang-shao (Painted Pottery) Period. Later more deposits were found in Gansu representing continuing cultural development between about 2500 B.C. and the Zhou Dynasty. Yang-shao culture was of particular importance in Chinese history, directly influencing the later Shang, or Xiaotun culture. At this time China had already entered into a period of agriculture and domestication during which the nomadic life was abandoned, and human settlements, villages and various types of houses were erected.

The most valuable find, consisting of remains belonging to the Yang-shao Period, was made in 1953 at Banpo, east of Xian in Shenxi Province. Banpo village, built approximately 6,000 years ago, covers an area of 50,000 square metres. The village was composed of three distinct parts: a residential area, the pottery kiln, and necropolises. In the residential district, four layers of houses have been discovered, representing several centuries of tribal occupation. Excavations to date have revealed 45 huts, two tents and about 200 caves, covering a total of about 3,000 metres. The earlier house plans, possible descendants of the nomadic tents, were circular in shape with wattle and daub walls, a reed roof and a centrally located fire pit for heating and cooking. Later houses developed square or rectangular floor plans and had southern exposures. Constructed with a framework of wood columns, some of the rooms had areas ranging from 20 to 40 square metres with rammed earth floors sunk a metre below ground level. The entire residential area was surrounded by a moat-like ditch of five to six metres in depth and width, constructed to provide protection from both enemies and wild animals. A 300-metre length of this moat remains today. The pottery making area, lying east of the residential quarter, is one of the oldest sites of its kind ever excavated in China. The burial ground, concentrated to the north of the settle-

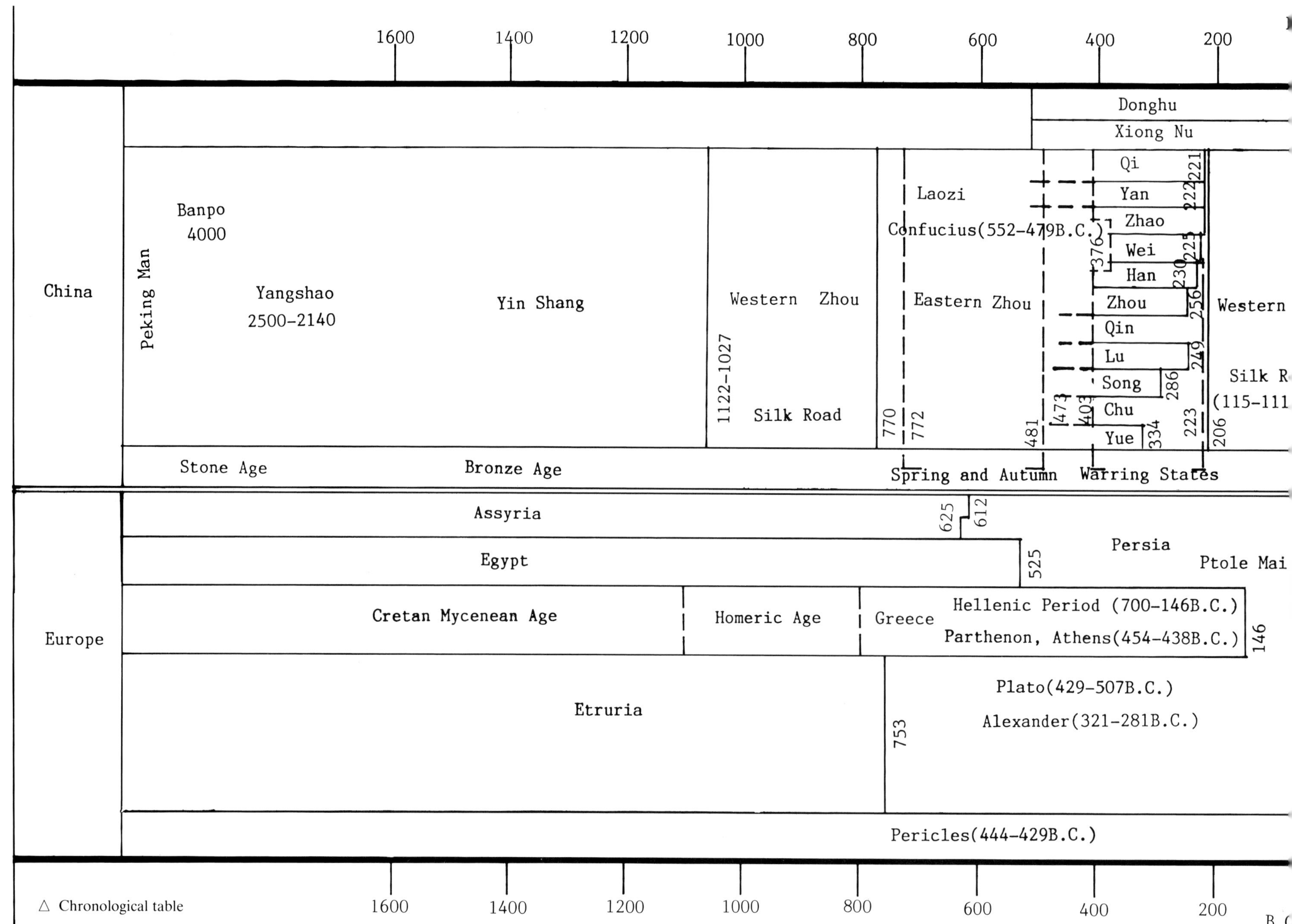

△ Chronological table

ment outside of the moat, contains 250 graves, indicating a belief in life after death and the expectation of living together in the afterworld.

Legends and myths aid us in determining the beliefs and distribution of the ancient people of northwestern China. According to the historical documents *Shang Shu* and *Yao Dian*, recording the legends of the mystic figures Yao, Shun and Yu and the Dynasties following them, the Xia Dynasty (21st-16th C B.C.) was the first dynasty in Chinese history. Historians have traditionally believed that before the Xia only tribal cultures existed. After many years of struggle and mutual influence, the tribes gradually merged and developed a dynastic concept.

According to legend, before the days of the primordial giant, Pan Ku, the universe was an enormous egg. One day Pan Ku split the egg, from which emerged human beings and tribes. The tribal heads were the Three Emperors (San Huang) and Five Emperors (Wu Di). The San Huang (Sui Ren, Fu Xi and Shen Long) were either legendary or symbolic figures. Legend indicates that Sui Ren invented the way to light a fire by drilling wood and taught the eating of cooked food. Animal domestication, farming, fishing, and hunting all began in the time of Fu Xi. It was said that he also invented the 'Ba Gua' (The Eight Diagrams). The symbols contained within the Ba Gua, which are formed by the male (yang) principles and female (yin) principles, could be used to record celestial and terrestrial forces. Later, Ba Gua was used by the Daoists (Taoists) as part of their teachings which run through the entire history of Chinese religions, philosophical and artistic thought. Fu Xi married Nu Wa, a goddess with a serpent's tail, and, through their union, produced human beings. The third San Huang, Shen Long (also called Yan Di) was believed to have taught agriculture and herbal medicine.

The mythical emperors were Wu Di, believed to have reigned between 2,550 and 2,140 B.C., Huang Di (Yellow Emperor), Zhuan Zu, Di Ku, Yao and Shun. Yao and Shun were later considered by Confucians to be model sovereigns. Legends indicated that Huang Di

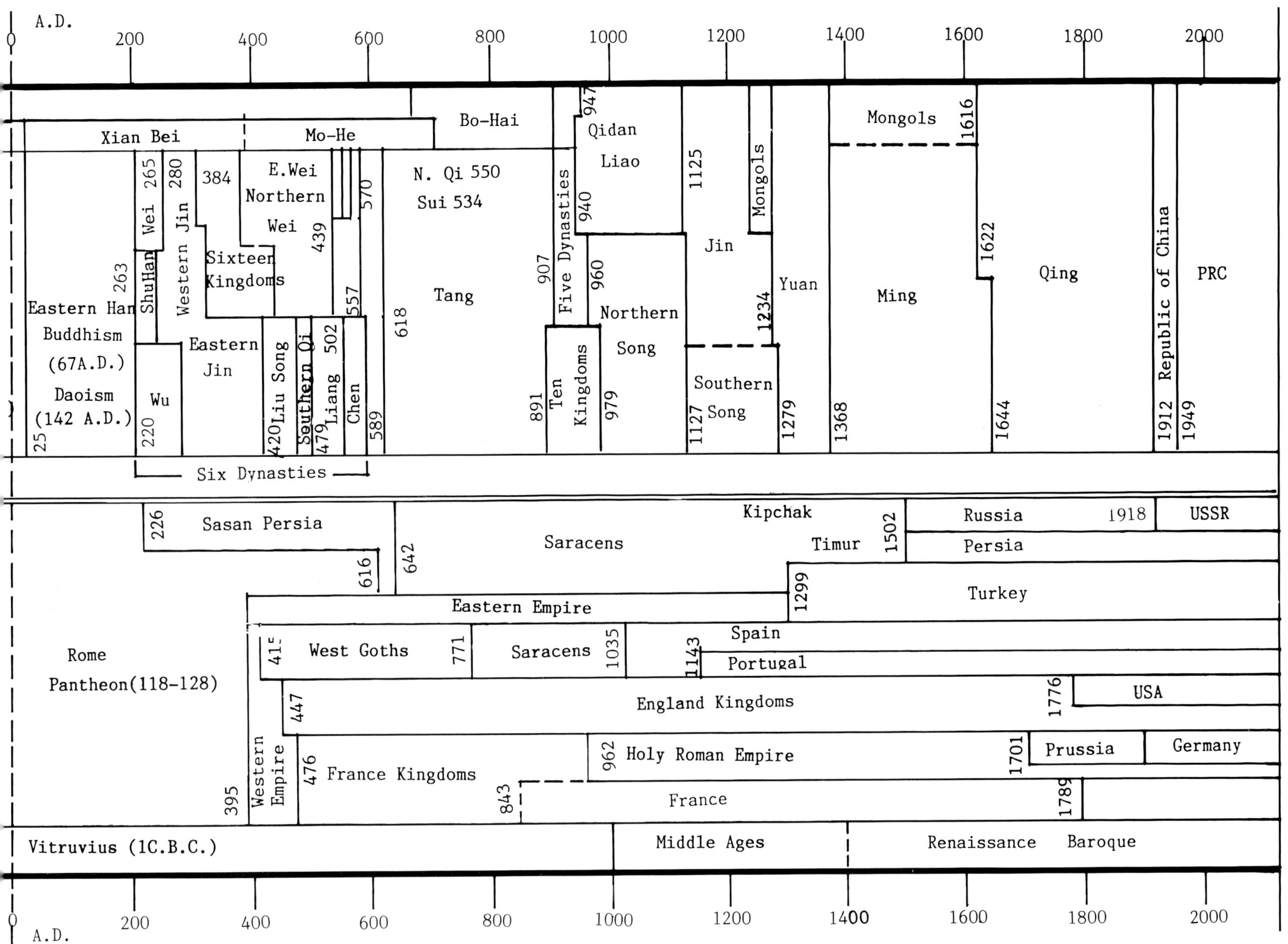

was a tribal head who lived in northern China where, after defeating the Yan tribe, he settled near the Yellow River. His reign was known for the building of boats, carriages, bows and arrows, jade weapons and the dyeing of the multicoloured clothes. Also attributed to Huang Di is the authorship of *Huang Di Nei Jing*, known in the west as *The Yellow Emperor's Classic on Internal Medicine*. His wife, Lei Zhu, is said to have introduced the rearing of silkworms and the use of the loom. Ancient scholars maintained that Huang Di was the ancestor of the Hua nationality.

If so much space has been devoted to the mention of these legendary figures, it is because they were considered heroes in the eyes of those who believed they were their descendants. It is difficult to determine whether they were real persons or legendary figures, but like any cultural myth, their importance lies in that they lived on as god-like guardian heroes in the hearts of the people. As an example, Yandi, who was said to be a human being with an Ox head, inspired and influenced the tribe into using an Ox totem. The Yan and Huang Di (Bear and Tiger totems) had three major battles at Ban Quan (now Huai Lai, near Beijing) with Huang Di being victorious. Another tribe, living in eastern China, had the legendary leader Tai Hao (family name, Feng), who was a man with a snake (or dragon) body. This tribe became known for its traditional snake (or dragon) totem.

It is not necessary for us to determine if, in fact, these legendary individuals were real persons, their importance lying, as stated, in the traditions they represented. It is known that the myths and legends of a nation profoundly influence that country's history, for they form, and then represent, cultural traditions, philosophical thought, political concepts and religious beliefs. From the very beginnings of history, heroes, those political religious leaders who had merit in the eyes of the people, were the object of worship. Thus, it was only natural to build cities and dwellings for them. These political and religious edifices, from the viewpoint of architectural history, then became the significant monuments of their country or nation. Structures developed under the influence of politics and religion – cathedrals, temples and palazzos of the west, pagodas, temples and palaces of the east – are seen everywhere in every period. In China, the most important architecture from the Yin Shang through the early Zhou Dynasties is of three kinds:

> The Mingtang, equivalent to a palace, the office of the kings; the second is the Piyong, a school; the third is the Taimiao, or ancestral hall, the place of ancestral worship.[1]

XIA DYNASTY (21stC B.C.-16thC B.C.)
SHANG DYNASTY (1562?-1066 B.C.)
THE DAWN OF CIVILIZATION

Historians generally maintain that what we term 'civilization' began after tribal society had entered into a class society with a state government ruling over cities which functioned as political, economical and cultural centres. Written characters were developed, creating a means of communication, recording commercial transactions and documenting history. In China the Xia and Shang Dynasties had all of these characteristics and thus could generally be accepted as the dawn of civilization in China. The location of the Xia and Shang, near the Yellow River Valley, is traditionally known as the cradle of Chinese civilization.

The Xia was founded by Qi, son of Yu the Great. Legend indicates that Yu harnessed the flood stages of the Yellow River. As a result, during the Spring and Autumn Period (770-476 B.C.) people were known to say '... if not for Yu, here we could only have fish and no human beings'.[2] Because of his flood control, irrigation and engineering works, Yu was worshipped as an inspired sage. The legend of Yu was an old myth that has been generally accepted as fact; however, there exist very few remains of the Xia Dynasty, making confirmation of its architectural and engineering developments difficult.

The Shang Dynasty, following the Xia, constructed cities at many locations. One site, dating from circa 1500 B.C., north of Zhengzhou, Henan, covers an area of 25 square kilometres surrounded by a rammed earth wall four to nine metres high and four to eight metres wide. Remains of dwellings and a variety of shops have also been unearthed at Zhengzhou. The tenth Shang emperor, Pangeng, moved the dynasties' capital to a place called Yinxu, between Xiao Tun and Anyang in Henan Province, around 1300 B.C. An excavation report of the 1928 Academia Sinica indicated that a large area of the palace, as well as burial grounds, were unearthed. Of primary scientific/archaeological importance were the exhumation of the grave sites. The tombs, about 20 metres square, were dug into the ground with below grade ramps in the four directions, or, in some cases, to the north and south. The ancient Chinese believed in a life after death. Consequently, the spirit of the departed was to be provided with all that he possessed, or would have liked to possess, in his earthly life, leading to the savage immolation of both human and animal sacrifices, as well as the inclusion of utensils and weapons in the tombs. Although barbarous, such customs have provided many artifacts, enabling the study and interpretation of Shang Dynasty social conditions. Recent excavations have revealed another city at Yanting in the west part of Henan Province. It could be Xi Hao, built around 3,000 years ago. The city is rectangular in plan, 1,200 metres from east to west; 1,700 metres from north to south. The city wall is 18 metres thick, constructed of earth. There are three rows of house foundations, the biggest is in the middle which is 200 square metres and faces south.

△ The Ming Dynasty Great Wall

ZHOU DYNASTY
West Zhou (1066? - 770 B.C.)
East Zhou (771 - 256 B.C.)

Wu Wang, of the vassal state of the Zhou Dynasty, conquered Yin Shang, moved its capital from Anyang to Hao, and initiated the transition from a slave society into a feudal society. The political organization of this period was a combination of familial and religious concepts. The Zhou enforced the Law of Succession to the throne, handing down the power of state to the deceased emperor's eldest son. This law helped to stabilize political and social order, taking advantage of the people's inclination towards ancestral worship. Zhou feudal society and its clan system, based on the family relationship, also became a major influence on the art and architecture of following dynasties.

The Zhou also decreed that the 'sacrificial ceremony be performed only by the eldest son, indicating his relationship to heaven and affording him universal respect. Although the other sons could not perform the ceremony, they were required to attend this veneration of their ancestors'.[3] Logically and forcibly they revered the eldest son, for the rule had become to worship ancestors; one needs to pay respect to the heir, and to respect the heir is the same as the worship of ancestors. In this way, the ceremony, status of the heir and the ancestral temple all became important elements in political stabilization. These regulations were further developed and concretized by Confucius. During the East Zhou many philosophers and politicians were produced, the most important being Confucius and Laozi (Laotzu). Living during the later part of the East Zhou, around 500 B.C., Confucius, of the Kingdom of Lu, was respected as a sage even during his lifetime, as well as during the entire 2,500 feudalistic

△ The Ming Dynasty Great Wall

years to follow. Confucianism adapted to the needs of both the controlling clan and the common people. Never overpowered by other schools and always dominating Chinese culture, Confucian thought was, undoubtedly, the epitome of ancient Chinese philosophical development.

The great philosophers of this period were Confucius and Laozi (500 B.C.). They represented the organization of two great systems of thought. The one trying to reconcile individualism with institutionism, and the other demanding a complete reversal of the existing order and a return to the 'natural state'. These two attitudes were represented by what came to be known as Positivism and Negativism. For the first time in Chinese history, precedent existed for the conscious and systematic reflection of thought. A few generations later, there appeared such men as Mencius (about 325 B.C.) to represent Positivism and Zhuangzi (a contemporary of Mencius) to represent Negativism.

The Period of Warring States or Stress and Strain (403-221 B.C.) came to an end when Shi Huang Di amalgamated the small principalities and established the Qin Dynasty (221 B.C.). Under his reign occurred that memorable event called the 'Fires of Qin' – the burning of classical writings. The event marks the close of the Ancient Period and the dawn of the Middle Ages in Chinese philosophy, between 246 B.C. and 960 A.D.

Upon the accession of the next dynasty, the Han Dynasty, a search was made for the lost classics. And the energy that would have been used in creative activity was absorbed by the work of collecting the newly-recovered writings. It is this fact that accounts for the traditionalism of the Medieval Period.

In this period, Buddhism was first introduced into China. About this time Chinese thought became pessimistic, and an eclectic tendency appeared in Chinese philosophy. Confucianism, Daoism, and Buddhism began to borrow from one another until a new synthesis was reached in what is called Spiritual Institutionism. The rise of this new system marks the beginning of the Modern Period in the history of Chinese thought (960 A.D. to this day). An excessive subjectivism and emphasis upon inwardness was characteristic of this period.

Confucius (552-479 B.C.) was born during a period of rivalry and uprisings when the vassal states were constantly at war, later known as the Spring and Autumn Period. He desired to restore the order of Wen, Wu and Zhou Gong's administration as well as the social peace of the early Zhou Dynasty. Confucius's theory was that those in power should practise an autocratic benevolence to the common people, while those at the bottom should respect, and be obedient to, the kings and emperors. His fundamental teachings consisted of a moral code centred on adherence to the Will of Heaven, harmony with nature, and behaving according to De (virtues). Like Jesus, he had never written any books but accumulated a huge following of disciples who recorded his teachings in, among other works, the *Classic of History*, the *Analects* and the *Zhou Ritual*. One document, the *Book of Songs*, has traditionally been attributed to Confucius. In all of the chapters accepted as authentic, the focus is on 'Tian (Heaven), obedience to the will of Heaven'. Since Heaven was represented by Tianzi (Son of Heaven) or the emperor, it followed that everyone should obey the emperor. Heaven also had a mystic power called 'Qi' (breath) on which the prosperity of the nation depended and everyone, from the Emperor to the common people, should be in harmony with this Qi. Since nature provided both food and health, the followers of Confucius worshipped heaven, earth, sun, moon, stars, hills, rivers – indeed, all discernible elements of the natural world. This logical attunement to, and worship of, heaven, was a form of animism which shall be described in later chapters. However, here it should be understood that, in Ancient China, the guiding factor of attuning to nature in the siting and planning of cities, buildings, and tombs was a major reason why Chinese architecture experienced very little change. Nature consisted of predictable cycles, and from year to year differed very little, a principle expressed in the arts and architecture of the nation. It was an accepted fact that obedience to the Will of Heaven and attuning to nature would eventually lead to the achievement of both personal and dynastic harmony. Confucius firmly believed that Harmony within the court would result in a prosperous and powerful reign. Harmony within the family and with nature would bring good fortune and health to the household. Inner harmony and moderation of one's self could bring a well-balanced character, and it is the aim of self-cultivation. Attuning to Heaven came from harmony with nature, obedience to elders brought harmony to the family, therefore, it could be said that the most important of Confucius's teachings, which also influenced architecture, was harmony.

Confucius related every aspect of human activity to the word 'Rite' or 'Reason' (in Chinese, both are pronounced 'Li') which represented his moral ideas governing the categories of daily life, regulating court ritual and directing art, literature and architecture. A scholar's responsibility was to abide by reason or observe rites, producing a rational philosophy with political implications. While 'De' was interpreted as benevolence and righteousness, rite produced order. Confucius taught the people with De but put them in order with rite, establishing an hierarchy of love, respect and filial piety. Confucianism established the rules and regulations to provide order in the complicated relations between men, thereby creating a stable social order. Achieved through education, the goal was to be faithful and obedient to nature and rulers, but his true aim was fundamentally ethical-spiritual, concern for spiritual health in the inner man, the fullness of internal life of the spirit.

Confucius' teachings maintained an influence over the people's minds for 2,500 years, disseminated through books as well as by verbal transmission of his quotations. Within architecture his influence can be seen in the *Zhou Ritual*, which required the use of imposing buildings expressing a dignity inherent in the concept of the state. In Chinese architecture, the unchanged form and construction methods, southern exposure, harmony with the site and building hierarchy were all controlled by these conservative ideas. Though conservative, these principles were not necessarily negative. Studied carefully, much could be learned from the manipulation and application of Confucian principles to contemporary architectural problems.

The other great philosopher of the period, Laozi (Laotzu), whose family name was Li, was believed to be a little older than Confucius. His book, the *Dao De Jing*, or *Laozi*, expressed a philosophy which was the complete antithesis of Confucianism. While Confucianism was essentially conservative, rational and adapted to the orthodoxy of an imperial state, Daoism was anti-rational, anarchical, mystical and taught the study and veneration of nature. Together, both philosophies exercised complementary influences upon Chinese thought, especially as expressed in art and architectural layout and selection of site. Related to witchcraft and the practice of alchemy, essentially a form of proto-science, Daoism had its roots in the ancient *I-Ching* or *Book of Changes*. Although Laozi became known as the founder of Daoism, it should be noted that he was that brand of sage which, in keeping with his philosophy, avoided public recognition, preferring the life of a minor court official and finally that of a hermit.

Though no Zhou Dynasty buildings have survived, these 'inheritors of the culture of Yin' are known to have used fired bricks and tiles for houses, palaces and city walls. Perhaps the greatest architectural heritage of the Zhou Rituals were the size, scale and hierarchy standards which would be applied to city planning and building design during subsequent dynasties.

▷ Beijing, Ju Yong Guan Gate of The Great Wall, Yung Dynasty, 1345, bas-relief

▷ Beijing, Ju Yong Guan Gate of The Great Wall, Yung Dynasty, 1345

▷ Kansu, the Great Wall, remains of Han Dynasty

▷ Kansu, Jiayu Guan Fortress and the western end of the Great Wall, Ming Dynasty, 1368

QIN AND HAN DYNASTIES
Qin Dynasty (221-206 B.C.)
Han Dynasty (206 B.C.-220 A.D.)

The final years of the Zhou Dynasty existed in a state of turmoil with the power of the Emperor deteriorating. Though the Emperor, in theory, wielded absolute authority, the kings of the vassal states were growing stronger and had split the country into seven kingdoms. This era, with a weakened emperor unable to exercise control over the kings, became known as the Period of Warring States (475-221 B.C.). Known for rapid advancements in science, art and literature, as well as the use of iron to make weapons and instruments, the Period of the Warring States produced a flourishing economy, great irrigation systems and many new cities. Finally, the king of the Kingdom Qin, having defeated the other kings, and the Zhou emperor established the Qin Dynasty in 221 B.C., assuming the title of Qin Shi Huang Di or the First Emperor of Qin.

The new dynasty immediately inititated many new construction works including, within the capital city, a palace complex (the A Fang Gong) and the Emperor's tomb. When excavated in 1973, one portion of this tomb yielded more than 7,000 life-size pottery figures of warriors and horses. It was also during the Qin that the already existing, but segmented, walls defending the country from the northern Huns were connected, creating the Great Wall of China. Though all of these efforts were undertaken with the desire to create a new era, the Emperor, in order to strengthen his control, persecuted the great feudal families. The books of Confucius were burned, and around 400 Confucian scholars were buried alive for supporting the Zhou Dynasty and preaching a return to the golden age of the Wen and Wu era, of the Zhou Dynasty.

To produce his gigantic works, Shi Huang Di mobilized hundreds of thousands of workers. Although this resulted in an abundance of architectural and engineering works, it proved too much of a financial and physical burden to the people. The cruelty and tyranny of the Emperor resulted in a short-lived dynasty, less than twenty years, before its overthrow by the Han. The unification of China and the tyrannical example of the Qin provided the Han with excellent lessons on how to control the country and its people. During the early Han, few public works were assigned to the people, providing a period of relative rest and establishing an air of gratitude toward the benevolence of the new regime. However, the administration realized that great architecture was an important factor in maintaining the government's authority as well as being a symbol of power. Thus began a period in which the Han endeavoured to create great cities and large buildings. The first concentrated effort was the building of Changan (now Xian, Shenxi Province) and the palaces and houses contained within the city. Following the completion of Changan, the wealthy from every part of the country were ordered to move to, and live within, the city. It was in this way that Changan became the largest city in the world during its day, and was a model of capital city design for the following dynasties.

Wudi (140-87 B.C.) of Han was an ambitious emperor. During his reign, Western Han became very powerful, with many battles fought and won. In the north he defeated the Hun invasion while, to the west, he sent a great expedition force (115-111 B.C.) headed by General Zhang Qian which opened a road of commerce and culture with the Central Asian countries. This road was identified in 1877 by the German geographer, Ferdinand Von Richthofen, which he named the 'Silk Road'. Beginning at Changan and following the Yellow River, the road travelled along the southern side of the Great Wall until reaching the oasis at Dunhaung, its major junction where the road split into two. One avenue proceeded north to Turfan, running along the Tian Shan Mountains (Celestial Mountains), through Aksu, She He Zi (New Town), Kashi and on to Samarkand. The southern fork travelled along the Kunlun Mountains to the north, through Yutian, Hetian (Khotan) and Jiohe, on to the west of Afghanistan and, finally, terminated in India. Under the Han and the later Northern and Southern Dynasties as well as the Tang, countless Buddhist pilgrims travelled these two routes to India. Chinese decorative arts, architecture, music and dance were subsequently enriched by this close link with Central Asia provided by the Silk Road.

Many gardens were also planned and constructed in Changan during the Han Dynasty. The most famous, the Imperial Garden, called Shangling, which included the first zoo to be founded in Chinese history, was attached to the magnificent palace complex. The Han also decreed building regulations controlling building size, colour and height for both government and common buildings.

During the Eastern Han, Buddhism was introduced from India to China in 67 A.D., bringing not only new spiritual elements, but also a variety of building types, including the Indian stupa, caves temples and new forms of sculpture and decorative arts. These gradually merged with traditional Chinese architectural styles, creating numerous new forms. Buddhism, after arriving in China, was influenced by the indigenous Confucianism and Daoism, creating many new sects of Buddhism. Each individual sect had its own ideas, having great impact upon art, literature and architecture, as shall be discussed in the chapter concerning religious buildings.

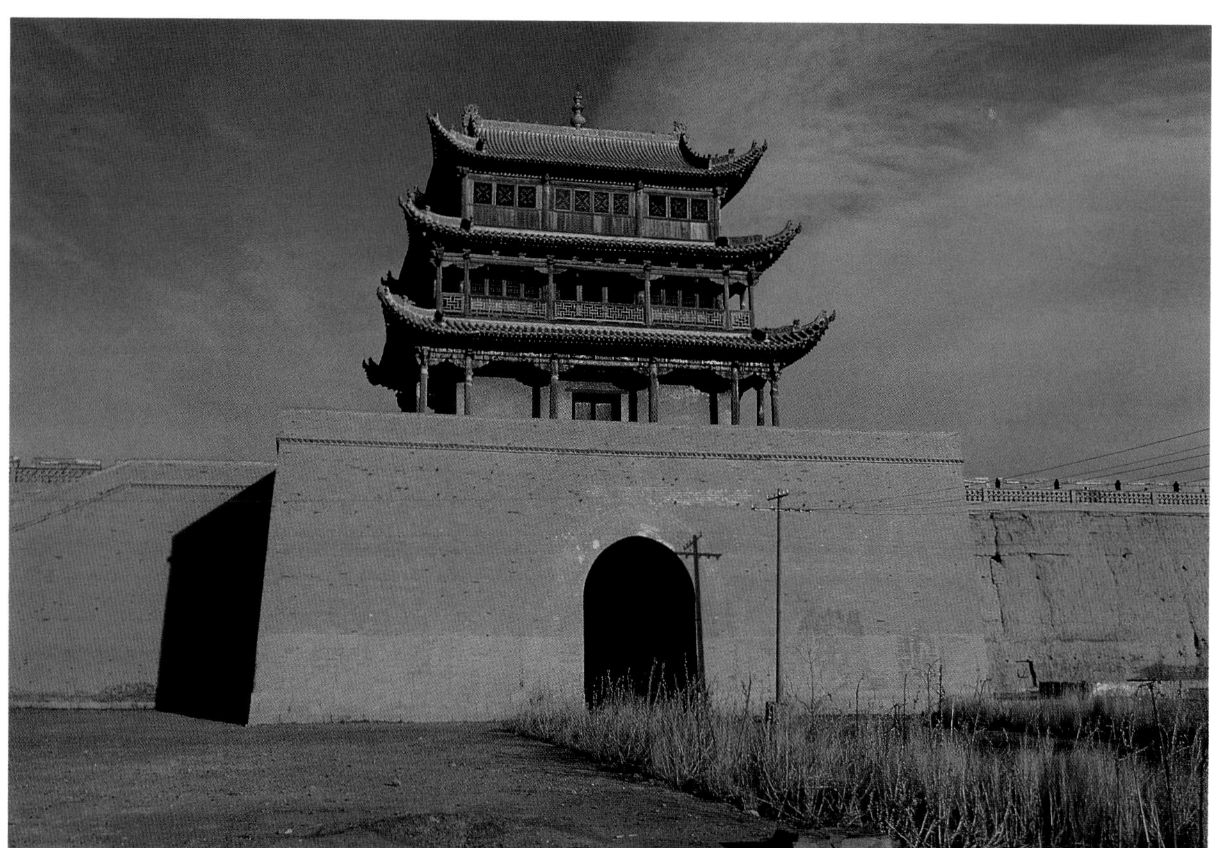

△ Kansu, Jiayu Guan Fortress, watch tower

From the many relics unearthed during archaeological digs, it has been determined that important buildings constructed in this period used Duogong (a cluster of brackets) to support roof structures. Wooden, multi-storeyed pavilions were built while kilned brick and tile construction was developed and widely used. Classical Chinese architectural systems were basically formed during this period and continually developed for the next 2,000 years.

Government corruption at the close of the period, combined with frequent warfare, weakened the Han Dynasty, which was finally conquered by the Western Jin (265-316 A.D.), a short-lived and undistinguished dynasty. A stronger northern people existed at this time, composed of sixteen small kingdoms. This effectively divided China into two sections, creating an era historically known as the Northern and Southern Dynasties.

NORTHERN AND SOUTHERN DYNASTIES (317-581? A.D.)

From the reign of the Western Jin, through the Northern and Southern Dynasties, until the Sui unified all the small kingdoms, stretched a period of 316 years marked by immense struggle and national infusion. Although the main portion of China (the northwestern part of China today) was occupied by the militarily stronger north, after many years it was assimilated by the culturally stronger south. Thus, it could be said that although China's Han people were conquered by the military power of the north, it was the culture of the south which was finally the victor. The sixteen small kingdoms in the north were eventually defeated and united by Toba Wei, a Northern Turkish national who founded his capital at Datong, Shanxi Province. The Wei abandoned their nomadic life, settled down, adopted Chinese writing and clothing, observed Chinese customs, adopted Chinese religious beliefs, and reopened the Silk Road. In 494 A.D., the Northern Wei relocated its capital in the city of Luoyang, where they improved the Han city plan by moving the palace further north and adding east and west markets outside of the city. As Buddhism was the national religion, many religious buildings were erected and cave temples hollowed out. In Dengfeng, Song Shan, Henan Province, a great, twelve-sided brick pagoda was constructed. Meanwhile in Datong, Taiyuan and Tianlong Shan (Shanxi Province), Longmen (Luoyang) and Mogaoku (Dunhuang), many Buddhist grottoes were hollowed out, sculptures carved and frescoes painted. Today they remain as magnificent examples of Indian and Central Asian arts blending with Chinese culture,

△ Guan Xian, Sichuan, Dujiang Yan, water irrigation works, 3 B.C.

illustrating the fact that whenever China had access to other arts and cultures, their influences proved beneficial to the Chinese.

When the Toba occupied the north, the Han people of Western Jin fled south, and made Jainkang (now Nanjing) their capital, thus creating two distinct political centres. Those in the south, however, also believed in Buddhism, and it was reported that in Jainkang alone, 480 temples were constructed. Though none of these exists today, many of the extant temples in Nanjing were built upon their foundations. During the Northern and Southern Dynasties, numerous foreign concepts and architectural forms were imported to China, examined and tested, and eventually assimilated by the Chinese culture. However, as this process took place during a period of unstable political conditions and an underdeveloped economy, it was difficult to express these influences entirely. Works of art and architecture were crude and unpolished, but they did, however, establish a foundation for the developments of later dynasties.

SUI AND TANG DYNASTIES
Sui Dynasty (581-618 A.D.)
Tang Dynasty (618-907 A.D.)

Sui, succeeding the Northern and Southern Dynasties and unifying China for only 27 years, was followed by the Tang Dynasty. The prosperous Tang Dynasty was a culturally sublime and militarily powerful period in China's history, which historians compare with the Han. Since the days of the Han and the Tang, the Chinese have called themselves the Han people, as this ethnic national group has always represented about 95% of the total population of China. Even today, in America, overseas Chinese call their section of town the Tang Ren Jie or the Street of the Tang People. Both the Sui and the Tang founded their capitals at Changan, which, together with Luoyang, were the largest cities in the world at the time, as well as being the greatest cities based upon the grid plan. The flourishing culture and economy of these dynasties made such large scale planning and construction possible. The Sui planner, Yu Wenkai, who worked through the Sui and into the Tang, constructed the western capital to the southeast of Han Dynasty Changan (Daxing City). Later, he designed the Tang eastern capital at Luoyang.

Both the Sui and Tang Dynasties continued communications with the west, sending monks to India to learn the language, translate sutras from sanskrit into Chinese and import Buddhist architecture, art and sculpture into China. The remaining Sui and Tang tombs, wooden temples, cave temples, pagodas and bridges stand as examples of the high technical standards employed in their sculpture, frescoes and calligraphy. These structures can still be seen and appreciated today.

SONG, YUAN, MING AND QING DYNASTIES
Song Dynasty (960-1279 A.D.)
Yuan Dynasty (1279-1368 A.D.)
Ming Dynasty (1368-1644 A.D.)
Qing Dynasty (1644-1911 A.D.)

The last days of the Tang, called the period of the Five Dynasties (907-979 A.D.) and ten kingdoms, was an era of turmoil in which these small kingdoms were fighting with each other, to be unified eventually by the Song. The Song, a weak and corrupt dynasty, was constantly invaded from the north, though miraculously their art and literature flourished. The first Chinese manual of building construction, comprising of thirty-four volumes and known as the *Ying Zao Fa Shi*, was written in 1100 and published in 1103. In it, the author, Li Jie (also known as Li Ming Zhong), an officer and builder in charge of architectural projects, combined descriptions of traditional construction methods with technical information on materials and workmanship. Another book, the *Mu Jing* (*Book of Wood*) by the carpenter Yu Hao, dealt with wood construction and carpentry methods. It was during this time, through the joint efforts of both administrators and builders, that building became increasingly refined in both form and construction. Products from the Song Dynasty include the tallest wooden tower standing in the world today, the Fogong Pagoda (in Yingxian), the first city plan of Pingjiang (now Suzhou) carved on a stone tablet, and the Youguo Temple Pagoda (in Kaifeng), which was completely covered with brown, glazed terra-cotta tiles.

In 1279, the cavalry of Kublai, grandson of the Mongolian Genghis Khan, defeated the Song, founding the Yuan Dynasty which located its capital city at Beijing. The Mongolians followed the Zhou ritual of city planning and named the capital Dadu, or Cambulac, the City of Khan. The militant Mongolians penetrated as far as Europe, with the returning officers and soldiers introducing Islam religion and culture into China. Kublai commissioned an Arab to construct the imperial palace in Cambulac, and a Nepalese to do the carvings, using primarily stone as a building material instead of the more traditional wood.

The Mongolians as invaders were never favoured by the Han. Thus, in order to appease the Chinese, they adopted Buddhism and constructed many Buddhist and Lama temples, such as the five-stupa pagoda in Beijing. In spite of their effort to integrate, the sup-

pression of the Han by the Mongolians caused much hatred and eventually produced a national revolt led by the Han majority resulting in the defeat of the Yuan and the founding of the Ming Dynasty. The Ming Dynasty has been perceived by some historians as a period of degeneration in administration, arts and literature. However, during the three hundred years of its rule, architecture experienced tremendous progress. The Great Wall, in its final form, was completed during the Ming. Now Nanjing and Beijing city planning still retain the scale of that period. The Forbidden City Palace, as it exists today, was of Ming style and creation. All of these architectural activities reveal that the Ming favoured grand and monumental buildings. The design of the structures emphasized symmetry, horizontal line, and the use of kilned brick and tile as building materials.

The Qing Dynasty, founded by Manchu nomads, a militaristic national minority from notheastern China, followed the Ming. During the Qing, another book on building construction, the *Qing Gong Bu Zho Fa*, was written, giving us a considerable amount of technical information on the materials, construction methods and decorative elements used during that period. In its final days the regime had become weak and suffered invasions by other powers. Corruption finally brought the dynasty to an end and the Republic of China was founded by Dr. Sun Yatshen in 1912.

SUMMARY

This brief chronological cultural background of historical Chinese dynasties is based upon the chief architectural developments of each period. It is easy to discern through study and Chinese history that, from the Xia Dynasty until the present, city planning and architectural design have been particularly influenced by specific political ideas and religious beliefs. If one were to study the architecture independently of these two factors, it would be almost impossible to explain the evolution of Chinese architecture. Within this architectural context can be discovered two characteristics in China's history: continuity and assimilation.

CONTINUITY

The Chinese cosmology has long been influenced by Confucian philosophy. Benevolence, hierarchy of class and seniority, the concept of 'sky does not change, so everything does not change', natural phenomena (hills, rivers, trees), the feudalistic system grown from and adapted to the sky, all expressed a permanence which controlled Chinese thinking, forming the seemingly unchanged, unique Chinese architectural style. During the 19th century, a large-scale exchange of ideas and cultural relations with the outside world began to occur, resulting in the neglect of Confucian ideals. Unfortunately, the result has been that many valid architectural design principles have been discarded. The design of a humane architecture, utilizing architectural forms to express existential meaning, and adaptation to, and congruity with, nature and the landscape, are all concepts which could be utilized today to create a balanced architectural vocabulary.

ASSIMILATION

Because of the continuity maintained in Chinese architecture, careful study is required to discern its subtle relationship with the cultural influences of the outside world. This becomes most apparent in the nation's

◁ Zhao Xian, Hebei, Anzi Stone Bridge, 605 A.D.

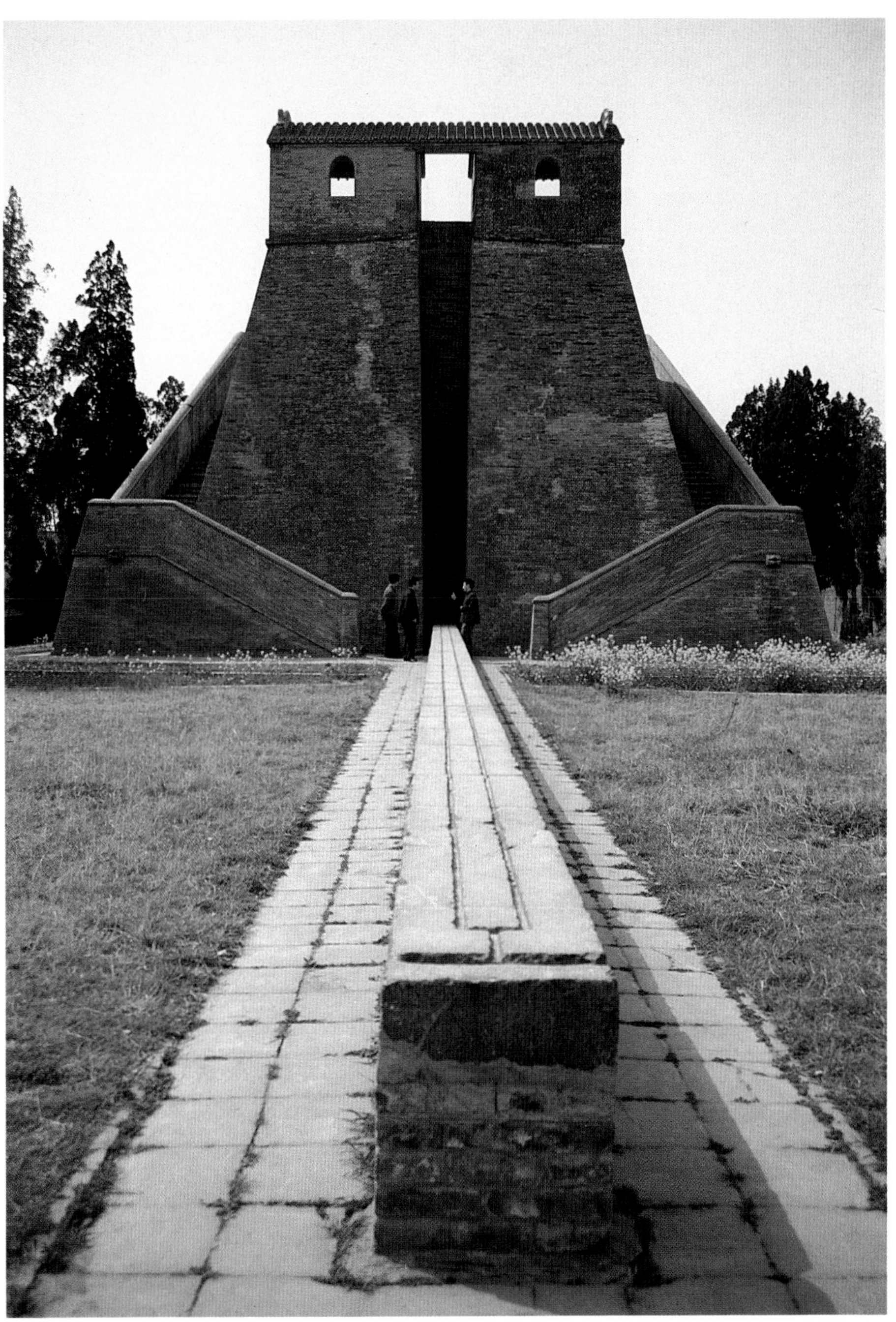

◁ Zhao Xian, Hebei, Anzi Stone Bridge, 605 A.D. bas-relief on railing

▷ Dengfeng, Henan, Shadow Measuring Platform, Tang Dynasty, 723 A.D.

historic assimilation of architectural types and forms, and in the decorative arts. For example, in many Buddhist pagodas and carvings, direct influences originating in Western art were not simply copied, but adopted, digested, absorbed and finally assimilated, gradually becoming integral features of the Chinese architectural idiom.

Assimilation was not only an architectural phenomenon, but also a characteristic of the nation's ability to absorb ethnic minorities and conquerors. During its long history China has been invaded and occupied by diverse foreign forces. Yet, in the end, this nation not only assimilated the conquerors, but also maintained its own unique cultural traditions. Many illustrious examples exist. The Tobas, Mongolians and Manchurians each invaded China as nomads, crossing the Great Wall wearing their ethnic clothes. Following a short gestation period, they were 'sinocized', changing to Han dress, learning Chinese culture, and adapting themselves to the indigenous building forms and city planning principles of the 'conquered' country. It was in this manner that classical Chinese architecture maintained its individual integrity, changing very little during several millennia.

In comparison Western architecture, also rooted in political philosophies and religious concepts, experienced great stylistic changes during roughly the same time span encompassed by the development of its Chinese counterpart. From Etruscan to the classical Greek and Roman, from Early Christian to Romanesque, from Gothic to Renaissance, Mannerism to Baroque, styles changed constantly, often radically, while Chinese architecture maintained its continuity. If one reason could be singled out to explain this phenomenon, it would have to be the stabilizing effect of Confucian thought and cosmology.

About fifty years ago, a group of Chinese architects gathered in Beijing to study classical Chinese architecture and city planning, forming an institute called the Zhong Kuo Ying Zho Xue She. Evidence from archaeological diggings, the measuring of buildings and archival research, when combined with a complete knowledge of the country's history, provided new insights into classical Chinese architecture. Through the efforts of the heads of institutes such as Lian Si Chen and Liu Dun Tseng a new, more comprehensive knowledge of the nation's classical architectural and planning developments was compiled and has continued to grow.

Not everything old or ancient can be defined as better or good. Each great work is an integral part of its own time, and can best express the ideas and technology of that particular period in history. However, many ancient works contain universal elements, often providing useful resource and reference material when applied to contemporary architectural problems. These are the elements, often containing subtle yet brilliant intuitive design solutions, which we should study, analyze and utilize in order to obtain maximum profit from our past. During the past two thousand years, in a vertical fashion, Chinese architecture has developed a tradition of continuity, expressing little change, whilst horizontally it has absorbed Western culture, integrating it with an inherent style, creating many new forms. This architecture, infused with the spirit of both the Chinese and the West, which neither copies nor rejects other cultural concepts, belongs to the whole world and all mankind.

China's civilization, spanning five thousand years, was developed in a territory encompassing roughly 3,125 miles from east to west and 3,440 miles from north to south, an area larger than the continent of Europe. Today, this land mass is inhabited by one quarter of the world's population. To pursue the entire architectural history of such a large country with a long and diverse history in one volume would be an impossible task. However, we shall take this opportunity to compile a record and depiction of Chinese architecture and city planning through typical examples. Hopefully, we will provide a comprehensive understanding of the continuous development of the character and essence of this classical Chinese architectural heritage, providing a tool to interpret the past, serve the present and define the future.

CHAPTER II

THE CHARACTER AND MEANING OF CLASSICAL CHINESE ARCHITECTURE

◁ Beijing, Temple of Heaven, Qinian Dian, 1889

THE UNIQUE CULTURE AND GEOGRAPHIC ENVIRONMENT of ancient China had worked together to produce an architecture which not only differed from the architecture of the rest of the world, but which also had retained its continuity for almost 2,000 years. From the form of a city to that of a single building, from construction to form, and from design concept to practice – that there was only minor changes made throughout such a long period is not only unusual within such a large nation, but is also a remarkable achievement worldwide. When discussing the history of Western architecture, we must describe the design concept, construction method, space, and meaning of architecture for each period of development. In contrast, in order to give readers a glimpse of the whole picture of Chinese architecture, we must describe the characteristics and meaning of Chinese architecture in general.

THE ORGANIZATION OF SPACE

Spatial organization in classical Chinese architecture is based upon both the daily needs and aesthetic requirements of the people. In China, standardized units were used to form interior and exterior space.

The Jian

The 'jian' is the unit of spatial organization. The organization of space in classical Chinese architecture is simple and straightforward. The basic concept involves the use of the jian, or bay room, as a standard unit which may be expanded or repeated to form either individual buildings or groups of buildings. The jian is a rectangular room or space defined by walls or columns which separate it from adjoining rooms or spaces. The jian can be extended to form a hall, or 'ting', by extending the standard unit (the jian) along a longitudinal or horizontal axis. A longer axis can be used to connect halls to form a building group, or even a city. Sometimes halls were grouped around a courtyard to form different types of building combinations.

The concept of the jian originated as far back as the Shang Dynasty. During excavations at Yinxu, the Shang capital at Anyang, more than ten buildings having rectangular foundations were discovered. Upon the foundations, laid out in straight lines and set at equal intervals, were bases for columns made of large, round stones bearing copper plates. Wood ashes were found on the copper plates, some of which were carved in a thunder-and-cloud design. The excavations at Anyang proved that even during the Shang Dynasty, both jian and wooden framing were used in building construction. The findings also indicate the beginning of standardization in building construction.

Except for a few examples, most of the ting have an odd number of bays, and the centre intercolumniation tends to have a larger span to emphasize the longitudinal axis. The axis is usually introduced by a frontal flight of stairs leading up to a big podium. The usual length of a bay was three metres, and the dimension of a jian was three by six metres, but after the Tang Dynasty the span was gradually widened. Important buildings, such as palace building groups or temples, would feature spans five to ten metres wide in their great halls.

The walls to the back of a hall, serving as the exterior walls of the building group, would have no openings to the outside. They are usually constructed of thick, kilned brick or rammed earth, protecting the building from fire while providing privacy and security for the occupants.

Thus, we see that the Chinese organization of space expands from a cell to a group, and from microcosm to macrocosm, adapting itself to different climatic regions. The same organizational concepts can be used for both public and private buildings. By varying the size of the hall or courtyard, the number of units, or the form and decoration, this uni-functional element could be adapted to different functional requirements.

The functionalist of today might be surprised to learn that the Chinese used the jian for many purposes. A hall could serve as a living space, an office, a study, a Buddhist worshipping hall, or even a throne hall. In a large complex, whether it functioned as a living space or an ancestral worshipping hall, the halls were all of the same form. Although separate and independent of one another, halls typically were interconnected by covered verandahs or walkways. This arrangement differs from the Western concept, which tends to unite all functions under one roof. Obviously, the Chinese multi-functional buildings do have some disadvantages. For example, it requires more effort to travel from one room to another, and costs are higher to build and maintain such structures. However, in a time when there were few people and plenty of land, the use of standardized designs and building elements was instrumental in speeding up construction. In addition, such structures could be easily expanded as needed.

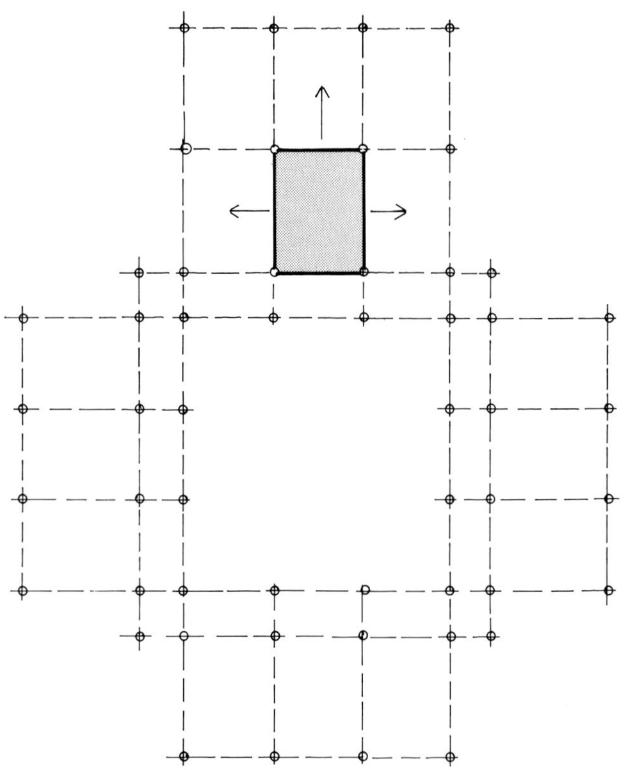

Axial Planning

The second characteristic of classical Chinese architecture, the symmetrical and orthogonal structuring of the plan and elevation, is obviously intended as a direct representation of the Chinese cosmos. Unlike Western axial planning, the Chinese place all the halls and courtyards along a longitudinal axis or path in orthogonal order. The halls are separated from each other by a courtyard, considered itself to be a major space in the composition rather than a subordinate part. Many major activities take place in the courtyard separating the halls. Usually, the longitudinal axis is considered to be the major axis and the horizontal axis the minor; however, at times, both function as major axes. Occasionally in a composition there will be only a partial axis, or the axis will be lacking entirely. These last two arrangements were primarily in landscape gardening.

There are three unit arrangements used in Chinese axial planning:

A. The first and most common arrangement of units placed the main hall at the centre of the major axis. Other halls were located to the left and right of this main structure, or in front and back of it. As a result of the hall arrangement, either one or two horseshoe courtyards were formed. Sometimes another minor hall would be located on the south side of the courtyard, allowing an enclosed courtyard to be formed by four halls and the walls which connected them. The most basic of Chinese courtyard forms, buildings continue to be grouped in this manner today.

A variation on this building arrangement, called Lang-yuan or verandah-courtyard, is formed by the placement of the main hall on the major axis with side halls to the right and left. These halls are connected to the main hall by covered verandahs, thus giving the arrangement its name. This composition has been widely used in China, beginning with the Han Dynasty and enduring until the Tang and Song Dynasties. After the Song Dynasty, very few structures were built using this form.

B. The second arrangement is called the central-building layout. After the Han Dynasty, a special plan was employed for monumental building layout. The composition, based upon perpendicular axes, placed the main building at the intersection of the two axes. The whole group was surrounded on all sides by minor halls, verandahs, and other buildings. In this way, a building complex which was symmetrical along both longitudinal and horizontal axes was achieved. The Han Ritual Building, Altars of Heaven of Ming, and Pule Temple of Qing were all planned in this way.

C. The third arrangement, used in large building group layouts, extended the building groups in one of three ways:

Longitudinal extension: when one group of buildings and one courtyard provided insufficient space to fulfill the functions required, the axis was extended further to form a larger building complex. Palace halls and courtyards were placed alternately along an axis, eventually forming a series of halls and courtyards. This type of longitudinal extension was first discovered in the palace remains of the Shang Dynasty.

Parallel extension: under this plan, when more room was needed, minor longitudinal axes were established

◁ Jian, the unit of construction and planning

▷ Spatial organization and axial planning

Key
1 Central building: a) Xian, Shenxi, Ritual Building Group, b) Beijing, Temple of Heaven, Round Mound, c) Xingping, Shenxi, Maoling Tomb, d) Chengde, Hebei, Pule Si. 2 Parallel Axis: a) Suzhou, Jiangsu, Cheng's House, b) Taiyuan, Shanxi, Congshan Si (based on a Ming Dynasty temple plan). 3 Central Axis: a) Beijing, East Mountain Si, b)Ronghe, Shanxi, Houtu Ceremonial Hall (based on a Jing tablet).

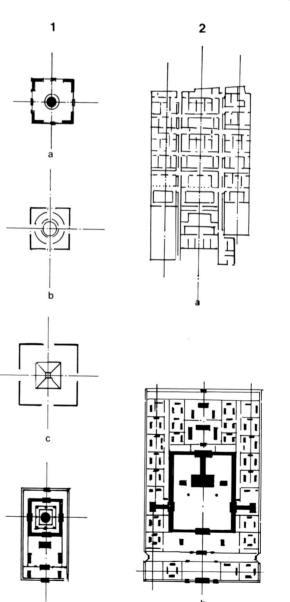

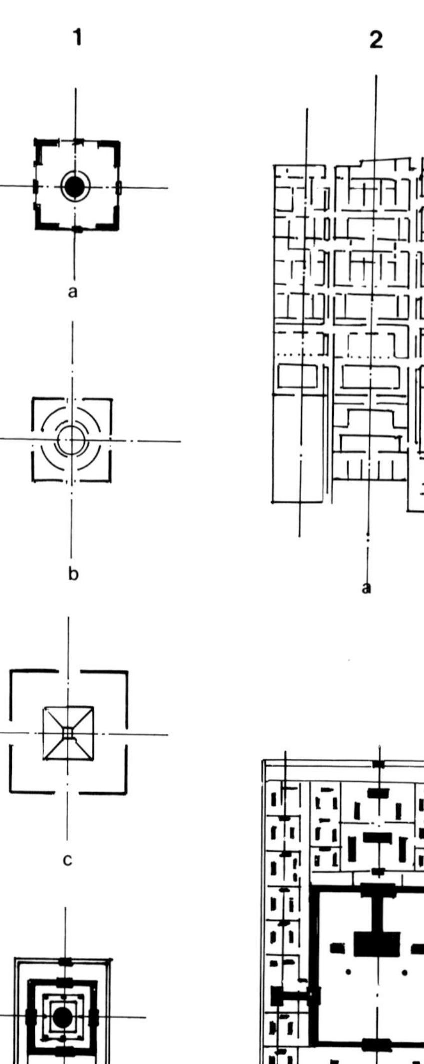

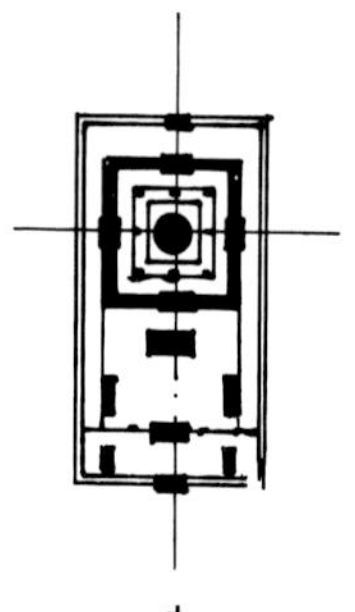

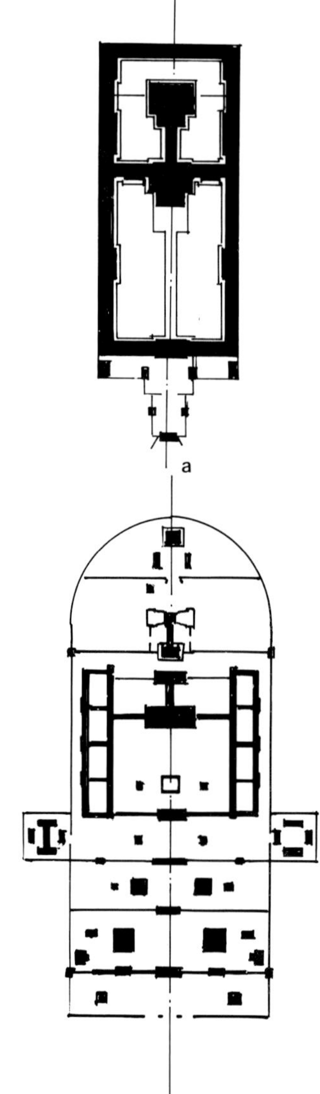

parallel to the main axis. Thus, instead of one longitudinal extension, more than two groups of building ensembles were established, each of which had its own specific function and size. This type of extension was developed in the palace and temple planning of the Tang Dynasty.

Cross extension: examples of this type are extended along both the horizontal and vertical axes. It is an appropriate form for the large building ensembles.

Axial planning provides the Chinese architectural group with a means of manipulating space. The use of space and minor halls to form contrasts with the final, culminating element – the main hall – is unique to Chinese architecture. The use of contrast is very different from what is found in Western architecture. In Chinese architecture, as one enters the main gate and steps into the courtyard, considered a transitional space, one can see that the entire building complex is composed of alternating solid and void. In passing from a hall to a courtyard, and then from a courtyard to a hall, one experiences a series of spatial sequences. The axis in a Chinese building complex acts as a path. One follows the path through a complex, unlike in the West where one follows the path into a building, the terminus of the axis. In contrast, in China one enters the building, experiences its interior, and then steps through the door to a courtyard. The Chinese courtyard is the centre of all kinds of activities. One could view the scenery and look at the other buildings, or join in the activities before following the path into the second building. By following the path, one experiences the continual contrast between solid (for example, a gateway) and void throughout the building. Whether in an exterior space or an interior space, both solid and void are part of the spatial organization and are complementary to one another rather than independent. In a rather long sequence, one might bypass a building to step into another courtyard, but the sequence always tends to induce one to enter and explore every building located along the axis, so that the interior and exterior spaces might be experienced as a harmonious whole.

The courtyard, enclosed as it is by the walls or buildings around it, takes on a special introverted quality. The seclusion of the courtyard, separated from the outside world, is another characteristic of Chinese architecture not found in Western architecture. This ensemble forms a small world by itself, a private space especially for the people who use it. This conforms with the Chinese custom of Feng Shui, (Wind and Water) to concentrate Qi (Breath) in the building group. Thus, in a Chinese building group, all of the buildings tend to face a void rather than the public street.

Geometry and order also control spatial organization. Under the influence of the simple, geometric buildings, the courtyard naturally took on a square shape. All of the one-storey buildings, both big and small, were erected in an orderly manner around the courtyard. This plan conforms to the Chinese people's 'close to the earth' idea, or the belief that when man is close to the earth, health will prevail. The ordered variety and the unification of scale and form enable the people who live there to experience the comfortable, tranquil, living environment provided by the space.

In Chinese building plans, the most important building was always placed at the most northern, that is the last part of the site. The sizes and heights of the surrounding structures gradually increased as the main building was approached, and the courtyard was proportionally enlarged as the climax of the plan was reached. Thus, through the utilization of spatial organization, the practical needs and cosmology of the Chinese people are unified in a functional, tangible symbol.

ORIENTATION – FENG SHUI

Another important feature of classical Chinese architecture is its attention to the concept of orientation. Buildings, except for those designed for special requirements or conditions, invariably face south or a little to the east. Because China is situated north of the equator, the climate is, for the most part, cold in the winter and warm in the summer, with a southeasterly prevailing wind. By orientating buildings to the south or southeast, the Chinese take advantage of the southeasterly winds and sunshine to provide the people living in the halls and courtyards with a pleasant microclimate. This idea of orientation developed into a special branch of art called Feng Shui, or Wind and Water. In a courtyard grouping, planned either in a horseshoe shape or with a quadrangle courtyard, at least half of the rooms face east or west. Those facing east and west are usually minor rooms, and are shaded by a wide overhang, verandah, or large trees, which act as a huge canopy over the place for living in all four seasons. Because of the special orientation requirements, the horizontal axis of the rectangular hall is always parallel to the east-west axis. In this way, the courtyard is elongated to provide more sunshine.

According to orientation requirements and Feng Shui, not only buildings faced south, but cities and tombs also faced south, for the ancient Chinese believed tombs were the dwellings of the deceased in the other world.

Since the dawn of history in China, man has been accustomed to considering the cosmic aspect of nature. The layout of cities and important buildings represented an ideal image, and it was only natural to choose a site facing towards the sun, the south or southeast, as these directions were considered to be the best orientation both practically and spiritually. Within ancient cities such as Xian, Beijing and Nanjing city roads run mostly north-south and east-west. In these cities the main entrance of buildings and courtyards usually faced south, forming complementary parts of the typical city plan of the period.

Feng Shui, although not a part of religious teachings, was almost universally considered and applied in all localities and with different building types. Guo Pu, a scholar of the Jin Dynasty said that:

> Qi (breath), if it rides the wind, would be scattered, but it would stop at water. Ancient people would concentrate Qi, so this was called wind and water, or Feng Shui.[1]

Another scholar, Wang Zi, of the Song Dynasty, wrote:

> . . . for a grave, a wide river in front, a high cliff behind, with enclosing hills to the right and left, would constitute a first class Feng Shui position. Houses and graves faced the south because the annual animation of the vegetable kingdom with the approach of summer comes from the quarter, the deadly influence of winter from the north.

In Feng Shui, it was believed that a site should be surrounded on three sides by higher land, like the crook of the elbow in a curved arm, to provide protection from inclement weather or an enemy. The lie of the land should be gently sloping and, if possible, there should be a river or valley nearby to allow surface water to drain easily. The concept of Feng Shui, the art of adapting a building so as to harmonize with the local environment and its climatic conditions, was based on the idea that people should live and work in harmonious surroundings, a principle of almost universal appeal.

CONSTRUCTION – WOOD

Classical Chinese architecture was constructed mainly of wood. When wood was abundant in the old days, the climate was mild and the land covered with verdant forest. Wood, as a building material, was natural and had many advantages: it is light in weight, easy to obtain, easy to work with, easy to transport, and most important, easy to standardize. When a wood structure was well protected from moisture and vermin, and occasionally painted with wood oil, it could last a long time. We can still find some well preserved wood buildings built more than a thousand years ago. Although durable when well maintained, there is one very great disadvantage. Wood buildings are easily destroyed by fire, and for this reason there are not many old wooden buildings extant in China today. In

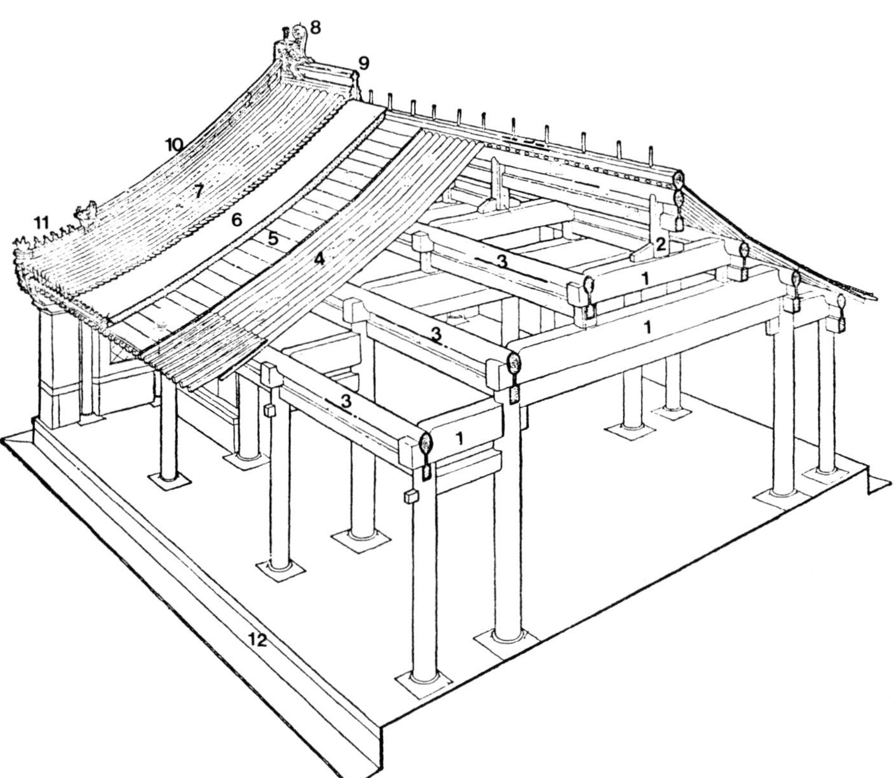

◁ Raised beam construction

Key
Raised beam construction:
1 Beam. 2 Strut. 3 Purlin. 4 Rafter. 5 Plank. 6 Lime scratch. 7 Pan and cover tiles. 8 Wen. 9 Main ridge. 10 Sloping ridge. 11 Decoration of mystic animal figures. 12 Taizi.

addition to wood, the Chinese used kilned brick and stone to construct large structures such as pagodas, tombs, bridges and walls. The reasons for such limited usage include: lack of good quality stone in quantity; the weight of stone made transportation difficult; and stone is not easily worked.

Obviously, the Chinese sensed the advantages of wood construction. The wooden frame system has some obvious advantages. The span of a wooden beam is wider and the plan freer and more flexible. In addition, wood is warm to the eye and touch, making it more acceptable to the occupants.

The wooden frame construction is of two particular types, both are of beam-and-column construction.

1. *Tai-liang*, or raised beam construction, was widely used in the Spring and Autumn Period and improved with time. Beams are placed on top of columns erected along the depth of a building. Shorter beams are placed on top of the struts on the lower and longer beams. Through the diminishing length of the beams, a triangular wooden framework is erected. Then purlins are placed on top of the struts on top of the beams to support the weight of rafters and the roofing. This is the basic structure of raised beam construction.

In classical Chinese architecture, a group of delicate fabricated cantilever components called 'duogong' are usually incorporated with the tai-liang system. These consist of a cluster of brackets used to support the roof on the inside of the building and the wide overhanging eave outside. According to the building regulations of the Tang Dynasty, duogong can only be used in palaces, temples and other important buildings.

Duogong is basically composed of two different types of structural elements. The first, a block placed on top of a column called 'duo', looks like a capital. Above it, and transverse to the direction of the depth of the building, are bow-shaped elements called 'gong' placed on smaller wooden blocks called 'sheng'. No nails or glue are used, as both duo and gong are assembled by mortice and tenon joints. This combination is called duogong. Originally used to support the beam ends and eave purlins, later duogong were used at the joints of frames to reduce the shearing stress and strengthen the joints. In general practise, the wider the overhang of the eave, the more layers of brackets are needed.

Until the East and Western Jin Dynasty and the Tang Dynasty, the form of duogong and its elements was gradually standardized. The duogong is really the most unique and special element in world architecture, both as a decorative and functional element. It seems hardly conceivable that this small bracket with delicate elements can support a gigantic roof structure with its wide overhang. It calls for men of high skill and rich imagination to produce anything like this, but the real merit lies in the nearly imperceptible modular system. The height of duogong was used as a ratio to determine the dimension of beam and tie beam after the Jin Dynasty. Until the Qing Dynasty, the width of the joint of the duo was standardized and used as the module. During the Song, the module was called 'cai'. In the *Ying Zao Fa Shi* there were eight cai grades, each further divided into 15 parts. The ratio of breadth to depth of a beam was standardized as 10:15. Before construction work started the standard procedure was to decide on the grade of cai. Then, according to the cai, the selected size and length of each member was established as were the height and curve of the roof respectively. A width of cai is called a duo kou (the mouth of duo), and it has 16 grades. The sizes of beam and height and diameter of a column are all decided by the module. This system simplified the procedures of architectural design, made estimation easier and facilitated 'prefabrication' on site. Many buildings could be built or assembled at the same time so as to speed up construction work.

The duogong, primarily a structural element, was of huge size both before and during the Tang Dynasty, but was progressively reduced in size during each of the dynasties following the Tang. It gradually ceased to function as a structural element, and finally became a purely decorative element in the Qing Dynasty.

2. *Chuan duo* is a construction method widely used in residential buildings and is still prevalent today in the countryside of southern China, in areas where timber is available. The advantage of this type of construction lies in the use of small size timber for beams and columns, thus making it more economical. Chuan duo type connects closely arranged columns lined along the depth of the building by small beams let into the columns to form a framework. First used during the Han Dynasty, it forms a light and delicate construction. The eave is supported by 'tiao' or 'cheng gong', a slanting bracket of various types. It is much simpler than the duogong, but very pleasing to the eye.

From the type of construction mentioned above, we can see that from the early days the Chinese separated

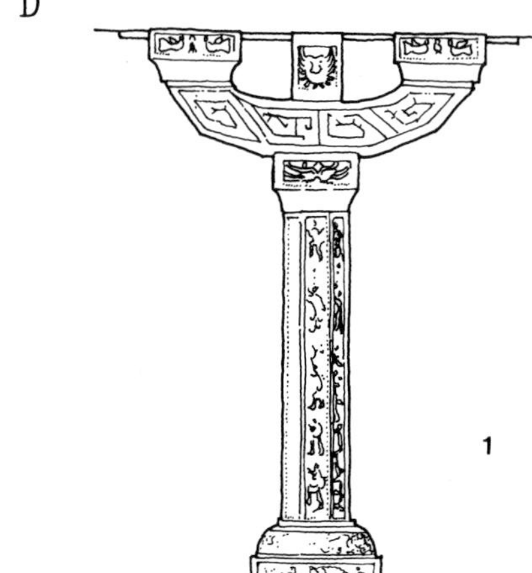

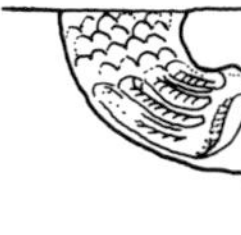

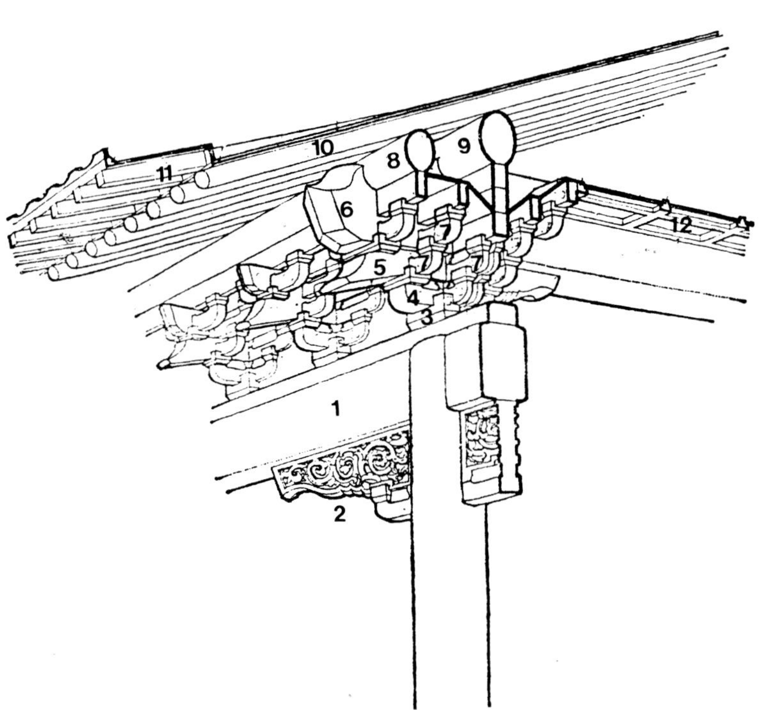

A

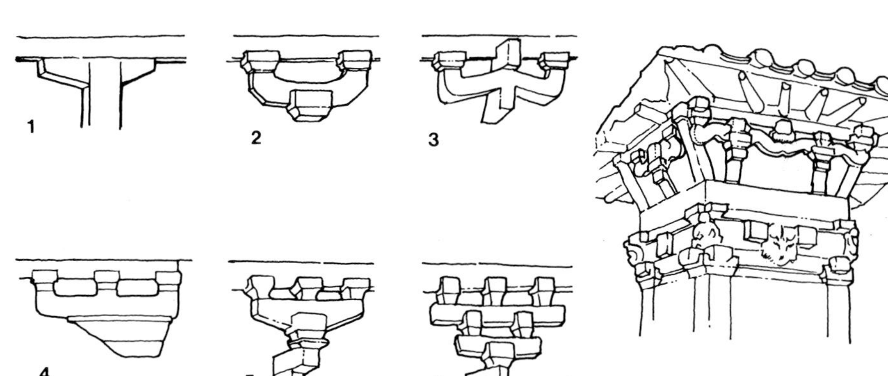

△ Duogong

Key
Duogong:
1 Beam. 2 Queti (bracket). 3 Duo.
4 Qiao. 5 Ang. 6 Head of a beam.
7 Gong and shen. 8 Eave beam.
9 Beam. 10 Rafter. 11 Cantilever rafter.
12 Ceiling.

Key
Different types of duogong:
A: 1 Gong (Guangzhou). 2 One Duo and two shengs (Sizhuan). 3 One Duo and three shengs (Sichuan). 4 One Duo and three shengs (Shangdong). 5 One Duo and three shengs (Henan).
6 Duogong (Hebei). 7 Corner duogong (Sichuan). B: 1 Renzi gong (Datong, Yungang). 2 Renzi gong and centre strut (Luoyang, Longmen). 3 Curved renzi gong (Gansu, Maiji Shan).
4 Renzi gong and one duo and three shengs (Dunhuang, Gansu).
C: Duogong and roof. D Duogong and column. 1 One duo and three shengs and octagonal column. 2 One duo and two shengs and octagonal column.
3 One duo and three shengs and square column. 4 One duo and three shengs and reed column. 5 One duo and round column. 6 Engaged twin square columns and duogong.

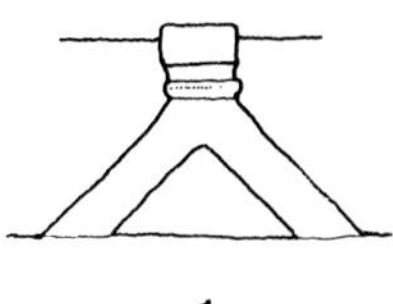

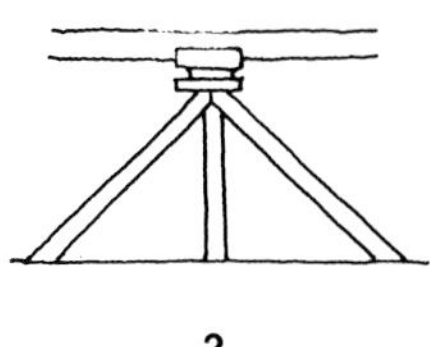

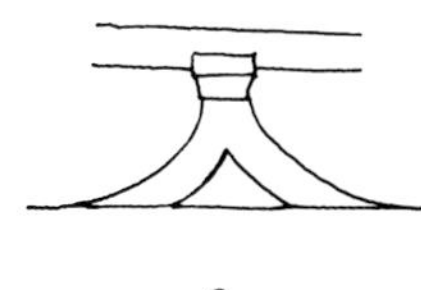

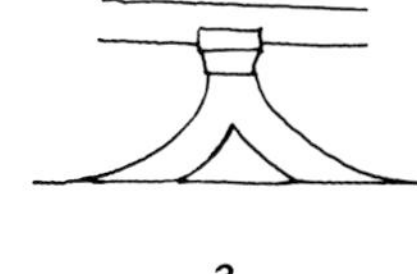

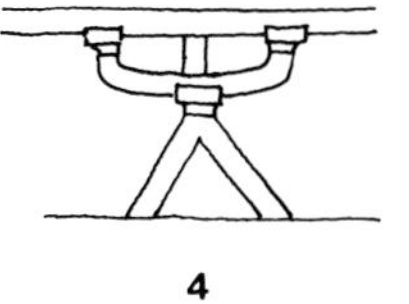

B

C

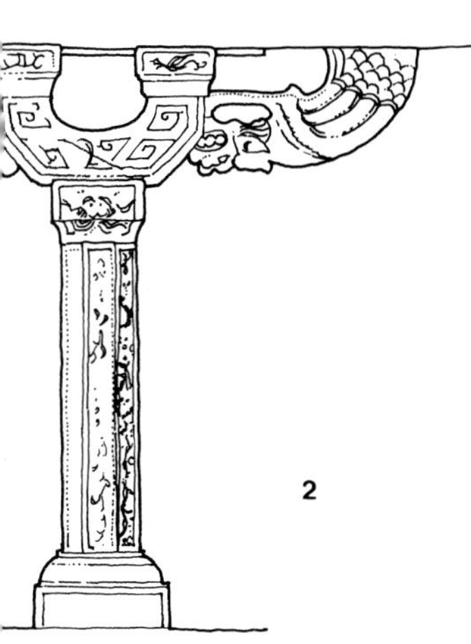

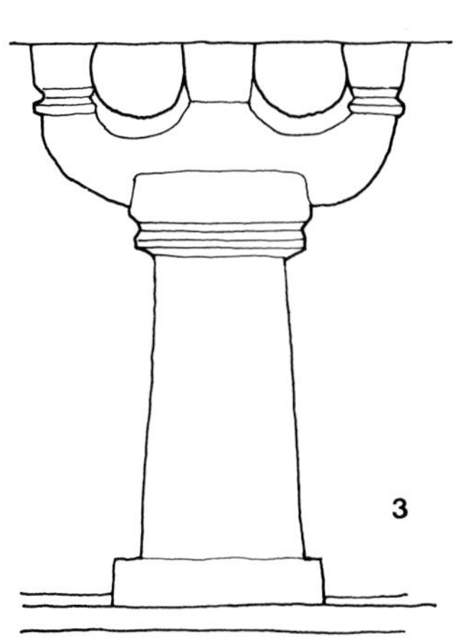

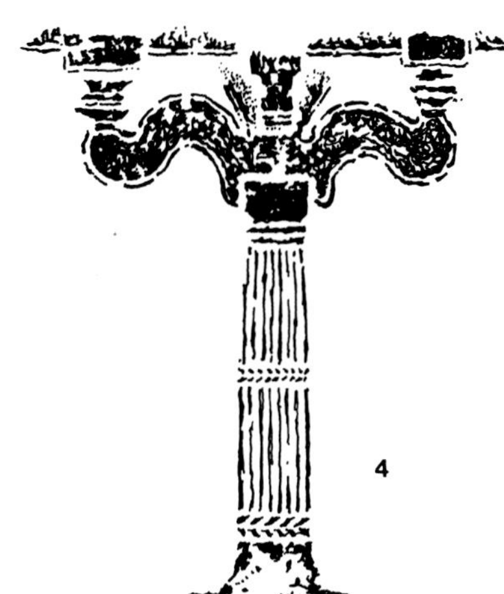

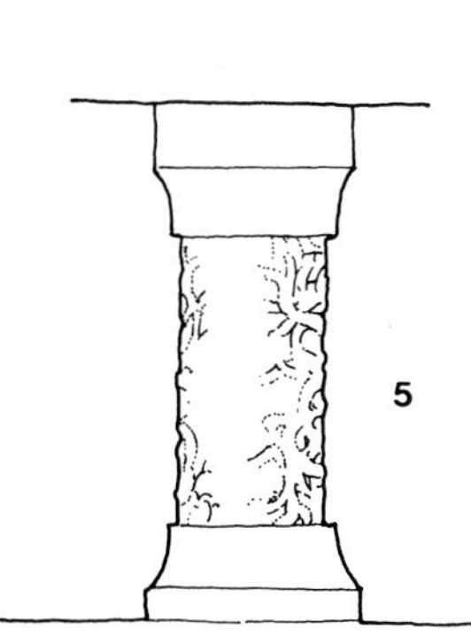

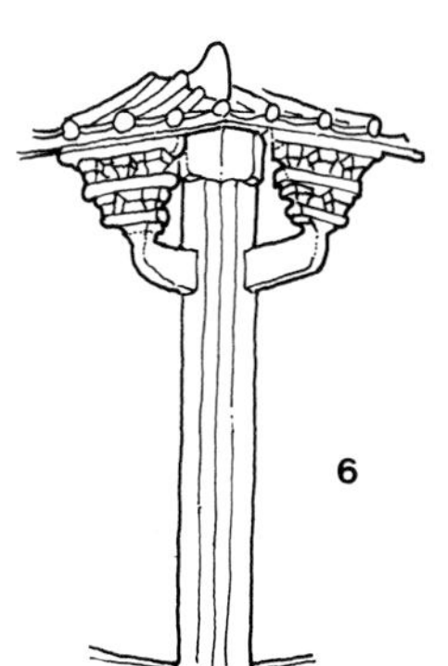

the supporting and the enclosing elements of a building. This enables them to open windows and doors of any sizes, on any walls and to any direction, and even to design a pavilion without walls. The thickness of the wall can be decided by the weather and not by its load-bearing strength. Interior partitions, usually formed from light-weight wood sash, can either make the interior a big space or separate it into small cells at will, thus ensuring great freedom and flexibility in planning.

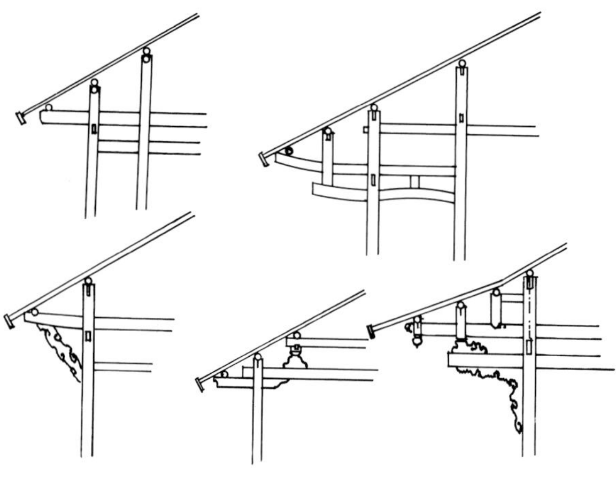

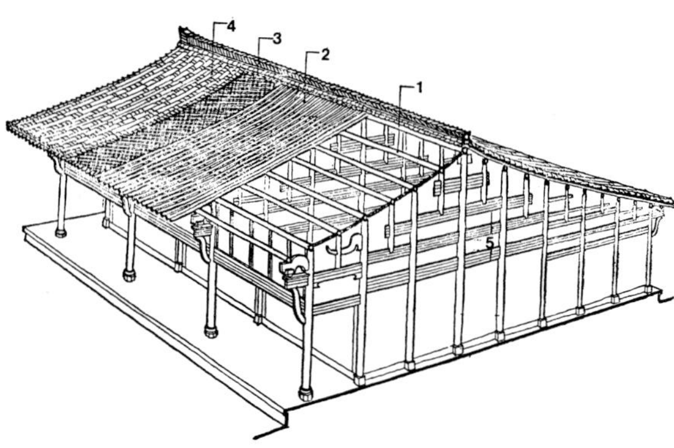

△ Chuan duo construction type

Key
1 Purlin. 2 Rafters. 3 Bamboo mat. 4 Pan tile. 5 Beams let into columns.

ARTICULATION OF CLASSICAL CHINESE ARCHITECTURE

We have dealt with the planning principles and construction features of classical Chinese architecture, which are indeed unique but difficult to differentiate. The easiest way to tell the difference between one architectural type and another, no matter whether the viewer is an expert or a layman, is by an analysis of the elevation and decoration of a building. The elevation of a classical Chinese building basically has three distinct portions: the podium underneath; the wall and column in between; and the big roof on top of the columns.

The last is the most prominent of all elements. Not only do public buildings like temples and palaces have big roofs, but residences have them too.

Roof

The first feature of a Chinese building that impresses a visitor is its beautiful and gigantic roof. Resting on top of columns the roof is a prominent feature, for the Chinese never had any intention of concealing it. Although richly decorated, the function of the roof is, naturally, to keep the rooms beneath it safe from rain, snow and weather. The wide spread of the roof and overhanging eave protect the building interior from hot sun in the summer while allowing sunshine to enter in winter when the angle of the sun is lower. It protects the wall and column from rain water. Important buildings have colourful glazed tiles or even gilded tiles as roofing materials, making for a brilliant display under the bright northern sun.

There were four basic roof types used in ancient China:

a. *Fudian roof* (hip roof). The Fudian roof was used only for important buildings according to a regulation which was instituted during the Yin Shang Dynasties, and continued in effect for more than 3,000 years until the Qing Dynasty. The roof form is essentially a very beautiful, dignified, larger hip roof, and is characterized by an inward curve and upturned corners. Since this type of roof had five ridges – that is a main ridge and four sloping ridges – it was called the 'hall of five ridges' during the Song Dynasty. All the ridges are decorated with sculptures. Important buildings, such as the main hall of a temple or the throne hall in a palace, not only use the hip roof, but also employ a double eave hip roof. During the Jin and Yuan Dynasties, the topmost portion of the hip roof was sometimes made flat, with the rest of the roof remaining the same as a hipped roof. This variation was called the Lu Ding roof.

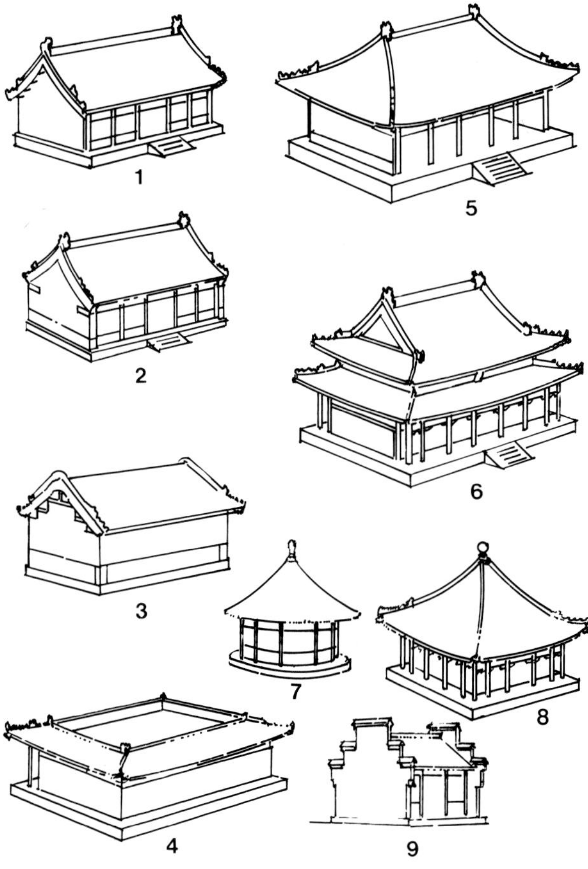

▷ Nine types of roof form

Key
1 Renzi Xuan shan. 2 Renzi yin shan. 3 Juan peng. 4 Lu ding. 5 Fudian. 6 Xie shan. 7 Conical cuan jian. 8 Pyramidal cuan jian. 9 Renzi with parapet wall.

b. *Xie Shan roof* (half-hip roof). The Xie Shan roof, mainly used in buildings of secondary importance, appears difficult to construct because of its complicated fabrication. In fact it consists of a hipped roof surrounded by a peristyle, and so is very simple. Instead of five ridges, the Xie Shan has nine ridges and so became known in the Song Dynasty as the 'hall of nine ridges'. At each end of the gable is an eave board and Xuan Yu (hanging fish) Ru yi (symbol of happiness) decoration. Until the Ming and Qing Dynasties, a decorated board was added to the gable end as decoration, making the gable end very pretty.

c. *Cuan Jian roof* (conical roof). A conical roof is unique in that it can be placed on top of almost any compact, symmetrical building plan of square, hexagonal, octagonal or circular form. Either pyramidal or conical, the top of the roof is sometimes flattened like a Lu Ding roof or may have a cross ridge. The latter has gables to all four directions and is most beautiful. Conical roofs are used in pavilions or tall buildings.

d. *Ren Zi roof* (gable roof). Ren in Chinese writing is '人', the form of a gable end, and so the gable roof was called 'Ren'. Easily constructed, this kind of roof is widely used in less important buildings such as the houses of the common people. There are two types: one in which the roof hangs over the end wall and another with the wall flush with the roof. Sometimes the wall reached around one metre above the roof, like a parapet wall. The parapet wall type has many variations, and the silhouette is very beautiful.

The gable roof or half-hipped roof has one main ridge at the junction of two sloping roofs. The main ridge also serves as the construction joint of the roof tiles. One special kind of gable roof is called the Juan Peng (rolling top), where the ridge is replaced by a curve. The construction of this kind of roof is made possible by the insertion of two struts on top of the top beam of the wooden frame, thus supporting two ridge purlins instead of one ridge purlin. The top of the roof can be rounded up and shaped into the form of a smooth curve. The wooden frame with the struts and purlins could be placed at any position so as to produce either a straight roof line or a slightly curved roof line. The Chinese have used the variegated roof forms for many years not only to produce an interesting silhouette, but also to give meaning to architecture.

Column

The second important feature of Chinese architecture is the column. As mentioned above, the function of the wall is to shield the structural elements of the building: from elevations, we can see that columns are also the components which divide the facade to give rhythmic effect to the building. On a long building, whether a great hall or a simple house, there is a verandah or porch in front or it is surrounded by a verandah. In contrast to the gigantic roof, the slender columns under it seem too delicate to support the heavy roof above. The wider the overhang, the larger will be the shadow cast on the wall; because of this illusion, the roof looks like a big canopy hovering above the podium and earth below.

The Chinese have never intended to cover up or hide structural elements. The intention has been to achieve the unity of structure and art by exposing and decorating structural elements. Sometimes a screen wall would only reach a foot or so below the eave, so that the upper part of a column and beams are exposed and visible. In the southern part of China where the weather is warmer and the walls thinner, all columns and beams are exposed, or separated, or half embedded in the wall, making the framework an integral part of the composition.

There are several variations in columns. Another characteristic of column arrangement, called Zhe Jiao, is the inclination of columns at either end to the centre. From the structural point of view, this inward slanting can prevent the column from leaning outward. In some buildings the columns have different heights, with the lowest ones in the middle. The columns gradually increase in height towards each end of the wall, naturally forming the main roof ridge and the eave below in concave curves. Complete harmony between structural means and aesthetic aims is achieved in this way. We can compare this arrangement with the optical correction of Greek architecture, which has the same effect, but we cannot find any written record that shows the Chinese were aware of the Greeks.

Employment of colour is another feature of Chinese architecture. From very ancient times, the pillars for palaces and temples were painted vermilion or red, and those of houses a chestnut colour. The walls of structures were also painted – those of palaces were red, the temples yellow, and black and white for houses. The most spectacular feature was the beam, as beautiful designs were painted on and even applied with gold foil to the beam. The chrome yellow glazed tile roof, the colourful beams and red columns, and the window and door sash make the elevation a magnificent colour composition. Chinese architecture is really an architecture of colour.

Taizi (Podium)

Important buildings in China generally sit on a wide podium. The original purpose of the podium was to prevent moisture penetration of the column foot and wall. Gradually, the podium became an indispensable symbolic element of building.

The outline of the podium was simple and unadorned in the beginning. The *Zhou Ritual* specifies the height of a podium as three chi (equivalent to one metre), an example being at the palace at Anyang, the Yin Shang capital city. During the period of the Six Dynasties, which accompanied the introduction of Buddhism into China, the Zumizuo form, rich in ornamentation, came to China.

Balustrades, used to prevent occupants from falling from the high platform, also imparted a decorative effect to the buildings. The oldest balustrades were made of wood, but later marble was used. The great halls of the Ming and Qing Dynasties have a three-tiered podium and balustrades, a response to the huge roof above. The roof, columns and podium are not individual parts but rather function as elements of a system, each part being subordinate to the superior idea of the system.

CITY PLANNING PRINCIPLES

When production was raised to a certain level, cities were born for the sake of controlling production. In China, probably the first city in history emerged in the Xia Dynasty, and larger cities were built in the later Shang and Zhou Dynasties. Historical records prove that during the Spring and Autumn Period planners focused the city proper – consisting of roads and houses – on the palace, and the city had regularly planned streets. Recent excavations at Hou Ma and Han Dan, both ancient capital cities in the northern part of China, have discovered the remains of rammed earth podiums and evidence of regularly planned streets and building blocks. Since the vassals were fighting with each other, city walls and moats around them were necessary for defence. In written Chinese, the word for city is 'Cheng', which also means city wall. The same word indicates that a city has a wall around it and was enclosed. A gate or several gates opened to each direction from the city, leading to the countryside and connecting the city thoroughfares. The layout of the streets was regular and in a grid pattern, with the palace or office at the centre. Important streets ran in a north-south direction.

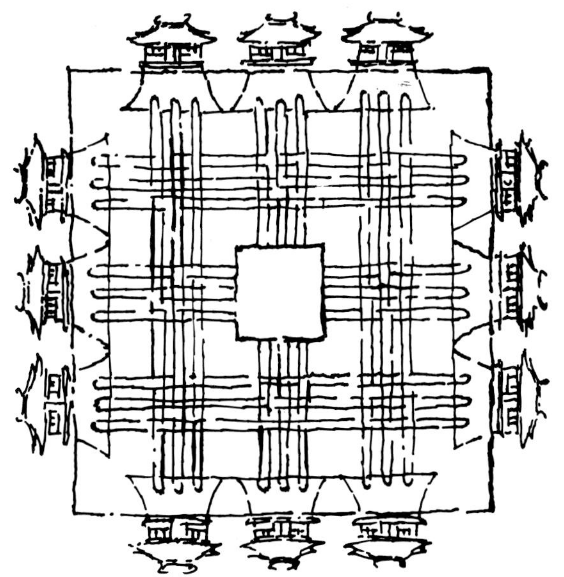

The book *Kao Gong Ji*, written during the Spring and Autumn Period, records the planning principles of the Zhou Dynasty capital city, clearly based upon Confucian doctrines. The primary thesis of the book was to place the palace or government building at the centre of the city, symbolizing the centralized power of the emperor and authority of the dynasty. According to *Kao Gong Ji*:

> The master builders who laid out a capital, made it a square and nine li (about three miles) on a side, each side having three gateways. Within the capital city there were nine lengthwise and nine crosswise avenues (or this clause can be interpreted as three lengthwise and three crosswise avenues, each avenue being composed of three parallel roads),with the width of each avenue nine chariot tracks or axle widths. On the left (east) was located the Ancestral Temple, on the right, the Altar of Earth. The court and palace were placed in the front (south), and to the rear, the market place (north). The market was around five hundred chi square.[3]

It was the Chinese custom to place important things, or an important guest, to the east. Thus the Ancestral Temple was placed at the east, for it was considered more important than the Altar of Earth.

Curiously enough, the city built entirely according to the *Kao Gong Ji* was not an ethnic Han city, but the Mongolian city of Cambulac (Beijing). Inside the city were 50 housing blocks. The plan of Ming Dynasty Beijing was to cast five li to the north and extending one li to the south, producing the form of today's Beijing. China also had irregular city plans, as indicated

◁ Wang Cheng, a model capital city plan

by the sites. Nanjing's plan is an example, although its palace ensemble was axial and symmetrical.

MEANING IN CLASSICAL CHINESE ARCHITECTURE

From the beginning of civilization, man has continually sought to reform and improve his environment according to the needs of basic physical existence. As culture was raised to higher levels, man was no longer satisfied with simple physical existence. Hence symbols, as employed in language, art and music, were used to express the deeper meanings of daily life. With the Chinese, art is a kind of symbolism. Architecture's specific symbolic language was developed to represent the character, spirit, feelings and ideas of both the builder and beholder.

Architectural symbolism creates a dialogue between man and architecture. Through this dialogue man experiences, understands and uses architecture. Symbolism was an intrinsic part of ancient Chinese culture. Through the perception of symbolic meanings in architecture, man began to understand and participate in deeper cultural activities. Some buildings have obvious semiotics to achieve this end, making them easily understood, while others are more complex, requiring a deeper comprehension of Chinese cultural traditions in order to be fully experienced.

Classical Chinese architecture in essence symbolized many levels of meaning: axial and symmetrical planning expressed ethics and ritual; orientation and Feng Shui depicted deeper religious meaning; the form of an individual structure characterized the Chinese spirit; while private garden planning expressed a philosophical content. In short, the Chinese world view was embodied in the symbolism of both architecture and site planning. Chinese symbolism,

> is not imitation, . . . not an adjunct to existence, a reduplication of the actuality, but a hint, an adumbration of what lies in the artist's mind.[4]

If we scrutinize these principles fully we can clearly perceive the essence of classical Chinese architecture and planning, not only the necessities of structural and existential requirements, but also – through sociology, art and philosophy – the agents which shaped the form and character of Chinese buildings.

The lasting culture of any nation is not formed in a short period. Drawing from the past creates the new, developing history and makes existence more meaningful. The study of cultural symbolism clarifies this process of growth and development.

Philosophy

The ancient Chinese also had a primitive concept of religion, unlike the religions of other ancient civilized countries. They worshipped all that could lessen their troubles and provide spiritual compensation for life's difficulties. A form of animism prevailed: hills, trees, rocks, rivers, sun, moon and wind all had spirits or were looked upon as gods. The sun and sky, responsible for growth, production and good health, were especially worshipped. Gratitude was also expressed to the spirits of departed ancestors, without whom successive generations could not exist. The emperor, self-proclaimed 'Son of Heaven', not only lorded over the people, but his spirit – which represented the heaven that produced the bumper harvest – was highly worshipped.

From the above it can be understood that the people of ancient China worshipped both man and nature. The elements of nature, manifestations of the infinite order of the universe, were viewed as the spirits which assured life's necessary cycles. Thanks was given to the spirits of departed ancestors, while the emperor was worshipped in the belief that he could pray to the gods on the people's behalf.

The scholars of ancient China, like the priests of India, Persia, Egypt or Babylon, were privileged individuals and functioned as a constituent part of the ruling class. As scholars assisted the emperors in praying to heaven, temples and altars of worship were an integral part of the palace. In all capital cities, there were ancestral halls as well as altars devoted to both heaven and earth.

City

The orthodox thought of the master scholar Confucius had a major impact upon the people and rulers of ancient China. The documents and regulations of the Zhou Dynasty were well preserved in Lu, the place where Confucius was born, enabling him to learn from, and adhere to their principles and become a major assistant to the emperor. According to the *Zhou Ritual*, based upon Confucian philosophy, there were specific planning arrangements of capital cities, palaces, government buildings and mansions. We have already mentioned that the majority of cities in China, except those limited by natural topographic features and rivers, were sited to the south, as dictated by proto-science, the art of Feng Shui and the principles set forth in the *Kao Gong Ji*. In Feng Shui, the cardinal points of the compass were represented symbolically: north was the Black Tortoise; south, the Fire Bird; east, the Green Dragon; and west, the White Tiger. Undoubtedly, the colour and character of animals were used to represent good or evil orientations. The Fire Bird or Scarlet Bird were mild creatures and were used to symbolize sun and warm climate, bringing life and animation to all beings. The Green Dragon represented rain water, indispensable to the growth of life. The black and white of the Tortoise and Tiger were evil and unlucky colours, symbolizing misery and invasion by enemies. Since most of the enemies of ancient China came from the north, as did the chilly winds which destroyed crops and impaired health, it was natural that the main city gate opened to the south.

The capital city, according to the *Kao Gong Ji*, ideally was square in plan with the palace at the centre. There were three gateways in each cardinal direction with the main gateway facing due south along the primary axis of the city and palace. The streets ran north, east, south and west creating square grid residential blocks symbolizing the 'round sky and square earth' concept. Thus, the land was organized into a large block with the palace at the centre and the small squares of the city housing blocks surrounding it, all contained by the large square, earth. The system expressed order, subordination and obedience, and a symbolism derived from the square also had many practical applications in building.

Starting from the Scarlet Bird Gateway, the city's axis ran through the centrally-located palace or government buildings, terminating at the north or Black Tortoise Gateway. This carefully planned axis symbolized the greater axis from heaven to earth, which connected the supernatural god to the human emperors, who were the channel of authority. This axis not only expressed dignity, but also indicated that the emperor, as heaven's representative, was to be obeyed. High massive walls, the wide, deep moat around the city and palace, and the high tower above the wall served to symbolize security and protection, while imparting the feeling that the emperor was not approachable by the common people.

To the surprise of Westerners and unlike Western cities, there was no public square in the Chinese city as the government or emperor discouraged public gatherings. The only natural place for gatherings was within the halls of large houses or in the courtyards between the halls. Although it was convenient for each family to use their own home for weddings, birthdays, funerals, festivals and other celebrations, the lack of public gathering areas indicated that in the autocratic system of ancient China there was no place (or reason) for individuals to express their political opinions.

Houses

Symbolism not only existed in city planning, but its presence was felt in every cell and the overall texture of the city. The house, the basic unit of the city, represented a microcosm of Chinese private life, which was based upon Confucian ideas of hierarchy of generations and code of ethics. Like the city plan, most

Chinese houses had a central axis with the main halls facing south. The entire house was enclosed by high, solid walls with only one or two doors leading to the streets outside. The high wall which enclosed the house served as protection against fire and theft, and also gave the occupants an immediate feeling of privacy and seclusion to make the house the domain of one family. As one walked along a residential street, only the high, brick walls and doorways were visible. Usually the only decoration visible on the house exterior was at the doorway. The most conspicuous markings of a doorway were the tablet and couplets, which gave identity to the house. The tablet, serving the same purpose as a coat of arms, was hung on a beam above the doorway to denote the importance or status of the house, such as the mansion of a scholar of merit like Zhuan Yuan Di. Couplets, found on the pillars at either side of the doorway in a larger house or painted on the door panels of a smaller house, usually expressed the religious belief or philosophy of the family. Mottoes were also used as a remembrance or to simply express the wishes of the people who lived in the house, though some of them were pretentious and only for show.

The major principles which influenced the house plan were reflected in the Confucian ethics code of patriarchal family structure, and harmony among the members of the family. In China's feudalistic society, the head of the family was invariably the male, and within the hierarchy of the family, it was the older generation which ruled. According to filial piety, also based on Confucian doctrine, children and descendants were obedient to the oldest generation of the family. The house was planned according to the same principle. The hall for the oldest generation was situated at the north of a courtyard farthest from the entrance to the south, while the quarters of the children faced east or west in the side halls. The first hall of a house was used as a reception and ceremonial hall where, on special occasions, the tablets of the ancestors were centrally displayed.

The general plan of a house reflected ancestral worship and authority, symbolizing the power elders had over the younger generations. But a house was different from a palace or a city. The scale of the halls and courtyard within the complex was comparatively much smaller, subtler and of human proportions, making them more intimate and humane.

Gardens

Parks or public gardens never developed in ancient China, and thus all gardens were private or attached to an institution, such as a temple, or adjacent to government buildings. The principle of axial symmetry was not applied to garden planning. Free and organic spatial manipulations were introduced to the general garden plan while individual buildings were usually symmetrical in form. This pluralistic approach was based on the philosophies of Daoism and the Chan Sect. The chief features reflected a love of, and integration with nature, with the intention of creating a poetic, picturesque, irrational setting. They were very unlike Mannerism or Baroque gardens, which were coordinated by an axis, expressing authority, extending from the main building to infinity. Chinese gardens were a place for family gatherings, an environment designed for relaxation and contemplation without the presence of authority, axis or rigid geometrical planning. Upon leaving the rigid ceremony of society and entering the naturalistic realm of a garden, a man could wander carelessly and unrestrained, without the bonds of ritual, in a dream-like escape from reality. Here, the arrangement of plants, flowers and rock forms were all abstracted from nature, requiring imagination to associate the garden with the naturalistic landscape.

Each garden reflected the ideology of both the owner and the designer or painter. In the halls, an owner designed formally to indicate dignity and prestige. However, in a garden he expressed his individuality. Few people enjoyed living in the restrained atmosphere of the tall and dignified halls prepared for the emperors and empresses. History records that royalty chose, instead, to retreat to the more simple environments of the Summer Resort at Chengde, the Summer Palace in Beijing or to one of the side halls in the Purple Forbidden City. This desire to retreat from formality, into the abstract world of the garden, was manifested by the ancient Chinese in the planning of the houses in which they lived and the gardens which they enjoyed.

In gardens, plant forms were not only selected for foliage, fruit, blossom or scent, but also for symbolic significance. Bamboo was an emblem of longevity, durability and unbending character which flourished throughout the winter, symbolizing the upright character and moral standards of a gentleman. Pine, also a token of longevity because it is an evergreen, symbolized lasting friendships which do not wither in adversity. The plum tree, whose flowers appear on leafless branches, was also regarded as a symbol of longevity. The many-seeded pomegranate symbolized the desire for many offspring. Peony Mou-tan, because of its large, rich flowers, was regarded as a sign of spring as well as an omen of good fortune. Narcissus blossoms on New Year's day foretold good fortune, numerous offspring, longevity and friendship. These blessings, symbolized in the garden by these plants, were what the ancient Chinese cherished most dearly in the world.

Buildings

It may be assumed that social conditions are the primary factors which create and change architectural form. Obviously, the development of form does not take place independently of building materials, construction techniques, climate and geography. However, identical materials, techniques and climates do not always necessarily produce similar architectural styles. Social, political, aesthetic and religious concepts more often dictate the growth of form and the development of style. The unchanging religious and philosophical beliefs, stagnant economies and political systems of ancient China, brought few changes in building forms. In China, wood frame construction has been used since ancient times with only very minor stylistic changes. In the West, the building material was primarily stone. However, as a result of religious and political fluctuations, architecture exhibited many great changes.

Since the emergence of its earliest buildings, the primary characteristics of Chinese architecture have been a large roof above slender wooden columns and beams resting upon a podium. Each element had specific structural functions while contributing special symbolic meanings to the whole. The roof form, including a portion of the ridge of both large and small structures, looked like a gentle, sweeping cantenary curve, much like a slightly sagging rope. Historic documents indicate that this form was developed to shed water away from the building foundations while permitting a maximum amount of light to enter the building. As ancient buildings were constructed upon platforms of sun dried brick or rammed earth, the concern for shedding water away from the structure can be easily understood. However, the curve of the roof and ridge cannot be justified by structural and practical requirements alone, since a straight slope would produce the same results. The choice seems to have been both aesthetic and symbolic. A curve would resemble the great tent of a nomad and be graceful to look at. Japanese carpenters determined a straight line with a tightened string, which naturally forms a graceful curve, a technique they may have inherited from the Chinese. The roof may also have represented heaven; the Yang, the light and upper principle; the platform symbolizes the earth, the dark and lower principle. Since the Chinese worshipped heaven, perhaps they employed the large, sweeping roof as a sign of respect for the 'Son of Heaven', and as a link between heaven and earth while, at the same time, expressing aspirations to enter an afterlife.

During the feudalistic period roof forms, as well as the type and colour of roof tiles, were strictly governed by codes indicating use and status. The most important buildings, such as ancestral and throne halls, used a hip roof form. Secondary structures had a half-hip roof, while smaller halls and private residences usually had a gable or an overhang gable roof. The colour and type of roof tile indicated the relative importance of the structure. In ancient China colours symbolized the five directions: green represented east; red, the south; white, the west; black was north; and yellow symbolized the centre, considered a direction in ancient Chinese cosmology. For almost 2000 years, during the Han and until the Qing Dynasty, 'fire represented the emperors, therefore yellow and red were the colours of the imperial family'.[5] The central location of the palace, together with the symbolism of fire, dictated the use of yellow roof tiles and red columns throughout an imperial palace.

Yellow was used long before the Han Dynasty as a colour of dignity. The *Zhou Ritual* records that 'ancient people wore yellow clothes and hats during sacrificial ceremonies, while the emperors used yellow silk for the interiors of their carriages'.[6] Yellow roof tiles and clothing gradually became reserved for imperial use. The imperial palace of the Ming and Qing Dynasties, covered with yellow glazed tile, must have appeared spectacular under a bright sun and blue sky in contrast to the greyish roofs of the common people's houses.

The height and number of tiers of the podiums also became a means of differentiating the character and significance of a structure. Important buildings, such as ancestral halls, praying halls and throne halls (the halls used most by emperors), had more than one, and as many as three tiers to the podium. In the Purple Forbidden City in Beijing, all platforms and balustrades were carved of white marble. One unique example in this palace complex, the three Great Halls, was erected on a single large marble podium.

Having accompanied Buddhism when it was introduced into China, the Zumizuo form, rich in ornamentation, came into use. According to Buddhism, a specific Himalayan mountain was known as Zumi Mountain, the seat of the Buddha. Although the use of the Zumizuo form for the base of a palace eventually lost its original religious significance, it continued to lend magnificence and rich symbolic meaning to the building above it. The commonly used Zumizuo form had the central portion setback from the front, a cyma-reversa moulding connecting with the base. Often, as a symbol of Buddhism, they were decorated with lotus petal designs. It is thought that this style of podium was first introduced from Greece to Gandhara, and then to India. From India, the form travelled to China through the Buddhist pilgrim monks. The posts, which projected above the handrail of the balustrade, exhibited capitals carved with symbolic dragon, phoenix and cloud designs. Such designs were restricted, by code, for use only in imperial buildings. Structures belonging to common people could only have a one-tier podium and geometrical patterns for the capital decoration.

To the common man, the symbolism of the planning and siting of a building was not easily perceived or understood in its entirety. However, architectural details, developed from the desire of the immediate meaning to the structure and to convey this meaning to the beholder, were usually placed close to the human eye and were easy to read. Classical Chinese architecture generally used plant, animal and geometric designs as well as colour to indicate the intended use of a building. Although each decoration had a meaning of its own, the decorations and details were interdependent rather than independent. The use of decoration on the roof, beams, columns and railings belonged to a well-developed system of symbolic vocabulary.

The decorations on the roof of a classical Chinese structure were symbolic construction details. In classical Chinese architecture, the construction details and structural elements were boldly exposed and decorated rather than concealed. The duogong was not only decorative, but imparted special symbolic meaning to the building. In the old days, only imperial buildings were permitted to use duogong, and the hipped-roof structures did so unanimously.

The decorative elements on the roof of important buildings differed from those used on the more common structures. On important buildings, the roof tiles, end tiles, ridges, ridge-ends and even the animals on the ridge were originally structural elements.

With time, decorations were developed to impart symbolic meaning. For example, wen, the end decoration of the main ridge, usually had some relation to water and water-borne plants or animals. The earliest wen were fish-shaped and named Chi Wen. Because the majority of classical Chinese structures were constructed of wood and were highly inflammable, any symbolism connected with water indicated a desire to extinguish flames. Such symbolism was amplified by legend. According to *Shou Wen*, 'a dragon ascends to the sky in spring, hides under the sea in the fall, representing rain and dew,'[7] in order to give rain in the spring for planting. The animal figures often found perched in single file on the roof's sloping ridge are led by Prince Min, a notorious state of Qi tyrant, who rides a hen. Legend relates that Prince Min, as a punishment for his crime, was strung up to the end of a ridge and left hanging there, without food and water, until he died. The symbolic use of Prince Min may have been intended to remind emperors not to act accordingly. The sculptural figures were always odd in number, an indication of masculinity. The more important buildings had a greater number of sculptures. The Taihe Dian in the Forbidden City, for example, had eleven of them.

Dragon and phoenix designs were most often used on the end roof tiles of imperial buildings. However, sometimes a coin motif was used symbolically to bring monetary fortune to the dynasty. The common people, forbidden the use of these imperial designs, utilized more humane and easily understood motifs. One such decoration, widely used for ridge ends, was the 'dove' design. The dove, in China, always symbolized faithfulness, peace, filial piety, numerous offspring and family happiness. Geometrical designs, such as the Ru-yi Head represented happiness. The 'Hui Wen' in the form of a meander, resembling a cloud design, may have symbolized the downpour that brought rain water for a bumper harvest. This symbolic vocabulary gave meaning and the blessings of comfort and happiness to the people.

In China, harmony in the family, based on the Confucian philosophy of family piety, was considered the primary source of happiness of one's life. The elders were respected, and the young were loved, producing a harmony in which happiness and prosperity prevailed. The symbolism inherent in classical Chinese architecture expressed and reinforced this philosophy.

We cannot say that roof top designs related to water were used exclusively. Sometimes brilliant designs representing fire were also used as decoration on the finial of a pyramidal, circular, hexagonal or octagonal roof. The finial was made in the form of an urn, sometimes made of metal, to cover the wooden members connecting all the slanting beams. During the Han and Tang Dynasties gilded bronze urns and sculptures were also used. Historical records indicate that the finial top of the Yongning Temple Pagoda of North Wei was entirely gilded. Empress Wuzetian of the Tang Dynasty constructed a hall with the roof consisting of a gilded top in the form of a ball surrounded by flames, which 'sparkled with a dazzling golden light equal to that of the moon and the stars'. However, such an ornate decoration of a building was rare.

The imperial buildings and temples of classical China formed an architecture of colour. The bright red columns and shining yellow glazed tiles of the Purple Forbidden City provided an impressive site for visitors. During the Tang and Song Dynasties, columns, beams and other wood elements were painted red with little or no decoration on the beams. After the Song Dynasty, decorated beams were used extensively.

Two styles of beam decoration, forbidden for common use, were used only on imperial buildings. One

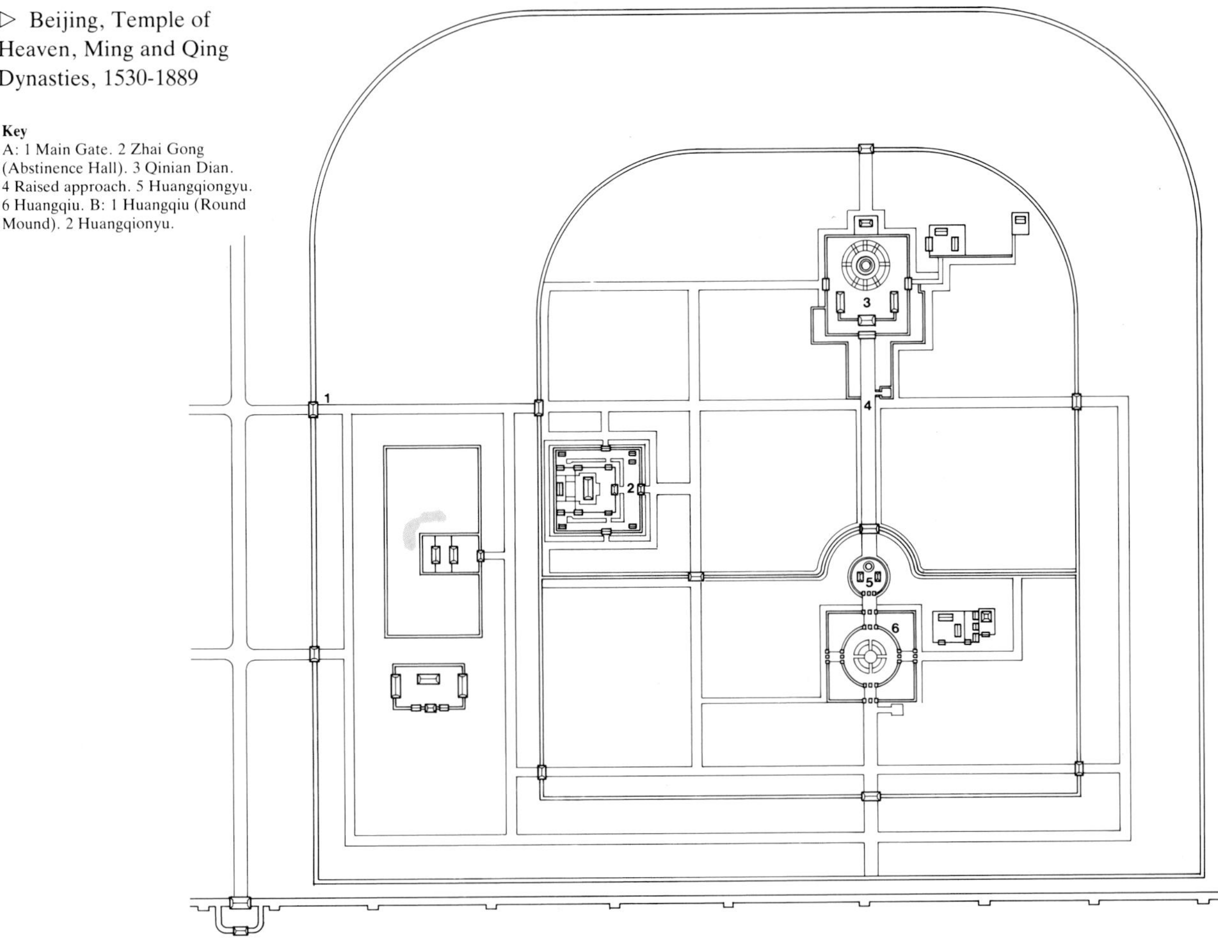

▷ Beijing, Temple of Heaven, Ming and Qing Dynasties, 1530-1889

Key
A: 1 Main Gate. 2 Zhai Gong (Abstinence Hall). 3 Qinian Dian. 4 Raised approach. 5 Huangqiongyu. 6 Huangqiu. B: 1 Huangqiu (Round Mound). 2 Huangqionyu.

was a dragon design, the He Xi painting, the other was the Xuan Zi painting. Elaborate and grandiose coffered ceilings, indicating importance and adding character, were also used for imperial structures. The design was either a dragon or dragon-and-phoenix motif, with the dragon representing the emperor and the phoenix the empress.

Since the Zhou Dynasty, an officer called the Si Kong has been appointed to enforce planning principles and building regulations. Such control of building practises facilitated construction. Officers regulated the construction of palaces, temples, royal tombs, cities, fortresses – even hydraulic irrigation works. Regulations controlling hierarchy of importance were particularly crucial, 'a rule not to be overridden by the common people.'

Tian Tan (Temple of Heaven): an example of symbolism

We could possibly say that the building complex which best exemplifies the symbolic nature of classical Chinese architecture is the Tian Tan in Beijing, where the emperors of the Ming and Qing Dynasties made sacrifices and prayed to heaven annually. From the general plan to the specific details of each structure of the Temple of Heaven, the conscious desire to use architecture to express the meaning of the building and build a dialogue between man and heaven is visible. Some of the symbols are easily interpreted, while others, being more obscure and complex, require careful study and observation. For these reasons it is an excellent example for illustrating the classical Chinese architectural vocabulary.

The primary use of the Tian Tan was the worship of heaven:

> In ancient times, Tian, or Heaven, was considered the dominant element, dispensing happiness or misfortune. Floods and drought were the will of the gods; Heaven decreed whether each year's carefully nurtured crops would thrive or fail, whether there would be fears of famine throughout the land. The emperor was regarded as 'Tian Zi' or the Son of Heaven. As such, he interceded with the gods at the Temple of Heaven on behalf of the people, guided by a strict, unvarying ritual, which was centuries old.[8]

The general layout of the Tian Tan was based on this concept of rigid ritual devoted to the uncontrollable process of nature.

Planning

According to the ancient *Zhou Ritual*, the Tian Tan should be sited at the southern part of a capital city. In this case, it is located at the southern part of Beijing, east of the city's main axis. The shape of the temple's site plan is square at the south and round at the north, expressing the ancient 'sky round and earth square' concept. There are two important building groups in the Temple of Heaven. The one at the south is called Huangqiu (the Altar of Heaven or Round Mount), while the other, at the north, is the Qinian Dian (the Hall of Prayer for a Good Harvest). Both are connected by a north-south axis approximately 400 metres long. Each year, in ancient times, one day before the Winter Solstice, the emperor stayed in the temple's Abstinence Hall, where he bathed and fasted. Early the following morning he walked to the Huangqiu through a grove of pine trees, the symbol of a bumper harvest because of its evergreen colour, to pray.

Huangqiu

Huangqiu, a round terrace enclosed by two courses of square courtyards with low parapet walls and higher peifangs (ceremonial arches), one inside the other, also symbolized the 'sky round and earth square' concept. The Huangqiu terrace consists of three concentric circular tiers, each with a balustrade of white mar-

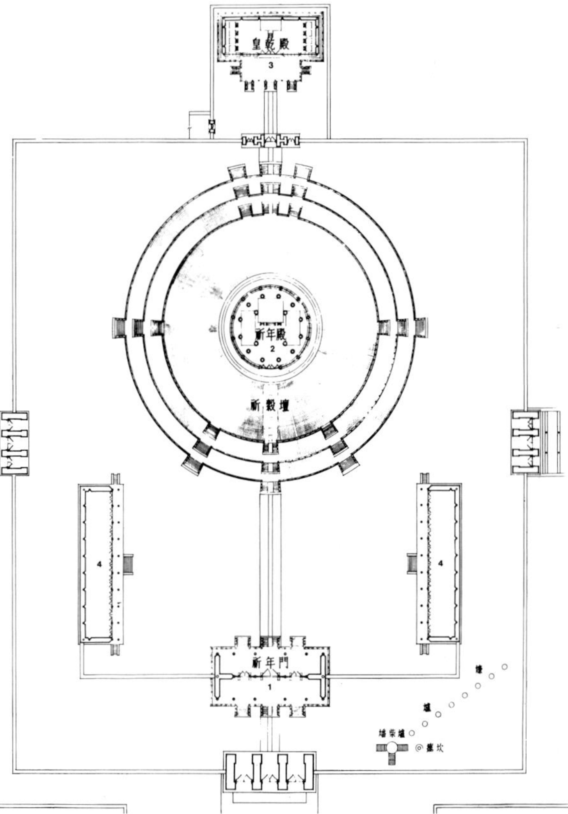

▽ Beijing, Temple of Heaven, Qinian Dian, 1889

Key
1 Qinian Men. 2 Qinian Dian. 3 Huangqian Dian. 4 Side hall.

◁ Beijing, Temple of Heaven, Qinian Dian, 1889

▽ Beijing, Temple of Heaven, Huangqiu, 1530

ble. The three tiers have diameters of 21 zhan (each zhan equivalent to approximately 11 feet), and triple staircases are used to ascend to the upper terrace.

Since the time of Spring and Autumn, the Chinese have used odd numbers as the Yang (male) symbol, representing the sun. Nine, which is the largest and most extreme of the one-digit numbers, represented the highest or greatest Yang. Here, at Huangqiu, each of the three terraces is composed of nine concentric courses of marble pavement. The balustrade posts are also multiples of nine. On the first tier there are 180 posts, the second tier has 108 posts, and the third consists of 72, totalling 360, corresponding to the 360 degrees of a geometrical circle of heaven.

Qinian Dian

Like the Huangqiu, the Qinian Dian stands inside a square courtyard and on top of a round white marble platform of three tiers. The hall has a complementary triple roof of blue glazed tiles capped with a golden finial. The blue, conical roof, supported by two concentric rings of 12 pillars each and four large centrally-located columns, symbolized the round, blue sky.

The columns are related to astronomy. The outer columns symbolized the 12 months of the year, and the inner ring, the 12 hours of the day (the ancient Chinese divided the day into 12 units of time instead of 24) while the four larger columns represented the four seasons of the year. When these symbols are understood, the Chinese desire to associate man with heaven and the greater natural rhythms of the universe can be easily discerned.

The coffered ceiling is supported by a series of blue and green brackets and beams. In the centre is a dragon and phoenix design. The inner ring of 12 columns is painted with a cloud design, representing the Tianzi

▽ Beijing, Temple of Heaven, Huangqiu, 1530

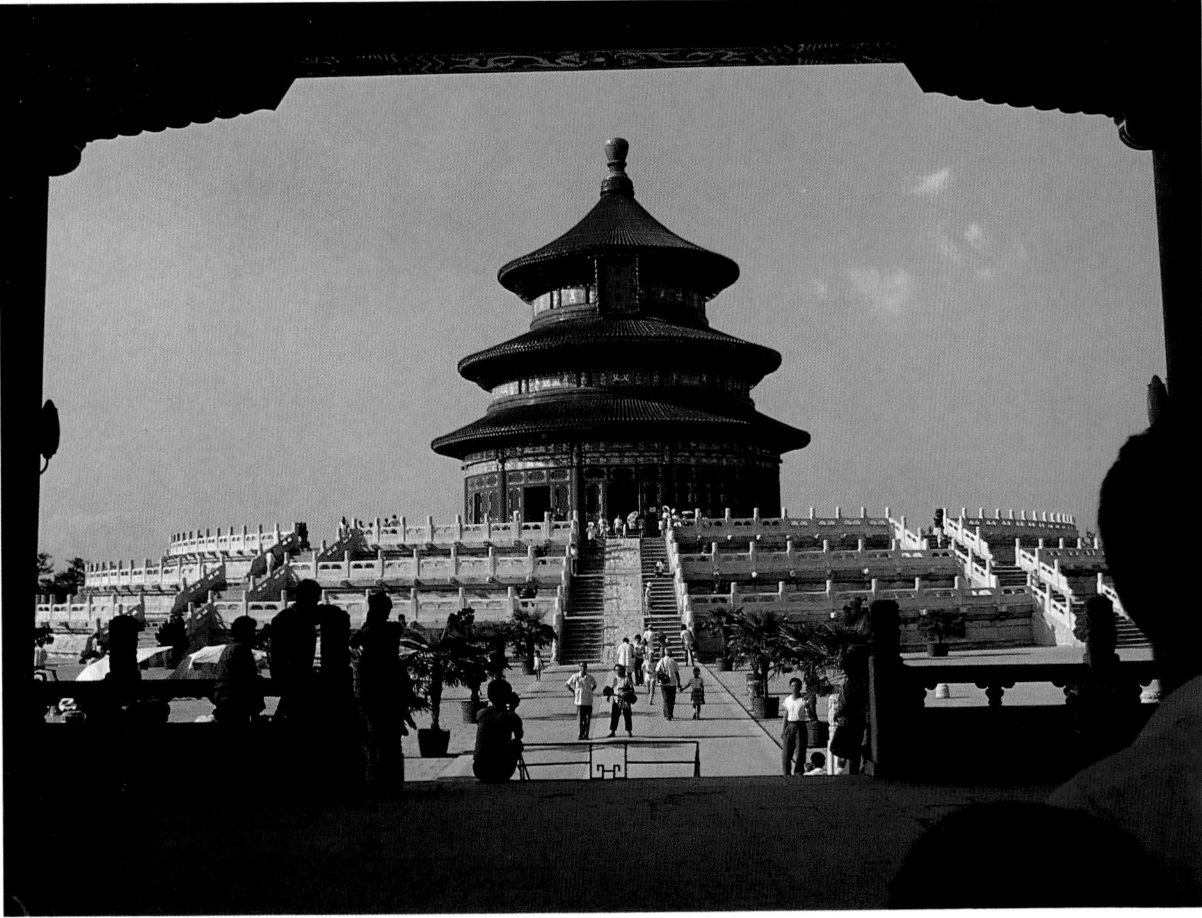

△ Beijing, Temple of Heaven, Qinian Dian, 1889

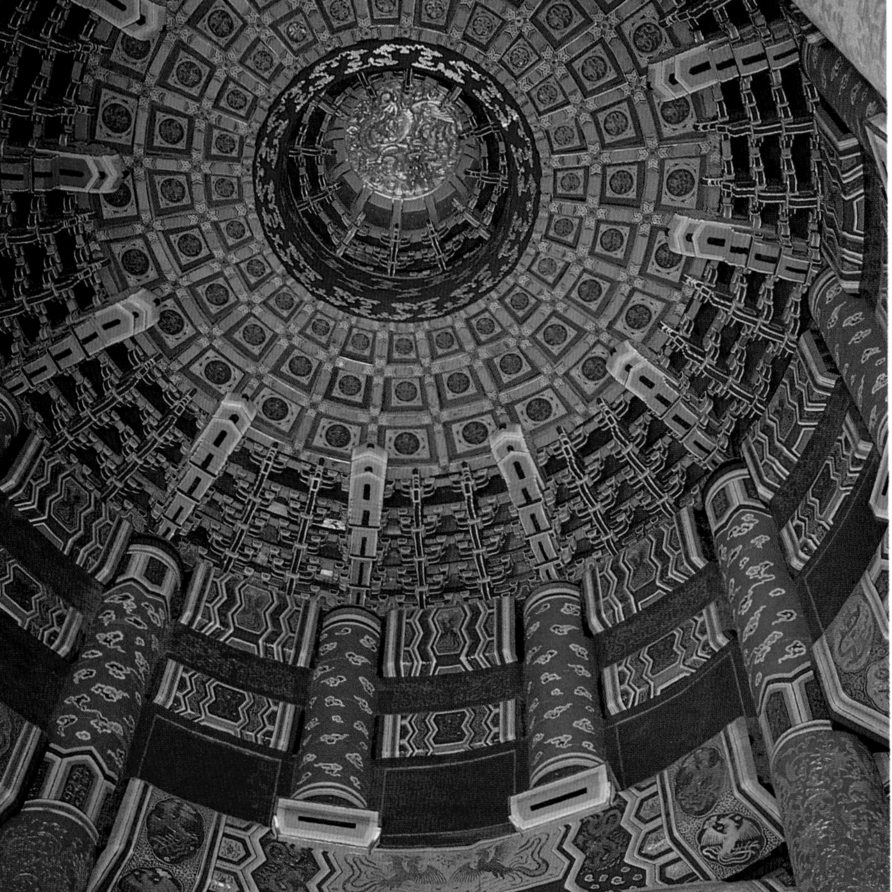

▷ Beijing, Temple of Heaven, Qinian Dian, 1889

high above the clouds among the blue heavens. In ancient times, the tablets of deceased emperors were placed on a table under the coffered ceiling. Approaching from the long, raised terrace, one crossed the high threshold of the great hall, gradually approaching the centre under the elaborate 60-foot ceiling. The designer of this temple may have intended the emperor to experience an integration between himself, the heaven above and his ancestors.

Classical Chinese architecture was more than a practical building system. Its added purpose was to use symbols to impart meaning to the harsh human existence. The aim of this chapter has been to give an indication of how the Chinese developed and used this symbolic vocabulary. Beginning with the general environment and working towards the development of details of individual structures, the ancient Chinese attempted to make their environment more meaningful. By examining this example, we may begin to understand classical Chinese architecture, while simultaneously, expanding our general knowledge of the relationships between man, his architecture and environment.

For Western readers, we can now make a comparison between Chinese and Western architecture. The Chinese city plans are more regular, following the ritual code. In the West, the main buildings are generally exposed as compared to the enclosed character of the Chinese plans. The West tends to concentrate all buildings in one area, while the dispersed structures and courtyard layout of Chinese architecture relates more to nature. In terms of building materials, the Western builders are apt to use stone and masonry, applied to the arch and vault system, so there are more high-rise buildings of a similar greyish colour. In comparison, the wooden framework of low rise buildings in Chinese architecture is painted with brilliant colours. In design works, standardization was implemented, but it was possible to still preserve the flexibility of planning. From a single building to building groups, not only are the structures unified in a hierarchical system, but they are also unified in composition and style.

If we review classical Chinese architecture from its early period until about one hundred years ago, we realize how rich and unique it was. As compared with the architecture of other countries in the world, the rate of evolution and development from the primitive days onward was much slower in China, and because of this it has retained its uniqueness.

Subtle and magnificent, delicate and grandiose, flexible and standardized, full of symbolic meanings, these are the chief characteristics of classical Chinese architecture.

CHAPTER III
CITY PLANNING PRINCIPLES

◁ Gaochang, Xinjiang, Buddhist temple

DURING THE FIRST DYNASTY IN CHINESE HISTORY, THE Xia Dynasty, there was a saying: 'To build city to protect the emperor, to build wall to watch the people.'[1] We can assume that during that time, there were walled cities to watch the people. Since that time, the Zhou Dynasty cities were enclosed with walls. In China the word for city (cheng) and wall (cheng) are the same. If a place was not walled, it was not really a city. A city must be a walled enclosure, and this was a fundamental feature of all Chinese cities. But we are not sure when the Chinese first built their cities.

The Shang Dynasty, which followed the Xia Dynasty (17-11thC B.C.), located its realm in the middle and north part of present-day Henan Province, near the middle reach of the Yellow River. The Shang people began a city at today's Zhengzhou, and another city called Yinxu (Xiaotun, Anyang). These cities are representative of city building activities of a slave society, and indicated that its economy and culture had developed so rapidly that cities were needed and had, therefore, emerged. The next dynasty, the Western Zhou, built two political centres, the Feng and Hao, located on the east and west banks of Feng River in the southwestern part of present day Xian. Because their locations were far from the cities of the previous dynasty, it was not possible to control them efficiently. Thus, Wuwang of the Zhou Dynasty ordered Zhou Gong (The Duke of Zhou) to build two new cities, the Wangcheng and Chengzhou, near Anyang. Wangcheng was used as an army post to watch the people and Chengzhou was used to control them. Wangcheng, later called Luoyi, was used as the capital city of Eastern Zhou. From the ruins, we can see that the city had a square plan covering an area of 2.9 by 3.3 kilometres. If we convert these figures to the Zhou measurement, the city was almost nine li square. The central buildings were located a little to the south of the city centre. We know that the Zhou cities were planned according to the rigid requirements recorded in the *Kao Gong Ji* of *Zhou Ritual.*[2] *The Ritual* was written in the Spring and Autumn Period and Warring State days, as compared with Luoyi, in which the form and locations of palaces basically corresponded with this regulation.

Kao Gong Ji also ruled that the 'longitudinal avenues have nine chariot tracks, a ring road has seven tracks, a suburban road has five.' This indicates that even 2,500 years ago the width of roads varied to accommodate different levels of traffic. Those in the city were wider and the ring roads were narrower, while suburban roads were the narrowest. Inside the city, the layout was axial, symmetrical, and very formal. The requirements stipulated that each side should have three gateways, the court of state should be placed at the centre, and that the locations of the Altar of Society and Ancestral Temple should be placed at either side of the main avenue. These regulations were used as the guidelines for the planning of cities of the following dynasties, even the Dadu of Yuan Dynasty and Beijing of Ming Dynasty. These were planned some 2,000 years after *Kao Gong Ji* was written.

Chinese city planning was closely linked with ideas of real and ideal social order, and a structured vision of the universe. Builders aimed at making the city a true image of the universe as an ordered whole, a symbol of power, order and attuned to nature.

From the above, it is clear that the characteristic features of ancient cities were as follows:

a) All cities were enclosed by walls.

b) Cities exhibit axial symmetry, with the palace located at the centre.

c) All major buildings face south. The roads were laid out running north-south and east-west, forming a checker-board grid.

d) Cities were designed with a square plan, and gateways opened to all four directions.

From 770 B.C. on, the Western Zhou Dynasty moved the capital from west to east until the Qin emperor unified China. This was the period of Spring and Autumn and Warring States, and was also the period in which China progressed from a slave society to feudal society. During this time, land became privately owned, and iron was used to make tools, promoting city development. The number of cities as well as the population as a whole increased. Some cities prospered as business centres because of the boom in trading. The city had become a political and economic centre as well as a centre of defence.

To choose the site of a city, Guanzhong had summarized that 'The land should be high but not too close to a hill then there will be water for use, land should be low enough but not near a river so there will be easy drainage.'[3] This passage shows he paid a lot of attention to water supply and drainage in the choice of a site for a city.

During this period, most of the important cities moved from west to east or were founded in the east. For instance, the Xiadu of Yan (4th-3rd C B.C.) was founded in Hebei, and Linzi (4thC B.C.) of Qi in Shangdong. This last city was the largest and most prosperous city of the Warring States Period. A famous politician of that period, Suqin, mentioned that 'In Linzi there are seventy thousand families . . . all rich and solid . . . chariots and people were crowded and mingled in the streets'.[4] It was indeed a bustling town. In China, as it is customary to estimate that each family had five persons, this city could have had a population of 350,000, not a small figure in that period.

After Qin Shi Huang, the tyrant annihilated the other six kingdoms during the 3rdC. B.C., and a series of changes were undertaken. First, he ordered that the city walls of the capitals of the six kingdoms be demolished so that it would be difficult for them to defend themselves. He then made Xianyang the capital city of Qin (northwestern part of present-day Xian), and ordered the relocation of 120,000 rich families to Xianyang to make it a prosperous city. According to records, for every kingdom he defeated Qin Shi Huang ordered that a palace be built based on the planning of the palace of the kingdom in Xianyang. He also ordered the construction of a palace of grand scale named A Fang Gong Palace. Dumu (803-852? Tang Dynasty), a famous poet, described the magnificent and richly ornamented palace in his *A Fang Gong Prose*:

> The six kings perished and the land within the four seas was unified. After all the timber of Sichuan mountains was cut, the palace called A Fang Gong emerged. It covered an area of more than three hundred square li, the sun and sky could not be seen, for every five steps there was a lou and ten steps a ge, verandahs winding and meandering, eaves extended high above, each building occupied a special site, almost touched each other . . .[5]

The construction of A Fang Gong used all the timber in Sichuan mountains. It showed that there was no good timber for construction purposes near Xianyang. By the last days of the Qin Dynasty, A Fang was razed to the ground in a battle. Now, at A Fang village near Xian remains a big rammed-earth platform with a perimeter of over 200 metres. Three big granite column bases are on it, each with a diameter of over one metre. These remains of the grand palace give us an idea of the column height and size of the building.

The Han Dynasty followed the Qin, making Changan (Everlasting Peace, south of Xianyang, also northwest of present-day Xian) its capital. The city was built in grand scale and used architecture as a means to show the central power of the state.

Gaozhu (206-195 B.C.), the first emperor of the Han Dynasty, built several walled palaces for himself. Because of the irregularity of the site and the locations of the palaces, the city had an irregular shape and consisted mostly of palace buildings. It had 12 gateways, each of eight metres in width, a pavilion served as watch tower placed on top of each gate, each gateway had four chariot tracks. The parallel avenues leading to the gateways were almost as wide as the gateways. The middle lane was called Shidao and was used exclusively by the emperor. Trees were lined along the road sides.

During its most prosperous days, Changan had a population of around 300,000:

> Nine markets were lined along the east and west sides of the major thoroughfare which ran from north to south, six to the east and three to the west, representative of flourishing trade. The residential blocks, surrounded by gridiron roads, were called Luli, (where Lu means gate and Li neighborhood) and were placed between the palaces. According to records there were as many as 160 Lulis in Changan, comprising the basic units of the city planning. Inside the Luli there were straight lanes with houses built in rows along the lanes.[6]

The houses were courtyard houses placed so that one was attached to another. All Lulis were enclosed by walls, with a doorway opening to each direction. Every residential lane had an officer to govern the people.

At the southern part of Changan were large-scale ruins of Ritual Buildings, consisting of more than ten building groups. The ritual building groups were axially and symmetrically planned. Each group was enclosed by walls with a door at each side, and at each corner was an L-shaped building to support the central one. At the centre were the remains of rammed earth platforms, some of them having column bases. From

▷ Changan (now Xian, Shenxi), city plan, Han Dynasty, 2ndC B.C.

Key
1 Changan (Han Dynasty). 2 Ritual Building Group.

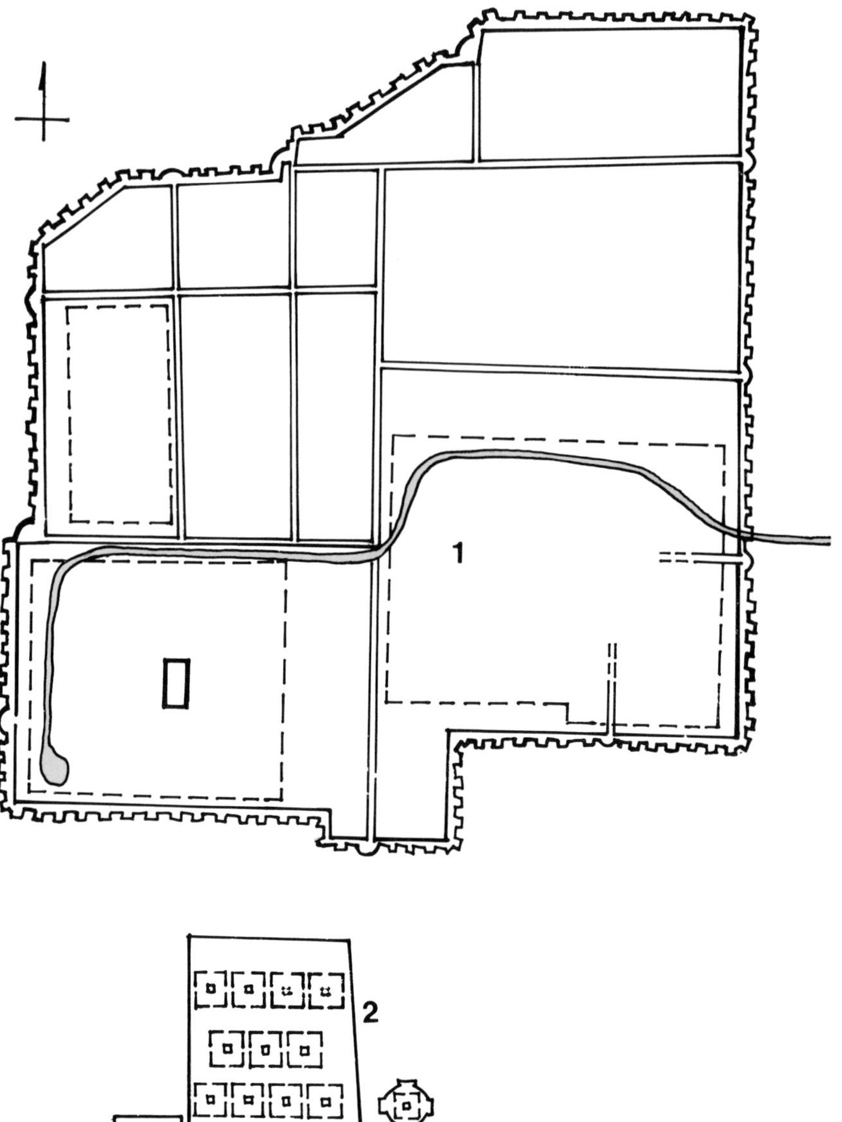

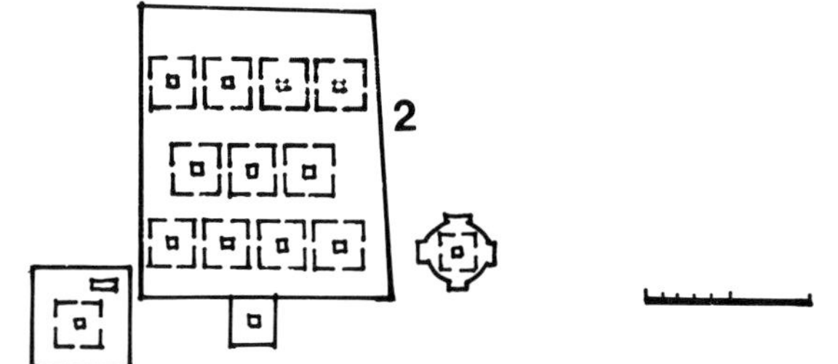

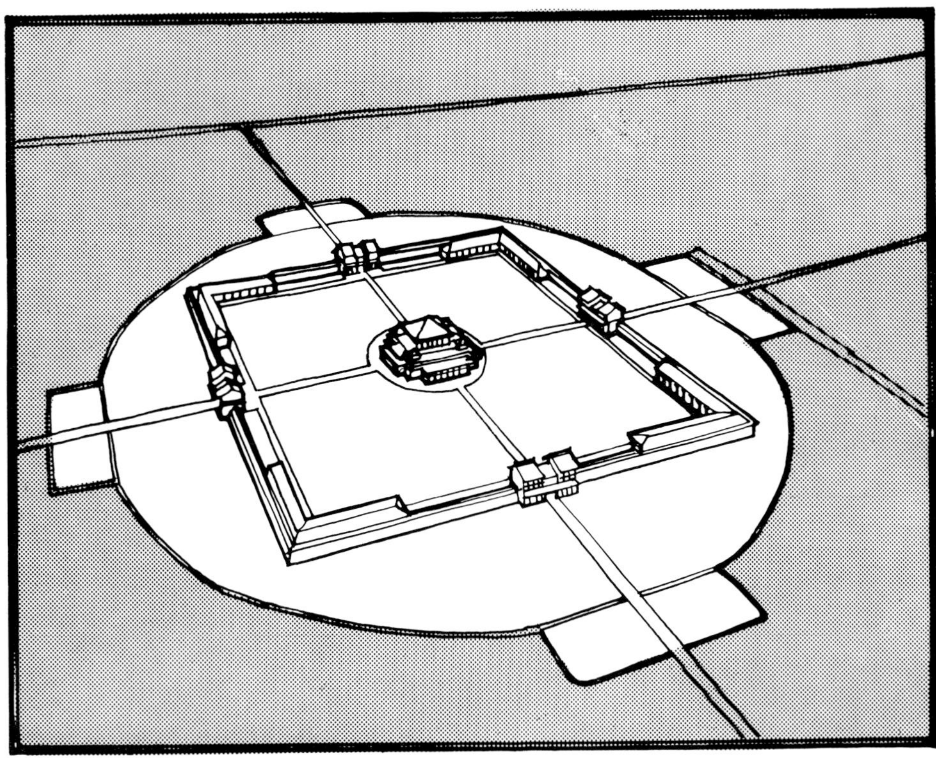

◁ Changan (now Xian, Shenxi), Ritual Buildings, reconstruction, Han Dynasty, 2ndC B.C.

this arrangement we can infer that there had been formal buildings of timber construction upon the platforms. The building at the east end could have been Mingtang (school).

The planning of these buildings was entirely different from placing buildings along a central axis. It reminds us of the central building layout of the Late Renaissance, but this was almost 1,500 years earlier. This particular layout had its influence on funeral buildings, the Buddhist temple of northern Wei and some of the ceremonial buildings of later periods.

Guangwu (25-52), an emperor who was noted for his ambition, moved the Han Dynasty capital Chengzhou to the east of present-day Luoyang and started the so called called Eastern Han Period.To the south of the city was the Luo River,to the north the Mang Hill, and the land had a gentle slope to the south providing good drainage. Luoyang was of rectangular shape, around nine li from north to south, and six li from east to west. It had 12 city gateways, 24 avenues, and possibly contained 140 Lulis.

During the last days of the Eastern Han there was continuous warfare between the warlords. The dynasty split into three and was called the Three Kingdoms, each of which occupied a large section of Han's territory. The largest among them was the Wei Kingdom headed by the very crafty Cao-cao. He founded this capital near present-day Lingzhang and named it Yecheng. According to *Shuijingzhu*, a classic book on geography written by Li Daoyuan at Niwei, the dimension of this city was seven li from east to west and five li from north to south. A wide avenue running from the east gateway to the west gateway divided the city into equal parts. The north part was for the court of state and at the centre were the palace buildings. The southern part was a residential district, subdivided into three square Fangli and three markets.

In general the Han cities had the following features:

1. *Axiality:* all cities adopted the north-south axial planning with the palace in the centre, as most of them inherited the tradition of the Warring States. Yecheng was especially distinctively zoned to provide easy communications between each part. These two features influenced the later city plans of the north-south, Sui and Tang Dynasties.
2. *Luli unit*: all the capitals had used the Luli unit to organize residential districts. Each Luli unit is one residential district. Officers were appointed to rule over people who lived inside. Luli was later called Fangli.

Market: from *Kao Gong Ji* we learned that 'in front lay the court of state, at the rear the market place'.[7] It is not difficult for us to speculate that the cities in the Warring States Period had concentrated market places. Changan of Western Han had nine markets. Inside were multistorey buildings, some of which were built along the streets. Following the growing varieties of goods, specific streets were formed for specific trades. As with residential districts, officers were appointed to control the markets. Some of the markets moved from the north part to the south, forming an important element of city planning before the Song Dynasty.

In the year of 494, Xiaowen Di, emperor of the Northern Wei Dynasty, moved the capital city from Pingcheng to Luoyang. First he ordered Jiang Shaoyou to visit Luoyang of the Han Dynasty to investigate the foundations of the palace, and next to make a survey of the Southern Qi palace in Jiankang. After the surveys, he started to plan and build a palace on the remains of the Western Jin Palace. The city thus planned had two enclosed city walls. The outer one had a dimension of 3,100 by 4,000 metres.

The palace was located centrally and a little to the north, basically built on the location of the northern palace of Cao-cao. The imperial garden to the north of the palace was built upon the remains of Cao-cao's Fanglin Yuan Garden. The wide avenue leading from the south gateway to the palace was called Tongtuo Kai (Copper Camel Street), and ministries and temples were placed along the street. The famous Yungling Temple, demolished long before, was situated to the west of the north end of this street. The ancestral Hall was placed at the east of the south end.

The rest of the city was filled with Luli blocks. Streets were of checker-board pattern. The famous Luoyang Market was located at the west side near the present day White Horse Temple. Nearby were shops of handicrafts and the houses of craftsmen and tradesmen. The houses of the nobility were concentrated in the northern part. Sitong Market, located outside the south gateway, was a market planned specially for international business transactions. Foreign merchants gathered and did business with local people there, making it an interesting place. Agricultural products were bought and sold outside the east gateway.

Overall, the city had a dimension of 15 li measured from north to south and 20 li from east to west. Inside were 320 walled residential blocks – the Luli. It was recorded that 'they were expensive to build but were secure from robbery';[8] apparently the aim was to protect those living inside to facilitate government.

▽ Yecheng (near Anyang, Henan) city plan, Wei Dynasty, 220-265

Key
1 Tongqiao Yuan (Copper Bird Garden). 2 Palace. 3 Luli (Residential Blocks).

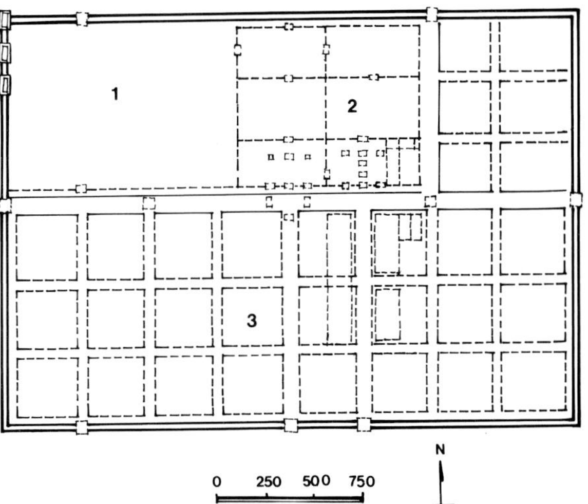

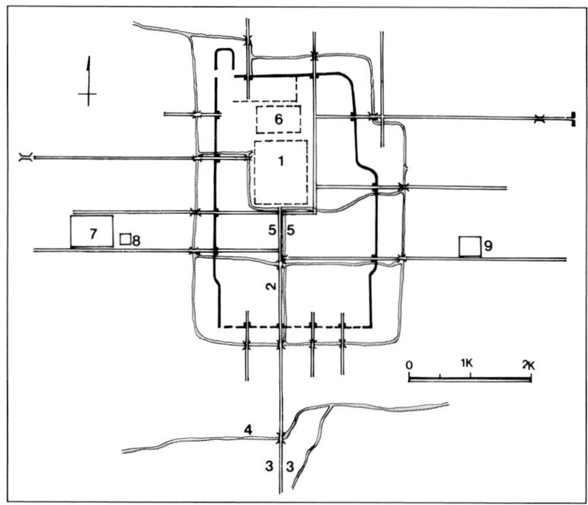

◁ Luoyang, Henan city plan, Northern Wei, 368-534

Key
1 Palace. 2 Tongtuo Street. 3 Siyi Li (Foreigners' Quarters). 4 Luo River. 5 Governmental Buildings. 6 Hua Qing Yuan. 7 Big Market. 8 White Horse Si. 9 Small Market.

▷ Jiankang (now Nanjing), Jiangsu, city plan, Southern Dynasties

Key
1 Wu Palace. 2 Jiankang Palace (Six Dynasties). 3 Qinhuai River. 4 Yudao (Royal Road). 5 Shitou Cheng (Rock City). 6 Xuanwu Lake. 7 Zhong Shan.

Jiankang (present-day Nanjing), the capital city of the Southern Dynasties, was built on the Yue Cheng at the end of the Spring and Autumn Days along the banks of Quinhuai River in the southern part of Nanjing. King Sunquan of Wu, which was one of the Three Kingdoms of the Han Dynasty in 211, moved his capital to this location. Sunquan took advantage of the natural rocky highland overlooking the Yangtze River and built Shitou Cheng (the City of Rocks), which had a perimeter of seven li. In addition, he selected the east side of this city to build Jiankang. To the north was a small hill and Xuanwu Lake, while south was Qinhuai River. The city itself was a tiny one of rectangular shape, only two li in perimeter. A palace was placed at the centre with an avenue proceeding from the palace to the south gateway. At both sides of the avenue were houses, shops and temples.

As Buddhism flourished in the Southern Dynasties, especially during the Liang Dynasty, there were hundreds of Buddhist temples in Jiankang. Dumu, a famous poet of the Tang Dynasty wrote: 'There were four hundred and eighty temples in the Southern Dynasties, many pavilions and high terraces amidst the misty rain'.[9] This passage gives us a general idea of how widespread Buddhism was at that time. Since Jiankang was located among the mountains on a site near the Yangtze River, the city grew to be irregular in shape. Rivers, lakes and hills influenced the directions in which the city gradually expanded. The builders did not have a general plan, resulting in a city which had the typical irregular plan of ancient China. The centre of the city was nevertheless in square form.

The dynasty following the Liang, the Southern Tang of the 10th century, also founded its capital at Jiankang. The residential district was moved further south. The Ming Dynasty also established its capital in Nanjing, and in 1366 large scale planning and construction works were started. First, a group of palace buildings were built at the south of the Zhong Mountain (Purple Gold Mountain) with the Taimiao (Ancestral Hall) and Shejitan (Altar of Society) in front of the palace. Nanjing at this time was a city of three city walls: the outer wall; the irregular Yingtianfu wall (the city wall of present day Nanjing); and Huangcheng (the Imperial City). The outer wall and Huangcheng were demolished during a battle fought in the time of the Taiping Celestial Kingdom.

The second wall had a length of 33 kilometres. The foundation of this wall followed the contours of the Yangtze River, lakes, and hills and was designed according to the functional requirements of all defensive works. It had 36 gateways, making it the longest city wall with the most gateways. The walls were strongly built, using hills and natural rock as its foundation. Where there was no natural rock, large stone blocks were used as the foundation. Robust timbers were used as the bed for the foundation when the wall crossed rivers and ponds, and the stone blocks were laid upon the timber. All the walls were built of large kilned greyish brick weighing around 20 kilograms each. The mortar was composed of lime mixed with juice of glutinous rice, making a very adhesive cementing material. The top of the wall was covered with a mixture of wood oil and clay so that it was waterproof and impregnable. The wall had a width of 10-18 metres at the bottom, tapering to 7-12 metres at the top. The construction work of this wall exceeded the quality of any other walls before it.

Nanjing during the Ming dynasty was also the cultural and economic centre, as well as the religious and recreational centre:

> During this period, there were shops and hotels lining the river, and the playing of musical instruments and singing could be heard all through the night. The population of Nanjing at that time was over half a million. There were two centres: one was the palace, the political centre in the northern part of the city; the second was the business, cultural and recreational centre located along the banks of the Qinhuai River in the southern part of the city.

The lower reach of the Qinhuai River passes through the southern part of the city of Nanjing. The famous Fuzimiao (Confucius Temple) district and Gongyuan (the School of Examination) were situated on the north bank of the river. Every three years, students all over Jiangsu arrived here to take an examination. Those who passed were admitted to a higher examination taken in Beijing; the

> others, who did not pass the examination usually prepared for the next examination given three years later. The examination of course was easier for those who came from well-to-do families, for they were not worried about their income and could devote all their time to study. Although economically disadvantaged, scholars from less well-to-do families could sit for the examination and, when they passed, they too could go to the capital to take the higher examination. Because of the nearby School of Examination, Fuzimiao district always had thousands of students together with their retinues gathered here. Bookstores, restaurants and even whore houses were established. The scholars and merchants made this area prosperous both culturally and financially. Although the examination system was abolished long ago, the business and handicraft trade still prospers to this day.[10]

This is probably why this district is so famous and distinguished from other cities.

Since the Western Zhou Dynasty, the Changan region has served as the political centre of Zhou, Qin and Han Dynasties. For instance, the Feng and Hao capitals and Western Zhou were founded on the banks of the Feng River, to the west of Changan. The Qin capital of Xianyang, located on the north bank of the Wei River, is to the north of Changan. To the northwest of the Changan region was the Western Han capital of Changan. After Sui unified China, the emperor was not contented with the small size of Han Changan, the salty water, and the mixed development of palace and houses of the common people. He decided to build a new capital to the southeast of Han Dynasty Changan, called in Chinese history the Sui Tang Changan (the present-day Xian). The planner of this new capital was Yuwenkai, and the capital was named Daxing after its completion. After the short-lived Sui Dynasty, Tang emperors continued to build following the original planning principles and changed the name of the city back to Changan. Now this great city has the Wei River to the north and both the Chan and Ba Rivers to the east, providing convenient water transportation. Changan had a dimension of 9,721 metres from east to west and 8,651 metres from north to south, forming a rectangular city plan. The city wall was 12 metres in thickness, with three gateways to each side. Each gateway had three layers, except the south Zhengde gateway which had five layers. Each gate was crowned with a high-rise watch tower.

The plan of Changan was a combination of the experiences of Yechang of the Eastern Han, Luoyang of Northern Wei and Yecheng of Eastern Wei. Constructed according to axial and symmetrical plan, the imperial city and palace were placed along the north-south axis. The lengthwise and crosswise roads formed a checker-board pattern, subdividing the residential area into 108 Lifang (neighbourhoods, same as Luli). The city had a clearly zoned land-use plan, a very regular road system, and expressed fully both order and power – the ideas and aspirations of the ruler.

The Imperial city inside Changan was placed on the axis and to the north. To the east and west of the axis and in front of the imperial city were the east market and west market. This arrangement was different from the requirements of *Kao Gong Ji* but was convenient for the people to go to the markets. Each market had an area of 1.10 square kilometres and was enclosed by a wall with doors opening on all sides. At the centre were the administrative office and the office of measurement. The west market was used exclusively for merchants who arrived over the Silk Road, and for international trade. The west market had a '#' street pattern. The width of the street was 16 metres and had drainage ditches and sidewalks. The east market had shops, housing 120 trades. The concentration of all handicraft shops in a permanent market was another feature of ancient Chinese city planning, the advantage being that it was easy to control.

Inside Changan were 14 north-south avenues and 11 east-west avenues. This orderly street pattern facilitated transportation and easy movement within the city. The centrally-located Zhuque Avenue (Scarlet Bird Avenue) was 150 metres wide; the others were 134 and 20 metres wide. Chinese parasol trees and Chinese scholar trees were planted along the avenues. The street pattern naturally divided the residential area into 108 Lifang, each of a retangular shape. The small Lifang had a dimension of 520 x 510-560 metres, while large ones were 600 x 1100 metres. All were enclosed by tall, rammed earth walls. Larger Lifang had a cross street leading to four gateways. Smaller ones had only one crosswise road running from east to west, and had only two gateways. The streets measured 12-20 metres wide. Doorways were closed after sunset, which, in addition to the enclosed walls effectively imposed a night curfew on the people. The lands lying outside the Lifang walls and along the streets were mainly used for the buildings of officers and for temples, as these structures were permitted to open their doors directly to the streets, and the occupants were not controlled by either officers inside the Lifang or by the night curfew.

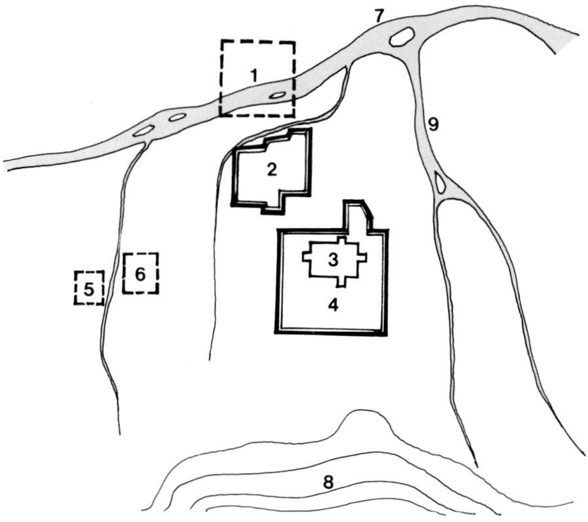

△ Changan (now Xian) Shenxi, city plan, Sui and Tang Dynasties, 581-907

Key
1 Xian Yang (Qin). 2 Changan (han). 3 Xian (Ming and Qing). 4 Changan (Sui and Tang). 5 Fengjin (Zhou). 6 Hawjin (Zhou). 7 Wei River. 8 Qinling Mountain. 9 Ba River.

Irrigation works and waterways were planned to guide water to the inside of the city for daily use and gardening. For instance, they supplied water to the famous Qujiang (Winding River) and Fuyong Garden (Peony Garden) at the southeast of the city and in front of Dayen Pagoda (Big Wild Goose Pagoda) which was an imperial garden often used in Tang Dynasty.

Dongdu (the East Capital) Luoyang of the Sui and Tang Dynasties was also a great, regularly planned city. After the Sui emperor unified China in the 6th century, he founded its capital city at Changan. This placed the political and military centre to the west while the economic centre was located to the east, making them difficult to control. Yangdi, the first emperor of the Sui Dynasty, started to build the East Capital at Luoyang. The emperor himself stayed in the East Capital most of the year. By the time the construction of the East Capital was begun, Sui's political power was at its zenith. Because of his wealth and the luxurious inclinations of Yangdi, the smaller East Capital was no less magnificent than was the West Capital.

Yangdi began construction with the imperial palaces. The city axis started at Man Mountain in the north, running down to the Yique Gate in the south. It commanded a grand view and was a good example of utilizing existing landscape. The city was seven li square, and city streets formed a checker-board pattern. The road leading from the palace to the south gate, the widest in the city, was 120 metres wide while other roads varied from 30-60 metres Lifang, generally of 450 metres square, each had a crossroad of around 14 metres wide. There were three concentrated markets in the city. The city was completely damaged during the battles at the end of the Sui Dynasty and again at the end of the Tang Dynasty and has not been renovated since.

These two capital cities, Luoyang and Changan of the Sui and Tang Dynasties, were used as prototypes

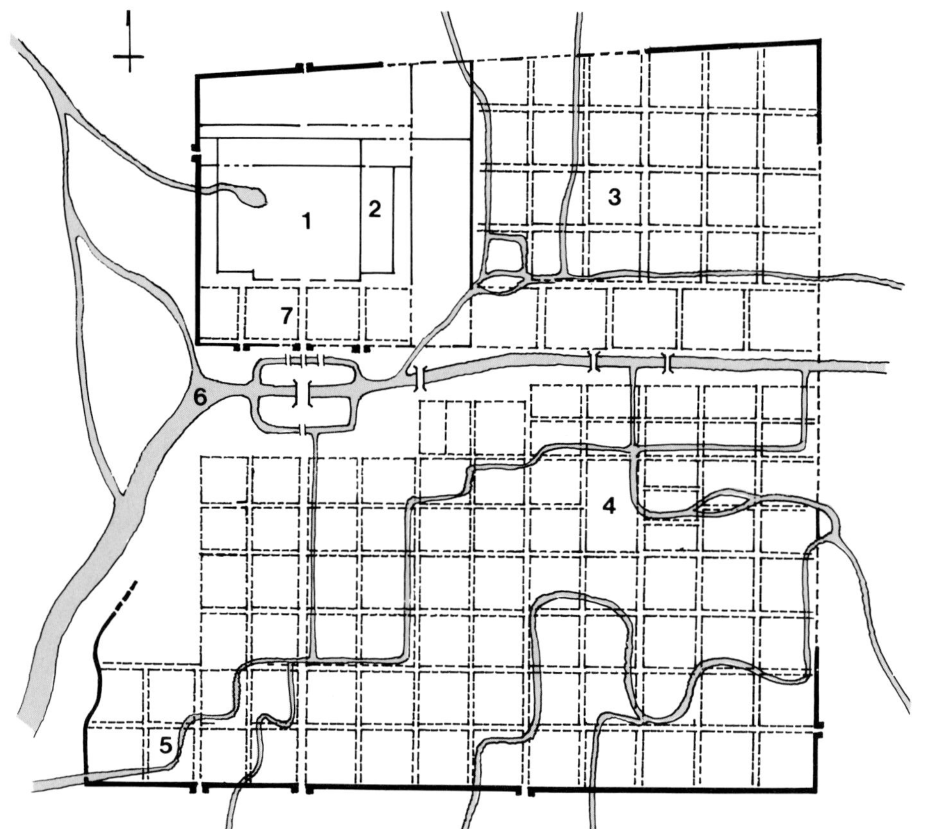

▷ Luoyang, Henan, city plan, Sui and Tang Dynasties, 581-907

Key
1 Palace. 2 Eastern Palace. 3 North Market. 4 South Market. 5 West Market. 6 Luo River.

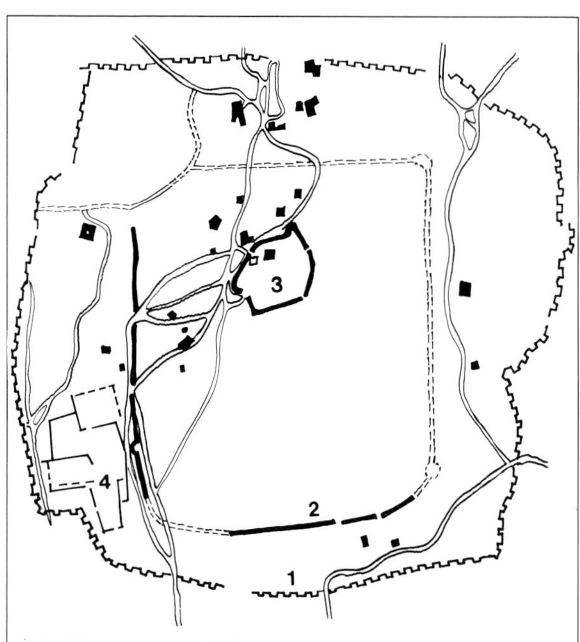

△ Gaochang, Xinjiang, city plan, Tang Dynasty, 2nd-14thC.

Key
1 Tang city. 2 Song city. 3 Palace. 4 Residential district.

for the planning of large cities built after them. They even influenced the design of, and were copied by, some large cities of Japan. The careful and magnificent planning of great cities like Changan was not only hitherto unheard of, but was also unprecedented worldwide. *Changan Zhi (Record of Changan)* recorded: 'The streets looked like checker-board and lined with buildings was straight like an arrow, was hitherto unknown in the imperial cities.'[11] This was not in the least an exaggerated remark.

From the above historical descriptions of city buildings it is clear that, from the Shang Dynasty until the Sui and Tang Dynasties, there was continuous warfare in the northwestern region. Buildings and cities were demolished, and excessive deforestation made the northwestern part a barren land. Because of this situation, the political and economical centres were moved eastward, making the southern part of the Yellow River and the Yangtze River valley the national political and economic centres. For instance, during the Tang Dynasty there were three large commercial cities, namely Guangzhou (Canton) of Zhujiang (the Pearl River) river valley, Yangzhou of Yangtze River valley, and Bianzhou (Kaifeng) of the Yellow River valley. Among them, Yangzhou was the collection and distribution centre for salt and iron, the largest commercial centre of China in its day. In the heyday of Yangzhou, the city was 7.5 kilometres long and 3.5 kilometres wide.

There was another important factor in the development of Yangzhou which should not be overlooked. Yangdi of the Sui Dynasty was a pleasure-seeking emperor who was obsessed by the beautiful scenery and luxurious life of Yangzhou. In 605 he ordered the building of a pleasure palace in Yangzhou. In order to reach this city by boat, a more comfortable way of travelling, he ordered the widening of an old river bed and made it a part of the Great Canal. When finished, it had a total length of around 1,800 kilometres and was 60 metres in width. Huge boats were constructed for him and his court to travel to Yangzhou. Eventually, this canal became the arterial river connecting the Yellow River and the Yangtze River. So it was said that 'Yangdi had exhausted his resources, but was a benefit for the later generations.'[12] Of course, this was not his original intention.

The criss-cross canals and waterways of Yangzhou made it a metropolitan centre of water transportation. From here boats could sail to the famous Slender West Lake which, with Guanying Hill as a backdrop, formed a charming landscape.

Jianzheng Monks of Yangzhou in the Tang Dynasty had travelled to Japan several times, bringing medical books and achievements in Buddhist architecture and art to Japan. The Golden Hall (759) of Nara, the oldest timber construction building in Japan, was built under his direction. It is a pity that although the magnificent temple he designed in Nara is still standing, the Dam-

▽ Yangzhou, Jiangsu city plan, Sui-Ming Dynasties, 581-1644

Key
1 Tang city. 2 Song city. 3 Yuan and Ming city. 4 Ming and Qing city. 5 Shouxi Lake (Lean West Lake).

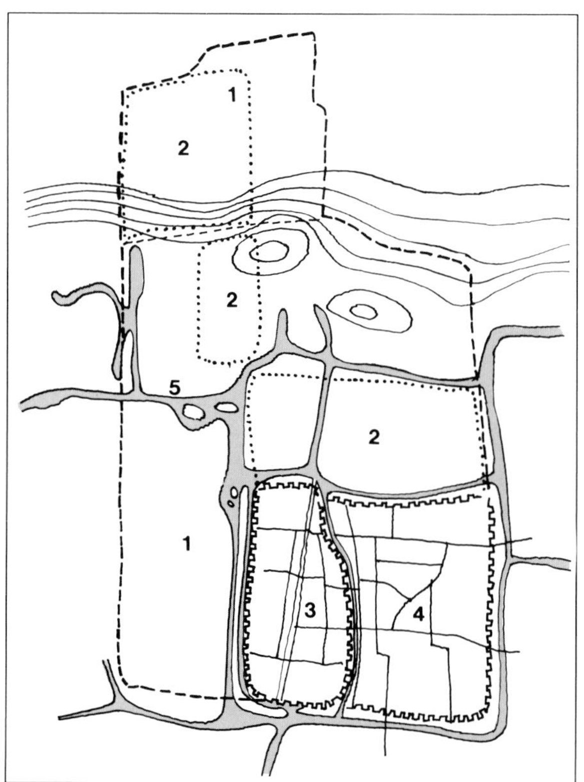

ing Temple where Jianzheng lived in Yangzhou was demolished during the Tang Dynasty.

The Tang Dynasty in China continued its trading and cultural communications along the Silk Road with the Western Region. Along the Southern route and in Turfan of Xinjiang Province many cities and shrines were built. Numerous monks, including the Master Monk Xuanzhuang, travelled along this route to India to study Buddhism. So along the road were many Buddhist temples and grottoes, such as the Tuyu Grottoes near Gaochang. Owing to either the discontinuation of communications or the lack of water, the desert area gradually expanded. Eventually the city dwellers moved away and the city was deserted altogether. Ironically, because of lack of precipitation and dry weather, some of the buildings, relics, and tombs have been preserved.

Gaochang or Xichang is one of the ruined cities. According to history, 'Gaochang was located in the land of Chexi . . . when Wudi of Han sent an expedition force to invade the west part of China, many soldiers were sick and tired, the sick soldiers were hospitalized here. Because the land was high and spacious, the city was prosperous, so it was named Gaochang (high and prosperous).'[13]

▷ Gaochang, Xinjiang, praying hall

▽ Gaochang, Xinjiang, interior of praying hall

The present ruins indicate that Gaochang had three city walls: the palace city to the north; the outer city; and the inner city. The entire city was of a square shape and enclosed by rammed earth walls 12 metres wide. The remaining sections of wall measured 11.5 metres high. A conical building and high platform at the centre of the city served as a Buddhist praying hall and a shrine. The shrine had many niches which held Buddhist images. The conical building had only one doorway and was open to the sky, an arrangement which is unique in China. Gaochang had been abandoned by the beginning of the Ming Dynasty, which lasted about 1,500 years.

Another ancient city built in the 1st century, called Jiaohe (River Intersection), was also located in the Turfan area. The site of the city, at the intersection of two rivers, was ten metres above the wide river bed. As Jiaohe was a naturally fortified city, city walls were not needed at most points along the perimeter. There were only two gateways to the city. The one facing south was the only approach to the city, while another facing east was an auxiliary gateway but was never used. Because of the shape of the natural site, the city had a longitudinal, leaf-shaped plan, 1,650 metres from north to south and a width not more than 300 metres. There were many temples inside the city, one of which resembled a five stupa pagoda. Between the streets were neighbourhood buildings, also enclosed by walls. During the 14th century, the rivers ran dry and the city of Jiaohe was abandoned.

Like the other cities in this area, Gaochang and Jiaohe used indigenous materials like rammed earth and sun dried bricks as building materials. From the remains of house foundations and the walls of dwellings, we know the houses were half sunken into the earth, a building method still used in this area. Arches and vaults of sun dried bricks were used for roofs and above doorways. Although these fortified cities were built in remote places far from the centre of culture, some of the planning principles of the Han were observed.

During the period encompassed by the Sui and Tang Dynasties, Kaifeng developed gradually into a handicraft, trading, and communications centre. During the middle of the Tang Dynasty, 100,000 soldiers were stationed here to protect water transportation. The rapid population growth caused a critical housing shortage and deteriorating sanitary conditions. In 955, a Late Zhou emperor ordered the redevelopment of Kaifeng. The plan included: construction of a new outer city (Luocheng), making the original city four times larger; the widening of roads; dredging the Bian

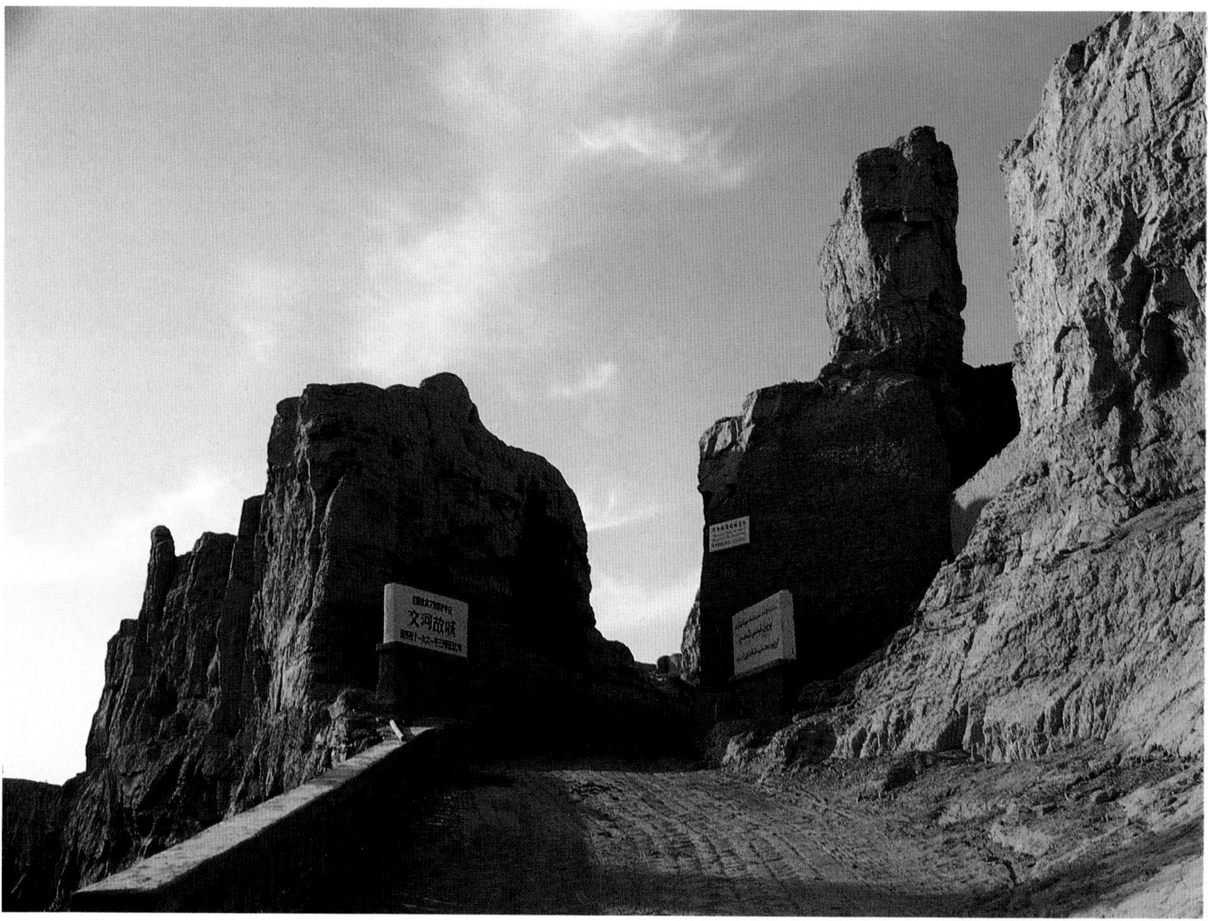

▷ Jiaohe, Xinjiang, city gate, 1st-14thC.

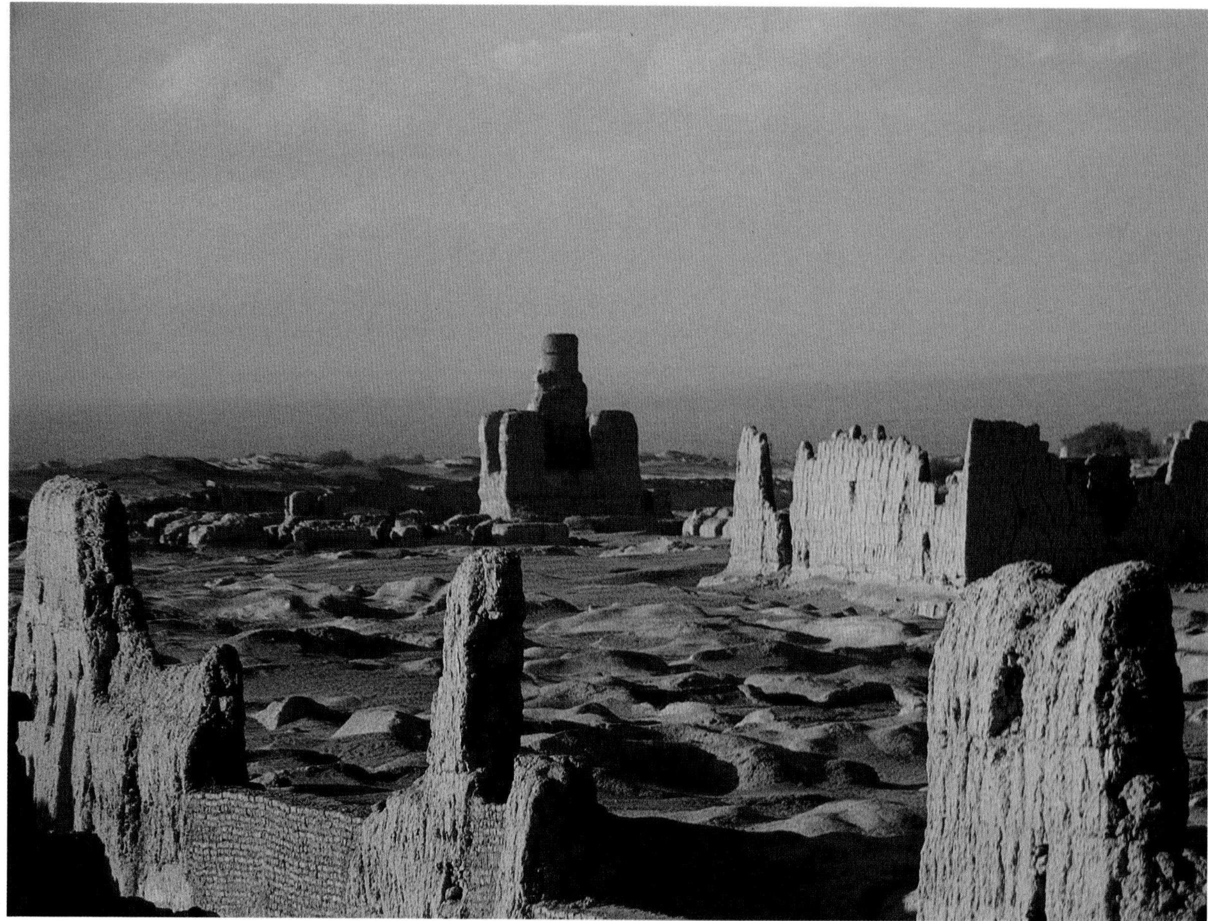

▷ Jiaohe, Xinjiang, bird's-eye view

▽ Jiaohe, Xinjiang, remains of a Buddhist temple

River; drawing up fire regulations; and the planting of trees along roads. Although there were no scientific city planning principles, a lot of attention was paid to the sanitary conditions of residential districts within the city, and emphasis was placed on the solving of practical problems.

According to a Song Dynasty block-print, *Dongjin Bianliang Map*, cut in the Yuan Dynasty, Kaifeng had three layers of city walls which wrapped around one another. The city plan was of rectangular shape, with the east-west axis longer than the north-south axis and a perimeter of around 45 kilometres. The centrally-located palace layout largely influenced the planning of two other cities called Jin Zhongdu and Yuan Dadu. The second city wall had a perimeter of ten kilometres and ten gateways. The several layers of walls were called Licheng. All three of the walls had wide moats around them. Kaifeng, a city featuring three layers of city walls and three moats, illustrated the importance of defence in those days.

Inside Kaifeng were many rivers. A Northern Song painter, Zhang Zeduan, painted *Boating Along the River at Qingming*, depicting Kaifeng's street life. In this scroll painting, the streets were not very wide in comparison with the houses built along it, but it did show that the walls around the neighbourhood had been torn down. The street then became a corridor street lined with shops. This arrangement, entirely different from the previous examples, was another feature of the planning of Kaifeng. Besides this shopping street, there were several concentrated market places. For example, the Xiang Kuo temple was the site of the largest market place in Kaifeng because of its convenient centralized location. This market opened five times a month. Other markets were also assigned to specific trading purposes for specific goods.

The planning of another city of the same period, Pingjiang (now Suzhou), was apparently influenced by both the natural landscape and historical development. Suzhou was said to have been built by Wuzixu, who served as Prime Minister of Helu, the King of Wu, 2,500 years ago. According to the history of the Han Dynasty, Wu Zixu inspected 'the Yin and Yang (the sunny and shaded sites) of the land, tasted the water, examined the vegetation, then he planned and built the city'.[14] The city was later burned down by Qin Shi Huang Di, the tyrant.

Located on very fertile land on the lower reach of Yangtze River, Pingjiang enjoyed a mild climate and abundant crops. The Great Canal of Early Sui passed through here, making Suzhou one of the centres of water transportation, handicrafts and trades. Intellectuals as well as merchants swarmed to this place; thus, during the Sui and Tang Dynasties, it became the

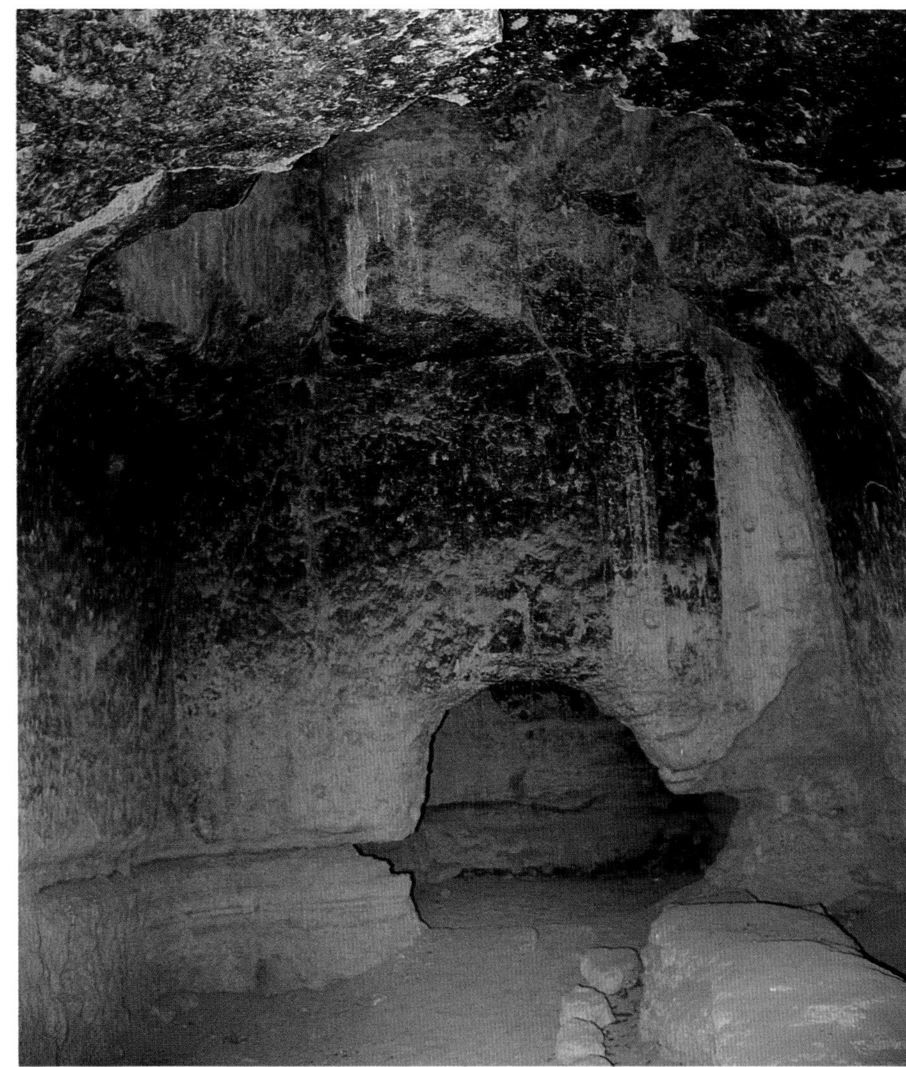

△ Jiaohe, Xinjiang, remains of dwellings

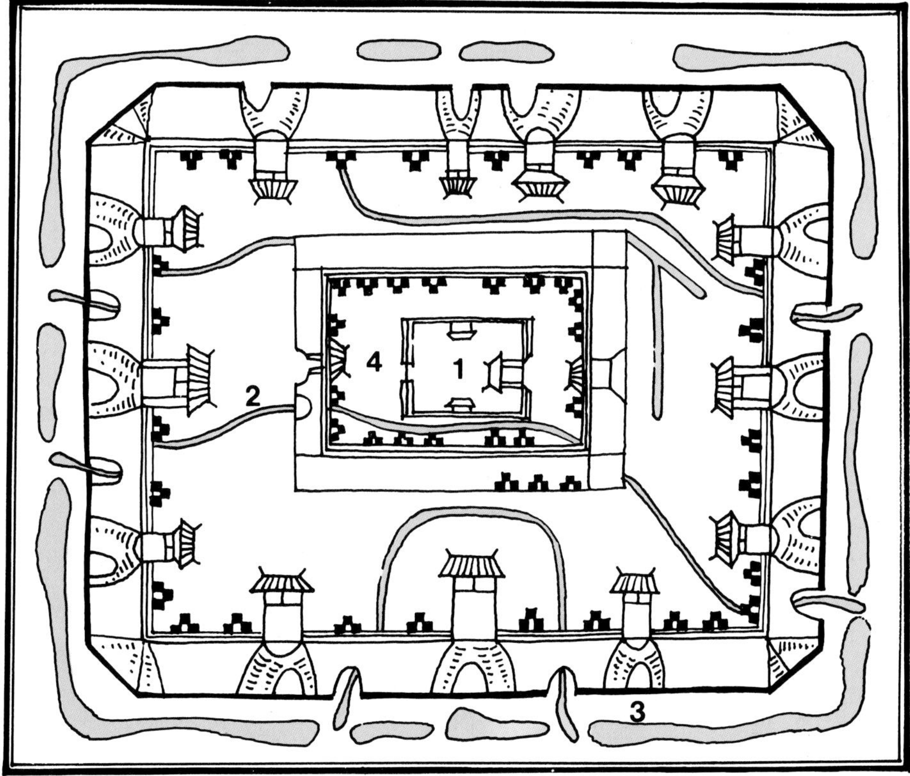

▽ Kaifeng, Henan, city plan, Song Dynasty

Key
1 Inner court. 2 Bian River. 3 Hulong River. 4 Old capital.

political, economic and cultural centre of this region once again.

The site of Pingjiang was selected after careful deliberation. Not only did it have transportation facilities, but crops were not threatened by drought or excessive rain, and the site was easy to defend. According to the *Song Dynasty Chronicle*, which recorded the selection of the site of Pingjiang:

> There should be walls and moat to defend the city . . . there are rivers and canals, they provided water transportation . . . although it was called a water-borne city, yet it was never troubled by flooding, that was due to the wisdom of the builder.[15]

Even today, more than 1,500 years after its erection, this evaluation still records the actual situation.

The city map of Song Dynasty Pingjiang, carved on a stone tablet, is still well preserved in Suzhou Museum. It is the earliest existing city map in China. When comparing modern Pingjiang with the Song Dynasty city, we find that the existing locations of roads, canals, buildings, such as the Confucius Temple or the Baoensi Temple Pagoda (Beisi Pagoda), the Pingjiang municipal government, the twin pagodas, even the city walls and gateways, all correspond to this map.

We can say with certainty that this is an important document in the study of both Song Dynasty city planning and Pingjiang city itself. The planning principles followed in Pingjiang included the placement of a government building group at the centre of the city, and important high-rise buidings at the intersections of main streets which served as identifying landmarks. For instance, the tallest structure, the Baoensi Temple Pagoda, is at the north end of a main thoroughfare. It can be seen from miles away, providing an interesting view from far off. The Xuanmiao Guan Temple, a Daoist Temple, was placed at the north side of a busy street and a square was provided in front of it. These and other buildings composed a very interesting skyline and formed the architectural composition of Pingjiang.

Pingjiang, with a city plan of rectangular shape, was entirely enclosed by a brick wall and wrapped around by a deep moat. There were altogether six gates (not 12 as ruled by *Kao Gong Ji* in the wall. One of the six, the southwestern gateway, was a water-gate built across a canal designed to handle water traffic. The streets leading to the other five gateways were made wider than others. There were three east-west roads and four north-south roads, an arrangement customarily called the 'three crosswise and four lengthwise avenues'. Since all the roads, lanes and canals in the city were laid out in the north-south and east-west direction, they were perpendicular to each other. Residential lots

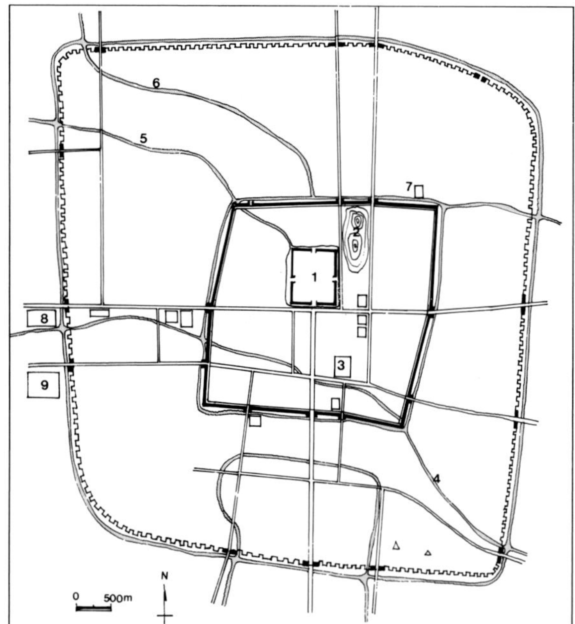

△ Kaifeng, Henan, city plan, Song Dynasty, reconstructed

Key
1 Inner court. 2 Gen Mount. 3 Xiang Kuo Si. 4 Bian River. 5 Jinshui River. 6 Wuzhang River. 7 Iron Pagoda. 8 Jinming Pond. 9 Qiongling Yuan Garden.

▽ Pingjiang (now Suzhou), Jiangsu, city plan, Song Dynasty

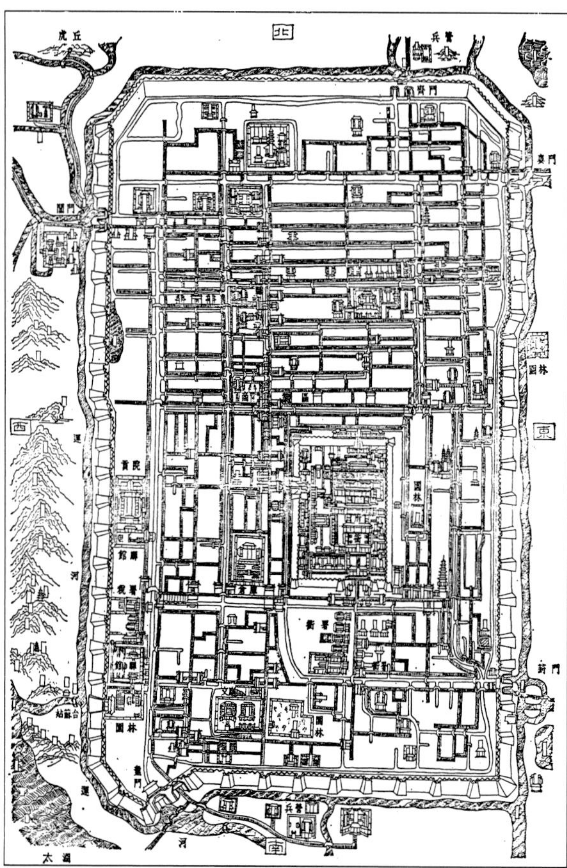

were located between the road and canal providing two entrances to each house: one to the small lane at the front (south); the second to the canal at the back. The front door was used as the family and guest entrance to the house, while the back door was used solely as a service entrance where provisions were brought into the house and wastes were removed to the countryside. The opening of a house directly to the street proved once more that in the Song Dynasty the Luli system had been abandoned. Because of the clement weather and abundant crops many retired officers, landlords, and merchants built their mansions here. These homes were the designs of artists and intellectuals who were supported and patronized by the rich. Adjacent to these houses were private gardens. The principles of garden planning used were closely linked to poetry and traditional painting; thus, both the master of the house and the intellectual collaborated in garden design. Sometimes, the master himself was a literate and created gardens of a unique style. Garden planning will be further discussed in the chapter about private gardens.

The planning principles of the Yuan Dynasty capital Dadu (Beijing), or the Ming and Qing Dynasties' capital of Beijing, were entirely different from the previous example, Pingjiang. The former capitals inherited the criteria of the *Zhou Ritual* and the experience gained in the construction of Kaifeng. The builders wielded their immense financial power which when combined with political ambition enabled them to concentrate several hundred thousand workers on the project to finally create a magnificent capital for a powerful empire. The building reflected the aspirations of the ruler, as well as the wisdom of the planner. Both the formal character of the city plan and the construction were unique in architectural history, making it worthy of its reputation as one of the greatest capitals in the world.

As mentioned above, the deterioration of the ecological environment moved the political and economic centres gradually to the east. During the 13th century, Kublai Kahn of Yuan stormed Jin Zhongdu and occupied the northern part of China. After his ascension to the throne, he ordered Liu Binzhong and an Arab to take charge of the planning and construction of a new capital next to Zhongdu. These two planners relied upon the ancient Han traditional city planning principles to build a city of 7,400 x 6,665 metres which was enclosed by a city wall and a moat. The wall had 11 gateways, three gateways on each side with the exception of the north side, which had only two gateways. The palace was centrally located. All the major roads led to the gateways, and between the major streets were residential lanes. Temples, offices and shops

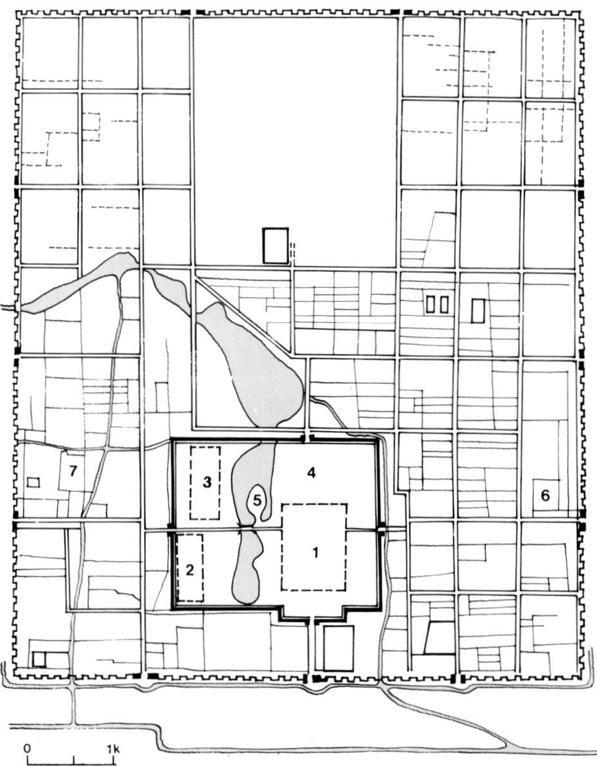

△ Dadu (now Beijing), city plan, Yuan Dynasty, reconstructed

Key
1 Inner court. 2 Longfu si. 3 Xinsheng Gong. 4 Imperial Garden. 5 Qionghua Isle. 6 Taimiao (Ancestral Hall). 7 Altar of Society.

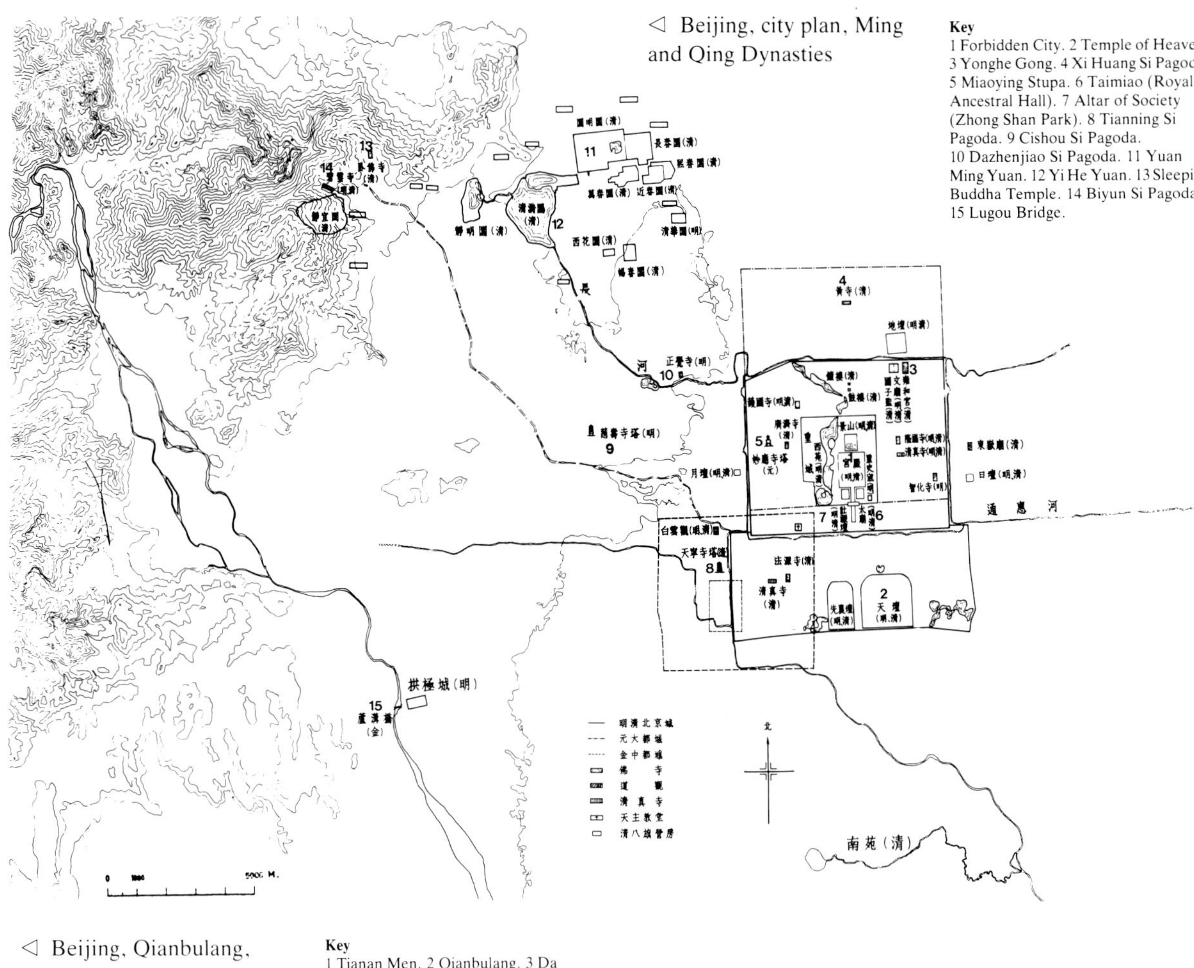

◁ Beijing, city plan, Ming and Qing Dynasties

Key
1 Forbidden City. 2 Temple of Heaven. 3 Yonghe Gong. 4 Xi Huang Si Pagoda. 5 Miaoying Stupa. 6 Taimiao (Royal Ancestral Hall). 7 Altar of Society (Zhong Shan Park). 8 Tianning Si Pagoda. 9 Cishou Si Pagoda. 10 Dazhenjiao Si Pagoda. 11 Yuan Ming Yuan. 12 Yi He Yuan. 13 Sleeping Buddha Temple. 14 Biyun Si Pagoda. 15 Lugou Bridge.

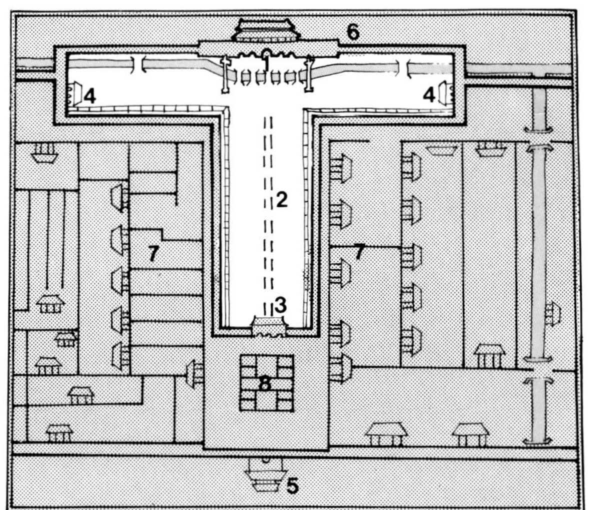

◁ Beijing, Qianbulang, Ming and Qing Dynasties

Key
1 Tianan Men. 2 Qianbulang. 3 Da Qing Men. 4 Changan Men (left and right). 5 Zhengyang Men. 6 Imperial City. 7 Ministries. 8 Qipan Street.

mingled among the residential blocks. The city was divided into 60 Fang, but was not enclosed by walls. The major building groups were, of course, the palace ensemble with the court on the main axis. The Ancestral Hall and Altar of Society were located at its sides, completely conforming to the requirements of the *Zhou Ritual*.

The two dynasties which followed the Yuan Dynasties also used Beijing as their capital. In 1553 the Ming emperors redeveloped the Yuan capital on the foundations of Dadu. In order to reinforce the defence works, an attached city was built towards the south, which enclosed the handicraft trading market, the Temple of Heaven, and the Altar of Earth. Thus Beijing, too, had three cities: the Imperial City; the Inner City; and the Outer City. Unlike the city of Kaifeng, which was wrapped by layers of walls, the outer city of Beijing was attached to the south wall of the inner city. Inside the Imperial City was the Forbidden City, which had a dimension of 960 x 760 metres from east to west and was enclosed by heavy walls and a deep moat. At each corner of the wall was a corner pavilion, and at each side a gateway. When the Manchus of the Qing Dynasty occupied Beijing, they continued to use the Ming Palaces and street pattern. Present-day Beijing, therefore, inherited the features of many dynasties. The Imperial City, built utilizing Ming Dynasty Nanjing planning and conforming to the idea of the *Zhou Ritual*, created a magnificent, grand unity with the palace as the centre. Such an integrated whole, with its great scale and regular pattern is extremely rare worldwide.

The planning of Beijing demonstrated the importance of the emperor by including palace buildings which symbolized his power. Their design expressed the idea that the emperor represented heaven, and symbolized his domination over the people. This idea was first expressed by the south-north axis representing a road from heaven to earth. This axis connected the palace with other important buildings and the axis of Beijing. The most southern gateway, Yongding Gateway, was next to the impressive Temple of Heaven and Altar of Earth. Stopping short of the Zhengyang Gateway of the Inner City, this axis provides a solemn introduction to the palace. Inside the Zhengyang Gateway, Daqing Men (now Tianan Men Gate) and Qianbulang (Corridor of One Thousand Steps) formed the prelude to the Imperial City.

In Qianbulang the space was contracted. The equally-spaced colonnade, which lined the corridor, utilized uniform rhythm and gradual crescendo to lead one towards the monumental Daqing Men of the Imperial City. The corridor, together with the Promenade, extended to the left and right forming a T-shaped, enclosed square. A number of features – the moat in front of the gateway with its beautifully carved Wulong Bridge (Five Dragon Bridge), the Huabiao (Dragon Pillar), stone carved lions of white marble placed against the massive dark red wall of the lower portion of the gateway – echoed the rhythm of the pavilion and white marble balustrade above to effectively create a play of scale, of form and of multiple colour. In addition, the horizontal lines as emphasized by the river, by the base and parapet of the wall, and by the extended double eaves and ridge, created a feeling of peace as well as of monumentality. This, when added to the emotional impact, impressed upon the visitor the supreme power of the Son of Heaven through the use of symbolic architecture. The well-proportioned mass and space, a place both beautiful and stately, functioned well and at the same time manifested the power of the emperor. It was a place of the highest architectural quality, a crystal of urban design and architecture. Unfortunately, in the 1950s, the Qianbulang was widened and the promenade opened. Under this ignorant design concept – big is great – the space was changed from enclosed to open, and an inhumane, bleak wilderness was created at the centre of this ancient capital. It is not 'whole', but rather an ugly 'hole'.

The supreme power of the emperor was also expressed in the mass of the buildings and by the employment of colour. All the palace buildings were enclosed in high, heavy red walls surrounded by a wide, deep moat. The palace was not only of great dimension, but was covered with a yellow glazed tiles which symbolized the imperial family. The low-lying houses of the common people outside the wall could only use greyish tile roofs and walls. Large crowns of green trees dotted the stretch of greyish colour. The visual effect produced by this use of colour allowed the palace to stand out from the houses, symbolizing the status of emperor and his control over the common people. The centralized location of the palace created a lack of communication between the east and west sides of the city. Today, this would be considered a sad mistake; however, in those days the intention was to prohibit easy communication and the circulation of ideas among the people. The arrangement could have worked as planned, or could have been an unplanned bonus.

Datong, the capital of the Northern Wei was the home of many Buddhist Shrines, including the world famous Yungang Grottoes. Built between the Outer and Inner Great Walls, the city was also a military fortification. It was called Pingcheng during the Wei. During the Ming Dynasty, in 1372, a kilned brick wall was built to take the place of the original rammed earth wall. It is a small city with a square plan and a perimeter of only 6.3 kilometres. Four gateways led into the city where they formed a crossroad. This is the typical form of many small cities. Governmental offices were placed at one side of the cross street, so making it convenient to control the whole city.

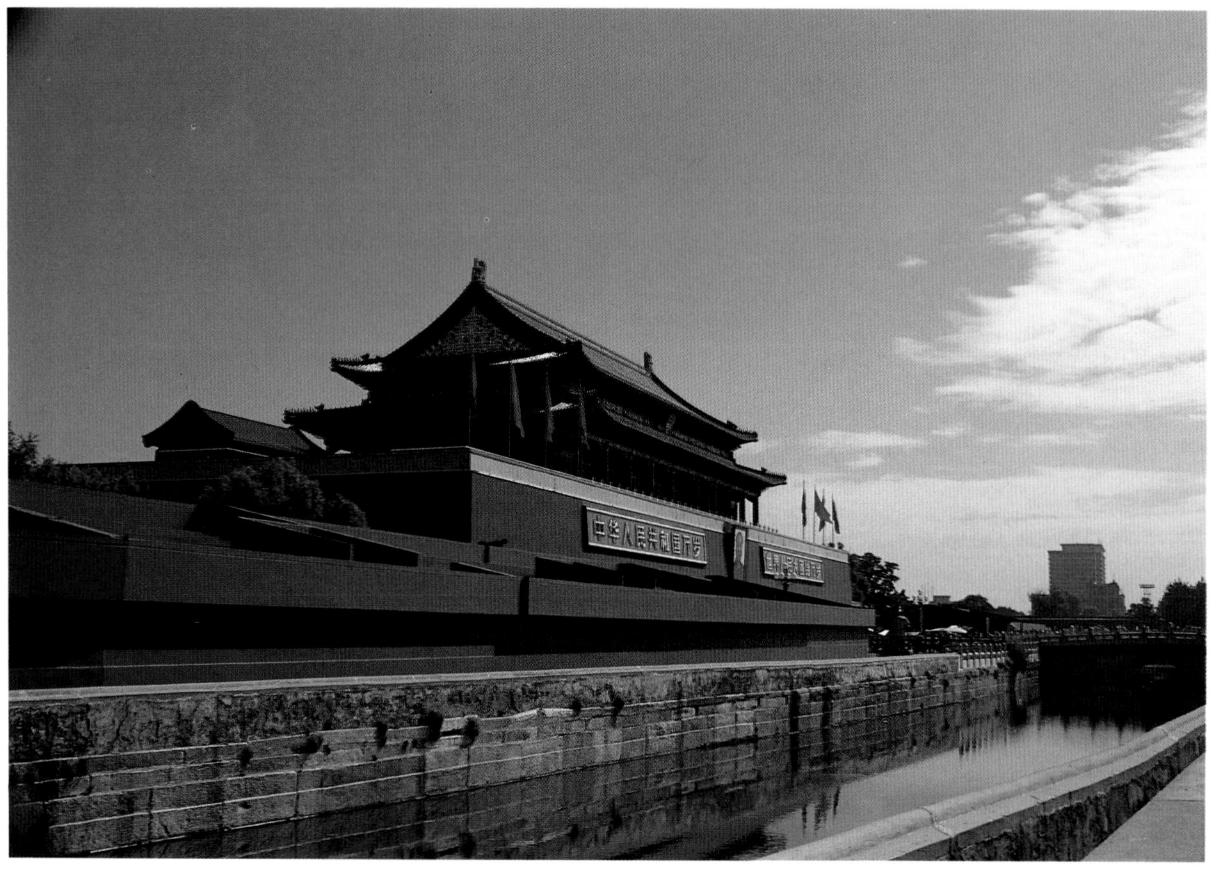

△ Beijing, Tianan Men Gate, Ming and Qing Dynasties

▽ Beijing, Tianan Men Gate, Moat, Ming and Qing Dynasties

◁ Beijing, Tianan Men Gate, Huabiao Pillar, Ming Dynasty

▽ Datong, Shanxi, city plan

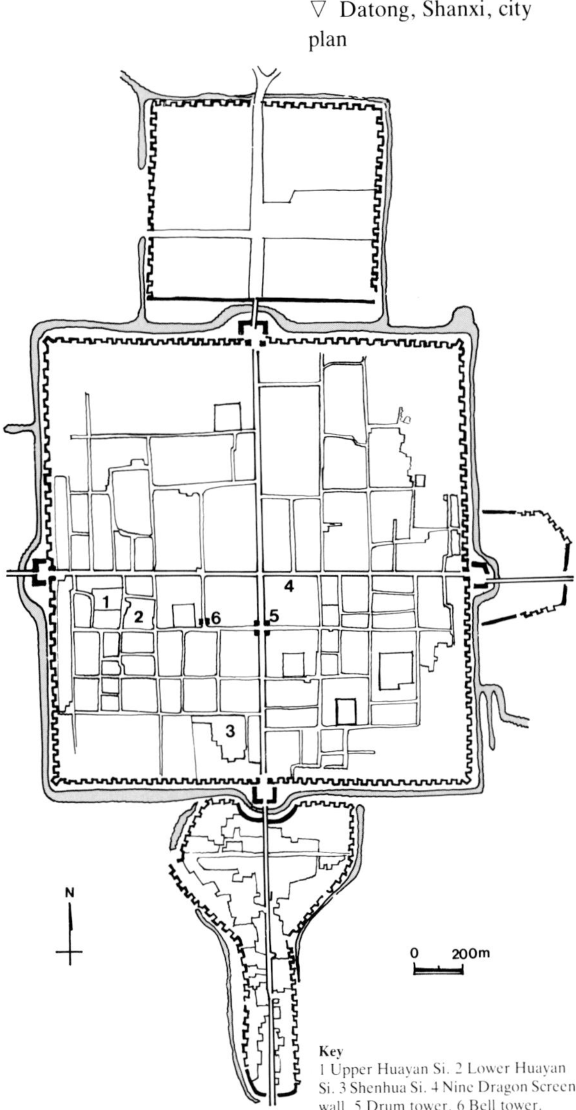

A BRIEF SUMMARY

We have dealt with the planning ideas and some typical examples of major ancient cities above, illustrating that from the dawn of civilization until the 19th century there were no great changes in city pattern. The *Zhou Ritual* required manifestation of the power of the Son of Heaven through the erection of a palace representing him; thus, the palace and court were placed on the axis, and high city walls and moats were built to protect the occupants. Landscape was also very important. The early civilization first developed in the northwestern district, where the land was usually flat. When building on a piece of flat land, a regular geometrical shape was usually deemed convenient. However, not all ancient cities were of square form. South of Yangtze River region, the landscape includes hills and lakes. Beginning with the choice of site, it was necessary to 'inspect the land and taste the water', and to 'suit the local conditions'[16] when designing such irregular cities as Nanjing and Changan of Han.

For a long time, the shape of the city plan went without any considerable changes due to the stability of Chinese feudalistic society, technical underdevelopment following the tenth century, and conservative thought. But if we examine the plan carefully, it was not without changes. Take the location of the marketplace. According to *Kao Gong Ji*, it ruled: 'in front lay the court of state, at the rear the market place.' The arrangement provided easy market access for the offices. During the Tang Dynasty, cities were more populated and had more affluent inhabitants who lived and did business inside the city. Thus, the marketplaces were placed in front of the palace near the residential area of the common people.

In the late Tang Dynasty the walls around the market were demolished in some cities, and shops opened directly on to the street. The ancient block rule was eradicated. This trend was further legalized during the middle of the Northern Song Dynasty. Lufang rule was also changed and dwellings had doors which opened directly on to the streets. The change in the market location and the dismantling of the walls were not important changes in planning principles, but as these reforms had taken four long centuries, they were considered to be major changes in the past 2,500 years. This illustrates that under the feudalistic system, it was not possible to make even a minor change in city planning principles. Only through change in the social system is the reform of city planning possible. That is why architects always say that city planning and city image are true reflections of the social system of a country.

When comparing Chinese city planning with its European counterpart, we can easily see where the great difference lies. In Western cities, from ancient Greece and Rome till the present day, the city centre has always contained the agora, forum or squares for the circulation and exchange of ideas of the people. Squares were created from democratic ideology, symbolizing the civil and religious rights of the people. In ancient China, these rights were non-existent. The common people were accustomed to the political thought: 'I work after sunrise, I rest after sunset, what do I care about the emperor and politics?'

The square city plan symbolized the 'sky is round and land is square' idea. It placed the palace at the centre of the city and also symbolized the idea that the Son of Heaven was the centre of the universe by facing the sun to the south.The high walls around the palace or city also represented the seclusion and control of the people. This was also expressed in the fabric of Luli and the houses inside it.

Throughout history cities have been rebuilt on old city foundations, then renovated, reconstructed and sometimes redeveloped. We can just as well say that cities have been built collectively through the ages. The sense of unity came from a splendid historical heritage and city planning, not just the use of one or two monumental edifices or one or two religious towers or palaces to dominate the cityscape. The Chinese city was organized horizontally, and the aim was simply to create a harmonious whole.

CHAPTER IV
RELIGIOUS BUILDINGS

◁ Song Shan Mountains, Henan, Shaolin Si Pagodas, Tang and Song Dynasties

DURING THE ENTIRE HISTORY OF CHINA, THE PRIMARY forces involved in developing a national architecture were political power and religion. Religious beliefs, being more popular among the common people, were more influential in daily life in the development of architecture and the arts. Consequently, during the past 1,600-plus years, many temples were constructed, Buddhist caves were hollowed out, and Buddhist sculptures carved, moulded and cast. These activities left a variety of buildings, sculptures and literature, enabling us to determine the original ideas and roots of the arts and architecture of individual dynasties within the greater context of Chinese history.

INTRODUCTION

Buddhism and Daoism (or Taosim) were the two major religions in China. Daoism, however, having had fewer believers than Buddhism, was less influential; Chinese culture and architecture had closer ties with Buddhism. Buddhism is believed to have been introduced into China during the 2nd century, during the last days of Western Han. Arriving from the 'Western Regions', Central Asia met with the highly developed Chinese culture of the Han Dynasty, the philosophy of Confucianism and the religion of Daoism. As Chinese culture absorbed Buddhism, many new sects or schools were founded. Although the believers of all sects worshipped Sakyamuni, the Buddha, the Lesser Vehicle and Greater Vehicle of Indian Buddhism failed to retain its original character among Chinese believers. The ultimate result was the development of more practical schools, including the popular Chan Sect (the Zen Sect of Japan) and the Pure-land Sect, all existing in China at the same time.

BUDDHISM

During the early days of the Eastern Han, Liu Ying, the King of Chu, believed in Buddhism and started to build Renci, i.e. Buddhist temples, thus showing that Buddhism was prevalent at that time and was favoured by the royal family and nobility. By the end of the Han Dynasty, there was sustained warfare, famine and plague, and Buddhism was turned to as one way to suppress the riots and uprising of the people. Ze Yong, a monk, was ordered to build many temples of 'multi-storeys, and on top of the roof was a golden disc, during the Buddha's birthday, free meals were given, tens of thousands of people watched;'[1] it was a very spectacular and grand occasion. For almost 300 years, there were occasional wars, even after the Jin Dynasty, and the common people were troubled by conscription and hard toil. One way to be exempted from these hardships was to shave one's hair and become a monk. Thus, Buddhism flourished during the Jin and became even more prevalent during the later Sui and Tang Dynasties. During this period, numerous temples and pagodas were built throughout the country. The early temples followed the form and style of India and the Western Region but, gradually infused with the indigenous Han style, building appearances changed. Since we do not have any existing buildings of the Han and only a few existing temples of the Tang, it is difficult to determine the extent of the Indian influence over these buildings. Fortunately, there exist cave temples, pagodas of the Northern Wei period of the 5th century, and from the frescoes and carvings in these buildings we are provided with ample documents to study the specific appearance of Buddhist architecture of that period.

DAOISM

Daoism is the only religion originated in China. The originator of Daoism is said to be Li Er of Laozi (Laotzu in English) and Zhuanzi after him. Laozi was an ancient Chinese philosopher of great wisdom. Zhan Dao-ling of Easter Han (142) of Sichuan called himself 'Tian Si' or 'Heavenly Master' and founded the religion of Dao, worshipping Laozi as Patriarch. The Daoist Religion, however, has nothing to do with Dao; the rituals and trappings were borrowed from Buddhism. During the Tang Dynasty, Buddhism was persecuted as unproductive and exploitative, and since the family name of Tang emperors was also Li, Daoism was placed in a more important status than Buddhism. Many mystic figures and stories were created and Daoist temples built. The architecture of Daoism was not as monumental and imposing as that of Buddhism, and this could be one of the reasons why this religion, originated within China, was not as popular and influential as Buddhism. Nowadays, the most important Daoist temple in China is Yongle Gong (the Palace of Everlasting Happiness).

ISLAM

Islam was introduced to China from Central Asia in 628, first arriving in Canton, then progressing to the northwestern provinces of China. Most of its followers lived there and in Xinjiang province. Many mosques have been built since then, the earliest existing being built in the 14th century. These buildings formed an important component part of Chinese architectural heritage and an evidence of friendly contact and cultural intercourse between East and West.

In the early Islamic examples, strong influence of Central Asiatic practice can be seen in the use of materials, construction methods and architectural treatment. Arches and vaults, even domes, are used in construction. The mass of the buildings were in simple geometrical forms with distinct axes. But as compared with mosques of Central Asia, they are less monumental and less elaborate. After the Ming and Qing Dynasties, mosques adopted the coutyard plan of traditional Chinese planning.

Of the above three religions, almost all had adopted the Chinese Han national form; only through details can we see the difference between them.

BUDDHIST ARCHITECTURE

Most religious buildings in China are Buddhist architecture and are designed as pagoda, cave temple (grottoe) and temple.

THE PAGODA

The Chinese pagoda was in origin an ancient Indian tomb, the word 'Ta'[2] (pagoda) denoting a Buddhist pagoda only. It is a new Chinese word put into use after Buddhist Sutras were introduced to China and translated from the Sanskrit 'stupa' or 'dagoba' and phonetic translation of 'topes'. We may assume that the concept and form of the Chinese Buddhist pagoda was originated in India. "Stupa" in India means "a heap", as to put dirt and stone on top of a tomb to mark the place."[3] The tradition goes that after Sakyamuni died, his body was cremated by incense wood and the remains of his bones were cracked like beads. Each bead was called 'Sarira' or 'Sheli' in Chinese, and each bead was buried in a stupa; hence the heap was called 'Sheli Ta'. A stupa is constructed mainly of four portions: the podium; the body; a precious box used to keep the sarira in; and the canopy, an umbrella-like disc. The whole is constructed of brick and stone and filled with dirt. A stupa was actually a monument.

Another kind of pagoda was generally believed to be evolved from the Chinese high-rise building, the Lou or Ge. On top of the roof, a small stupa was added; hence it was called the pavilion-type pagoda. There are different opinions about this assumption. For instance, Liu Zhiping maintains that 'the only real Ta is stupa, which is a tomb'[4] or the Lama stupa of Yuan Dynasty, and that 'pavilion-type pagoda and close-set eave pagoda are not pagodas but the multi-storeyed pavilions of Indian Buddhist halls'.[5] It would be difficult to determine now which is true, but one thing which is acceptable to all is that the conception and form were originated from India. After the Ta was introduced into China and infused with some of the features of Chinese architecture, the Chinese pagoda was created. During the 3rd century the pagoda existed in India. Xuanzhuang, the master monk of Tang Dynasty (602-664) who stayed in India for 17 years, must have been familiar with this type and could have introduced it to China.

The pagoda in the early days was the central building built on the axis of a temple. Generally, a pagoda was erected before other temple buildings and was the most important of a temple complex. However, since the rise of icon worship in Buddhism, halls were built for chanting sutra in front of statues, and the importance of the pagoda was decreased. At one time, the pagoda and hall were of the same importance. The pagoda was first built in front of a hall, then later behind it or in a side courtyard. Sometimes pagodas were built on high land outside the temple complex to give directions and guide the pilgrims, and were called 'guiding towers'. The tower on top of high land or a peak gave faraway pilgrims a sense of arrival in a land of Buddhist shrines. Sometimes a pagoda was built on higher land at the end of the axis as a terminal building. The forms of pagoda can be classified as the close-set eaves type pagoda, the multi-storeyed pavilion type pagoda, the Lama stupa, the single-storey pagoda, the Diamond throne pagoda and the jin zhuan pagoda.

The earliest extant example of Chinese pagodas are in Yungang (Cloud Hill Grottoes), Buddhist Grottoes and Longmen Grottoes. In Yungang there are multi-storey pagodas which were carved out of stone in the form of three, four, and nine storeys. There are bas-reliefs of pagodas too, complete with structural elements like posts, beams, tie-beams, duogong, and inverted V-shape gong. From these examples we are sure that the pagodas of India were Sinocized even as early as the Northern Wei Period.

In Northern Wei, on Song Shan Mountain in Henan, was built the Songyue Temple Pagoda (523), which has a plan of 12 sides and is of the close-set eaves type. During the Tang Dynasty, most of the pagodas were of square plan form, and in the later Song Dynasty, pavilion-type pagodas were built for lookouts as well as to be looked at. Beisita (North Temple Pagoda) in Suzhou, a wooden tower at Yingxian, are examples of this type of pagoda. During and after the Yuan Dynasty, many Lama stupas and Diamond Throne pagodas were built. We shall deal with them separately in the following examples.

△ Datong, Shanxi, Yungang Cave, stone pagoda, measured drawing

▷ Song Shan Mountain, Henan, Songyue Si Pagoda, Northern Wei, 523

1. *Miyan (Close-set eave) Pagodas.* During the Northern and Southern Dynasties, many Buddhist temples and pagodas were built in the northern region – the oldest surviving brick pagoda is Songyue Temple pagoda built in Northern Wei on Song Shan Mountain in Henan. It has a 12-sided plan of fifteen storeys high, and the outline of this pagoda is a graceful curve, the profile resembling the curve of the Sikhara tower of India. It is the first and only one of its kind in China. The tower measures 39.5 metres high, and the diameter at the base is 10.6 metres. Hollow inside and without staircase and floors, it is impossible to climb. The elevation is divided into three distinct parts. The lowest part is a high double-plinth storey, very simple in form and decoration, with an opening facing south. On top of the plinth is the second portion, which has a

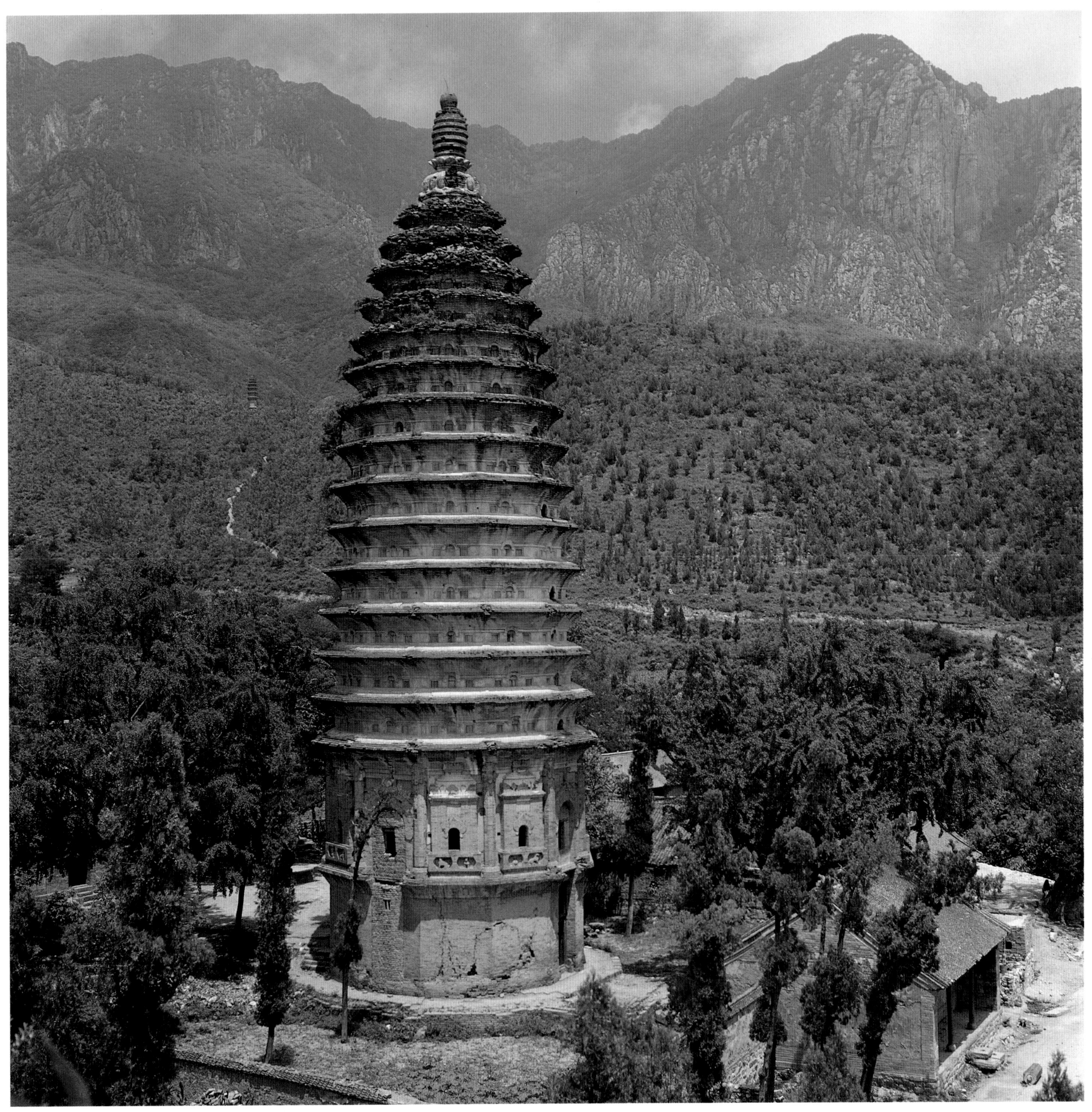

greater diameter than the lowest one, with arches, recesses and niches, like Boddhgaya Tower in India. The arches are decorated with lion reliefs; at each of the 12 corners is an octagonal corner column, with a base of lotus petal design; the capital is decorated with lotus petal and flame-like designs. Above this portion are 15 close-set eaves corbelled out of solid brickwork, and since the walls between the eaves are so short, only very tiny windows could be opened. The stone sha (finial) is held by inverted lotus petals, very bold, robust and pretty. We can assume from the remaining finishing lime plaster on the wall surface that the original colour could have been white, and this is a unique feature of the brick tower of that period. The white walls must have stood out distinctively from the enclosing purplish rock hills and green woods. The outline and details of this pagoda show definite influence from India. Lions were not indigenous to China; they were imported to China from Persia as a present to the emperor, and were taken as a symbol of strength. Using lion sculptures to guard the opening was symbolic of warding off evil elements.

Songyue Temple Pagoda is located in a secluded place facing a valley. Judging from its location it was not possible to build many buildings in front of it, so it became a centralized pagoda. It is beyond doubt that this tower preceded all the early Tang Dynasty brick towers and other close-set eaves towers of the following dynasties.

In a valley near the Songyue Temple Pagoda is a Tang Dynasty brick pagoda, very graceful in outline, called the Fawang Temple Pagoda (The Pagoda of the King of Law). Its plan, like all Tang Dynasty pagodas, is square, its high plinth devoid of any decorations and its outline a graceful curve like the entasis of a Greek column, the middle portion bulging a little and gradually tapering to the top. Its 15 corbelled brick eaves, one upon another, was typical of the Tang Dynasty pagoda.

Xiaoyan Pagoda (Small Wild Goose Pagoda), located inside Xian, is very much like the Fawang Temple Pagoda. Built in 707, it also has 15 storeys and is 45 metres high; the plan is 11.38 metres square. Built on a platform extending to all four sides, two stone staircases extend to the north and south, and the beams of the north and south doorways have delicately carved scrolls of plant designs and Buddhist images. Inside is a staircase only 60 centimetres wide which can no longer be ascended, since the top storeys and finial were damaged by several earthquakes; but the fine and graceful outline is still evident.

During the Liao Period, Tianning Temple Pagoda (The Pagoda of Heavenly Peace) was erected in the southwestern part of Beijing; it stands on a piece of flat

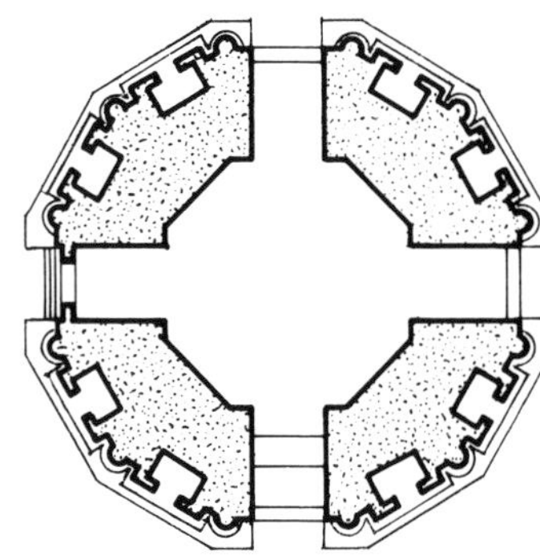

0 1 2 4 6m

△ Song Shan Mountain, Henan, Songyue Si Pagoda, Northern Wei, 523

▷ Xian, Shenxi, Xiaoyan Pagoda, Tang Dynasty, 707

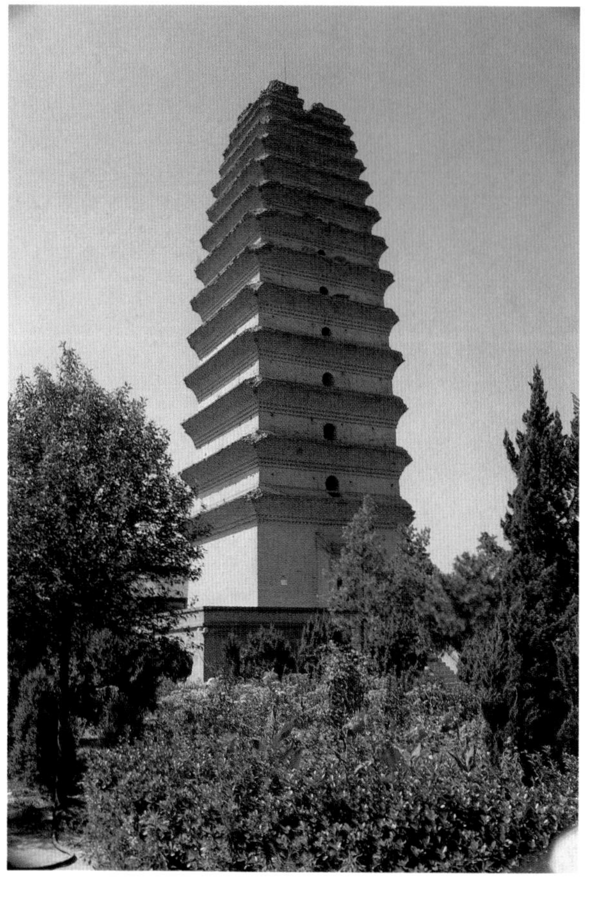

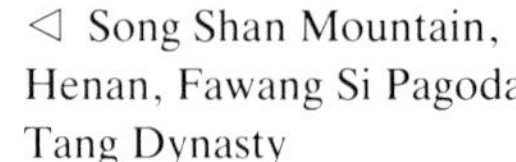

◁ Song Shan Mountain, Henan, Fawang Si Pagoda, Tang Dynasty

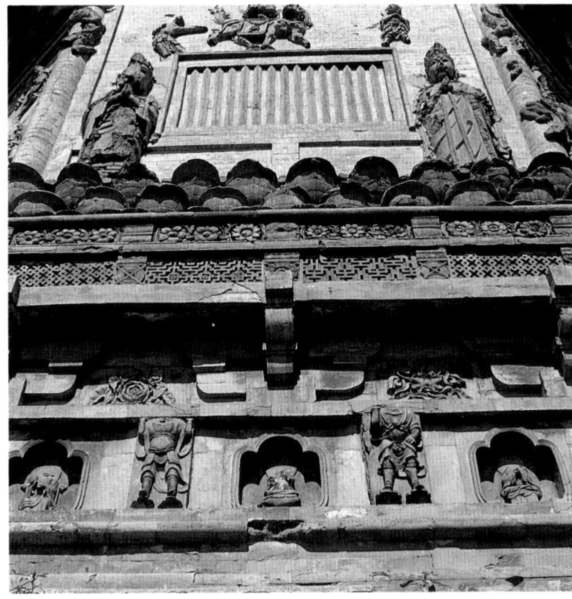

△ Beijing, Tianning Si Pagoda, Liao Dynasty, detail

◁ Beijing, Tianning Si Pagoda, Liao Dynasty

land with a height of 57.8 metres. Octagonal in plan, it is 13 storeys high and built entirely of brick. The pagoda was erected on a platform; above are two tiers of zumizuo, the entire surface covered with Buddhist images. Above the second tier zumizuo are duogong which support a cantilevered balcony above. The main portion of the pagoda is built on top of the balcony with a base of lotus petals. At each of the eight corners is an engaged column, the wall between columns having blind doors and windows; it is guarded by carved reliefs of warriors and Buddhas. Above this portion are the close-set eaves, each supported by brick duogong. The pagoda is covered with a pointed roof and finial. The tall and tapering outline of the pagoda makes it look very tall, erect and straight. The decorations, from the plan and simple platform up to the delicately carved zumizuo, then to the comparatively flat body, and on to the elaborate eaves formed in a transition form simplicity to complexity, make a very graceful silhouette and lend a spiritual uplift to the supernatural beings above.

In the western suburb of Beijing is another pagoda of the same type built during the Ming Dynasty. Only the details are different between these two, and many have mistaken it for the Liao Pagoda. Built in 937-975, Qixia Temple Pagoda at Nanjing is a smaller stone pagoda, very elegant and refined. The railing surrounding the platform is an imitation of wood construction, the geometrical pattern representing the railing of that period.

In comparing the close-set eaves pagodas of the Tang and Liao Dynasties, it is not difficult to tell that during the Tang the plan forms were unanimously square with very simple decoration, and the plinth was

◁ Nanjing, Jiangsu, Qixia Si Pagoda, Southern Tang, 937-975

▽ Nanjing, Jiangsu, Qixia Si Pagoda, Southern Tang, 937-975

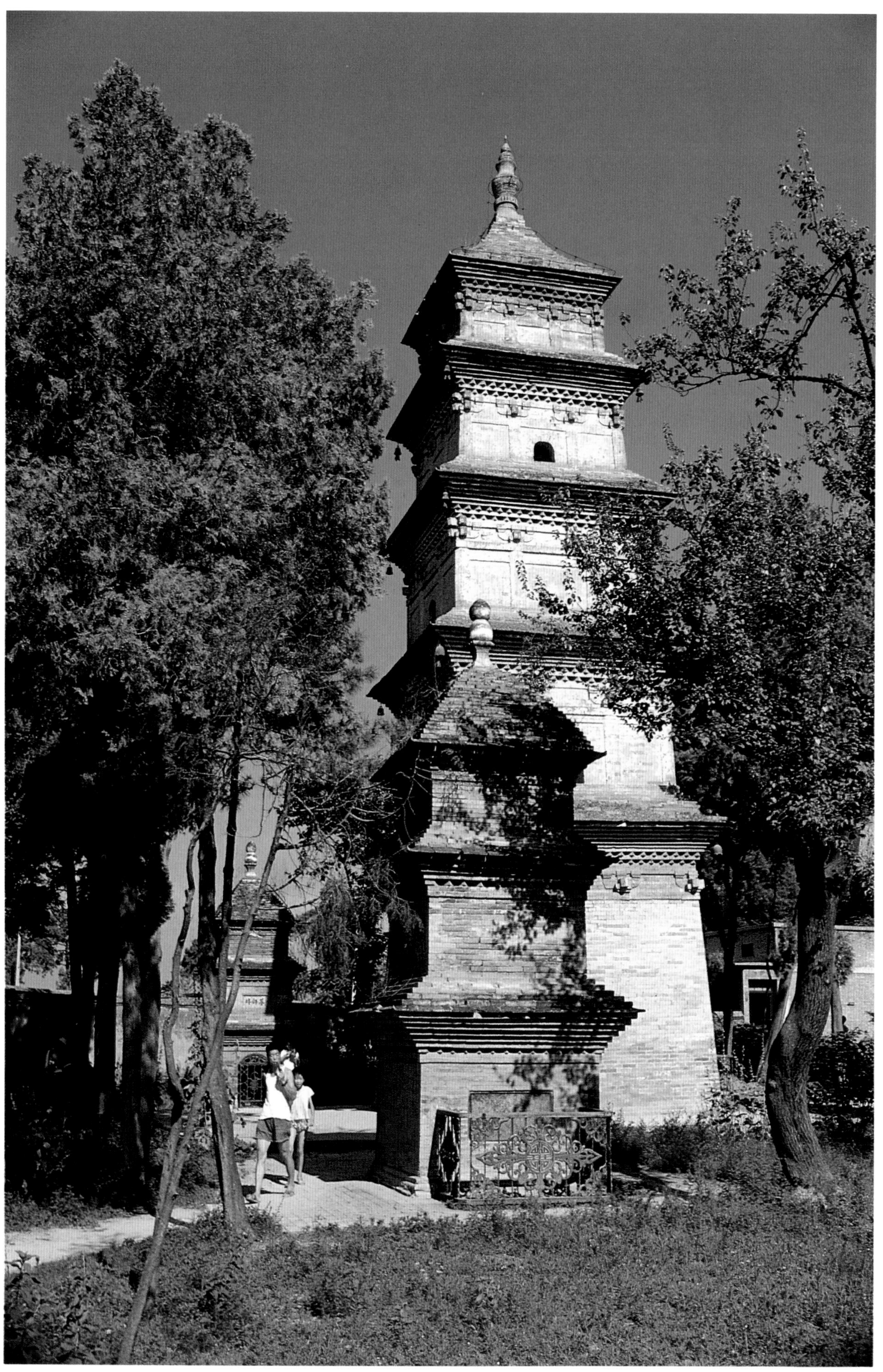

◁ Xian, Shenxi, Xuanzhuang Pagoda, Tang Dynasty, 669

plain and simple. In contrast, the Liao pagodas have octagonal plans, adopted zumizuo, employed duogong, and were embellished with lotus petal carvings. The main portion has blind doorways and windows, and guardians. The eaves are also supported by duogong, and the entire structure is richer and more refined in form.

The main features of close-set eaves pagoda are that they were made of brick and stone, could not be climbed up, and were intended purely as monuments of worship or as a tomb of a monk. The eaves, with some exceptions, were always in odd numbers.

2. *Louge Pagoda (Multi-storey Pavilion Type Pagodas).* The second big category of pagoda is the multi-storey pavilion-type, and most Chinese pagodas were of this kind. They first appeared in the Yungang Grottoes, and were called Caitya in India. These pagodas were carved out of stone, but the details shown represent wooden construction. The base is a square block; above are podium, engaged pilasters and duogong to support the cantilevered tile roof. The outline is tapered from bottom to top.

Chronologically, the first existing pagoda built of this kind is the brick Xuanzhuang Pagoda at Xian (669, repaired in 681). Master Xuanzhuang died in 664 and the pagoda was built for his remains. It is situated on a high terrace overlooking the southern plains. There are altogether three towers placed symmetrically, with the central one the tallest; it is a unique case in pagoda layout. Xuanzhuang's pagoda plan form is square in shape, the central one stands 21 metres high and has five storeys. With the exception of the first storey, all four eaves above were corbelled out at the corners with brick laid diagonally called Yazi (teeth). Since the first-floor walls were repaired, it is difficult to determine whether there were pilasters here or not.

The largest and most imposing pagoda of this kind, however, is the Dayan Ta (Big Wild Goose Pagoda) in Cien Temple, Xian. This pagoda stands on a piece of highland, facing Qujiang (The Winding River) nearby and the Nanchan (South Mountain) faraway, the tower commanding a grand view; it overpowers the surrounding buildings in a superb and monumental way. Situated within the enclosure of Cien Temple, founded in 652, the tower was first erected in 704 at the request of Monk Xuanzhuang for the storage of the sutra he had brought back from India and for the translations of sutra done by him. The tower was rebuilt during the Ming Dynasty and did not retain its original appearance, but the layout is original. Here we can see how

▷ Xian, Shenxi, Cien Temple courtyard

▽ Suzhou, Jiangsu, Yunya Pagoda, Song Dynasty

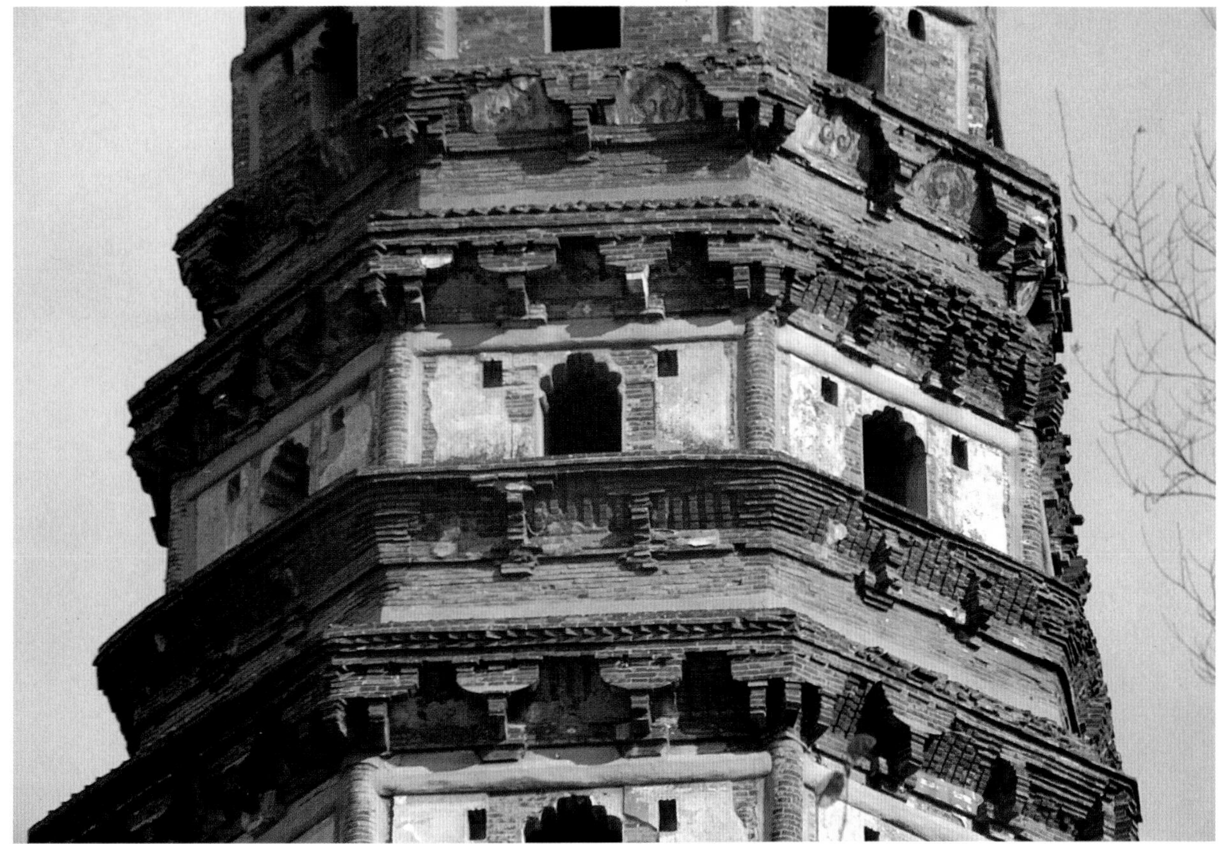

the planners of Tang Dynasty used the natural landscape to build terraces one about the other and how they used the axial courtyard planning principle. Finally, the huge 64 metres-high pagoda was used as both terminal and climax, a statement well expressed.

Inside the pagoda are wooden staircases, and stacks are placed near the outside walls, showing that the multi-storey pavilion-type pagoda is different from the former closer-set eaves pagoda. The former's practical functions are to place the sutra in a high, dry and well-ventilated space, where they are easily preserved; other functions were pertinent to the Tang Dynasty, during which time pagodas and temples were used for secular purposes and had no connection with religion. This temple was used once a year as the place for the emperor to examine the scholars as they passed the merit of Jinshi. Here they were gathered and ordered to compose poems, and banquets were given; it was a big event of that day. Other secular use was made of the temples as well, including vegetarian restaurants and tea houses. In this sense, a temple was also a building for public activities.

Yunya Temple Pagoda (Cloud Cliff Temple Pagoda) in Suzhou is a brick pagoda on top of the Huqiu Hill (Tiger Hill); so situated, it is also called the Tiger Hill

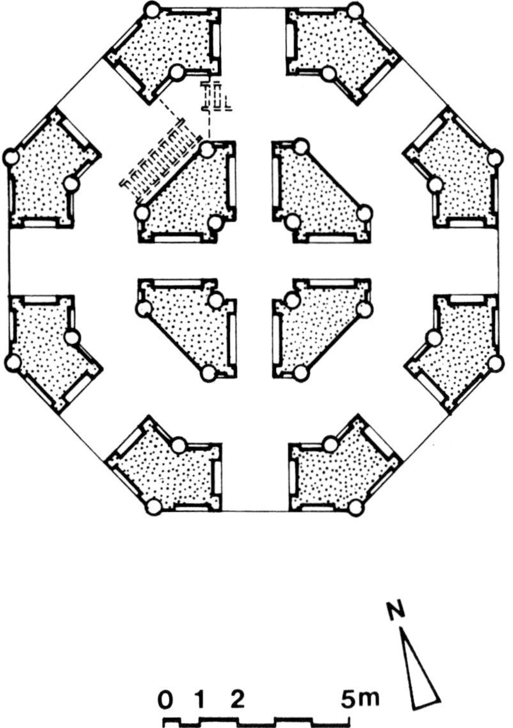

△ Suzhou, Jiangsu, Yunya Pagoda, plan

◁ Suzhou, Jiangsu, Lohan Yuan Pagoda (Twin Towers), Song Dynasty, 982

▽ Kaifeng, Henan, Youguo Si Pagoda (Iron Pagoda), Song Dynasty, 982

Pagoda. From the Five Dynasties until Song Dynasty, there were a lot of warfares in the northern part of China; thus a great deal of pagodas were built in the South of Yangtze River district. One of the largest was the Yunya Temple Pagoda which has a base diameter of 13.68 metres and stands seven storeys high, with a total height of 47.26 metres. The difference between this and the other northern pagodas of the same period is that the main body, eaves and duogong were brick-works, supported by brick duogong, but on the outside of the brick eaves wooden eaves were added, which now had been lost; only the holes of the joints of wooden beams and rafters of the body of the tower can be seen. This tower had an octagonal plan; a wooden staircase was constructed to lead to the top. Due to the fact that the foundation was on a sloping rock bed slanting to the north, the whole tower is leaning in a northeast direction and is 2.30 metres off centre. The details show it is an imitation wooden structure; there are round columns at every corner, and the beams above all show wooden construction methods. From the remaining plaster comes evidence that the original colour of the walls was rusty red, but there is no indication as to the colours of the eaves.

Beisi Pagoda or Baoen Temple Pagoda (Pay a Debt of Gratitude Temple Pagoda) situated at the centre of Suzhou, is another example of the multi-storey pavilion-type. First built in the Southern Song, but subsequently burnt down several times, the present one was repaired during the last days of Qing Dynasty in 1900. Octagonal in plan, it has nine storeys with balconies and eaves. The duogongs are original but were painted white. From a wooden staircase one can reach the top floor. It is a great place for a lookout.

During the Song Dynasty, and also located in Suzhou, two Wang brothers built two towers of similar design in Lohan Yuan. Commonly called the Shuangta (Twin Towers), they are seven storeys high, octagonal in plan, and are unique in China.

In 1049 at Kaifeng in Henan, then capital city of the Song Dynasty, a wooden pagoda was built at Youguo Si but was struck by lightning and burnt down after 15 years. In 1109, another pagoda was built at the same location. Consisting of 13 storeys and measuring 54.66 metres high, the pagoda is brickwork clad throughout with dark brown glazed tiles with green dots; these tiles give it the look of rusty iron, and as such it is commonly called the 'Iron Pagoda'. Almost nine hundred years have passed, and still the glazed tiles have retained their new appearance – evidence of an excellent technique. Each glazed tile is decorated with apsara, dragon, unicorn, lion or flower design; all were representative of the Mi Sect of Buddhism. The pagoda is a valuable example for the study of Song Dynasty brick carvings.

The most outstanding pagoda, and built entirely of wood, is the Fogong Temple Pagoda (The Pagoda of Buddha's Palace) in Yingxian. Built in 1056 in the Liao Period, the tower occupies the centre of the temple with the gatehouse to the front, drum and bell towers at the sides, and a hall behind it. This gigantic tower is not only the climax of the temple, it is also a majestic and monumental climax of the whole city and is the tallest wooden structure in the world today.

Like other pagodas of the same period, it has an octagonal plan, five storeys and a height of 67.3 metres. In between storeys are structural storeys without windows, making it altogether nine storeys high. The diameter at the base is 30.27 metres. The lowest floor is surrounded by covered verandahs which strengthened the whole edifice. The structure of the tower has two rings of columns firmly connected from floor to floor but inclined slightly to the centre, so the outline also tapers towards the top. This feature added structurally to the stability of the tower and visually to its height. The eaves and floor beams are supported by over 60 different giant duogongs.

The structural system of this pagoda was advanced for the period. The columns formed two concentric rings, unlike the towers before it, which had square plans and were stabilized by the heavy walls and a central column or staircase. Here the octagonal plan is more compact, with a core in the centre. It enlarged the earlier type of central column to a core of columns,

△ Kaifeng, Henan, Youguo Si Pagoda (Iron Pagoda), Song Dynasty, 982

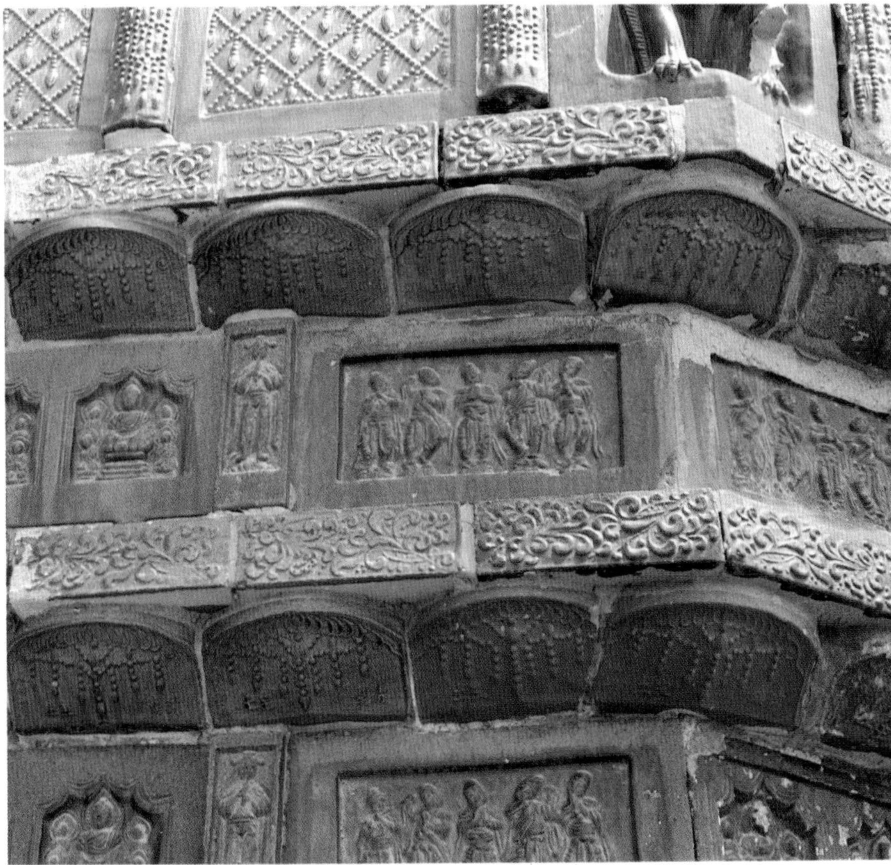

◁ Kaifeng, Henan, Youguo Si Pagoda (Iron Pagoda), Song Dynasty, 982

△ Yingxian, Shanxi, Fogong Si Pagoda (Great Wooden Tower), Liao Dynasty, 1056

▷ Yingxian, Shanxi, Fogong Si Pagoda (Great Wooden Tower), Liao Dynasty, 1056

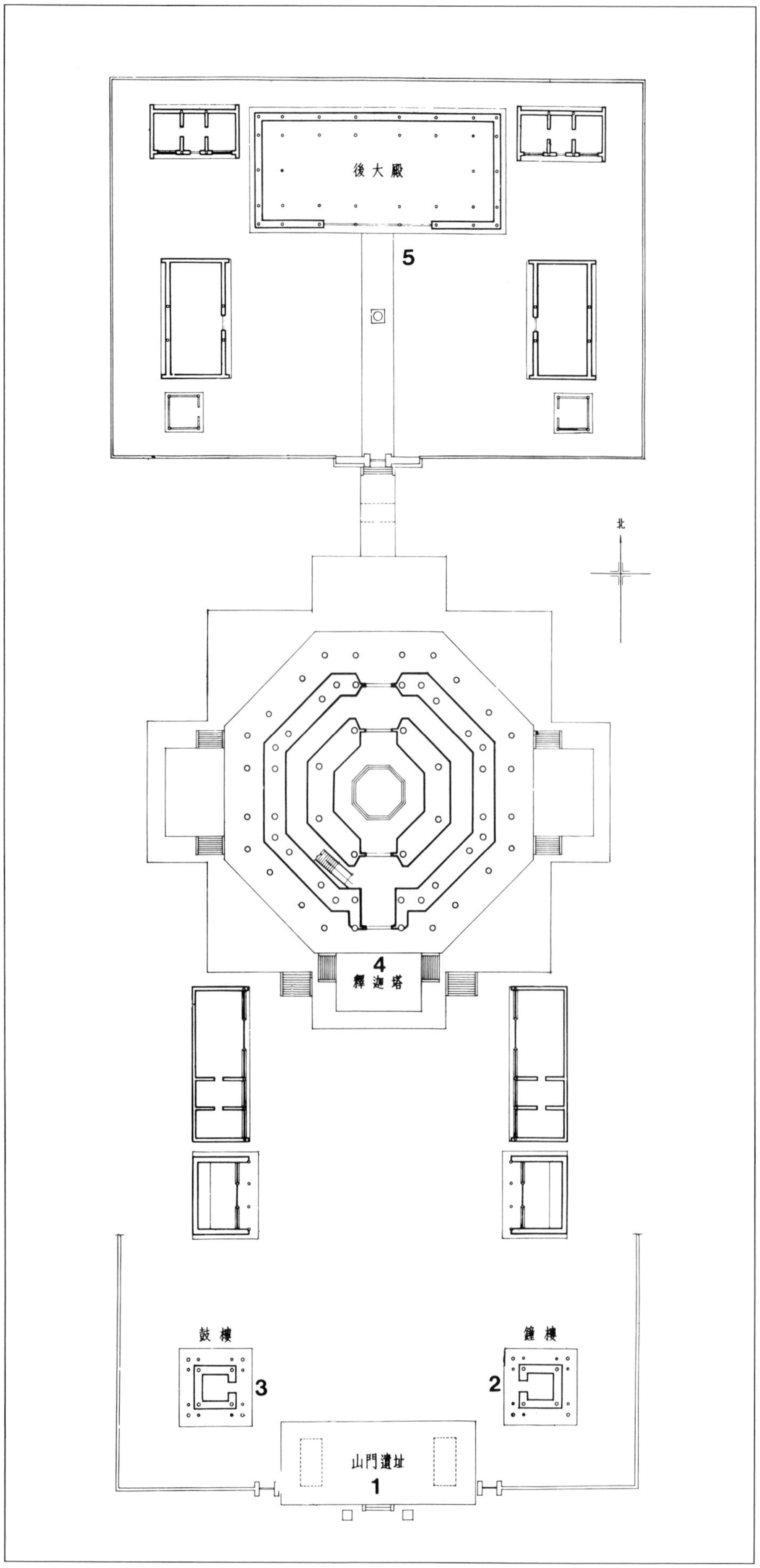

◁ Yingxian, Shanxi, Fogong Si Pagoda (Great Wooden Tower), Liao Dynasty, 1056

Key
1 Gatehouse (demolished). 2 Bell tower. 3 Drum tower. 4 Fogong tower. 5 Main hall.

enlarging the inner space for the placement of Buddhist images, and using the space between the two rings for worship. During the Jin Dynasty, bracings and members were added to the structural storeys, which further strengthened and rigidified the entire building. Between the joints are little gaps which, for more than 900 years have enabled this pagoda to endure numerous earthquakes, bad weather and even a cannon ball. The pagoda still stands in the middle of the old city, the roof pinnacle looming above the low buildings and piercing into the sky as if to enhance the faith and communications with the supernatural forces above.

Although the pagoda is massive in form, there are balconies cantilevered at every floor which, together with the verandah at the lowest floor and the very high sha piercing the sky combine to help relieve the heaviness of the body of the structure. The graceful outline, changing rhythms and stability, illustrate that both Chinese wood construction and art were indeed sophisticated and superb at this time.

From the opening of the peifang (ceremonial arch) in front of the pagoda, one can catch a view of the whole building with the columns and beams of the opening serving as a picture frame: this is a method widely used in the site planning of buildings. As one passes through this peifang and the space enclosed on both sides by side halls, approaches the foot of the tower and looks upward to the finial, the experience gained from space and time and spiritual movement generates a communion with heaven above. Inside, the pagoda is dimly lit and a seated Buddha is seen under the coffered ceiling, as if the Buddha looked condescendingly upon the believers. This circumstance again reinforces the supernatural circulation between man and god, thus enhancing man's faith in religion.

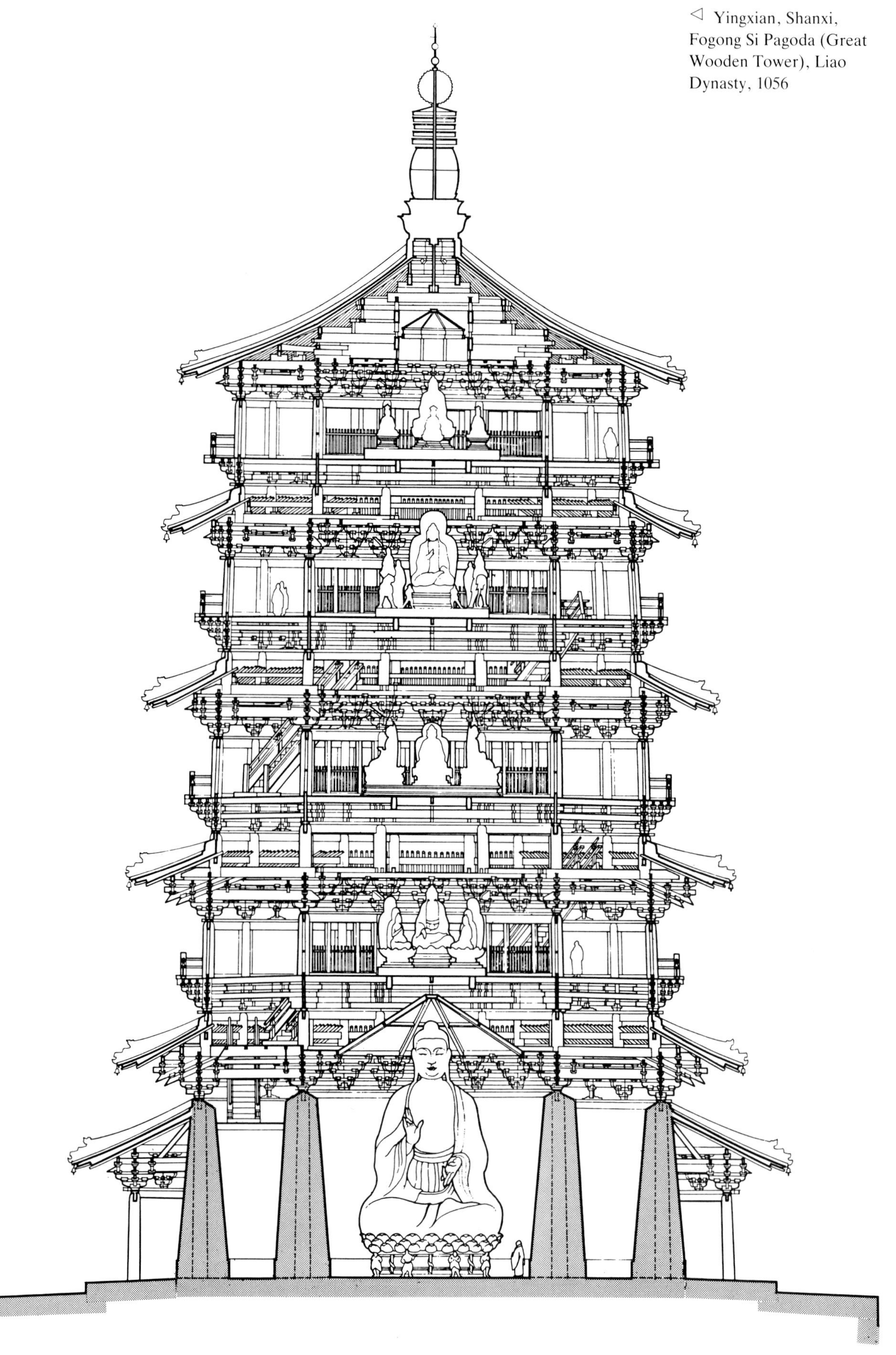

◁ Yingxian, Shanxi, Fogong Si Pagoda (Great Wooden Tower), Liao Dynasty, 1056

Through a narrow staircase worshippers tortuously climbed to the floors above, worshipping the Buddha image in each floor and, looking out, felt both fulfilled and relaxed.

During the same period, and in the southern part of China in Fujian, two stone towers were built in the Kaiyuan Temple in Quanzhou. Unlike the twin towers in Suzhou, which were built very close to each other, these are standing far apart and are much larger in size. Each is five storeys high and has an octagonal plan form. At each corner is a column, and the duogong and eaves above the column are all made of stone. Each intercolumniation has three jians (bays) and a door in the centre to walk out to the balcony. The other details are like that of the other Song pagodas. In the vicinity of Shaolin Temple (Little Forest Temple), Dengfeng, Henan, there is a group of tombs built in the style of pagodas which are the tombs of monks called Talin (Forest of Stupas).

3. *Single storey pagoda.* In the third category is the single-storey pagoda which are monks' or nuns' tombs, and which were built of brick or stone. The plan forms were usually square or octagonal and 3-4 metres high. The earliest example of this kind is Jinzan Monk Tomb Pagoda in Song Shan Mountain, built in 746. The tomb was built of brick with an octagonal plinth; as it was ruined and repaired, the original form cannot be discerned. The main body followed the wooden construction with octagonal pilasters, and beams and brackets of inverted V-shaped supports. The doors and windows in-between columns and the vertical mullions also imitated wood construction, the vertical mullion having been a prevalent type used especially for temples. The upper portion is a finial.

As mentioned above, during the Tang most of the pagodas had square plans, so the octagonal plan of this pagoda is a rare case. After two centuries, however, octagonal plans became commonplace and square ones rare.

4. *Lama stupa.* We have noted that some scholars in China believed that the only pagoda introduced from India to China was the stupa. The emperors of the Yuan Dynasty believed in Lama Buddhism, and were especially influenced by the magical and esoteric practices, so Lama Buddhism was prevalent and many Lamaseries were built in Tibet, Qinhai and in Beijing. The white stupa of Miaoying Temple in Beijing, built in 1271, is an important example of this kind and was designed by the Nepalese architect Anige. It has a height of 50.86 metres and is stuccoed with white lime. This big stupa was erected on top of a T-shaped platform, and above it are two tiers of zumizuo. On top of the zumizuo, huge lotus petals support a pot-bellied jar-like stupa with a neck, which was called the Thir-

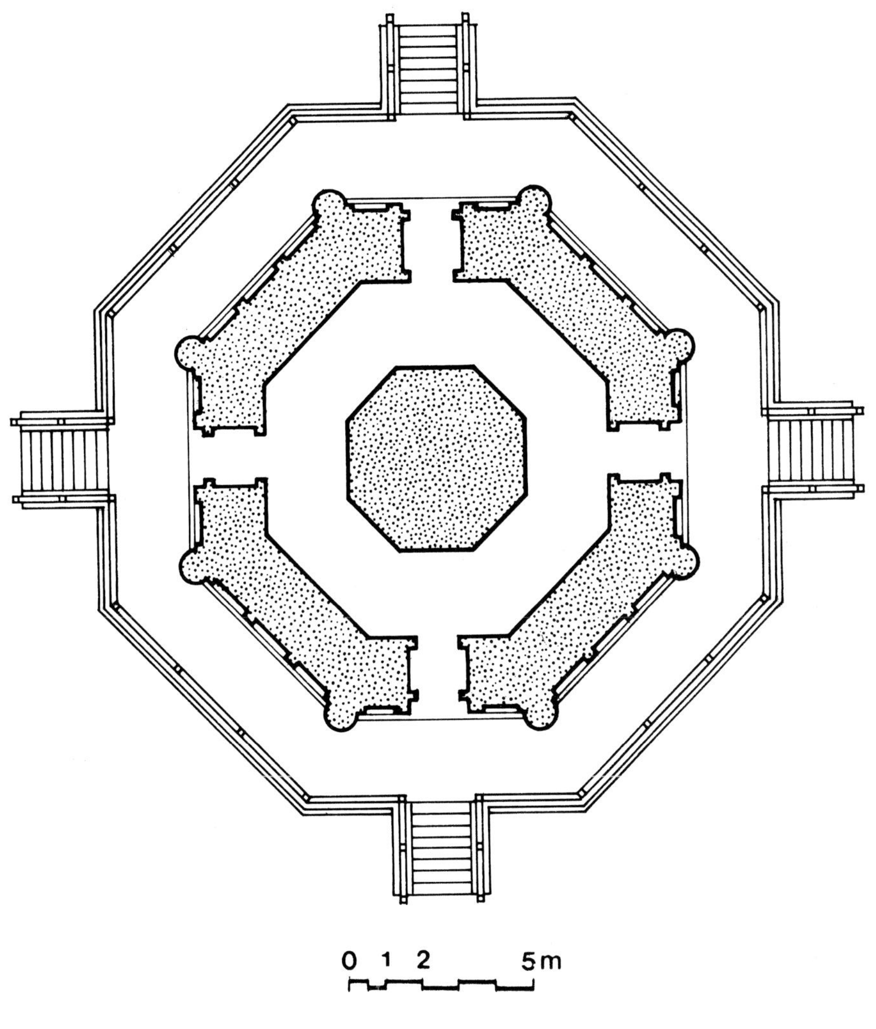

◁ Quanzhou, Fuqian, Kaiyuan Si Pagoda, Song Dynasty, 1228-50

N

0 0.5 1m

◁ Song Shan Mountains, Henan, Jinzan Monk Tomb, Tang Dynasty, 746

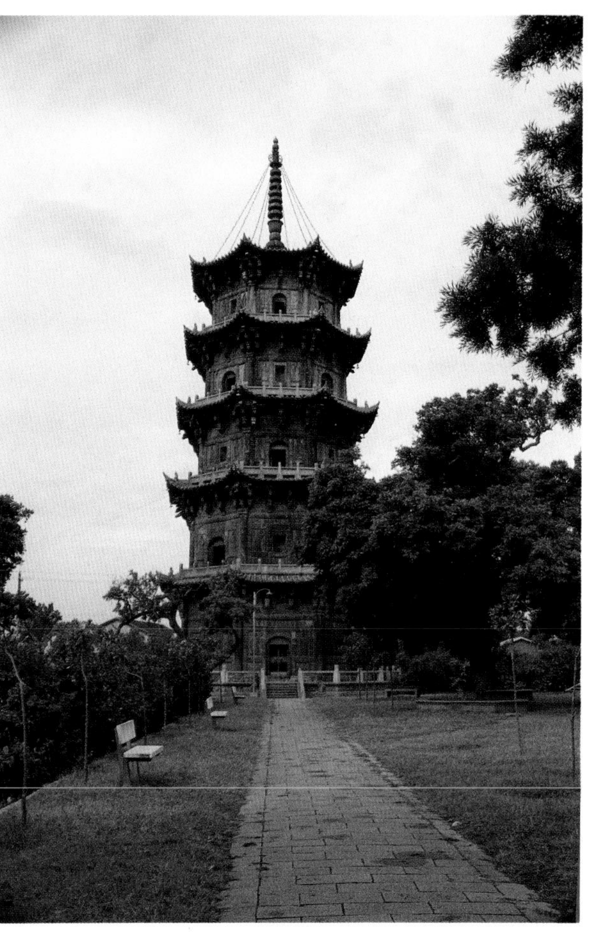

◁ Quanzhou, Fuqian, Kaiyuan Si Pagoda, Song Dynasty, 1228-50

▽ Song Shan Mountains, Henan, Jinzan Monk Tomb, Tang Dynasty, 746

◁ Wutai Mountain, Shanxi, Datayuan Stupa, rebuilt in the Ming Dynasty

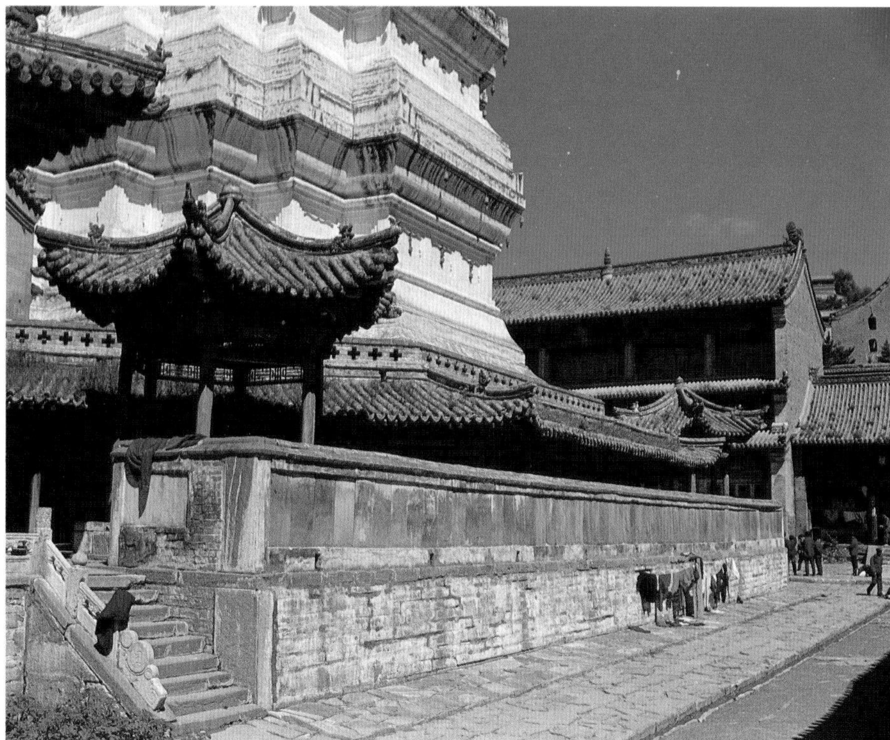

▷ Wutai Mountain, Shanxi, Datayuan Stupa, rebuilt in the Ming Dynasty

teen Heaven, while an umbrella-like disc crowns the whole. This stupa is well proportioned, very majestic and monumental, and an excellent example of its kind. Since it is located in a densely built-up residential district at the west side of Beijing, it cannot be seen in its entirety.

The second stupa worthy of note is the Datayuan Temple Stupa (Stupa of Big Stupa Courtyard Temple) of Wutai Mountain, Shanxi Province. The stupa was built in the fifth year of Yongle of Ming Dynasty (1407). The central feature of the temple is a gigantic white stupa 75.3 metres high, which looks very much like the Miaoyin stupa of Beijing, but is thinner and much higher. The lower portion is surrounded by verandahs and halls. When viewed from a distance, it stands majestically among the green mountains. The tall and massive form, the white body and golden disc are a spectacular sight, and form a most important landmark to this Buddhist shrine.

5. *Jinkong Baozuo Pagoda (Diamond Throne Pagoda).* In addition to the Lama stupa, another kind of pagoda called the Jinkong Baozuo Pagoda, or Diamond Thro-

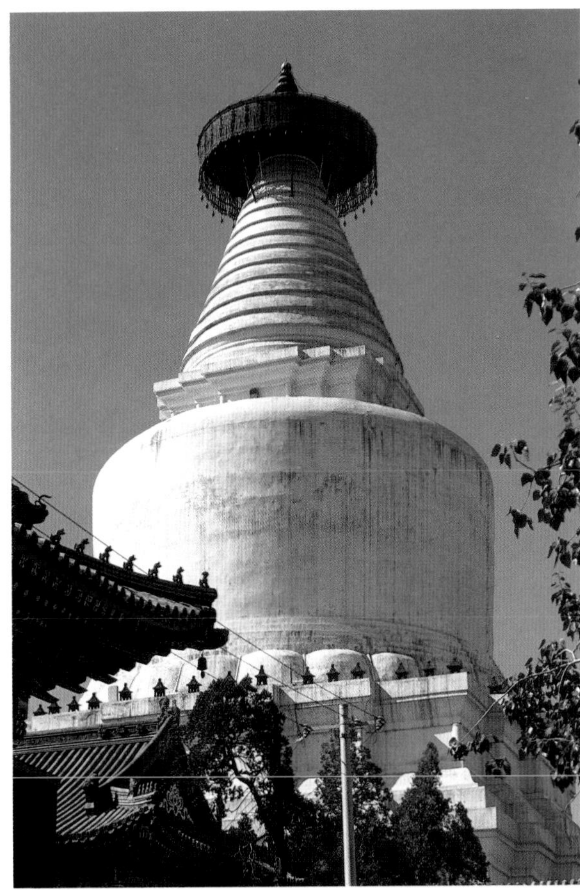

△ Beijing, Miaoying Stupa, Yuan Dynasty, 1271

▷ Beijing, Dazhenjiao Si Pagoda, Ming Dynasty, 1473

ne Pagoda, also originated from India. Its parent was the Diamond Temple of Boddhgaya, the place where the Buddha lived. The prototype of this temple is on top of a square platform on which five towers were built, the central one being the tallest and the four corner towers being smaller. The earliest example of this type could be the Yunju Temple Pagoda of Jing, but it is in a ruinous state. The pagoda at Jiaohe in Xinjiang could be a relic of the Tang Dynasty, and is also ruined. The most important examples of this kind are concentrated in the vicinity of Beijing and strongly resemble their Indian predecessors. However, the best of them are the Dazhenjiao Temple, Xihuang Temple, Biyun Temple in Beijing, and Ciden Temple in Huhehot of Inner Mongolia.

Dazhenjiao Temple Pagoda (Temple of True Awakening) is situated in a secluded place off the highway at the western suburb of Beijing. During the reign of Emperor Yongle of Early Ming an Indian Buddhist monk, Pandida, presented to him 'Five Golden Statues of Buddha and a model of the Diamond Temple'.[6] Yongle then ordered this temple to be built to receive

▷ Beijing, Biyun Si Pagoda, Qing Dynasty, 1748

△ Beijing, Dazhenjiao Si Pagoda, Ming Dynasty, 1473

◁ Beijing, Dazhenjiao Si Pagoda, Ming Dynasty, 1473

△ Beijing, Biyun Si Pagoda, Qing Dynasty, 1748

▷ Beijing, Xihuang Si Pagoda, Qing Dynasty, 1780

this religious object. In 1473 a pagoda was built after this model. It has a rectangular terrace of 15.7 x 18.6 metres composed of six horizontal layers and a base; the total height of this terrace is 7.70 metres. It has a zumizuo base of about 0.5 metres, and on top of it are five horizontal layers, the facets elaborately carved with motifs of Lama Buddhism and covered with slightly cantilevered eaves. The platform is slightly tapered towards the top, and the top is 0.5 metres narrower than the bottom at each side. The cantilever has 13 eaves nearly eight metres in height, others have eleven eaves nearly seven metres in height, and all are very delicate and refined. In front of the central one and between the two smaller ones is a small hall with a conical yellow glazed tile roof. Since it is placed in this important position and is colourful, it stands out from the greyish stone structures to add a finishing touch to the pagoda, bringing it to life. Although the pagodas followed their Indian origins, the close-set eaves of the pagodas are in the Tang style: this is an excellent example of cultural circulation and assimilation.

On the axis of the platform and to the north and south are two arched doorways; inside is a staircase leading to the top of the terrace. The carvings on the facets are high-reliefs of the Garuda, a bird with a human face (Golden Wing Bird), a lion, a horse, a peacock and the Lama Eight Instruments, a Bodhi tree, guardians, and Arahats. They are outstanding examples of Buddhist carvings.

In 1748 under the reign of Qianlong of Qing Dynasty, another Diamond Throne Temple Pagoda was built at the east side of Xiang Shan (Fragrance Hill) in the west mountains of Beijing. This is the Biyun Temple (Azure Cloud Temple). Built of white marble, the total height of the pagoda is 34.7 metres. The platform is fully covered with niches and Buddhist images. On top of the terrace are five 13-storey square towers of close-set eaves, two small stupas, and a little Diamond Throne Pagoda. The silhouette is rich and picturesque, but with order. Biyun Temple faces a southeastern valley; from the meandering upward road and from faraway, the white pagoda stands out among the clouds and dark green trees. Along the road were ancient pine trees and a stream of rapid torrents; doubtless, the choice of site was influenced by the 'Fairyland' idea of Daoism. After the gatehouse, the halls, arches and courtyards are laid along a central axis, and gradually move upward according to the slope of the site. After several beautifully carved peifangs, the pagoda is finally reached. This tortuous path has the same meaning as other temples. Although the sculptures of this pagoda are not as reticent and refined as the former one, the siting and space manipulation is far better than all other pagodas of the same kind.

Another Diamond Throne Pagoda built under the reign of Qianlong is Xihuang Temple Pagoda (West Yellow Temple Pagoda) in Beijing. Built in 1780, it was erected to house the personal effects of the deceased Panchan Lama VI. The pagoda is a jewel of Qing Dynasty architecture. The height of the platform is only about three metres, and instead of pagodas, five Lama stupas sit atop the platform.

Between 1727 and 1732 in Huhehot in Inner Mongolia, a Diamond Throne Pagoda was built in the Cideng Temple. It has the same form as the former ones, only the platform is covered with carved, dark brown blocks. Each layer has a glazed tile eave. The platform is bordered with white stone, so the colour is richer and more sedate. Like the Dazhenjiao Temple Pagoda, five towers and a small pavilion were built on top of the

◁ Huhehot, Inner Mongolia, Cideng Si Pagoda, Qing Dynasty, 1727-32

▽ Zhending, Hebei, Duobao Pagoda, Jin Dynasty 1161-89

▽ Zhao Xian, Hebei, Tuo Luo Ni Sutra Pillar, Song Dynasty, 1038

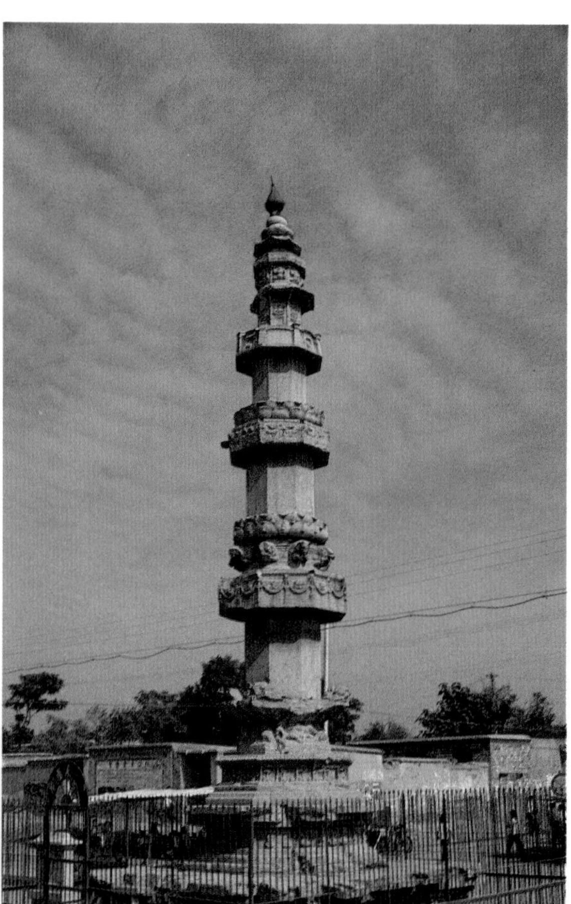

platform; the middle one is seven storeys high, the rest are five storeys high. Its total height is 16.5 metres. Although the outline and proportion of each tower is not as good as the former ones, the carvings of Buddhist images and the Bodha tree are of Indian style and very refined.

The Duobao Pagoda of Guanhui Temple in Zhending was built between 1161 and 1189, and because of the numerous sculptures on the pagoda, it is commonly called the Huata (Flower Tower). This pagoda is made of brick and plaster, the central pagoda several times taller than the four others. The pagoda now lies in a yard and is in a deplorable state of ruin but some of the sculptures on the central pagoda are still discernible.

6. *Jin zhuan (Sutra Pillar)*. Jin zhuan is a vertical pillar like the memorial column or obelisk, and its aim is to use sculpture and sutra inscribed on the surface to preach and educate people in Buddhism. The earliest examples are found in Foguang Temple. One is at the front of the temple, of octagonal shape with a base and finished with a roof. Erected in 857, it has a height of 3.24 metres. The base also has an octagonal plan with lotus petal designs. Between the petals are lion carvings in the round. The pillar is fully carved with sutra; the tassels on the capital could have been introduced from the West. Another pillar erected in 877, also in

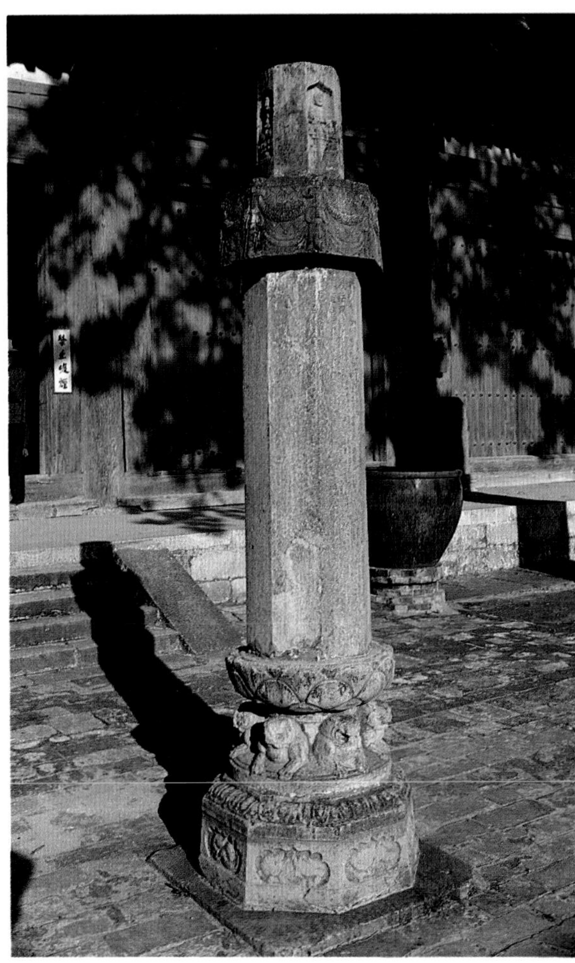

◁ Wutai Shan, Shanxi, Foguang Si Sutra Pillar, Tang Dynasty

Foguang Temple, has a height of 4.90 metres and, as with the former one, the canopy is widely overhung, a reflection of the base.

During the Song Dynasty a great deal of zhuan was erected. The tallest as well as the most magnificent is in Zhaoxian, Hebei Province. It was erected in 1038, and has a height of more than 15 metres, completely carved of stone. The base has three layers of zumizuo, and each is carved with warriors and dancing girls of vivid and lively movements. The upper zumizuo depicts a house of three bays, and shows columns and beams. On top of it is the sculpture of a hill used to support the pillar, which is carved with Buddhist stories. The purpose is obviously to use the refined art form and carvings to educate people, especially the illiterate. The pillar and some of the carvings are now weather-beaten, and some parts of the pillar have been ruined.

BUDDHIST GROTTOES

Grottoes, which are cave temples, or stone shrines, make up another important building type of Buddhist architecture. In Buddhism, the grotto is called Caitya, and it resembles a stupa in form. The difference is that in the latter the remains of Sakyamuni were preserved, whereas there were none in the former. Since Caitya is an object of worship in a cave temple, cave temples can

▷ Zhao Xian, Hebei, Tuo Luo Ni Sutra Pillar, Song Dynasty, 1038

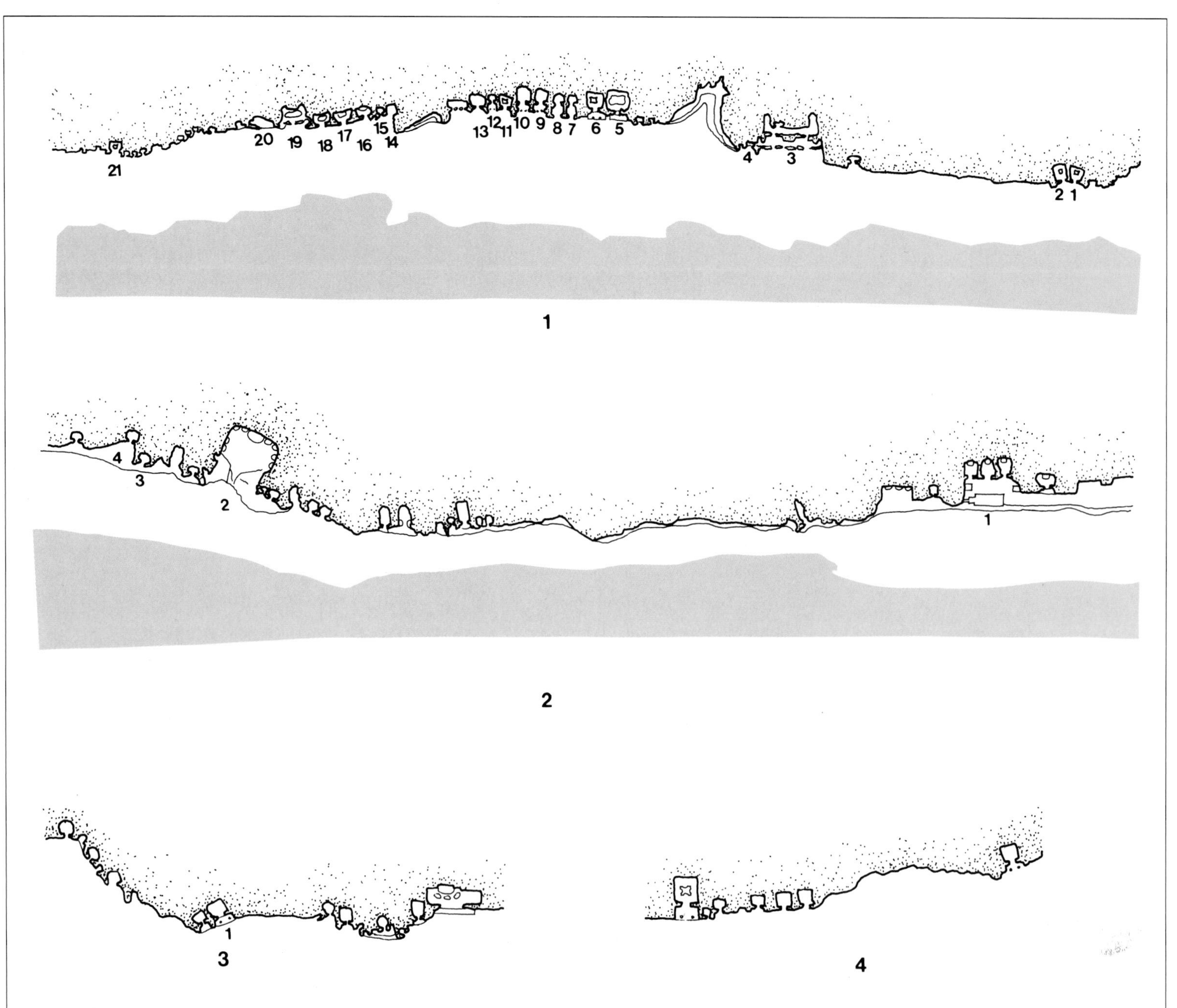

▷ Dunhuang, Gansu, Mingsha Shan Hill

◁ Comparative plans of Yungang, Tianlong Shan, Longmen Caves

Key
Yungang Caves. 2 Longmen Caves: (1) Bin Yang Caves, (2) Feng Xian Cave, (3) Yao Fang Cave, (4) Gu Yang Cave. 3 Tianlong Shan Caves, West Bank. 4 East Bank

sometimes be called Caitya too. The earliest cave temple is Mogao Grottoes at Dunhuang, hollowed out during the 4th century. Next are the Yungang Grottoes (Cloud Hill Grottoes) in Datong, Shanxi, built between the 4th and 5th century, and the Tianlong Mountain Grottoes, Longmen Grottoes and Dazu Grottoes. Almost all grottoes are built against a cliff and face a river or a valley; inside the caves are Buddha images.

Hollowed-out shrines were undoubtedly influenced by Indian Buddhism and became prevalent in China after the 4th century. When Buddhism was introduced into China through the Silk Road, it first came to the western part and arrived at Dunhuang, a crossroads and oasis in the desert where monks and merchants came to rest. Natural cave temples were hollowed out in this area, since this was much easier than building temples. The Bamiyan of Afghan was situated on the Silk Road where, on a cliff 1,500 metres in length, many caves and images were carved; this may have had a direct influence on Dunhuang.

The Mogao Grottoes, commonly called One Thousand Buddhist Caves, lies at the western end of the Great Wall, the Jiayu Guan Fortress, and at the edge of Mingsha Hill (a sand dune) there are remains of the Great Wall of the Han and Sui Dynasties. Although Dunhuang was hollowed out some 1,500 years ago, it was not discovered until the beginning of this century. In 366, during the Northern Wei Dynasty, caves were dug out on the west bank of Dunhaung River. These caves were first financed out of donations from believers and with official support in the Early Tang Dynasty. The caves are in two to three tiers and are reached by external cantilevered wooden walkways and staircases. The early caves were comparatively smaller, about 40 square metres in size; the bigger one is about 200 square metres. Porticoes of wood were built in front of the caves in order to protect the inside. The surviving porticoes were built during the Song Dynasty with very few robust wooden duogong. The walls and ceilings of the caves are covered with fresco paintings on plaster, with sculptures in clay and wood, and a few of stone; they represent the plastic art of that period. After the Song and Ming Dynasties, more images were added in the caves. The central nine-storey hall was built in the Qing Dynasty

◁ Dunhuang, Gansu, Mogao Caves, Main Hall and a tomb

▷ Dunhuang, Gansu, Mogao Caves, wooden portico

▷ Dunhuang, Gansu, Mogao Caves, fresco

◁ Dunhuang, Gansu, Mogao Caves, duogong, Northern Song

▷ Dunhuang, Gansu, Mogao Caves, Buddhist statue, Sui Dynasty

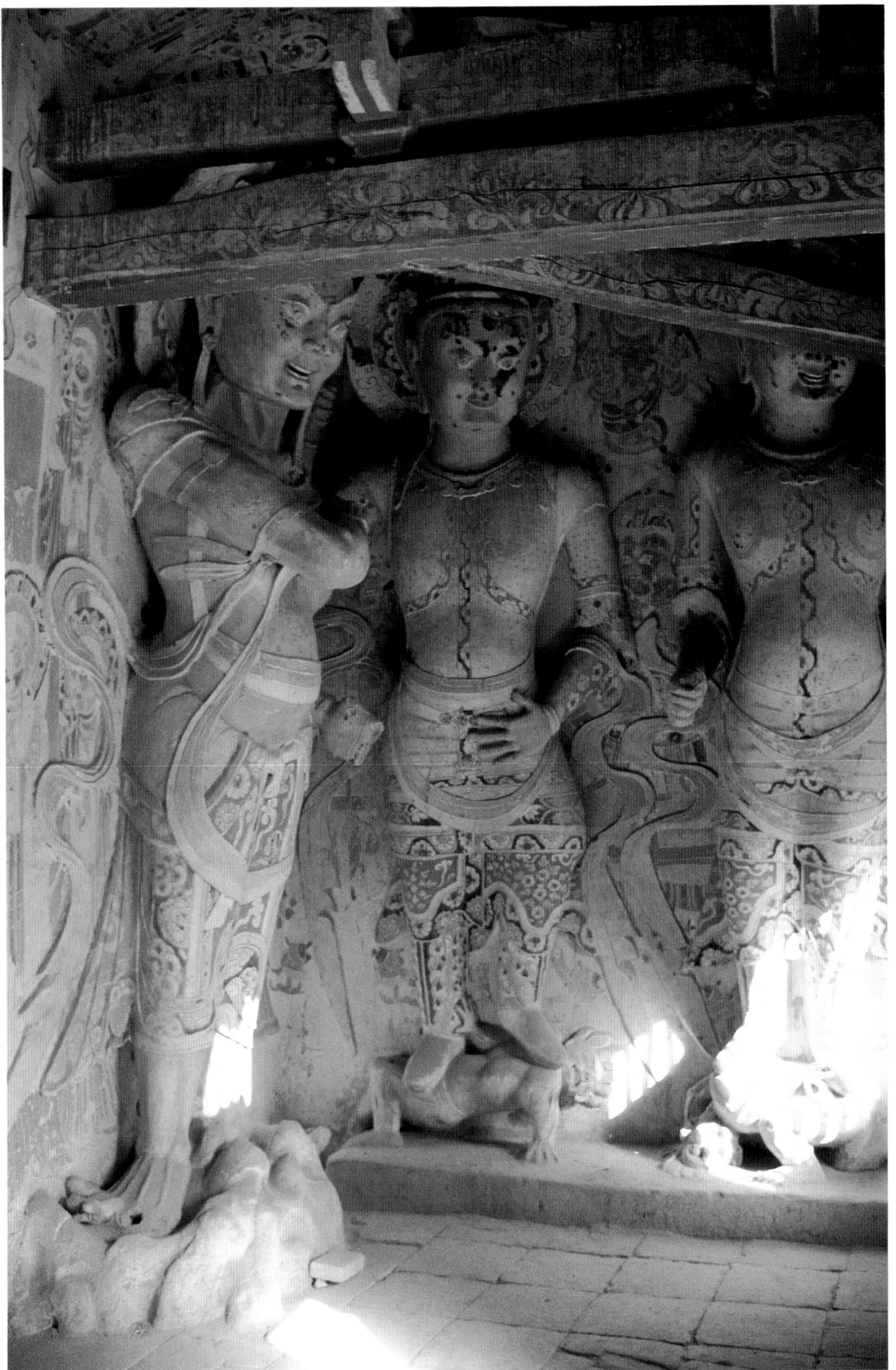

to cover a gigantic Tang seated Buddha statue.

The major achievement of Dunhuang religious art was the use of lively fresco to depict the Buddhist stories from ancient India. They preached the concepts of eternal life, Karma, or cause and effect Samsara, or transmigration, the performance of good deeds, how to reach a peaceful nirvana state, and finally how to get into the Western Paradise, or Pure-land. The Northern Wei paintings retained some of their Indian precedent and until Sui was Sinocized.

In China today there are almost no buildings erected before the Tang Dynasty extant, but the fresco paintings inside the caves provide us with much documentary evidence concerning building layout, architectural style, and construction methods of that period.

Halls and pavilions were of wood construction and roofed with tile; they were of hip roof form and half-hip roof form. In the planning of houses high walls were used to create several courtyards and were built on platforms. Widespread eaves were held by duogong; large scale temples used axial planning and symmetrical layout. The roof pitch was low and railing details were delicate.

Ceilings in the caves are in truncated pyramid form; the centre is a square or rectangular shape. Decorations are generally concentrated in the centre and on the border and are of brilliant colours, which have lasted until today. The design in the middle is generally a lotus flower on a pair of dragons. The borders are bands of 'hill and water' design, like those on bronze utensils before the Zhou Dynasty started to use fish scales, cloud patterns, and scroll leaf decorations. From the Jin, Wei, and down to Sui and Tang, the early designs are of geometrical form or animal figures, but until the Tang, plant-life forms were used throughout and are more vivid than geometrical ones. They served as foils for the theme and enriched the entire composition. Brighter colours were used too, and gold colours were added to accentuate the theme. The scroll leaf flower pattern took the place of dragon and tiger motifs. These free forms were inherited from the lively art of the Han Dynasty, as in a continuous band. The flowing lotus, grapes, and pomegranate specimens introduced from central Asia were used as a decorative pattern; rhythmic as well as dynamic, this constituted a new aritstic development of the period.

The coffered ceiling inherited the canopy and curtain form also from the Han Dynasty, a departure from the reticent hill pattern and the pearls and tassels which enriched Tang Dynasty design. The rendering of the patterns was also changed from flat wash to gradation, which added a three-dimensional effect. The coffered ceiling is something to look up to from below, and the design should bring the eyes from the border, or the lowest part, gradually up to the centre. Here the combined forces of the composition and the pattern carry the eyes forward to the central structure; it is a vertical upward force, formed by the pattern on the one hand and by the horizontal free-scroll plant life form on the other. The interaction of the combined forces form a canopy that looks as if it is revolving in the sky, finally ending at the lotus motif, symbol of the flower which is not foiled by the mud, and the eternal state was reached. The colours used in the frescoes and designs are usually blue, jade green, red, black, white and gold, which correspond to the colours specified in the *Ying Zhao Fa Shi* of the Song Dynasty.

Dunhuang is famous for its frescoes, and Yungang is famous for its sculptures and carvings. Both are important milestones of Buddhist architecture and the crystallization of the circulation of art between East and West. In Yungang the Buddha image, the decorations and architectural details all represent the cultural circulation between China and India as well as Central Asian countries. The art form of the West had been circulated absorbed, infused, and assimilated, and finally resulted in a new form completely without precedent, which eventually became a part of the precious heritage of ancient Chinese culture. Chinese historical development shows that whenever an open door policy is enforced, a flourishing culture is sure to follow.

The importance of the Yungang Grottoes, as compared with the other grottoes of the same period, lies in the fact that not only were Buddhist sculptures carved, but also a large number of architectural construction and decorative details were depicted as well. They help us to understand the architectural and sculptural art of the 5th century. It is in this sense, then, that Yungang is more important than the Dunhuang, Tianlong Shan and Longmen grottoes.

Yungang is located on the west side of the historical city of Datong, in Shanxi Province. During the Warring State Period (475-221 B.C.), corresponding to the ancient Greek and Hellenistic period, and down to the Qin and Han Dynasties, it was:

> an important fortress and crossroad between the outside and inside of the Great Wall, and the Hun from Shanyu down were all friendly with the Han people, they frequently met under the Great Wall . . .[7]

The Tobas was another nomad ethnic minority of the northern part of China. From the 1st century they migrated from the northeast, crossed the Great Wall to the southeast, and controlled the northern portion of the Yellow River by force, finally founding the Northern Wei Kingdom. In 398, Emperor Daowu made Datong its capital, which became the centre of political, cultural and religious life for nearly 100 years. Yungang caves were carved in this period. From

△ Datong, Shanxi, Yungang Caves, Northern Wei, 460

▽ Datong, Shanxi, Yungang Caves, halls

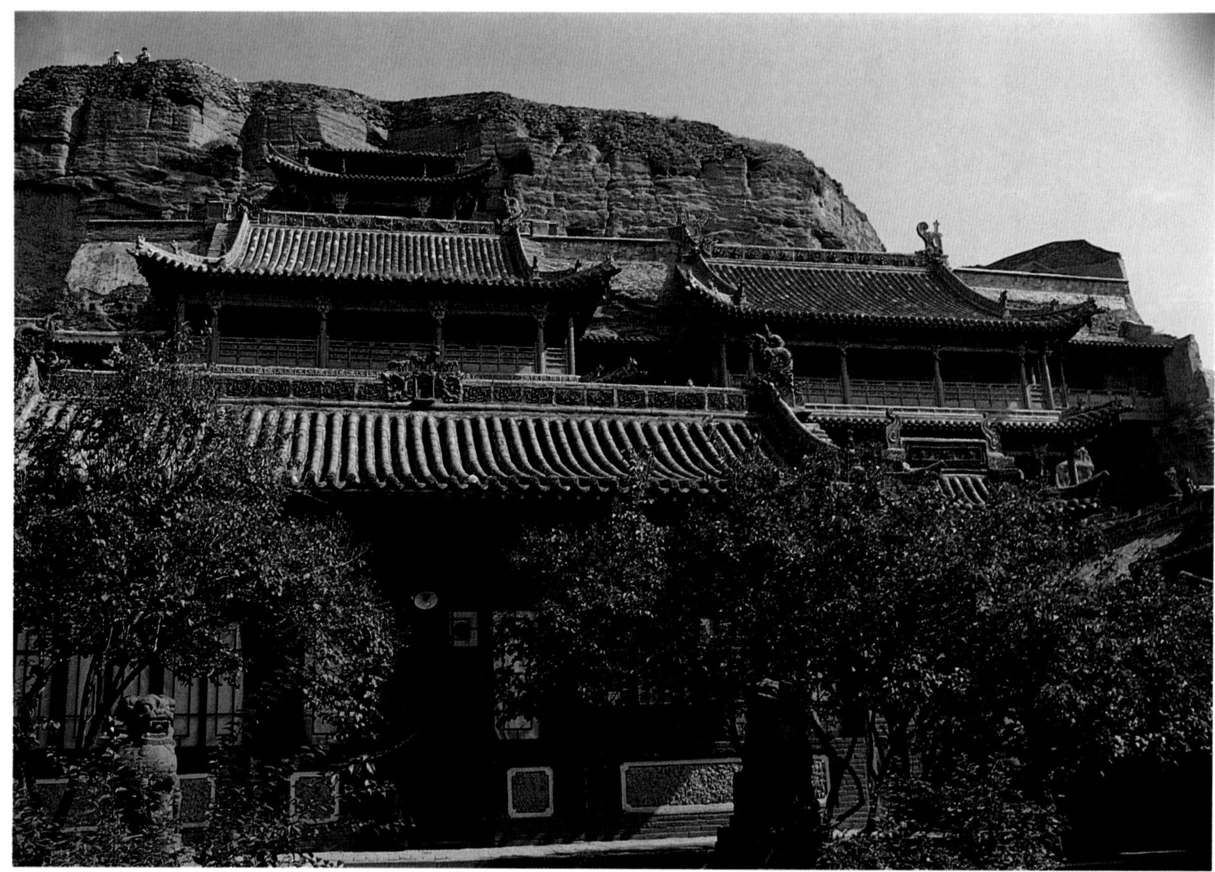

Emperor Ming Yuan on, the emperors of Wei came here to worship and pray, and it became the 'Holy Mount' and a Buddhist shrine.

Yungang caves were carved at the south side of Wuzhou Mountain nearly one kilometre in length from east to west. The largest of ancient China, there now exist 53 large caves, as well as 1,100 small caves and niches. There are altogether 51,000 images, all of different expressions and beautifully sculpted. It deserves to be called an artistic treasure of the world, a wonder of Buddhist art. The main force of workmen who hollowed out the caves and sculpted the images were captives of Northern Wei. Most of the caves were carved within the 30 years between 460 and 494, and the smaller ones were carved up to 525. They can be divided into three stages according to type, image expressions, and chronology.

According to the Wei Shu (*Book of Wei*, Chronicle of Wei)·Shi Lao Zhi:

> At the beginning of the He Ping Period, Monk Tanyao appealed to the emperor to carve the west side hills . . . Five grottoes were hollowed out of rock, inside were five Buddhist images, the tallest is over 70 feet in height, the second tallest was 60 feet, they were elaborately carved and mesmerizing in their beauty.[8]

Cave numbers 16-20 represent the first stage. The main features of these caves are an eliptical floor plan, the dome-like ceilings, and a small window facing the top of the image, which lends light to the head.

The sculptures were influenced by the Greco-Indian Buddhist carvings of Gandhara, which were developed in north India from the 1st century onward, and spread throughout all Central Asia. Details of Iranian, Byzantine, Roman provincial, Greek and Indian carvings influenced those found in these caves. The sculpted Buddhas in these caves are simple in style; garments have little decorations, the carvings of cloth arranged in processions, following the lines of the folds. The material has a woollen look and shows a trace of Middle Eastern, Pakistani and Afghanistani costumes. The Buddha sculpture in cave number 20 is a perfect example of the style of the first stage: the expression is severe and immobile, with a strong and geometrically-shaped mouth, protruding nose, and colossal ears; the shoulders, of immense width, are almost two thirds of the total height.

The second stage has five groups of caves, numbers 7-8, 9-10, 5-6, 1-2, and 11-13. In front of cave numbers 5 and 6, four-storey buildings were built giving shelter to the caves behind. The largest are numbers 3 and 11. Most of the caves in this period have square floor plans and are divided into adjoined caves. Some have a Caitya in the middle which is also used as a pillar to

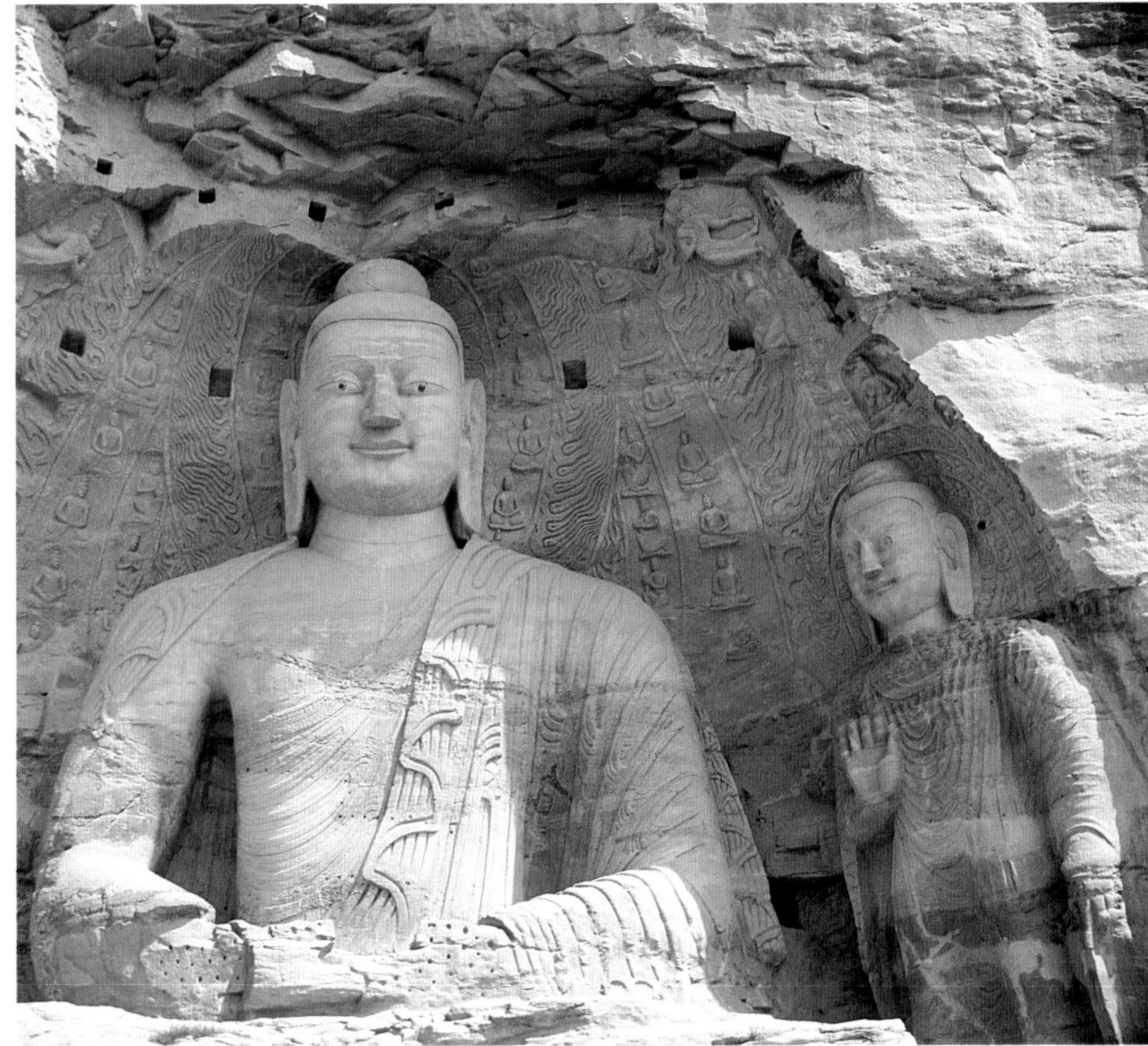

△ Datong, Shanxi, Yungang Caves, Giant Buddha, Northern Wei

◁ Datong, Shanxi, Yungang Caves, carved ceiling and wall surfaces

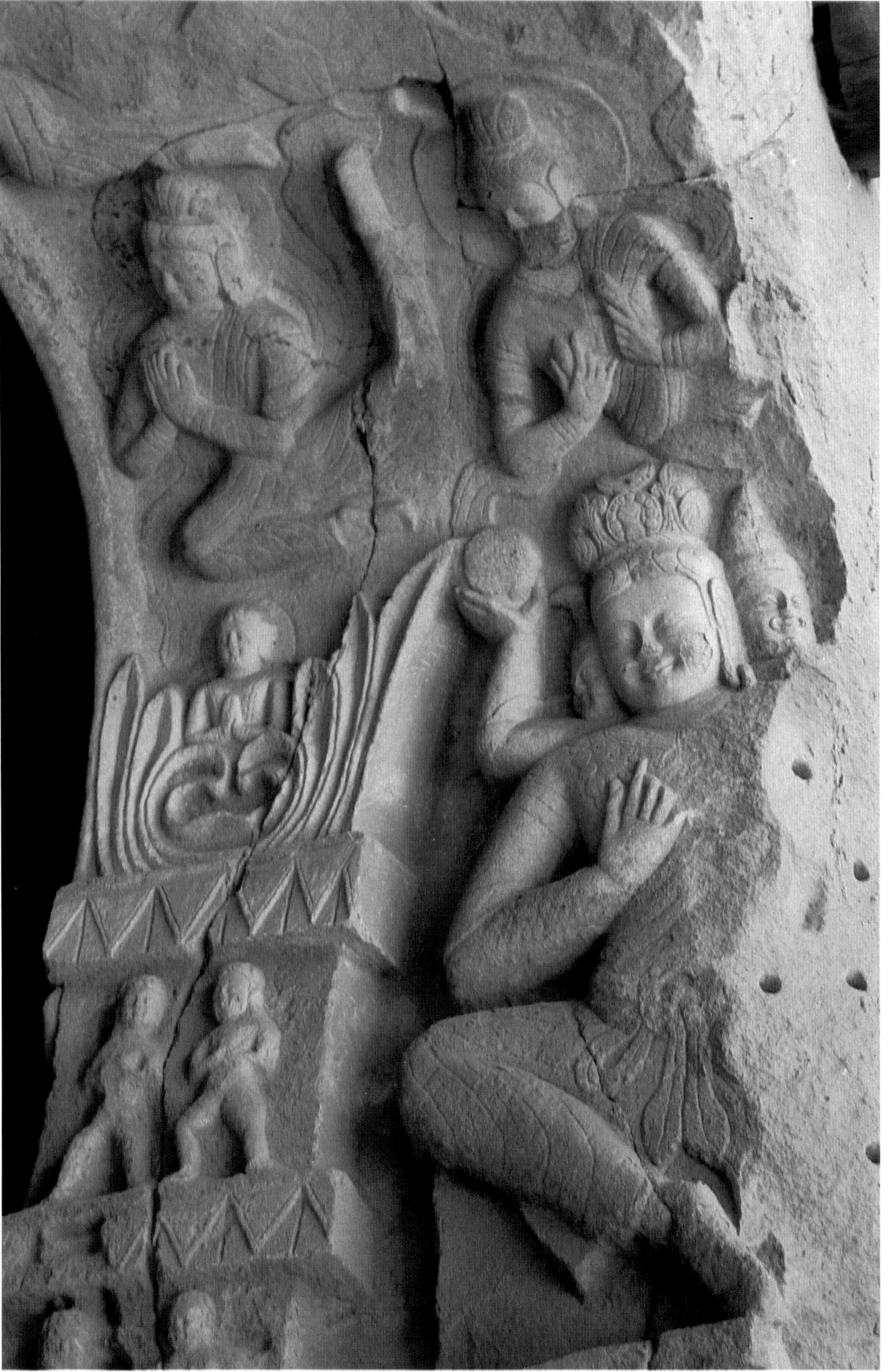

◁ Datong, Shanxi, Yungang Caves, bas-reliefs

▷ Datong, Shanxi, Yungang Caves, carved ceiling and wall surfaces

support the ceiling. Ceilings are curved and decorated, some in the form of a dome, some of square shape and coffered. The full length of the interior walls are covered with niched, Buddhist images, and are richly decorated with plants, lotus or other flowers, scrolls of vines, flames, and apsaras; animal figures like phoenixes, dragons and tiger motifs are also used.

Indian influences can be seen in the clothing, the head dress, and the appearance of the elephant; the Iranian and Byzantine influence in the wearing of beads, the weapons and lions; the Greek influence in the trident and the acanthus leaves.Broadly speaking, the iconography is taken from Greco-Buddhist style. Numbers 9 and 10 should be noted particularly where in front of the caves are peristyles of three spans divided by richly carved columns. Some animal sculptures at the bottom resembled lions, but because of weather-beating they are barely legible. The loggia resemble wooden post and lintel construction; here the Indian-influenced caves were combined with traditional Chinese architecture. The fusion of Chinese aesthetics and foreign themes can be seen in rounded niches, and in the ornamental motifs where acanthus foliage is used alongside curtains held back by beading, and in the Chinese style roof.

The bas-reliefs are also noteworthy. Decorations above doorways and niches reveal the construction and detailing of the Northern Wei Period. Here one sees the roof tiles, the inverted V-shaped Gong, and the symmetrical scroll decoration and plant design at the sides of the doorway with Ionic columns; there is definitely a Greek influence. There are countless whirling apsaras, some are Indian with short robes and feet appearing beneath them; some are Chinese, of a more serial build, their robes ending in long trains flying out behind them. Most of the wall and ceiling surfaces are also painted with red, blue, yellow and white opaque colours.

Most of the caves carved in the third stage are small niches, their plans nearly square and more ornate. The faces of the Buddhas are thinner, and there are also pagodas serving as pillars.

Yungang is a dry, deserted spot. For centuries the weather has been eroding the sandstone of the cliff, threatening the caves as well, whose rows of openings now look like a deserted beehive. These Buddhist caves rank as one of the greatest monuments of Chinese religious art, marking a crucial moment in the history of Chinese art. Countless fertile influences were brought to China by the Central Asian people,

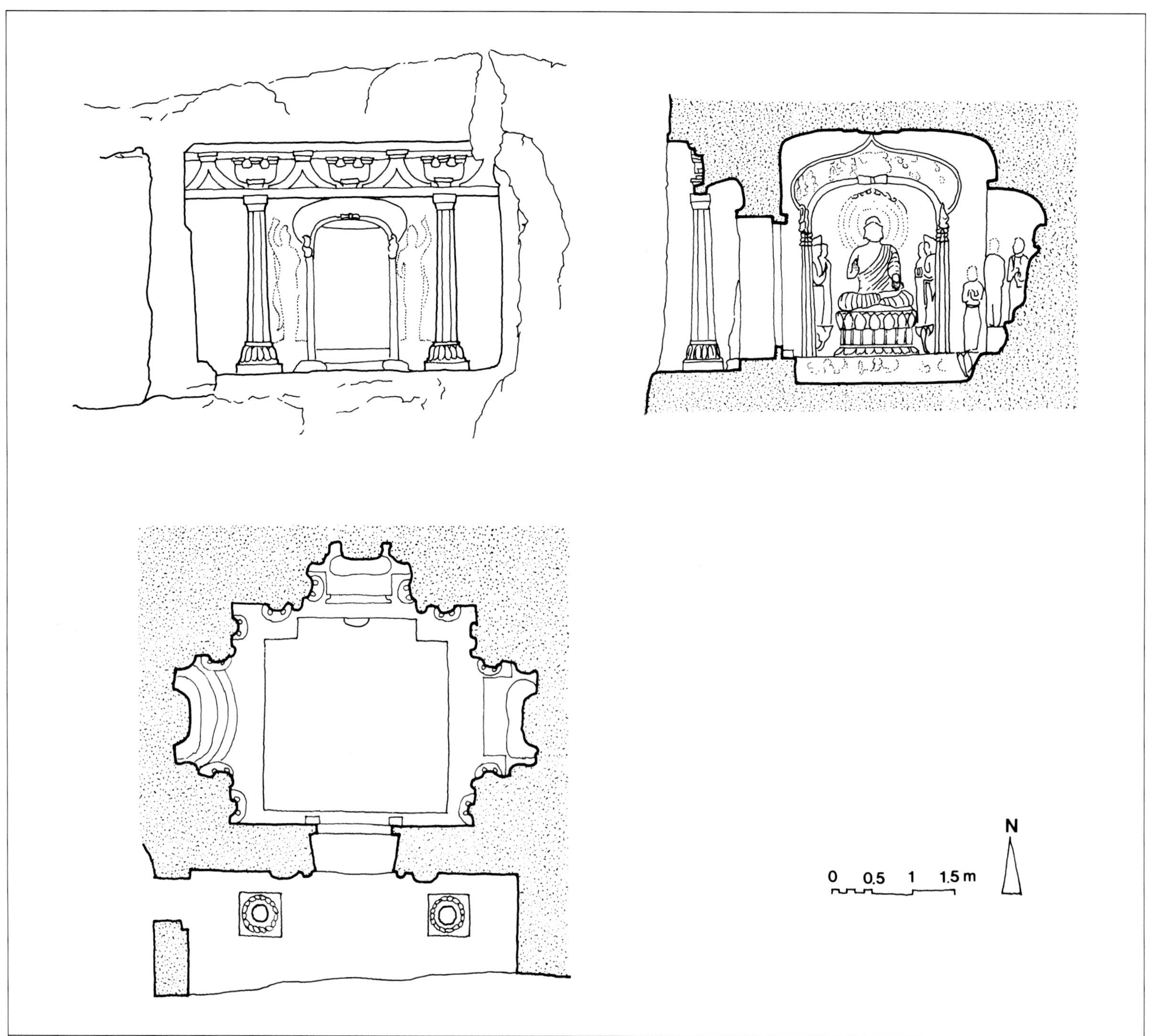

◁ Tianlong Shan, Taiyuan, Shanxi, Tianlong Shan Caves, No. 16 cave, plan and section

inspiring a great renewal in the creative spirit at a time of social and political upheaval.

Tianlong Shan (Heavenly Dragon Mountain Grottoes) is located to the south of Taiyuan, Shanxi Province. The grottoes were hollowed out along two opposite cliffs with a valley in between. The earliest caves were hollowed out at Northern Qi (550-577); the others are works of the Sui and Tang Dynasties. Number 16, hollowed out in 560, is worth special notice. In front of the cave is a carved stone portico of three bays, the middle span supported by two, octagonal-section slender stone columns with a big duo placed on the top as the capital. Above the lintels stand duogong and an inverted V-shaped gong. The elevation is well proportioned. Here the statues were carved in the round; the cloth seems as though it was poured over the voluptuous bodies; the figures seem to have a mobility of movement, unlike the static expression of Yungang. Here the Indian feeling for swelling form and the Chinese expression in terms of linear rhythm are finally amalgamated in a style which was used for the later Buddhist sculptures.

In 494, Northern Wei moved its court from Datong to Luoyang, Henan, where Emperor Xiaowen commissioned similar Buddhist caves to be done in Longmen Cliffs. The work was carried on until the Tang Dynasty. Altogether there were carved 1,352 caves, 785 niches, 39 small carved pagodas, 97,306 statues and 3,608 inscriptions. Most of the caves are on the west bank. The Longmen Grottoes are situated about 15 kilometres south of Luoyang at a spot where the Yi River, on its way northwest towards the Luo River, flows for about 600 metres between two high cliffs, which resemble two giants posts. Hence the name Yi Que, 'The Yi Gate' or Dragon Gate, was introduced.

The most famous caves are on the west bank, among

▷ Tianlong Shan, Taiyuan, Shanxi, Tianlong Shan Caves, sculpture

△ Tianlong Shan, Taiyuan, Shanxi, Tianlong Shan Caves, Northern Qi, 560

them the Fenxian Temple, the Bingyang Cave, and the Guyang Cave. Fenxian Cave is by far the biggest cave of them all. From east to west it measures 40.7 metres, and from north to south 36 metres. It was carved in 672 and was approached through a vast wooden hall built up against the cliff. The hall disappeared long ago, but the holes for the supporting beams can still be seen. According to the Tang Record, the Buddha has a height of 17 metres; the two Buddhas at either side are smaller in size. They are not only of colossal build; their value lies in the sculpture art. The seated Buddha in the middle dominates and unifies the whole com-

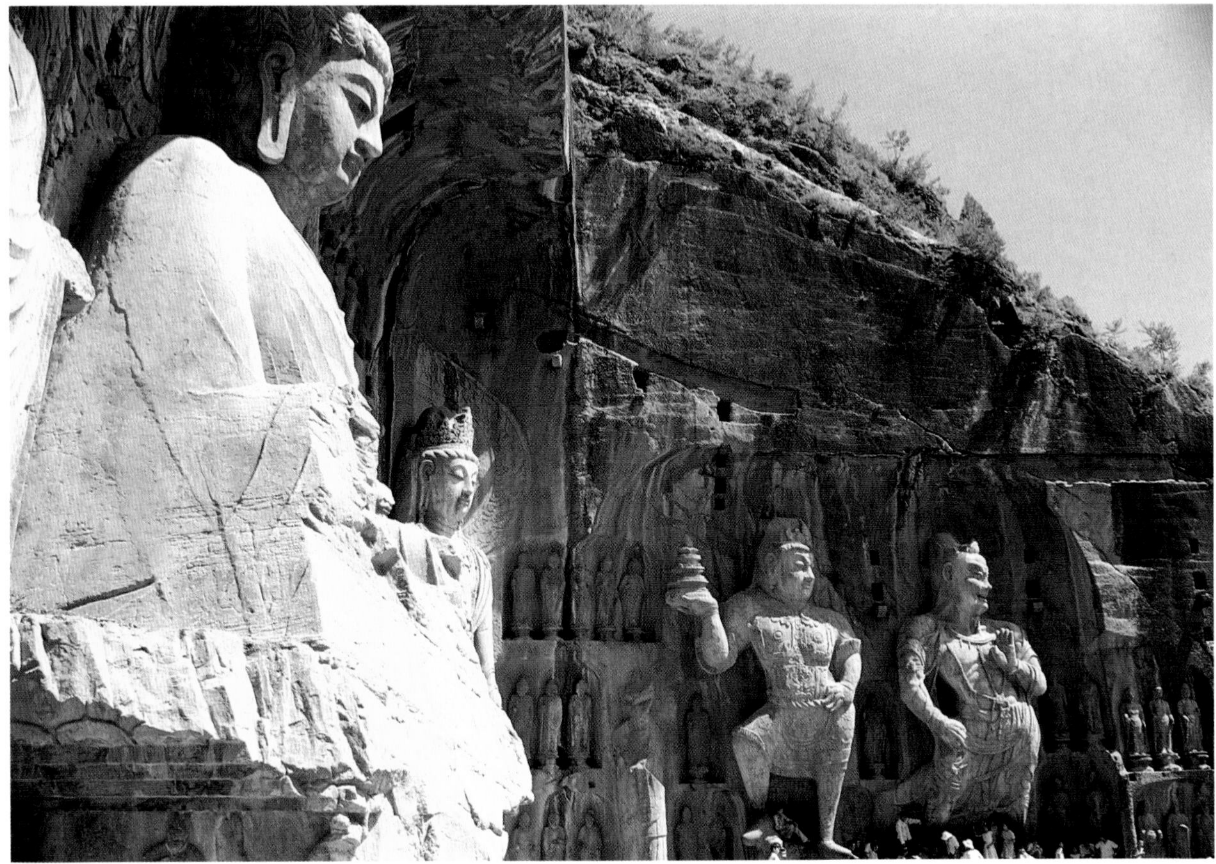

◁ Luoyang, Henan, Longmen caves, 6th C

◁ Luoyang, Henan, Longmen caves, the Giant Buddha

▽ Luoyang, Henan, Longmen caves, Guardian and Celestial King

position, whilst the other images are subordinated to it. The Tianwang (Celestial King) on the north wall is most striking; his left hand is on his hip, and he carries a pagoda in his right hand, while with his right foot he tramples on an evil spirit. The other one is the Defender of the Buddha. The mystic gentleness of Wei faces give way to calm majesty and a condescending air, which portrays something of the emperor himself. Tang Dynasty sculptures generally are in a reposed and reticent mood; eyes and eyebrows are thin and curved, with prominent nose and mouth. The corners of the lower lip are turned a little upward, and the facial expression is one of feminine gentleness. The ceiling in one of the caves has a lotus design which is also typical of this period.

Dazu lies 60 kilometres away from Chongqing in Sichuan Province. It is another wonder of the monumental religious art of stone sculptures. Unlike the above-mentioned three groups of caves, Dazu sculpture began only about 1,000 years ago, continued through the Northern Song and Southern Song Dynasties, and was completed in the Ming Dynasty. About 50,000 sculptures of Buddhist figures are well preserved in 290 honey-combed niches and grottoes spanning half a kilometre.

During the late Tang Dynasty, Chinese society was thrown into turmoil by war in the north. Emperors Xuanzong (712-756) and Xizong (873-888) fled to Sichuan to take refuge. Along with them came a great number of monks, intellectuals, painters, and sculptors. Their presence made Sichuan a centre for the culture and art of Buddhist monasteries, religious paintings and sculptures. The cliffs of northern and eastern Sichuan were ideal for bas-relief carving.

Dazu stone sculptures are divided into two areas; one is on the Northern Hill, where the cliff is sheltered by a long gallery. There is a 'revolving repository' (1142-1146), except that it is made of stone and is not actually revolvable. It is octagonal in plan, and the pedestal is a lively twined dragon poised in flight. The stack also supports the ceiling, and the eaves have greater curves than their northern counterparts. They are the style of the southern part of China, where it seems they were formed in this period.

Boading Hill is covered with ancient cypresses and verdant bamboo and has a cliff covered with numerous carvings. At the entrance of Boading Hill is the Shengshou Temple. One can easily tell the difference between a northern style temple and this one, as the curves of the roof and eaves are more apparent.

According to the development of Buddhist Grot-

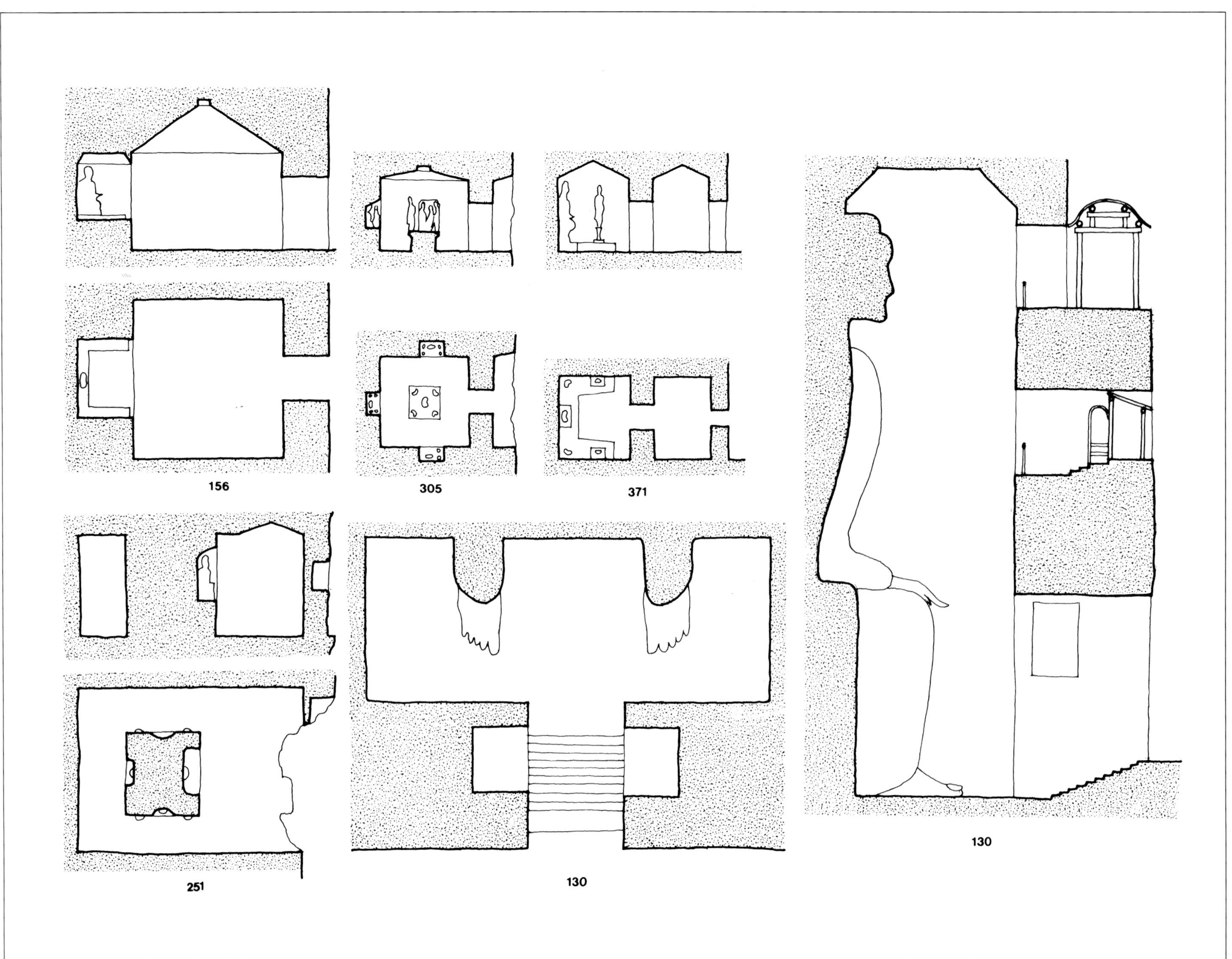

toes, we can summarize the character and layout into three categories:

i. For almost all the grottoes, from Dunhuang down to Dazu, the site chosen was orientated towards a valley or, in most cases, a river where the cliffs were usually perpendicular and, as such, were easier to hollow out. The caves orientated to a river or valley command an open view and a symmetrical layout, with the river as the central axis.

ii. The plan forms of most of the early caves are elliptical, with a dome-like ceiling; the door to the cave faces the river, and a square opening on top of the doorway serves as a window to give light to the head of the statue. There are no architectural treatments on the walls, their only purpose, apparently, being to emphasize the image. Later caves have square plans and are larger, some consisting of two adjoining rooms or 'jian', which are divided by walls or a Caitya. The ceiling looks like a truncated pyramid, or a coffered ceiling. The walls are fully covered with bas-reliefs.

iii. After the 5th century, porticoes were added to the fronts to protect the caves. They were either made of wood or carved from stone, imitating wood construction. The sculptures, bas-reliefs, are elaborate and rich in style and motif. From the development of cave buildings we can also find the progression of process from the simple and primitive to a state of maturity.

BUDDHIST TEMPLES

Early examples of Buddhist temples in China were based on Indian tradition which used the pagoda as the central building, it in turn being enclosed by praying halls, lodgings and other buildings. During the Han and Wei Dynasties, these were called Fu Tu (pagoda) and not temples, for the pagoda was the major building. After the Eastern Jin Dynasty, because of iconic

△ Comparative study of cave plans, sections and details of Dunhuang

Key
Dunhuang, cave 156, Mid-Tang; Dunhuang, cave 251, Wei; Dunhuang cave 305, Sui; Dunhuang, cave 371, Early Tang; Dunhuang, cave 130 Mid-Tang. 1 Dunhuang cave 331, coffered ceiling, liusu (tassels). 2 Dunhuang, cave 322, putao (grapes). 3 Dunhuang cave 197, scroll flower. 4 Coffered ceiling, lotus design. 5 Yungang cave 312, Apsara. 6 Yungang cave 1 tassels. 7 Dunhuang cave 9, tassels and Apsaras. 8 Dunhuang cave 9 Lotus petals. 9 Dunhuang cave 9 lotus petals. 10 Dunhuang cave 6, scrolls. 11 Dunhuang cave 13, Apsaras and curtain. 12 Longmen, Guyang cave, Lion design. 13 Yungang cave 8, Golden Wing Bird. 14 Tianlong Shang cave 2, Apsara. 15 Dunhuang, cave 185, hood over a nich.

worship, Buddha images were placed in the halls for worshipping; hence, halls took the place of pagodas as the major building in the enclosure. The side halls – living quarters – were either placed after the main hall or at one side of the main hall, according to courtyard-hall planning principle; this arrangement was entirely of the Chinese Han tradition. Until the Northern Wei Period, princes and noblemen believed in Buddhism. They gave up their mansions for temples, since houses and temples had the same plan, and no more pagodas were built inside the temples. Thus, during Tang Dynasty, many temples had no pagodas in them. The largest one of this period had many courtyards; some had as many as 48 courtyards and more than 4,000 rooms. The courtyards were surrounded by covered verandahs, and frescoes were painted the full length of the verandah walls. It would not be difficult to imagine that there were superb collections of paintings and calligraphy exhibitions arranged in the temple. It is a pity that most of the Buddhist temples were demolished during the Empress Wuzetian's days. Luckily, however, two Tang wooden temples, the Nanchan and Foguang at Wutai Mountain, escaped the disaster, and they are valuable examples of this period.

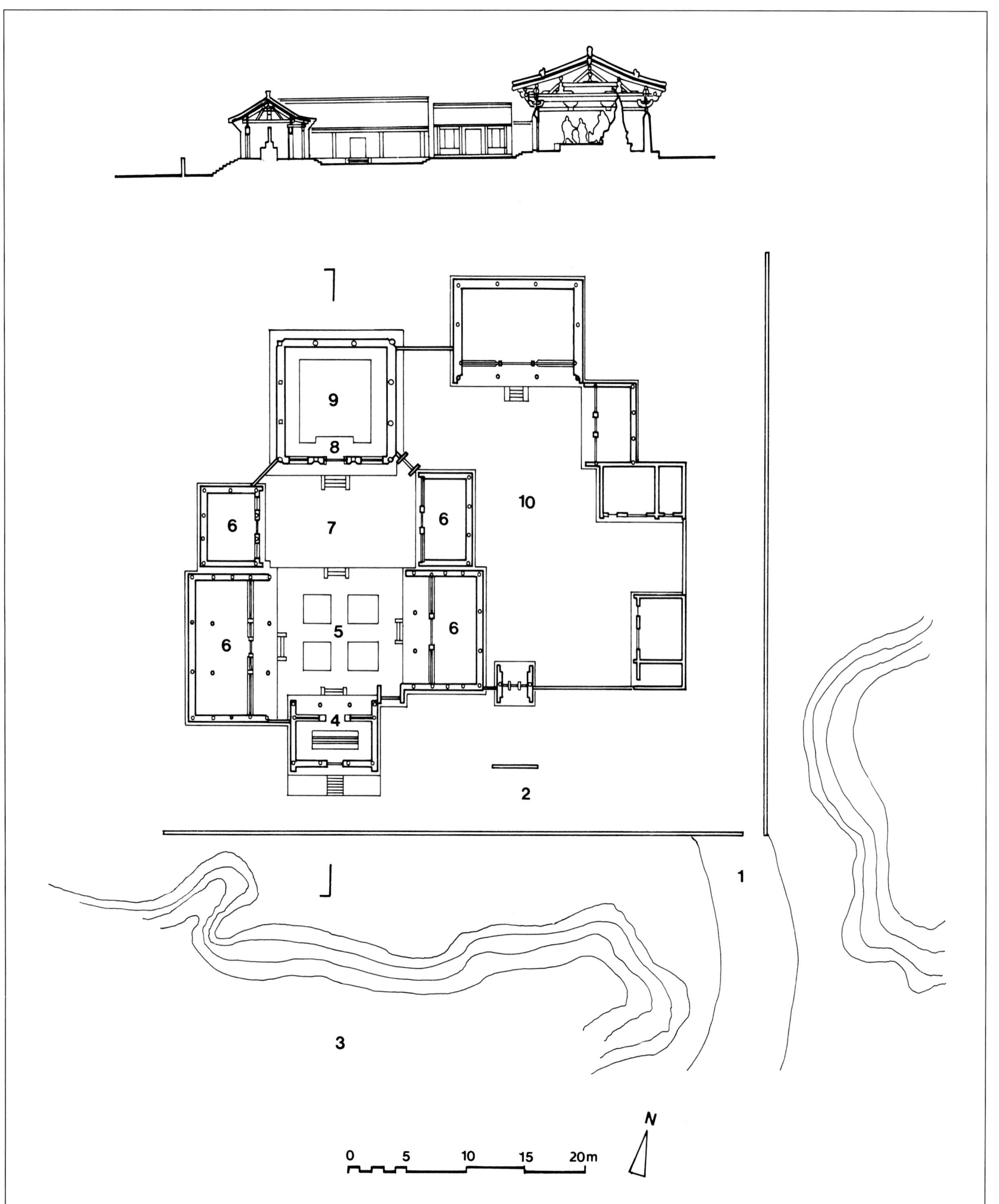

◁ Wutai Shan, Shanxi, Nanchan Si, Tang Dynasty, 782

Key
1 Approach. 2 Terrace. 3 Valley. 4 Gatehouse. 5 Courtyard. 6 Side Halls. 7 Terrace. 8 Main hall. 9 Platform for Tang Dynasty moulded Buddha statues. 10 Zusi Tomb. 11 Monks' residence.

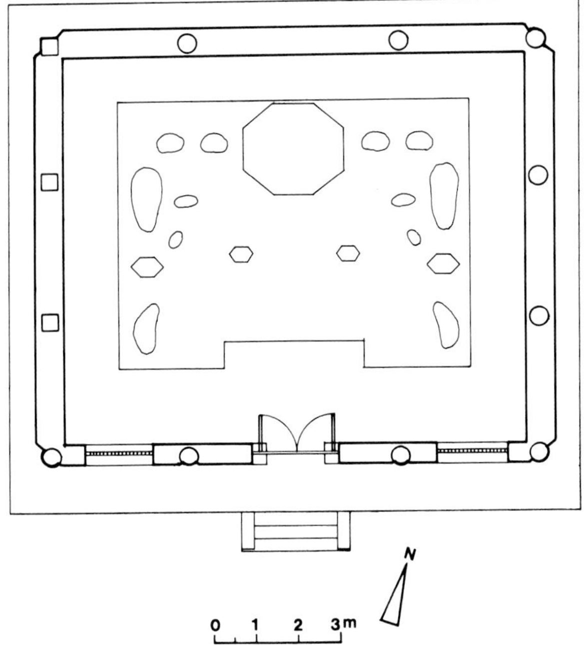

△ Wutai Shan, Shanxi, Nanchan Si, Tang Dynasty, 782

▷ Wutai Shan, Shanxi, Nanchan Si, Tang Dynasty, 782

▽ Wutai Shan, Shanxi, Nanchan Si, Tang Dynasty, 782

▷ Wutai Shan, Shanxi, Nanchan Si, Tang Dynasty, 782

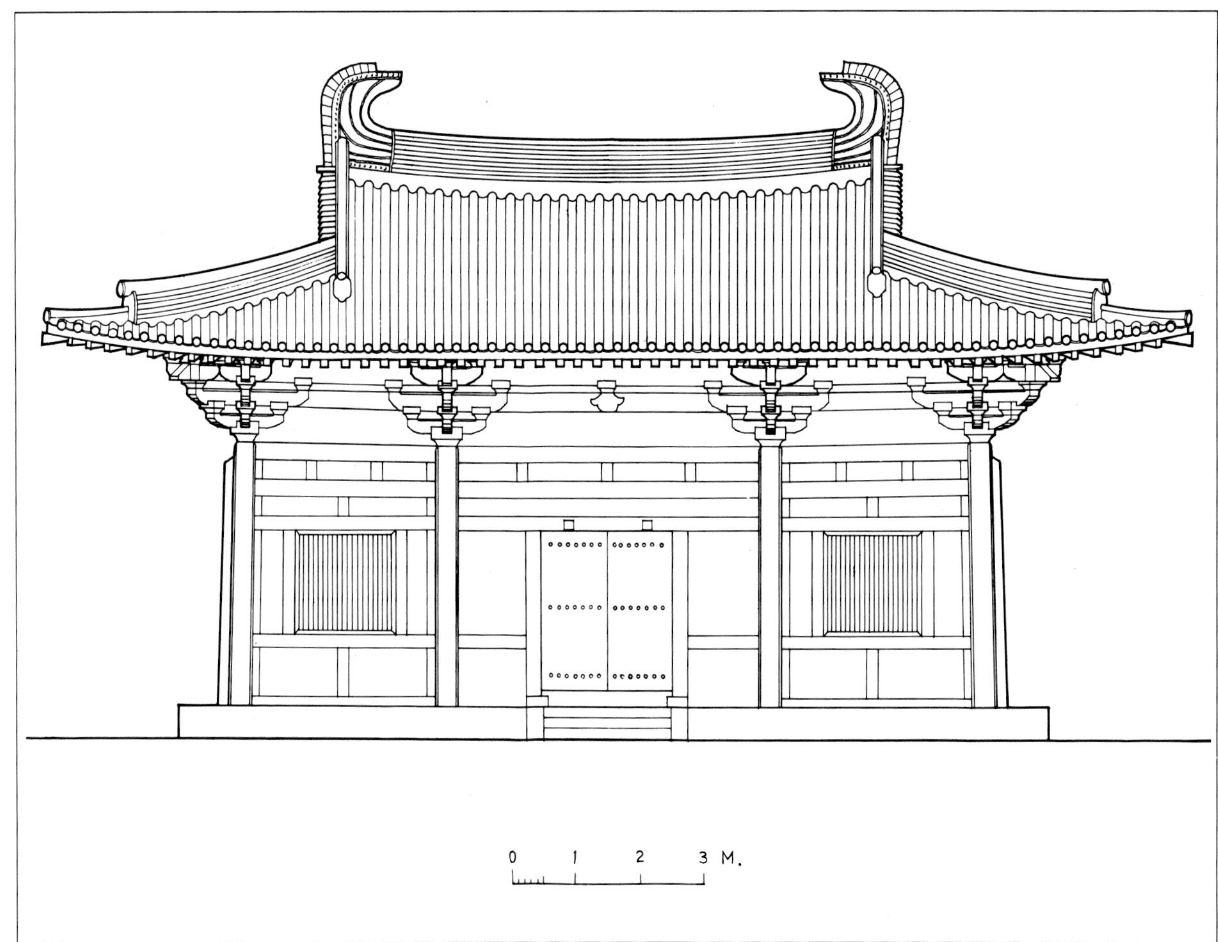

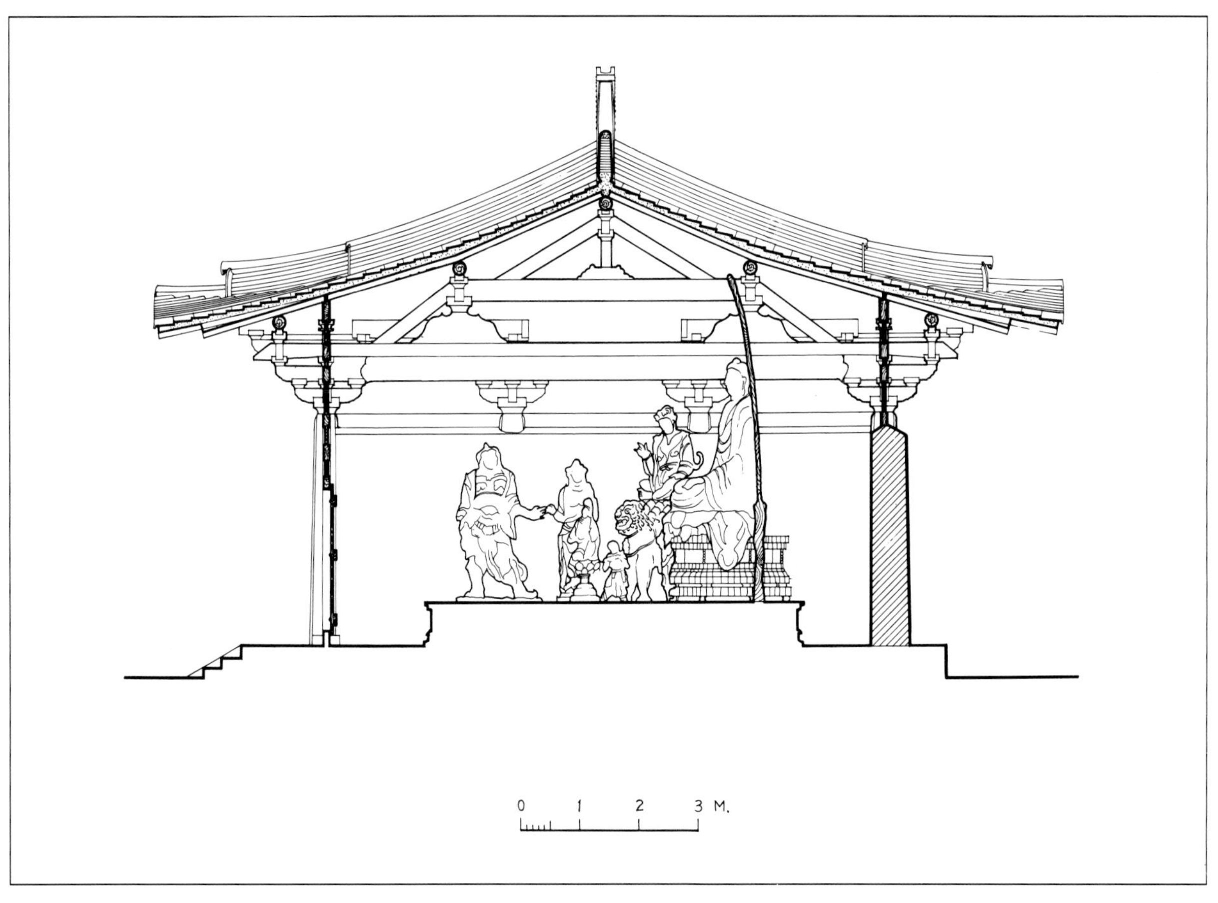

Nanchan Temple is the older but smaller of the two, built in 782. It is situated in a secluded valley and was forgotten, thus escaping the destruction of Buddhist temples. This small temple has only three bays, and is covered with a single eave half-hip roof. Situated to the north of a courtyard, well proportioned to the size of the hall, it has an intimate, serene atmosphere. The detailing of this small hall is simple and it is modestly adorned. Outside the gatehouse is a valley. The beams, eave rafters and brackets are original, and are good examples for the study of Tang Dynasty design

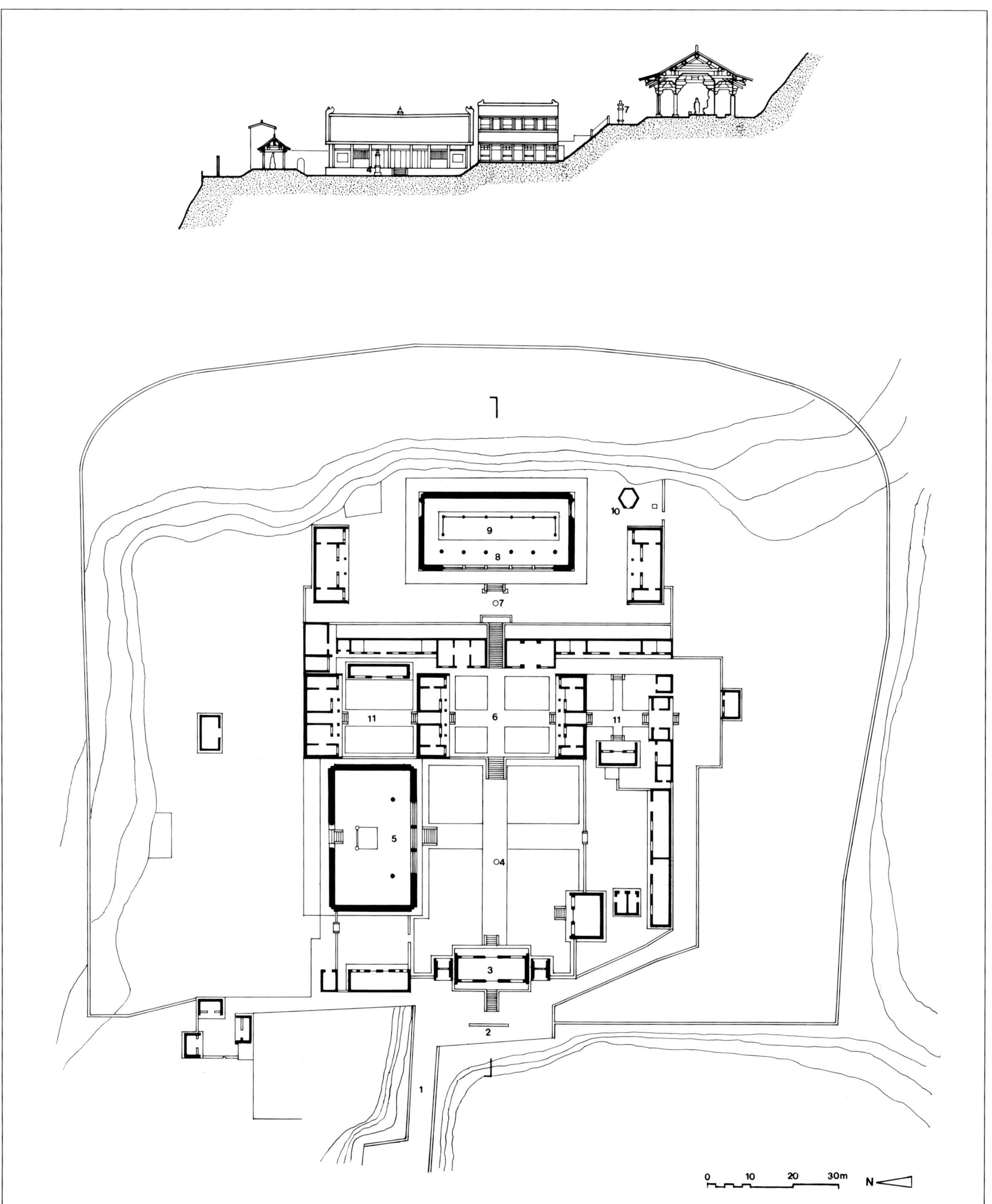

◁ Wutai Shan, Shanxi, Fo Guang Si, Tang Dynasty, 857

Key
1 Approach. 2 Screen wall. 3 Gate house. 4 Sutra pillar, Tang Qianfu. 5 Hall of Manjusri. 6 Terrace, was site of main hall. 7 Sutra pillar, Tang Dazhong. 8 Main hall. 9 Platform for Tang Dynasty moulded Buddha statues. 10 Zusi Tomb. 11 Monks' residence.

◁ Wutai Shan, Shanxi, Foguang Si, Tang Dynasty, 857

△ Wutai Shan, Shanxi, Foguang Si, Tang Dynasty, 857

▽ Wutai Shan, Shanxi, Foguang Si, Tang Dynasty, 857

and construction. The building, with its big roof and wide overhang over the pillars, is very imposing. Inside it contains a fine collection of Tang Buddhist statues, representing the plastic art of the time.

The other wooden temple is Foguang Temple (Temple of Buddha's Light), also on Wutai Mountain. Built in 857, it was one of the 'Ten Big Temples' of the Tang Dynasty. It is situated on a gentle slope facing west so it has an east-west axis, and is built on three terraces. On the first terrace is the Wen Shu Hall (Hall of Manjusri) built during the Jin Dynasty (1137). The main hall is on the third terrace and is considered by most scholars of classical Chinese architecture to be the best example of Tang architecture. The hall has seven bays in width, four in depth and is of a rectangular plan, measuring 36.27 metres in length and 20.26 metres in depth. It has a single eave hip roof, and a very wide overhang of 4.20 metres, about one half of the height from ground level to eave. The height of the duogong is also about one half of the height of the pillars, the roof curving slightly upward towards the ridge.

The appearance of this hall includes many typical features of Chinese architecture. The big sweeping roof and wide overhanging eaves are supported on a wooden frame, with a podium under it; the proportion

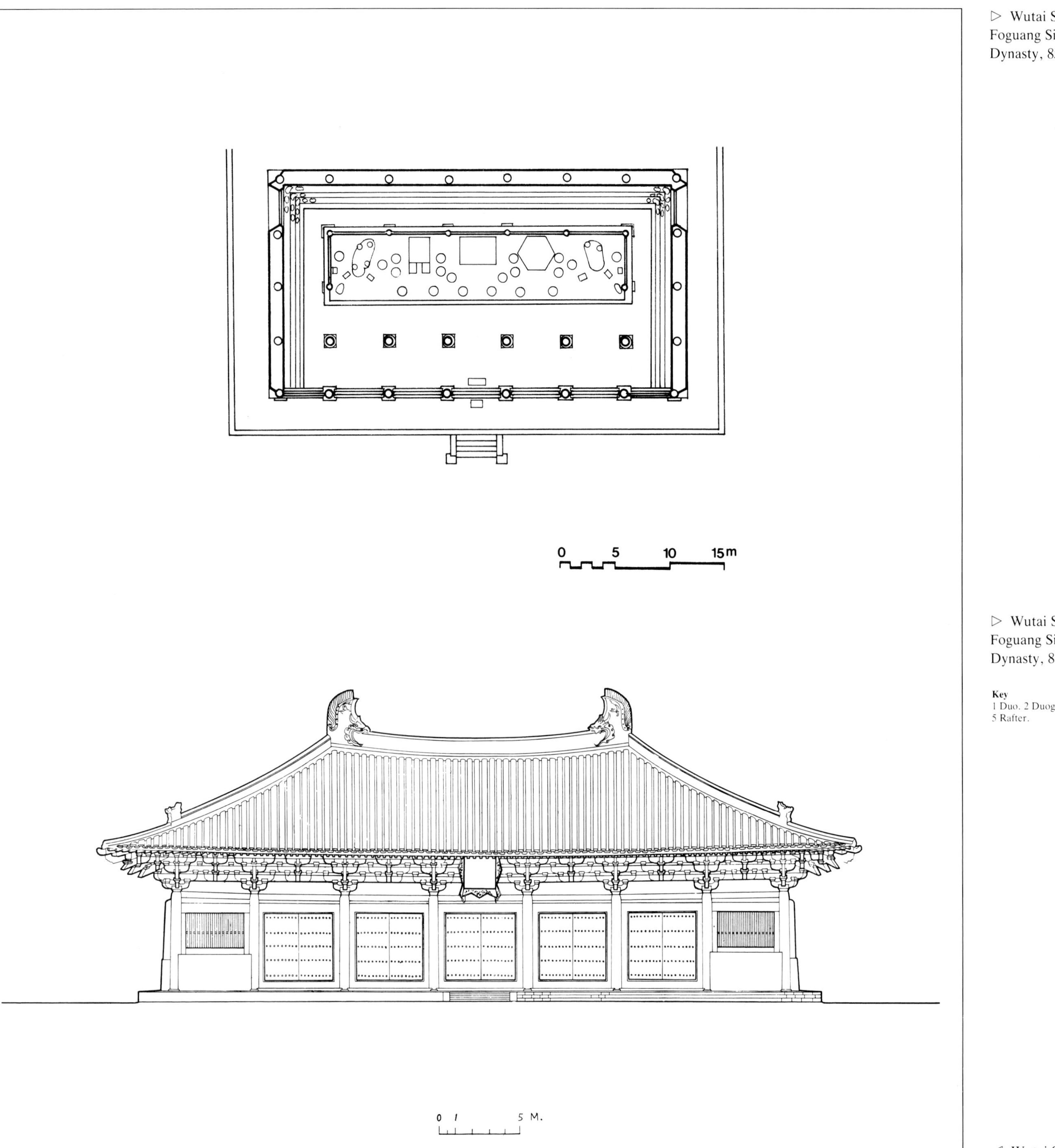

▷ Wutai Shan, Shanxi, Foguang Si, Tang Dynasty, 857

▷ Wutai Shan, Shanxi, Foguang Si, Tang Dynasty, 857

Key
1 Duo. 2 Duogong. 3 Ang. 4 Ceiling. 5 Rafter.

◁ Wutai Shan, Shanxi, Foguang Si, Tang Dynasty, 857, main hall

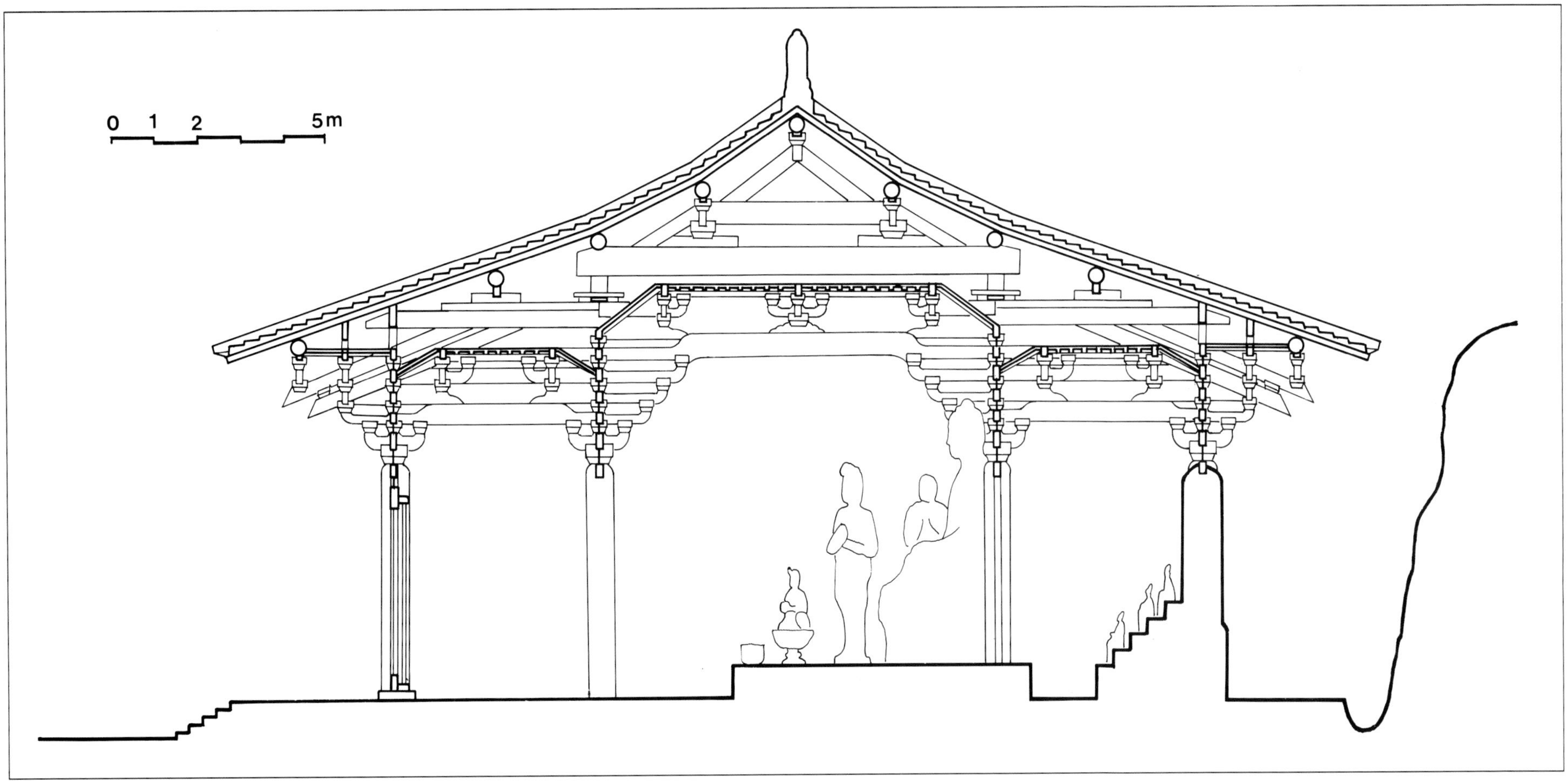

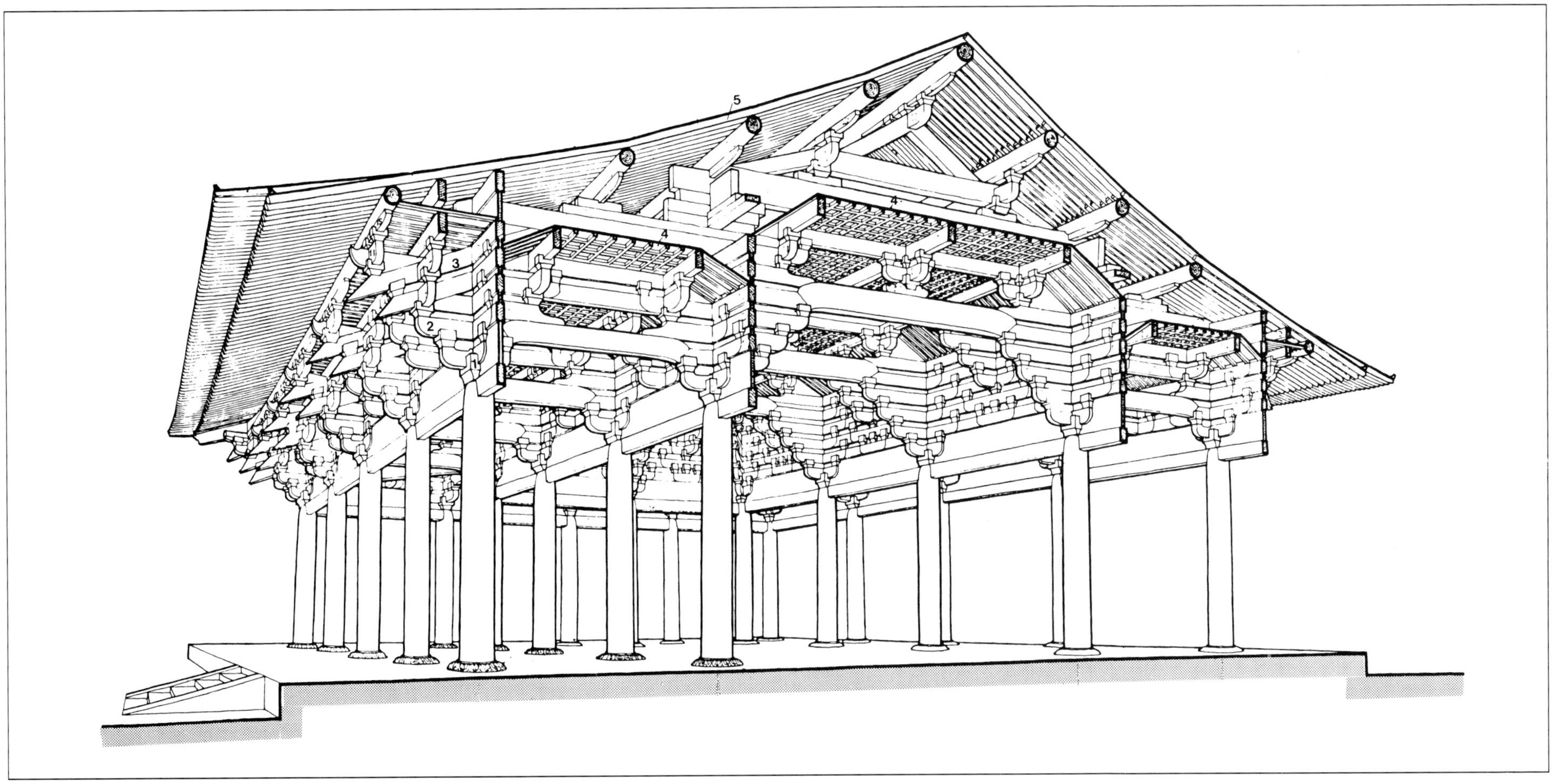

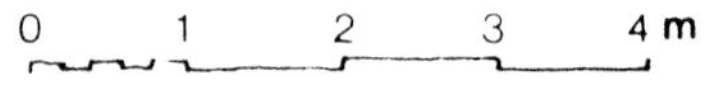

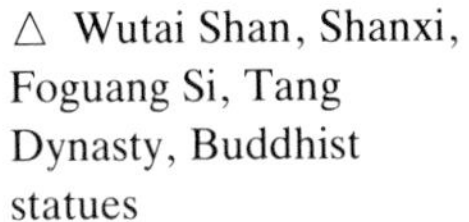
△ Wutai Shan, Shanxi, Foguang Si, Tang Dynasty, Buddhist statues

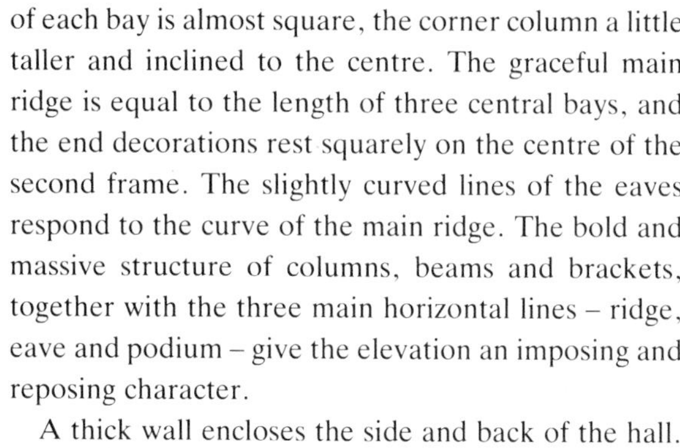
of each bay is almost square, the corner column a little taller and inclined to the centre. The graceful main ridge is equal to the length of three central bays, and the end decorations rest squarely on the centre of the second frame. The slightly curved lines of the eaves respond to the curve of the main ridge. The bold and massive structure of columns, beams and brackets, together with the three main horizontal lines – ridge, eave and podium – give the elevation an imposing and reposing character.

A thick wall encloses the side and back of the hall. The five centre bays are of equal width, and the two end bays are smaller, corresponding to the ambulatory at two sides and behind the long dais in the central portion of the hall. On top of the dais are more than 30 clay figures of Buddhist images, about 20 of them sculpted during the Tang Dynasty. Their faces are round and soft; supple clothing reveals the curve of the body, the folds following the lines of the body; the plain folds with horizontal lines are softened to graceful curves. Some of them were painted recently.

At the right side of Foguang Temple is a hexagonal plan Zusi Tomb (The Tomb of the Patriarch), built in the Tang Dynasty. On top of the arched doorway is a pointed flame-like decoration. The eaves were corbelled out and used inverted lotus petals to support the top. The tomb is plastered and whitewashed throughout.

Longxing Temple (Temple of Flourishing Buddhism) at Zhending, Shanxi, was first built during the Sui

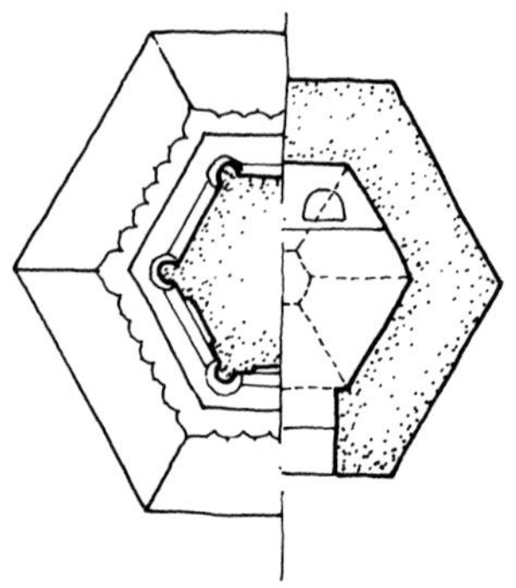

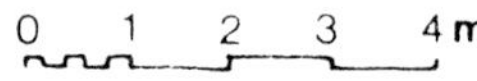

△ Wutai Shan, Shanxi, Foguang Si, Tang Dynasty Zusi Tomb

◁ Wutai Shan, Shanxi, Foguang Si, Tang Dynasty, Zusi Tomb

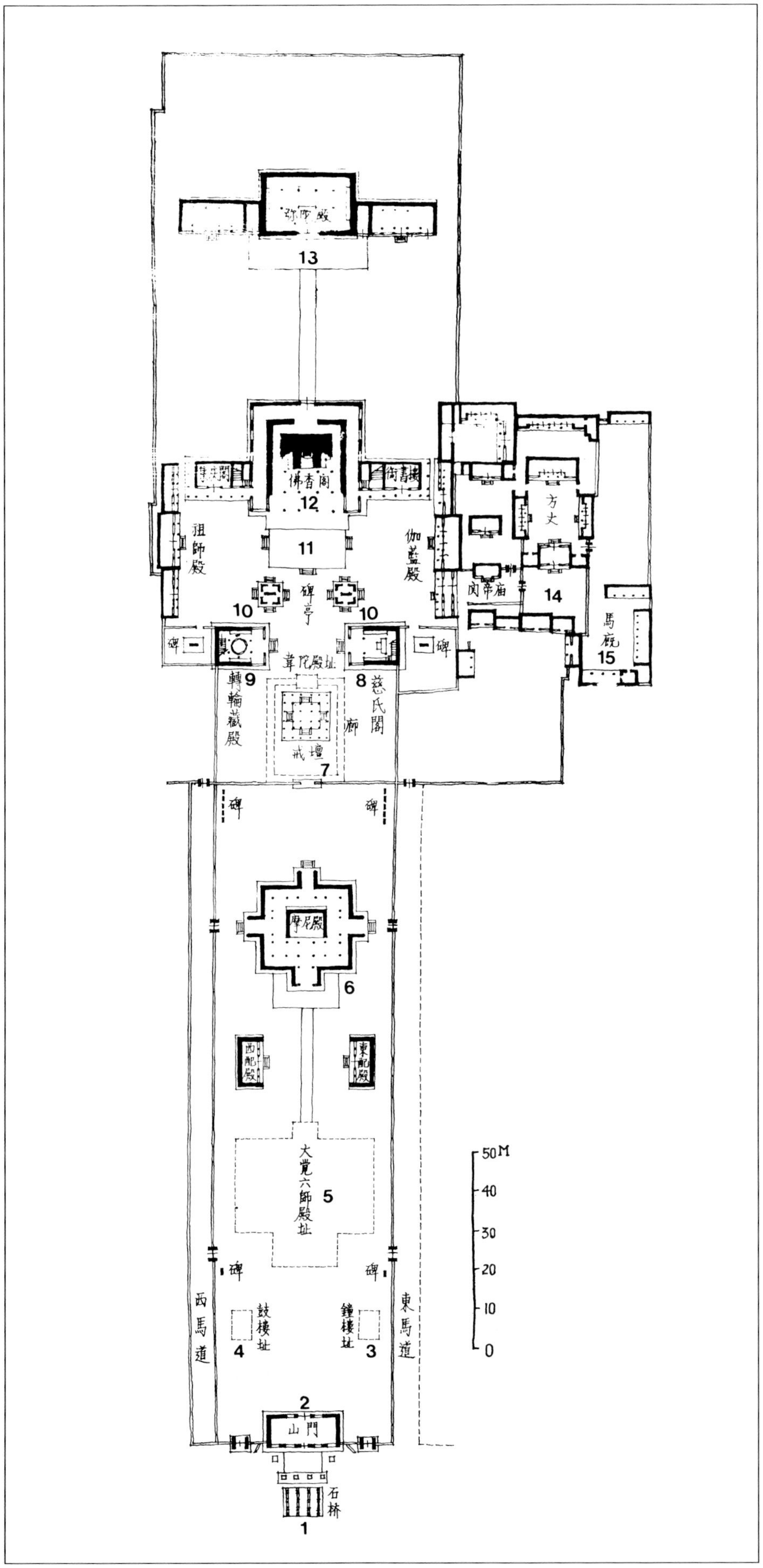

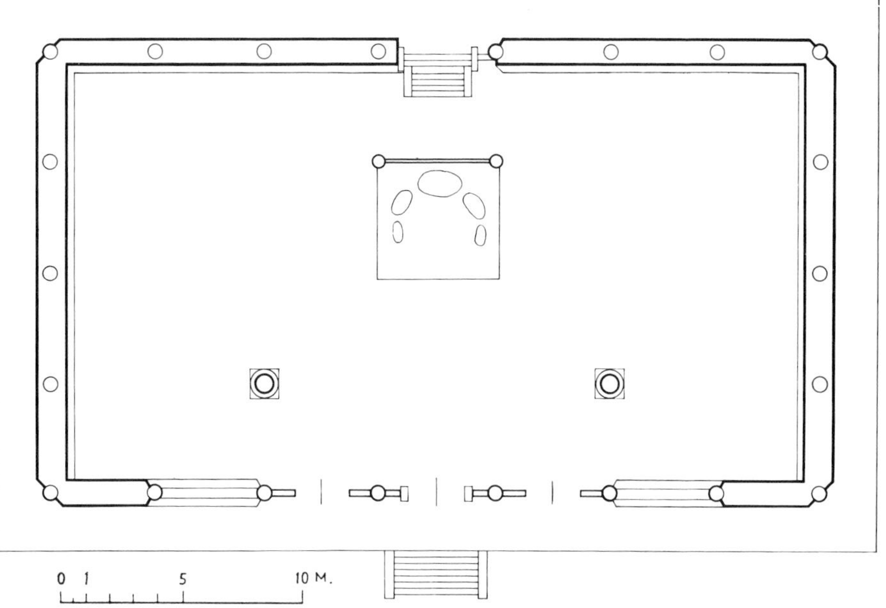

△ Wutai Shan, Shanxi, Foguang Si, Tang Dynasty

▽ Wutai Shan, Shanxi, Foguang Si, Hall of Manjusri, Jin Dynasty, 1137

◁ Zhending, Hebei, Longxing Si, Song Dynasty, 971

Key
1 Stone bridge. 2 Gatehouse. 3 Bell tower (demolished). 4 Drum tower (demolished). 5 Hall (demolished). 6 Moni Hall. 7 Altar of Abstinence. 8 Cishi Pavilion. 9 Sutra Repository. 10 Pavilion of tablet. 11 Platform. 12 Foxiang Ge (Dabei Ge). 13 Mituo Hall. 14 Monks' quarters. 15 Stable.

Dynasty (971) and has been successively repaired in the years since then. The Moni Hall, Repository Pavilion and Dabei Pavilion are representative of the architecture of that period, and each is rare in China. The layout represents the temple planning adhered to during the Song Dynasty.

After the gatehouse is the Moni Hall, which is noted for its construction and complicated roof form. Moni Hall was built in 1052 of Northern Song Dynasty. The floor plan is close to a square and has five spans; a foyer is thrust out to each side, so the plan form is a cross. The hall is enclosed by heavy reddish colour walls.

△ Zhending, Hebei, Longxing Si, Song Dynasty, Moni Hall Section

◁ Zhending, Hebei, Longxing Si, Song Dynasty, Moni Hall, 1052

◁ Zhending, Hebei, Longxing Si, Song Dynasty, Guanying statue

▽ Zhending, Hebei, Longxing Si, Song Dynasty, Cishi Ge Pavilion

Only the front of the foyer has doorways, so there is a strong contrast of solid and void. Because of the cross-shaped plan, the roofs of the foyers, with their gable-ends, protrude in all four directions. This was a rare configuration before it was erected, and remained so afterwards. Similar manipulation could only be found in Song Dynasty paintings; perhaps this was a common practice of that dynasty. With the doors of foyers opening to the front, and the gable-ends thrusting to the four cardinal directions, it is as if the doors first attracted everyone into it and then radiated them to all four directions. The combination of the cross-plan and the tier half-hip roof, with gable ends facing different directions, created a roof of 16 corners and 33 ridges. It is a form not used after the Song.

Inside, the hall is dim, the dais enclosed on three sides by massive walls. Although this furnished a rigid construction, one can barely see the face of the Buddha image in it. This kind of construction was also a common practice of the Song Dynasty. To the back of the image and on the wall is a plaster-moulded image of Guanying (Goddess of Mercy, Avalokitesvara), considered to be one of the finest modelled sculptures of the Song. Sitting on the waves, one of her feet is on a lotus flower while the other leg crosses it. The facial expression is kind and gentle, pure and noble, as if she is listening carefully to the prayers of the common people. In Buddhism, sculptures and the halls that contain them were always closely integrated, ideally forming an organic whole.

Behind Moni Hall and to the left of the axis is Zhuanglun Zhang, a revolving repository:

> This ingenious device was invented as early as 544 A.D. by a pious believer named Fu Hsi. When he saw that the number of sutras was multitudinous and that it was questionable if men would be able to read them all, he built a large shrine which had a pillar in the centre; its eight sides being hollowed out and filled with sutras. He promised that those who visited his repository, possessed of full enlightenment and able to make the repository revolve, had merit which was one with that of those who recited many sutras. A very popular practice through the Song, Yuan, and a great part of the Ming Dynasties, seems, in fact, largely to have influenced the general conception of how a Buddhist library should be built.[9]

Here it is a two-storey building which housed the revolving repository. It looks like a small pavilion, and truly reflects Song Dynasty construction.

The last of the building groups is Dabei Pavilion or Foxiang first built in 971 and rebuilt in 1944. It has a height of 33 metres to house a 42-hand bronze Guanying statue, 24 metres tall. The statue was cast and

▷ Zhending, Hebei, Longxing Si, Song Dynasty, Taizi of Guanying

▽ Zhending, Hebei, Longxing Si, Song Dynasty, Dabei Ge, 971, rebuilt 1944

sculpted when the pavilion was first built, and is the largest in China today. After the middle of the Tang Dynasty, statues of large size were cast and placed in large temples. In order to house the tall statues the major buildings became taller too, this practice forming a special feature between the end of the Tang and Early Song. The plan of Foxiang Ge is also rare in China. It is attached by two lower buildings at each side and forms a special 'hall with two wings' layout. The lower wings enrich the outline and the scale of the central building. Inside, the zumizuo under the large Guanying statue is also unique in China. Besides the commonly used lotus petals, vivid winged apsaras were carved on the upper band; on the attached columns are high-reliefs of warriors and twined dragons; in the panels are bas-reliefs of dancing and singing girls. All these help to define the pleasant, merciful character of Buddha, the Goddess of Mercy.

We have already described three special buildings in this temple, each with a specific usage and a specific form. Moni Hall is especially beautiful in form, and the repository and the pavilions behind Moni Hall are two identical buildings facing each other. The Foxiang Ge is a high-rise building, its construction just like the putting of one building on top of another. The interior of this building is a large hollowed-out vertical space, with galleries around the void, but from the exterior it looks like a three-storey building, the eaves and balconies reflecting the galleries inside. The lowest floor is made wider by a portico, its balcony and another portico; the top building has a double eave half-hip roof. Although it is a high-rise building, horizontal lines dominate the elevation, giving it a reposing feeling. The layout of this temple will be discussed in the context of the layout of Buddhist temples.

△ Jixian, Hebei, Dule Si, Liao Dynasty, gatehouse, 984

▷ Jixian, Hebei, Dule Si, Liao Dynasty, Guanying Ge

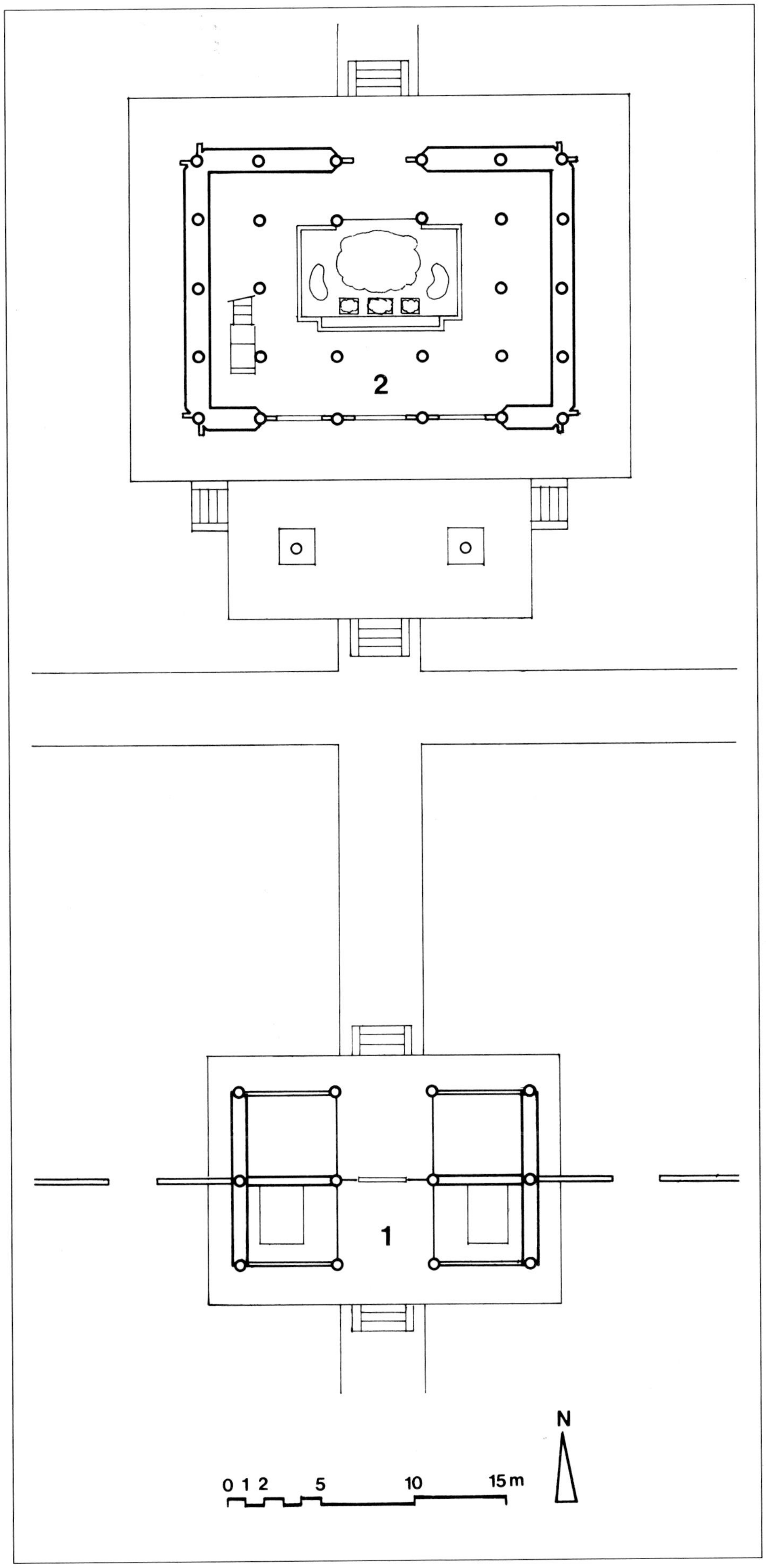

◁ Jixian, Hebei, Dule Si, Liao Dynasty, 984

Key
1 Gatehouse. 2 Guanying Pavilion.

The other temple built to enshrine the Guanying, and also a masterpiece, is Dule Temple (Temple of Unique Happiness), built in 984 in Liao Dynasty in Jixian in Hebei Province. The surviving main hall and the gatehouse were both built in the 10th century. A covered verandah originally connected these two buildings but disappeared long ago; there is now only a visual connection between the two.

The gatehouse has three bays, a hip roof, a low podium, a wide overhanging eave, and a bold end-ridge decoration, giving it an imposing feeling. Typically, the gatehouse is divided in the middle by pillars and door sashes into two equal parts. The main hall is best viewed from the centre inside the gatehouse. Here the centre bay, framed by columns and beams, serves as a picture frame; and just like the opening of a peifang, it is a way to create a visual tension between buildings across space.

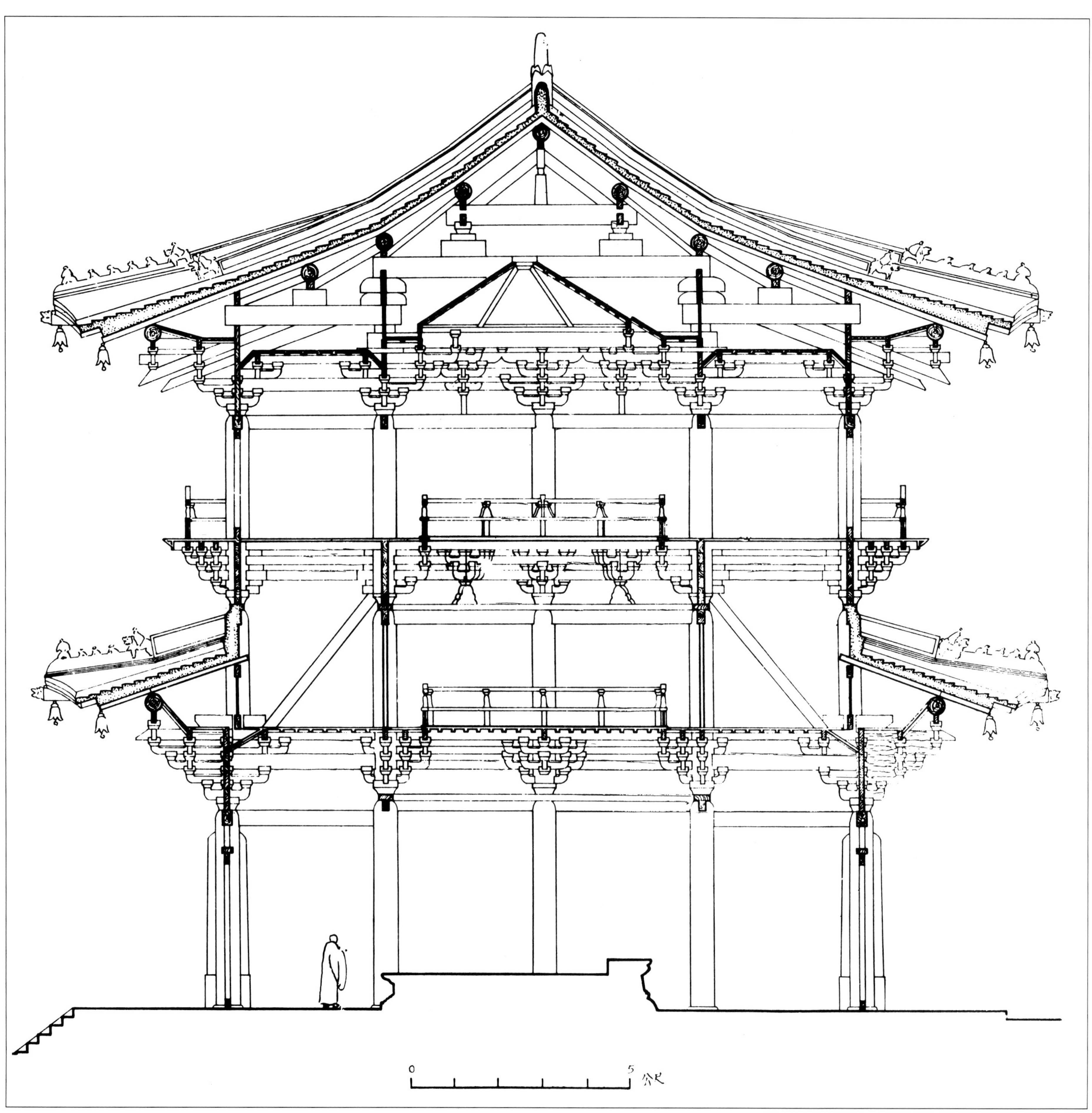
0
5
公尺

△ Jixian, Hebei, Dule Si, Liao Dynasty, coffered ceiling

▷ Jixian, Hebei, Dule Si, Liao Dynasty, Jade Girl

◁ Jixian, Hebei, Dule Si, Liao Dynasty, section

The main hall is a building three storeys high and with five bays. Actually, it is a two-storey building with a structural floor sandwiched in between; thus, it looks like a two-storey building from the elevation. The interior is a vertical space three storeys high, surrounded by two tiers of galleries, which houses a 16-metre high Liao Dynasty moulded Guanying with 11 faces. On top of its head an octagonal dome called 'Duo Ba' (interlocked octagons) rose up to the top and formed a dome-like recession, forming a focal point of the hall. The segmental carved laths of this dome are resting on octagonal base frames. Usually placed above a Buddha image, they were made of wood and painted, probably evolved from the prototype of the canopy.

Although this is a three-storey building, the construction principle is the same as the one-storey hall of Foguang Temple, which is to divide the plan by columns into central part and ambulatory part, and place three one-storey buildings one on top of the other. This arrangement resembles three tables, placed one on top of the other, with the exception that the columns above are not directly resting on the ones below but rest on the duogongs below; this is called cha zhu zao of staggered column construction. Thus the elevation is tapered upwards, with the reposing horizontal lines of the balcony, eave lines and main ridge all helping to make it a feature with the robustness of the Tang but softness of the Song. The attendants of Guanying is a very good example of Liao Dynasty plastic art.

Datong, the capital city of Northern Wei is not only famous for its Yungang Grottoes; there are also several important temples of the later Liao and Jin periods. They are the Upper and Lower Huayan Temples, and Shanhua Temple.

Since the Liao emperors were sun worshippers, Huayan Temple in Datong was built on an east-west axis in order to face the rising sun. The Upper Huayan

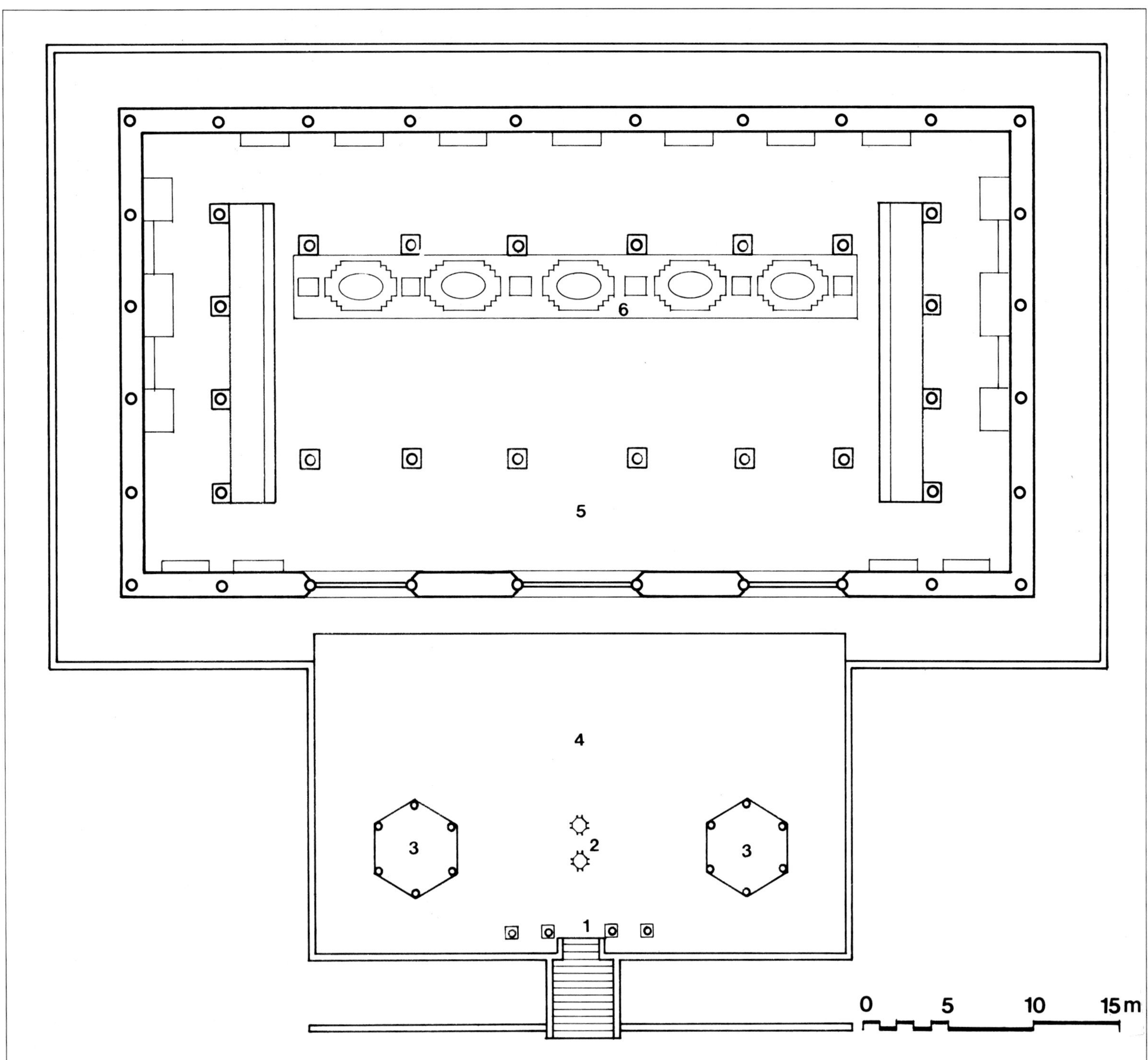

◁ Datong, Shanxi, Upper Huayan Si, Jin Dynasty, 1140

Key
1 Peifang. 2 Incense burner. 3 Pavilion. 4 Platform. 5 Main hall. 6 Podium for Buddha statues.

temple was built in 1140; its main hall has nine bays, and its hip roof is the largest single eave wooden construction in ancient China. The interior of this great hall is a masterpiece of interior architecture. On the low dais parallel to the longitudinal axis of the hall are five standing Buddha statues, luxuriously clothed and shining brilliantly against the dark background illuminated by the candle light in front of them. Along the walls are frescoes of bright colours in the dim light; the gods and goddesses seem to be circling, dancing, moving around the Buddha statues in the air. The building models in front of the Buddha images are scaled models of buildings. The interior design, which has combined architecture, sculpture, and frescoes in one space, is a successful rare example of this type.

Inside the Lower Huayan Temple, the main hall, rebuilt in 1038, is the Bojiajiaozang, a repository for sutras; it is famous for its stacks and Liao Dynasty sculptures. The sutras were stored in 38 stacks made in the style of miniature buildings and pavilions connected by a flying bridge at the centre. The stacks are in fact scaled models of buildings and from these models, the building construction and style of Liao can be studied. The dais is low and wide, and apart from the three principal Buddhas of the present, past and future, there are attendants of various postures; they were the most elegant sculptures of China at that time. The stacks and sculpture represent the Pure-land Sect idea.

Shanhua Temple is located a little to the south of Datong, and was rebuilt in 1128. The gatehouse, Sanshen Hall (The Hall of Three Sages) and Puxian Ge were built in the Jin Dynasty. This is the largest existing Jin temple. Here the planning principle of Liao can be examined.

The Pure-land Sect has a small temple built in Yingxian called the Jintu Temple (Temple of The Pure-land)

△ Datong, Shanxi, Upper Huayan Si, Jin Dynasty, 1140, main hall

△ Datong, Shanxi, Upper Huayan Si, Jin Dynasty, 1140, interior

◁ Datong, Shanxi, Lower Huayan Si, Bojiajiaozang, Jin Dynasty, 1038

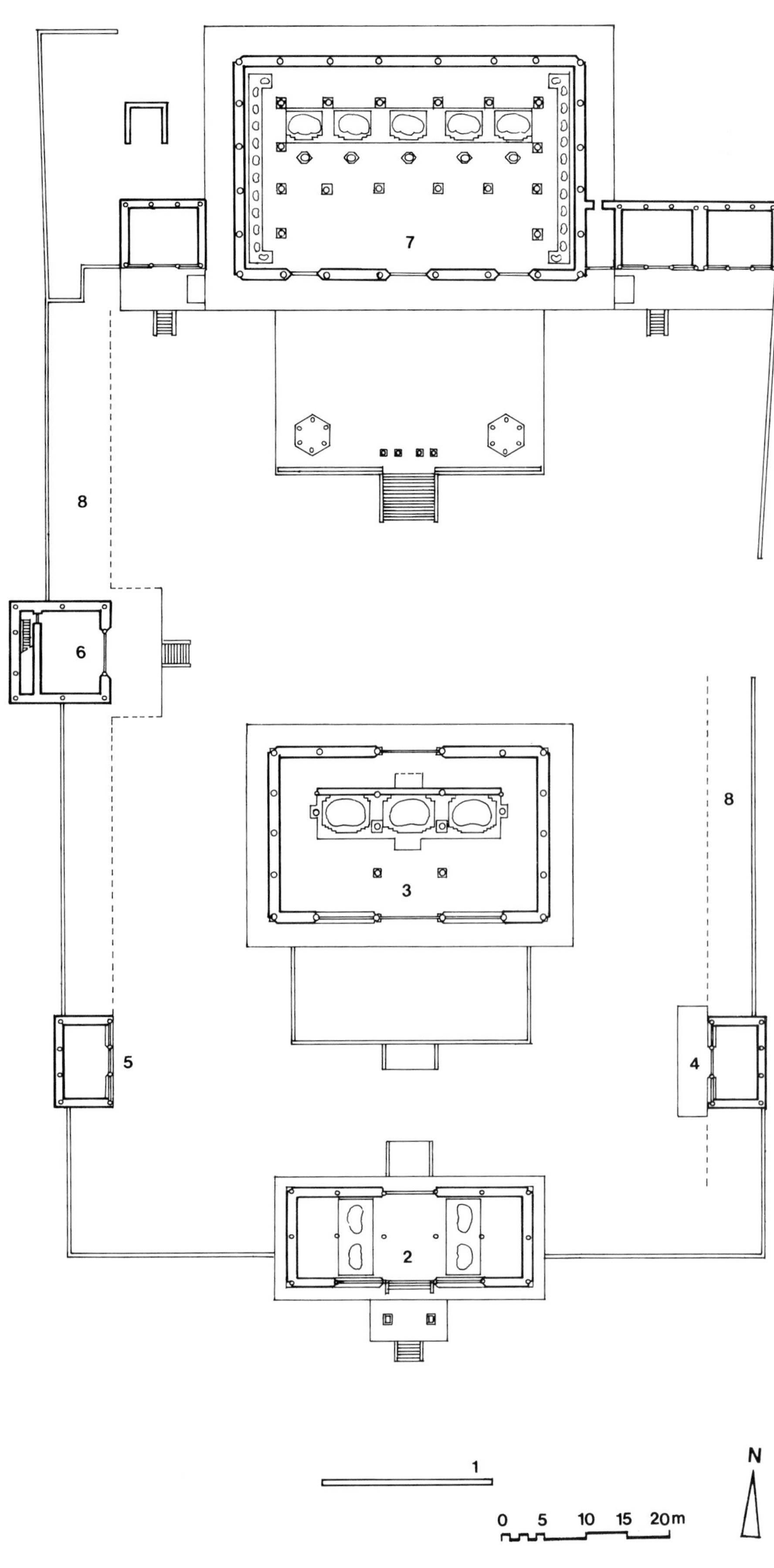

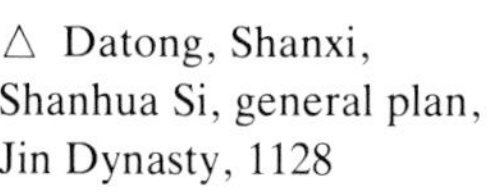

△ Datong, Shanxi, Shanhua Si, general plan, Jin Dynasty, 1128

Key
1 Screen wall. 2 Gate house. 3 Sanshen hall. 4 East Side hall. 5 West Side hall. 6 Puxian Ge. 7 Main hall. 8 Verandah (demolished).

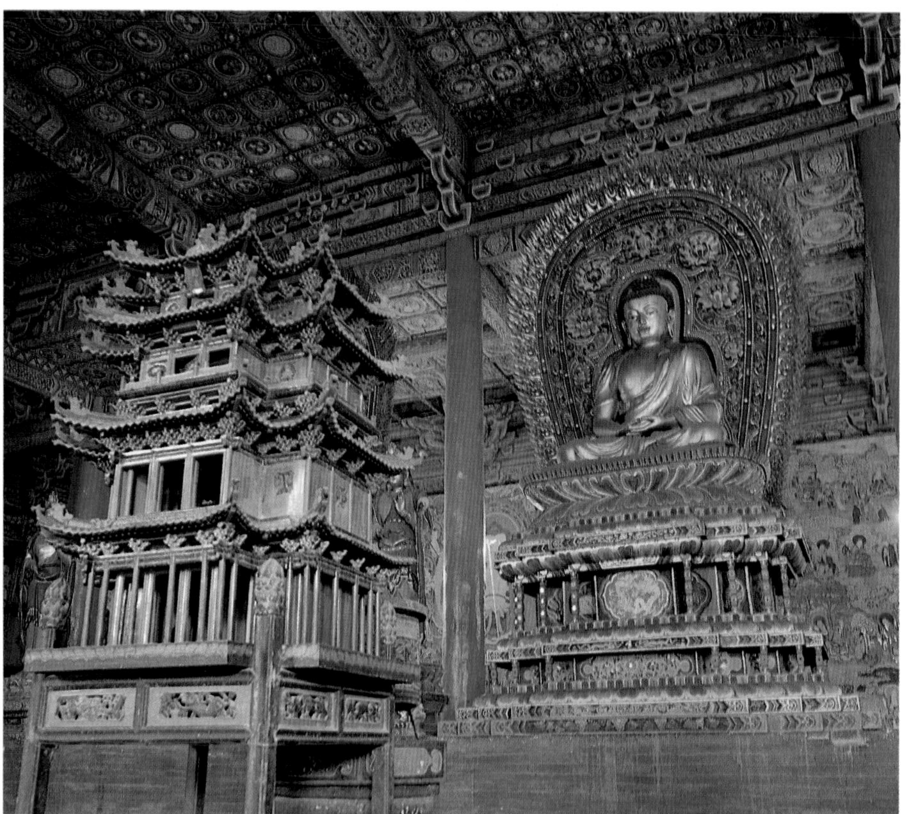

△ Datong, Shanxi, Shanhua Si, main hall interior

▽ Datong, Shanxi, Shanhua Si, Puxian Ge

△ Datong, Shanxi, Shanhua Si

▽ Qhanzhou, Fuqian, Kaiyuan Si, Southern Song Dynasty

△ Qhanzhou, Fuqian, Kaiyuan Si, Southern Song Dynasty

which is noted for its beautifully carved and modelled coffered ceiling. The ceiling design depicts a heavenly palace, the idea of the Pure-land. The ceiling consists of several square panels, each of which has an exquisitely colourful roof built at each side. The Pure-land use these images to confirm the happy afterlife and preach devotion of good deeds during their lifetime.

During the latter half of the Song Dynasty, because of continuous invasions from the north, the court was moved to south China. Many temples were built; in Fuqian, for instance, the famous Hualin Temple in Fuzhou, and the Kaiyuan Temple in Quanzhou, a seaport. Here can be seen the difference in construction and style between the northern and southern buildings. Since Fuqian's weather is warm and humid, natural ventilation is considered an important requirement and special attention needs to be paid to produce natural ventilation in the halls. For instance, the main hall of Kaiyuan temple was a Song construction, and although it was burnt down and rebuilt in the Ming, it still retained the Song style. It has a hip roof of gentle slope, and the curves of the ridges and eaves are more apparent as the southern people liked a soft and graceful appearance. The columns were made of stone, which is indigenous and affords easy upkeep in a humid climate. The spaces between eaves are open to the outside, a device allowing warm air to circulate.

The Zusi Temple (Hall of the Patriarch) in Shaolin Temple is a departure from the Pure-land Sect. It was built in 1125 at a place claimed to be the meditation place of Boddhidarma, the Creator of the Chan Sect (Zen in Japanese). The story goes that when the Indian Monk Boddhidarma came to Canton by sea and travelled to Nanjing in 520, he had a dispute with Emperor Wudi of Liang and he 'crossed the Yellow River on a reed',[10] landed at Shaolin Temple, and there he sat and faced a bare wall for nine years and died in 535. His teachings included the mystic knowledge of 'nothing-

◁ Song Shan, Dengfeng, Henan, Shaolin Si, Zusi Hall, Song Dynasty

△ Song Shan, Dengfeng, Henan, Shaolin Si, stone pillar, 1125

▷ Song Shan, Deng Feng, Henan, Shaolin Si

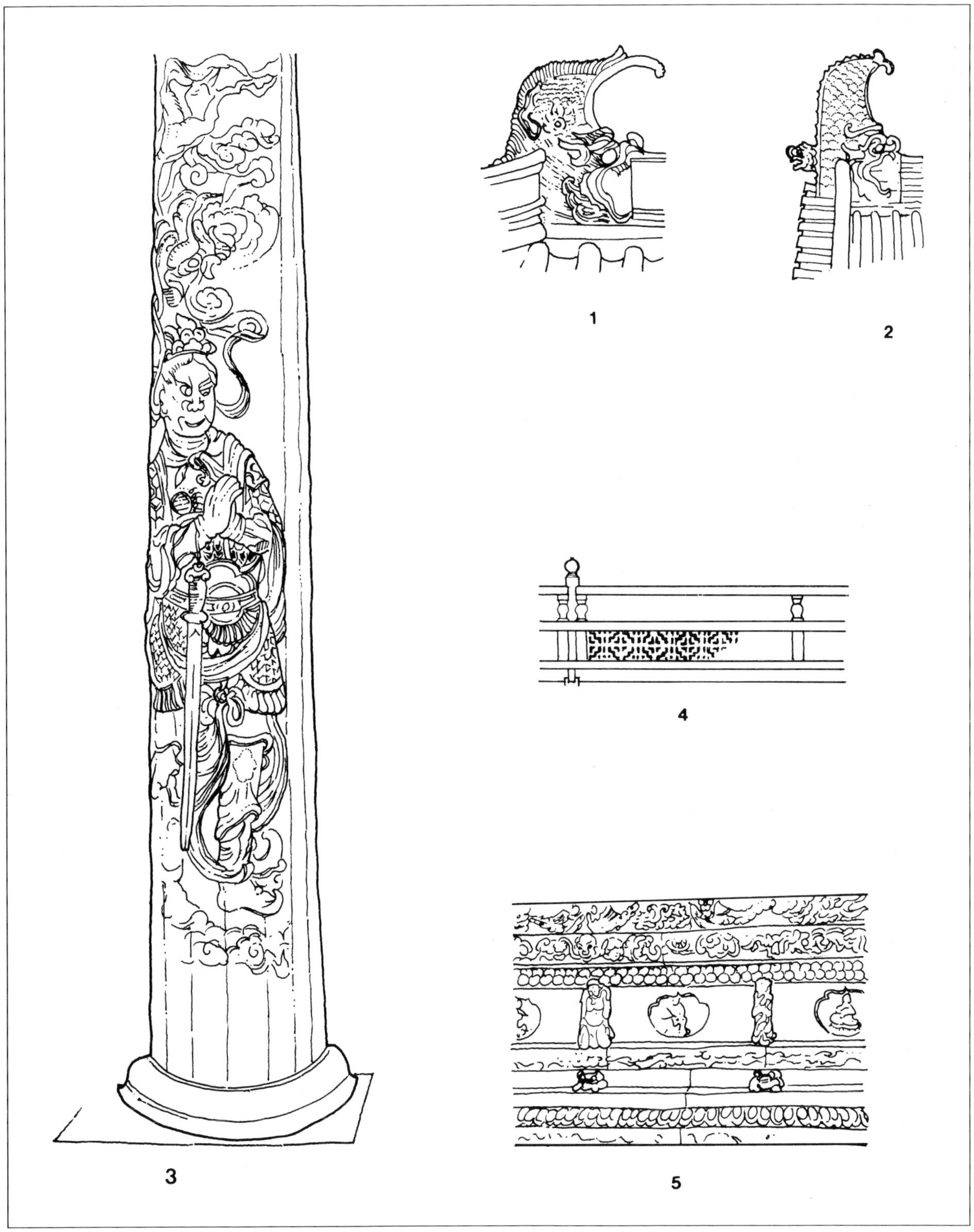

Key
1 Jisian, Dule Si, Wen of gatehouse (Lian Dynasty). 2 Datong, Lower Huayan Si Sutra stack (Liao Dynasty). 3 Dengfeng, Shaolin Si, Zusi Hall, Stone pillar. 4 Datong, Lower Huayan Si, sutra stack, railing. 5 Zhending, Longxing, Foxiang Ge podium (Song).

ness of everything'[11] and to sit in meditation (dhyana); therefore the site must be secluded and quiet. The architectural feature of the building was on the fluted stone columns where the Four Celestial Kings and plant life were carved. The structure was almost identical to the specification in *Ying Zao Fa Shi*, and therefore a good example for study of Song Dynasty architecture.

Another small temple worth mentioning here is the Xuankong Temple (Hanging Temple) at Hunyuan in Shanxi Province. It was first built in Northern Wei, and was repaired many times afterwards. The building has since lost its original appearance, but the peculiar site selection and the superb workmanship is unique in China. Instead of being hollowed into the cliff, this temple of more than 30 rooms and halls was built on the surface of a perpendicular cliff of rock, as if it is set in the rocks. The construction started by pre-cutting all the elements which were then carried to the top of the cliff. Workmen and elements were hung from the cliff to each designated position and they then fixed the elements into the rocks; beams were braced against the rock, which then formed an integral structural system. Several earthquakes occurred after its completion, but the structure was not affected; it proved that it has a sound and stable structural system and superb workmanship.

◁ Hunyuan, Shanxi, Xuankong Si, first built in Northern Wei, reconstructed during the Ming Dynasty

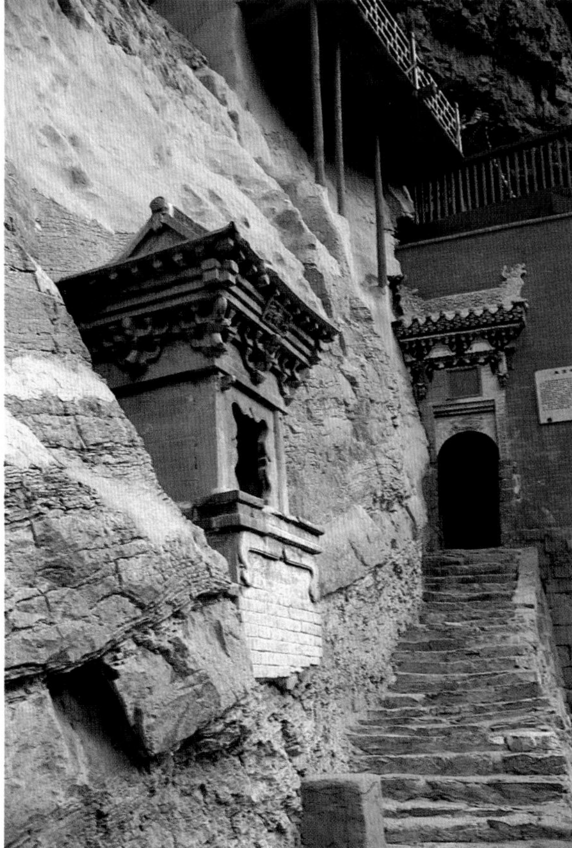

△ Hunyuan, Shanxi, Xuankong Si, first built in Northern Wei, reconstructed during the Ming Dynasty

▽ Hongdong, Shanxi, Lower Guansheng Si and Shui Shen Miao, Yuan Dynasty

Key
1 Pavilion of tablet. 2 Covered bridge. 3 River. 4 Stage. 5 Gatehouse of Water God. 6 Ming Ying Wang Hall. 7 Gatehouse of Lower Guansheng Si. 8 Front Hall. 9 Bell Tower. 10 Drum tower. 11 Rear great hall. 12 Wei Tuo Hall. 13 Cave dwellings for monks.

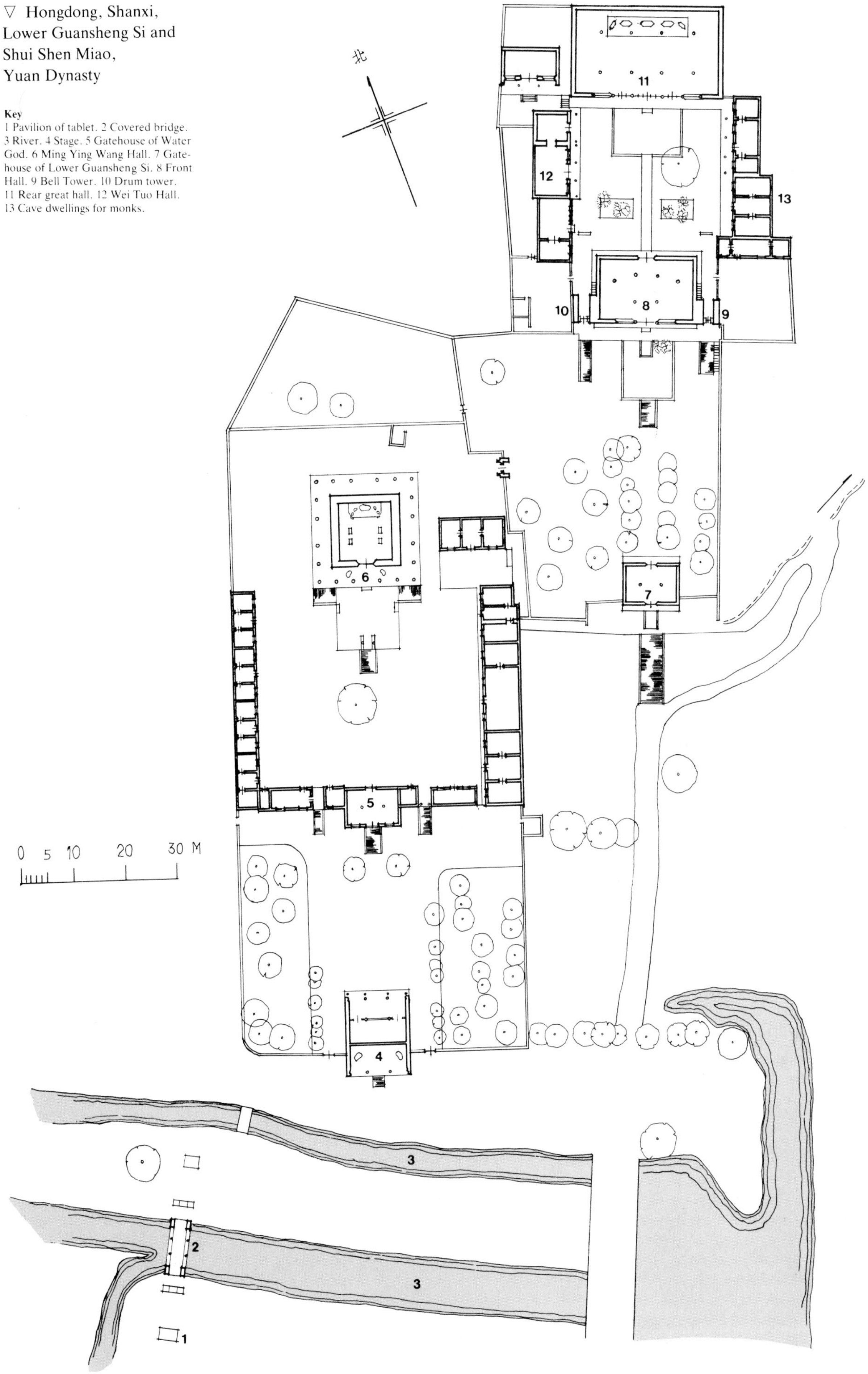

Guansheng Temples at Hongdong in Shanxi Province are important examples of Yuan Dynasty Buddhist temples. The temple which is situated at the top of a small mountain is called the Upper Guansheng Temple, and the one at the foot of the hill is called the Lower Guansheng Temple. To the southwest of the lower one is a small temple called Shuishen Temple (Temple of the Water God).

The lower temple was built on a sloping site with a gradual ascent; through a steeper slope, the gatehouse is reached. Unlike ordinary planning, the bell and drumtower were not built independently but were attached to the front hall. The rest of the temple is the same as other temples.

The main hall of the temple of the water god was completed in 1324. It has a double eave half-hip roof, surrounded by ambulatory columns, and was one of the types of ceremonial buildings of the Yuan Dynasty.

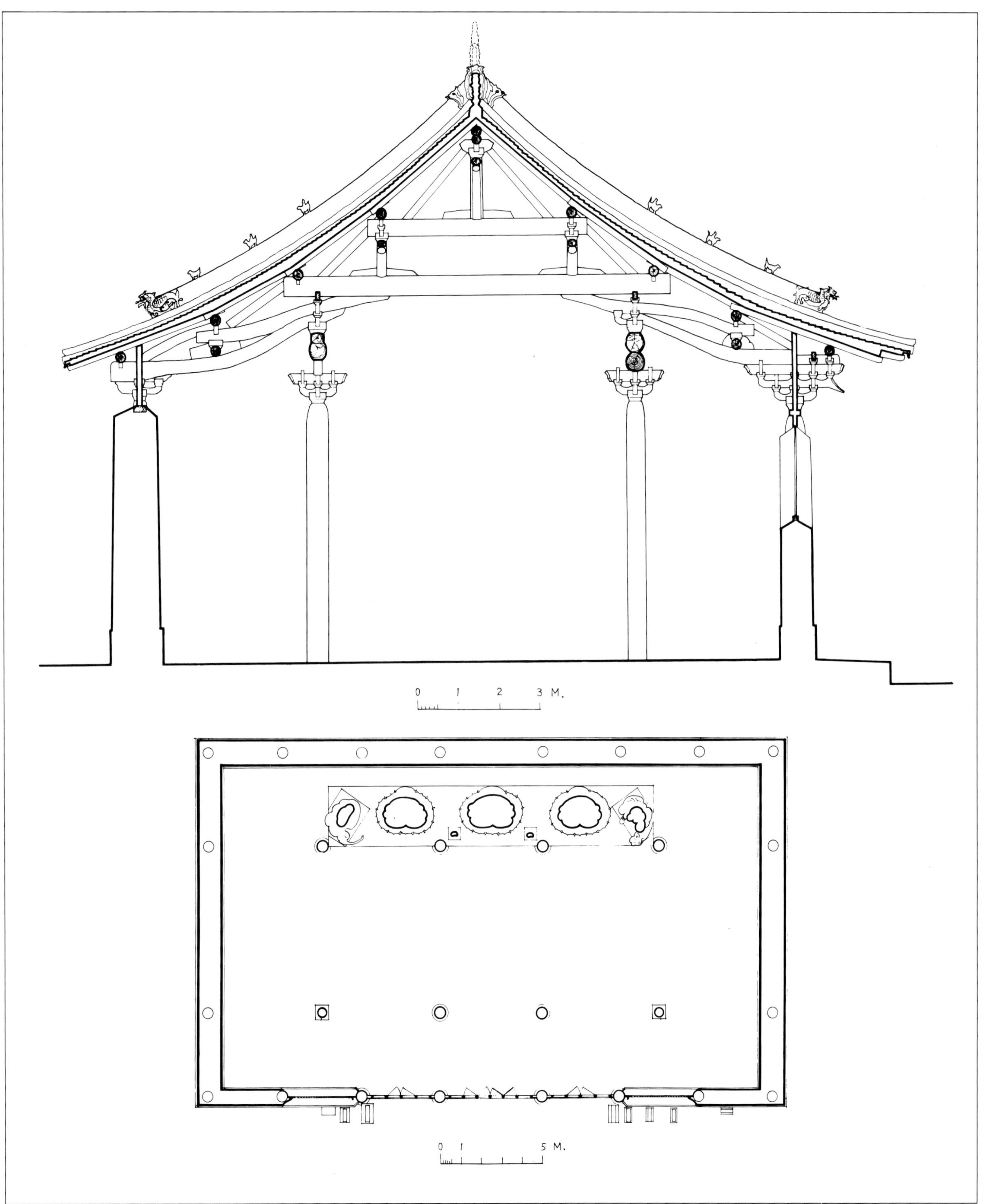

◁ Hongdong, Shanxi, Lower Guansheng Si, main hall, 1309

△ Hongdong, Shanxi, Lower Guansheng Si, main hall, 1309

In front of the temple is a stage facing a courtyard for people to sit and watch the performance. The Yuan Dynasty is famous for its development of theatrical art; the most famous plays and dramas in historical China were written during the Yuan, and people liked to go to theatres. It was customary that stages were built opposite temples, and hence it became a special element of Yuan Dynasty temple layout. Inside the main hall is a famous fresco painted on a side wall which depicts a performance, and this is the earliest fresco about this activity ever discovered. It shows that there was no definition between stage and backstage, but during the performance a curtain was hung between the two. It is a valuable record for the research of Yuan Dynasty performing art. Not until the Ming and Qing Dynasties were the performing arts developed further,

◁ Hongdong, Shanxi, Shuishen Temple, Yuan Dynasty, 1324

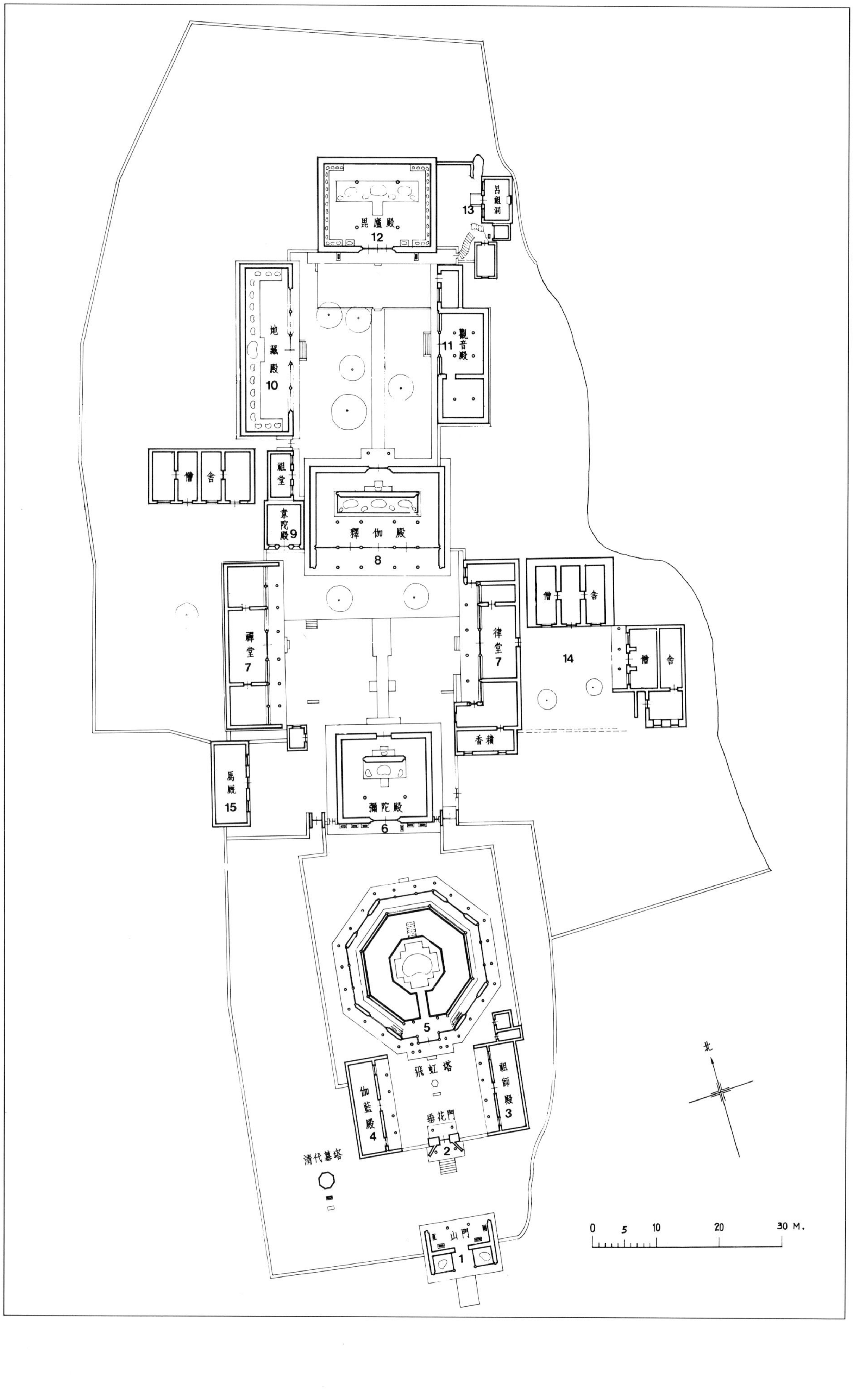

△ Hongdong, Shanxi, Upper Guansheng Si, Ming Dynasty

△ Hongdong, Shanxi, Upper Guansheng Si, Feihong Pagoda, 1505-17

◁ Hongdong, Shanxi, Upper Guansheng Si, Feihong Pagoda, 1505-17

Key
1 Gatehouse. 2 Gate. 3 Zusi Hall. 4 Jialan hall. 5 Feihong Pagoda. 6 Mituo hall. 7 Meditation Hall. 8 Sakyamuni Hall. 9 Weituo Hall. 10 Dizang Hall. 11 Guanying Hall. 12 Pilu Hall. 13 Luzu Cave. 14 Monks' residence. 15 Stable.

▷ Hongdong, Shanxi, Upper Guansheng Si, Feihong Pagoda, 1505-17

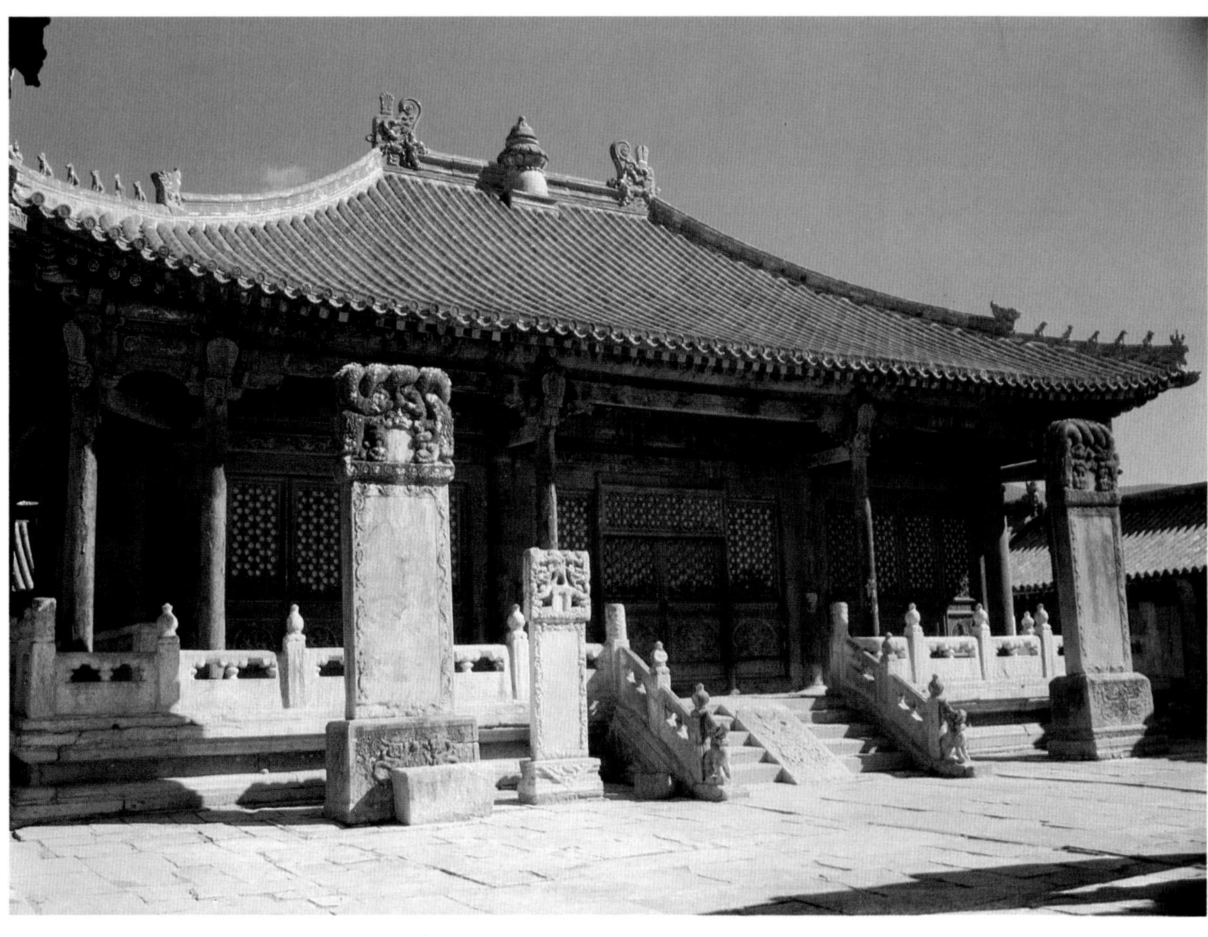

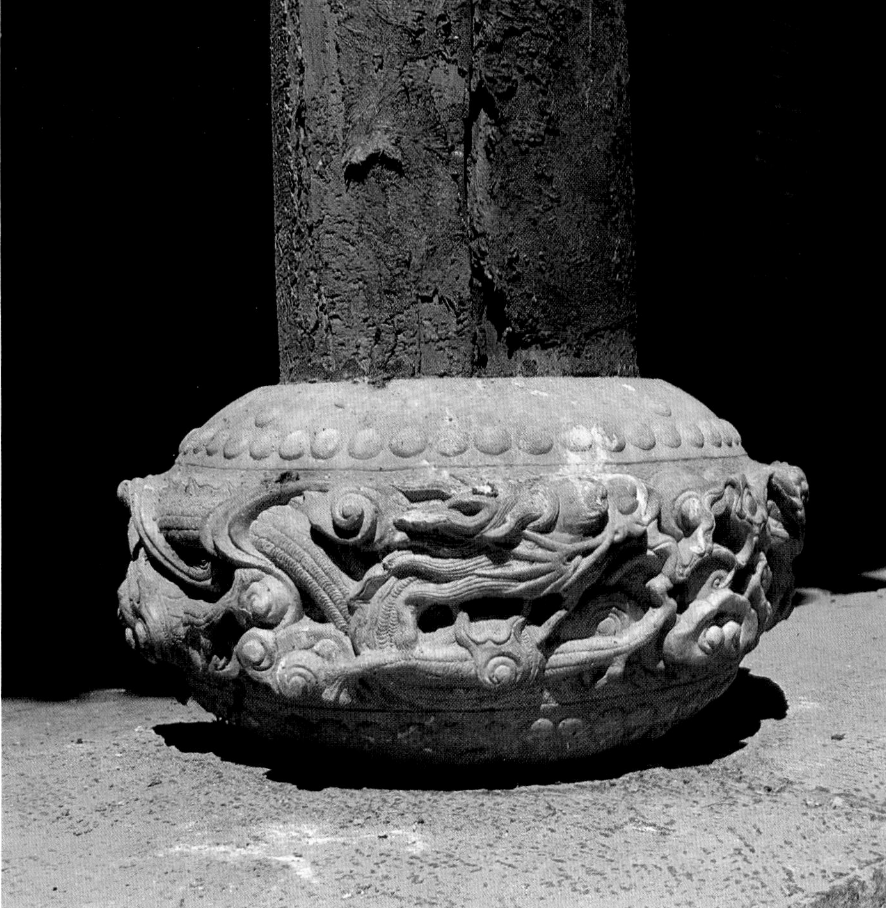

△ Wutai Shan, Shanxi, Buddha's Peak, main hall

◁ Wutai Shan, Shanxi, Buddha's Peak, column base

and then there were stage, backstage and side stages at left and right for accompanying musicians. In front of this temple is a pool and two water channels, and the reason for building a temple of a water god here was probably due to the lack of water resources for irrigation.

From the lower temple can be seen the glazed tile pagoda and the upper temple on the hilltop. The temple was of the Ming Dynasty but the Buddhist images were modelled in the earlier Yuan Dynasty. On axis is the glazed tile pagoda, which is 13 storeys and 47 metres high, and has an octagonal plan. Because of its multi-coloured surface and its position in the ancient pines under a blue sky, it looks like a brilliant rainbow, and so it was called Feihong Pagoda (Flying Rainbow Pagoda). On the surface all the duogong, columns, panels, and niches were made of glazed tiles. The large degree of tapering makes the top too slender and out of proportion. Inside the pagoda on the second floor is a small hall with a dark green glazed tile dome, also exquisitely made.

LAMA TEMPLES

Lama Buddhism is a sect of Buddhism founded in Tibet during the Tang Dynasty in 747, but it was particularly favoured by the Yuan Dynasty emperors. The head of Lamaism was honoured as Fawang (the King of Law or God king), and for the sake of unifying Tibet with the rest of the Mongolian Empire, Lamaism, which was prevalent only in Tibet, was brought to other parts of China and continued its influence in the Ming and Qing Dynasties. The Qing Dynasty rulers, activated by political motives, also claimed belief in Lama Buddhism in order to control the Tibetans and Mongolians; thus it became an instrument of political rule. In the end, there was a close alliance of politics and religion. A great number of Lama temples – stupas of peculiar form – were built and Lama Buddhist buildings developed rapidly. During the Yongle Period of Ming Dynasty (1403-1425) the Lamas divided into two factions: the old faction wore red cassocks and was called the Red Sect; the other wore yellow and was called the Yellow Sect. Qianlong Emperor of the Qing Dynasty favoured the Yellow Sect, and so most of the Qing Lamaseries belong to the Yellow sect of Lamaism.

The most magnificent of Lama temples is the Potala Gong (Potala Palace) of Lhasa, Tibet, which is also the centre of Lama Buddhism. The building group was started during the 7th century in the Tang Dynasty, but the present one was built in the Qing Dynasty (1645) by the 5th Dalai Lama and took 50 years to complete. The palace was built on the Red Hill to the north, and is divided into two parts. The central, red coloured part is

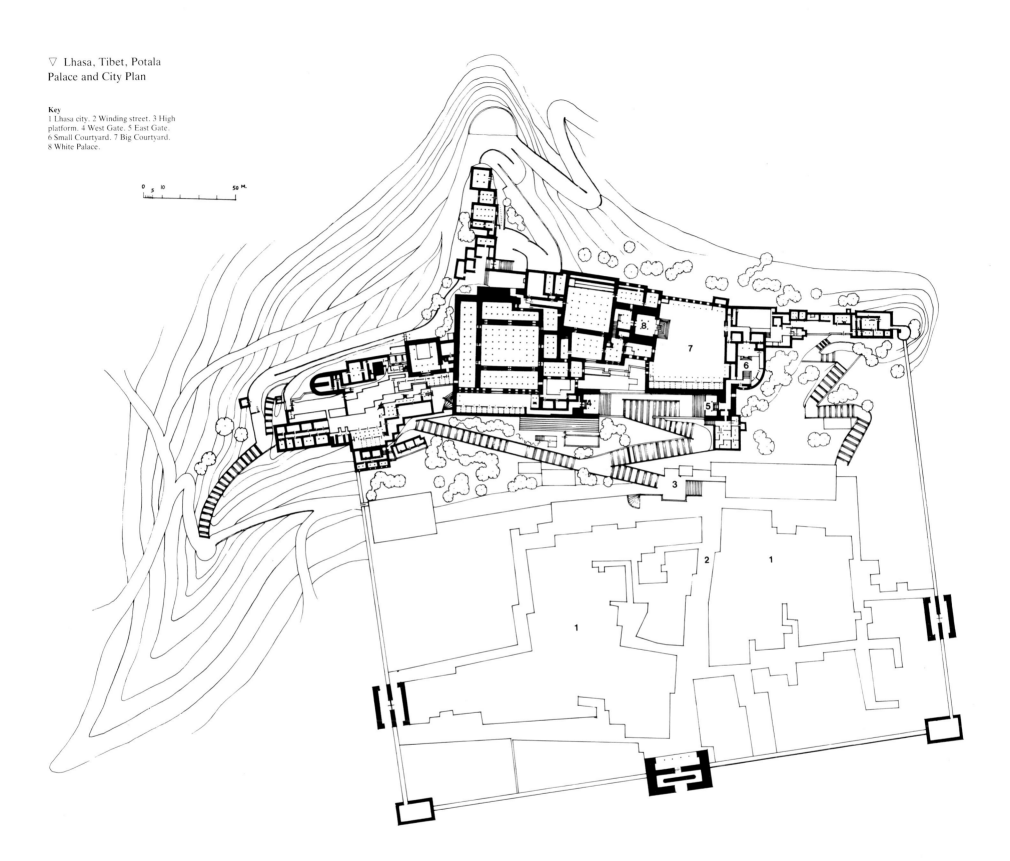

▽ Lhasa, Tibet, Potala Palace and City Plan

Key
1 Lhasa city. 2 Winding street. 3 High platform. 4 West Gate. 5 East Gate. 6 Small Courtyard. 7 Big Courtyard. 8 White Palace.

called the 'Red Palace' and was the place for the relics of the deceased Dalai Lama of each generation as well as for worshipping Buddha. The other part flanking the Red Palace is the 'White Palace', and is used for bedrooms, dining halls, office and storage. Altogether more than 200 metres high and 360 metres in length, it is enclosed by a massive stone wall. The artistic achievement of this palace is that indigenous building materials were used to create a great work which integrates the Han and Tibetan architectural styles.

Potala faces the small town to the south. The city's winding streets resemble the Medieval towns of Europe, and this is the visitor's introduction to the palace. Above the rooftops of dwellings the majestic silhouette of the palace can be seen while threading through the streets, the only approach to the palace; and at the end is a high platform, which marked the beginning of the divine palace and end of the secular world. As one followed the road built almost parallel to the contour lines with myriads of stone blocks, first the west gate and then the east gate were reached. It is the only gate

◁ Lhasa, Tibet, Potala Palace, Qing Dynasty, 1645 (courtesy H.S. Guo)

△ Lhasa, Tibet, Potala Palace, Qing Dynasty, 1645 (courtesy H.S. Guo)

△ Lhasa, Tibet, Potala Palace, Qing Dynasty, 1645 (courtesy H.S. Guo)

through which the palace is accessible. Here vistas were provided at every turn to attract the eyes. The last gate is the first climax of the palace. Inside the gatehouse and enclosed by massive stone walls was a stone staircase in darkness. After several tortuous curves a small courtyard of irregular shape and various levels was reached, first descending and then climbing. Then there is the sacred gateway, which has a large portico, from which a very big courtyard (1,600 square metres) called the East Terrace comes into view. This is the second introduction, which guides one to the White Palace to the east and the magnificently decorated gateway. Here a gold pagoda, trapezoidal windows, and a grand staircase dynamically invites one to step into the dark interior of the palace to worship the mystic King of Law. East Terrace is called 'Dayangshar' in Tibetan. On festival occasions, religious rituals were performed here.

The space sequence thus planned is from small to large, from crooked to straight, from contraction to relief, from light to dark, and from up to down. Following this sequence of spatial varieties and the attendant physical exhaustion, the emotion of the believer changes accordingly. There are minglings of expectation, apprehension, fear, anticipation and, finally, fulfillment and reverence. Here on the balcony of the last courtyard 70 metres above ground level one commands a grand view of the whole city as if one is on top of the world, and heaven has been reached.

The other architectural feature of Potala is that its

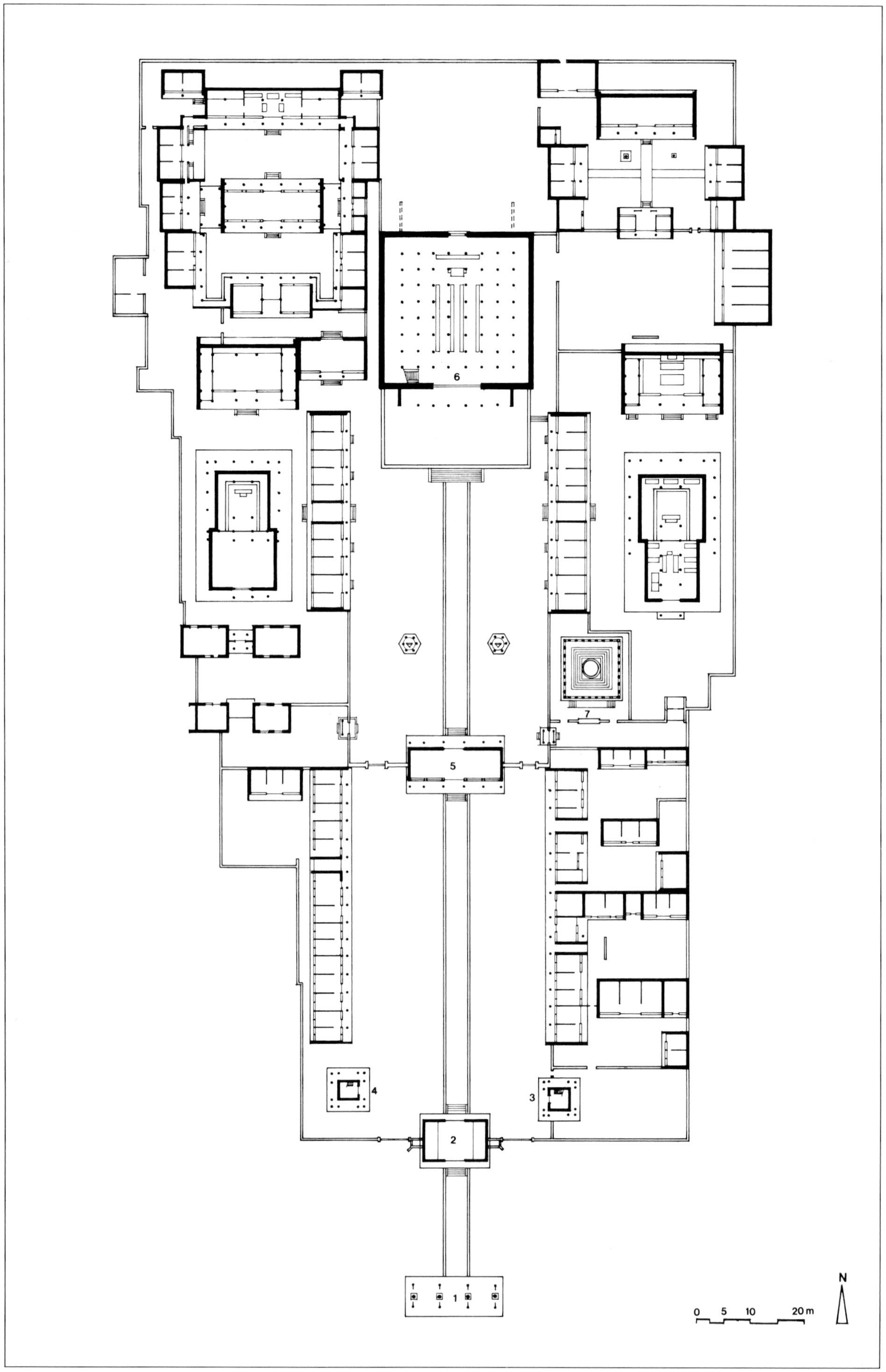

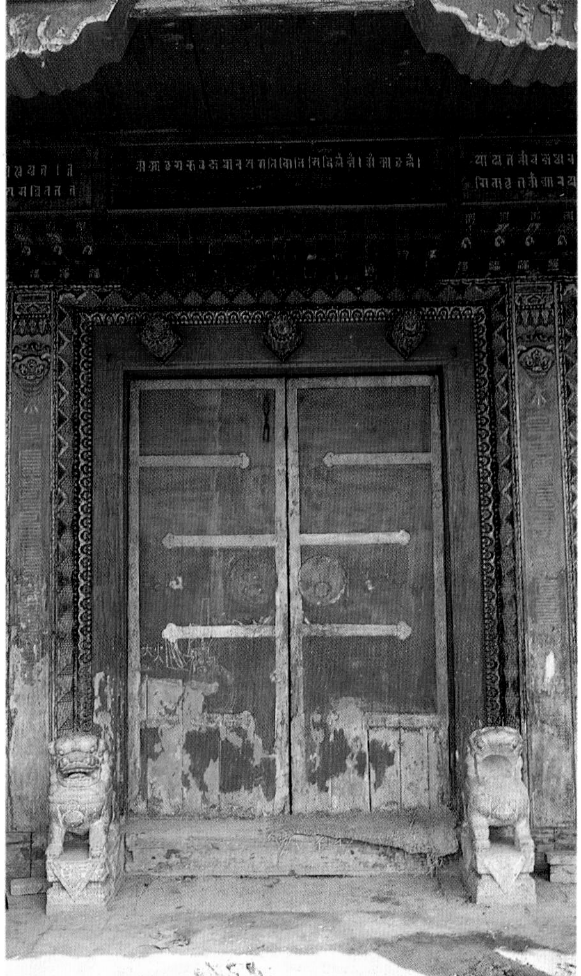

◁ Xilituzao, Huhehot, Inner Mongolia, Ming Dynasty, enlarged in 1688

△ Xilituzao, Huhehot, Inner Mongolia, Ming Dynasty

Key
1 Peifeng. 2 Gatehouse. 3 Bell tower. 4 Drum tower. 5 Hall. 6 Main hall. 7 Stupa.

building is so closely related to the site. The palace seems as if it had grown from the hill and become an integral part of it: they are harmonious and in unison. The building material used changes from the indigenous stone of the basement wall to the whitewashed wall with trapezoidal windows, then to the upper red wall with the golden roofs above it. The stone foundation merges with the site, and no distinct definition can be seen. The windows are larger at the top and smaller down below, as if they are graduated watercolour wash. Standing powerfully and majestically on the hill, it is not difficult to understand its symbolic meaning. The God King grew from the land to wield his supernatural majestic power to control all human beings, and the king is the representative of God. Heaven is high above; one has to pass all the hardships in order to reach it.

The Xilituzao Lama Temple at Huhehot, inner

Mongolia, is a large temple, first built during the end of the Ming Dynasty and enlarged in 1688 in the Qing Dynasty. It followed the Han planning layout, and except for the Dajin Tang (the Great Lecture Hall), the buildings were all in the Han style. The hall was formed by a front portico, praying hall and Buddha hall. Inside the hall, the wooden columns and brackets reflect the Tibetan decoration, being more resplendent than Han Buddhist temple decorations. The roof is mostly flat except for the middle portion, which has a half-hip roof. Nearby to this temple is Dazhao (Great Temple), built in 1580. The front elevation is of two storeys and is a rare case in temple architecture.

In present-day China, however, the greatest and most glorious of Lama Buddhist temples groups are in Chengde, Hebei, and all were constructed during the early part of the Qing Dynasty. They are unique, not only because the buildings and building groups combined the Han and Tibetan architectural styles, but they also symbolized the unity of all nationalities within China. It is in this sense that the city and buildings can be called a 'Symbol of Unity'. During the reigns of Emperors Kangxi and his grandson Qianlong, the Qing Dynasty was at its zenith; and out of political reason, together they built these most monumental relics outside the Bishushan Zhuang (Summer Mountain Resort) in Chengde. These two ambitious emperors were not only great warriors who defeated the aggressors who invaded China, but also patrons of art and literature, and through their talents Chinese literature developed rapidly. Suffice it to say that they built these buildings for the reason of unifying China rather than for enjoyment and religious belief. Even after the Qing emperors made Beijing the capital city, they still maintained their marital relationship with the Mongolian nobility, thus taking control of the Mongolians.

Another policy was to invite those who were loyal to the Qing emperors to the vicinity of Chengde for a hunting party every autumn, and sumptuous feasts were thrown afterwards. The hunting ground covered an area of about 100 kilometres in length from north to south and had a perimeter of 700 kilometres. The real purpose behind these hunting parties was a display of power to the nobilities and the training of the Army of Eight Banners (the Qing Dynasty army differentiated their armies by eight colour banners), as well as to defend themselves against invasion by Czarist Russia. Kang Xi in one of his poems expressed that his idea was 'to have an everlasting peace and a bumper harvest'.[12] The Summer Mountain Resort and the Outer Eight Lamaseries are an architectural unity. The central axis of all the Lamaseries are focused on the centre of the resort, and from the hills inside the resort the front elevations of the Lamaseries can be clearly seen, so that visually and spiritually they are an integral part. The Lamaseries were built consecutively from 1713 to 1780, a duration of almost 70 years.

△ Xilituzao, Huhehot, Inner Mongolia, Ming Dynasty

▷ Chengde, Hebei, Puning Si, Dacheng Ge, Qing Dynasty, 1755

In 1755 the Qing Dynasty defeated aggressors from the north. Emperor Qianlong threw a celebratory feast in the Summer Resort in honour of the four nobilities loyal to the Qing Dynasty and titles were bestowed on them. Since the Mongolians believed in Yellow Lamaism, Qianlong tried to conciliate the nomads and made Lamaism the national religion. The same year the Puning Temple was built (The Temple of Universal Palace) as a replica of Sanmoya Temple of Tibet at the southern part of a hill to the northeast of the resort. The Dacheng Ge was built to house the 22.28 metre high cedar Buddha statue of Guanying, so the temple is also called the Big Buddha Temple. The first part of the plan was laid out on the Han principle, i.e. symmetrical and axial. There is a gatehouse, bell and drum-towers, and the windows and archway of the gateway have beautifully carved architraves of foliate designs. Inside the gateway are the stele pavilion, the Hall of Four Heavenly Kings, and the Great Hall of the hero, the last with a Lama stupa centred on top of the main ridge. The stupa is made of bronze and is gold plated; the base is of glazed tile and of the same material as the ridge; it was probably used to suggest to visitors that

◁ Chengde, Hebei, Puning Si, Dacheng Ge, Qing Dynasty, 1755

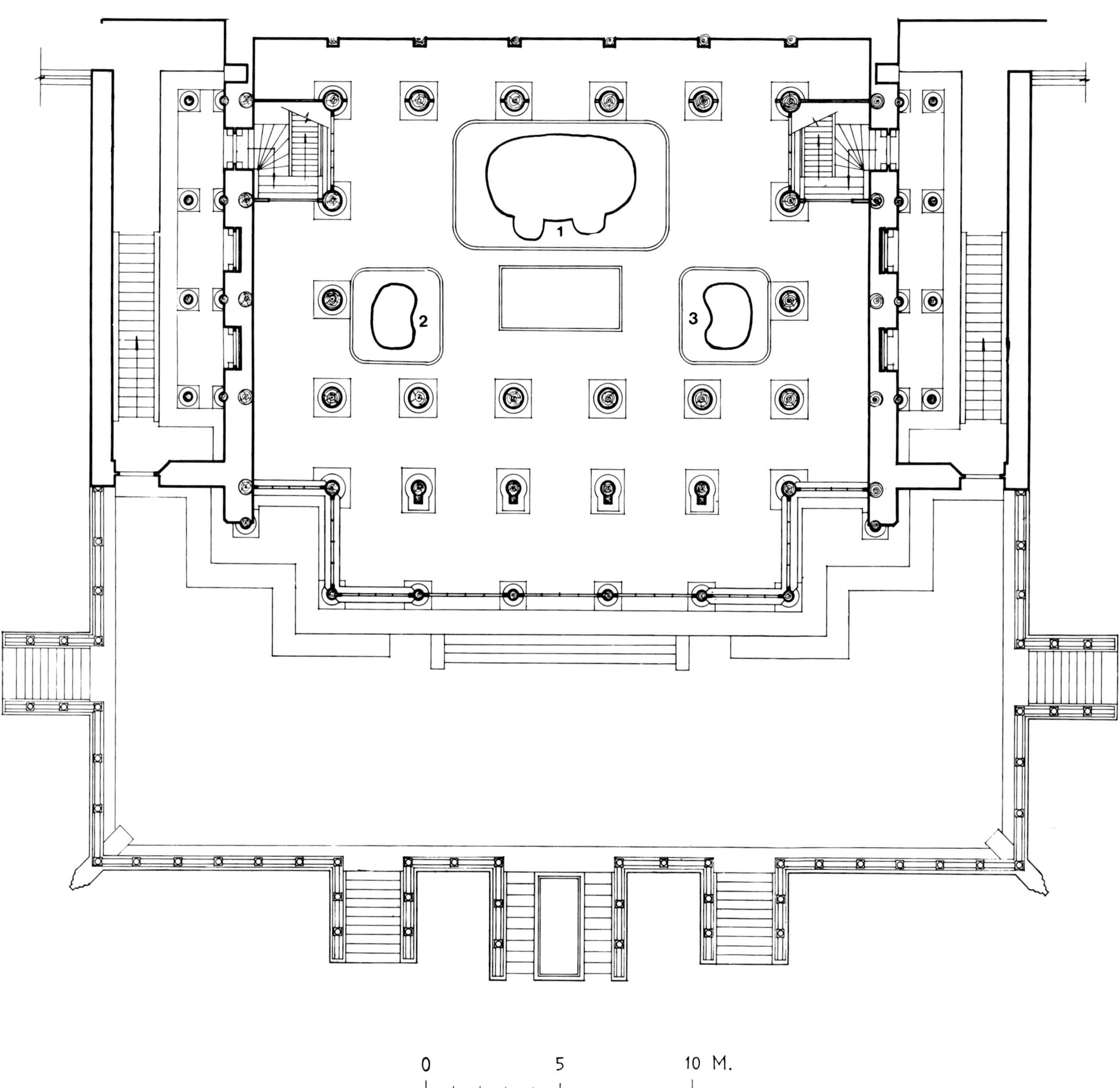

▷ Chendge, Hebei, Puning Si, Dacheng Ge, Qing Dynasty, 1755

Key
1 Statue of Guanying. 2&3 Statue of attendant.

the rest part of the temple would be of Tibetan style.

The ground at the back of the great hall rises up about eight metres, and the 39 metre-high Dacheng Ge is located at the middle of this platform. A steep staircase leads to a hall which controls the entrance to the platform. This hall has a trapezoidal plan, and hence was called the 'Triangular Hall'. One is able to see through the arched opening the soaring roof of the high-rise pavilion behind. In between these two halls is a spacious terrace; many Beitai (White Platform) and Hongtai (Red platform) and stupas of Tibetan style were placed at random on the terrace. They contrasted in height and scale with the ge and made it more monumental in scale. The Tibetan temples were characterized by heavy walls which tapered a little inwards, and small windows which made walls appear much thicker. There are also horizontal bands on the wall and at the top of the parapet to give the buildings a stable effect. It was the rule to paint the monks' residences and minor halls white and the main hall red, but there are special cases; some of the buildings had a red top and white base or vice versa.

Dacheng Ge occupies the central location of the terrace, and is an excellent example of Chinese wooden construction. It not only dominates the entire building group, the form is also most remarkable and creative. The plan is of a simple rectangular shape with the central portico thrust out and erected on a white marble podium. The elevation shows five tiers of eaves, but the inside is one large, tall space 24 metres high, surrounded at different levels by two galleries. The big statues of Avalokitesvara together with attendants are housed here.

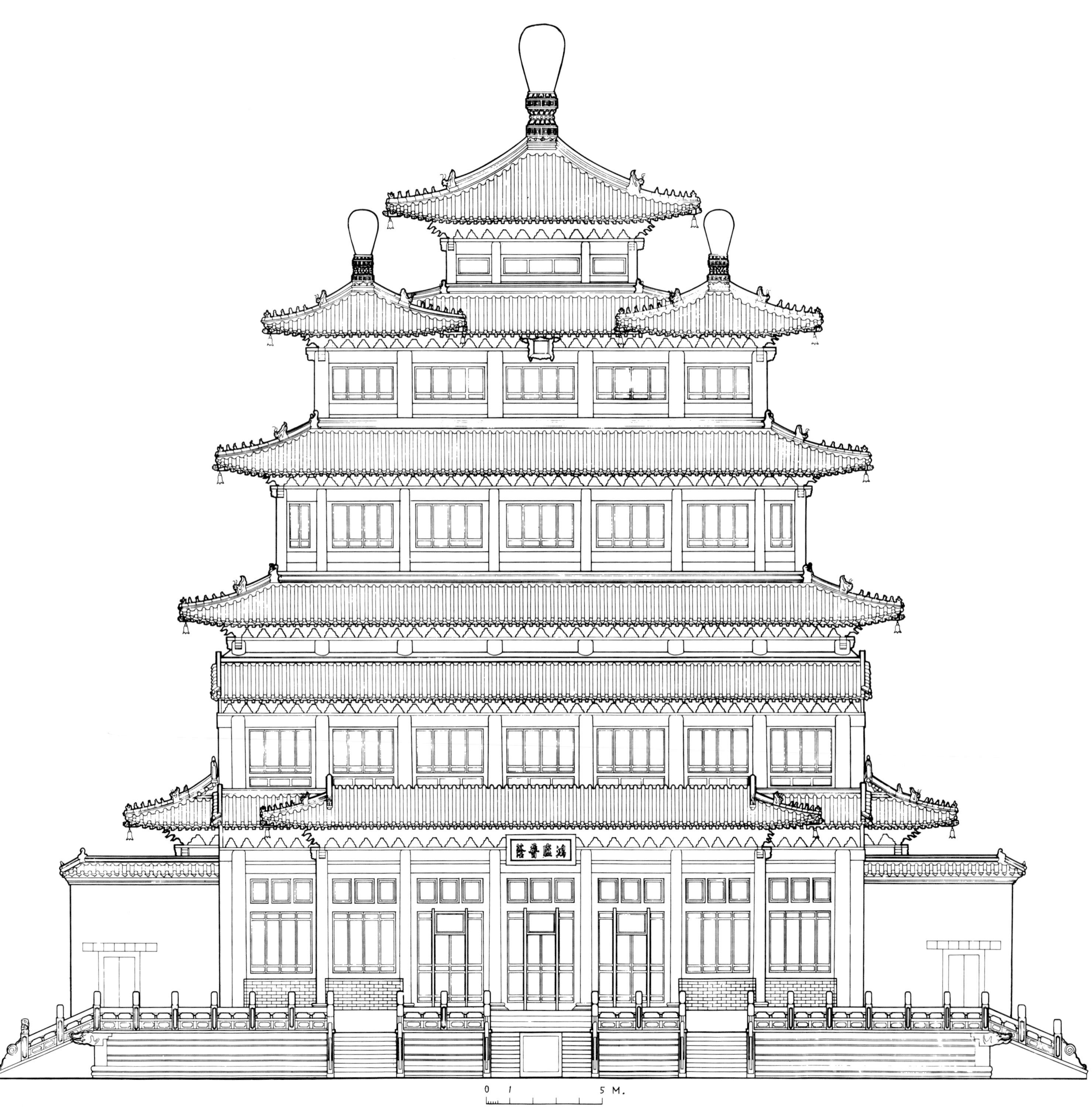
0 1 5 M.

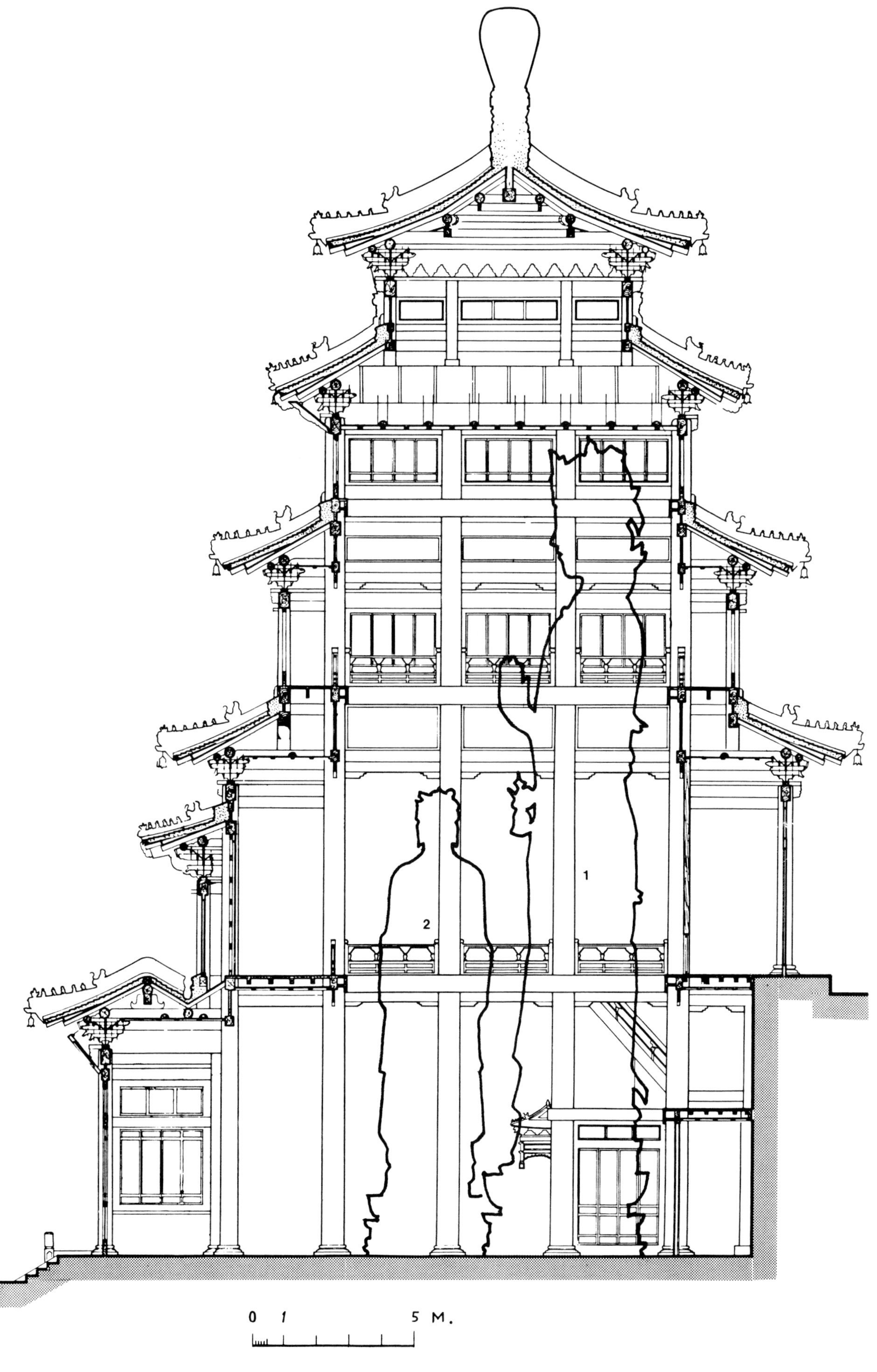

◁ Chengde, Hebei, Puning Si, Dacheng Ge, Qing Dynasty, 1755

▷ Chengde, Hebei, Puning Si, Dacheng Ge, Qing Dynasty, 1755

Key
1 Statue of Guanying. 2 Statue of attendant.

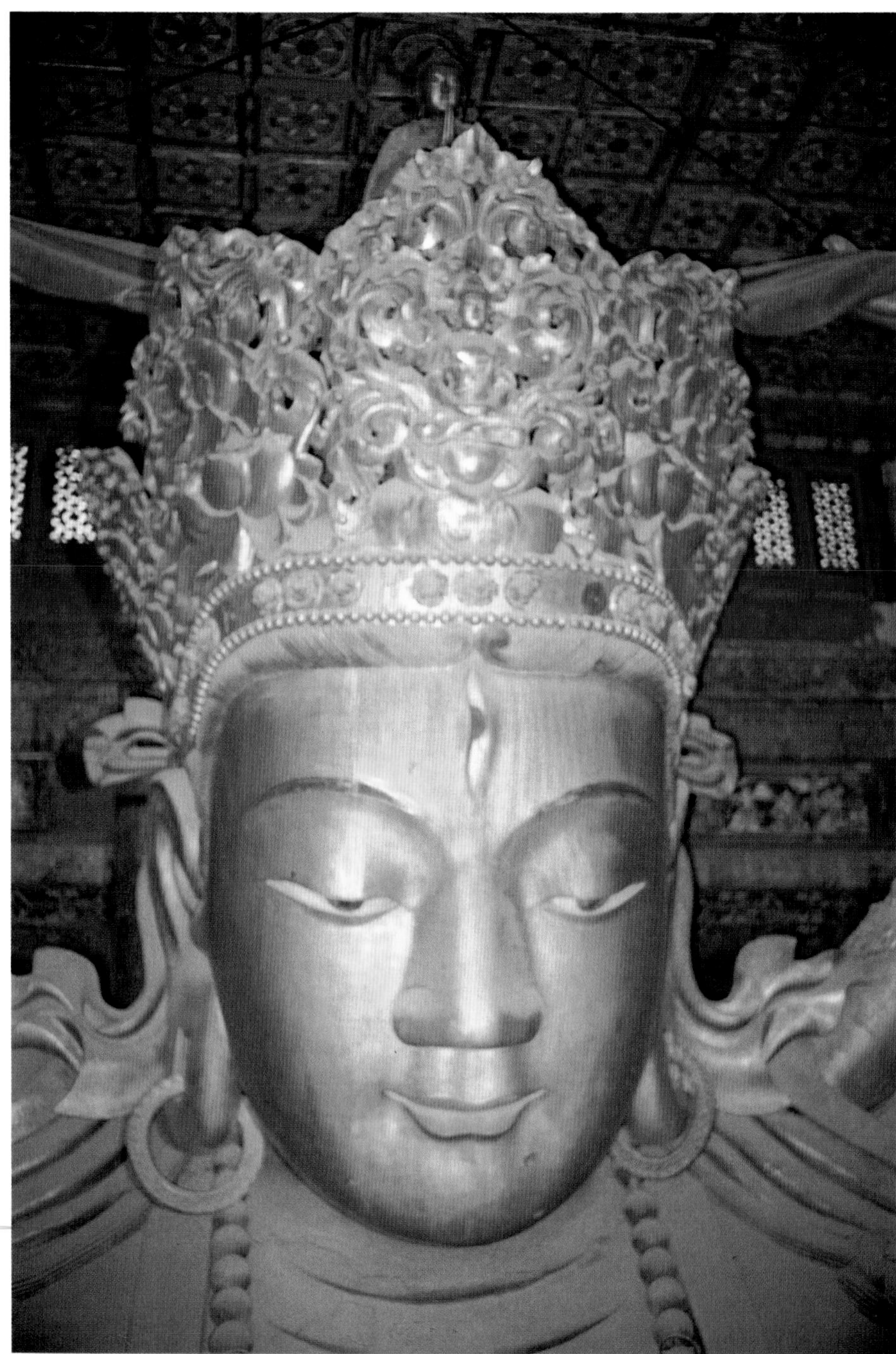

◁ Chengde, Hebei, Puning Si, Dacheng Ge, head of the Great Guanying

The next remarkable feature of the elevation is the roof design. Instead of a single big roof, it was composed of one big roof in the centre and four small ones at each corner, all of pyramidal form; thus the scale of the roof is minimized and this produces a soaring upward efect. Unlike the traditional horizontal lines of most Chinese architecture, here vertical feeling is emphasized. It produces an effect like that of the medieval Gothic style, which brings the eyes and the spirit of the visitor to the apex, and makes one feel that the God is high above and the Law of Buddha is boundless. The roofs were arranged in a '#' form plan, according to Buddhism. The middle space of the cross represents the Xumishan of the Buddha, and around it are four minor Buddhas. The finial of the central roof raises up to one storey high; this finial and the four smaller finials form a tension with the pyramidal space. Under the bright northern sun and azure sky, and above the many red and white platforms, they combine to produce an attractive and lively effect.

The galleries inside the hall provide the best locations in which to study the giant Buddha. One can appreciate the whole sculpture and the attendants from the ground floor, while at the first gallery the body and arms, with the instruments held in the hands, are in sharp focus. As one climbs to the second gallery, the facial expression and details can be clearly seen. The entire void is dimly lit. Only from the top most windows is the faint light directed into the kind golden face of the giant Buddha, and the eyes of the visitors are attracted to the face at once.

To the west of Puning Temple, and facing the Resort in the south and on the southern slope of a hill, is the Xumifoshou Temple. In 1780, Banchan Lama, the Living Buddha, came all the way from Tibet to pay tribute to Emperor Qianlong, who ordered a copy of the form of Zhashi Lunbu Lamasery in Tibet and built a temple here. Literally translated from Tibetan to Chinese 'Zhashi' means 'happiness and longevity' or 'foshou'. To the west of the Big Red Platform or main hall is 'Jixiangfaxi', or the Hall of Luck and Happiness, which was used as the temporary abode of Banchan.

A glazed pailou in front of the Big Red Platform was used to emphasize the entrance and define the space. It has three arches, with rusty red walls and white marble architraves, and not far from it is the Big Red Platform. This three-storey building, with Han style glazed window hoods, dotted the massive wall; the roofs of pavilions above the parapet wall seem to support the pyramidal gold roof in the centre. They are an exquisite integration of Han and Tibetan architectural styles.

The Big Red Platform is a building with a square courtyard in the middle, in which the praying hall Miaogaozhuangyan was built. A narrow space was left between the praying hall and the surrounding building. The golden roof is the climax and attracted people from the very beginning. The vivid movement of the golden lively dragons climbing on top of each ridge was arrested and anchored by the heavy golden stupa at the apex.

The Jixiangfaxi, too, has an elaborate gilded roof with delicately sculpted mystic ornaments, scale-like roof tiles, the Lama stupa at the middle of the main ridge and the 'Sea Elephant' decorating the end of the ridge; all produce an exotic feeling.

The last of the main axis is a seven-storey glazed tile pagoda, which serves as the finale of the sequence. The pagoda was faced with green glazed tiles, and trimmed with yellow eaves of the same material, colours used widely during the Qing. There are Buddha images on every facet. However, the main feature of this pagoda is its podium at the first floor. 'To build a wooden ambulatory at the first floor, with balconies above it, the topmost being the main portion of the pagoda'[13] was a typical Qianlong practice and a richer articulation of form. Shading under the roof of the ambulatory and looking towards the sublime and magnificent Putuozhongcheng Lamasery to the west and Puning to the east, one feels as if the sequence does not terminate here since they beckon one to go further.

Putuozhongcheng is another eminent example of integration of the Han and Tibetan architectural styles.

◁ Chengde, Hebei, Xumifoshou, Qing Dynasty, 1780

◁ Chengde, Hebei, Xumifoshou, praying hall

◁ Chengde, Hebei, Xumifoshou, gold roof

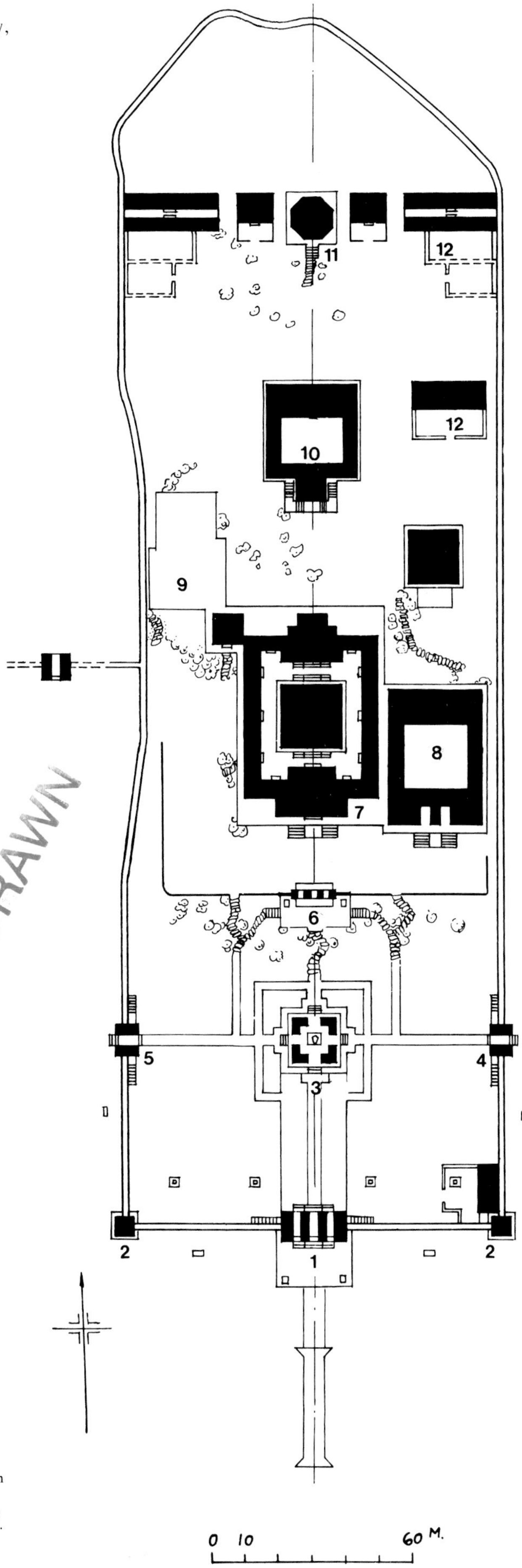

▷ Chengde, Hebei, Xumifoshou, Qing Dynasty, 1780

Key
1 Gatehouse. 2 Corner tower. 3 Pavilion of stele. 4 Bell tower. 5 Drum tower. 6 Glazed peifang. 7 Big Red Platform. 8 East Red Platform. 9 Jixiangfaxi Hall. 10 Jinhe Tang Hall. 11 Glazed tile pagoda. 12 Monks' residence.

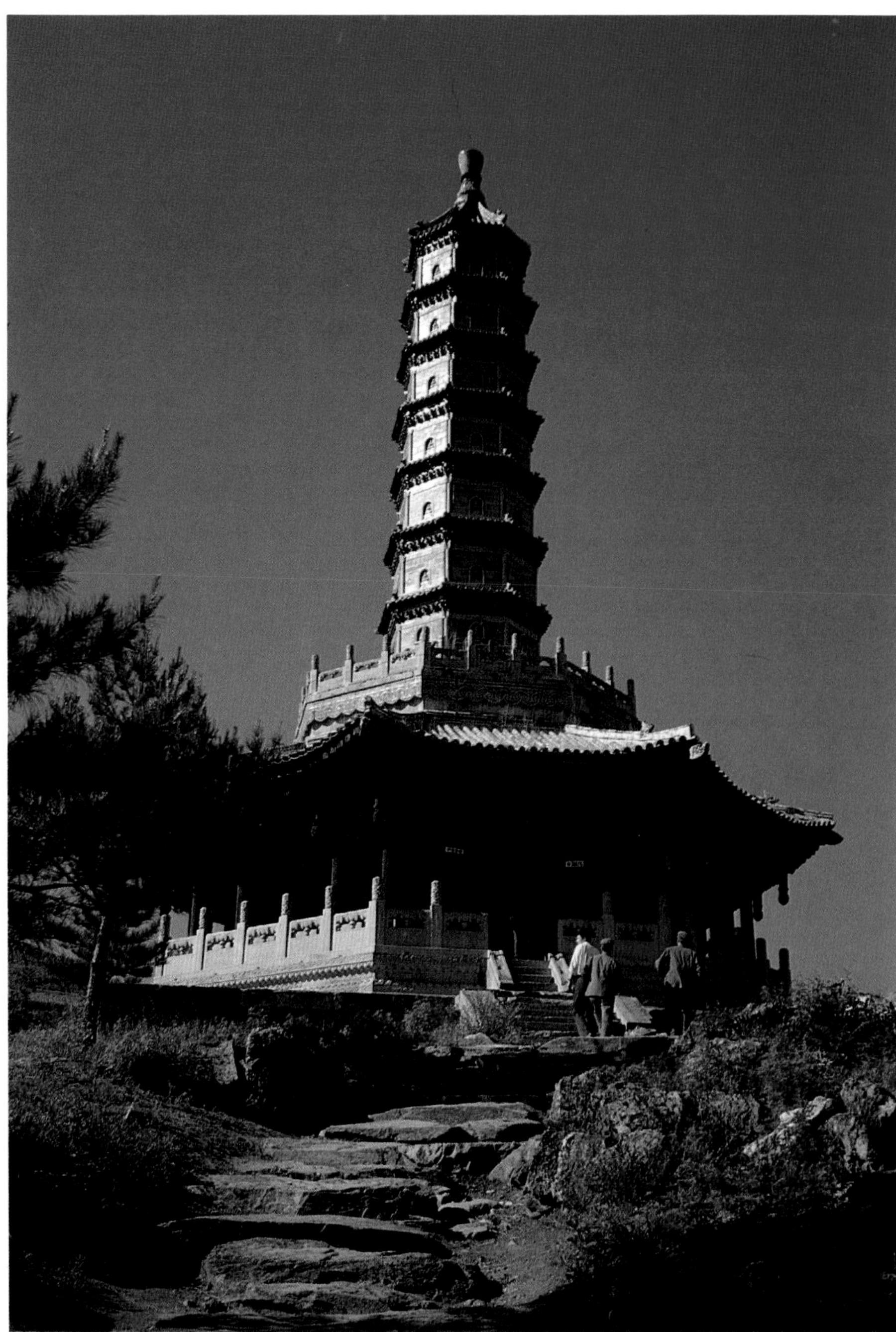

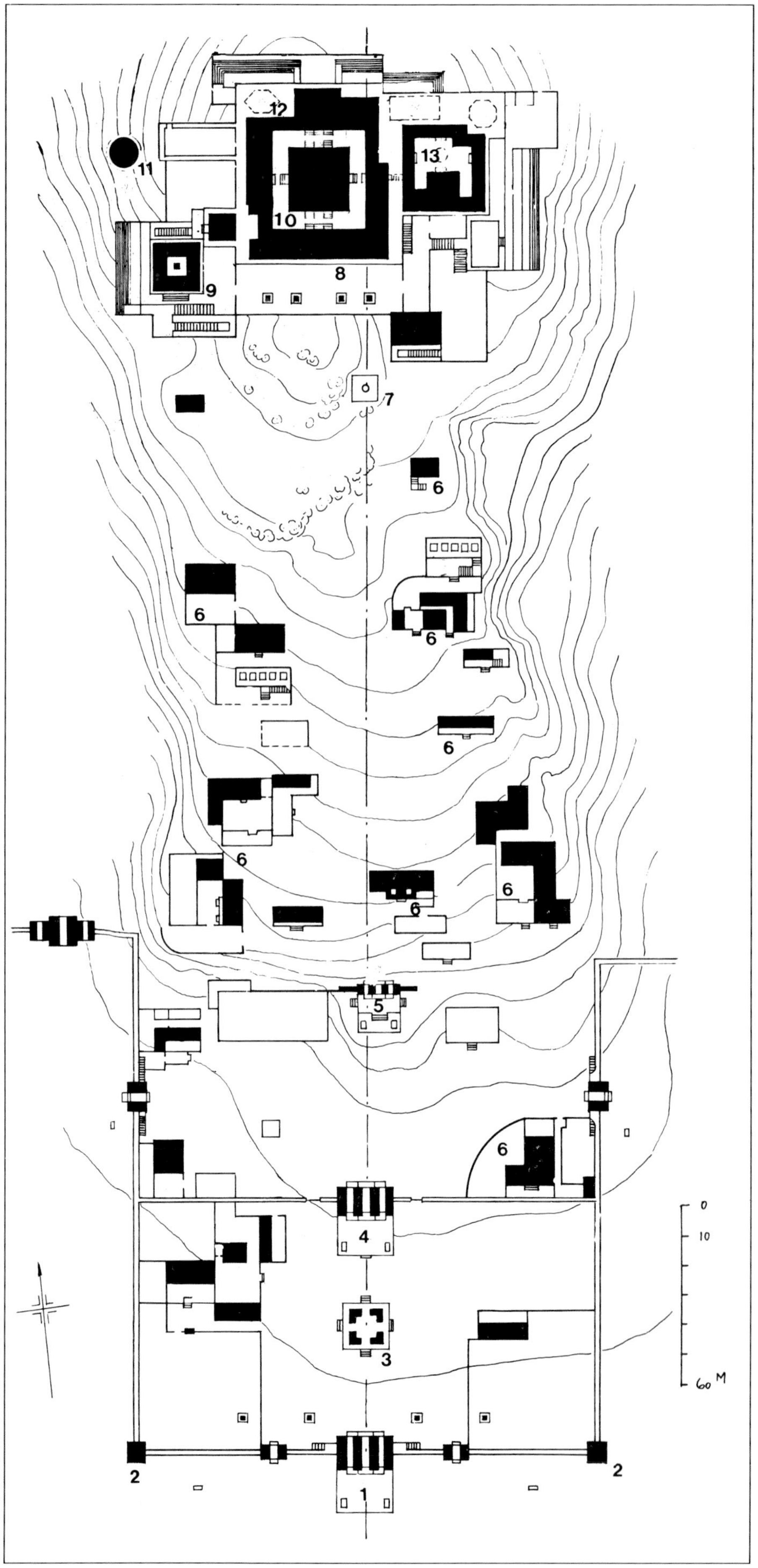

△ Chengde, Hebei, Xumifoshou, glazed tile pagoda

The spatial sequence is formalistic but does not adhere to the axial and symmetrical layout; it creates an entirely new sequence. Here the excellent concept of the old masters left a lot of inspiration for us. Shortly after the rebellion of a northern tribe was settled, the princes and nobilities of the Gobi desert assembled in Chengde and the whole country was united again. Between 1767 and 1771, in just four short years, the Qing emperors built this temple after the concept of Potala (Putuozhongcheng is the Chinese translation of Potala). Covering an area of 220,000 square metres, it is the largest of all Chengde temples and the richest in form.

Dahongtai (the Big Red Platform) represents the combination of Han and Tibetan architectural styles;

▷ Chengde, Hebei, Putuozhongcheng, Qing Dynasty, 1771, plan

Key
1 Gate. 2 Corner. 3 Pavilion of stele. 4 Gate of Five Stupas. 5 Glazed tile peifeng. 6 White Platform. 7 White Stupa. 8 Big Red Platform. 9 Qianfo Ge. 10 Wangfaquiyi Hall. 11 Yuan tai. 12 Hexagon Pavilion. 13 Stage.

▷ Chengde, Hebei, Putuozhongcheng, Qing Dynasty, gateway

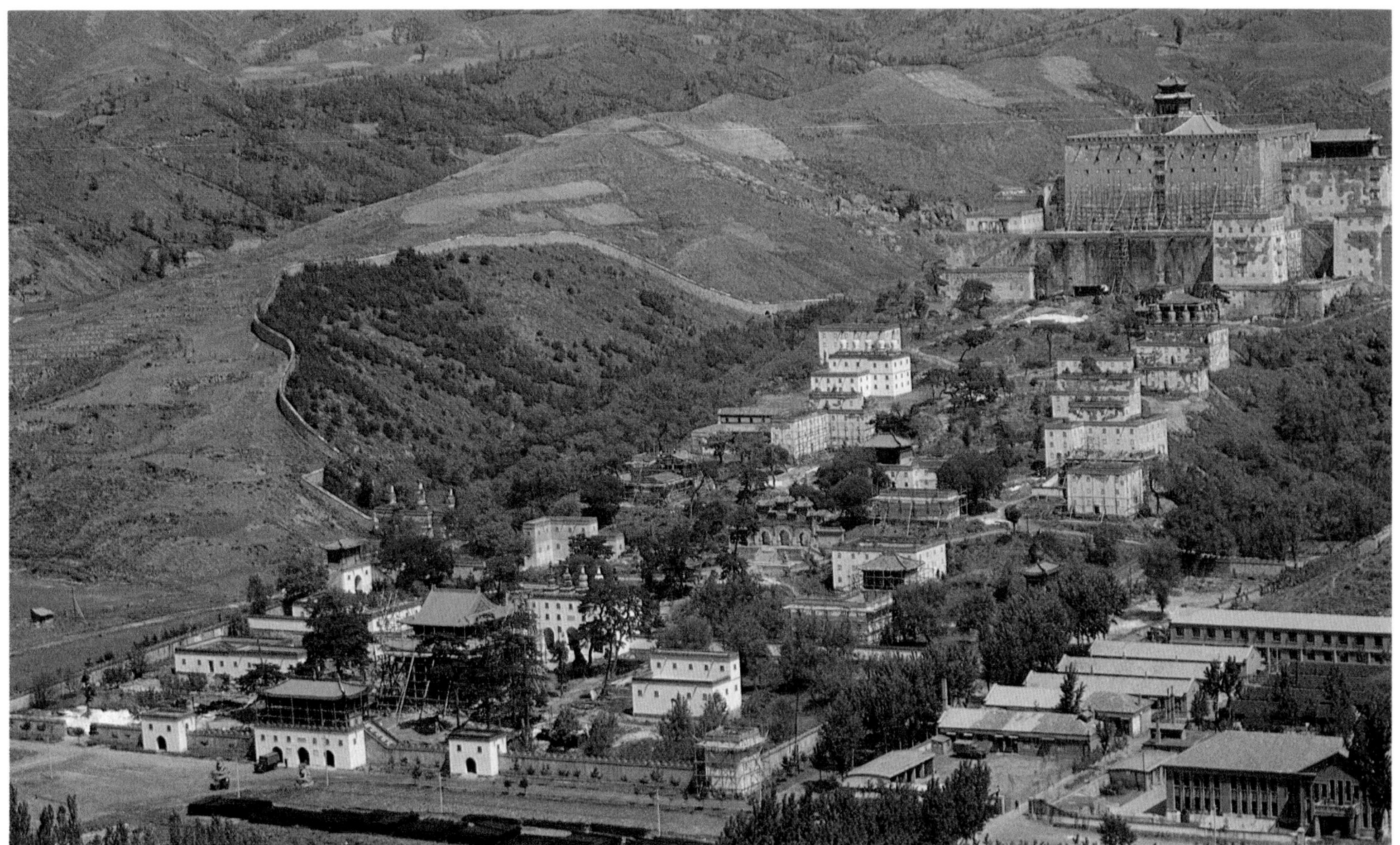

◁ Chengde, Hebei, Putuozhongcheng, Qing Dynasty, 1771, bird's-eye view

◁ Chengde, Hebei, Putuozhongcheng, Qing Dynasty, the Big Red Platform

Key
1 Big Red Platform. 2 Qianfo Ge. 3 Wangfaquiyi Hall. 4 Yuan Tai. 5 Hexagon pavilion. 6 Stage. 7 Pavilion.

◁ Chengde, Hebei, Putuozhongcheng, Qing Dynasty, eave detail

▷ Chengde, Hebei, Putuozhongcheng, Qing Dynasty, coffered ceiling

the golden roofs of the pavilions at the northeastern and northwestern corners are of the Han style. These pavilions seem to have been placed at random, but are actually in harmony and organically integrated with the solid red wall below. The Buddha niches placed at the centre of the south facade and running along the parapet wall not only attract the eyes of visitors but also give meaning to the character of the building. It demonstrates beyond doubt that different styles can be fused together if this is done wisely.

To the east of the Resort is the Pule Temple. Since the main hall has a circular plan and a conical double eave roof, it is commonly called the 'Yuantingzi' or Round Pavilion. The pavilion is built in a terraced city called Ducheng, a city of three layers of walls. The first layer is a square city wall; inside is a raised platform, the Ducheng. Stupas were placed at four corners and centres of the square platform. The central building is a circular pavilion, the Xuguangge (the pavilion of Morning Light). Inside the pavilion is a small temple of Tibetan style called the Mandala, which contains a bronze Happy Buddha. The coffered ceiling of the pavilion follows the roof line and is supported by many brackets which ascend gradually; every inch of the ceiling is decorated and covered with gold foil, and in its centre is a dragon design. This ceiling is an excellent example of its kind.

◁ Chengde, Hebei, Pule Si, 1766, Mandala and coffered ceiling

△ Beijing, Yonghe Gong, 1644

▽ Chengde, Hebei, Pule Si, 1766

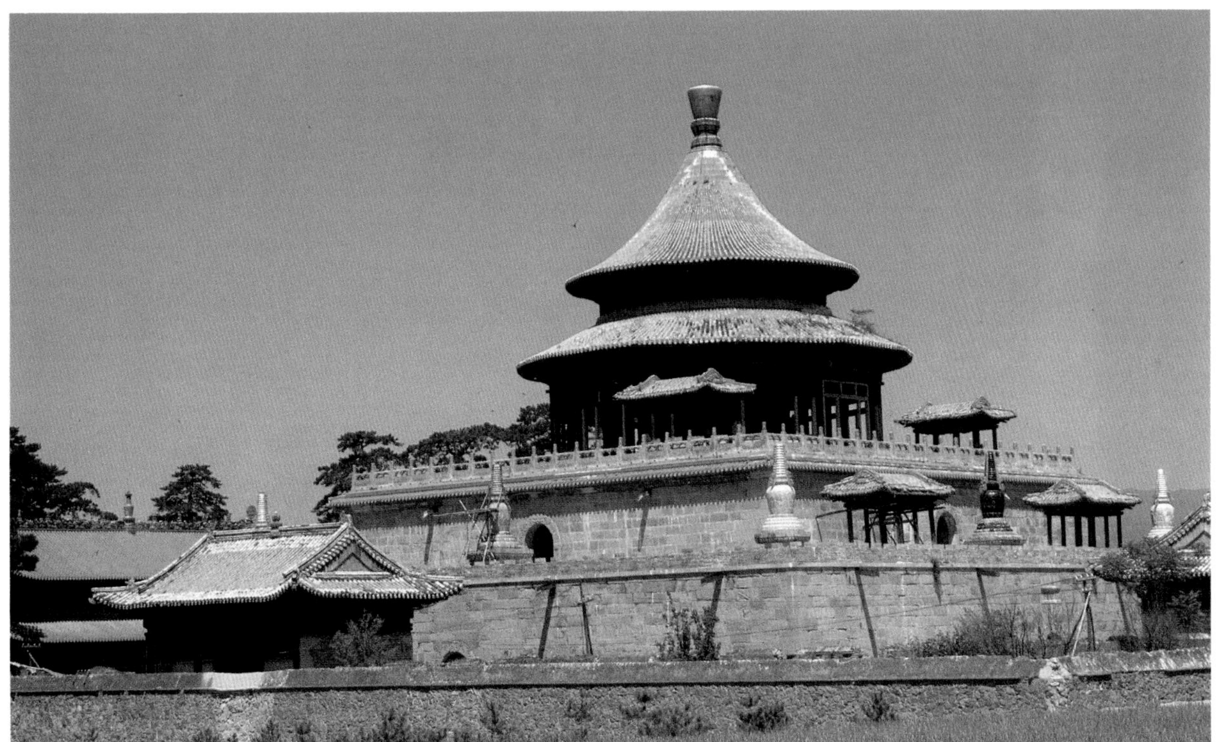

There were eleven Lamaseries in Chengde, of which there now exist only seven, the others having been demolished either in warfare or by fire. Their design infused the Han and Tibetan architectural styles, but each has its own identity and is a rare case in the history of Chinese architecture. Architectural treatment and skill in manipulating space were also varied so as not to adhere to the letter of architectural laws; they represent a wealth of Chinese culture.

Constructed in 1694 as the palace for a prince, the Yonghe Gong, located on the east side of Beijing, is the largest Lama temple in the city. During the reign of Qianlong it was turned into a temple, so the entire plan followed the Han planning principle. The last and largest building of this enclosure is Wangfoge (the Pavilion of Ten Thousand Buddhas), three storeys tall; two two-storey wings flanked it and were connected to the central building by flying bridges. It is unique in China.

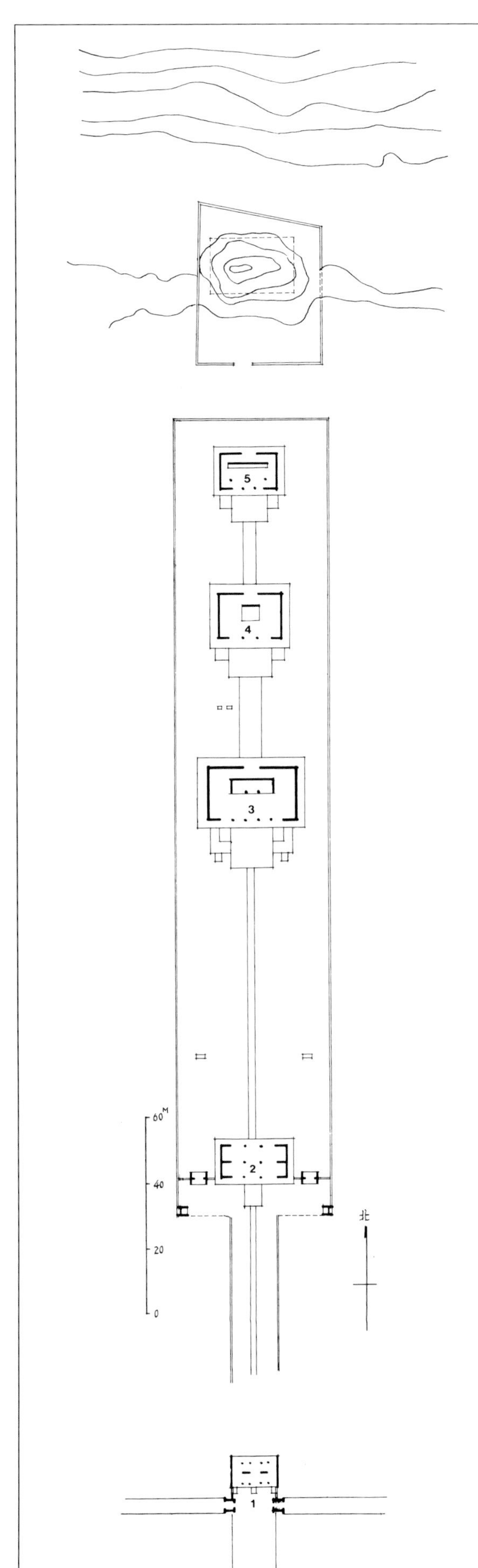

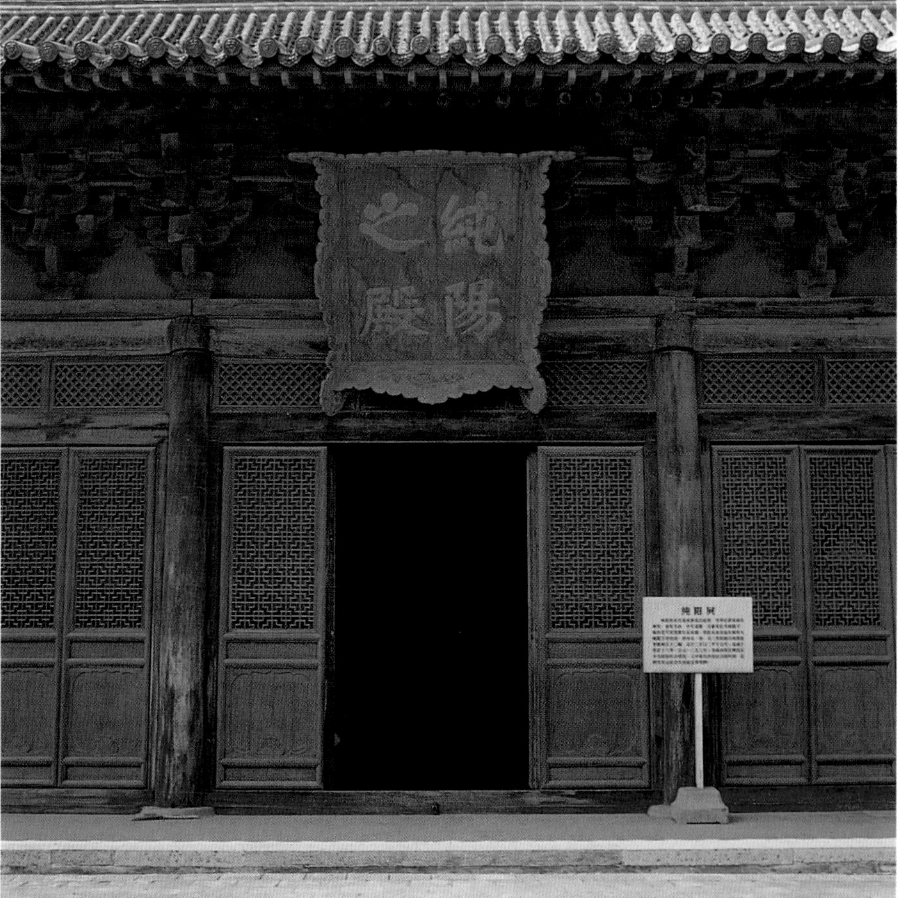

△ Ruicheng, Shanxi, Yongle Gong, Sanqing Dian

▷ Ruicheng, Shanxi, Yongle Gong, Chunyang Dian, door sash

◁ Ruicheng, Shanxi, Yongle Gong, Yuan Dynasty, 1212

Key
1 Gatehouse. 2 Wuji Men. 3 Sanqing Dian. 4 Chunyang Dian. 5 Chongyang Dian.

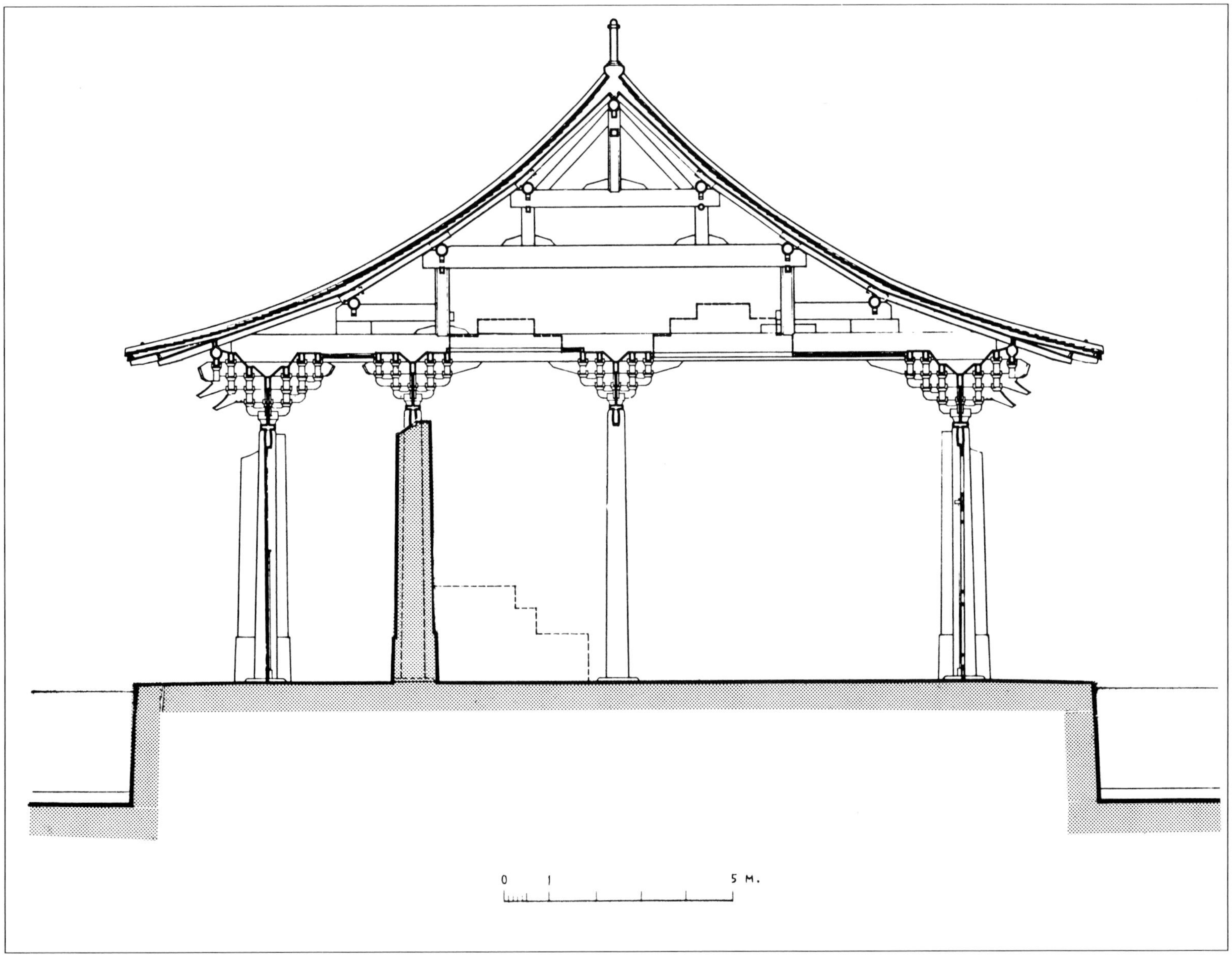

◁ Ruicheng, Shanxi, Yongle Gong, Sanqing Dian

0 1 5 M.

DAOIST TEMPLES

The name 'miao' was used exclusively for temples of Buddhism. The Daoist has another word, 'Guan' or 'Gong' (palace), for their shrines. But the general layout of a guan followed exactly the Han temple layout, the only differences being their decorations and frescoes. The most distinguished Daoist shrine is, nevertheless, the Yongle Gong (Palace of Everlasting Happiness) in Ruicheng, Shanxi Province. The original location of this palace was in Yongji, also in Shanxi, legendary home of Ludongbin, one of the Baxian (Eight Immortals) of Daoist beings, but it was removed to Ruicheng, 45 kilometres away, in the 1950's because a big dam, the Sanmexia (Gorge of Three Gates) was to be built at the Yellow River and Yongle Gong would have been under the raised water level. The present ensemble followed axial planning principles. There are four halls: the Wujimen (Gate of the Ultimate Extreme), Sanqing Dian (Hall of the Daoist Trinity), Chunyan Dian (Hall of the Pure Positive), and Zhongyan Dian (Hall of the Double Positive). The Yuan Dynasty style of 1212 is well preserved here, and the whole is an excellent document for studying the architectural style and construction of that period. Inside the halls, elegant frescoes covering 960 square metres in area depict Yuan Dynasty spiritual beings and sovereign gods and buildings.

Sanqing Dian, the main hall, is the largest of all. Although it was built during the Yuan, and has been repaired several times, it still retains the features of the roof curve and duogong of the previous Song Dynasty. It has a hip roof with yellow and green glazed tiles on the ridge, animal decoration, a very lively wen, columns painted a dark bluish colour and a door sash of dark burnt sienna. These are departures from Buddhist temples.

▽ Ruicheng, Shanxi, Yongle Gong, Chunyang Dian, duogong

▷ Ruicheng, Shanxi, Yongle Gong, Sanqing Dian, frescoes

◁ Ruicheng, Shanxi, Yongle Gong, Chunyang Dian, frescoes

The four interior walls and niches were painted thoughout. On the east wall are depicted more than 300 spiritual beings. Among them are the stalwart majestic kings; the Yunu (Jade Girl) holding lingzhi, a kind of fungus which was supposed to have an elixir effect; celestial gods and heavenly warriors, all different facial expressions. Inside the Chunyan Dian, frescoes depicted a conversation between Lu Dongbin and Zhong Lichuan. Only two seated persons were painted with a simplistic flow of brush; others were painted in the same artistic style and depict villages, palaces, and people, all united by trees, rockery, cloud and water. The coffered ceiling and beams of Sanging Dian were also of the same bluish grey and white colour, the design of the ceiling is octagonal which might suggest the shape of Ba Gua (the Eight Diagrams). From this ensemble we can see that the Daoist as well as the Buddhist used frescoes rather than words to preach, allowing the illiterate to understand the teachings of the religion as well. The higher the artistic value, the higher the effect. In Yongle Gong the frescoes are in harmony in terms of both colour and literary content, and to this day people have been enlightened by their artistic value.

The Xuanmiao Guan in Suzhou is another large temple situated in the centre of the city. The Sanqing Dian (Hall of Pure Trinity) was built in 1176. Although the structure has been repaired from time to time, it still retains the Song Style. The brackets were made in the Song and are a rare case in China.

ISLAMIC MOSQUES

Many Islamic Mosques were built following the introduction of the religion to China. The Muslims came on the Silk Road and lived together in the northwestern part of China where the Huajiao Lane Mosque in Xian, Shenxi, is now the largest mosque in present-day China. Islam is prevalent in Xinjiang, and almost every street has a mosque of small or large size; most of them preserved in the Central Asian style, and some are very exquisite. From the sea, Muslims landed at Canton or Guanzhou, and mosques were built there too. In Quanzhou in 1009, a mosque called the Shengyou (Qinjin) was built. During the early Song Dynasty, Quanzhou was already a seaport, and Muslims, using the local stone, built a comparatively large mosque right in the centre of the city. Now it lies in ruins except for the front part which still exists. From this fragment one can still see preserved, in the pointed arch of the main entrance and the extrados, the style of Central Asia.

Huajiao Lane Mosque is called the Great Mosque for it is the largest in China, having been built in the 8th century. The present mosque, however, was mainly a

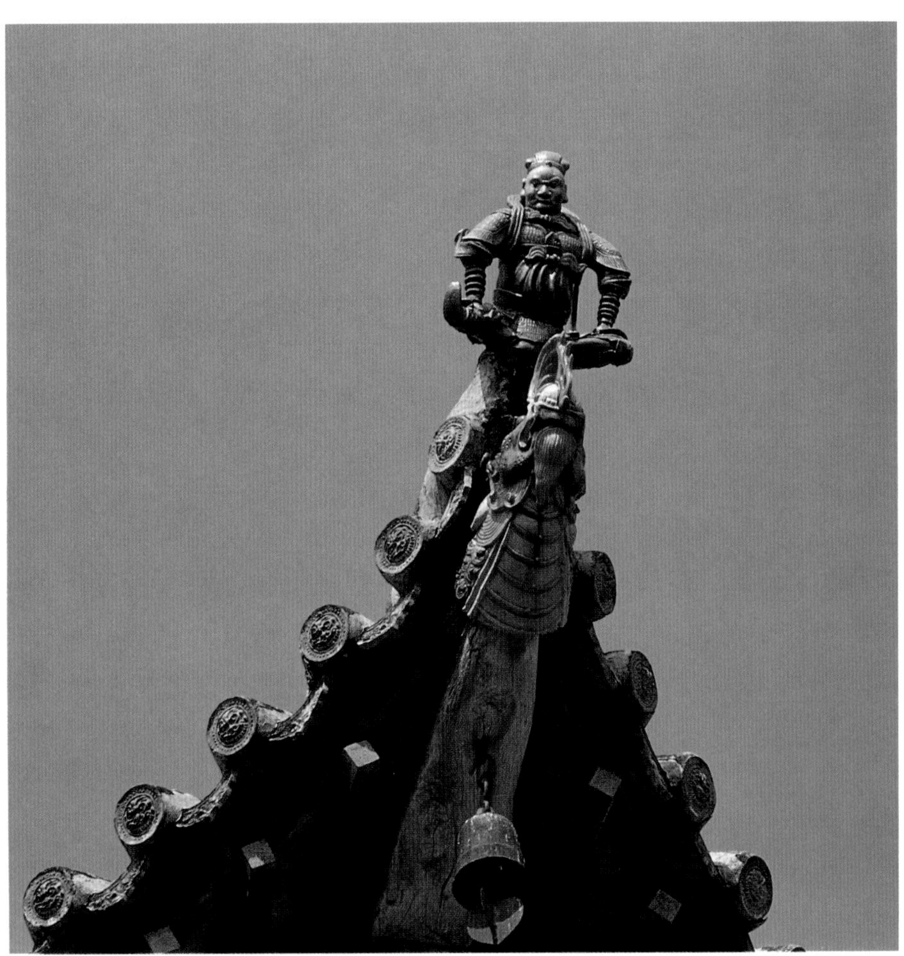

◁ Ruicheng, Shanxi, Yongle Gong, Sanqing Dian, eave decoration

▽ Ruicheng, Shanxi, Yongle Gong, Sanqing Dian, coffered ceiling

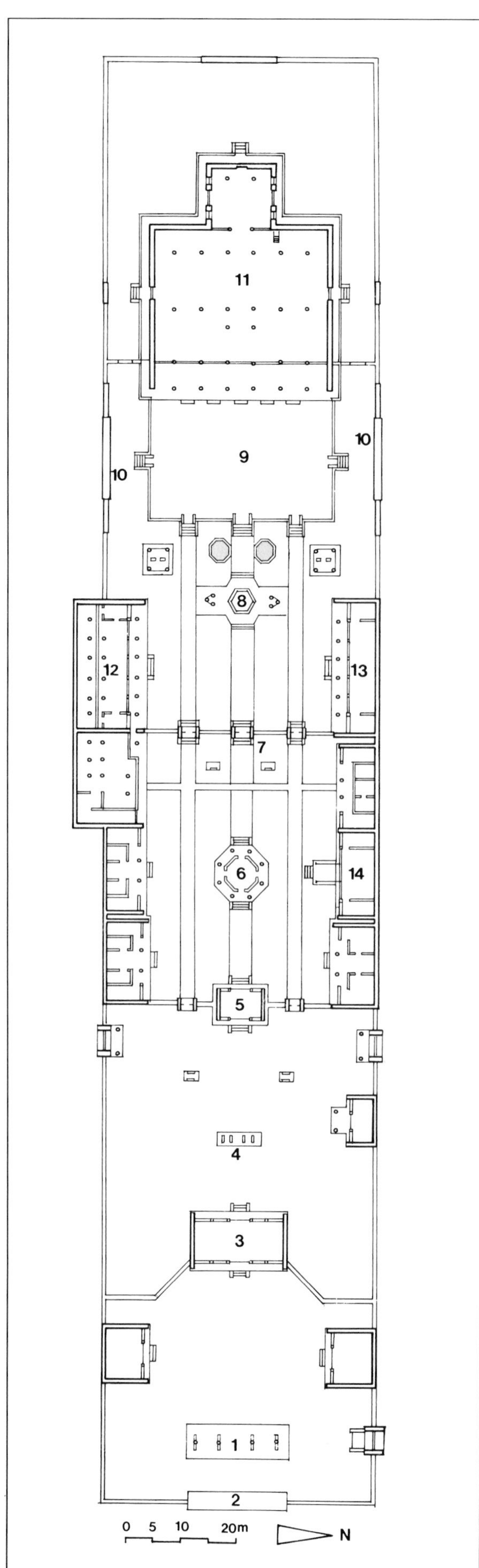

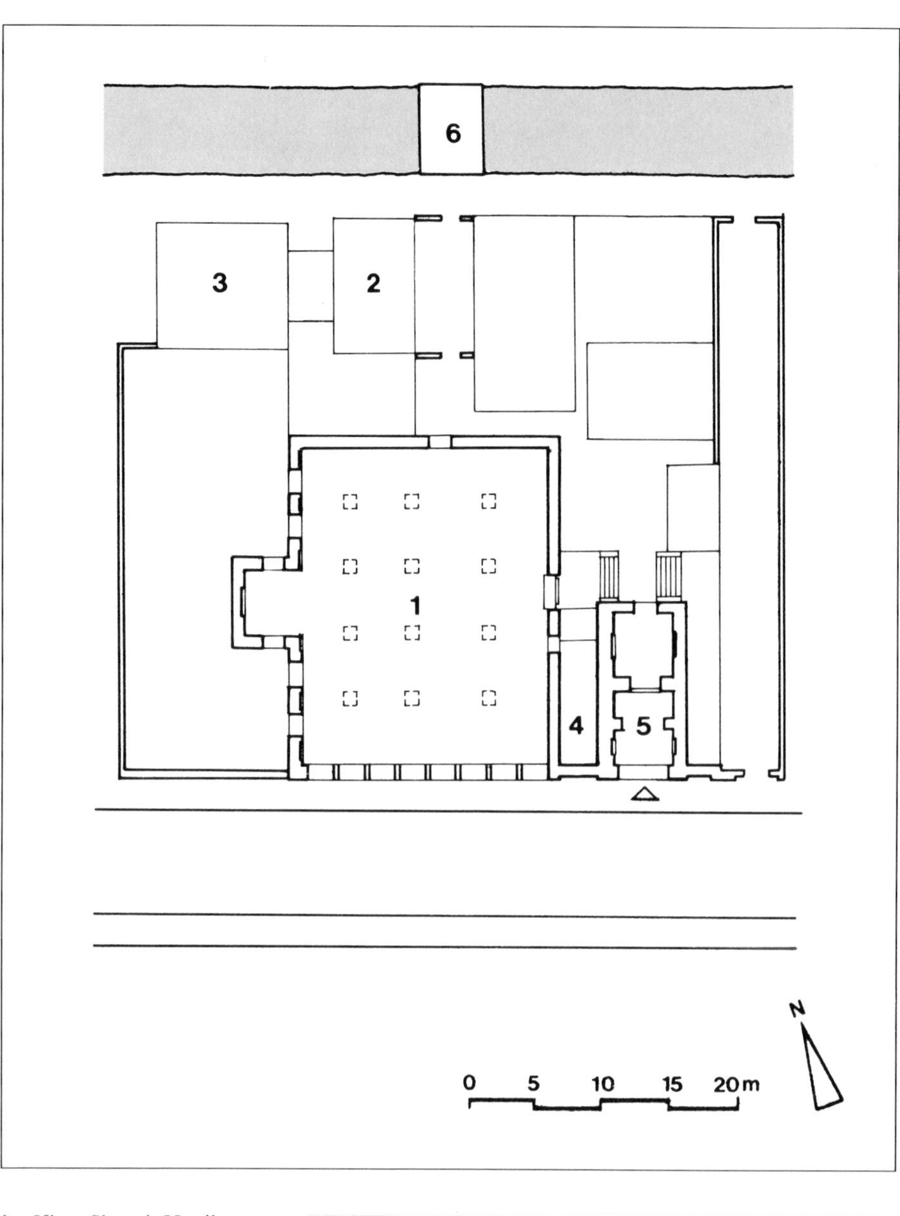

▷ Xian, Shenxi, Huajiao Lane Mosque, Shengxin Lou

◁ Quanzhou, Fuqian, Shenyou Mosque, Song Dynasty 1009

Key
1 Fengtian Tai. 2 Ren Shu Gui Yi Tang. 3 Ming Shan Tang. 4 Minaret. 5 Wangyue Lou. 6 Bridge.

▷ Xian, Shenxi, Huajiao Lane Mosque, Yizheng Ting

◁ Xian, Shenxi, Huajiao Lane Mosque, Ming Dynasty, 1392

Key
1 Peifeng. 2 Screen wall. 3 Main gate house. 4 Stone peifeng. 5 Second gate-house. 6 Shenxin Lou. 7 Wall. 8 Yizheng Ting. 9 Yuetai. 10 Screen wall. 11 Praying hall. 12 Bathhouse. 13 Guest hall. 14 Lecture Hall.

▷ Beijing, Ox Street Mosque, Pavilion, Qing Dynasty, 1699

◁ Xian, Shenxi, Huajiao Lane Mosque, side hall

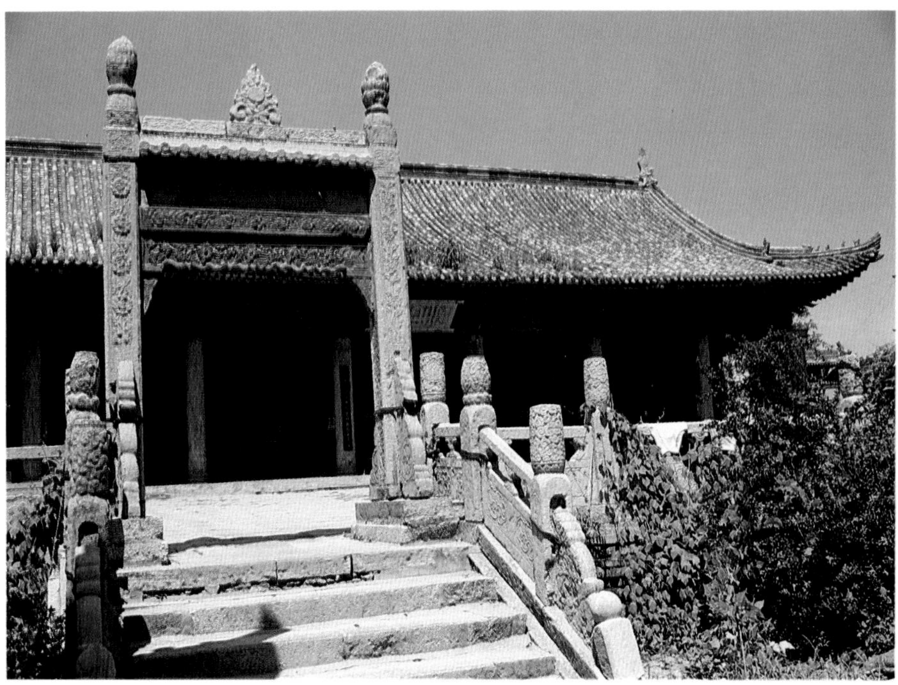

▷ Xian, Shenxi, Huajiao Lane Mosque, praying hall

Ming construction of 1392. The axis runs from east to west, for Muslims face Mecca – or west in this location – while praying; thus the main entrance is at the east end. The temple adopted the traditional axial and symmetrical planning principle: starting from the east are peifang, gateway, Shengxin Lou, a minaret in the Han pavilion style and lastly the praying hall. Shengxin Lou is a three-storey pavilion with an octagonal plan used to take the place of the minaret. The pavilion after this is called Yizheng Ting which has a special plan form. The plan looks like a bird spreading its wings, so it was also called the Phoenix Pavilion. After this pavilion, and on a platform, is the praying hall which has a square plan and a front terrace. Inside, all the panels are carved with plant scrolls, arabesque characters and vines, and are painted dark red, brown and gold. The darkened room presents an atmosphere which is mysterious yet quiet and serene. The small side halls along the axis used wooden sashes as partitions which are both simple and undecorated.

清真古教
牛街清真寺

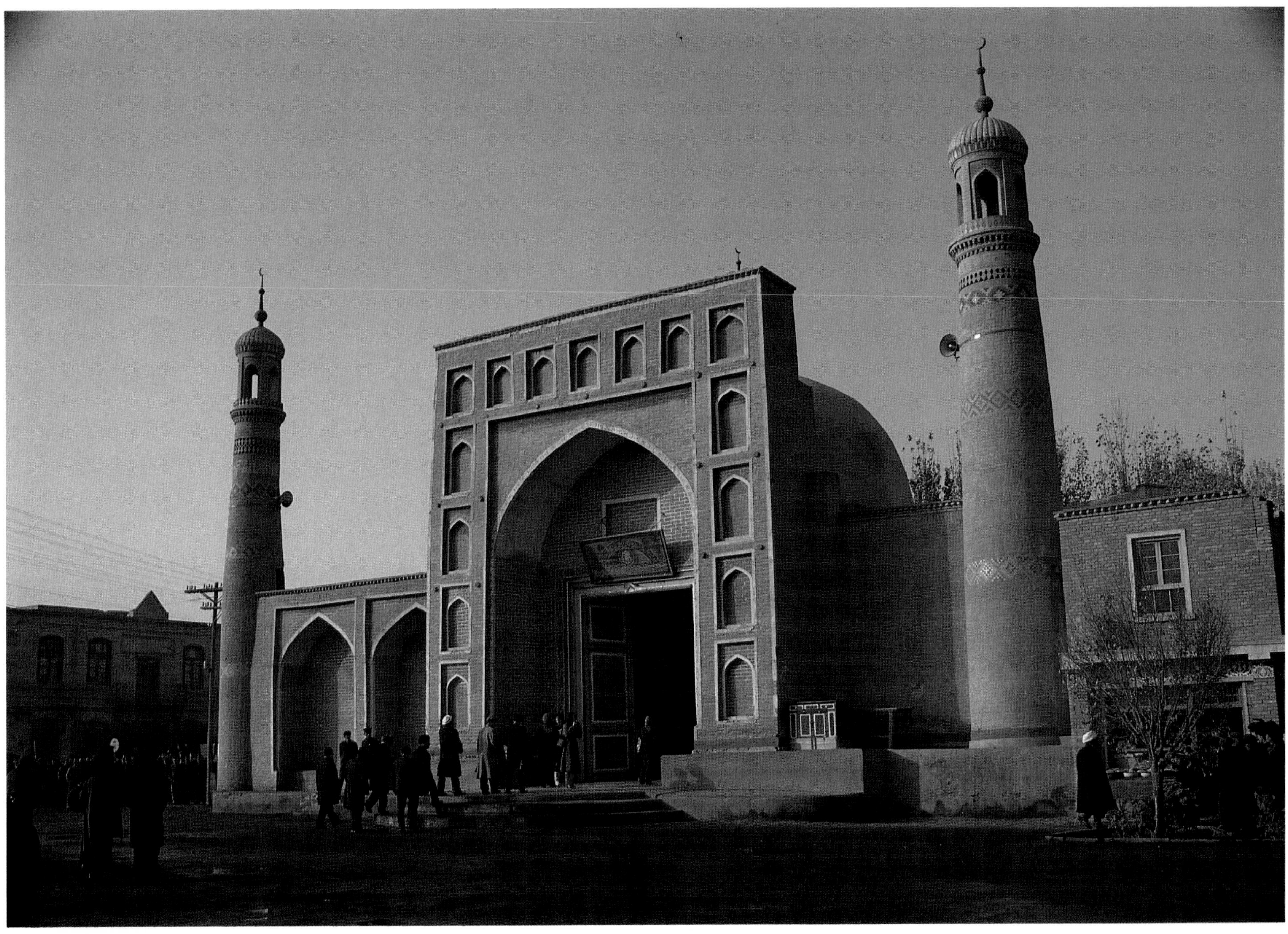

◁ Beijing, Ox Street Mosque, praying hall

△ Kashi, Xinjiang, the Great Mosque, 1861

The Niujie Mosque (Ox Street Mosque) in Beijing, built in 1699, also used the traditional courtyard plan, but more elaborately decorated. The minaret is a two-storey pavilion with yellow and green glazed roof tiles. Inside the praying hall, the beams and columns were also carved with plant scrolls, with arabesque inscriptions from the Koran in gold on a red ground. From these two mosques we can see that when Islam was introduced to the interior of China, the arabic architectural style was also introduced, but after about a hundred years they were adopted, assimilated, and infused, and a Chinese Islamic architectural style was created. This demonstrates the ability of the Han to absorb foreign elements and create a new style based on the foundation of both traditions.

Although Islam came to Xinjiang between the 10th and 11th centuries, it was not until the 15th century that it became the major religion of Uygur nationality. The largest mosque in Xinjiang, the Aitika at Kashi (Kaskan), was built in the 17th century. The main entrance has a pointed arch opening on a rectangular facade, very much like the Shangyou Mosque in Quanzhou, but it has two small minarets at either side of the doorway and retains the Central Asian style. The Imin Mosque at Turfan was built in 1778, the tower constructed of kilned brick and having a height of 44 metres. The diameter of this tower is 11 metres at the base and 3.8 metres at the top, and inside is a spiral staircase leading to the top floor. The tower is famous for its geometric decoration constructed of kilned brick. Although the tower tapers towards the top, the number of patterns is the same, the workman having dexterously reduced the sizes of the bricks to this end. The mosque itself was made of sun-dried brick, and the domed roof was supported by arches, a kind of construction widely used in Xinjiang.

◁ Turfan, Xinjiang, Imin Mosque, Qing Dynasty, 1778

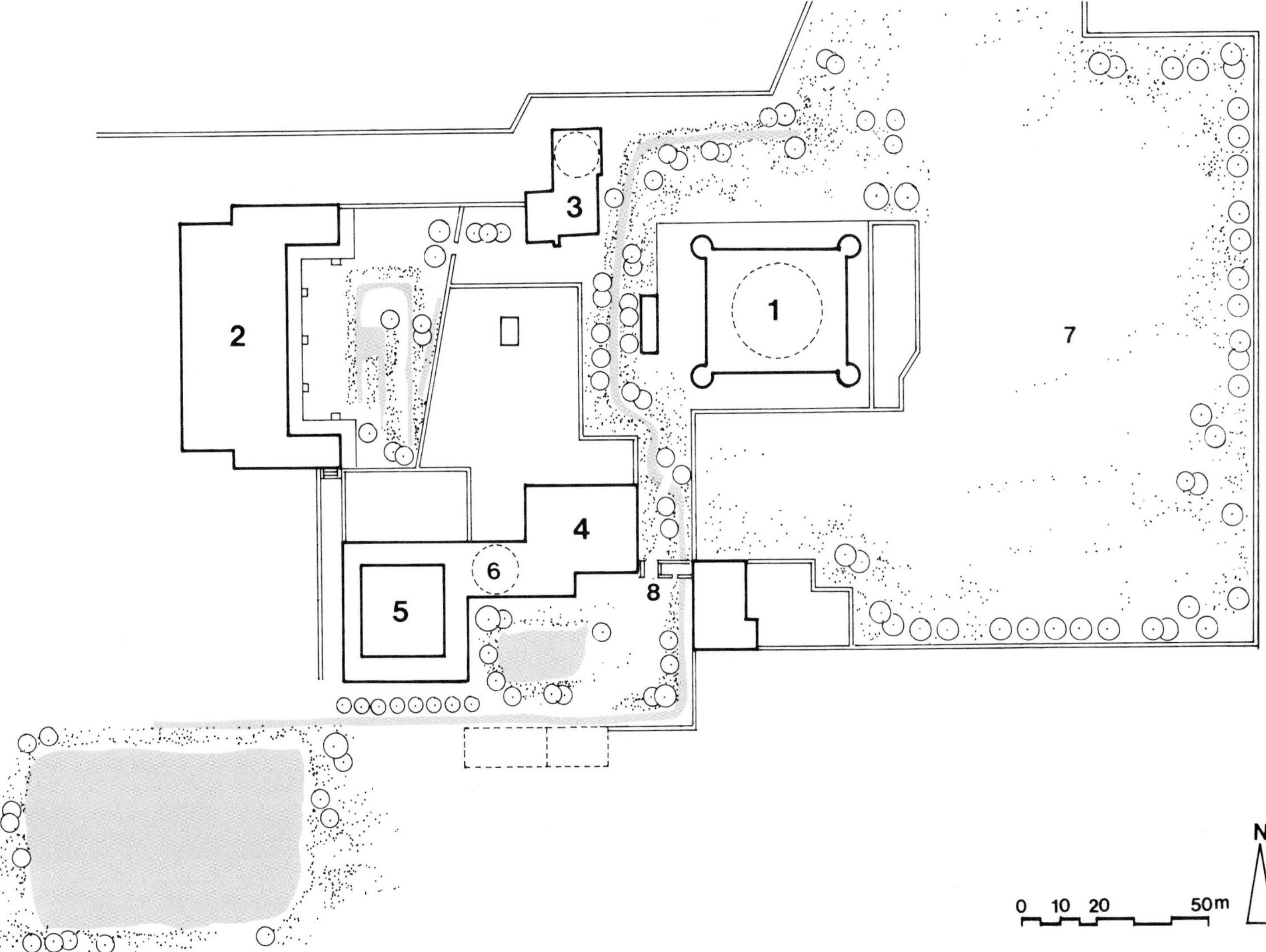

△ Kashi, Xinjiang, Aba Khoja Mosque, mausoleum, Qing Dynasty

Key
1 Mausoleum. 2 Great Praying Si. 3 Luding Si. 4 High Si. 5 Lecture Hall. 6 Low Si. 7 Cemetery. 8 Archway.

▽ Turfan, Xinjiang, Imin Mosque, minaret detail

◁ Turfan, Xinjiang, Imin Mosque, Qing Dynasty, 1778

△ Kashi, Xinjiang, Aba Khoja Mosque, mausoleum

◁ Kashi, Xinjiang, Aba Khoja Mosque, mausoleum, gateway

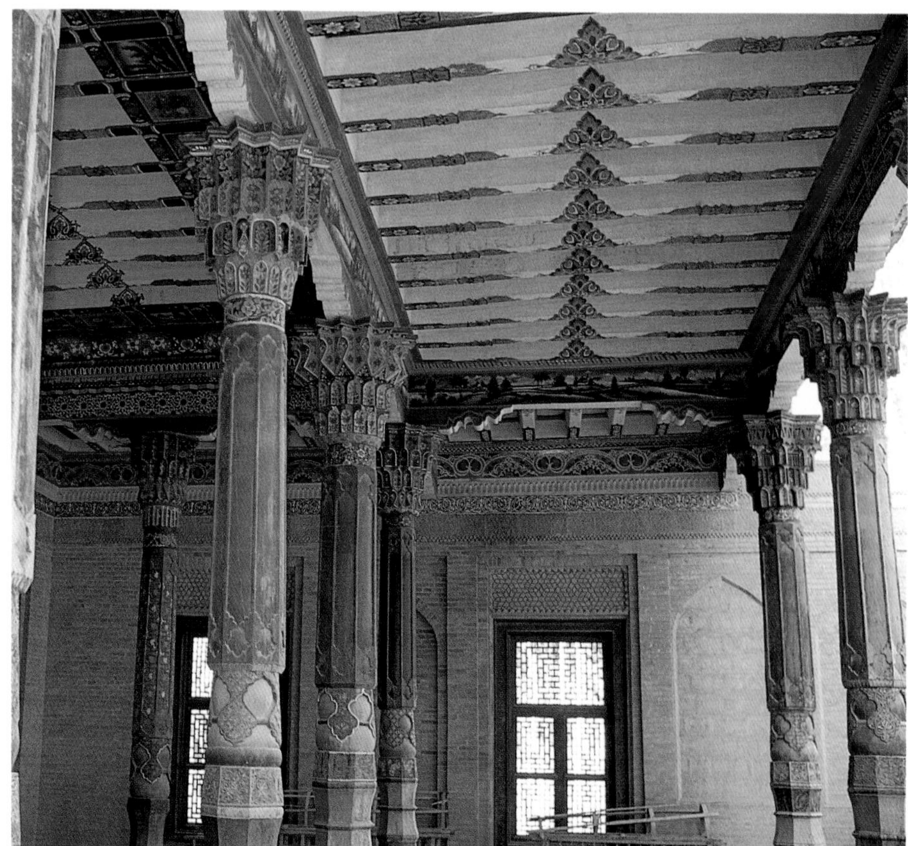

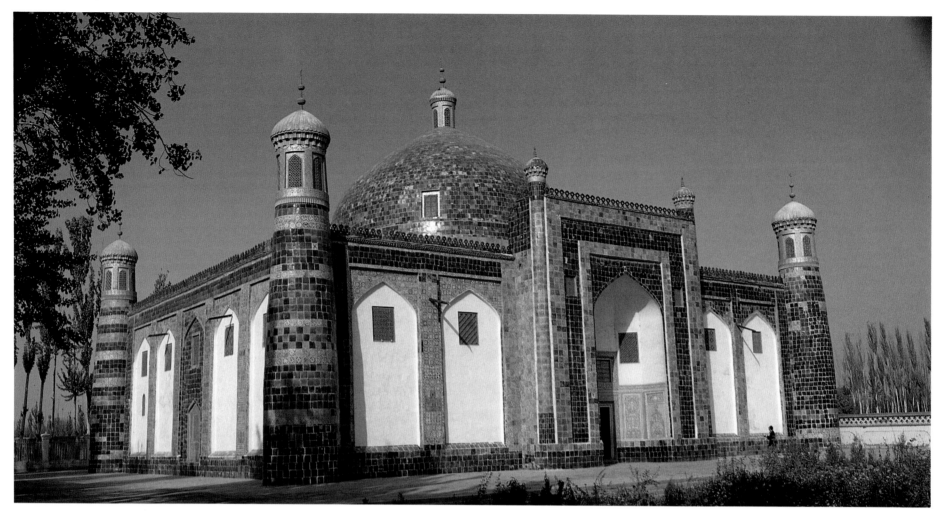

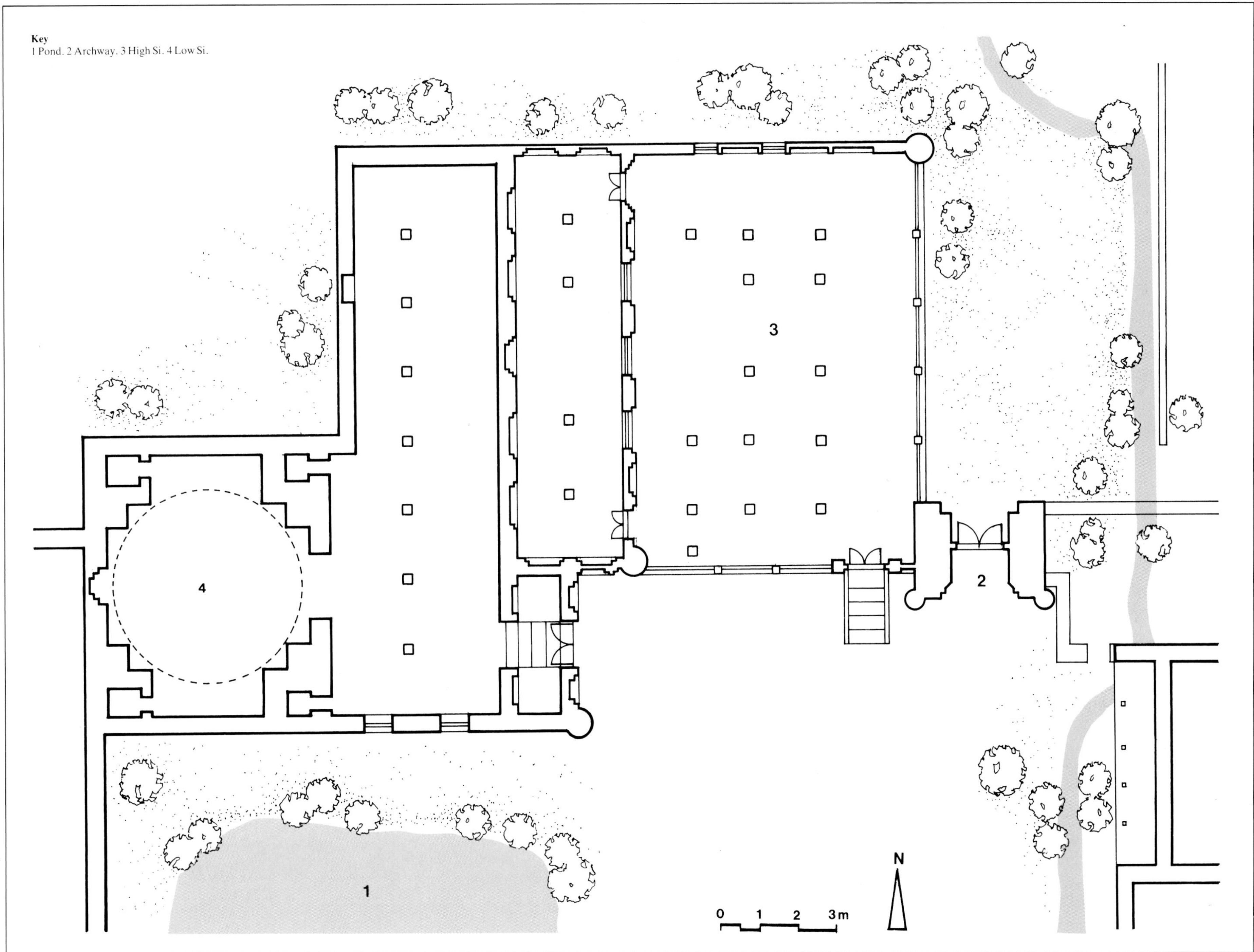

◁ Kashi, Xinjiang, Aba Khoja Mosque, mausoleum, beam and column

△ Kashi, Xinjiang, Aba Khoja Mosque, mausoleum, high and low praying hall

The Aba Khoja Mausoleum, Mosque and Cemetery in Kashi, Xinjiang, is a large architectural ensemble consisting of a Mausoleum, four service halls, and one Lecture Hall. Thousands of tombs surround the Mausoleum. The work started in the 18th century and has undergone continuous expansion and renovation. The pond in front of the main entrance expresses the idea to bathe and clean oneself before going into the mosque, for God loves a clean body. The gateway also has a rectangular facade with a pointed arch opening and two minarets flanking the entrance. It is faced with glazed tiles of white and blue which gives a feeling of cleanliness. To the left and inside the entrance is the High Mosque with minaret and variegated column designs and decorated beams. To the right of the entrance, through a narrow path and another entrance is the Mausoleum, the main building of the group. It has a large dome of green glazed tiles, supported on four sides by pointed arches which are in turn supported by brick walls. Minarets were placed at the four corners of the building. The walls, except for those areas faced with glazed tiles, were painted white. The side walls of the main entrance were decorated with pastel blue, green and silver plant scrolls. The feeling is delicate and refined, unlike the monumental and mournful feeling usually associated with a mausoleum; maybe it is a premonition to the people that when they leave the body they will arrive in the paradise of everlasting happiness promised by the Prophet. Inside the great hall and under the dome is a low rectangular platform where symbolic tombs of important members of the family were placed.

As the building group was built over a period of time, the buildings were only loosely integrated and lacked unity of space. Fortunately all retained the same style so at least a unity of form was achieved. It remains to this day the most distinguished example of all of Islamic architecture in China.

In general, the architectural characteristics of Islamic mosques in China are as follows.

The plans of the early mosques bore some resemblance to the traditional courtyard plan of the Han. Coincidentally, Islamic mosques in the Central Asia region also used the courtyard plan exclusively, which is usually square in shape, supposedly after the basilica churches of Byzantine. The praying hall was situated at one side of the square courtyard and was enclosed on three sides by colonnades. The Cordova Mosque in Spain, built between 785 and 987, still retains this basic pattern.

The praying hall in all Islamic mosques is orientated so that is has its back to the Kaaba (Caaba), the Black

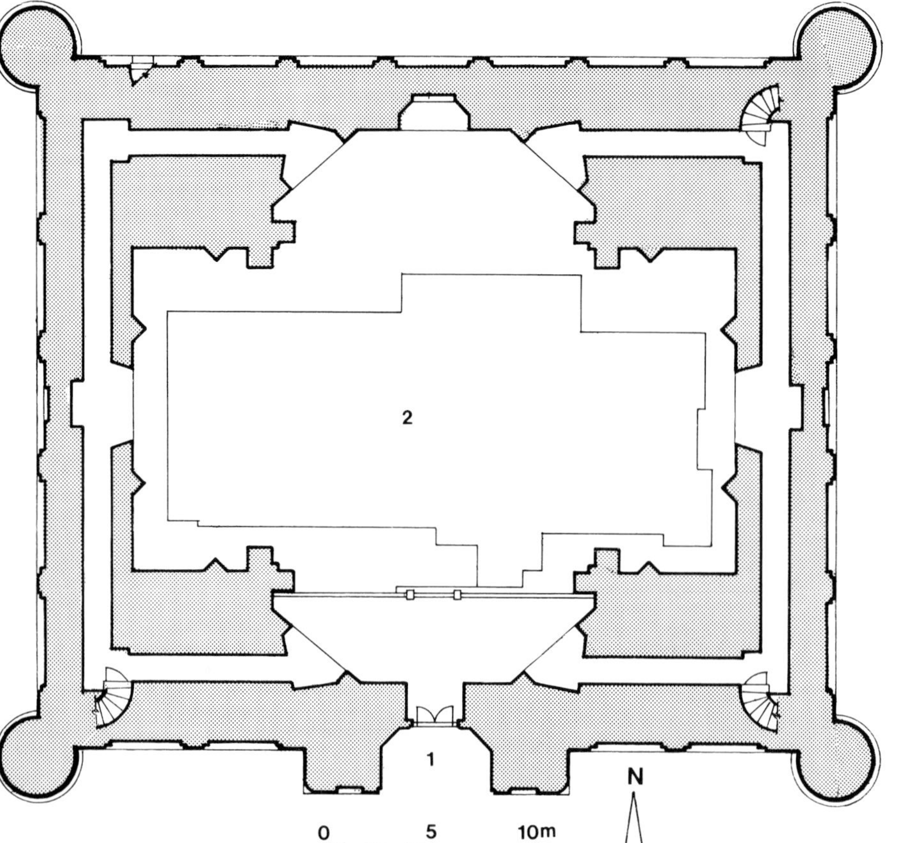

◁ Kashi, Xinjiang, Aba Khoja Mosque, mausoleum

Key
1 Doorway of Mausoleum, 2 Platform.

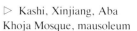

▷ Kashi, Xinjiang, Aba Khoja Mosque, mausoleum

◁ Kashi, Xinjiang, Aba Khoja Mosque, cemetery

Stone, in Mecca. In this way, while praying all the believers could face Mecca, the birthplace of Mohammed, the prophet, and of Islam. If we draw the axes of all the mosques in the world, we would find that all of them are focused on this point, as if they are radiated from the centre of Islam. For instance, the main entrance of the Great Mosque in Xian faces east, the axis back to the kaaba in the west. The Shengyou Mosque of Quanzhou has its main entrance at the west, while to enter the enclosure one has to turn to the left to reach the entrance of the praying hall. The entrance of Ox Street Mosque is orientated to the west and one has to turn 180 degrees to reach the praying hall.

As a rule, Islam requires all believers to come to the mosque to pray, so a great courtyard and a great hall are needed to accommodate all the worshippers. To use wooden frame construction methods to build such a large hall would be both difficult and expensive, so the solution was to connect several longitudinal halls with gutters in between the sloping roofs for drainage. The Ox Street Mosque praying hall has a width of five bays and a depth of seven bays, and the roof is made by three connected sloping roofs each two bays in depth.

The Sacred Record says that one day while Moham-

0 1 5 M.

med and his wife were praying in the wife's room, Mohammed discovered that there were flying-bird patterns embroidered on the window curtain. In order not to distract their piety to God, he ordered that the curtains be taken down. It is also forbidden in Islam to worship any living thing in the mosque. Islam is not an icon worshipping religion; therefore, only paintings of plants like trees, flowers and fruit are permitted to decorate a mosque. Arabic characters and calligraphies are beautiful artistic works, and they were also used to decorate mosques. For these reasons there are no animal figures or similar images found in Islamic mosques.

THE LAYOUT OF RELIGIOUS BUILDINGS

Religious beliefs commonly existed in the minds of people, and had great influences on daily life and, therefore, on the development of arts and architecture. As mentioned above, various religions and different philosophies, in turn, had a major impact upon temple site selection and planning arrangements. It has been a commonly held belief that the planning principles of all Chinese temples were the same; however, this was only true to a certain extent. If scrutinized carefully, we find that no two Buddhist temple layouts are identical.

While we cannot state that there was a typical Buddhist temple plan, we can, in general, determine that all temples embodied distinct characteristics of Chinese planning; specifically, an axial symmetry with halls and enclosed courtyards.

Choice of Site

As has been stated, the primary influence in the choice of a temple site was the newly developing variety of religious beliefs. Among these, three stand out: 1) the Daoist influence; 2) the beliefs of the nobility; 3) the ideas of the Shan Sect.

1.*Daoist Influence*. Formed during the Han and Tang Dynasties, it was during the Eastern Jin Dynasty (317-420 A.D.) that Daoists began to seek serene, secluded locations for their abodes. Always scenic in nature, these inaccessible, mountainous retreats represented the 'fairyland' or heaven-like ideal of Daoism.

Following the Northern and Southern Dynasties (420-589 A.D.) and Tang Dynasty, Daoism reached its zenith. It was during the next dynasty, the Song (960-1279 A.D.), that Buddhism, Daoism and even Confucianism gradually merged in ideology. As the Buddhist sects absorbed the Daoist 'fairyland' concept, they began to choose mountainous sites, integrating temples with landscapes and even developing more formally planned, attached gardens.

2.*Beliefs of the Nobility*. During the Jin, and Northern and Southern Song Dynasties, the nobility and high officers in the government believed their souls could be saved from sin and the sea of misery by giving their mansions and estates to Buddhist sects for temples. A book titled *The Buddhist Temples in Luoyang* tells us that:

> . . . the mansions of princes and all ranks of the nobility were given to the Buddhist and made temples.[14]

This practice, especially prevalent in the north in Kaifeng, the then capital, and Louyang, was also followed by the nobility in the southern areas. It was at this time common in the north for private houses, mansions and estates to have attached gardens. The individual owners often competed in terms of both elegance and extravagance in garden design and building. The general concept was to make the garden as natural as possible, exhibiting a variety of building types, pools, and false hills of rocks, and planted with rare trees and flowers. This philosophy of garden design eventually extended to the selection of beautiful, naturally landscaped, temple sites.

3.*Ideas of Different Sects of Buddhism*. During the disorder, discontent and decay at the close of the Eastern and Western Jin Dynasties, one sect of Buddhism, led by the monk Huiyuan (334-416 A.D.), retreated to the south of China, finally taking refuge in Lushan, Jiangxi Province in 381. Following the Wei and Jin philosophies taught by Laozi and Zhuanzi, they sought to inspire thoughtful contemplation through withdrawal from the active world. Stressing the reunion of man with nature, finding his place in the ultimate cosmos and developing a sensitivity to natural phenomena, the aim was to stand above and not be bound by conventions, finally overcoming material desires and, ultimately, attaining sainthood. Living in a *laissez-faire* peaceful spirit, this Buddhist sect even surpassed Daoism in its aversion to illusory earthly matters. Stressing complete withdrawal from the world, they chose isolated sites for their retreats, which made contemplative wandering in picturesque environments possible.

Huiyuan remained in Lushan for more than 30 years, eventually being named as the patriarch of the Pure-land Sect. Through his disciples his doctrine spread, with its greatest influence being felt in the southern part of China. This influence continued during the Tang Dynasty with other Buddhist sects seeking beautifully landscaped sites to build temples.

Boddhidarma of the Chan Sect also practiced meditation, teaching the rejection of books, doctrines and reflection, and is founded on introspection alone, that:

> All reasoning should be rejected, all doctrines are simply as many useless burdens imposed on the mind, salvation rests in a sudden realization of the vanity of everything.[15]

The spirit of Chan is very close to the Daoist thought of Zhuanzi in some respects: rejection of all intellectual speculation, all worship, social restraints, etc.

During the later days of the Tang, as Buddhism became sinocized, there emerged a distinct southern school, the Chan Sect. Headed by Huinen (638-713 A.D.), the sixth monk of the sect, they preached Dhyana, that is, the deprivation of all trivial desires, accomplished by sitting in quietude, eventually achieving a peaceful state of mind. As meditation required a quiet setting, the followers of the Chan sect selected secluded settings for their temple sites. The four major Buddhist shrines constructed in China during that period, the Wutai Mountain in the north, centrally located Jiuhua Mountain, Emei Mountain in the south, and Putuo Island at the east coast, were all in remote locations.

Situated with its back to a hill or high land, sometimes on the peak of a mountain amidst the clouds, hidden in a valley or wooded setting, built into a natural cave, or facing a river or lake with its back against a cliff, each Buddhist temple had a different plan, but because of the intermingling of the previously discussed concepts, all are situated in secluded, scenic places.

Orientation and 'Feng Shui'

Since the dawn of history in China, man has been accustomed to considering the cosmic aspects of nature. The temple place, as well as the layout of other important buildings, represented an ideal image and it was only natural to choose a site facing towards the sun, the south or southeast, as these directions were considered the best orientation both practically and spiritually. Buddhist temples located in the countryside and in mountainous places did not strictly adhere to this rule. More often, the Chinese Feng Shui dictated the orientation and plan of temples. The chosen site often made a southern orientation impossible, so there are famous temples facing east, west and even north. The reasons for such decisions were to harmonize with the cosmic forces of the environment and orientation to a particular view. Whenever a monk selected a site, his aim was that the landscape should be used without making large-scale transformations. This philosophy not only saved manpower and cost, it took maximum advantage of the landscapes features while preserving the view.

The Nanchan Temple, located on Wutai Mountain in Shanxi, is the oldest existing wooden temple in China. Enclosed on three sides by higher ground, it faces south and is erected on a terrace. The road leading to the front approaches from the east and terminates at the square in front of the temple gateway. According to the art of Feng Shui, it is an ideal location. Since the winding road is the only path leading to the temple, there is no through traffic, providing a well protected and quiet setting.

Foguang Temple, on the same mountain as the previous example, is the next oldest existing wooden temple in China. Because of Feng Shui, the temple faces west. The site is enclosed on the north and south with highlands, a higher hill to the east, while at the west is a valley with a river running through it. The road leading to the temple was built on the hillside to the north, terminating at the front of the temple, which is on a terrace many feet above the valley.

The Upper and Lower Huayan Temples, however, were influenced by other factors. These two temples, constructed by the Toba Wei during the Liao Dynasty, are facing east because the Toba worshipped the rising sun. Islamic mosques in China unanimously face east, so that worshippers can face west or Mecca while praying.

Hierarchy of Deity

The general characteristic of Chinese architectural sequence is an axial symmetry. The smaller temples have a single axis while the larger ones have a major axis and one or two minor ones. Most often the axis was a straight line along which all the main halls and monuments were erected. If the temple was constructed on a hilly site and a straight line was not possible, the halls followed the contour of the site. Whether straight or curved, there was a distinct line of movement which was the processional route, the spiritual axis of the temple. It was along this spiritual axis, the path that the believer travelled along from before the gatehouse to the main hall, that the halls and other buildings were arranged according to a specific Buddhist hierarchy and ceremonial order.

Every temple has a gateway like a ceremonial arch, or, if a larger temple, a gatehouse. Often there were sculptures at each side of the gatehouse. Fierce looking and borrowed from Daoism, they are called the Heng Ha Two Generals, one being Heng and the other Ha. With weapons in their hands, as if to guard the entrance and forbid trespassers, they always give the visitor a sense of security and the feeling that the temple is not a place for pleasure but a place of worship.

The subordinate spaces in the centralized axis were not just repetitions of the central cells but were related to form in a rhythmical group. Designed for different purposes, individual space sizes were proportional to the hierarchy of functions performed in them, with the scale of the main hall dominating the entire group.

Usually directly opposite the gateway was a pavilion of stele or an incense burner. At either side of the courtyard there was often a bell-tower to the east and a drumtower to the west, coinciding with the idea of 'strike bell in the morning and beat drum in the evening.' As the sun arose, a monk would ring the bell and all the monks would gather in the main hall, beginning their morning service of sutra chanting and worship. At the end of the day, after sunset, the drum was struck signaling everyone to retire to their rooms.

The use of both instruments in religious ceremonies dates back to prehistoric times. Adopted by both Daoists and Buddhists, this practice, inaugurating the day and closing it, constituted one of the most essential features of a Buddhist temple. The bell, rung first in the morning, was the foremost of the two instruments. However, not all temples contained bell and drumtowers. Evidence indicates that some had no towers or, occasionally, only the belltower, such as Ninggu Temple in Nanjing which had only a belltower at the east, and the Fengxue Temple near Luoyang which has only a drumtower at the west.

In the courtyard between the gate and the main hall is the Tianwang Dian or the Hall of the Heavenly Kings. In Buddhism the Four Heavenly Kings rule the continents lying at the four corners of the universe, with the centre being the abode of the Gods. The four kings protect the Three Precious Things, which are the Buddha, Law, and Sangha (the body of believers). In the Patriarch Hall at Shaolin Temple at Dengfeng, the images of the kings were carved on the four stone pillars surrounding the inner shrine of the main hall. In the centre of the hall usually stands an altar with the fat and smiling image of Mile Fo (Maitreya), the Buddha who is to succeed Sakyamuni to govern the world. This hall provides the first climax of the temple.

Daxiong Boa Dian, (the Precious Hall of the Great Hero) following the Hall of Heavenly Kings, is the climax of the entire plan, both spiritually and architecturally, for it is the largest building in the complex and the hall of the Buddha. Inside the hall and on an altar is usually a huge image of the Buddha or a triad of Buddhas seated on lotus thrones. With Sakyamuni sitting in the centre, the three images represent the Buddha past, present and future. Sometimes, Sakyamuni may be accompanied by two standing images of smaller size, that of a young man, called Anam (Ananda), on his right and an old man with long eyebrows, called Jiaye (Kasyapa), on his left. They were the tenth and third of his ten great disciples as well as his two favourites. Anada is to reappear on earth as Buddha in another Kaipa and is responsible for compiling the Buddhist scriptures. Kasyapa is the keeper of Buddhism's esoteric tradition.

The Articulation of Form and Space

A Buddhist temple was a holy place for both the common believer and the saint. The believer's aim was to transcend the secular world, entering the Pure-land or paradise. This required an emotional/transitional environment, and the space experienced before one reached the temple was the appropriate place for such a transition. It was in this space, in preparation for receiving the religious spirits, that since the believer's emotional transition could not be immediately effected, time became an important factor in the transformation. The length of the road leading to the temple and the expanse and character of the space helped to fulfil this religious requirement.

Usually between the highway or city thoroughfare and the road leading to the temple, there was a landmark defining the first space of the temple. The landmark could be a pair of door posts, a peifang, a tablet or, in some large temples, a free-standing doorway. Between this landmark and the gateway of the temple is usually a meandering path and natural landscaping.

After entering the main gateway or gatehouse, the halls and the courtyard in front were designed according to a traditional architectural layout as well as a hierarchy of religious and functional requirements. As

▽ Yangzhou, Jiangsu, Guanying Hill archway

△ Wutai Shan, Shanxi, Foguang Si

we can easily see, the utilization of the natural landscape and views makes the space between the two gateways most interesting. Yet, when considering the articulation of form and space, the buildings inside the second gateway become more meaningful, since both of these spaces represented an integration of the philosophies of Buddishm, Daoism and Confucians, and both embody the Buddhist dogmas of hierarchy of importance. Confucian ideas of man-made order, symmetry and the Daoist irregularity and imitation of nature help the visitor experience the mystic, religious character of the temple. The integration of the three beliefs is the essence of the concept of temple layout.

The monks, influenced by Daoist principles, were interested in finding serene landscape environments for temple sites. In China that usually means a place with hills and water, without which there was no landscape. The monks then utilized the advantages of the rippling stream, verdant woods and precipitous cliffs as natural material, tastefully designing quiet, beautiful spaces.

Here we shall use Foguang Temple to illustrate the organization of form and space. This temple is approached from the southwest with hills to the left and a valley to the right. The long, sinuous, gradually ascending path was experienced as an uplifting process. The temple is hidden behind profuse trees until, suddenly, the great screen wall bursts into view and the square in front of the temple is reached.

Often a square is placed in front of a temple. The square in front of Foguang is approached by a gentle ramp and is enclosed on two sides by the gatehouse (originally the Hall of Heavenly Kings) and the screen wall. In addition there is higher land to the north and south which forms a quiet, enclosed space, corresponding to the quiet nature of the Buddhist spirit. This front square becomes an independent space when the gatehouse doors are closed. It seems to me that the designer, not intending to incorporate this space with those inside, created an enclosed space which does not penetrate the temple proper. A visitor, or believer, when climbing by foot, usually panting after the long walk, would reach this space and take a rest by the retaining wall near the screen wall and, looking back on the path he has just trudged, experiences a feeling of fulfilment, pleasure and, perhaps, reverence.

The screen wall was designed to create a quiet space and was supposedly able to ward off evil spirits attempting to enter the gate, in addition to functioning as a work of art. Most were made of brick or stone with a coping of tile, and constructed on a platform. At the centre of the wall was, often, an exquisitely carved-brick or glazed tile bas-relief of a plant or a calligraphy such as the word 'Fo' (Buddha) or a very elaborate one with nine dragons. In this case the big characters 'Foguang Temple' were written on the wall to identify the temple.

The builders of Foguang Temple utilized the slope of the east-west axis, creating three terraces. On the lowest terrace is a long approach where the Hall of the Manjusri, the first space used to make preparation for worship was erected. Through the door frame of the gatehouse, the main hall on the third terrace comes into view. The door frame and the right and left side walls emphasise the three-dimensional effect of the space.

On the second terrace was the hall of Mile Fo (Hall of Amida) which was burned down during the Tang Dynasty. As the third terrace is very high, visitors on the second terrace can only see the roof of the hall above. It is only after climbing the steep steps between the second and third terraces that the facade of the great hall and the stone pillar comes into full view. It is not known whether this was the intentional idea of the designer or was formed naturally, but the artistic effect created by the view from the third terrace, experienced after the anticipation of the first and second terraces, is a very dramatic one.

The space in front of the main hall on this third terrace is narrow, with two large ancient pine trees flanking the entrance to the main hall. There, the visitor can appreciate the simple, sturdy, honest, unadorned elevation and the wide eave supported by the gigantic duogong cantilever 13 feet out from the facade. The wide overhang, equivalent to one half of the height between the platform and eave, and robust duogong elements are indicative of the bold and stable Tang Dynasty architectural style. Here, in front of the temple and under the great eave, it is as if the believer is sheltered by the power of Buddha. The Chinese used the roof to symbolize heaven and platform the earth; here this gigantic roof seems to cover whoever is under it, making people feel that all living things are under the aegis of heaven, and that man must believe in Buddhism in order to avoid evil fortunes and have his soul released from purgatory. The function of the big duogong is not only to support the wide overhanging eave, but one of its elements, the 'ang', starting from the outside and carried to the inside, also has the function of guiding people from outside into the interior. Inside, after crossing the high threshold into the dimly lit hall, the smoke of burning incense wood, the gigantic candles in front of the 30 Tang Dynasty statues, and the curved halo of the Buddha almost touching the ceiling above, all help to make the images and the space blend into one entity.

Within the city of Zhending the Longxing Temple is a rare example of Song Dynasty architectural layout. Constructed on a flat piece of land, the front of this temple contains a screen wall, bridges, a peifang and gatehouse. The original first hall was destroyed by fire many years ago; now, the second hall, the Moni Hall with its unique roof form, is the first climax of the group.

The climax, however, of Longxing Temple is the Foxiang Ge (Fragrance of Buddhas Pavilion). After the Moni Hall there is a long approach. The designer manipulated the long space with high and low buildings, making it more interesting. First there are two high-rise pavilions, then two lower stele pavilions, all flanking the approach and serving as the frame of the taller main hall at the end. Then past two closely related lower and smaller stele pavilions, the space is further contracted. Some small elements, like stone bridges and an incense burner were added and the movement was arrested; lastly, Foxiang Ge was reached. The ge is situated at the middle of a transverse rectangular courtyard space. This high-rise hall was designed and erected to house a 24-metre bronze statue of Guanying. The dimly lit interior of this hall, with the only light rays shining on the head of the Buddha image, seems to produce a divine effect.

Upper Guansheng Temple at Hongdong, constructed during the Yuan Dynasty, has an entirely different plan. The climax of this temple is a glazed tile pagoda. Originally, in China, the pagoda anticipated the halls in temple planning. It is recorded of Yongning Temple that:

> major buildings were built along the axis, first the gatehouse, followed by the pagoda and then came the Buddhist halls.[16]

This type of plan was common in India, where the pagoda was built to house relics of the Buddha or a saint. The relic was a major object of worship; therefore, erecting a pagoda at the centre of the temple had a distinct religious meaning. Upper Guansheng Temple is located at the top of a small hill while under it is the lower Guansheng Temple. From the lower temple the tower of the upper one can be seen, enticing the visitor to climb the winding path to the gateway. Through the opening of the gateway, an elaborate doorway, the entrance to the pagoda, and the delicate and colourful detail of the glazed terra-cotta tiles covering the entire body of the pagoda, come into view. The gatehouse, doorway and entrance are so close to each other they become unified in appearance, creating a force whch attracts the visitor to go beyond. Inside the tower is a small sanctuary where, under a greenish glazed tile dome, there sits a Buddha image. It is so dark inside, with only the head of the image discernible, that it seems that the visitors to this unseen world find the power to govern their lives.

Yongquan Si (Bubbling Spring Temple) is located on Drum Hill at Fuqian. The approach leading to the temple is an excellent example of the sensitive combination of landscape and temple. As one follows the stone steps to the temple, the ancient trees give shade to the walks and spring below. The doorway is of special interest, for it does not have door panels; instead, a pair of couplets were hung on the post, saying: 'Pure-land is clean and need not be swept, opening has no doors need not be closed'. Such sayings of Buddhist teachings were meant to invoke a religious response in the visitor.

The road leading to the temple is surrounded by outcroppings of rocks into which more than 300 tablets were carved with poems and calligraphy. With its moss-covered stone bridges and rocks, this cool place, especially in warm and humid weather, produced in the visitor an out-of-the-world feeling, becoming the ideal 'fairyland' environment of Buddhism.

▽ Fuzhou, Fuqian, Yongquan Si, Drum Hill, stone carving

禪林幽趣
官方子容觀察推官趙瑾
川節度推官趙諮節度推
通判錢昉權簽判宋球東
總靈源洞知福州燕度題
同賓僚遊鼓山登大頂峯
嘉祐辛丑歲七月十八日

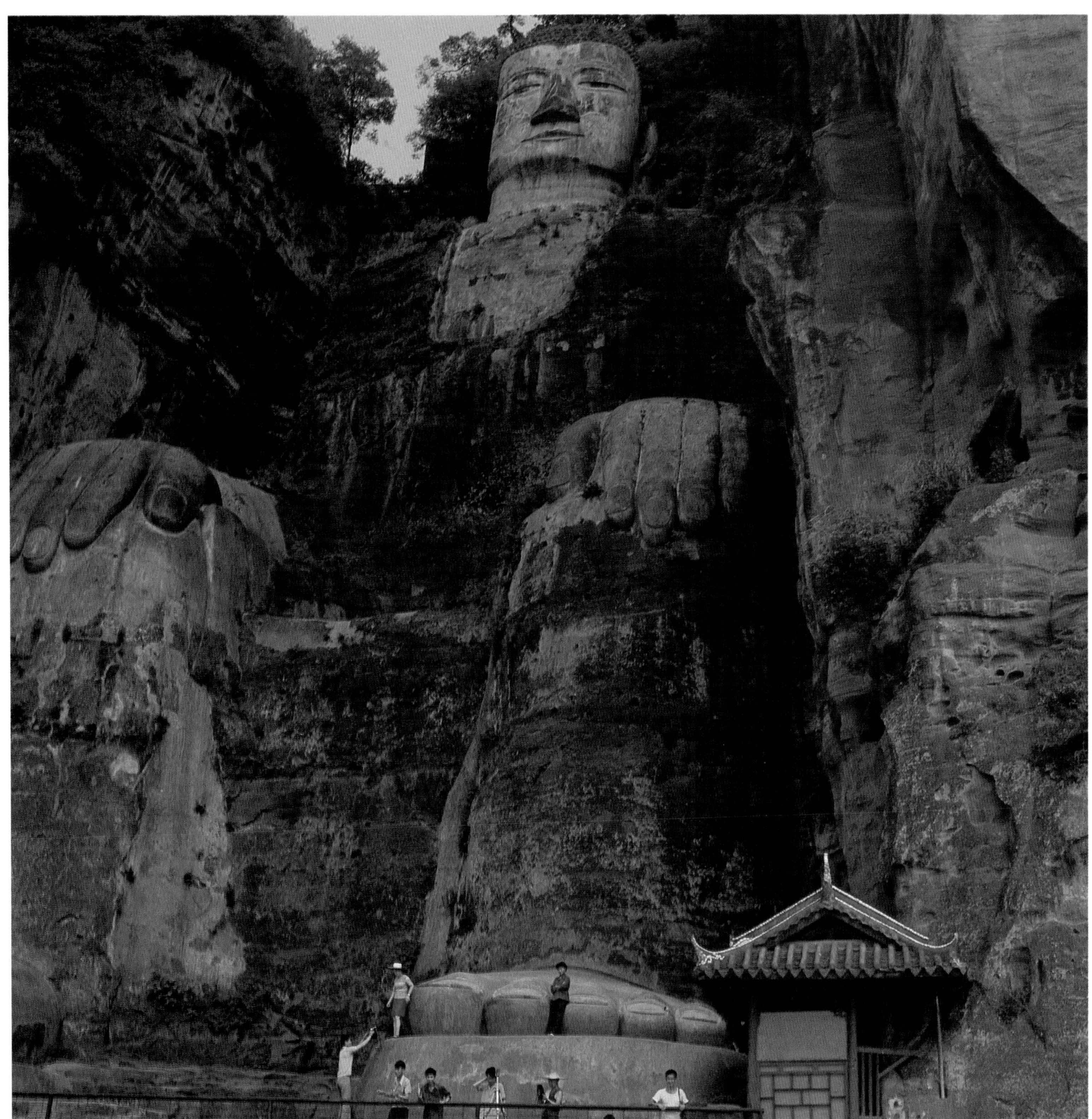

◁ Fuzhou, Fuqian, Yongquan Si, Drum Hill, stone carving

▷ Leshan, Sichuan, the Great Buddha, Tang Dynasty

The spirit path leading to Yunya Temple on Tiger Hill at Suzhou is a very long one. It is also well combined with the landscape like the Yongquan Temple, but with the Yunya Pagoda always in view. The path to the pagoda is dotted with platforms, pavilions, rock outcroppings, and staircases until, finally, through a moon doorway, the tower is reached.

Wuyou Temple in Sichuan faces the Ming River and is approached from a 73–metre high image of a Tang Dynasty seated stone Buddha. From the feet of the statue one climbs nine flights of stone steps carved out of a rock cliff in order to reach the gateway of the temple. Along the steps are small caves and niches, each containing one or more Buddha images. Here instead of calligraphies, sculptures were used to teach the visitors Buddhist beliefs.

Also located in the mountainous Wutai is the Datayuan temple. The road leading to Datayuan involved an entirely different concept. Once inside the gateway, the visitor was led by a long and narrow winding road enclosed by two heavy, high, red walls which go upwards towards the Great White Stupa. The stupa, the largest in China, looms above the top of the walls and is only visible behind the trees; the long narrow path may

◁ Wutai Shan, Shanxi, approach to the Great Stupa

▷ Wutai Shan, Shanxi, Longquan Si, staircase and peifang

▷ Wutai Shan, Shanxi, staircase leading to Buddha's Peak

have been suggestive of the torturous spirit path to the Pure-land.

To the north of Datayuan and on top of a small hill is the Buddha's Peak Temple. First erected in Northern Wei and repaired continuously, visually this temple integrates with the Big Stupa and becomes an inseparable component of the composition. The road leading to the temple first started from a ramp and stopped at the gatehouse. Inside is the first part of the temple, then a very steep staircase of 108 steps leads to a peifang and a platform with the doorway to the temple. On top of the platform and against the parapet wall, one commands a good view of the Big Stupa and the whole valley.

Longquan Temple is sited on a hill facing a wide, shallow pebble bed river at Wutai Mountain. The great

◁ Chengde, Hebei, Putuozhongcheng, the Big Red Platform

▷ Jiuhua Shan, Anhui, Taintai Si

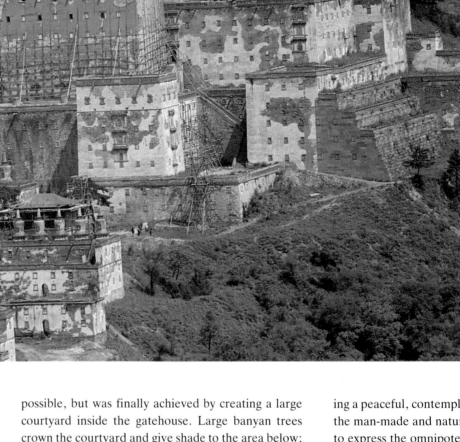

stairway leads to the elaborately carved white marble peifang of the steep space enclosed by trees. On top of the platform and under the peifang is a panoramic view of the entire valley, an excellent example of the art of Feng-shui. Although the space behind the peifang and the gatehouse is cramped with the stone bridges, stone lions and flagpoles, the short distance and narrowness of the space is not noticeable. Many similar examples exist on Wutai Mountain and elsewhere in China.

Tiantai Temple (Heavenly Platform Temple) of Jiuhua Mountain in Anhui Province is situated on a prominence and is surrounded by an abundance of trees. In front of this small, humble, residential-like temple is an excellent view of the valley and temples below.

The way to create a serene space in front of Kaiyuan Temple in Quanzhou is entirely different from the above and is practised in temples located in the heart of a city. Kaiyuan is situated in the city and along a main thoroughfare where a serene environment was not possible, but was finally achieved by creating a large courtyard inside the gatehouse. Large banyan trees crown the courtyard and give shade to the area below; stone stools and tables were placed under the trees. Two granite pagodas were placed widely apart symmetrically, and in between the courtyard and pagodas are paved areas and flower beds. As this large space is enclosed by high walls from the outside street, the space in front of the main hall actually served as a transitional space, enhancing the emotional transformations.

The preceding examples illustrate the variety of spaces in front of temples. Though each is different, all serve to create a transition from the secular world to the spiritual world. The long walks aided the visitor in the elimination of worldly concerns while at the same time stabilizing the emotions.

The natural landscape along the road, the rustling sound of the leaves and the murmuring of the rippling stream established a refreshing sensation, while the verdant woods provided serenity and quietude, creating a peaceful, contemplative aura. This integration of the man-made and natural landscapes was an attempt to express the omnipotence of God while at the same time illustrating the ever-changing, short-lived character of the material universe.

Located to the north of the Imperial Summer Resort, Changde Putuozhongcheng Temple illustrates another variation of temple planning. Mirroring the characteristics of the Potala of Tibet, the legendary palace of the Dalai Lamas, it is actually a giant castle built on top of a fortress on a rock hill. Steep ramps with 125 stone steps cut into the hillside lead the pilgrim to the portals.

At the Potala it becomes apparent that the lower portion of the temple is painted white (the White Palace). The Red Palace, containing the temples, monastic apartments and the monastery of the Dalai Lamas symbolized power and authority. As such the Potala was a structure which had all the functions of a Buddhist temple under one roof.

The Putuozhongcheng resembles Potala, but the front portion of the temple adheres to the traditional Chinese plan. As one passes the gatehouse and the stele pavilion, the gateway of five stupas is in view. This unique gateway serves as an introduction and anticipates the visitor's step into an architectural space from the Han style to Tibetian style.

> The gateway has three arched openings hollowed out from a massive brick wall of white stucco. On top of it are five Lama stupas of blue, white, chrome yellow, rusty red and black glazed tiles. They are colourful and brilliant under the sunlight . . . the change of colour and light and shadow is an enchanting experience, and visitors stopped and watched, and felt that from here on they would step into a mystic world of profound mystery and religious belief.[17]

Also, through the arched openings, the distant view of the massive red platform is seen, producing in the visitor an inspiration to probe into the truth of Buddhism. The gateway of five stupa declares the end of the introductory space on the one hand and announces the advent of the climax in the other. This is an everchanging colourful progression in space.

The manipulation of space after this gateway changes suddenly from axial symmetry to free planning according to the landscape. As the road follows the contour lines of the slope, and along the road were placed many low white residences of the Lama monks which contrast strongly with the Big Red Platform, the latter, with its towering and overpowering mass, dominates the entire space. By comparison, the small white platforms and gateway all turn to mere miniature decorations, the contrast symbolizing the supernatural power and lofty idea of Buddhism. The Big Red Platform is both the functional and sequential climax.

> If we looked back to history and found how this was used during the time it was erected, it would not be too difficult to imagine that the pilgrims, trudging slowly after the glazed tile pailou toward the centre niches on the 42-metre solid wall, had to kneel down, their foreheads touching the ground for every step they took. They might have firmly believed that after this tortuous path, how much spiritual consolation and freedom from the burden of sin they could get. The massive form of the platform affects the spirit, conveying how great is the Buddha and how little are the human beings. Now, even though we understand intellectually how deep was the religious influence on the mind of the common people, it would be difficult for us to feel the state of mind and the feeling of awe and veneration of those pilgrims.[18]

Of the niches embedded in the centre of the big red wall vertically, each has a glazed colour tile roof hood, duogong, door sash and Buddha image. Together with the brilliant Buddhist images, the long shadows of the extending water spout along the parapet create a lively, everchanging feeling, which is both magnificent and vivid.

But the sequence does end here, through the ramp enclosed on both sides by heavy walls.The hexagonal double eave golden roof of a pavilion suddenly emerges on top of the high masonry wall. This roof and the wooden hall create an irregular silhouette. Using the red plastered wall as a foil, one is brilliant and glittering, the other colourful and delicate; they set off each other beautifully. The believers, under the architecture of Wanfaguiyi Hall, which is a weather-beaten, motley, contrast of red and white, primitive and delicate, smelled the faint fragrance from the wood and the ash of the incense burner.

> Under the golden coffered ceiling and facing the Buddha image under the niche among the chanting Lama monks in yellow cassocks, the low rhythmic sound orchestrated with the sound of knocking of hollowed 'wooden fish' amidst the thin smoke atmosphere, one could experience how much effort the master builders of the past had spent in order to create an atmosphere like this. Here they had created an integration of form, sound, colour, and smell, and through art and sense a religious impact was attained.[19]

To the east of the Imperial Summer Resort and under two natural stones of unique forms, the so-called Big Upright Stone and Frog Stone, is the Pule Temple. The two natural elements and the man-made temple group admirably to form a triangular space which when

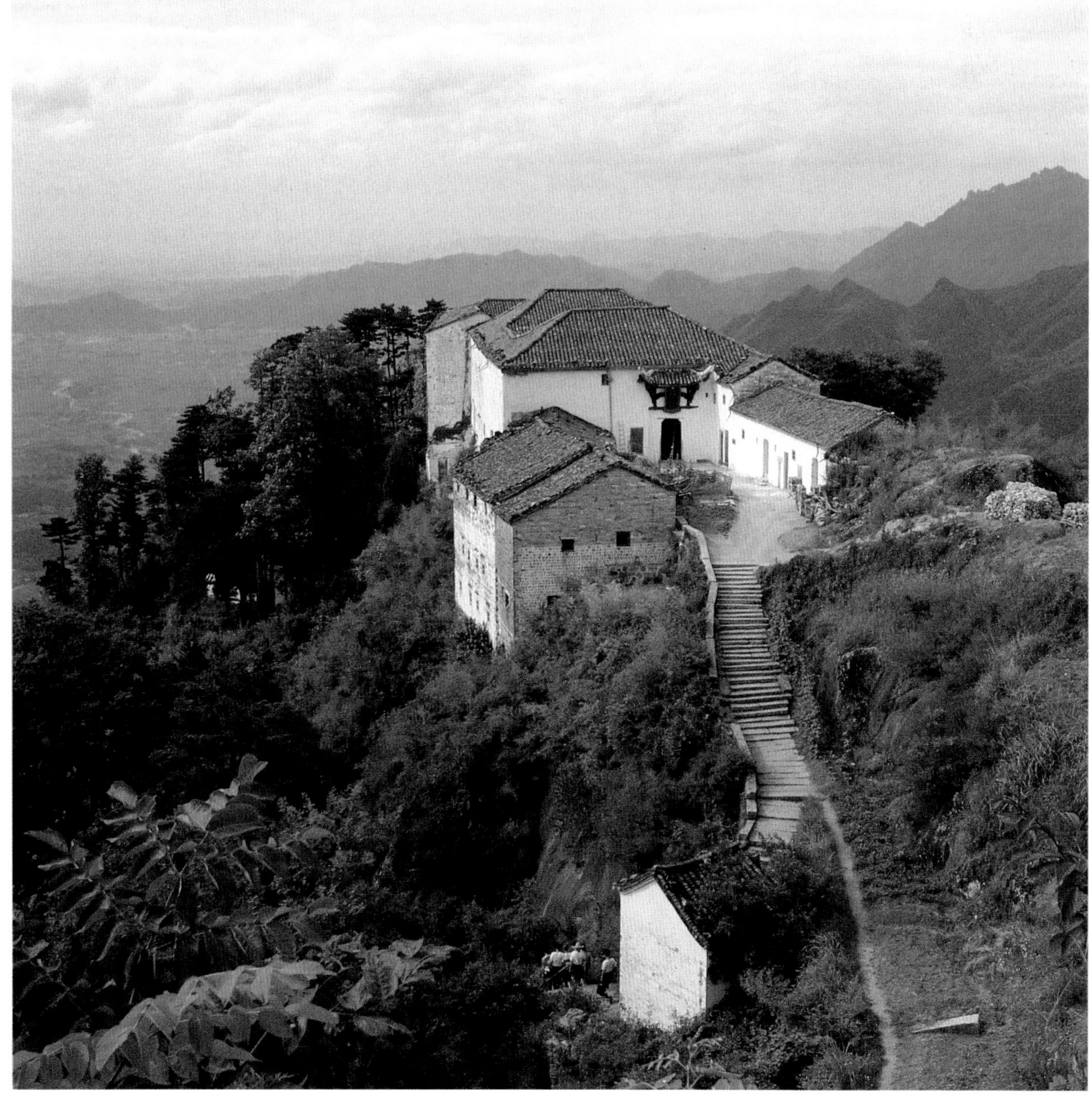

seen from the resort in the early morning and mountain haze, gives an ethereal feeling. The axis of this temple is pointed to the centre of the resort to create a unity, and a sense of subordination to the emperor was clearly manifested. The centre of this temple is a circular pavilion with double eaves of yellow glazed tile, situated on a high platform within a city wall. Inside the wall is a two-tier platform, both of square plan. The first tier has battlements, èight glazed tile stupas of various colours placed symmetrically on the four corners and centre of each side. They supported visually the big pavilion with a conical roof at the centre, the Xuguang Ge. This is a unique example of temple planning in China.

To summarize, the traditional Chinese religious buildings, from the choice of site to the final plan, were influenced by many different sources and ideas. The monks who chose the site because they liked to escape from city life into a peaceful, wooded setting, nevertheless liked the individuality of a place without the horror of isolated mountains. The humble pilgrim, who might also be an emperor or dignitary, toiled for a long time to reach the temple in order to worship the Buddha. Both experienced the tension which exists between man and nature.

The temple culminates in the harmonious grouping of the individual halls, courtyards and gardens, blending with their natural environment; they are both religious and poetic and must be seen and judged as one organic whole. The temple proper, always treated in an abstract order and as the centre of the religious world, especially in Buddhism, was dedicated to Sakyamuni, a symbol of Buddhism, and individual place. Although the intent of the designer was to make the halls and courtyards places of worship – and they actually achieved this particular purpose – it seems to me that the monks also intended to humanize this worshipping place by the use of floras, sculpture, and furniture, to provide a place for meditation and peaceful life.

The architectural traditions which have been described are of immense value when applied to contemporary design. Recently, many monumental buildings have been constructed throughout the world which boldly attempt to dominate their surroundings. Buildings vie for attention, each attempting to surpass its neighbours. They are no longer Chinese in character, the great traditions of the past having been lost to contemporary design considerations. There are many lessons we can learn from these excellent examples of the past. They can inspire, enrich and nourish our thinking. Utilizing design principles guided by these concepts, perhaps one day a simple, organic and unpretentious architecture will finally evolve.

▷ Chengde, Hebei, Pule Si and natural elements

CHAPTER V
HOUSES

CHINA IS A LARGE COUNTRY COMPRISED OF MANY nationals, of various climatic conditions and of diverse geographic environments. In ancient times, primitive man settled most parts of present-day China, where he cultivated crops, domesticated animals, and fashioned dwellings for protection. Some of the dwellings of later days were covered by roofs made of sticks and wattle supported on pillars, and thus larger spaces were created for living. Following social and technological developments, the largest group of Chinese nationals, the Han people, developed their unique wooden frame construction method. Their method later spread to Korea, Japan and reached as far as Indo-China.

We have already dealt with primitive cave dwellings and wooden frame construction in both the Introduction and the chapter discussing the characteristics of Chinese architecture. Here, the intention is to discuss the most pervasive and influential dwelling form of the Han people, the courtyard house.

The Han people were first scattered along the middle and lower reaches of the Yellow River, where the climate was mild and wood was abundant. The officers and merchants of the Zhou Dynasty are credited with the creation of the typical Chinese house with the hall and gatehouse along the axis, and development of the symmetrical layout,[1] around the end of the 12th century B.C. The gatehouse was divided by wooden posts and walls into two equal parts, which were used for the guests as well as for ceremonial occasions. There were east and west sections used for the arrival and departure of guests as well. The main hall was centrally located and larger in area than were the living quarters.

These examples illustrate the influences of the political system and thought of the feudalistic system on the design of dwellings. The existence of courtyard houses at this early date is difficult to verify archaeologically for lack of evidence. However, the divine characters used in the Yin and Shang Dynasties included a word written like " 亞 ", which symbolized four halls facing a central courtyard. A simplified version of the same word written like " 亞 ", explained that there were courtyard buildings in use,[2] but we still do not have actual archaeological evidence to prove their existence. According to carvings on old bronze vessels; there were two- to three-storey buildings in which the beams and overhanging eaves were supported by columns and duogongs. These, in turn, supported the cantilevered balcony and balcony seats above. Records indicate that buildings of that period were decorated with colourful paintings. It suffices to say that the economic and technological developments were well progressed at this time.

We do not have substantial evidence of housing in the Qin and Han periods. However, documents of this period record the existence of large-scale residential buildings and gardens built to imitate the natural landscape. From the incised brick funeral utensils found in the Han tombs, as well as in the ruins of Luoyang house foundations, and in the remains of the Western Han village at Sandao Gou of Liaoyang, we have some idea of the building forms of that period.

Most of the plans of the small houses of this period were either square, rectangular or L-shaped. The L-shaped house had two sides enclosed by buildings and the other two sides by walls, thus forming a courtyard.

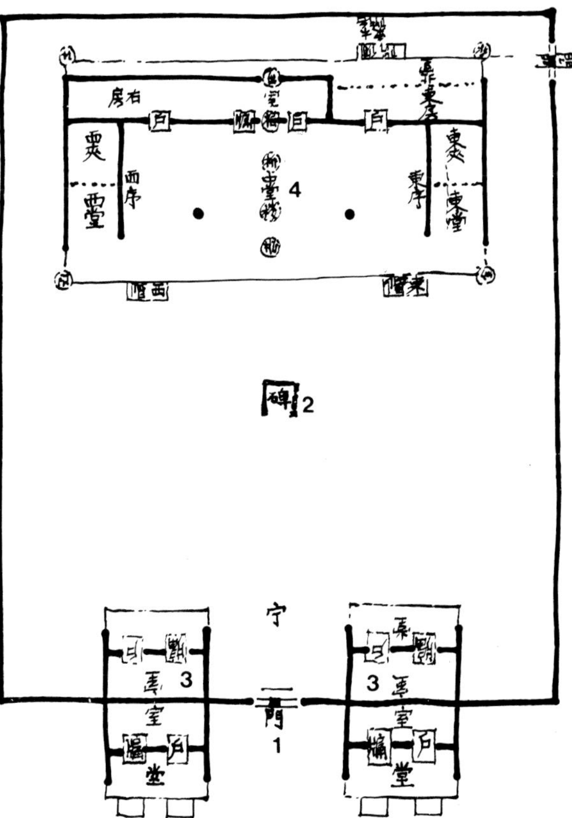

◁ Beijing, a courtyard house

△ House plan for an officer, Zhou Dynasty

Key
1 Entrance door. 2 Tablet. 3 Rooms. 4 Main hall.

Later houses were formed by two parallel rectangular buildings connected by walls at the sides to form a courtyard. These were single storey or two- to three-storey houses, all using frame construction and pitched roofs.

Incised brick dug from Sichuan Province is most significant[3] as they provide much vital building information. The incised bricks from Sichuan depict a house entirely enclosed by walls, the inside of which was divided into two different functional parts by a wall. To the left was a gate leading to a small courtyard, where there was a second gate opening into a larger courtyard with a hall of three bays. Inside the hall two persons were seated on a mat and a pair of cranes were dancing in the courtyard, indicating that this was the major living area of the house. To the right was another courtyard with a tower (possibly a watch-tower), a kitchen, a clothes-horse, and a well. A man was shown sweeping the yard, with a dog running near him. This scene explained that the master of the house was well-off, so he could afford to have a larger house and more facilities. The house apparently was of wood framed construction with covered verandahs running along the wall to connect the various places. From these fragmentary discoveries and through the study of the house plans, construction methods, and functional requirements we have a general idea of the life-style of the people of that time.

We are still unsure of when the well-known 'typical' Chinese house – the courtyard house – was first used. The earliest evidence, found in Shangdong of the Han Dynasty, consisted of incised brick which depicts a courtyard house consisting of two rather narrow, elongated courtyards wrapped on all four sides with halls,

▽ Chengdu houses, Northern and Southern Dynasties

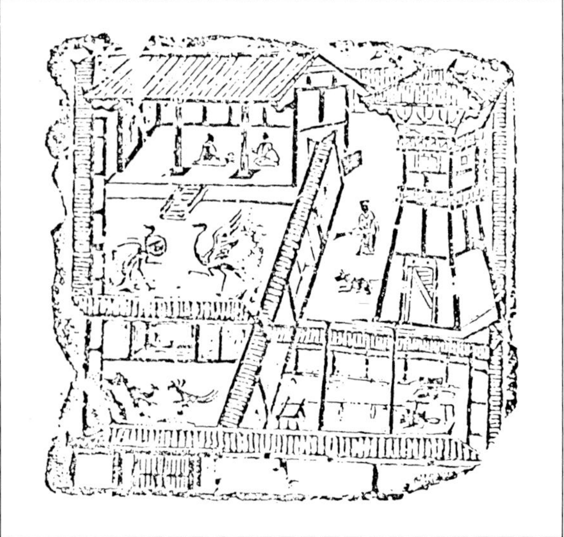

▷ Stone carvings of houses, West Han, Northern Wei, Tang and Sui Dynasties

Key
Stone carvings of houses:
1 House on stilts. 2 House with a courtyard. 3 L-shaped house. 4 House of three bays. 5 Yinan, Shangdong, stone carving in a tomb (Han). 6 Ningmao, stone carving, Luoyang, Henan. 7 Ningmao, stone carving, Luoyang, Henan. 8 Luoyang, Henan, stone carving, E. Wei. 9 Dunhuang fresco, Tang Dynasty, house with verandah. 10 Dunhuang fresco, Tang Dynasty, house with verandah. 11 House with a bed, Sui and Tang Dynasties. 12 House with a screen and tables, Tang Dynasty. 13 House with a dining table, Tang Dynasty.

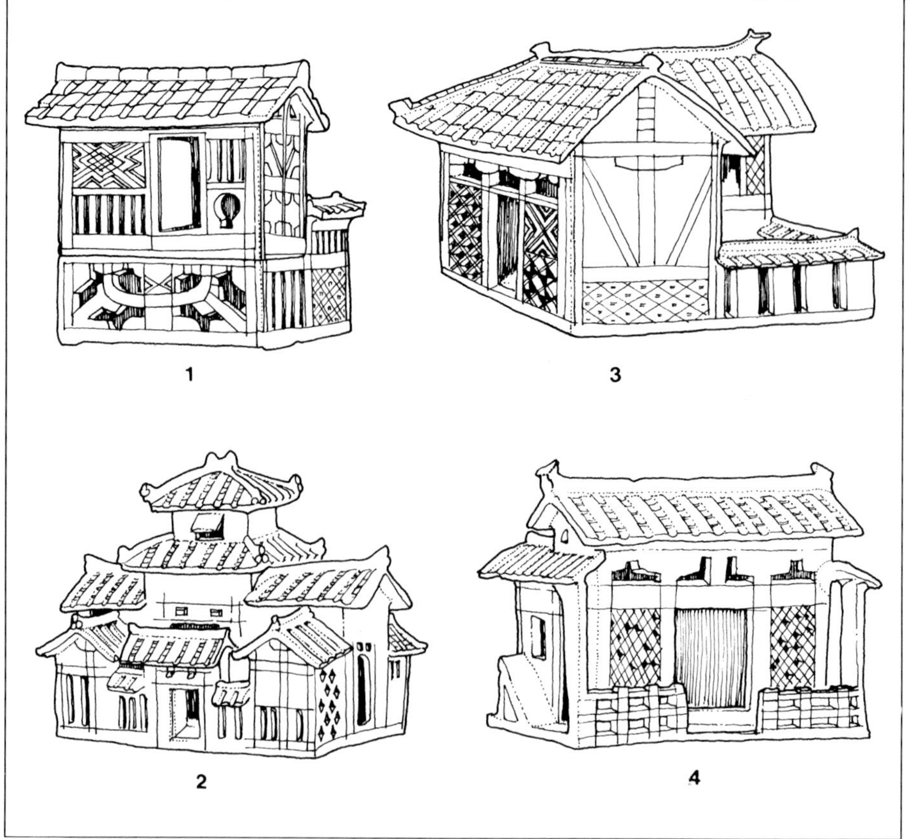

essentially a typical 'four-closed courtyard'. Although simply designed and built, this illustration on brick exemplifies the design concepts of that period: 1) the use of axial and symmetrical planning principles; and 2) the enclosure of space by buildings and walls.

These findings provided valuable documentation of house design in several periods. However, the examples only illustrate the layout of the houses and are insufficient evidence of scholars attempting to elucidate the idea and philosophy behind the formation of the house plans.

PHILOSOPHY GENERATES THE PLANNING IDEA

Houses which use the courtyard as the centre to form the 'three-closed courtyard' or 'four-closed courtyard' had their roots in Confucianism and in the rather rigidly feudalistic family tradition, which was also influenced by Confucian philosophy. One of the essentials of Confucianism is 'Harmony' – harmony within a family, inner harmony of one's self, and the ethical concept of deference to elders. Wang Guowei, in his *Ming Tang Qin Dian Tong Kao*, explained very clearly:

> In building a palace, the dwelling halls should be placed as close to each other as possible. Then there will be a close relationship and an intimacy between the members, and the house functions well. In order to make all the halls close to each other, a four-closed courtyard house eventually evolved. A four-closed courtyard house has halls facing north, south, east, and west which all focus on the central courtyard. This is not only the easiest way, but the most expedient and attractive.[4]

The key phrases are 'intimacy' and 'functions well'. By using the traditional 'jian' as a unit of building construction intended to inspire harmony and intimacy within the family, and to bring all material life and spiritual life to a focus, the courtyard house thus planned embodied the Confucian philosophy. The form encouraged emphasis and enforcement of the Confucian idea in daily life.

The moral code of Chinese feudalistic society was rigidly patriarchal. In the hierarchy of the family, the older generation has precedence over the younger, and the head of the family was always the male of the oldest generation. Confucianism encourages 'parents' kindness and filial piety,' meaning the parents should be kind to their children and the children should be obedient to their parents. There are many moral codes, but the highest is obedience, especially to the father, followed by the eldest son. Of course, there were examples where, after the father of the oldest generation departed, the wife became the head of the family. In olden days women were not supposed to express their ideas in public; thus, their ideas were usually carried out through a male, such as the eldest son.

In this rigid hierarchical family system, an axial, symmetrical courtyard or courtyard house was the

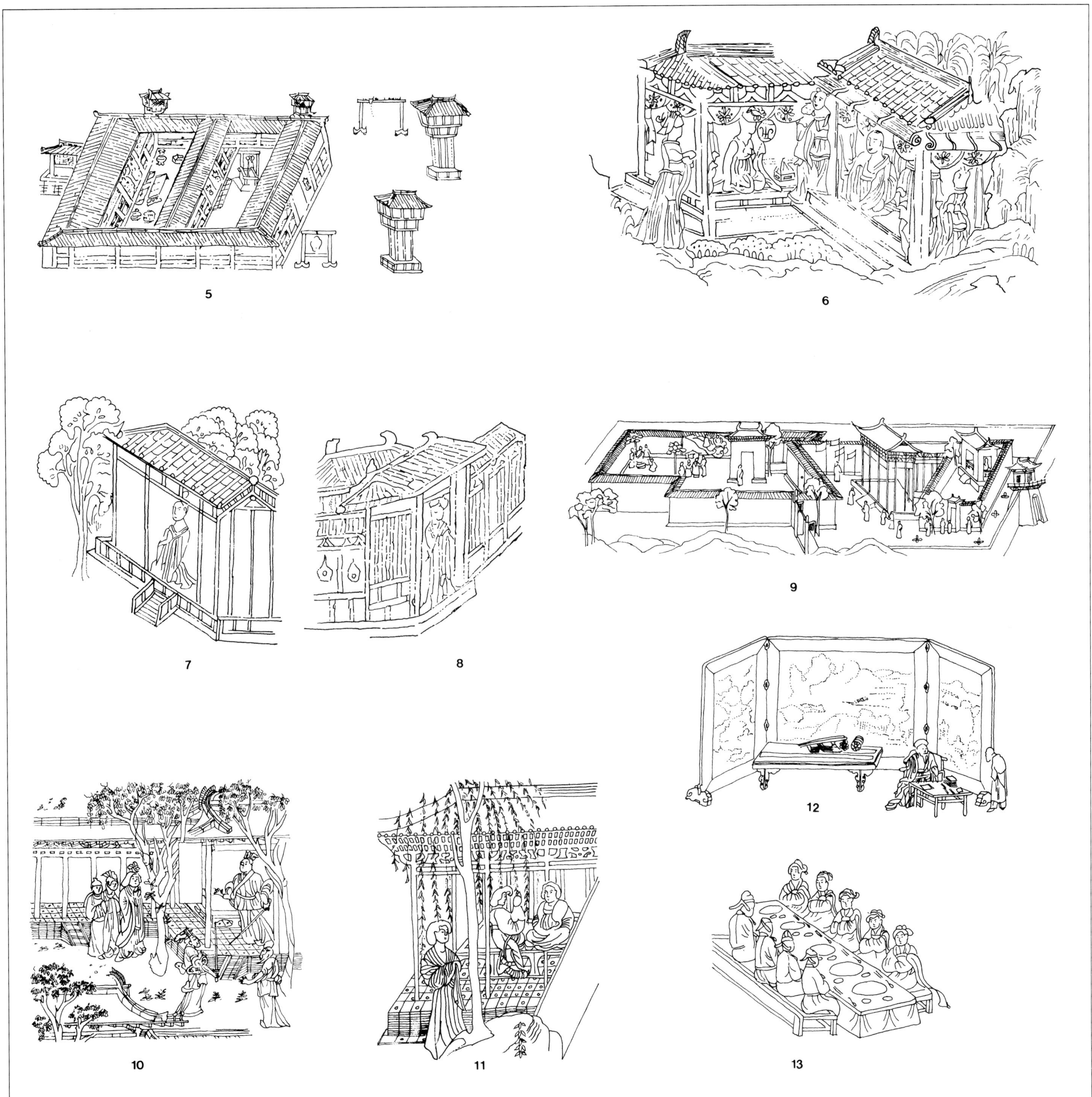
5
6
7
8
9
10
11
12
13

most suitable means of expressing this meaningful concept. The last hall on the axis of the courtyard served as the living quarters of the oldest generation, while the side halls facing east and west were for the children. The last hall would be the highest, most exquisitely decorated building in the whole enclosure. The side halls would be lower and were less decorated. Thus the form, symbolism and the location all gave importance to the main hall. In a large complex, composed of a series of halls and courtyards, the first hall was used as a reception hall. During important occasions, this hall served as a ceremonial hall for worshipping ancestors, or for other ceremonies. This arrangement represented the hierarchical family idea.

Harmony and ritual generated the layout and form of the courtyard house. Spiritually, a house like this has another meaning, that of a retreat which embodied an eternal meaning.

Socialists maintain that the spiritual life of a people is determined by its milieu; its social, economic and political atmosphere. The same is true of the Chinese. The 'communistic' character of the Chinese family-system society has played its role in shaping their philosophy.

> The Emphasis upon filial piety, deference to grey hairs, respect for institutions, and kindred virtues, is a direct outgrowth of their 'communism.'[5]

But while this may explain the rise of some of the ethical principles that govern the relationships of man to man, and the axial planning principles, yet it is never of itself sufficient to account for the peculiar character of the Chinese mind, namely, its ethico-spiritual interest.

Nor can we fall back upon the economic background of the people, as the advocates of the materialistic conception of history would have us do. It is true that the attainment of a high degree of culture by a people presupposes complete freedom from drudgery and concern over the immediate needs of life. But in the case of the Chinese, the fact is that their thought is not so much the effect as the cause of their particular economic development as has been suggested above. Plain living was enjoyed from the beginning. Inventions were rejected as devices calculated to foster licentiousness and effeminacy.[6]

We must, then, turn to examine political history for extraneous causes of their peculiar type of thinking. The course of historical development in China has not remained static, but has been full of changes of greater or less proportions. More than 20 dynasties have come and gone. Invasions of barbarous or semi-civilized tribes swept through now and then to disturb the established order. Adding to the confusion, internal dissension and factional strife broke out periodically. Now, this state of affairs could not fail to impress upon the minds of the thoughtful a sense of transiency of life, the lack of permanence in human affairs, and a consciousness of human suffering. Although the Chinese believed that 'Tian (Heaven) does not change, so Dao (way) does not change.' Reality, however, proved that people actually lived in an unstable, transient world. As a result, the thoughtful came to withdraw themselves, becoming entrenched within the safe barriers of the inner life against outward misfortunes, making true happiness depend entirely upon their own inward state. Thus the communistic character of the family system, the inward feeling of withdrawal from the outside world, and the idea of plain living did not stimulate the people to improve their abode and so contributed to the formation of the courtyard house. The house is not a castle in the minds of the Chinese, but a retreat from the real world outside, a place where all the members of the family could gain peace of mind, symbol of eternal stability in the transitional world.

As the halls were built around, and faced into a courtyard, a heavy masonry wall at the back of the halls separated them from the outside world. Because the centre of all activities was the courtyard, there was no privacy concerning the movement and activities of all family members. But as the house was completely cut off from the outside, it was an organization which had the distinction of seclusion. Futhermore, it created a layout and a form which rallied all the members of a family psychologically to live in a spiritual refuge together. During the feudalistic era, the family was a well-knit societal unit, with the members of the family closely linked. Only through unity of thought and the force of a family were they able to confront and survive the misfortunes of life.

The significant meaning of a courtyard house was thus manifested. Ethico-spiritual harmony and a ritual mode of living were the main forces created in the courtyard house. Conversely, this pattern influenced and reinforced the life-style and thought of all the family members. Physically, a courtyard was used chiefly for pedestrian circulation between halls. There were parterres and fish ponds to give life to the space. Large deciduous trees were planted in the courtyard for shade, scent and fruit. A pavement was provided for the placing of tables and chairs. Altogether, it was an ideal space for relaxation, circulation and recreation.

It was the habit of the Chinese that, unless it was unbearably cold, the rooms were not heated. In the south, a charcoal fire was built in a brazier to give warmth to the rooms, while in the north a 'kan' of a raised brick red or brick floor with flues inside gave warmth to the room in cold days. There was no great difference between room temperature and the outside temperature. People were used to wearing fur-lined or cotton-padded gowns to keep warm. Summertime was easier, more comfortable, as cross-ventilation was provided to remove warm air. In warmer climates, the courtyard plan had great advantages. The buildings around the courtyard served as wind barriers. On sunny days, the courtyard or the space under a verandah made pleasant living spaces. On snowy days, the people gathered to drink wine and appreciated the red plum blossoms or verdant green bamboo leaves flourishing in the snow. Spring and autumn were, of course, the best seasons to use the courtyard. In summer, the dense leaves of the trees provided cool shade and reduced the radiant heat from the pavement, walls and roof. Life in a courtyard was pleasant indeed. It was natural, outdoor living space shared by all. In as much as all the doors and windows of the halls opened toward the courtyard there was an interpenetration between inside and outside. People were inevitably attracted to the centre.

Some of the larger courtyards had verandahs wrapped completely around them, providing a transitional space between inside and outside. The function of the verandah was basically circulation between the halls during rain or snow; however, chairs and benches were also built-in or placed against the rail, forming a 'ringside seat' to watch both the landscape and the activities in the courtyard.

The high walls at the back of the halls protected the courtyard by keeping out noise from the outside and giving privacy to the occupants, thus creating a special tranquil atmosphere. These wall functions engendered a special serene mood for the people which also helped to preserve a peaceful mind.

When comparing the Chinese courtyard house with their European counterparts or the houses of other cultures, it is evident that the roots which formed the Chinese courtyard house were different. The Chinese used simplified construction methods and simple forms to create an entirely harmonious, holistic whole conforming to their particular world view.

COMPACT COURTYARD HOUSE

We have already mentioned that China is a country of multinationals and of various climatic conditions. The courtyard house is not the only house type in China; however, from north to south it was the typical form used by the majority of the population. In places where building density was high, the courtyard was made smaller, and the surrounding buildings could reach two storeys, but their design concept and meaning were unanimously the same.

For instance, in the mild and hilly provinces like Anhui there were small courtyard houses, and from

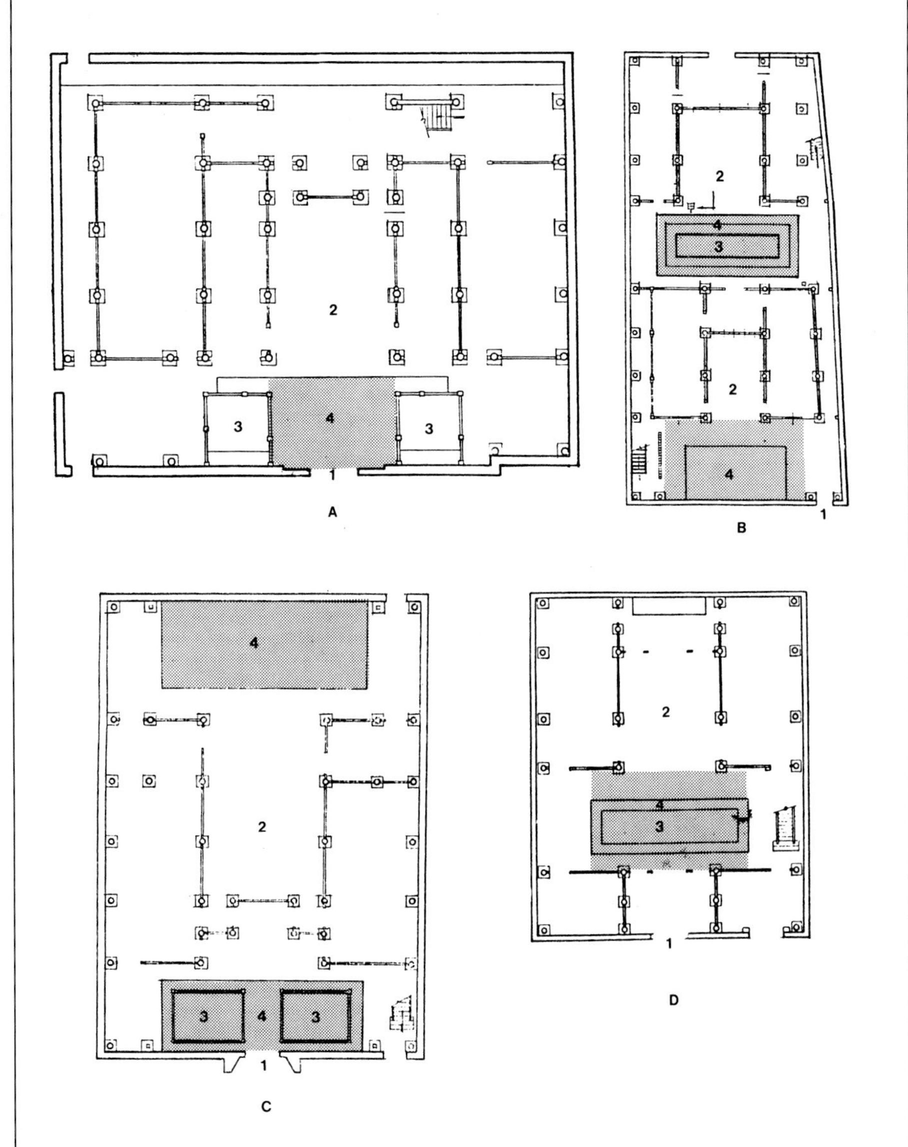

▷ Anhui, compact courtyard houses

Key
A: House with one courtyard at the front. B: House with two courtyards at the front and centre. C: House with one courtyard at the front and back.
D: House with one courtyard at the centre. 1 Entrance. 2 Hall. 3 Pavement. 4 Courtyard.

the funeral utensils of the Han Dynasty we know there were both U- and H- shaped houses.[7] The courtyard was comparatively small, and the middle portion of the house was raised to two storeys, perhaps to draw warm air from the rooms below. The small courtyard was used for pedestrian circulation, lighting the interior, ventilation, draining rain water, and for outdoor activities. In the south portion of the Yangtze River Valley, in provinces like Anhui and Guangdong where the climate is warm, many small courtyards are spatially combined with the hall. The only boundary between them was a threshold or a level change, as no doors or windows were used to separate the two. They were completely open to each other, so it was convenient to use the courtyard on a fine day and just as easy to move into the hall when the weather turned rainy. Most of the courtyard houses in Anhui were two storeys high, several of which were built during the Ming and Qing Dynasties. Although the life-styles of the local people and economic conditions of society have changed from when these were built, the small courtyard house is still loved today by the people in this district.

It should be made clear here that the small courtyard house is, by and large, a kind of courtyard house but, as they were shaped by a different set of circumstances, they are not entirely similar. The original concept of the small courtyard house provided comfortable quarters for smaller families and so were not meant for a whole family of several generations. It is most suitable for two generations, but can be extended to a large complex. No matter what the exact forms were, these two categories have their similarities. From the general concept to layout, from space to detail, both types of courtyard houses conform to human scale. By depending heavily on detailing and plants, the designers tried to humanize the harsh masonry construction and pavement, essentially the major contributions of courtyard or small courtyard houses.

'Three-closed' and 'four-closed' Courtyard Houses

Anhui Province is located at the lower reach of the Yangtze River, where the people enjoy a mild climate and an affluent life-style. In the region surrounding Huizhou, many small, compact courtyard houses were found which had been built by the affluent merchants of the Ming Dynasty. These houses, built within a square or rectangular enclosure, included a main hall which was generally two storeys high, and east and west rooms, which were usually small one-storey buildings. Because of the long main hall, the 'three-closed' courtyard was narrow too. Sometimes, a row of rooms was added to the front, thus forming a four-closed courtyard. Larger houses were extended along the axis, yielding '日' and '目' plan forms: these layouts provided more rooms for larger families, but the meaning did not change.

Courtyard houses, aside from a very compact plan, shared other features which affected general appearance: they were laid out according to the contour of the site; they were constructed in an area of high building density; they were orientated to south or southeast; they had whitewashed walls with very small windows; and had high and low greyish roofs or copings. The silhouette formed was picturesque and especially attractive, in the rather humid, hazy, hilly environment. Because of the high building density, for protection from fire and for security purposes only small windows opened on the exterior walls.

Most of the houses had only one entrance leading to the inside. As the rest were blank walls, the entrance became the centre of decoration and stood out distinctively against the flat wall. Because of their various designs the doorways identified each family. One kind of design featured a hood placed over the doorway. The beams and frieze were made of brick and carved with designs, the top was covered with roof tiles, and the doorway itself was lined with a variety of local black stone. Usually the opening was in rectangular shape, but some featured a semi-circular archway. More elaborate cases could be found, too, where brick or wood duogong and a covered doorway were used, but not painted with bright colours.

Another kind of doorway was called peifang (ceremonial archway) doorway. Peifang was used in front of important building groups and monumental buildings, but was seldom used in front of dwellings. When a peifang was used, it gave distinction to the house and indicated the status of the owner. There are numerous peifang in the Huizhou district, most of which were made of stone and beautifully carved, and there are a number of unique peifang forms and layouts, which we shall discuss in the chapter on ceremonial buildings.

A special feature found in the Huizhou district was

◁ Xixian, Anhui

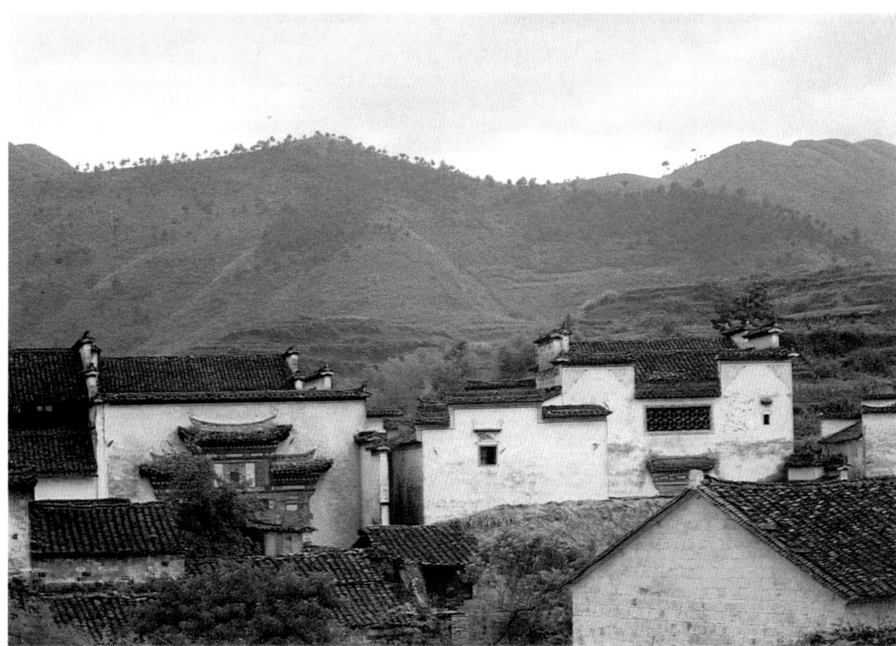

◁ Xixian, Anhui

◁ Xixian, Anhui

▷ Xixian, Anhui, doorhood

▽ Xixian, Anhui, doorhood

△ Xixian, Anhui, peifang doorway

◁ Xixian, Anhui, peifang doorway

△ Xixian, Anhui, window grille

△ Xixian, Anhui, window grille

the use of engaged peifang to mark doorways. These were made of stone, or stone and brick, and few were of wood. The carvings were usually delicate. Smaller peifang had only one opening, and larger ones had three openings. Regardless of the number of openings, there was only one doorway at the centre, and the other 'openings' were filled with brick.

Small windows were usually found only at second floor level for safety reasons. The window openings contained stone or brick grilles delicately carved with scrolled plant life, geometrical, lotus petal, and even dragon designs.

Wooden frame construction was widely used in the areas south of the Yangtze River, and facilitated cantilever construction. As the material was easily carved, the cantilevered parts became the centre of decoration. It is evident that the cantilevered balconies, the window sash, the railing, the overhanging eave above, and the spandrel below were the first things one noticed upon entering the building.

The idea of using cantilevered balconies might have originated from the need to get more sunlight into the upper rooms and for overlooking the courtyard. It was also used as a storage area for foods and other things. In another type of balcony, which was not cantilevered, the railing height was the same as the window sill. Both types have mullions which also serve as pillars to support the extended eave. The carving shown has symbols of happiness and longevity.

▽ Xixian, Anhui, section

The cantilevered balcony is comparatively richer in form and more practical than that which is not cantilevered. The space gained from the cantilever enlarges the usable area of the upper rooms. From section drawings, we can see that in the construction of the balcony the pillars and roof are organically connected. A seat was sometimes added to the balcony between the pillars, usually at a height of 50 centimetres from the floor. Outside the seat is a railing which is also about 50 centimetres high but extends further out, and thus has the name 'Goose Neck Chair'. To the south of the Yangtze River district it was commonly called a 'Beauty's Rest' or 'Flying Chair'.

The railing was attached to the eave pillars, which were aligned with the columns below. Under the bal-

◁ Xixian, Anhui, a Ming Dynasty house

▷ Xixian, Anhui, wood railing

◁ Xixian, Anhui, window sashes

▽ Xian, Shenxi, window sashes

▷ Anhui, beam and decorations

cony were exquisitely carved wooden brackets, and the upper part of the pillar supported the duogongs above. The balcony is by all means a special feature of the houses in this area. Anhui alone has numerous houses of this type, but the detailing of the railings are all different. The woodwork was painted with a kind of transparent wood oil which allows the grain to show, making the wood intimate and warm to the eye.

The walls facing the small courtyard were of wood. The decorative details on the window and door sashes were usually consistent with that of the railings. The spaces were interpenetrating. As one walked along the winding lane, paved with large stone blocks and enclosed on both sides by high walls, one passes various elaborately decorated doorways. Suddenly, one enters a realm of tranquility. A small pool is in the centre, enclosed by wooden walls and sashes. One feels that one has entered a secluded and intimate place. It was not difficult for anyone to understand that the design idea was also based on the creation of a miniature society, where the centre was the family and the ideal was harmonious living.

In the interior of the house, all the construction members forming the framework were exposed to the eye. The details, integrated with structural system, provided the special character of the dwelling among the houses in the nearby district. The wooden beams were shaped like a carved beam called the 'moon beam'. The central portion of each beam was slightly larger than the ends, and was curved a little upward, giving a soft outline yet retaining a feeling of strength. The joints where the beam ends joined the columns were again supported by a bracket carved with a flower, a motif featured in the mid-Ming Dynasty. Sometimes a curved block was placed on top of a beam to take the place of a strut or to add a lotus flower under a short strut or duogong. In short, since this place was far away from the capital of Beijing, the construction methods did not adhere rigidly to established formalities. As such, it was more flexible and could accommodate the wishes of the people. The incised crescent-moon shape was also a decorative feature of the period, used to emphasise the unity between bracket and beam.

The Ming Dynasty court decreed:

> Officers of the first grade to the third grade can build halls of seven bays, from the sixth to ninth grades, the beams can only be decorated with black colour . . .[7]

Thus, the interiors of the houses were painted black. Although the houses described above belonged to merchants rather than to officers from the sixth to ninth grades, they could have been patterned after the example of the officers. During the last days of the Ming, there was a relaxation of regulations, as Anhui is far away from the capital. It is a pity that the interior was made dull and gloomy because of this decree.

Details such as the base of a column, a hole under floors and brick eaves for air circulation all became a part of the decoration in the small courtyard houses.

In China, just like their Western counterparts, were numerous dwellings combined with shops. These combination buildings lined the shopping street, with the shops placed in the front. The living area was placed either above the shop or at the back, and was separated from the shop by a small courtyard. Because of high population and building density, the site of the house was usually long and narrow.

It was recorded during the Song Dynasty that be-

△ Anhui, beam and decorations

◁ Anhui, beam and decorations

▷ Anhui, column base

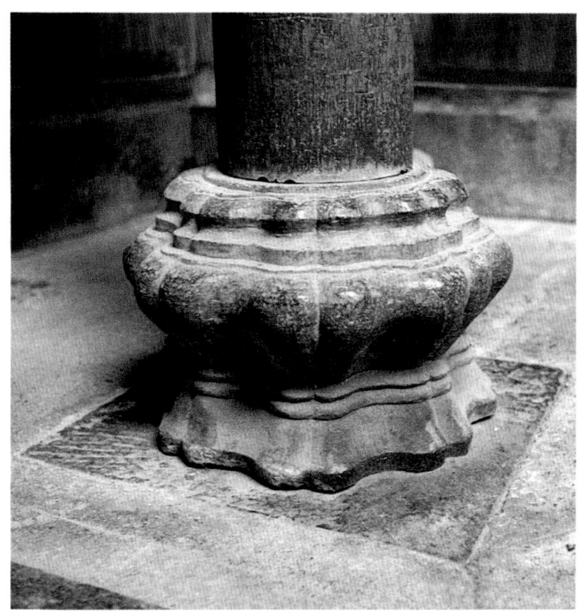

▷ Anhui, beam and decorations

▽ Anhui, brick carving

▷ *Life along a river in the Qing Ming District*, Song Dynasty painting

cause of flourishing business, the walls which enclosed residential blocks and shopping blocks were demolished. This allowed both houses and shops to line the street, and the streets became corridor streets. In addition, due to the rapid development of handicraft trades, some of the trades were concentrated along particular streets, and so many streets were named after the trade. Even today, some of the streets are called 'Cloth Lane', 'Ox Street', 'Hog Market', or 'Glass Tile Lane'.

Restaurants, teahouses, and 'pubs' were two to three storeys high, and had decorated gateways. The traditional painting, entitled *Life along a river in the Qing Ming District*[9], of the early 12th century depicts the market near a bridge and the city gate of Kaifeng, the capital city. The painting shows the forms of shops along the street and illustrates the market square in detail. Because of later developments, most of these streets and shops were demolished to make way for new buildings. Only in a few remote towns like Xixian, Anhui, did corridor streets and combination residential shop buildings survive. Here, if one threaded one's way through winding narrow shopping streets, only a little piece of sky is seen. Because of the narrowness of the street and the cantilever of the second floor, the eaves of the houses almost touch.

Because of the staggered nature of the street and gateways at either ends of the thoroughfare, the street itself becomes an enclosed longitudinal space. In addition, the flimsy appearance of the buildings, the delicate detail, and the rhythmic end wall all contribute to the light, peaceful, attractive character of the space.

The street is narrow, but because the shops open onto it, this actually enlarges the street space and forms many pockets for such varied activities as the transaction of business, tea drinking, working, and talking to friends. This arrangement helps to make the street life especially lively.

COURTYARD HOUSES

We have dealt with the philosophy and concept from which the courtyard houses were generated, but as a result of different natural conditions and the varied customs and lifestyles, there were several varieties. Usually the houses have entrances facing a narrow lane. Except for the entries to houses, the lane was enclosed on both sides by heavy masonry walls. Occassionally, high windows, a roof or a tree seen over the top of the wall, indicated that there was a courtyard behind the wall.

The entry doors were elaborately decorated as in the small courtyard house. Since most of the lanes were narrow, some of the entrances were set back from the street. A wide roof covered the doors, and was closed most of the time. It opened only when necessary; thus, the street itself was usually a quiet place.

According to Feng Shui and superstition, the entrance was not placed on the axis but usually at the southeastern corner. The northern Feng Shui School held that:

> A house is different from palace and temple (layout), so the door should not be placed to the south and on the axis. From innate Eight Diagrams, the northwestern is Qian (male) and southeastern the Kun (female), both are the luckiest directions, so they were used as the principles and bases to decide the location of the entry. Thus, when the house is located on the north side of a street, the entrance is located on the southeastern corner, and for those to the south, the entrance is placed at the northwestern corner. The northeastern corner, the next to the best location, was for locating the well and the kitchen. If need be, a door can be opened there too. Only the southwestern corner is ominous, thus storage rooms and the pithouse can be built there.

This superstitious and absurd formulation actually controlled the layout and the location of the doorway in the north.

Inside the entry is a small courtyard which serves as an open-air foyer. A screen wall was usually placed opposite the entry, also erected according to superstition. The ancient belief held that evil spirits and demons can only travel in a straight line. When they encountered the screen, they were bound to turn back and not enter the house. On the screen there are beautifully carved patterns symbolizing happiness. The combination of the entrance and the screen wall not only provides the visitor with a feeling of seclusion, but also gives identity to the house.

Turning left from this small courtyard and passing another doorway, a reception hall would be situated to the north of another courtyard, where sometimes a third doorway was built. This special courtyard and hall were used on special occasions like weddings, funerals, or ancestral worship as a ceremonial hall. The next courtyard and halls encountered, called inner

▷ Xixian, Anhui, a shopping street

◁ Xixian, Anhui, a shopping street

▽ Beijing, a residential lane

▽ Beijing, doorway to a house

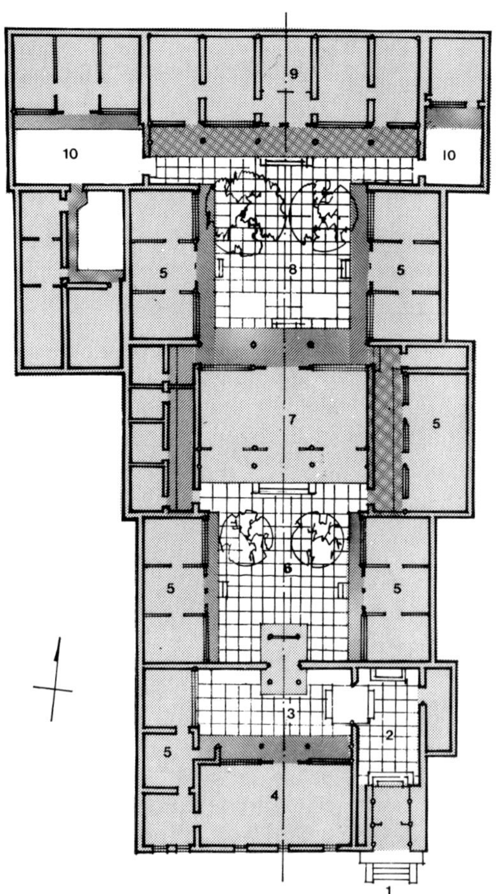

△ Beijing, plan of a four-closed courtyard house

Key
1 Doorway. 2 Entrance courtyard. 3 Second courtyard. 4 Hall. 5 Side hall. 6 Main courtyard. 7 Main hall. 8 Inner courtyard. 9 Chambers. 10 Service.

▷ Taiyuan, Shanxi, courtyard house

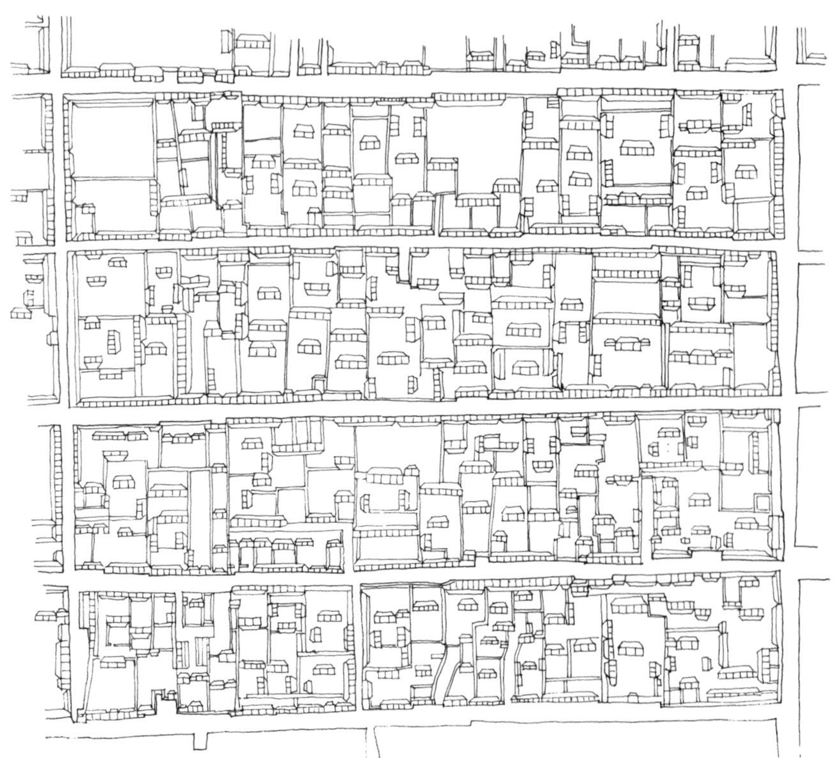

△ Beijing, typical residential blocks, Ming and Qing Dynasties

courtyard and inner halls, were the private living quarters. Male guests were not supposed to trespass upon the private area. Service quarters were usually placed next to or near the private quarters. Sometimes a back door was provided for bringing in fuel and provisions as well as serving as an entrance for servants.

Larger houses had two-storey buildings and an attached private garden. All the halls were connected by covered verandahs. The decorated columns, beams, brackets and doors contrasted with the greyish pavement brick and greyish roof tile, making the house especially attractive.

The courtyard house found in the southern part of China has an almost identical layout, the major differences being the elaborately decorated main entrance situated on the central axis. Sometimes a covered sedan chair hall was added inside the entrance just before the main hall. To compare the styles of the north and south, the northern houses were constructed in a colder climate and thus wall and roofs were thicker. Houses in the north were larger in size if built for higher officers and were richly decorated to make the homes more imposing to represent the status of the master of the house.

In the southern part of China, being warmer, the houses which were built for minor officers or merchants were constructed with thinner walls and roofs. Sometimes the columns were exposed, and the eave overhangs were wider for easy drainage. The colours used were generally warm grey and whitewashed walls. The woodwork was covered with a chestnut colour or dark red paint or transparent paint. The general feeling was sedate and subtle, designed to create an intimate, pleasant environment for peaceful and harmonious family life.

The characters and carvings on the frieze above doorways contained an auspicious sign, a propitious omen, a wish or a sentiment. For many dynasties, the Chinese endured the horror of warfares and turmoils. The people who grew up in this environment resorted to superstitious beliefs to obtain peace and happiness for their family. This was perhaps the reason why the Chinese loved to use symbols of happiness as decoration to bring the blessing and protection of 'super-beings' to the family.

Places like Fuqian and Guangdong enjoy a warmer climate; thus the houses have larger windows, the roof curve is usually greater, and the long ridge was divided into several sections to make the long line look shorter but somewhat overdone.

The most attractive features of the southern houses include the picturesque silhouettes, their harmonious relationship with nature, the contrast of wall and opening, of solid and void, and the subtlety of blended

△ Fuqian, a courtyard house

△ Wuxi, Jiangsu, a courtyard house

▷ Suzhou, houses facing a canal

▷ Changsha, Hunan, end walls

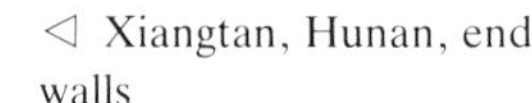

◁ Wuxi, a detached courtyard house

◁ Xiangtan, Hunan, end walls

▷ Yangzhou, Jiangsu, end wall

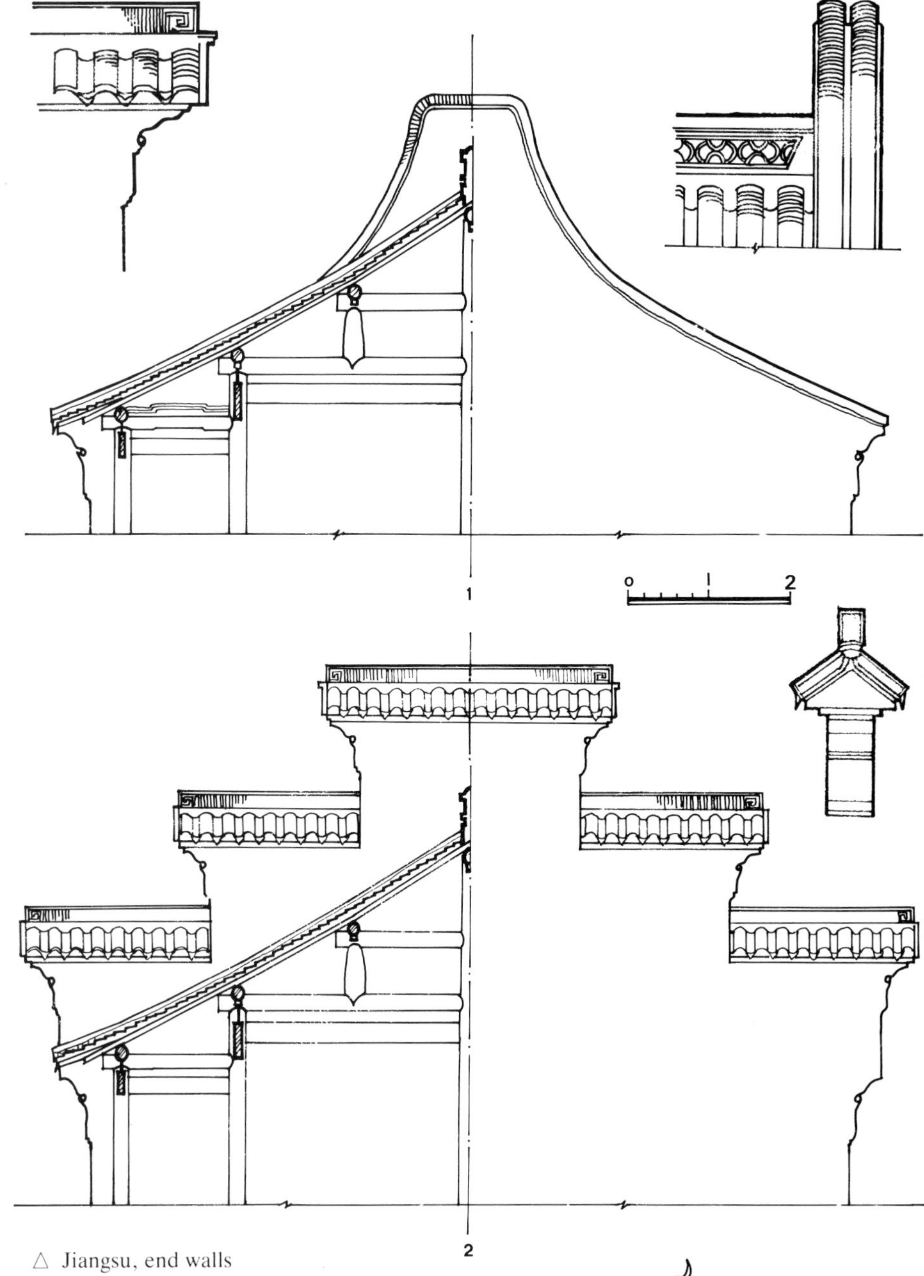

△ Jiangsu, end walls

Key
1 Guanying cape end wall. 2 Wushan screen end wall.

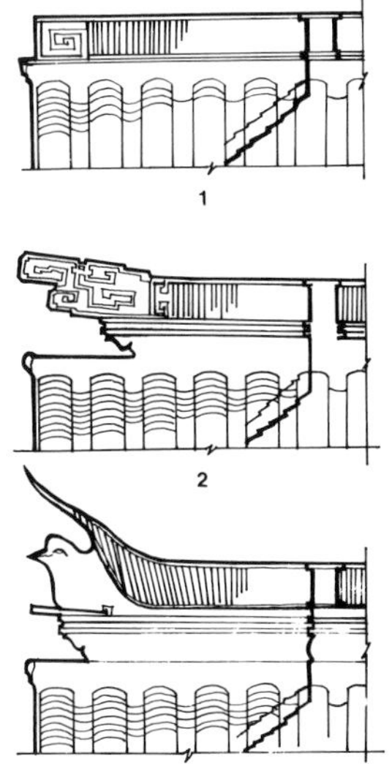

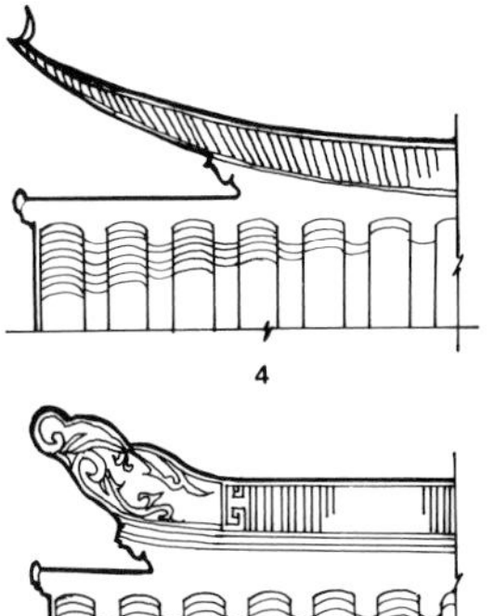

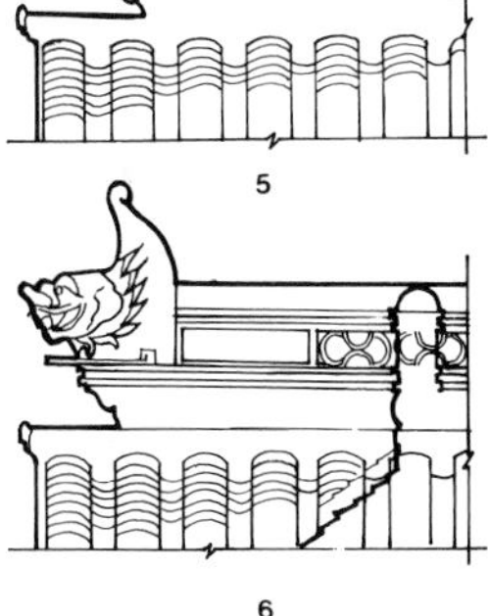

▷ Jiangsu, end walls

Key
1 Gaozhe ridge. 2 Wentou ridge. 3 Fuzi ridge. 4 Cimao. 5 Wentou. 6 Fulong.

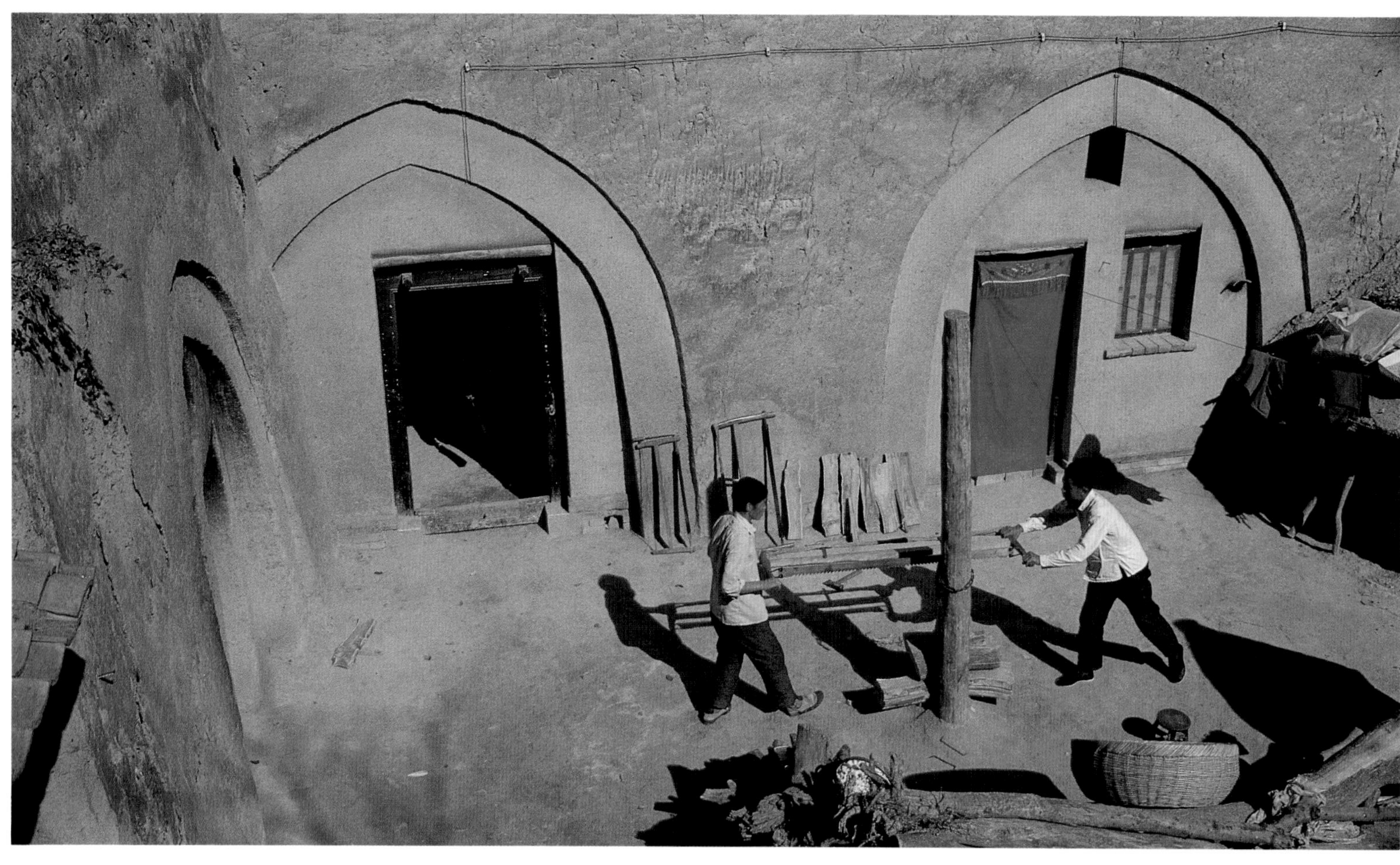

◁ Xian, Shenxi, cave dwelling

▷ Luoyang, Henan, ramp leads to a sunken courtyard

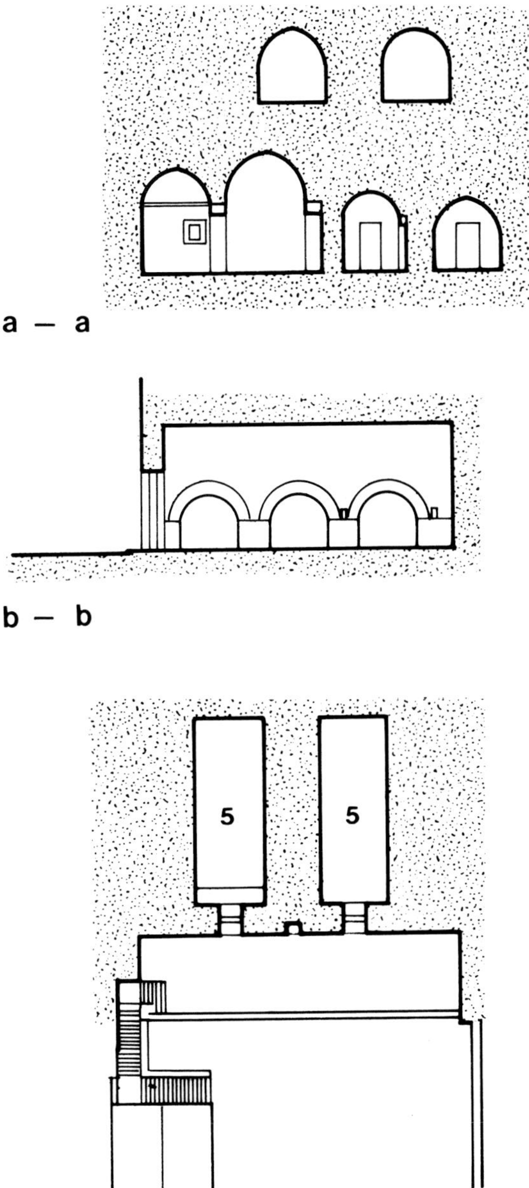

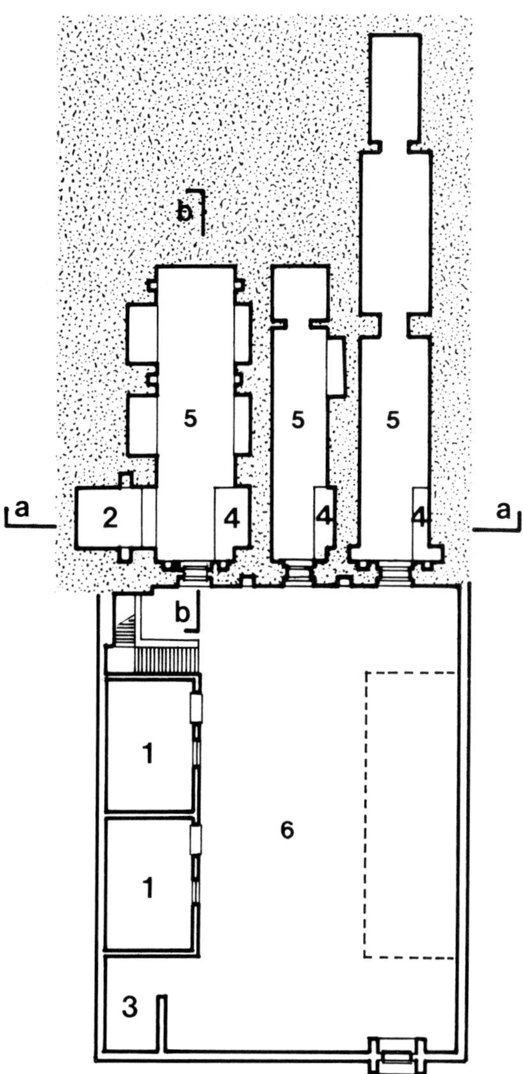

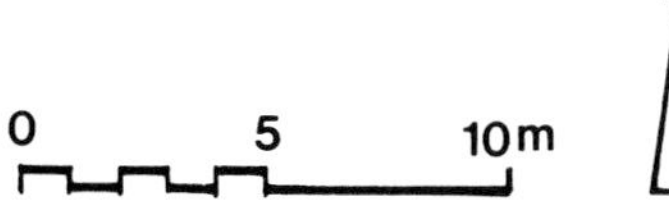

△ Cave dwellings, plan and section

Key
1 Guest room. 2 Storage. 3 Toilet. 4 Range. 5 Room. 6 Courtyard.

colour. The houses along the Suzhou canal near the Maple Bridge have one side facing the street and the other side facing the canal. Because they were built in different periods, the houses were sometimes set back or protrude forming an accidentally staggered building line as well as a high and low silhouette. They are pretty to look at, and much more attractive than if built on uniform building lines.

The rhythmic end walls of a group of buildings in Xiangtan, Hunan, have an interesting outline. The sedate colours blend beautifully with the natural landscape and the pool in front, creating a feeling of repose. The end wall of a large rural house in Wuxi, Jiangsu, and of another near Yuelu Institute in Changsha, are very attractive; the gradually rising wall of the former and the dynamic rhythm of the latter form beautiful outlines which were pleasing to the eye. One of the whitewashed walls in Yangzhou is decorated by the shadow of bamboo nearby. The solid and void contrast of the facades expresses the functional requirement and rigidity was thus avoided. These are good examples of design skills.

CAVE DWELLINGS

The cave dwelling is a special kind of house found in the loess area along the Yellow River in the northwestern part of China, where rainfall is scanty and timber scarce. The caves were dug into a loess cliff providing a dwelling with a narrow facade and extending into the cliff. The vaulted ceiling was sometimes strengthened by inner brick vaulting.

Where there were no cliffs, a sunken courtyard was dug and caves were dug in from the 'walls' of the sunken courtyard. A ramp was built to allow carts and residents down into the four-closed sunken courtyard. Since the cave dwelling had only one side facing the outside, there was insufficient daylight and poor ventilation. Some of the later cave dwellings have 'courtyards' at both ends of the cave to provide cross-ventilation. Some of the cave dwellings were integrated with regular houses built on the land in front, thus forming a combination of houses and caves.

The caves had the advantage of being easy to heat in cold weather and cool in warm weather. A recent survey shows that people living in the caves have enjoyed a longer life-span than those living in traditional courtyard houses.

CONCLUSION

The Chinese house, as represented by the courtyard houses of the Han nation, embodied the ethical thought of Confucius. The life-style of the people represented their physical and spiritual life. During long years of feudalistic society, this kind of house facilitated the control of the elders over the young and all the members of the family lived harmoniously together.

The courtyard, the focus and centre of all activities, was also an indispensable place for the circulation of ideas and for contact. The halls around the central courtyard are the 'private' sectors, the courtyard, the 'public' space, the focus of life; verandahs played the role of a transitional space. The main hall of a house was made obvious by its form, decoration, and location on the axis. The decorations of the frieze of the doorway, the bright colour, and the architectural sequence of the house all concentrated to express the social status of the family and the owner's position of control within the family.

This use of balanced symmetry and climatic layout based on the Confucian ethic was used for thousands of years, producing many attractive and functional houses. But due to conservative ideas and fixed design concepts, which did not encourage the adoption of improvements, the development of a stereotyped house form was unavoidable. This is the only blemish in an otherwise perfect design.

CHAPTER VI
PRIVATE GARDENS

◁ Wuxi, Jiangsu, Meiyuan pavilion

FOR MANY YEARS CLASSICAL CHINESE PRIVATE GARDENS, famous for their landscape art, were built attached to large houses, palaces and temples. Although the locations and the persons they served were different, they shared common characteristics. As Chuin Tung pointed out:

> The simplistic requirements of a garden were practically contained in the word ' 園 ' where ' 囗 ' symbolized a walled enclosure, ' 土 ' was similar to the plan of a building, but can also represent a pavilion, the middle ' 口 ' represents a pool, and ' 𧘇 ' looks like a rock or a tree from the front.[1]

Thus, a garden is a place enclosed by walls, inside of which are buildings, pond, flowers, trees and rocks.

Most importantly, private Chinese gardens were in all respects *private* gardens. The characters rest in 'serenity' and 'scenery', the objective of garden architecture. A quiet, serene environment provided the master of the garden with a place for contemplation, introspection and repose. Scenery helped to mould one's temperament and heighten artistic cultivation. Being interconnected and related, these two qualities were especially prominent in the design of southern gardens.

In the chapter outlining the characteristics of classical Chinese architecture I described how Chinese buildings and building groups employed axiality and symmetry to express monumentality. In contrast, the gardens were:

> A beauty of intricacy and fascination, and extremely skilful in manipulation.[2]

The layouts, mostly free, asymmetrical, and natural, were combined with poetic concepts and painterly ideas, thus creating a unique, humane architecture.

PHILOSOPHY

The content of Chinese poetry and painting was deeply influenced by Daoism and the Chan Sect. The philosophers of Eastern Jin drew deeply on Buddhism, but their literature reflected both Buddhism and metaphysical philosophy. Such men as the Seven Scholars of Jianan or the Seven Sages of the Bamboo Groves were greatly influenced by religious beliefs. When Zhuangzi was dying, he said concerning his burial:

> I will have heaven and earth for my sarcophagus, the sun and moon shall be the insignia when I lie in state, and all creation shall be the mourner at my funeral.

This excessively anthropopathic conception of nature made it possible for him to fully unite himself with nature.

Daoism studied nature, not for the purpose of practical use, but in the course of seeking personal salvation, the basis of its metaphysics.

> With Laozi and his school, moderation means diminution of desires. There is no greater sin than yielding to desire, no greater misery than discontent, no greater calamity than acquisitiveness.[4]

In the system of Laozi,

> the idea of peacefulness occupies a prominent place. He insists on non-action and non-interference with natural instincts.[5]

– by which he means not inactivity, as the term might suggest, but acting in accordance with the nature of things. Inactivity inspires quiet repose and confidence in the spiritual order. Through non-action everything can be accomplished. With Confucius, repose is a concomitant of moderation or inner harmony, and conformity to one's life circumstances is a condition of moral repose.

One of the Seven Sages of the Bamboo Groves wrote:

> Oh how short a time it is that we are here: why then do we not set our hearts at rest, ceasing to trouble whether we remain or go? What benefit is there in wearing out the soul with anxious thought? . . . Then let me stroll the bright hours as they pass, in my garden among my flowers, or I will mount the hills and sing my song, or compose my verse beside the limpid brook. Thus will I work out my allotted space . . .[6]

This is an expression of the sentiment of that age which greatly influenced the thought of the minds of scholars of the following years.

With the introduction of the Chan Sect of Buddhism, and Monk Huiyuan's emphasis upon inner contemplation, this sentiment was intensified and became even more pronounced; and in its fusion with Daoism, everything in the world is vanity, and the desire for escapism influenced the special spirit of Chinese gardens. However, we must point out that because of the turmoil and corrupt situations of the time, many scholars, poets and painters were discontented with reality. They were decadent in spirit, resorting to drink, or composing verses to vent their sorrowful, gloomy mood. Naturally this also influenced the healthy concept of garden design. Fortunately, not all garden designs were thus affected, continuing to employ the beauty of nature and landscape to nourish the human mind, to give repose to the spirit, and to cultivate lofty sentiments.

NATURE

Historically speaking, Chinese garden architecture has long flourished. For example, the Lingtai of Zhou Dynasty, and the Shanglin Garden of Han were built thousands of years ago. They were all imperial gardens. When Huizhong of Song (1102-1125) reigned, the Song Dynasty was in a period of political recession; but it was also a period of great artistic activity, as glorious in art as in poetry and philosophy. The writers had a passion for nature unmatched elsewhere in the world. The Song artists delighted in their portrayal of mountains, mists, plunging torrents, the flight of wild geese from the reed beds, the moonlit reveries of sages in forest solitudes, the fisherman in his boat on lake or stream. Huizhong, still very much devoted to art, sponsored literature. Futhermore, he integrated poetic and painterly feelings into garden design. These ideas influenced even the southern part of China; therefore, there were famous gardens in these regions.

> It was unique because they have used the inherent forms of nature as inspirations for the aesthetics; it was elegant because they use the elegant taste to remedy the luxurious.[7]

This passage explains that, under the influences of Huizhong, the aim of gardens in the southern part of China was to have poetic and painterly feelings, creating a place of natural beauty with a serene and elegant atmosphere. Through the uses of this concept, a unique garden architecture was created.

Most of the ancient imperial palatial gardens were built for the pleasure of hunting, so the scenery was comparatively natural in spirit. After the construction of the palaces of A Fang of Qin and Weiyang of Han, owing to the grand scale of numerous buildings, the gardens became extravagant and artificial. Quietness and elegance were sacrificed. During the Caowei and Jin periods, the Seven Sages of the Bamboo Groves wandered amidst mountains and rivers. They detested the world and its ways, and their thinking induced people to escape to natural landscapes. On the other hand, the famous calligrapher Wangxizhi of Jin Dynasty, in his eminent handwriting of *Preface to the Orchid Pavilion Collection* described the natural landscape around the Orchid Pavilion:

> Here are the lofty mountains and ranges, profuse forests and bamboo, clear water and rapid torrents, surrounded my left and right, guide it for floating cups (competitors had to compose a poem while a little wine cup floated along on the winding stream).[8]

Taoyuanming, a scholar of the same period, in his classical prose poem *The Homecoming* writes:

> Homecoming bound! . . . To ramble in my garden is my daily joy; its stillness is guarded by a constantly closed gate . . . the evening mist rises lingeringly out of the valleys; tired birds find their way home. The shadow floats out and soon they have disappeared; leaning with my hand against my solitary pine I still linger.[9]

Through the hills, water and woods of the unique and quiet landscape, once combined with the thought of standing aloof from worldly affairs and Daoist nature, mystics have long influenced the philosophical thought and concept of garden design. The Lantian Villa of Songzhiwen and Wanchuan Villa of Wangwei, both of the Tang Dynasty, were both influenced by this philosophical thought; thus, bamboo isles and sunken flower beds were built. Wangwei the poet-painter who lived his life as a hermit, an officer and a lay Buddhist, was especially sensitive to natural beauty. The famous Song scholar Sushi wrote in his *Dongpozhiling* regarding Wangwei's poem: 'Pondering Mojie's (nickname of Wangwei) poem, it is a painting, viewing Mojie's painting, it is a poem.'[10] The natural scenery depicted in his poem was poetic, and was a very high accomplishment. From one of his poems, *Overlooked*, we can experience his emotion:

> Beneath the bamboo grove, alone,
> I seize my lute and sit and croon;
> No ear to hear me, save mine own;
> No eye to see me, save the moon.[11]

His painting was highly esteemed by his followers as 'Scholar's Painting', and the atmosphere depicted in the painting was something the garden designer desired to create and even dreamt about.

Baijuyi, another Tang Dynasty poet, has given us in his prose *Caotangji (Record of the Thatched Hut)* a detailed description of his garden and the mountain view of Lushan Mountain in Jiangxi Province:

> Before the hut extended an open court covering about 100 square feet, and in the middle of this court rose a terrace. On the south side lay a square pond, twice the size of the terrace. Around the pond were planted bamboos from the hillside and wild flowers; white lotus flowers and white fish were placed in the water. Farther south wound a stony stream, and along this grew pines and other conifers; bushes throve at their feet. The paths, which led in and out, were paved with white stones. To the north of the hall, steps had been hewn in the mountainside, so that one could ascend to the top, and on cleared places, the stones were piled up in the form of 'mountains'. There was a stream, and a tea plantation, inviting to the pleasure of tea drinking. On the eastern side of the hall the water fell from a height of three feet, and on the opposite side it was led from the height by an open bamboo pipe to pond . . . Since my youth I have lived in varying circumstances, sometimes in a hut, sometimes in an elegant dwelling, but wherever I have lived, even if it was for some days, I have always built a terrace, piled up stones and excavated a pond, for my passion for mountains and water was irresistible.[12]

Baijuyi composed several poems and referred to the same topics. He had always utilized natural elements, sided by artificial works, and was evidently a devoted amateur gardener. In his small garden, he combined a terrace, a pond, stone paved paths, dense forests and tall bamboos, flowers and a waterfall. We can almost sense the charm of the garden from the descriptions above.

Liuzhongyuan, also a scholar of the Tang Dynasty, in its heyday, wrote in his *Gumtang Xiaoqiu Ji (Record of a Little Hillock at Gum Pond)* describing his garden creation:

> [Once I had] cut all the weeds and deteriorated trees and had them burnt; the fine trees stood erect, pretty bamboos showed and grotesque stone was exposed. Looking through the trees, I could see the mountain peaks, the floating clouds, and the flowing water.

After such efforts at clearing he could then:

> Sleep on a mat, watch the clear scenery, listen to the murmuring of the creek, feel the quiet cool atmosphere.[13]

Needless to say, the aim of the scholar was to have a natural atmosphere so that, through the senses of the eye and ear, he could finally attain spiritual enjoyment of the mind – not the worldly enjoyment of the emperors and kings, but a sense inseparable from the artistic accomplishment of the scholar.

Wangyucheng, in the *Huanggong Zhulou Ji (Record of Huang Gong Bamboo Pavilion)*, described how he used bamboo to build a small pavilion and, after its completion:

> I held a volume of *Zhouyi (Book of Changes)*, sat quietly among the smoke of burning incense, discarded all worldly concern. Outside were the river and mountains; only the sailing boats, flying birds and misty clouds, bamboos can be seen. While I sobered up from wine, and finished drinking my tea with incense extinguished, I saw the setting sun off and met with the rising pale moon. This was too a wonderful place for a relegated officer.[14]

All the literati mentioned above lived amidst a natural

landscape, as did Liuzhongyuan, either in a thatched hut or a bamboo house, solitarily thinking about faraway fantasies as if they were walking lightly like a fairy, and in a complacent, leisurely gentle manner. There were plenty of descriptions like this in Chinese literature; however, the emotions associated with the landscape could not be realized by vulgar persons. That was why gardens were built at the back or to one side of a house, following the forms of famous mountains and rivers to build a man-made natural landscape. Gardens were designed for repose and rest to attain mental tranquility and for meditation over spiritual matters. The essence of garden design is to draw beauty from nature, and so create a tranquil environment.

POETIC AND PAINTERLY CONCEPT

> Poetry was cultivated by the Chinese chiefly as a means of self-expression; a vehicle for expressing their inner conflicts, disappointments, aspirations of the inner man; in short, their spiritual experiences. . . that is the 'embodiment of one's spiritual expressions in symbols'.[15]

For instance, the falling of leaves in autumn symbolizes one's misery while the thriving trees encouraged one to go all out in a distressed situation.

> As for music, it is a means of purgation, which is conceived of as possessing that power of calming, purifying, and ennobling our affections, and regulating our desires. In these cases, the beautiful is subordinate to the spiritual.[16]

Poetry, prose, painting and music in China are interrelated and were used to express inner feeling through symbolism. Poets – most of whom were also painters – and literati all contributed to the art of garden architecture. The author of *Yuanye (Garden Planning)*, Jicheng, was a painter. The concept of Zhozheng Yuan came from the painter Wan Zhangming. Painter Shitao was an expert in piling hills, and painter Li Yunling planned Siziling (the Lion's Garden). These were by no means isolated cases.

The artistic concept of poetry, its artistic form, and the structure of prose can be borrowed for garden design. Qien Yong of the Qing Dynasty wrote:

> Designing a garden is just like composing poetry or prose, it must be a work of disciplined winding, in concert from beginning to end.[17]

To some extent, the Chinese and Westerners have had the same approach and reached equally satisfactory results. Poets and painters have to a great extent influenced English garden design. Westerners have examined Alexander Pope's garden as the garden of a painter (Pope declared that, 'all gardening is painting') seeking poetic and painterly concepts. Although the 18th-century gardener Lancelot Brown (1716-83),

> was never a painter, he compared his art to literary composition, setting a comma here, a full-stop there. Those are not the symbols that a visual artist would use; rather those of a literary mind. Brown did not acquire the painter's method of pictorial approach, except in a very generalized way. . . Brownian landscape was, therefore, aimed to create the gentle serenity that Richard Wilson infused into his contemporary landscape painting.[18]

How similar was his pursuit of serenity and scenery to that of the Chinese! However, in China, garden design did not seek to replicate the artistic form of poetry, but was inclined to the integration of its artistic conception with that of garden design. The feeling or sentiment seemingly floated in the air and was not connected to any specific object although through the artistic form of an object the lofty aspiration of the designer was expressed and communicated to the beholder.

Garden design, nevertheless, was different from poetry or prose. The media are not brush or paper, but rather a process, where there is never a final stroke of the pen or a last word, and which is in a continual state of change. It is the placement of the elements which make a garden – such as water, rocks, trees and flowers, buildings and space – and the utilization of the effects of natural phenomena – the change of seasons, light, colour, shadow and sound – to achieve aesthetic feelings, and to evoke associations between objects and the observer. Through these a communication between the designer and the beholder can eventually be reached.

The poetic feeling associated with garden design is basically aimed at creating a poetic atmosphere through the use of the above elements. The artistic form of poetry combines regularity, cadence and rondo. When comparing these characters with laws of architecture, regularity becomes axiality and symmetry; cadence is high and low, forte and piano and rhythm; rondo is repeat, reappearance. The Chinese garden embodies all these characters, the most important of which is rondo. A man, when strolling along a path inside a garden, repeatedly views the same object from different angles. He experiences different sceneries, views variegated artistic forms, and gains different artistic concepts. Chinese garden design resorted to these means to create a serene, elegant poetic atmosphere.

We can say positively that painting is the mother of garden design. Traditional Chinese landscape painting is called Shan Shui painting, or the painting of hills and water. Hills and water constitute landscape and are also elements of garden building; therefore, it is natural to associate painting with garden construction. Chinese landscape painting first started during the Caowei and Jin Dynasties. Landscapes were painted as a backdrop for a portrait to express the personality of the person depicted through hills, water, trees and flowers.

Zhang Ziqien of the Sui Dynasty was a virtuoso in painting. His paintings featured 'one thousand miles in a foot of paper'[19]. Under his influence, various facets of landscape painting were developed and had reached a sublime state during the heyday of the Tang Dynasty. The paintings by Wu Daozi, another virtuoso of the same period, were acknowledged as the Xieyi painting. He utilized a freehand brush stroke characterized by vivid expression and bold outline to communicate his feelings, thoughts and attitudes to those who look

◁ Taihu Lake, Jiangsu

▷ Wuyi Mountains, Fuqian, Sea of Clouds

▽ Wuyi Mountains, Fuqian, Jiuqu Stream

at his work, which served as a forceful vehicle for conveying ideals and aspirations, obsessions and impressions.

It was not a 'realistic style of painting, but a great departure from paintings of classical Western style or the present-day Chinese painting approach. Xieyi landscape painting was created after the painter had wandered among famous mountains and rivers. He was able to assemble and digest the quintessence of nature, even the momentary beauty through a highly generalized rendition of the landscape, expressed and recreated through his brush. So the landscape painters like to visit Lushan, Huangashan or Wuyishan, all famous mountainous places. Their unique forms and towering cliffs were sometimes hidden from view, or only faintly visible because they were partly covered by clouds.

To the Xieyi landscape painters, a panoramic view was not important. Rather, the important image was a creation of the painter's imagination and his abstraction of the view. Instead of making a quick sketch in the mountains, the mountain was only significant to him in the contemplating of it, wandering through it and painting it. After he returned to his studio, he wielded his brush to paint the momentary scenery on the two-dimensional paper, he collected in his mind that which

> shrinks the vastness of Nature to enhance the appreciation and comprehension of it through art.[20]

The painter's visual experience and artistic intention are expressed through brush, by painting the Shan Shui from his mind's eye.

In garden design, the designer took over the painter's intention in the application, usage and abstraction to the three-dimensional landscape painting. When visiting a garden, and stopping in front of a doorway, a visitor would be thrilled to resolve the scenery into a two-dimensional landscape painting.

> Chinese art is subjective rather than objective and in this respect differs from the Greeks. It is the personal element which is important in their conception of art. 'The secret of art', says a 12th-century critic, 'lies in the artist himself'. As a man's language is an index of his nature, so the actual strokes of a man's brush, in writing or painting, betray him and reveal the nobility of his personality or its meanness.[21]

In Xiehe's *Six Canons of Painting*, or principles of painting, he laid down one of the canons as 'Jing-yin-wei-zhi' or 'managing composition'. The painter should deliberately leave a large space empty on the paper; because we can never know everything, why paint everything? His landscape is not a final statement, but a starting point; it is implicative and not an end in itself.

Traditional Chinese painters have been criticized for their lack of knowledge of scientific perspective from the Western point of view. True, Chinese paintings do not utilize static viewpoints and vanishing points. Rather, in a painting, many viewpoints and vanishing points occur comparable to the shifting perspective of the West, which permits the visual description of the total landscape. The analogy of this Western technique is the long scroll painting, which sometimes reaches dozens of feet long. While looking at a scroll, the view unfolds gradually, just as though the viewer were strolling in a garden. Views change at every step, developing gradually through time and space, to reveal the hills and water, to discover the natural beauty and to admire the whole landscape. Through the layout and each element, the viewer comes to understand the meaning of garden design. Since it is a long scroll, viewed each day at a certain hour, one can only see a section of the painting and leave the rest to another day. Such an experience is comparable to looking out of a window or standing just inside a doorway to enjoy

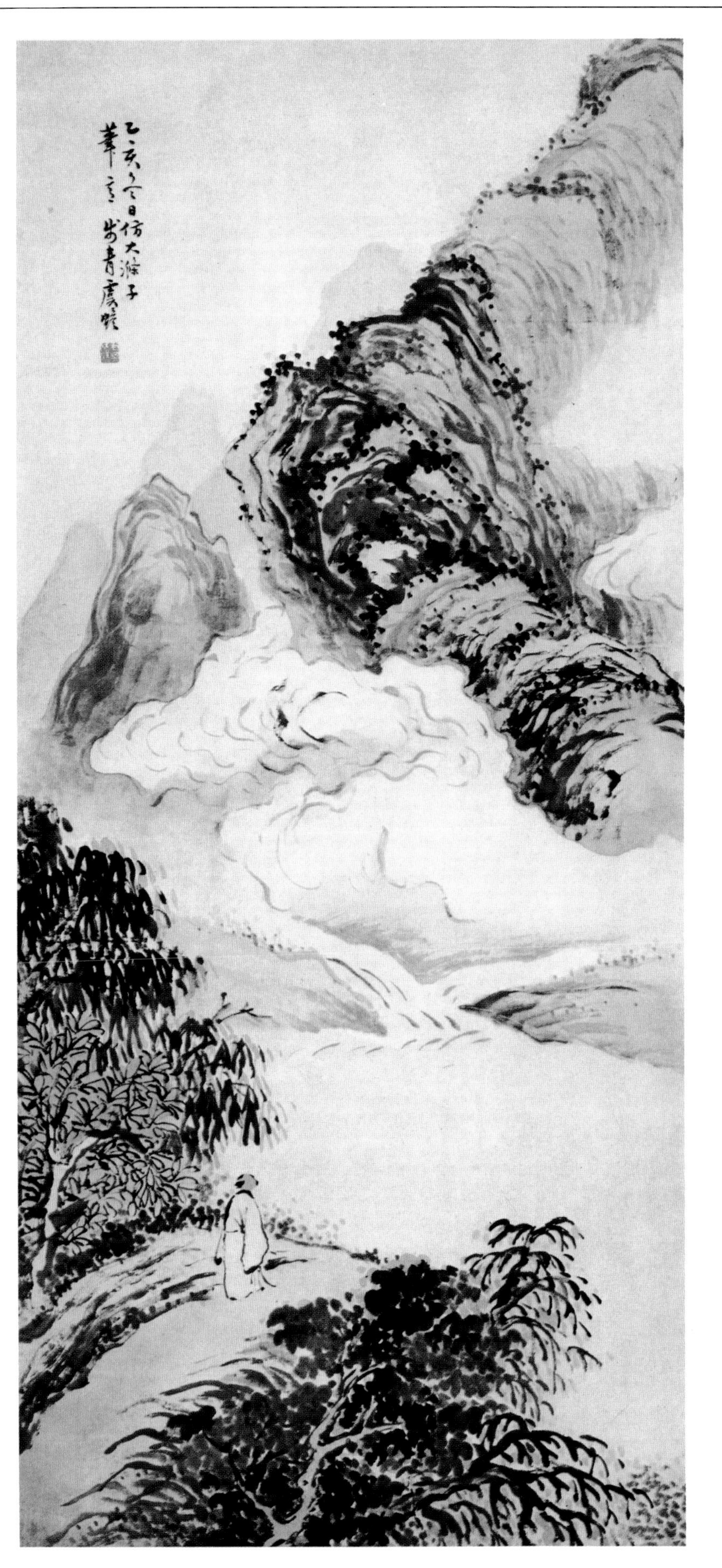

◁ Traditional Chinese painting, Qing Dynasty, Yuan Jiang, 17th-18th century

the beauty of light and shadow, trees and flowers, sunshine or rain, and seasonal changes. For these, poets composed many emotional poems. Such as Li Bai, a great lover of landscape, in one of his poems, *A Reply:*

He asks why I perch in the green jade hills,
I smile and do not answer. My heart is
comfortable and at peace.
Fallen peach flowers spread out widely, widely
over the water.
It is another sky and earth, not the world of man.[22]

Wangwei, in his *Where I Was Born:*

Still peeps the sun through my gauze window at
home.
The early plum blossom, Oh. Yet does it blow?[23]
(translated by Fletcher)

Wangjia, in his *A Storm:*

No rain, and lovely flowers bloom around;
Rain falls, and battered petals strew the ground.
The bees and butterflies flit, one and all,
To seek the spring beyond my neighbour's wall.[24]
(translated by Giles)

Zhangbi, in his *To An Absent Fair One:*

After parting, dreams possessed me
and I wandered you know where.
And we sat in the verandah
and you sang the sweet old air.
Then I woke, with no one near me
save the moon still shining on,
And lighting up dead petals
which like you have passed and gone.[25]
(translated by Giles)

The poems express their emotions, but also tell us that a garden is not just a place for strolling. The garden serves as a place to enjoy the scenery on a certain occasion, integrating one's emotion and elaborating it as in poems. The above poems, although showing a tint of melancholy, are not in the least vulgar. Famous gardens, like famous paintings, are a piece of art which move one's feelings, serving as a garden for meditation not for recreation. The gardens were created like a shifting perspective painting. After looking at recurring scenes, the viewer experiences an endless after-taste. Yet gardens are different from scrolls. The end of a long scroll was usually the end of enjoyment; although some scrolls did not have an end, it helped to guide the mind of the beholder to somewhere faraway. The twisting paths of the garden have the same effect, as they guide the visitor to almost endless variegated sceneries. The natural elements like rocks, trees, flowers or ferns change occasionally, but they exist in the mind almost permanently. Someone living in a city, who cannot leave his secular matters to others, can build a garden at the rear of his house where he might wander the paths of imagination, enjoy the beautiful scenery created by a painter, and nourish his mind.

Xiehe, in his *Six Canons*, described 'miao' (tracing), 'ling' (copying from the original) and 'fang' (imitating the manner of the masters). These are three ways to learn painting, in which the aim is to inherit from a model skill and contents, and then afterwards create. A reference to continuity has always been a part of the cultural tradition of Chinese painting, and garden designs, which imitated painting, also have continuity. The Suzhou gardens seen today were restored on the foundations of the past. The designers of today, who study the literature and documents of the past, so far do not want to change the location and form of a pavilion or a tree. This is not mere imitation, as the chief goal seems to be the restoration of the original atmosphere. For instance, Zhuozheng Yuan was first built in the Ming Dynasty. For the sake of accommodating more visitors and enlarging the garden, designers studied a multitude of literature and then restored the east garden to its original planning, which had covered a larger area. Of course, the designing of a new garden has a different approach, so as to absorb the quintessence of the old and inherit the traditional spirit rather than merely its form.

The typical way to learn calligraphy is to trace and imitate models of handwriting, and the way to learn the composition of poetry is to memorize Tang poems. To learn garden design one has to understand and learn from the spirit and layout of past examples. A garden is a place which makes one recollect the past and how people lived in the space. Only through the experience attained in the environment could one fully understand its meaning and acquire its feeling. So this 'imitation' is not an imitation of its form but of its intrinsic value.

THE CHARACTERISTICS OF PRIVATE GARDENS

The gardens that we are dealing with are the gardens of private houses, privately owned and not public in nature. The best private gardens are found mainly in Suzhou and Wuxi near Taihu Lake, and Yangzhou, all located at the lower reach of the Yangtze River. Enclosed and protected by walls, they are noted for their long history and high quality. The cities of this region enjoyed a mild climate favourable for horticulture, and the agricultural products contributed to a thriving economy. Canals and roads facilitated communication, laying the foundations for cultural activities. Induced by such propitious conditions, landlords, merchants, and retired officers flocked here. Writers, painters and craftsmen also came and lived under the auspices of the rich to make a living. Having pooled their talents for planning and construction, the gardens flourished. Suzhou gardens ranked foremost mainly because of this.

All kinds of gardens contain buildings. In addition, gardens are enclosed by pavilions, verandahs, hall and walls; in other words, a building is not surrounded by greenery, but the space is enclosed by buildings. Without buildings, there can be no garden. The main difference between Western and Eastern gardens and their

◁ Nanjing, Jiangsu, Xi Yuan, the main hall

◁ Nanjing, Jiangsu, Xi Yuan house boat

△ Suzhou, Jiangsu, Huqiu Hill stone pavilion

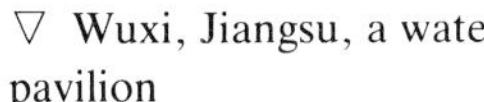

▽ Wuxi, Jiangsu, a water pavilion

basic elements lies in the use of buildings and not in vegetation. Buildings in a garden serve to 'frame' or emphasize a good view, and at the same time the form is a decoration for the garden. The buildings found in Chinese gardens are: 1) ting (hall), 2) ting (pavilion), 3) lan (verandah), 4) xie (den).

Ting, or the hall, functions as the main building and so is the largest in the garden. The site of important gatherings, such as the entertainment of guests or family members during festivals and other special occasions, the hall was usually placed at a prominent location. Jicheng said: 'When planning a garden, the first thing is to place ting'.[26]

Terraces were placed in front or at the back of a ting for activities on fair days. Most ting have windows opening on all four sides in order to capture scenic views and provide ample light to the interior. A southern orientation is best for scenic landscapes.

There is a special kind of ting, called 'Liangmian ting' which has two fronts. The plan features a partition in the middle which divides the hall into two equal parts; during the winter, the southern part is used to enjoy the warm sun and in the summer the northern part is used to catch a cool breeze. Since the ting is the largest building in a garden, 'very few walls are built around it, thus more space is provided, very few trees to avoid crowding and shield views.'[27]

Xie is also a kind of hall provided especially for enjoying views and smaller gatherings. 'Xie means borrowing, for the borrowing of scenery'.[28] Xie was sometimes built over water and so is called a water pavilion. Around it are seats and balconies for sitting and enjoying sceneries. The function of ting and xie are practically the same, only a ting (pavilion) is smaller in scale. The ting can also be placed near or over a pond, but is generally built on top of a hill. Ancient Chinese gardens were called 'Ting Gardens', indicating that the ting is an important element in garden design. 'Ting' in

Chinese means 'pause', a place where one lingers for relaxation and appreciation of scenery. When a pavilion with wing-like roof is placed on top of a hill, it becomes a place for resting after the climb and for looking into the distance where one can look quietly and ponder.

If there is no view, then what is the purpose of building a pavilion? Although the scenery is often 'borrowed' from faraway, it can also be scenery found in the garden nearby. Full blooming flowers, budding flowers, verdant trees, falling petals or leaves, fish swimming, birds singing, all contribute to scenery, and are all attributed to poetic feeling. In poetry ting and xie were the main subjects. Ge, a two- to three-storey building is also built as a lookout.

Xuan, used as a den or a study, is placed in a quiet location. Screened by evergreen trees such as laurel or bamboo to create a serene environment, the building generally has large windows to provide ample daylight to the interior. One kind of playful architecture is the fang, a house-boat, which is built over water and used as a hall.

Another element widely used is the hall, which provides security but is often used to define spaces and create different landscape. The wall in itself can also be a piece of art, composed of whitewashed masonry, of stone laid in random bond, or of weaved bamboo. A door opening is provided, serving both as a means of communication and as a picture frame attracting one to a view or drawing attention to certain objects – a corner of a building, an old tree, or a rock.

The shapes of the doorways are varied. The most commonly used, the moongate, is in a simple circular shape, symbolizing a full moon or happiness. Other spaces, such as the Chinese crabapple flower, begonia, and geometric shapes as the hexagon or oblong were also used.

Walls were also used to divide space into single pictorial courtyards. Many such courtyards may be found in a big garden. They are simply walled up and decorated with regularly-spaced tracery windows in geometrical or free-flowing forms. Besides decoration, the other function of dividing walls seems to be to give privacy to the courtyards. Through the numerous tracery windows, a corner or a part of the adjacent courtyard is in view. Although spaces were divided by walls, through use of tracery windows, the space seems to be limitless and was not confined to a small area. White washed walls, like the rice paper used by traditional painters, lends itself to the shadow of trees and flowers as if they were painted with ink on the walls. Sometimes rocks, ancient trees, and creepers use walls as a backdrop, or are encased in it to form a special bas-relief. Plant forms which change with the season are

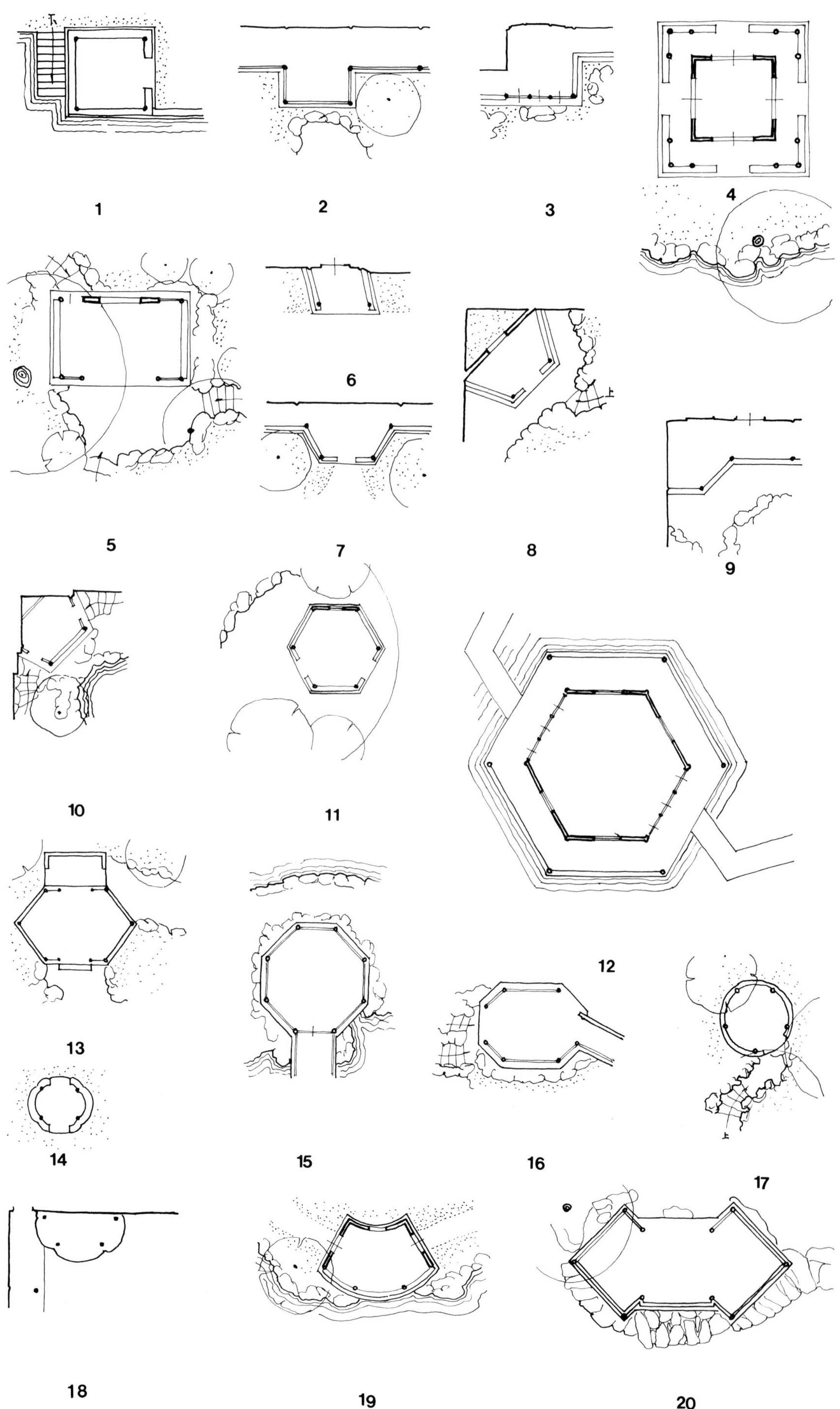

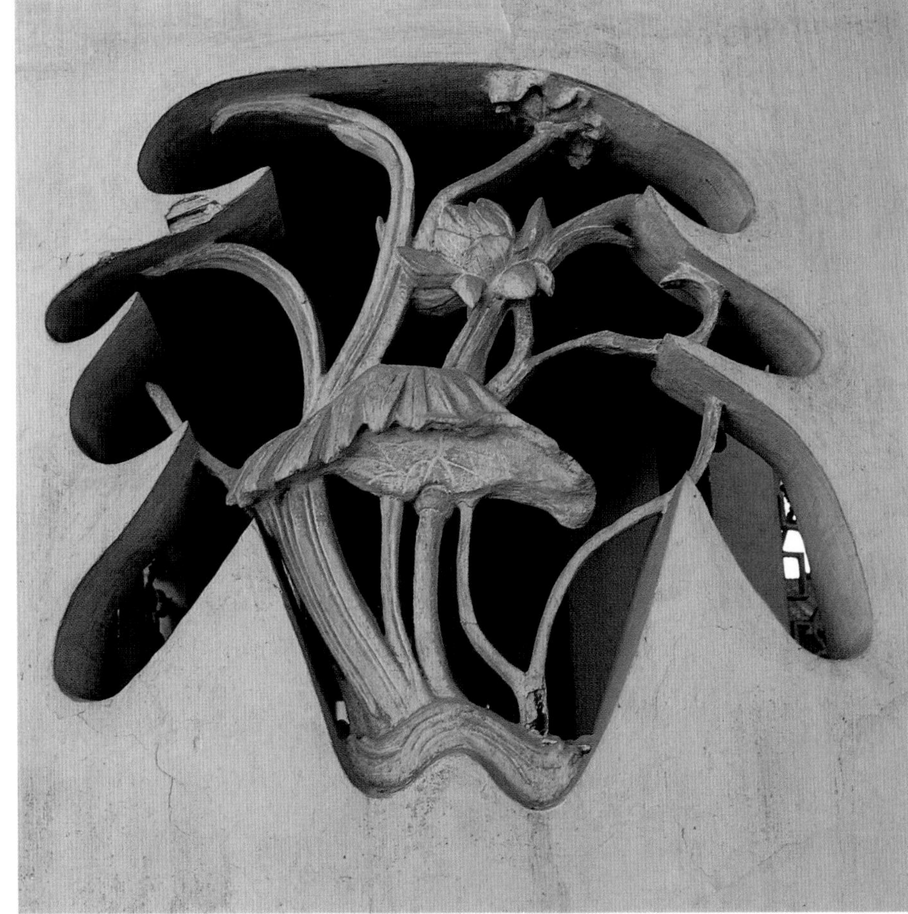

△ Suzhou, Jiangsu, tracery window

◁ Suzhou, Jiangsu, tracery window

◁ Suzhou, Jiangsu, tracery window

▷ Suzhou, Jiangsu, tracery window

▽ Nanjing, Jiangsu, Mochou Lake, moongate

◁ Various pavilion plans

Key
1 Zhuo Zhen Yuan, Luyi Ting. 2 Sizilin, Shuangxiang Xian Hall. 3 Wu Home, Ban Ting. 4 Zhuo Zhen Yuan, Xiuqi Ting. 6 Xi Yuan, Ban Ting. 7 Chang Lang Ting, Bei Ting. 8 Cheng Home, Ban Ting. 9 Sizilin Ban Ting. 10 Lu Home, Ban Ting. 11 Yi Yuan, Xiao Cang Lang. 12 Xi Yuan, Huxin Ting. 13 Liu Yuan, Zhile Ting. 14 Huangxiu Shan Zhuang, Haitang Ting. 15 Zhuo Zhen Yuan, Taying Ting. 16 Xiao Yuan, Octagon Ting. 17 Zuo Zhen Yuan, Li Ting. 18 Zhao Home, Ban Ting. 19 Zhuo Zhen Yuan, fan-shaped Ting. 20 Tian Ping Shan, Biayun Ting

most beautiful. To avoid monotony, the ridge or plan of a wall is curved to evoke a dynamic feeling.

The above elements of the garden are connected by covered verandahs. Obviously, the function of a verandah is to connect two buildings for sheltered circulation. A verandah can be used as a gallery, against a wall to divide two separate courtyards. The verandahs on both sides of the wall become what is called a double verandah, and the wall between them can be pierced with tracery windows to unite the two spaces visually. Sometimes a verandah is built over water on stilts, looking very much like a covered bridge. In some gardens, tablets were encased in the wall, and the corridor becomes a gallery. The tablets recorded pleasurable moments spent in the garden, and extemporaneous feelings in verse as mementos for later periods. Thus the elegance of the garden is enhanced.

Jicheng especially liked the winding verandah. He said:

> It is excellent when long and winding, ancient verandahs turn in right angles. My verandahs were in zigzag form, following the shape and slope of the site. Sometimes it will bend on the way up a hill, reach an edge of a pool, pass through flowerbeds, and cross valleys, twisting and seemingly there is no end. . .[29]

Although this verandah was built for circulation, it was not intended to reach its destination in a hurry. One could read the tablets, and watch scenery. The main purpose was to stroll leisurely and to while away time.

Another element in a Chinese garden is rockery. The success or failure of a garden usually hinges on the placement and form of a rockery. A rockery may serve as a central theme of a courtyard, where it is placed on a pedestal, in a pond, or cemented together to form caves and peaks. One kind of rockery is made from lake rock, quarried from a small island in Taihu Lake near Suzhou. This limestone, after years of washing and scouring underwater to remove the soft spots, features grotesque criss-crossed lines and furrows. When placed in front of a hall outside a window, or into a man-made hill, the transition from artifact to nature takes place and is unique in the world. Jicheng wrote:

> It is at its best while top heavy for its rugged, craggy form. Rock should be upright, and avoid placing it in the centre of a space. The best way is to scatter them.[30]

The good rock is grotesque, spare and porous. This kind of rock features abstract outlines, and positive and negative volumes of yin and yang.

Another kind of rock, yellow rock, was used mainly to pile hills, but its form is different from lake rock. It is not spare or porous, but a grotesque hill can be heaped.

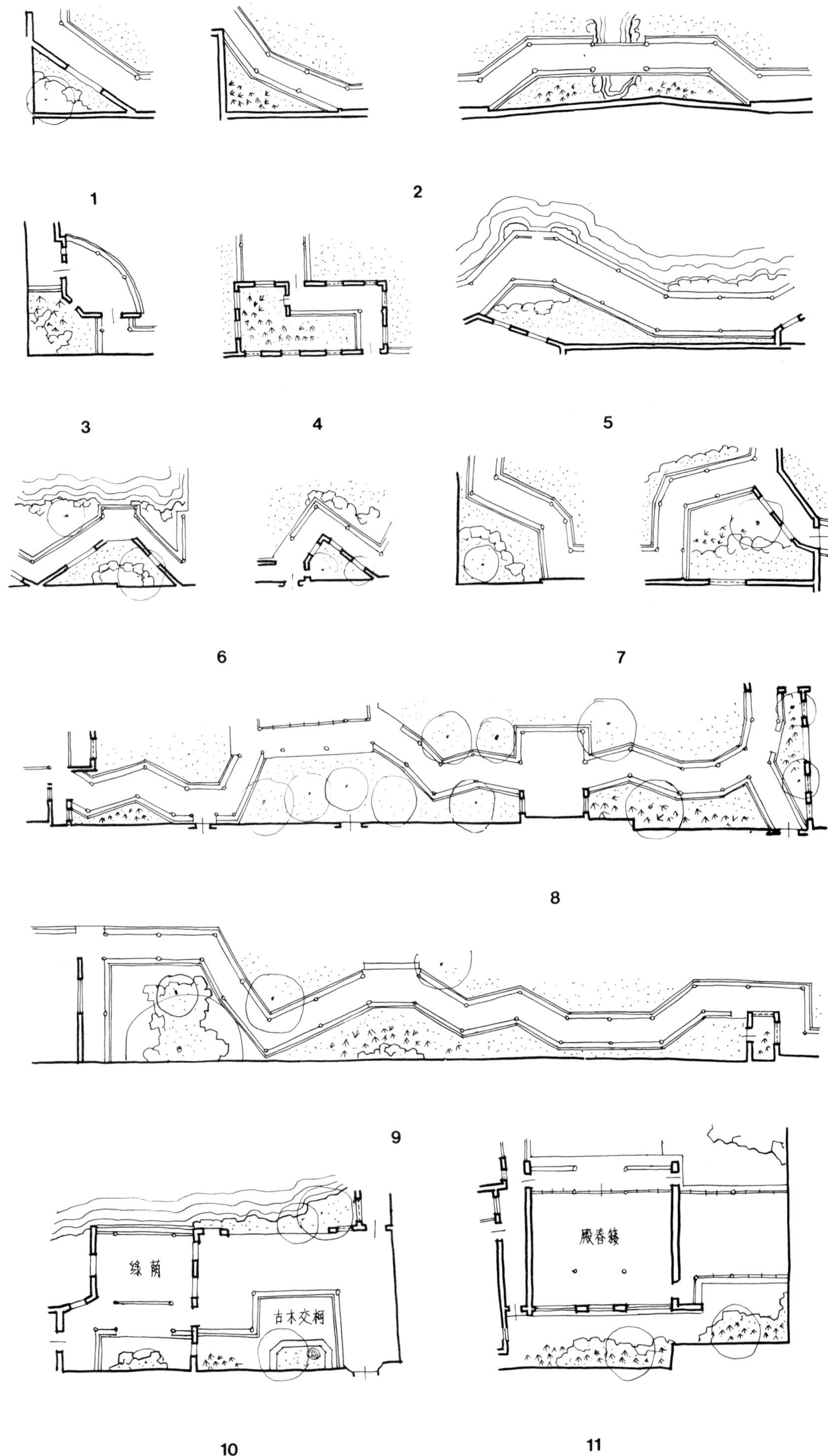

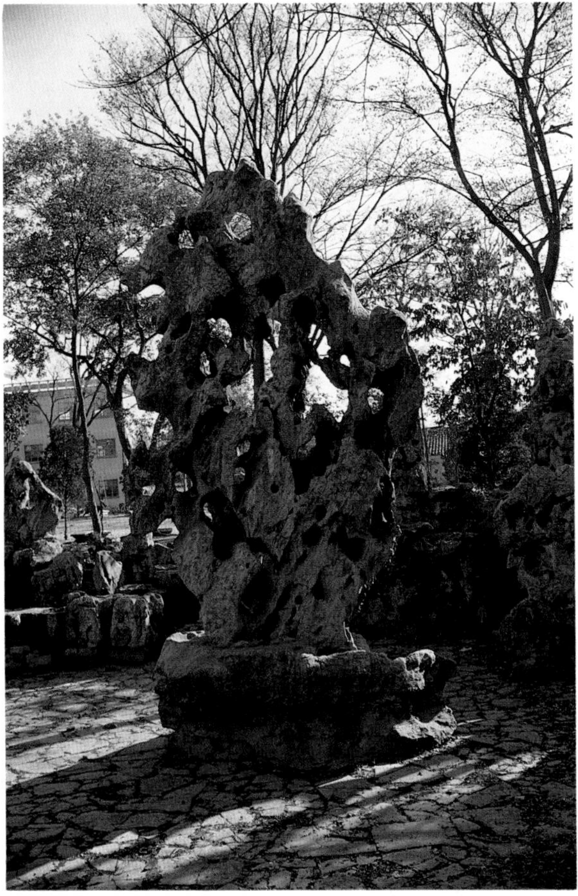

△ Suzhou, Jiangsu, Ruiyun Peak

▽ Suzhou, Jiangsu, Ou Yuan, yellow stone rockery

▷ Suzhou, Jiangsu, Liu Yuan dragon wall

◁ Various verandah plans

Key
1 Yang Home. 2 Liu Yuan. 3 Siziling. 4 Canglang Ting. 5 Zhuozheng Yuan. 6 Chang Yuan. 7 Liu Yuan. 8 He Yuan. 9 Liu Yuan. 10 Liu Yuan. 11 Wangshi.

Both lake rock and yellow rock can be used to pile a hill representing the hills in a landscape painting. In a painting, the hills are made for dwelling, for viewing and for wandering. The hill for viewing is a peak of perilous aspect and difficult of access. The 'hill' in a garden is similiar, so Jicheng said:

> While piling a hill, the grotesque concept produces a grotesque hill, the lofty idea produces lofty hills, a broad idea broad hills, a profound idea profound hills, primitive simplistic ideas produce primitive, simplistic hills, mediocre, vulgar ideas produce mediocre vulgar hills.[31]

However, a false hill is not a real hill. It only tries to help one to recall and visualize the real one, and to develop the imagination of the beholder. Some practices use rock to imitate animal or human figures. The more it resembles the real thing, the lower and more vulgar the quality and taste.

The natural landscape is marked by collections of water, namely a large water body, rivers, small streams, creeks, torrents and water falls. In the private garden, a large body of water is not possible but a pond is a must. Water is the complement of rock, so the saying goes: 'rock makes one feel primitive, water makes one feel remoteness.' Remoteness is an artistic feeling one gains from the presence of water. A broad body of water is connected with small winding streams, which meander among the pavilions and terraces. Set off by trees and bushes, the water cannot be viewed at a glance.

The following are the common practices of managing water:

Set off and twisting: the employment of trees, bushes, rocks, boulders, banks and buildings to create irregular, complicated banks. Water pavilions and verandahs are built over the water, as if the water was flowing out from under the buildings, or the use of protruding rocks combined with plants and willow trees to hide the bank, giving an illusion of a boundless body of water. The twisting of the bank, the small creek, and the pond edge is intended to break the monotonous borderline. Queer rocks, slender clusters of bamboos, and vines are used to cover the borderline. Some gardens use lake rock or yellow stone as banks to give a wild, natural feeling.

Definition: to define a large body of water and divide it into smaller areas, a bridge is built across narrow channels, or causeways are used as stepping stones to connect several smaller ponds and so enhance the depth of the garden.

Reflections made from a pool can enlarge the dimension of a garden visually. South of the Yantze River valleys, duck weed, lilies, goldfish and Manderin ducks in a body of water can create special effects.

SCENERY AND TRACK

Gardens differ in size and shape. The larger garden is naturally divided into more courtyards, and each courtyard has its particular theme and character in order to create a particular feeling of place, according to the idea of the master. For instance, in Liu Yuan (Lingering Here Garden), Suzhou, the Yifeng Xuan courtyard employed Guanyun rockery as the theme. The dynamic movement of the rockery contrasts sharply with the reposing horizontal lines of the eaves and railings. In Zhuozheng Yuan Garden, the Loquat Courtyard features loquat trees, and the pavement uses loquat leaf patterns.

Some gardens used historical tales to identify a courtyard. In the Siziling Garden (Lion's Garden), the idea of Li Xue Tang Courtyard was to encourage diligent study and respect for the teacher. According to the tale, one day a student sought instruction from his teacher on a snowy day, but he found his teacher was taking a nap. Instead of turning back or waking him up, the student stood reverently in the courtyard and in the open, waiting until the teacher awoke.

Because the courtyards are interconnected, they create a fabric of spaces. Each has a special meaning, each is different in size and in arrangement. The character is irregular, and there is no climax, no axis, and no monumentality. As one enters the small entry leading to a garden and walks into a particular space, although it is usually small in scale and wrapped around with winding verandahs, the feeling gained is always the same: repose, harmony, serenity and elegance.

From beginning to end, the activities of a person are subjected to the spatial form and character of the courtyard in continuity. Unlike the sequence of Western gardens, the path the person follows is fixed or always the same. In a Chinese garden, one can choose one's own route at will, strolling along the twisting path. Sometimes it appears that the walker reaches the end of a path, but with a sudden turn there is another path or another open space.

There is always something unexpected to see which will surprise the visitor. Recurring surprises are encountered in the garden along the twisting, recurring paths as if there is never an end. There is always the feeling that one is not able to cover all the garden, or to see every part of it. There is always a feeling of endlessness, always a lingering interest, and always something left for another day.

Evidently, to cover the whole garden in a single day was not the purpose. Although it is the same place with the same scenery, if one took a different path and viewed the elements from different angles, the scenery would be different. In addition, the experience gained

◁ Suzhou, Jiangsu, Huang Xiu Shan Zhuang Villa, rockery and bridge

◁ Nanjing, Jiangsu, Mochou Lake, water courtyard

differs from person to person. Most interestingly, even if one goes back to the same location from a different direction, it is as if one is experiencing an entirely new scenery.

This is the circumstance that is usually associated with Chinese gardens, and is of course most interesting. Although it is a small garden, it is of unlimited space. It is possible to enjoy oneself so much, and linger on and on. As mentioned before, it was not the intention of the designer to guide the visitor along a fixed, planned line, but rather to create an illusion through the use of variegated landscape in a small area.

EXAMPLES

When people speak of Chinese gardens, they mean the gardens designed and built in the Yangtze River style of the South among which the Suzhou, Nanjing, Wuzi and Yangzhou gardens enjoy the highest distinction and embody all the characteristics of Chinese landscape art.

NANJING, ZHANG YUAN

This garden is located in the southern part of Nanjing and was founded in the early Ming Dynasty. During the Qing Dynasty, Emperor Qianlong, in one of his southern tours, visited this garden and named it Zhangyuan. It was famous for its rockery, but due to numerous wars, most of the rockery has moved to other gardens. Only recently, Liu Dengzeng restored it to the splendour of the past.

As one enters through the small garden entrance at the south, and through another small opening, a rock is seen standing freely in the middle of a small court and serves as a vista. After the visitor reaches the moongate, not only has he had a glimpse inside the doorway, but was also enchanted by the bamboo shadow 'painted' on the whitewashed wall, the meandering covered verandah, and rockery. One sees the main hall in the midst of the garden. The covered porch faces south and overlooks a small pond. The rockery stands in the south, and forms a grotto to the north. Thus, one always sees the shaded part and observes the tiny waterfall falling down over the rocks to the pool below. The moist atmosphere and water encourage the growing of moss which hangs from the rocks above. The small grotto caved-in to symbolize the yin thus provides a contrast of positive and negative, of rough and smooth and of still, solid rock and flowing water. Also in the grotto are rocks resembling stalactites and stalagmites and false mountains. This rockery forms a screen so that the noise from the street beyond cannot be heard in the garden, but the sound of dripping water can still be heard. In the main hall, this management of sound creates a very quiet atmosphere. There are pines

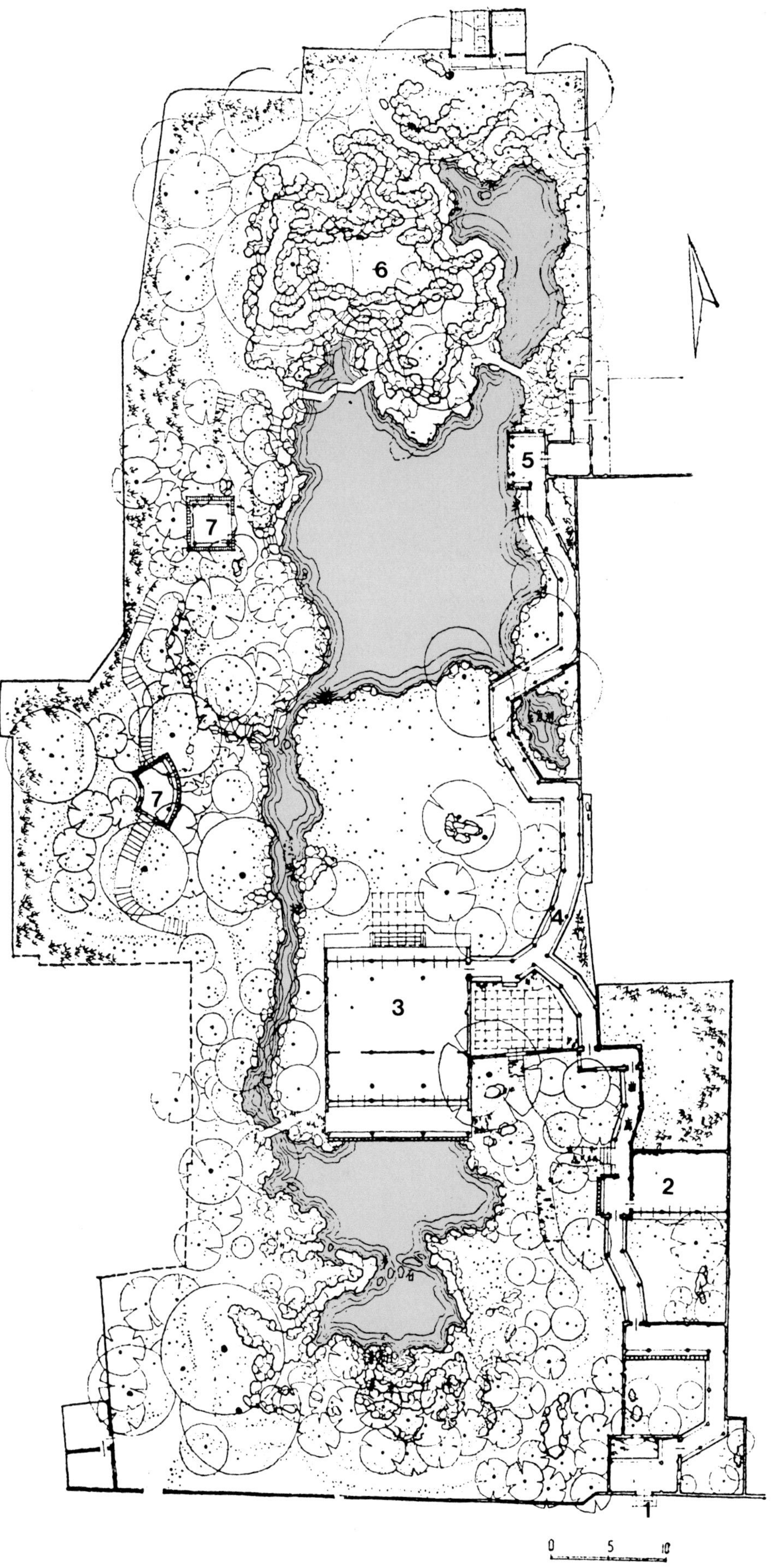

▷ Nanjing, Jiangsu, Zhang Yuan, plan

Key
1 Entrance. 2 Small den. 3 Main hall and water pavilion. 4 Verandah. 5 Water pavilion. 6 False hill. 7 Pavilion.

▽ Nanjing, Jiangsu, Zhang Yuan, moongate tracery window and bamboo

△ Nanjing, Jiangsu, Zhang Yuan, gateway and rockery

△ Nanjing, Jiangsu, Zhang Yuan, false hill

◁ Nanjing, Jiangsu, Zhang Yuan, water pavilion and bridge

△ Nanjing, Jiangsu, Zhang Yuan, rockery and creeper, a natural painting

◁ Nanjing, Jiangsu, Zhang Yuan, verandah

△ Nanjing, Jiangsu, Zhang Yuan, eave of verandah

and small maple trees on top of the false mountain to make it look more like an element of a Shan Shui painting.

The north side of the main hall faces a lawn and beyond it is a nearly-square shaped pond. A lawn is unusual in Chinese gardens, but here it resembles the scenery of the countryside. The edge of the pond is left in its natural condition; with the earth sloping down to the water surface and weeping willows nearby, it does give a feeling of the countryside. On one side of the pond is a winding covered verandah which leads to a small water pavilion, and on the other side is a small creek connecting this pond with the pool in the southern part of the main hall.

There are all kinds of flowers and blossoms near the covered verandah and inside the courtyard. In spring there are peach blossoms, begonias, cherry and maple in bright red colours, which provide a charming and pleasant sight for all visitors.

△ Wuxi, Jiangsu, Jichang Yuan, Huishan

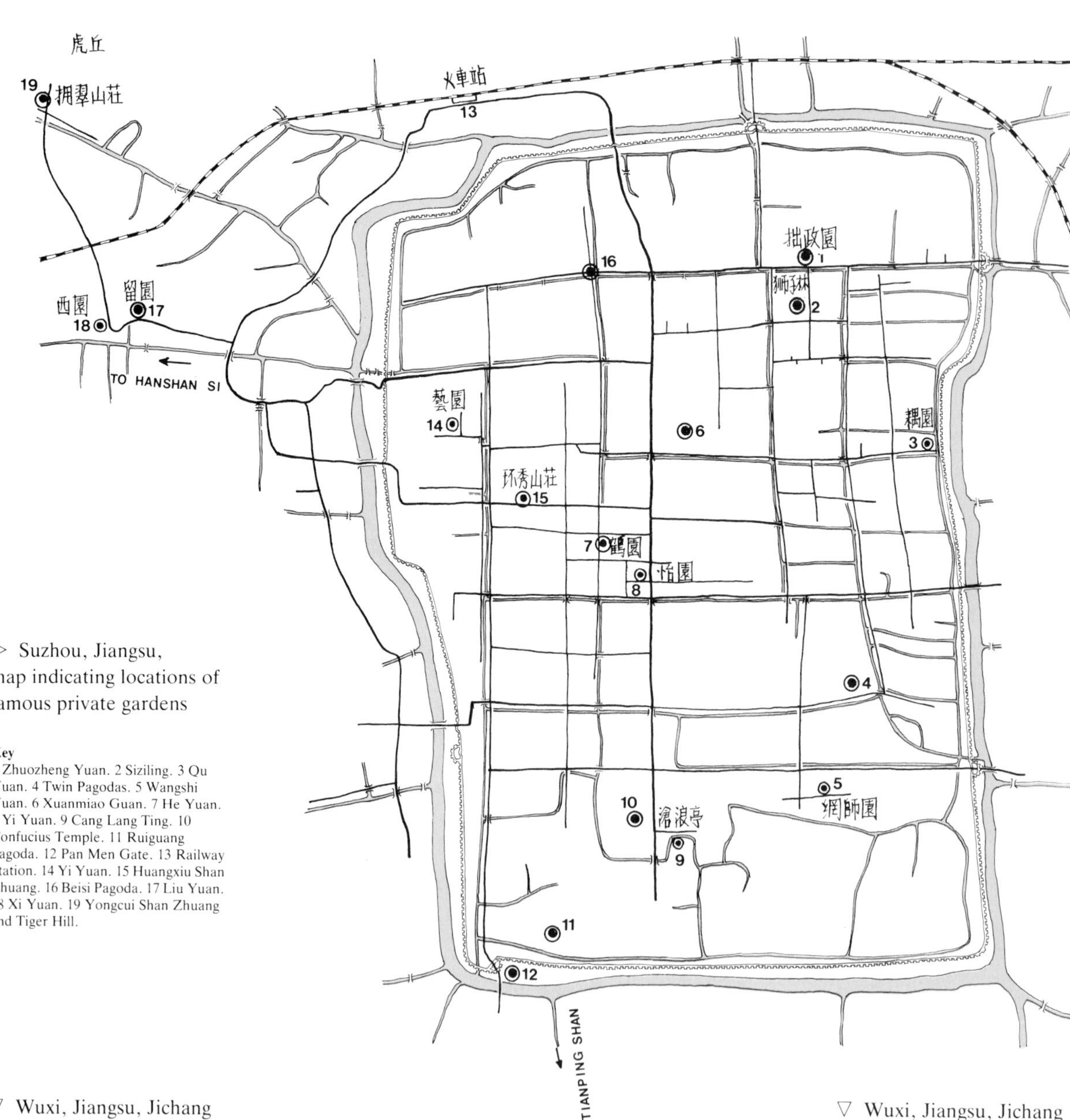

▷ Suzhou, Jiangsu, map indicating locations of famous private gardens

Key
1 Zhuozheng Yuan. 2 Siziling. 3 Qu Yuan. 4 Twin Pagodas. 5 Wangshi Yuan. 6 Xuanmiao Guan. 7 He Yuan. 8 Yi Yuan. 9 Cang Lang Ting. 10 Confucius Temple. 11 Ruiguang Pagoda. 12 Pan Men Gate. 13 Railway Station. 14 Yi Yuan. 15 Huangxiu Shan Zhuang. 16 Beisi Pagoda. 17 Liu Yuan. 18 Xi Yuan. 19 Yongcui Shan Zhuang and Tiger Hill.

▽ Wuxi, Jiangsu, Jichang Yuan, winding verandah

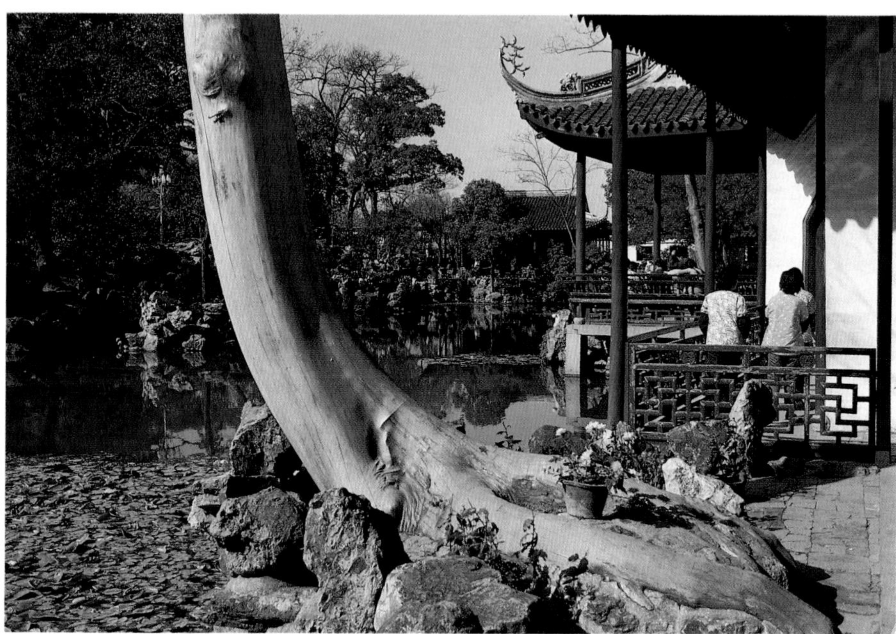

▽ Wuxi, Jiangsu, Jichang Yuan, water pavilion

Key
1 Entrance. 2 Wuzhuyouju Pavilion. 3 Biba Yuan and Linglong Hall. 4 Yuanxiang Tang. 5 Xuexiang Yunwei Ting. 6 Yiyu Den. 7 Xiao Cang Lang. 8 Xiaofeihong Bridge. 9 Xiangzhou House Boat. 10 Jianshan Lou. 11 Yulan Tang. 12 Yilang Pavilion. 13 Yushuitongzue Pavilion. 14 36 Yuanyang Hall (36 Mandarin Ducks Hall). 15 Daoying Lou. 16 Covered verandah. 17 Hefeng Simian Pavilion. 18 Middle Yuan. 19 West Yuan.

△ Suzhou, Jiangsu, Zhouzheng Yuan Garden, plan

WUXI, THE JICHANG YUAN

Both Wuxi and Suzhou are close to Taihu Lake. Many gardens were built near the lake, one of which is the famous Jichang Yuan located to the east of Wuxi under Huishan Hill. Jichang Yuan is dated to the early 16th century in the Ming Dynasty. During the Qing Dynasty, Emperor Kangxi and Qianlong visited this garden. The latter was inspired by the beauty of the garden and built Xiequ Yuan (the Garden of Harmonious Interest) in Yihe Yuan in Beijing. Jichang Yuan is visually connected to Huishan Hill and combined into a complex.

Jichang Yuan was famous for its old trees and rockery, but because of the negligence of the Qing Dynasty, the old trees withered, and the pool dried up. It has been repaired recently, but not restored to the splendour of the past. On entering the garden and turning to the right, there is a rockery which served as a screen. Wandering through the rock and turning back, one sees a big pool under shaded towering trees, the main part of the garden. It is just like other gardens in the south, where the main part is always a pool surrounded by a covered verandah and rockery. Planted in the pool are yellow lilies. On the east bank and at the end of the verandah is a water pavilion. Leaning on the balustrade, one watches the fish swimming idly beneath. Looking across the pond, one sees large trees on top of yellow rocks at the narrowest part of the pool. At the other side of this rock, there is a small creek formed by rock. It is an artifice: when the water runs down over the rocks, one can hear an octave of musical notes from the running brook while viewing the pagoda on top of Huishan as borrowed scenery. At the foot of Huishan is a group of buildings which climb up the hill, and are built in accordance with the steep site. Under this group is a small court with a deep pool. This is a good example of utilizing the form of the site.

SUZHOU

a. Zhuozheng Yuan (The Garden of a Humble Administrator)

Zhouzheng Yuan was first begun in the Ming Dynasty on the site of a temple in Suzhou. In the Qing Dynasty, the Manchu generals made it the headquarters of the Army of Eight Banners, so it was often called the Manchu Garden. The existing garden was built in the early 16th century (1506-21). Today, it combines the East Garden, the Middle Garden (i.e. Zhuozheng Yuan) and the West Garden into one. It is a typical Chinese garden, and is considered by most scholars to be the most beautiful garden in present-day China.

◁ Suzhou, Jiangsu, Zhouzheng Yuan Garden, Yuan Xiang Tang, door sashes

△ Suzhou, Jiangsu, Zhouzheng Yuan Garden, pavilion of four moongates

▽ Suzhou, Jiangsu, Zhouzheng Yuan Garden, Yuan Xiang Tang, main hall

▷ Suzhou, Jiangsu, Zhouzheng Yuan Garden, borrowed view

The best part of this garden is the middle portion. One third of the middle portion is water, a characteristic which is typical of classical gardens. It is described as bright and beautiful hills and water, with profuse trees and an extensive pool, the natural landscape embodying the style of the water country of the south part of the Yantze District. As one enters through the garden opening, one immediately notices the silhouette of the Beisi Pagoda looming above the weeping willow trees on the bank of the lotus pond, the winding stone bridge and the pebble-paved narrow path. To the right of this path is a little pavilion with four round openings. Looking out of the openings, one sees different views of bamboo, the pool, and old and grotesquely-shaped trees. As one follows the winding path with the pool to the right and a small hill to the left, one passes into a procession of colourful flowers. One finally reaches the main hall, the Yuan Xiang Tang (Hall of Far-off Fragrance), which stands almost in the middle of this garden. To the north of the hall is a spacious terrace facing the lotus pond.

Here it is evident that the planning of a Chinese garden usually placed a pond in the middle and the main hall at the south end rather than at the north end of the pond. Thus, during most seasons the scholar or the master could sit here with his guests while looking toward the lotuses or red fish swimming in the pond

and reciting poems, or composing parallel couplets phrases, or playing chess, or doing nothing – just sipping rice wine and listening to the pattering of raindrops on the umbrella-like dry leaves of the decayed lotus.There is a pavilion which is named: 'To retain the decayed leaves of lotus for listening to the pattering of raindrops.' It is romantic as well as melancholic.

In almost every private garden, water dominates the scene. In this garden, the central art is mainly of water, and by careful design it is broken up by bridges into many small areas. This exemplifies one of the principles of garden planning, which is 'divide and multiply'. In Zhuozheng Yuan, the water is divided into several small interconnecting pools. In fact it is like a water labyrinth, where the water flows over rocks, under bridges, or under a pavilion. The darkened shadows contrast with the bright water, and the reflections of the pavilions, old trees and shrubs along the shore make the landscape lively in a unique way.

Chinese scholars love landscapes. Traditional Chinese scroll paintings mostly represent mountains obscured by mists. Men sit in the mountains enjoying the view or meditating on the beauty of nature, either seated in boats, on rocks, or from the balconies of a garden building.

Another feature of gardens is the great care which was taken to plant flowers so that there should be some perfumed blooming flowers during every month and every season of the year. The most cherished flowers are plum bossoms and begonia for winter and early spring, peony and wisteria for spring, lotus and jasmine for summer and begonia, laurel and chrysanthemum for autumn. No garden was complete without bamboo, pine, juniper and cedar, because they are evergreens and symbolize longevity, lofty ideas and everlasting friendship.

The terrace of the pavilion juts out over the lotus pond, and across a zigzag stone bridge leading to the north embankment is a small pavilion, the Xue Xiang Yun Wei Ting (the Fragrant Snow and Azure Cloud Pavilion). In China almost every hall or pavilion has a name attached to it. For example, a pavilion set in a bamboo grove may be named 'Bamboo Grove'. Here the gazebo served as a place to view the big hall, or conversely, provided a scenic view from the main hall.

◁ Suzhou, Jiangsu, Zhouzheng Yuan Garden, bird's-eye view of central part

To the west of this big hall, through a winding covered verandah, one suddenly discovers an open space with water. A small, delicately carved, wood covered bridge, the Xiao Fei Hong (little Flying Rainbow Bridge), hovers over the narrow pond and through the pillars of the bridge one sees a small pavilion. Next to it is a stone boat, which was named the Xiangzhou (Fragrant Isle). It is one form of garden architecture which is built in the manner of a boat. In this case, it is an ornate house which looks like the raised deck of a big boat.

From the Xiao Chan Lang Pavilion (Little Surge Wave Pavilion), one sees through the covered bridge towards the He Feng Si Mien Ting (Lotus Breeze Pavilion) with the Jianshan Ting (Mountain View Pavilion) as its background. The jutting rocks and the flat water surface compose a tranquil environment.

▷ Suzhou, Jiangsu, Zhouzheng Yuan Garden, Xiao Fei Hong Bridge

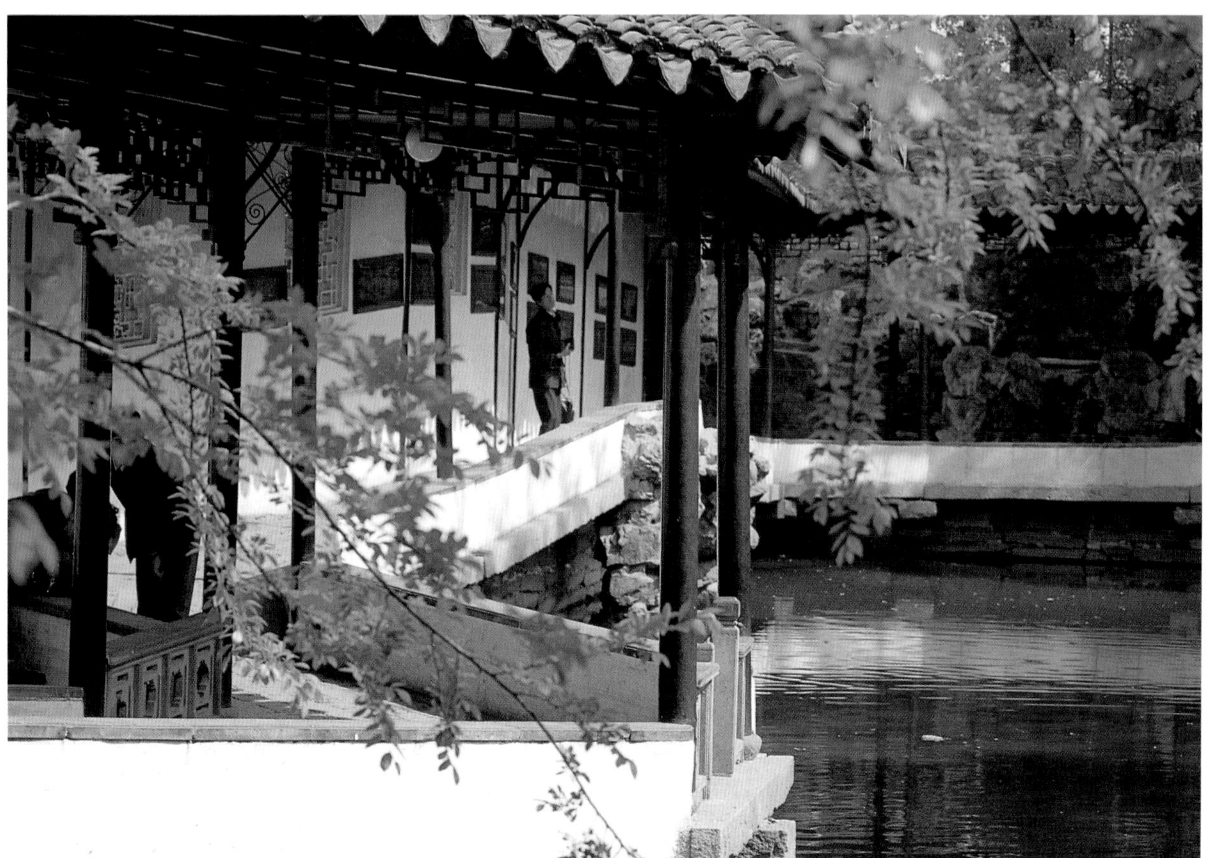

▽ Suzhou, Jiangsu, Zhouzheng Yuan Garden, covered verandah

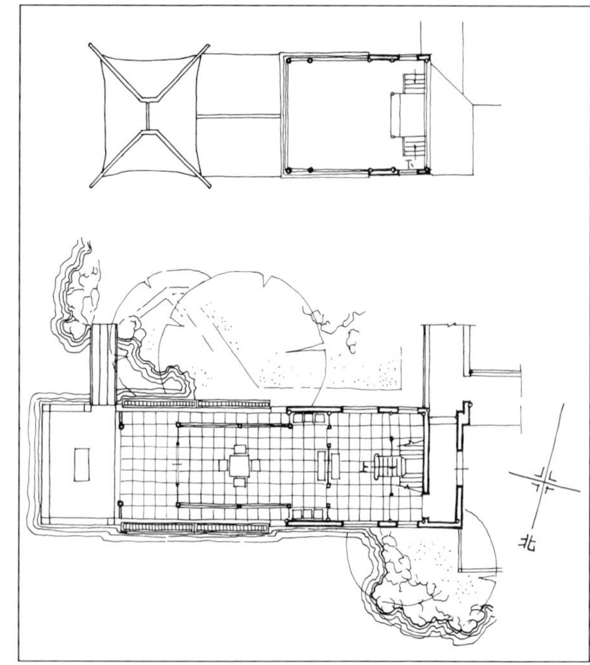

△ Suzhou, Jiangsu, Zhouzheng Yuan Garden, Xiang Zhou House Boat

▽ Suzhou, Jiangsu, Zhouzheng Yuan Garden, bridge and pavilion

Passing through the boat house, one goes along a dark and narrow covered verandah, through an octagonal doorway to find another small pavilion, the Yilian Pavilion (Pavilion For Two), crowning the top of a small mount. Here one comes to another enclosed water court, a narrow space. At the right of this space is a covered verandah. If one follows the verandah, one will find at the other end of the narrow water court another pavilion named Bai Wen Yi Shen Zhi Zhai (Hall with Mementos of Wen and Shen). Wen Zhengming was a famous painter, and the designer of this garden. The reflection of this pavilion in the water, the swinging willow branches and the zigzag covered verandah make it a serene space, where one is bound to gradually acquire a peaceful mind.

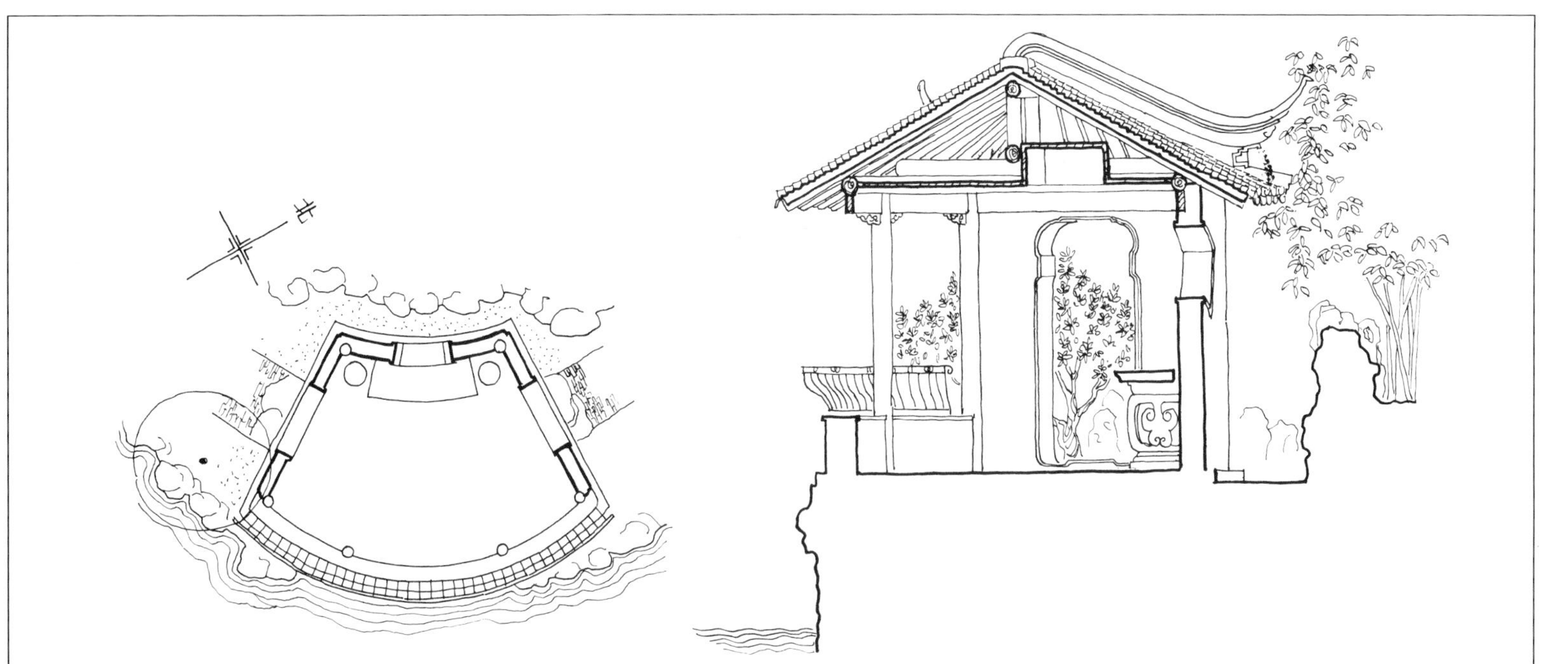

▷ Suzhou, Jiangsu, Zhouzheng Yuan Garden, fan-shaped pavilion

◁ Suzhou, Jiangsu, Zhouzheng Yuan Garden, detail of railing

▷ Suzhou, Jiangsu, Zhouzheng Yuan Garden, 36 Yuan Yang Hall

▷ Suzhou, Jiangsu, Wangshi Yuan, a den

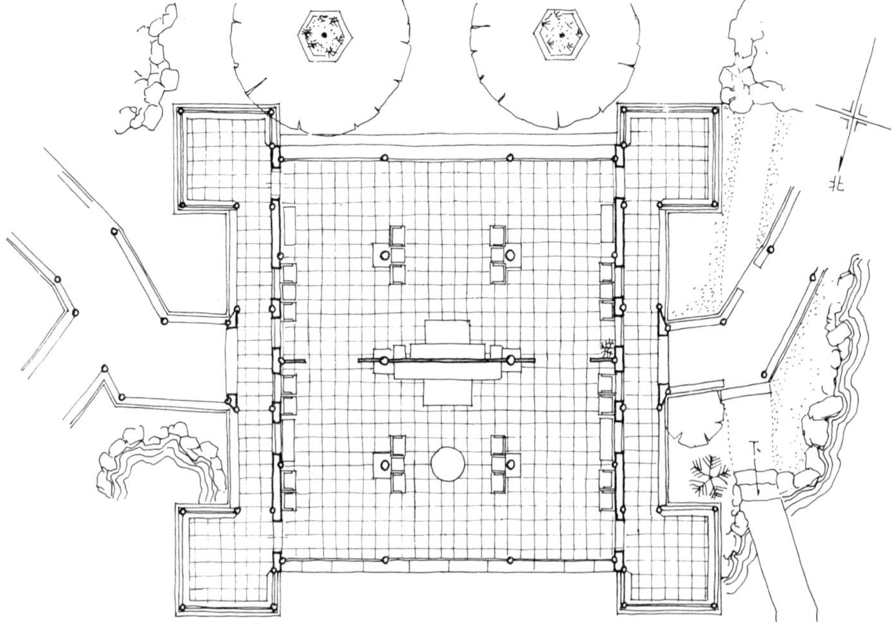

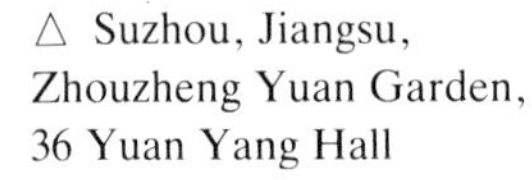

△ Suzhou, Jiangsu, Zhouzheng Yuan Garden, 36 Yuan Yang Hall

◁ Suzhou, Jiangsu, Zhouzheng Yuan Garden, fan-shaped pavilion

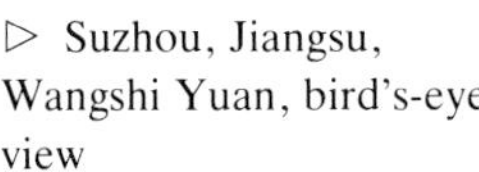

▷ Suzhou, Jiangsu, Wangshi Yuan, bird's-eye view

Opposite this verandah and facing the doorway is a fan-shaped pavilion, an unique plan shape. The name is Yu Shui Tong Zuo Xuan (With Whom I Sit Den). It was named after the poem: 'With whom I sit, the bright moon, the cool breeze and mine own'.

In the covered verandah there are tablets and stelae encased in the wall. As one wanders under the roof and casually reads the poems and inscriptions in fine calligraphy on the wall, these tablets not only serve as decorative motif but tell the history of the garden. They help one to understand why and how this garden was built. The tablets also record pleasurable moments spent in the garden; it is really an uplifting moment for those with a mind to read, and it will certainly add to the new visitor's delight. The walls of this verandah are pierced with attractive tracery windows through which one can see the plants and scenery of the neighbouring spaces.

Looking out from this narrow space, one at once notices the view of another large pavilion, the Sanshiliu Yuanyang Hall (the Thirty-six Mandarin Duck Hall). During the old days, there were colourful Mandarin ducks swimming near and under this pavilion in pairs as the ducks are really love birds. The plan of this pavilion is also of this nature, having a symmetrical plan with a screen in the middle dividing it into two equal parts, one looking to the north and the other to the south. Thus, during the summer months, the scholar and his household would stay in the north room, which is usually cooler, looking towards the lotus and enjoying their fragrance.

b. **Wangshi Yuan (The Garden of the Master of Nets)**
The area of this garden covers only some 5,000 square metres. It is one of the loveliest gardens in this city. Like every other garden in Suzhou, the middle part of this garden is a small pool with pavilions, halls, and covered verandahs around it. The most remarkable feature of this garden is that it is small, but it still has all the beauty and character of a traditional garden.

The east part was the residence and the garden was placed to the west. As the visitor enters the main entrance, passes through several halls, and goes through a narrow doorway, he finds himself in a hall called the Xiao Shan Cong Gui Xuan (Den of Small Hill and Laurel Grove). It is located among laurel trees and faces the little pool to the north. The densely planted evergreens and rockery form a natural screen for the hall, and give privacy to this secluded place. Through the leaves, over the rockery, and across the water surface, one can see the towering white bark pine and yellow stone piles. From this hall, after turning back to the east side of the pool and wandering on the narrow path of pebble stone, the visitor finds

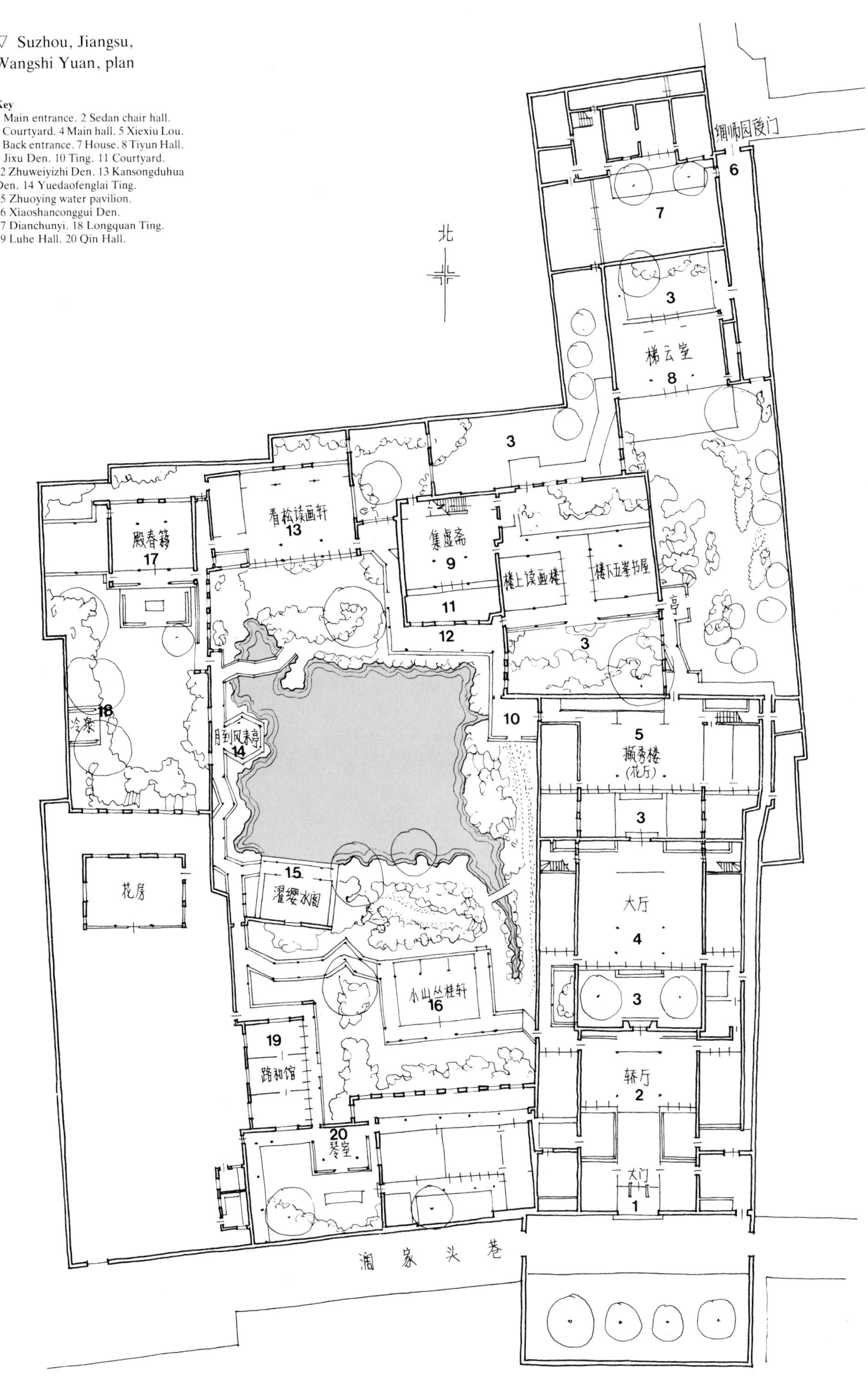

▽ Suzhou, Jiangsu, Wangshi Yuan, plan

Key
1 Main entrance. 2 Sedan chair hall. 3 Courtyard. 4 Main hall. 5 Xiexiu Lou. 6 Back entrance. 7 House. 8 Tiyun Hall. 9 Jixu Den. 10 Ting. 11 Courtyard. 12 Zhuweiyizhi Den. 13 Kansongduhua Den. 14 Yuedaofenglai Ting. 15 Zhuoying water pavilion. 16 Xiaoshanconggui Den. 17 Dianchunyi. 18 Longquan Ting. 19 Luhe Hall. 20 Qin Hall.

△ Suzhou, Jiangsu, Wangshi Yuan, central part

△ Suzhou, Jiangsu, Wangshi Yuan, water pavilion and picture openings

▽ Suzhou, Jiangsu, Wangshi Yuan, pool and surrounding buildings

◁ Suzhou, Jiangsu, Wangshi Yuan, verandah and pavilion

◁ Suzhou, Jiangsu, Wangshi Yuan, pavilion and pool

△ Suzhou, Jiangsu, Wangshi Yuan, Dian Chun Yi Den

▷ Suzhou, Jiangsu, Wangshi Yuan, picture window and living picture

▽ Suzhou, Jiangsu, Wangshi Yuan, picture window and living picture

▽ Suzhou, Jiangsu, Wangshi Yuan, tablet inside the den

himself alongside a high whitewashed fence to his right with the pool to the left. The high wall compels one to look towards the centre of this garden as well as at the gallery and pavilion situated opposite the hall. In the gallery, one is aware of different forms of windows. Rectangular, octagonal and circular at openings all face different directions, and each has justified itself as a picture window. One faces the slender bamboo cluster, a second faces the pine tree nearby, and over the balcony another has a view to the middle of the pool and faraway pavilion. Although there are many kinds of window frames in the gallery, one does not feel that there is disorder. Coming out of the gallery one finds oneself amidst rocks and under giant trees.

Through the trunks, one again sees the main hall and a stage by the pool with a pavilion in the foreground, the Yue Dao Feng Lai Ting (Breeze and Moon Pavilion). It is a small pavilion with a wide spreading roof. The corner is bent up in a sharp curve, just like a bird poised for flight. The pavilion is built over the pool on stilts, facing east. On a fine autumn night, one hears the Chinese flute playing on the stage while looking towards the moon hanging above the trees and roofs, where the sapphire sky and roofline meet. The dark shadow cast by the buildings and foliage, and the serenity of the entire atmosphere makes one feel calm and enchanted.

Hidden at the back of the pavilion is a small doorway which leads to a secluded court in front of a study, which is named Dian Chun Yi (Peony Hall). Inside the study and opposite the entrance is a beautiful picture window, outside of which is a cluster of thin bamboo planted against a whitewashed wall. The frieze is painted with peony flowers too. The window is a picture frame, and the picture is the ever changing bamboo, a living picture. Picture windows like this are used extensively in Chinese gardens. For instance, a window in another hall has a very elaborately carved wooden frame. The rope-like detail is winding, and does not have an end. It symbolizes longevity and eternal life. The maple tree outside is beautiful to watch as it changes colour in autumn. Tablets, used to identify a hall, also evoke a philosophical response in the visitor. Here, the tablets in the den read 'Dian Chun Yi'; in spring there are peony flowers, but on other occasions they are on paintings.

Coming out of the court, the visitor once again passes through the covered verandah. Looking to the east, there is a two-storey building surrounding the pool – a rare case in a garden. The reason is obvious. As the site is so limited, what else could one do except build higher! In the olden days, the daughters of the family lived on the second floor. When there was a show on the stage, as the daughters were not permitted

△ Suzhou, Jiangsu, Liu Yuan, plan

Key
1 Main entrance. 2 Luyin Den. 3 Quxi Lou. 4 West Lou. 5 Xiao Peng Lai. 6 Mingse Lou. 7 Hangbi Shan Fang. 8 Dragon wall. 9 Wufeng Xian Hall. 10 Linquan Qishuo Hall. 11 Guanyun Peak. 12 Guanyun Lou. 13 He Suo.

to come down and sit among the male guests, they hid behind a screen or a bamboo curtain enjoying the show from above.

c. Liu Yuan (Lingering Here Garden)

Liu Yuan was built early in the Ming Dynasty (1522-66) and was used for many generations as a private home. At one time the garden belonged to the Liu family, and was named Liu Yuan. Today, the garden is open to the public as it is no longer a private home. The name has been changed to Liu – which means lingering here – a word phonotypically the same as the name of the family which formerly owned it.

Like Zhuozheng Yuan, the central portion of the garden is a pond, around which are halls, pavilions, terraces, arbors and bridges. The sequential experience of this garden, almost identical to that of other gardens, is at first restrained, building the visitor's anticipation with occasional surprises and culminating in final satisfaction. One first enters an inconspicuous door, and passes into a narrow covered passage which sometimes widens into a small court. At the end of this narrow, dark passage, the pond and the open landscape suddenly burst into view. One is surprised to see the exuberant foliage, flowers and the beautifully designed garden architecture under the bright sun and greyish-blue sky. Contrary to Western gardens, where it is easy to visualize the sequence of spaces as one moves from the gate to the garden, the Chinese gardens intentionally limit one's view to a small space at a time.

Subtle is the series of views and sensations provided by the approach from the entrance to the water area. The verandah is bent so that one sees first a narrow shaft of space focused on a small court and then one shifts to another open space. The space widens into a courtyard, and finally reaches the central portion which contains the pool. It is not a large body of water but through the design, and through contrast 'to see in the little the great', it fits into Blake's conception: 'to see the world in a grain of sand and heaven in a wild flower.' There is an endeavour to make small things appear large, and large things small. Through contrast of narrow corridors and open spaces, one feels that the open space is larger than its actual size.

From Luyin Xuan (Green Shadow Den) one's attention is naturally attracted by the pergola of wisteria built at the middle of the pool. The pergola is actually a bridge, and in springtime the dazzling light green leaves and purple flowers are exciting to see. To the left, one can also see the big terrace in front of Hanbi Shanfang (Green Hill Den) and Mingse Luo. As one moves into the water space on the bridge, the vista is

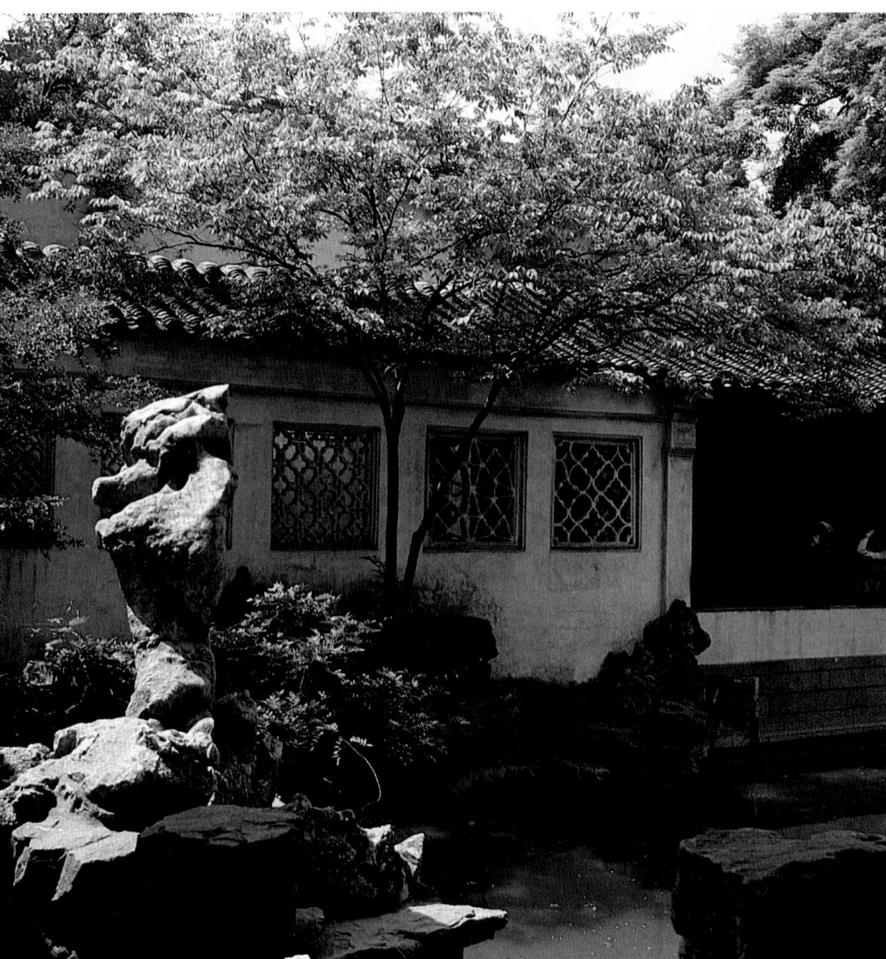

◁ Suzhou, Jiangsu, Liu Yuan, Luyin Den, the best place to appreciate the central part

▽ Suzhou, Jiangsu, Liu Yuan, Mingse Luo, Hanbi Shan Fang

▽ Suzhou, Jiangsu, Liu Yuan, Xiao Pen Lai pergola and bridge

△ Suzhou, Jiangsu, Liu Yuan, a winding bridge

▷ Suzhou, Jiangsu, Liu Yuan, Linquan Qishuo Hall, tracery doorway

▽ Suzhou, Jiangsu, Liu Yuan, Mingse Luo, Luyin Den and Quxi Luo

completely enclosed by the tall whitewashed walls so that there is no distraction from the street which surrounds the garden. One can catch a glimpse of the maples and gingko trees over the walls. When ascending the steps, the whole space is at the feet of the visitor.

The eye wanders through the trees and shrubs, finally reaching the pavilions, and once again comes back to the traceries on the wall. The total view is at one's command, and the harmony and unity of the whole work are remarkable. Here is an example, developed over time, of the full interplay of the many necessary elements of design-recession plans, penetration in depth, the meeting of the sky and the water, ascent and descent. . .

When crossing the pond, and passing a small doorway, one arrives at the largest hall of the garden, the Wufeng Xianguan (the Fairy Hall of Five Prominences). When the garden was in private use, the master and his household came out into the garden from a opening named Hesuo (Stock Gallery), which is located in a courtyard south of this big hall. In another big hall, the Linquan Qishuo, located to the east of the former hall, a giant monolithic stone was set up in the courtyard adjacent to it. In China a garden without a rock will not be complete. The rocks should appear

▷ Suzhou, Jiangsu, Liu Yuan, Guanyun Peak

▽ Suzhou, Jiangsu, Liu Yuan, Guanyun Peak, as seen from Linquan Qishuo, Hall

▽ Suzhou, Jiangsu, Liu Yuan, Linquan Qishuo Hall, window sashes

◁ Suzhou, Jiangsu, Liu Yuan, Linquan Qishuo Hall panels

△ Suzhou, Jiangsu, Liu Yuan, Linquan Qishuo Hall

natural, rather than artificial, and should give a picturesque feeling to the garden. The rockery inside the courtyard, which stands in a pool, is the tallest in Suzhou and so was named Guanyunfeng (Crown Cloud Peak). The rockery is a queer object, half natural and half mason crafted. In this case, it serves as the central motif of this courtyard; hence the main building in this courtyard is named the Guanyun Lou (Crown Cloud Lodge). The rock resembles contemporary sculpture by Henry Moore and Noguchi, who utilize the same abstract outlines, and positive (yang) and negative (yin) volumes and surfaces.

In the large halls the panels and doorways are exquisitely carved.

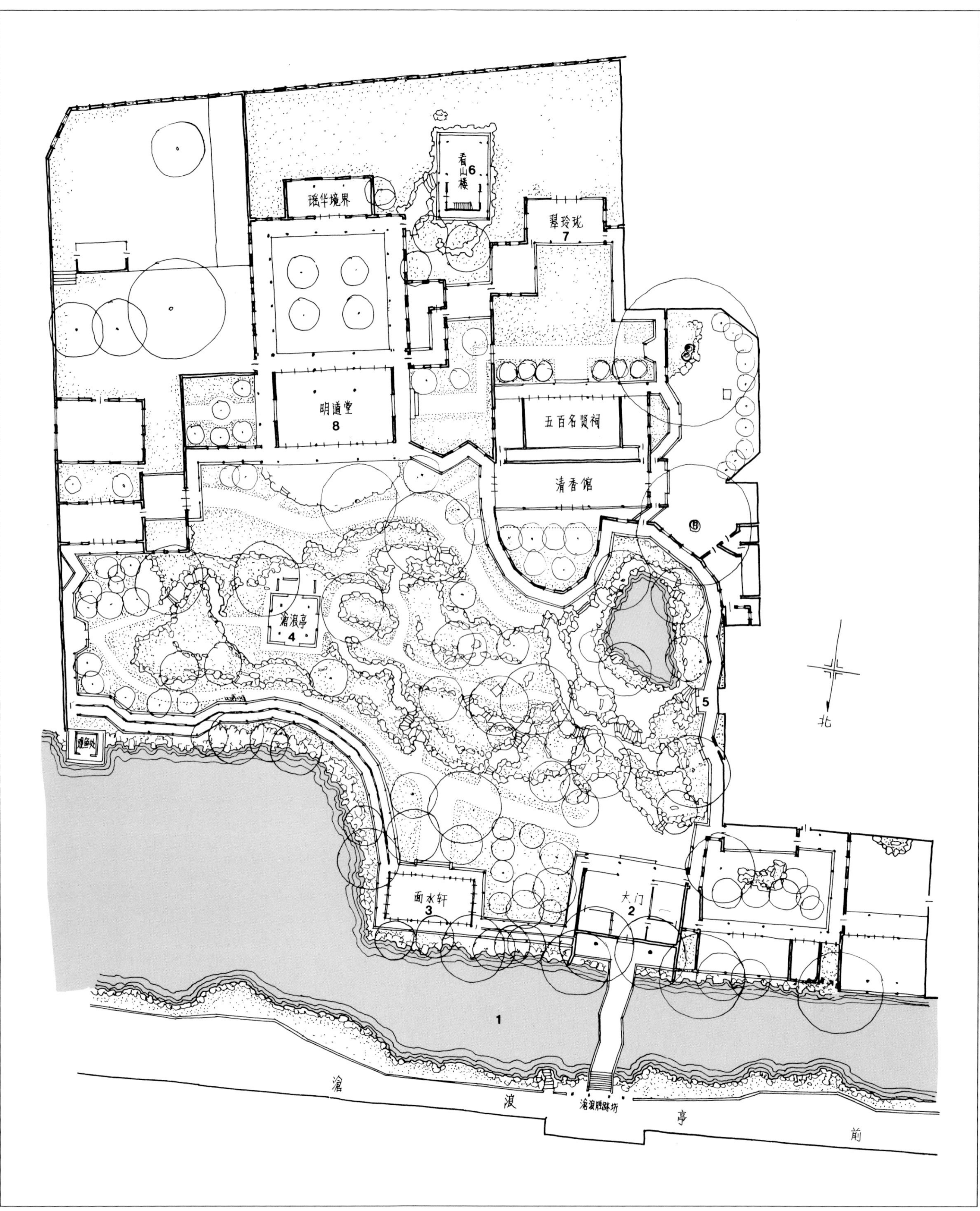

◁ Suzhou, Jiangsu, Cang Lang Ting, plan

Key
1 Canal. 2 Main entrance. 3 Mianshui Den. 4 Cang Lang Ting. 5 Ban Ting. 6 Kanshan Luo. 7 Cuilinglong. 8 Mingdao Tang.

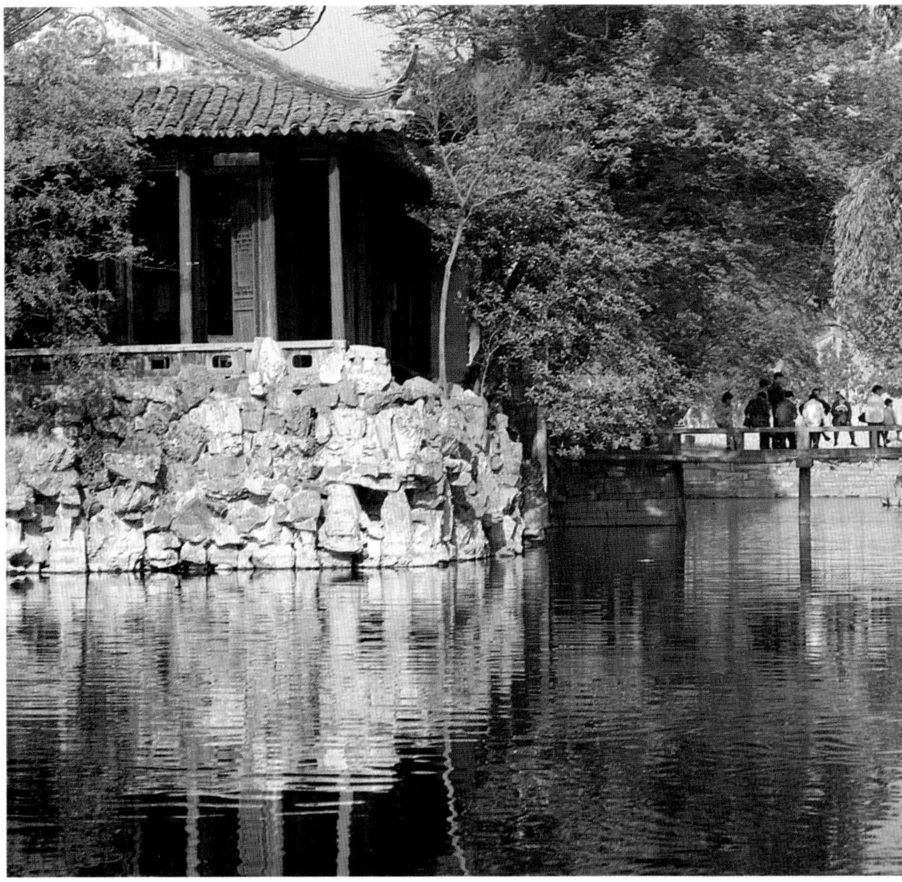

△ Suzhou, Jiangsu, Cang Lang Ting, pavilion facing canal

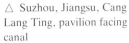

d. Cang Lang Ting (The Surging Wave Pavilion)

This is situated in the southern part of Suzhou. It was first built during the 10th century and belonged to an officer of Wu. In the Song Dynasty it was acquired by Su Shunqing, who erected the Sea Surge Pavilion on the very quiet water's edge. This pavilion 'borrowed scenery' from the broad water space and was set amidst flowers and slender bamboo clusters.

The unusual feature of this garden is that it is situated on a hill and 'it gathers about it several tens of acres of water' and a small canal leads to Pang Gate. The canal outside the garden separates it from the street, and a flat stone bridge gives access to the brick-carved entrance. Once inside the garden one is immediately attracted by the pavilion on top of the small hill. It is a natural one with yellow stone at the east and greyish lake rock at the west to retain the earth. A winding narrow path leads up the hill, under the shade of old trees. Slender bamboo plants line both sides of the staircase leading to the pavilion, which is situated on top of the small hill. Just as Shenfu wrote:

> . . .in all the world we thought, no life could be happier than this.

In the garden:

> beyond the eaves of the pavilion, an old tree raised its gnarled trunk; its branches throwing a dense shade across the window, dyeing our faces green. . .[32]

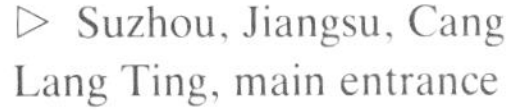

▷ Suzhou, Jiangsu, Cang Lang Ting, main entrance

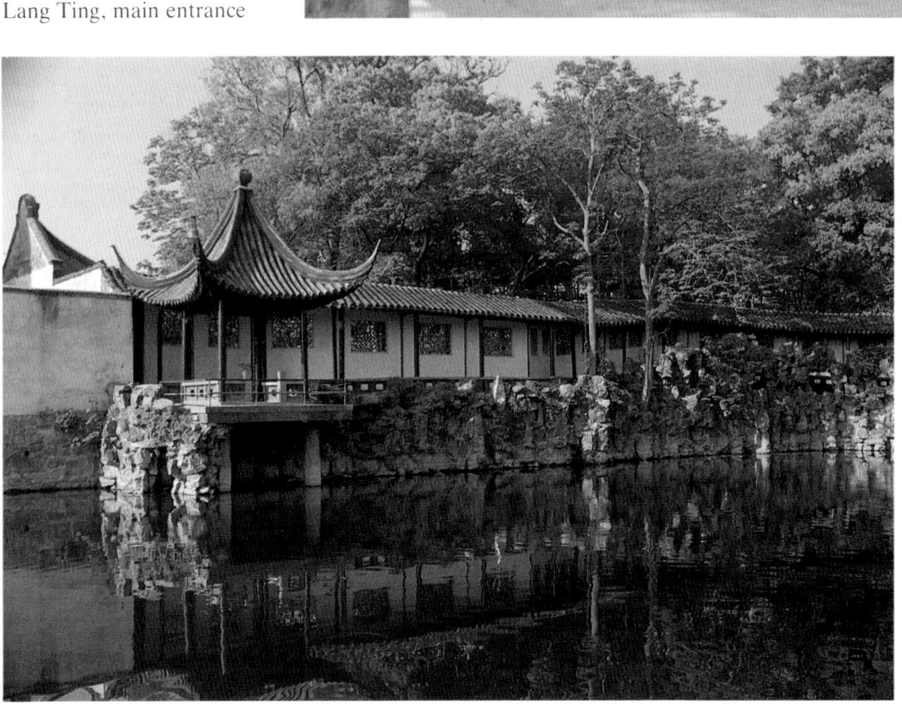

◁ Suzhou, Jiangsu, Cang Lang Ting, pavilion and verandah facing canal

▷ Suzhou, Jiangsu, Siziling, pool and rockery

e. Siziling (Lion Forest)

Close to Zhuozheng Yuan is the Siziling Garden, which originally belonged to the monastery next door. In the Yuan Dynasty, about 1342, the abbot of the temple erected the rock hill of this garden and in 1373, a painter, Nizan, made a painting of this garden which gives us a general idea as to what it looked like then. The garden passed into various hands and was finally acquired by the Pei family. It was lavishly restored, and soon became one of the famous gardens of the city.

The motif of this garden is the rockery hill, which occupies the southeastern part of the pond inside this garden. Most of the pavilions occupy the northern part of this garden, of which the total area is about one hectare. The beauty of this garden was supposedly attributed to its wealth of grotesque rocks which resembled lions, so dear to the scholars. These were assembled with great skill into a maze of winding paths, grottoes, hills, bridges and plantings of trees. Upon first seeing this, one would think the master had too much to spend and put too much in so restricted a space. One gets a sense of overcrowding and uneasiness instead of serenity and repose, which are the chief charms of the typical Chinese garden. Shenfu criticized Siziling thus:

> Although it was said that the rockery was the work of Nizan, the rocks were exquisite and delicate, and many ancient trees were in the garden. But the general sight, as if they are cinders heaped in a mess, piled up with moss, hollowed like ant hills and tunnels, entirely lack of the atmosphere of hills and woods.[33]

True, if the master's idea was carried out rather than the craftsman's, this would have become a much better garden.

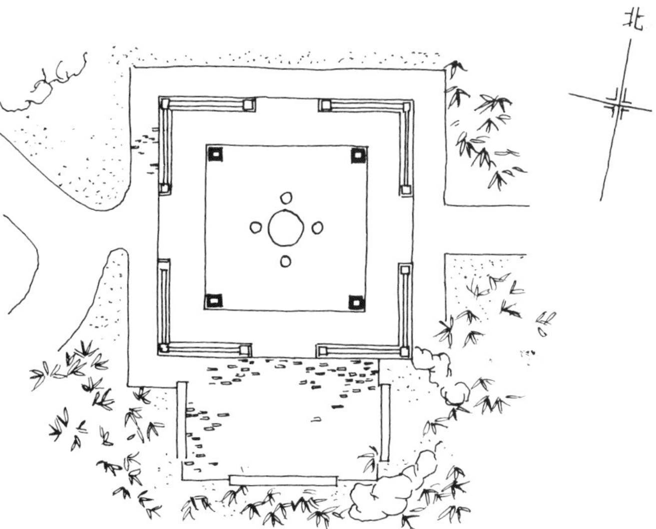

◁ Suzhou, Jiangsu, Cang Lang Ting, pavilion

△ Suzhou, Jiangsu, Cang Lang Ting, pavilion, plan and elevation

△ Yangzhou, Jiangsu, Ge Yuan, moongate and bamboo

▽ Yangzhou, Jiangsu, Ge Yuan, reflection of a pavilion

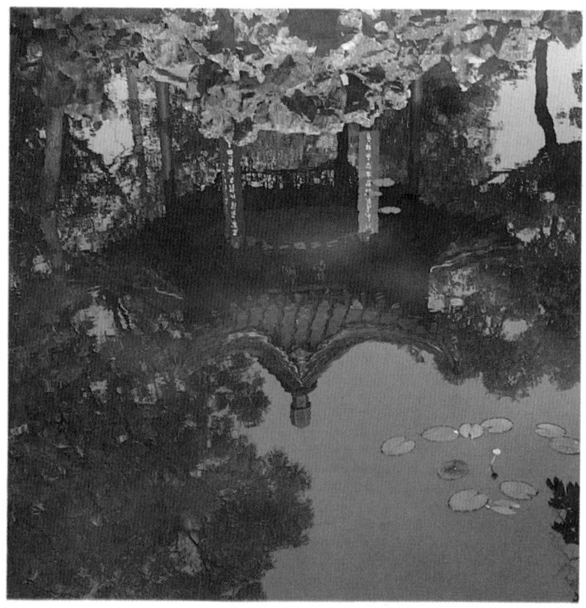

▷ Yangzhou, Jiangsu, Ge Yuan, begonia window and view

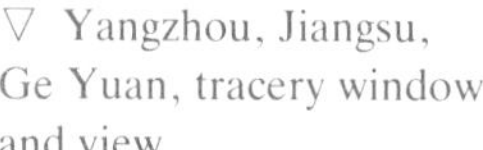

▽ Yangzhou, Jiangsu, Ge Yuan, tracery window and view

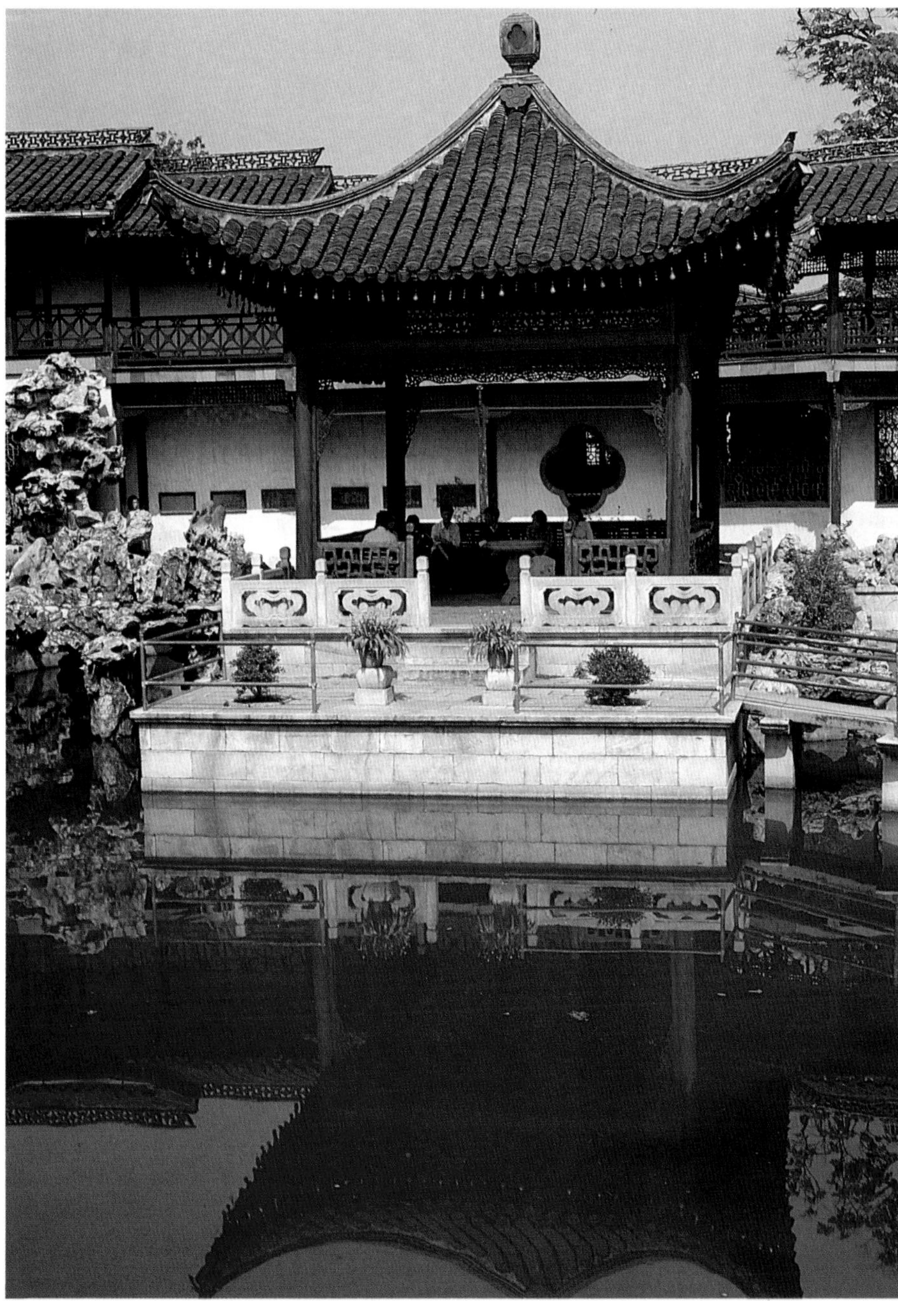

△ Yangzhou, Jiangsu, Ge Yuan, pavilion and pool

YANGZHOU

Ge Yuan

Ge Yuan (Bamboo Garden) is among the few well-preserved gardens in Yangzhou. The word 'Ge' (个) in Chinese character resembles the form of a bamboo leaf. As the garden was planted with a lot of bamboo, it was named after the bamboo. Through the tracery windows of the verandah one can catch a view of the main part, which is usually a pool. There is a two-storey building with a covered verandah and balcony wrapped around it. A stone boat is situated in the pool, its reflection enchancing the depth of the pool. This is one of the methods used in Chinese gardens to make the small appear large. The rippling waves, the yellow lilies and the quietly swaying leaves in the breeze all engender a peaceful and tranquil atmosphere.

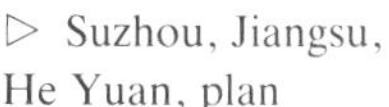

▷ Suzhou, Jiangsu, He Yuan, plan

Key
1 Gatehouse. 2 Simian Ting. 3 Main hall. 4 Den. 5 Half hall.

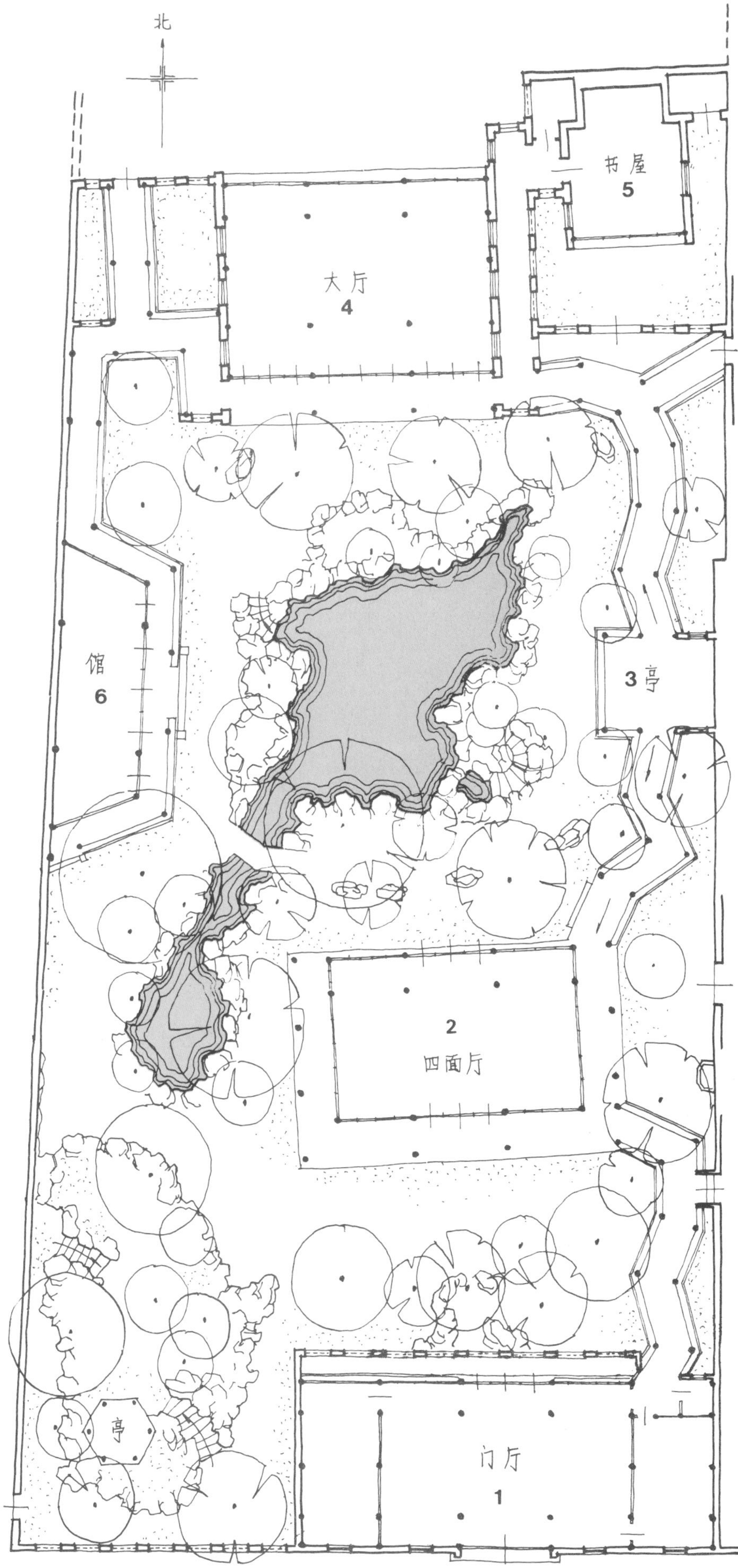

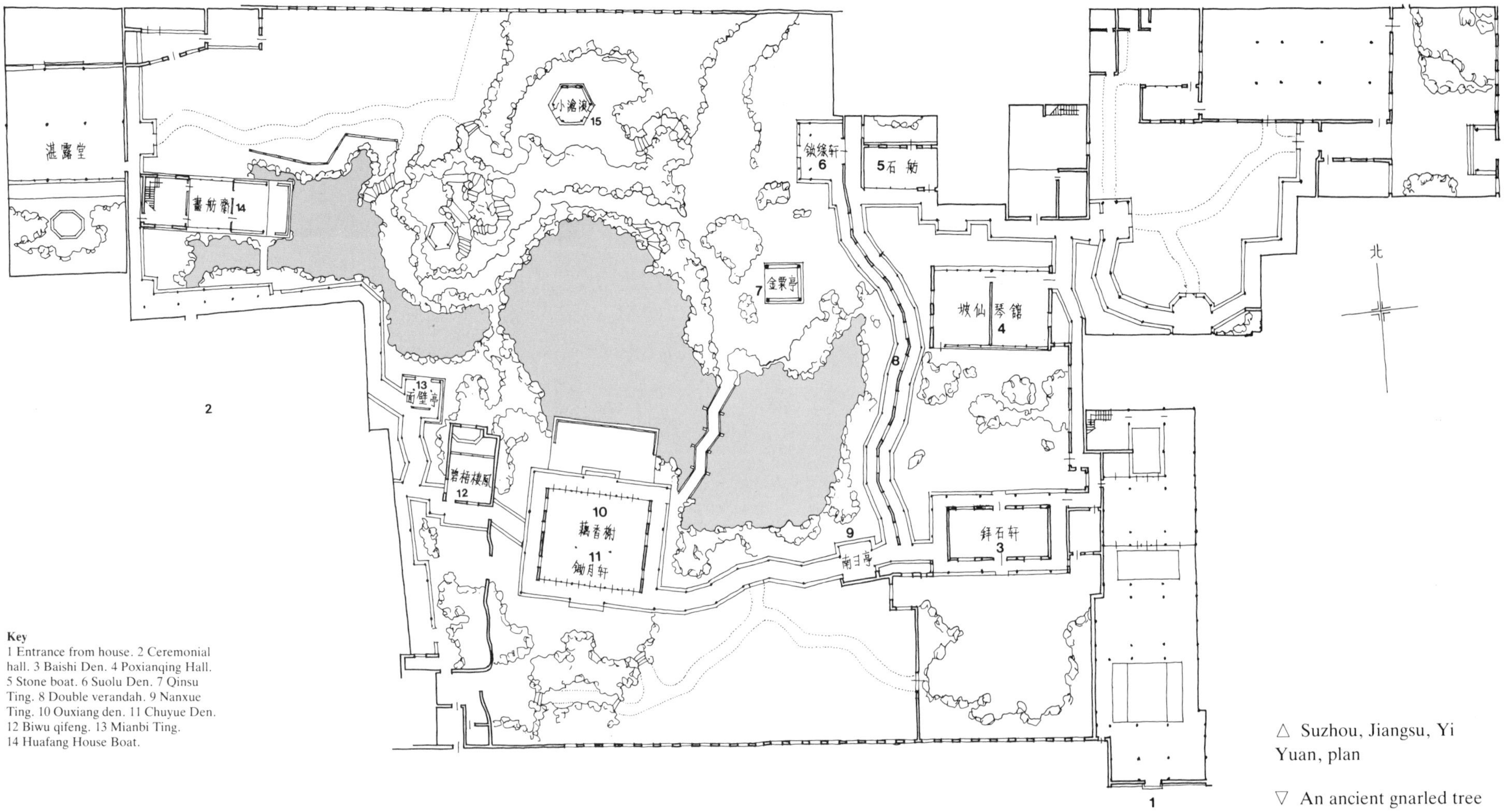

Key
1 Entrance from house. 2 Ceremonial hall. 3 Baishi Den. 4 Poxianqing Hall. 5 Stone boat. 6 Suolu Den. 7 Qinsu Ting. 8 Double verandah. 9 Nanxue Ting. 10 Ouxiang den. 11 Chuyue Den. 12 Biwu qifeng. 13 Mianbi Ting. 14 Huafang House Boat.

△ Suzhou, Jiangsu, Yi Yuan, plan

▽ An ancient gnarled tree

CONCLUSION

When designing a Chinese private garden, the first thing is to choose a quiet place and take advantage of the natural landscape: hills, water and trees. Man-made improvements may be added later. In this way, a garden of serenity and elegance can be obtained. 'A good design depends seventy percent on the designer and thirty percent on the craftsman.'[34] Ingeniously borrowing from nature and designing accordingly is the key to designing a beautiful garden. Since most Chinese gardens are small, borrowing from the outside is one way to enlarge the garden visually. When selecting a site or designing a garden, there are no guidelines. All one needs is elegant taste. In designing according to the intention of the master and natural landscape, significant alteration of the natural site is not encouraged, as such change can only result in a very artificial garden. The principle is to design according to one's mind and work intelligently.

Shenfu, a scholar of the Qing Dynasty, was very knowledgeable about garden design: In his *Six Chapters from a Floating Life*, he writes:

> In laying out garden pavilions and towers, suites of rooms and covered walkaways, piling rocks into mountains, or planting flowers to form a desired

shape, the aim is to see the small in the large, to see the large in the small, to see the real in the illusory and to see the illusory in the real. Sometimes you conceal, sometimes you reveal, sometimes you work on the surface, sometimes in depth. One need not waste labour in vain merely in terms of the well-known formula: 'winding, deceptive intricacy' or 'a broad area with many stones.'[35]

From his own feeling, Shenfu's descriptions are true revelations gained from many gardens.

To Westerners, Chinese gardens may seem irrational and have neither reason nor formulae. Winding verandahs were planned and the paths were covered with moss and are slippery. Safety is not required. The quaint rocks were either in the form of peaks, embankments, hills or grottoes which were not meant for climbing. A meandering stream flows under a low, zigzag bridge which is narrow and without balustrade, as if it was not meant for crossing. In the garden are old, gnarled trees, a few leaves, and a few flowers. The bamboo must be thin and sparse, as the aim seems to be to create something perplexing and irrational. The reasons for all these seeming absurdities include philosophic thought, the Chinese attitude on beauty, poetic feelings, and the painterly concept special to the Chinese. Man wanders about perplexed, pauses, then turns back. In a garden, naturally, the visitor is always expecting something. Is it not much more enjoyable to travel than to arrive? To the master, 'a pleasure delayed is a pleasure twice enjoyed'.[36]

When comparing the Chinese garden with its Western counterpart, the two are found to differ from design concept to planning skills. If one uses the Western concept of enjoying a Chinese garden, walking instead of strolling in it, it would be difficult to understand the Chinese garden. We know from history that even the master of a house does not go into it everyday. It is like a landscape scroll in a gallery; nobody goes to see it everyday. Only during different seasons, at different occasions, will he pause sometimes at the entry to the garden or facing a window, where through the window panes or screen he enjoys the scenery for a little while before turning back to the house. The scenery he gathered, the rock placed to represent cliffs, the creek, the river, the pattering sound of autumn rain, or the whispering of wind all lent to the poetic feeling of the person. He is wandering, not walking, in his garden, in a land of dreams. Just like Chuin Tung explained, the Chinese garden is 'a garden of deception, a realm of dreams and a little world of make-believe, and to find in the little the great, and in the evident the intangible'.[37] Only by sensing Chinese gardens in this way, can the true meaning be understood.

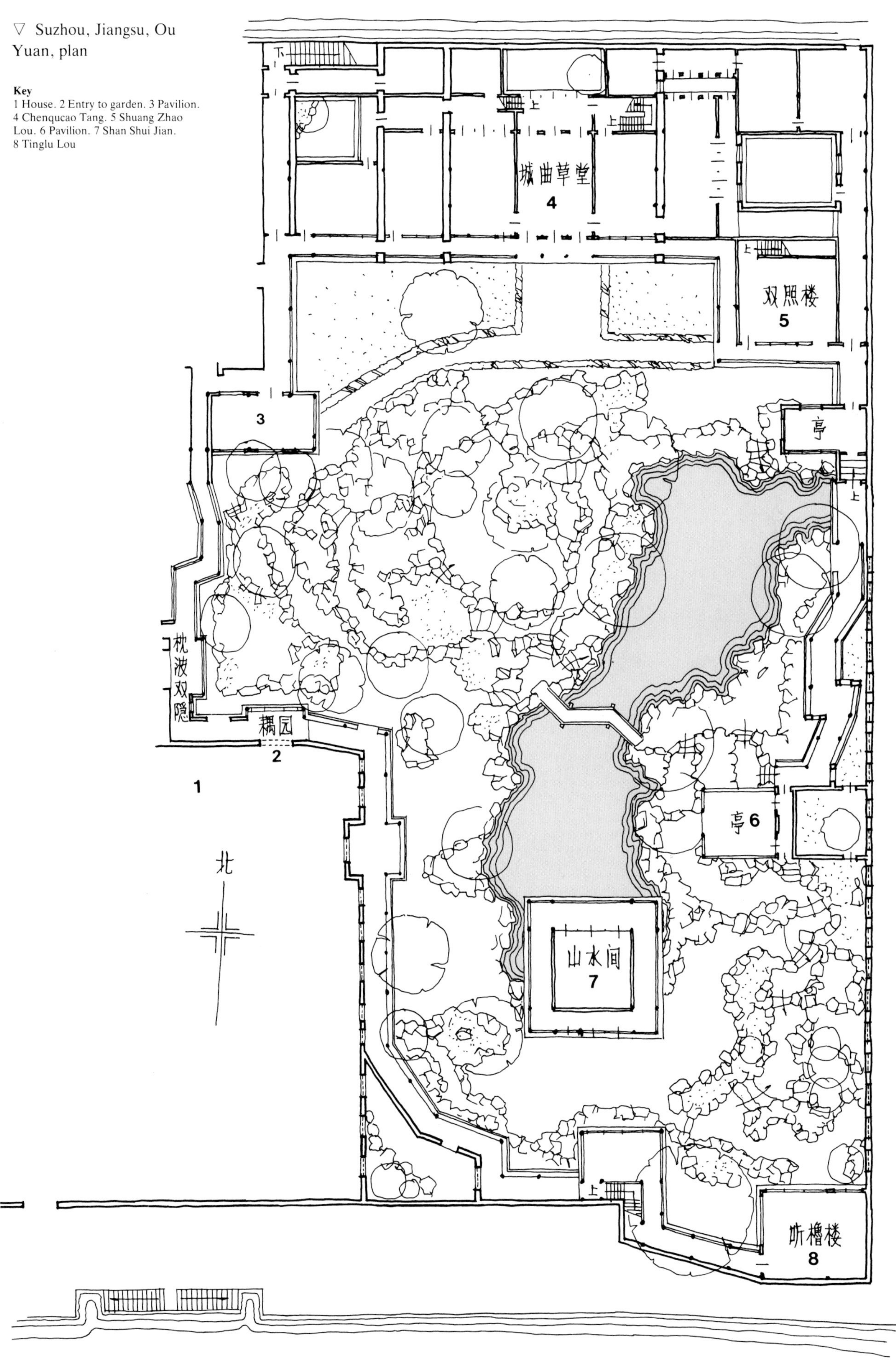

▽ Suzhou, Jiangsu, Ou Yuan, plan

Key
1 House. 2 Entry to garden. 3 Pavilion. 4 Chenqucao Tang. 5 Shuang Zhao Lou. 6 Pavilion. 7 Shan Shui Jian. 8 Tinglu Lou

CHAPTER VII
FUNERAL AND CEREMONIAL BUILDINGS

◁ Xian, Shenxi, Qin Ling, pottery soldiers, Qin Dynasty, c3rd century B.C.

STARTING FROM THE BRONZE AGE AND IRON AGE, THE people of China worshipped both man and nature, they believed in life after death and in reincarnation. For a long time, gratitudes were offered to the spirits of departed ancestors; master teachers were worshipped for their teachings; and emperors were worshipped in the belief that they could pray to the god on the peoples' behalf. There were ceremonial halls, praying halls and grand funeral architecture built to commemorate these activities.

FUNERAL BUILDINGS

Filial piety in China was considered a great moral code of the people. Confucius says: 'Filial piety consists of obedience; in serving one's parents when alive according to propriety; in burying them when dead according to propriety and sacrificing to them according to propriety.'[1] A tomb in China was treated as a dwelling as well as a place for worshipping the dead. A nondescript tomb was considered not in propriety to their ancestors.

The typical Chinese tomb is a mound, either square or circular in plan, its size according to the social status and wealth of the family. Some large tombs recently excavated had an underground chamber or chambers resembling courtyard houses. The body of the deceased was placed on a platform in the coffin chamber. The smaller ones did not have a chamber, and the coffin was buried deep underground.

Feng Shui also dictated the choice of site of a tomb. Apart from the landscape, the terrain, water sources, transportation and defense capabilities were also important factors. People made good use of the natural environment or changed it to suit their purposes.

For emperors and dignitaries, the site of a tomb would be located on high land with good surface drainage, a low water table, and orientated to the south, so that the body and the coffin would not rot easily. The site also had to be easy to defend from robbers or enemies. As there were treasures buried with bodies, they were subject to robbery. During or before the Shang Dynasty possessions liked by the deceased were buried together with the corpse. Sometimes, beloved concubines, horses, attendants, and slaves were also buried alive in the belief that they could serve him in the other world, to ensure that the next life is as pleasant as that on earth. In one tomb, recently excavated, more than 400 bodies were found. It meant nothing but the deep rooted superstition and cruelty of the ruling class of the society.

It was not until the Zhou Dynasty that wooden or pottery figurines were used to take the place of live persons. Pottery utensils replaced real objects. Confucius denounced this cruel practice openly by saying: 'Those who favour the institution of burying the living with the dead do not have children of their own.'

There are many examples to validate these conditions, which will be discussed in the following examples. There is evidence that many tombs were exhumed right after the corpse was buried and it is believed that many were robbed by or under the direction of the person who built them so they knew the exact location of the coffin and how to reach it.

Qin Ling

Before the Han Dynasty, large tumuli were of pyramidal form and were man-made. The best example of this kind is the Qin Ling of Shi Huang Di, the first Emperor of the Qin Dynasty. The tomb is located on the south bank of Weihe River one kilometre north of Mount Lishan. It is of pyramidal form having three terraces. After more than 2,000 years of erosion, the present tomb measures 345 metres (1,120 feet) from east to west and 350 metres (1,135 feet) from north to south. The walls of each terrace incline to the centre, and altogether have a height of 45 metres (146 feet). The tomb is enclosed by two layers of square walls, the outer one measuring 6.3 kilometres in length, and the inner one 2.5 kilometres. It is the largest tomb ever built in China. The walls and natural landscape were used for easy protection of the body. Although great care had been taken during Shi Huang Di's lifetime, the tomb was exhumed and robbed a few years later by Xiangyu, a general who removed all that it contained.

The Han Dynasty historian Sima Qian has left an excellent description in his *Historical Records* of this gigantic undertaking:

> The workmen sent there numbered over seven hundred thousand. They dug down as far as the water; bronze was poured in and the sarcophagus brought; marvellous tools, jewels and rare objects were brought there and buried . . . Artisans were ordered to make automatic crossbows and arrows; if anyone had tried to make a hole and enter the tomb, they would have immediately fired on him . . . The emperor ordered that all his wives should

▷ Mahao, Leshan, Sichuan, rock-hewn tombs, Han Dynasty, bas-reliefs

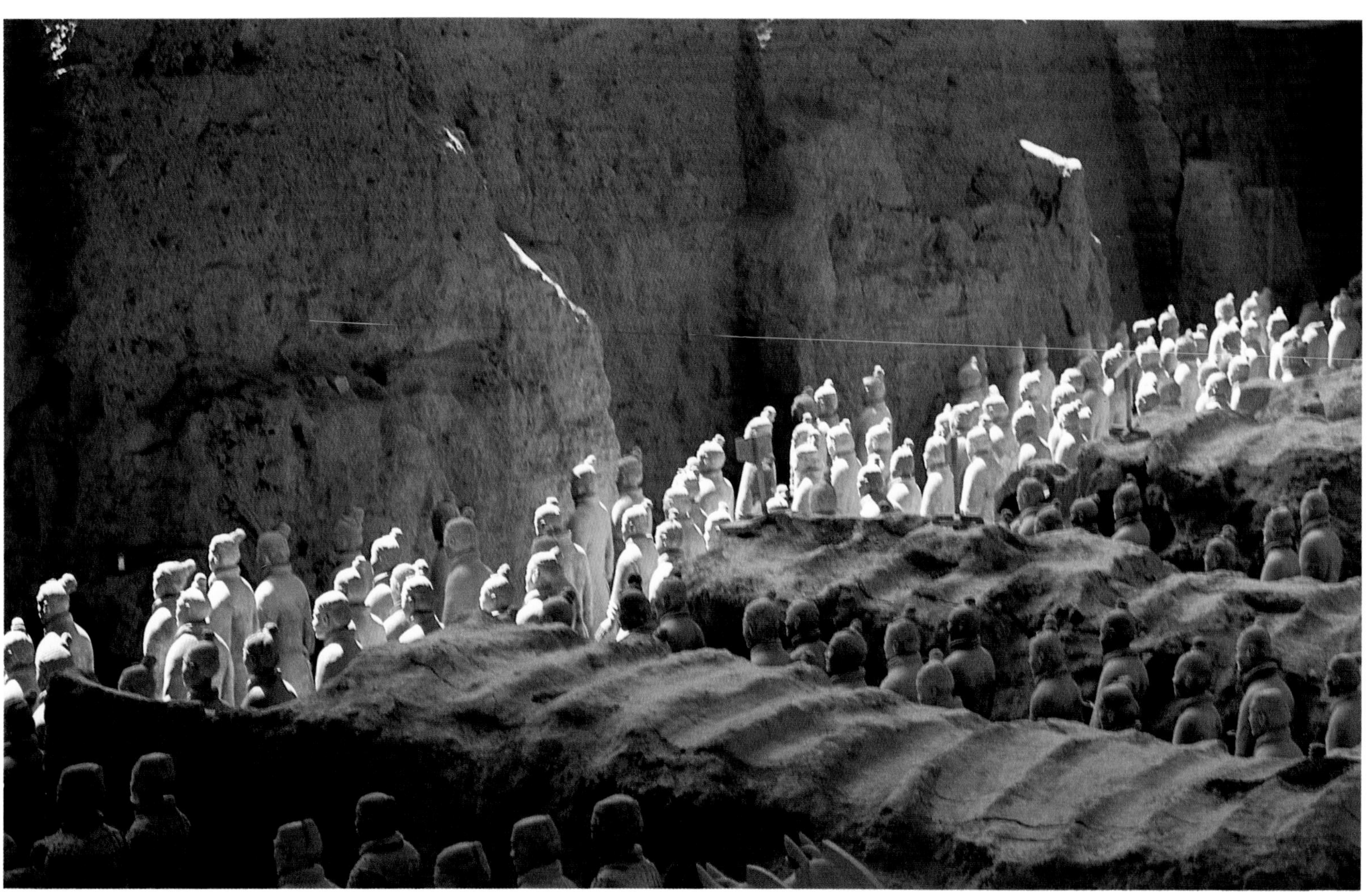

◁ Xian, Shenxi, Qin Ling, pottery soldiers, Qin Dynasty, c3rd century B.C.

> follow him when he died . . . When the work was over and the central passage leading to the tomb had been disguised and blocked, the outer door to it was dropped into place, shutting in all those who had been employed as workmen or craftsmen.[2]

The chambers were made of stone, trees were planted on the artificial mounds, and in front of the tomb were the sacrificial hall and worshipping hall; so it was called Ling Jin, tomb and halls.

In 1974, a peasant found some pottery fragments to the west of the mound of Qin. He reported his find to the local government and in that same year, large scale excavations began. Large massive army vaults were discovered where some 6,000 life-sized terra-cotta armoured warriors and horses were found in trenches. They are approximately 1.8 metres (6 feet) tall. The vivid warrior figures are clad in armour or short gowns, belted at the waist, and are holding real weapons. The figures are wearing different hair styles and their postures are full of power and grandeur. They represent a microcosm of the 'Strong soldiers and horses'. All stand in the formation of Qin army rule. The officers are lined abreast in the front row, soldiers, and horses follow in files. All the warriors have solemn facial expressions; they exude vigour and alertness. The horses have their ears erect, forelock lifting and heads up as if neighing on the alert. Since the vault of more than 8,000 figures lies about 1,711 metres (5,550 feet) to the east of the tumulus, too far away to protect the tomb, some historians think this could be the vault of Empress Xun of Qin, who ruled Qin for 41 years and half a century earlier than Shi Huang Di.

Rock-hewn Tomb of Sichuan

During the Han Dynasty, not only were there artificial earth mounds on top of deep buried coffins, but in Sichuan Province a group of rock-hewn tombs were found. The best preserved is in Mahao, Leshan. The tombs have rock-hewn chambers, and coffins were placed inside chambers like the tombs of ancient Egyptian dynasties. The tombs were orthogonal in planning, symbolizing a dwelling for the living. In one of the tombs, the front hall was used as a hall of sacrifice facing the Ming River. The walls inside were covered entirely with bas-reliefs, and on the left, it depicted a story of 'The Assassination of King of Qin by Jinke', a famous heroic story of the Warring States Period. At the far left, it depicted a warrior guarding the palace of Qin, next to that was depicted Jinke trying to pierce him with a sword, the middle right showed the warriors holding Jinke, and the far right showed Jinke's attendant, Qinwuyang, holding a map with a dagger hidden inside. To the right of the front hall are stone-carved pavilions and pagodas which show clearly the architectural style and construction method of that period. They employed robust beams and brackets together with the heroism of Jinke to symbolize the virtue of the deceased and the durability of the tomb through the conception of mass, solidity and sizes, as well as the durability of the living. The tombs were used for all the members of the family to be buried together and not for any individual.

As the axis extends into the cave there are halls and side halls, and inside the side halls were utensils used by the deceased and the chambers for coffins. The coffins in this tomb were lost, but from another tomb at Pengshan nearby we can see that the wooden coffins usually had an outer sarcophagus called 'Kuo'. It is well preserved and carved with symbols of the Green Dragon, White Tiger, Firebird and Black Tortoise, which symbolize east, west, south and north directions respectively. Other Han Dynasty tombs in the northern part of China used hollow brick tile to cover the tombs, the tiles measuring 1.10 metres (3.5 feet) in length and about 10 centimetres (4 inches) in thickness.

△ Mahao, Leshan, Sichuan, rock-hewn tombs, Han Dynasty, bas-reliefs

▷ Mahao, Leshan, Sichuan, rock-hewn tombs, Han Dynasty, bas-reliefs

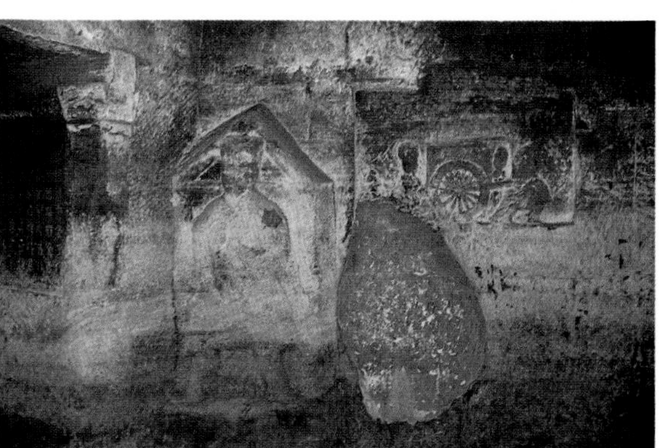

▷ bas-reliefs

◁ Mahao, Leshan, Sichuan, rock-hewn tombs, Han Dynasty

▷ Mahao, Leshan, Sichuan, rock-hewn tombs, Han Dynasty, stone coffin

◁ Nanjing, Jiangsu, stone Pixie, Northern Qi, 550-577

▽ Nanjing, Jiangsu, stone pillar, Northern Qi

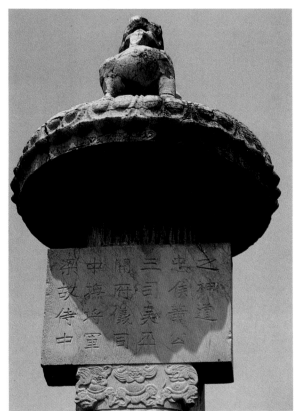

△ Nanjing, Jiangsu, stone pillar, Northern Qi

▷ Xian, Shenxi, Qian Ling, Tang Dynasty, 650-683

Pillars and Pixie

In Nanjing, and in the Northern Qi period (550-577), pillars and a mystic animal called pixie were used to mark the approach to a tomb of nobility. Pixie is a mystic animal which represented a lion.

Qian Ling Tombs, Xian (650-638)

Qian Ling Tomb is the joint tomb of Gaozhong, the third emperor of the Tang Dynasty and his empress Wuzetian, the latter acceding to the throne after Gaozhong died. According to records the tomb was enclosed by walls, gateways and buildings with 378 rooms. To the southeast of the tomb are 17 satellite tombs of princes, princesses, kings and high officers including the Princess Yongtai's tomb and Prince Zhanghua's tomb.

Unlike the Qin Tomb, the choice of the site of the tomb shows careful use of natural landscape and according to Feng Shui, the site has a natural main peak to the north and two smaller peaks to the south. The higher peak was dug out and used to house the bodies, the two peaks facing each other formed a natural gateway as Que to the tomb. An approach starting from the south, passing the two small peaks going upwards finally terminates at a large terrace at the foot of the higher peak. When looking to the south, it commands an expanse of landscape, and the monumentality is enhanced by the natural setting.

Starting from the south, exquisitely carved stone sculptures are lined along the approach. First there is a pair of stone pillars called the Cloud Pillars, carved with a lotus motif base and capital, the shaft of which is a peony flower design. There are winged horses, which are very robust and head-lifting, together with scarlet birds, horses, generals and officers. In front of the tomb and at the edge of the big terrace is a pair of lions. To my mind, they are the best carvings of all. They are strong, fierce looking and sturdy, giving an impression that they guard the entrance to the tomb and that no one should dare to enter. To both sides of the tomb stand 60 envoys from the Western Regions in their national costumes; they came here to pay their last tribute to the deceased emperor. It is a pity that their heads are lost. To one side of the approach is a tablet 6.3 metres (20.5 feet) high called the 'Tablet With No Inscriptions'. Records say it was erected by order of the empress, and it was her idea to leave it blank for the people after her to inscribe her works onto it, no matter whether they be of merit or a failure.

Princess Yongtai was a granddaughter of Gaozhong. Her tomb was built near Qian Ling and is outstanding for its murals. The murals present a wealth of images with few colours and an economy of forceful flowing lines, a character of Tang painting.

△ Xian, Shenxi, Qian Ling, stone pillar, base

◁ Xian, Shenxi, Qian Ling, stone pillar, capital

▷ Xian, Shenxi, Qian Ling, tablet with no inscriptions

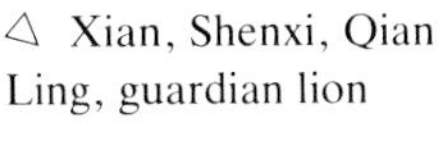

△ Xian, Shenxi, Qian Ling, guardian lion

▽ Xian, Shenxi, Qian Ling, winged horse

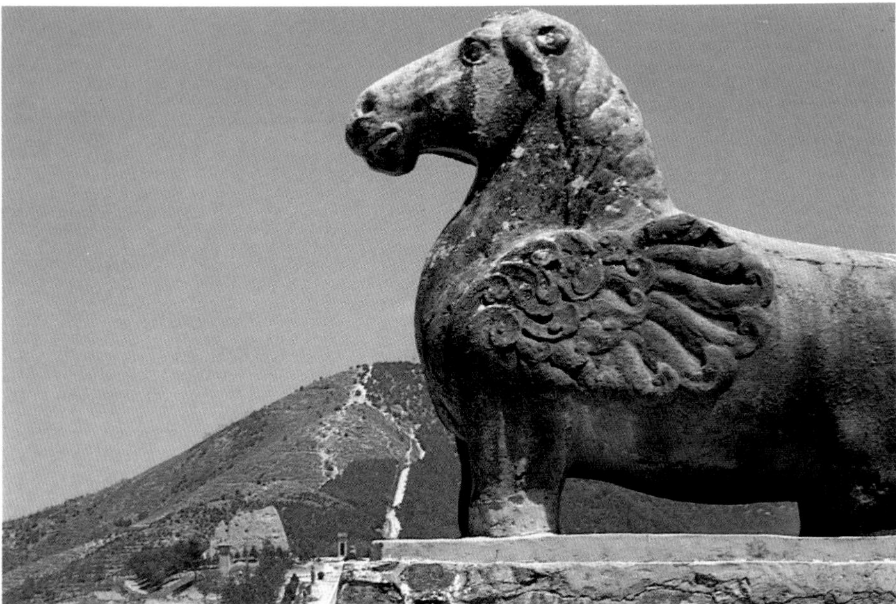

▽ Xian, Shenxi, Qian Ling, Princess Yongtai Tomb, fresco

▷ Xian, Shenxi, Qian Ling, Princess Yongtai Tomb, fresco

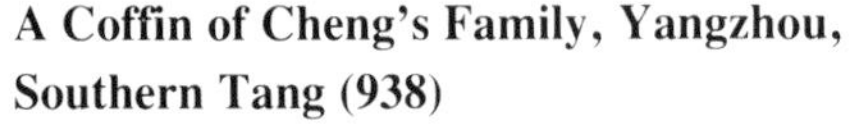

A Coffin of Cheng's Family, Yangzhou, Southern Tang (938)
Discovered in Yangzhou, this resembles a door leading to a dwelling of the other world.

Xiao Ling and the 13 Tombs of Ming Dynasty
Xiao Ling (1386), located in Nanjing, is the tomb of Zhu Yuan Zhang, the first emperor of the Ming Dynasty, and is also one of the best examples of site selection. The tomb is approached through a winding avenue, which turns according to the topography of the terrain. First there is a tablet, at the south where all the members of the royal family should dismount and walk to a pavilion called Fangcheng or Square City. They then follow an approach, first heading north, then turning to the west into a wide avenue lined at both sides with stone sculptures of elephants, lions and horses. After these two pillars mark another approach, which faces north; the approach is lined with stone sculptures of officers, both armed and in full court costumes. The avenue is paved with big flagstones and behind the statues are pine trees. The avenue ends at a river with five stone arched bridges across it, which is called the Five Dragon Bridge. Across the bridge is a

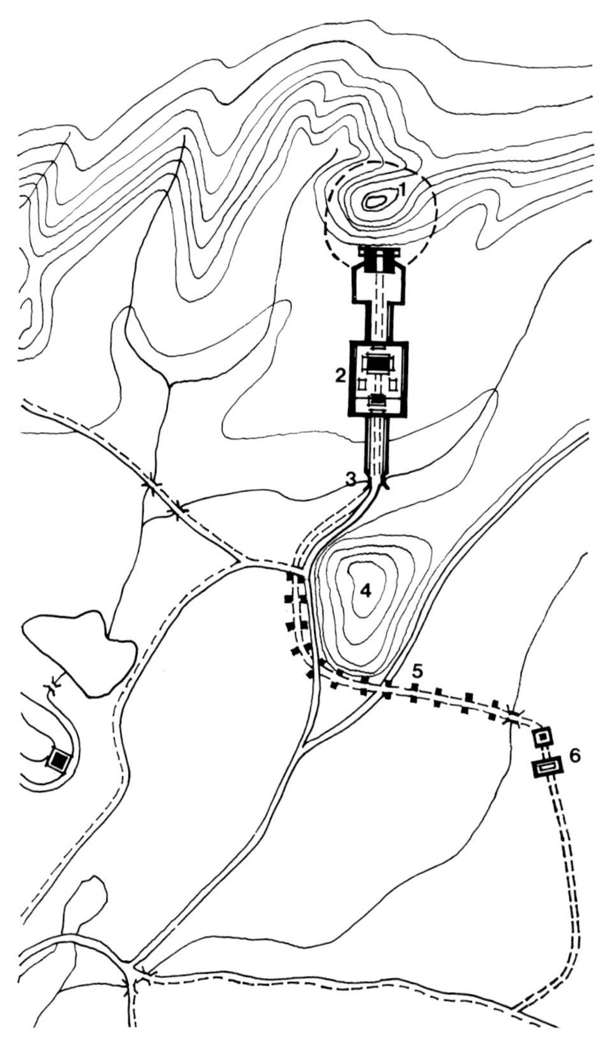

△ Nanjing, Jiangsu, Ming Tomb, Ming Dynasty, c.1368

Key
1 Tomb. 2 Ceremonial Halls. 3 Five Dragon Bridge. 4 Meihua Shan. 5 Statues. 6 Pavilion of tablet.

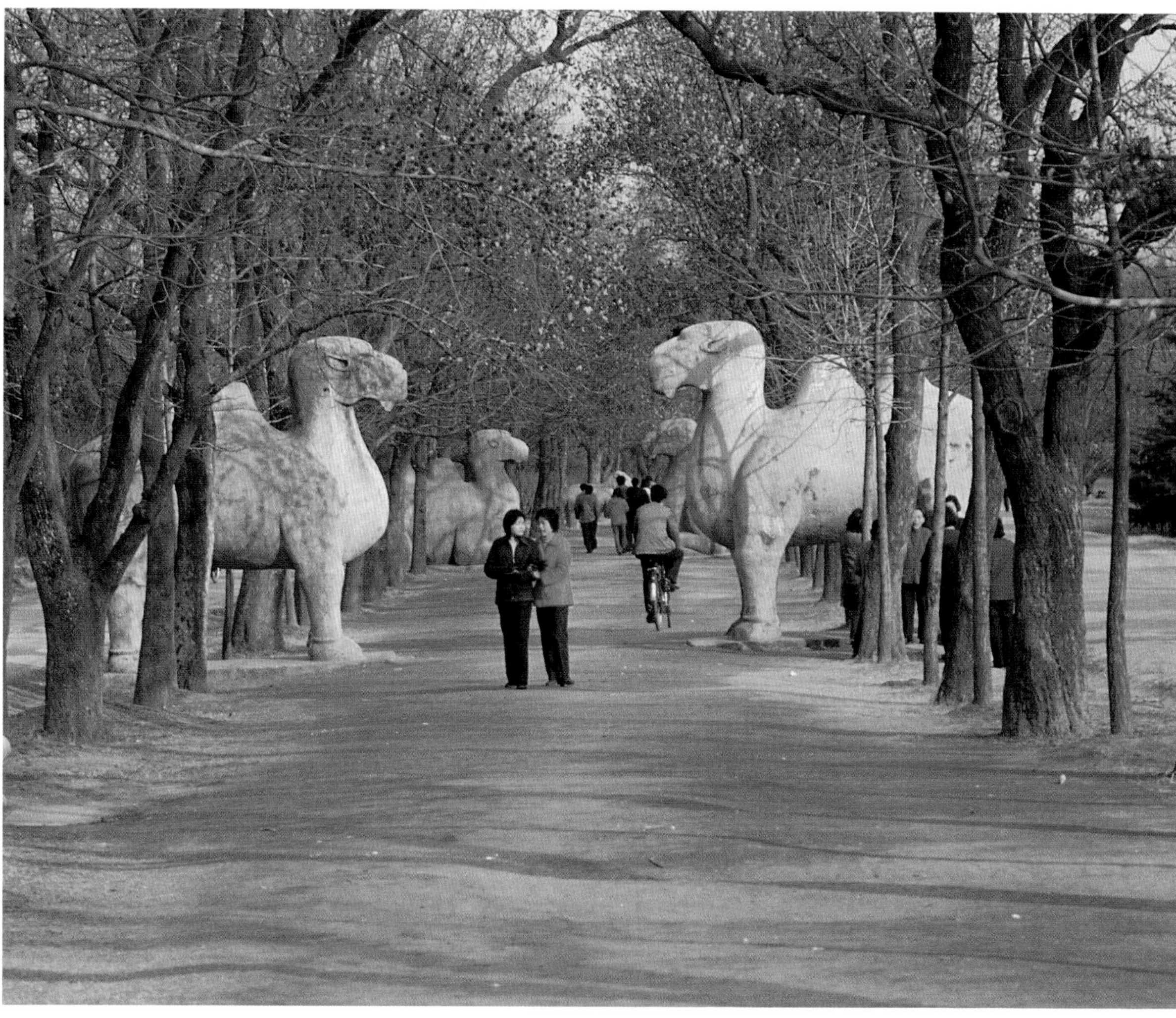

△ Nanjing, Jiangsu, Ming Tomb, stone sculptures

◁ Nanjing, Jiangsu, Ming Tomb, stone sculptures

◁ Yangzhou, Jiangsu, wood coffin and model of a building, Southern Tang, 738

▷ Beijing, Ming 13 Tombs, Ming Dynasty, 1409-1644

Key
1 Marble Peifeng. 2 Da Hong Men. 3 Pavilion of Tablet. 4 Statues. 5 Dingling. 6 Changling.

group of buildings laid out according to the requirements of ritual. The last building in front of the tomb is a high platform which was crowned with a pavilion, but only the ruined walks and column bases show that there are buildings on top of the platform. The platform was reached by a ramp with a vaulted roof, the ramp penetrated the platform and finally reached the platform above, which faces the large tomb hidden among the verdant trees. The ensemble, although simple and unassuming, represented the personality of the deceased emperors. It is far less imposing than the Tang or Song tombs, but it has a quiet dignity, subtlety and is full of surprises, and far superior to the Tang and Song tombs.

The third emperor Cheng Zhu moved its capital to Beijing in 1402. From 1409 until 1644, 13 tombs for the Ming emperors were built at the south foot of Tianshou Shan Hill in Changling, about 50 kilometres (35 miles) northwest of Beijing. The construction was scattered over a 40 square kilometre area. This is commonly called the Ming 13 Tombs.

The site was chosen for its excellent Feng Shui. The entire district was surrounded on the north, east and west by undulating mountains, forming a secluded, shielded environment. To the south, two small hills opposite each other were used as a natural gateway (Que) to the compound.

The entrance is marked by a five-bay white marble peifang, its centre aligned with the main peak, the Tianshou Shan Hill, 11 kilometres away, approximately in 1,300 metres north of the peifang in the Dahongmen (Big Red Gate). After the Dahongmen is the Pavilion of Tablet and the approach to Changling. This approach was lined up with 18 pairs of statues of ministers, warriors (all clothed in official costumes), camels, horses, lions and mythological animals. After

▷ Beijing, Ming 13 Tombs, marble peifang, details

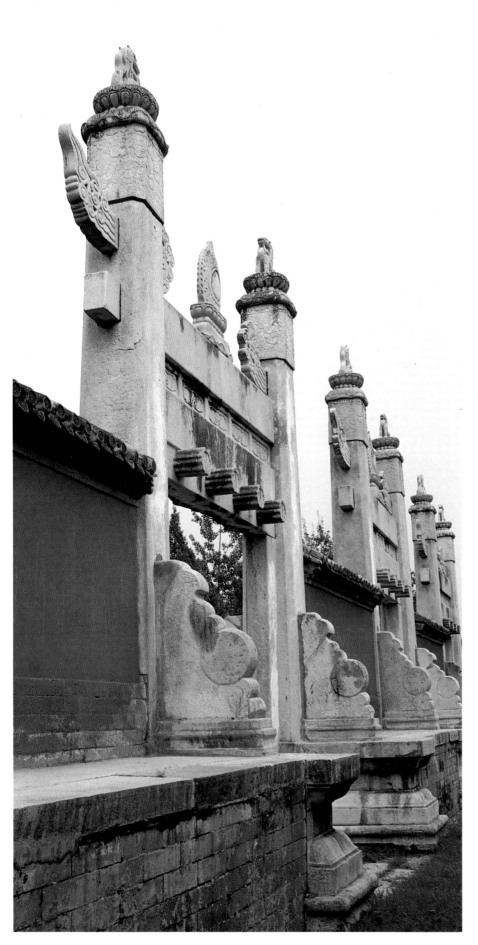

△ Beijing, Ming 13 Tombs, marble peifang

◁ Beijing, Ming 13 Tombs, Big Red Gateway

the Dragon and Phoenix Gate, the land gradually slopes upward and at the end is the Lingen Men, the gate of the main tomb, Changling. The main hall, the Lingen Dian, which is like the Taihe Dian in the Purple Forbidden City, is situated in a walled courtyard and on a triple marble podium of 3.2 metres with a yellow glazed tile, double-eave hip roof. Because it was used for worshipping and the offering of sacrifices to the ancestors of Ming Dynasty emperors, it is even larger than the Taihe Dian, being 66.75 metres by 29.31 metres and 30 metres in height. It seems to me that the podium is too low for the big hall above it. The columns were constructed of a single trunk of Chinese cedar, the Nanmu. The four largest central columns have a diameter of 1.17 metres each. The balustrades on the podium have pillars of a dragon and phoenix design. They symbolize the emperors and empresses respectively. To both sides of the courtyard are two small furnaces of glazed tiles in the form of miniature halls, complete with roofs and door sashes.

After that great hall and in another enclosed courtyard is a massive square tower, which is the entry to the tomb. In front of the tower is a long stone table, placed perpendicular to its axis. Five utensils were placed on it; the utensils are made of stone and were used while making offerings.

In 1957, one of the Ming tombs, Dinling, was excavated. It was the tomb of Emperor Wanli (1573-1620), the fourteenth emperor of the Ming Dynasty. The mound is about 76 metres (229 feet) in diameter and covered with pine trees.

The tomb was planned like a dwelling only it was underground and all the 'courtyards' were covered with limestone barrel-vaults. There are two side walls and one main hall. The approach to this tomb is a ramp

◁ Beijing, Ming 13 Tombs, stone sculpture

▷ Beijing, Ming 13 Tombs, Ningen Dian, 1424, interior

◁ Beijing, Ming 13 Tombs, Ningen Dian, 1424

▽ Beijing, Ming 13 Tombs, Ningen Dian, podium and railing

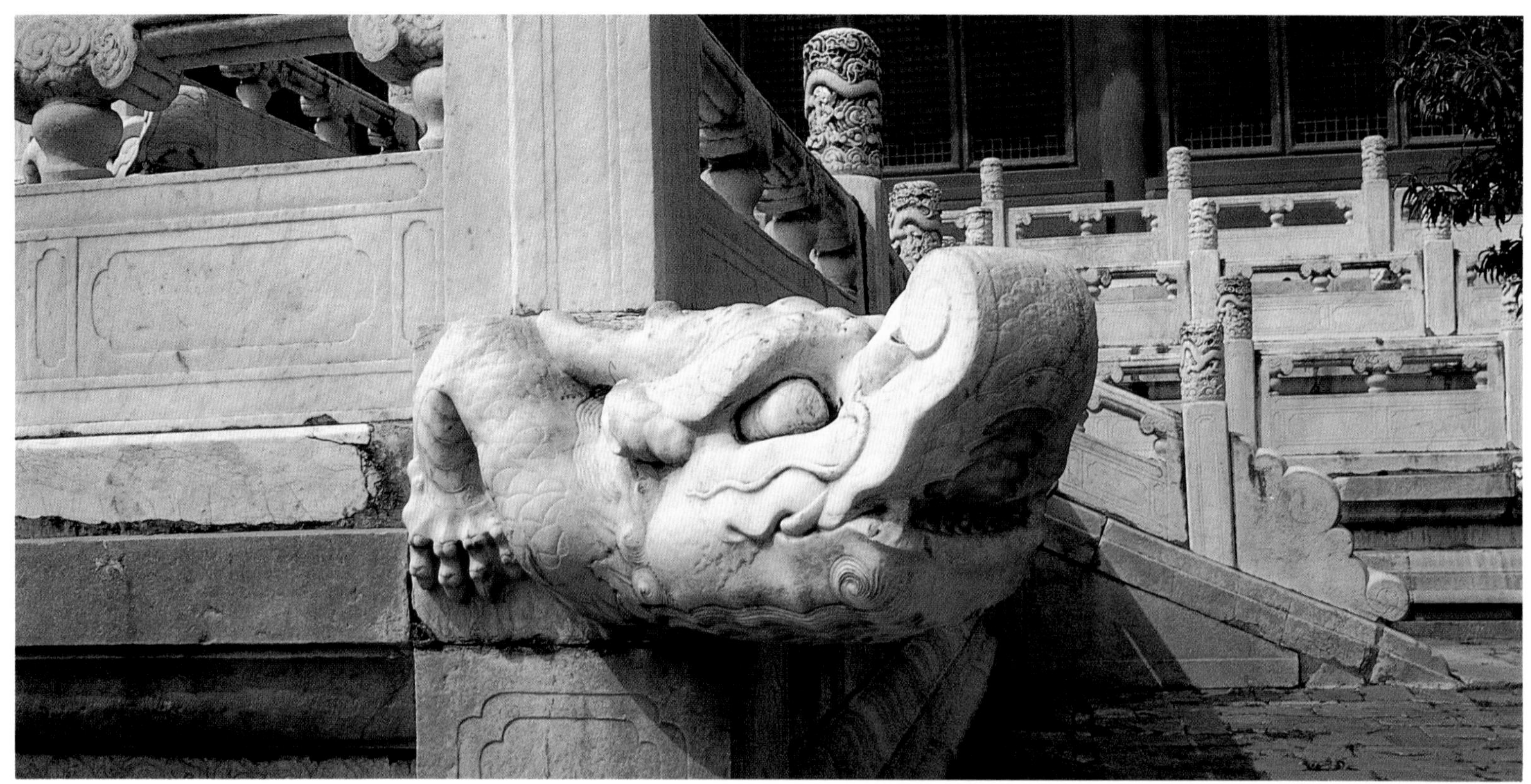

▷ Beijing, Ming 13 Tombs, Ningen Dian, Chi Head spout

▽ Beijing, Ming 13 Tombs, Ningen Dian, capital of dragon design

▷ Beijing, Ming 13 Tombs, gatehouse to Changling

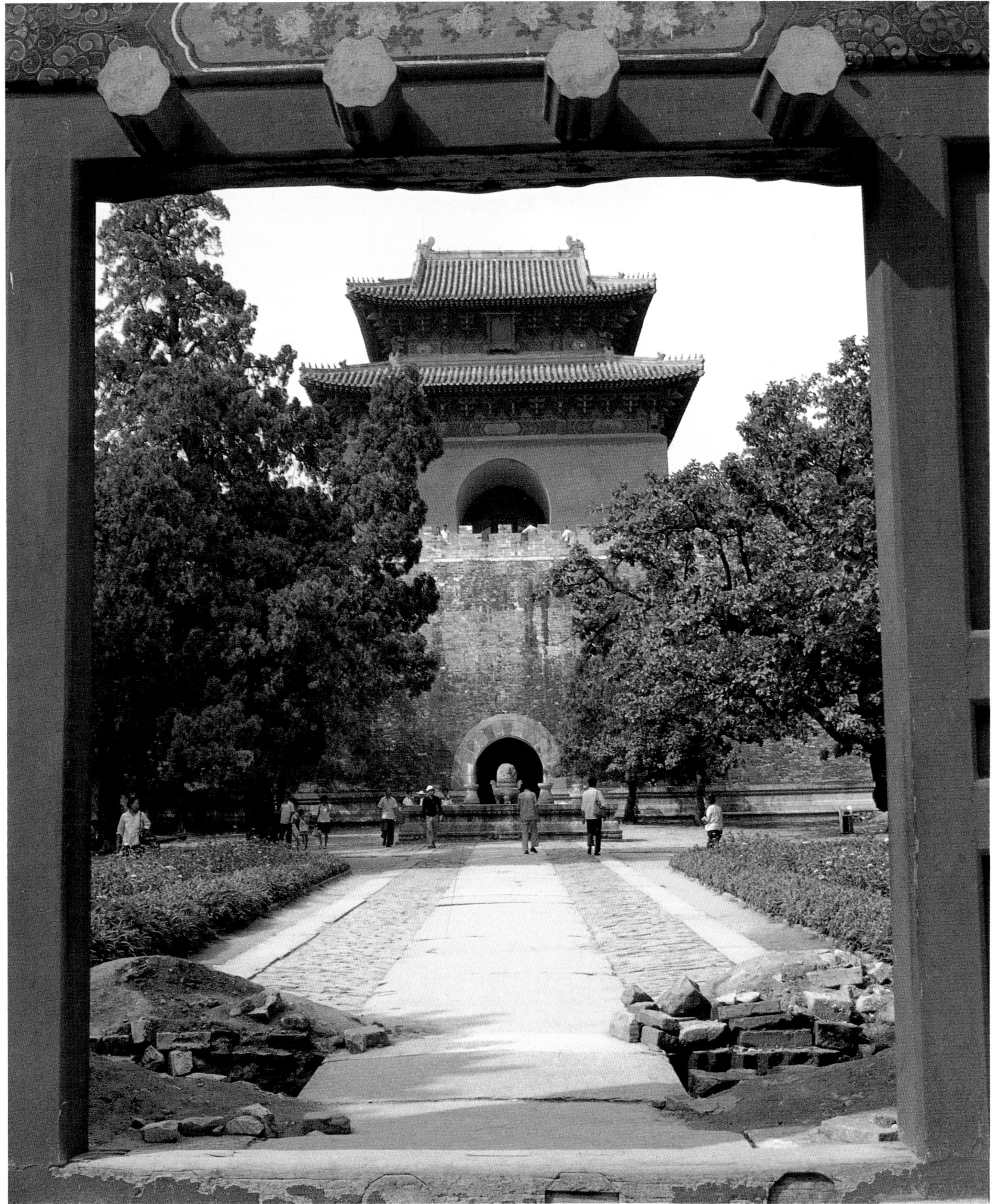

◁ Beijing, Ming 13 Tombs, Ningen Dian, capital of phoenix design

◁ Beijing, Ming 13 Tombs, Ningen Dian, a glazed tile furnace

▷ Beijing, Ming 13 Tombs, sacrificial table of five utensils

▽ Beijing, Ming 13 Tombs, Dingling, 1573-1620, plan and section

Key
1 Entrance. 2 Hall. 3 Side hall. 4 Main hall. 5 Platform.

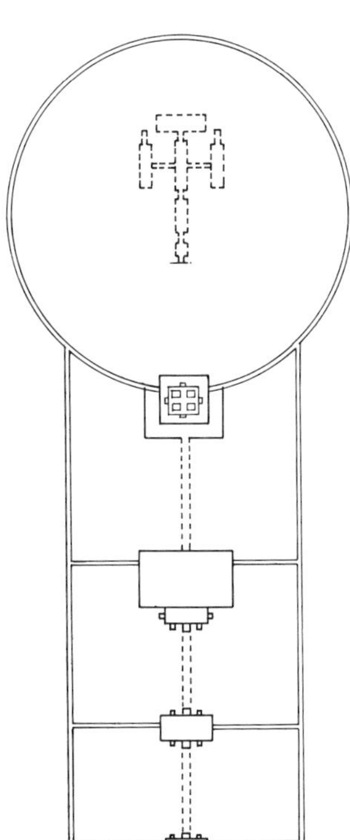

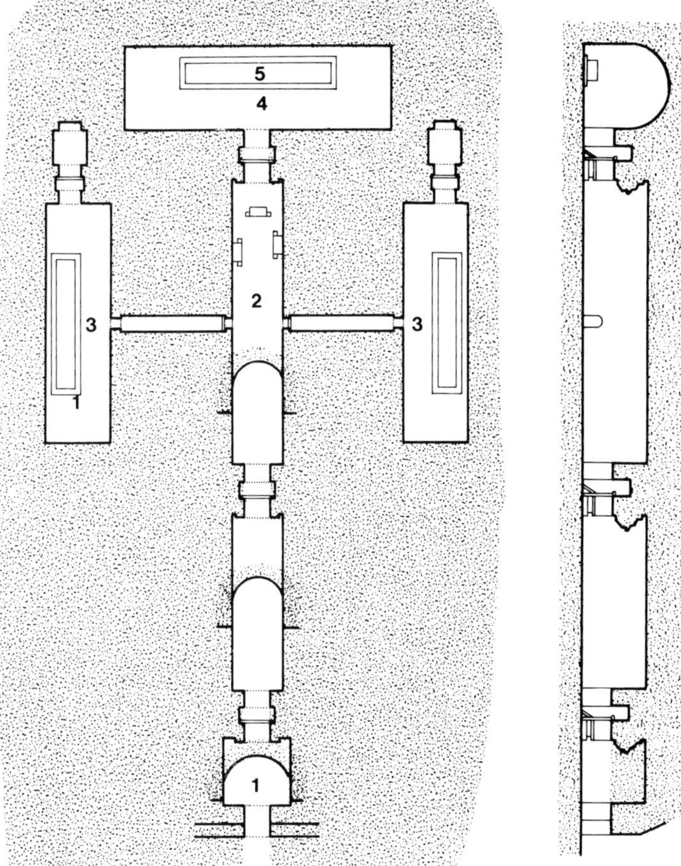

and has several massive self-locking marble doors, 19.81 metres below ground level. From the entrance to the end is approximately 83.82 metres in length. The first square space is a vestibule leading to an arched opening, and through another long 'courtyard' is the central hall, 32 metres long by 6 metres wide, and containing one big carved white marble throne and stools. A large porcelain urn of white and blue colour was placed in front of the throne. The urn was filled with oil and a wick, which was lit before the doors were locked. The last hall is where the coffins were placed. On a long marble podium stood three coffins in which the emperor and his two empresses were buried.

The side halls were originally built for the two empresses, also with self-locking doors leading to the outside, and would have been used if they had died after the emperor; but in fact they both died before him and thus their coffins were placed to await him in the main hall. The whole find has since been called the Subterranean Palace.

CEREMONIAL HALLS

Jinci (The Hall of the Sacred Mother, 1023-1032)

Located at the suburb of Taiyuan, Shanxi Province, Jinci was built to worship the mother of Shuyu. The planning of the whole ensemble took advantage of the wooded hilly terrain and a stream running diagonally across the main axis, thus creating an ensemble which integrated the landscape with monumental buildings. On the main axis, first there is a stage for performances, a stone bridge, a platform on which stand four cast iron warriors, a hall for sacrificial offerings, a cross-bridge, and at the end is the Hall of the Sacred Mother. Around this group, numerous halls and pavilions were built. All had their axes perpendicular to the main axis of the ensemble, and a unity was thus achieved. Among them, the hall and the cross-bridge in front occupy an important position in the history of architecture for their unique forms.

Repaired in 1102, the main hall has a big double tier half-hip roof. The building is surrounded by an ambulatory and the peristyle in the front is double depth.

▷ Taiyuan, Shanxi, Jinci, ceremonial hall, plan, Song Dynasty, 1023-1032

Key
1 Iron statues. 2 Hall of Sacrifice. 3 Cross Bridge. 4 Hall of the Sacred Mother. 5 Shuijin platform. 6 East Spring Pavilion. 7 Lotus Pond. 8 Zhibo Channel. 9 Stage. 10 Shengying Tai. 11 Tongle Ting. 12 Ceremonial Hall of Three Sages. 13 Tang Shuyu Ceremonial Hall. 14 Guandi Hall. 15 Wenchang Gong.

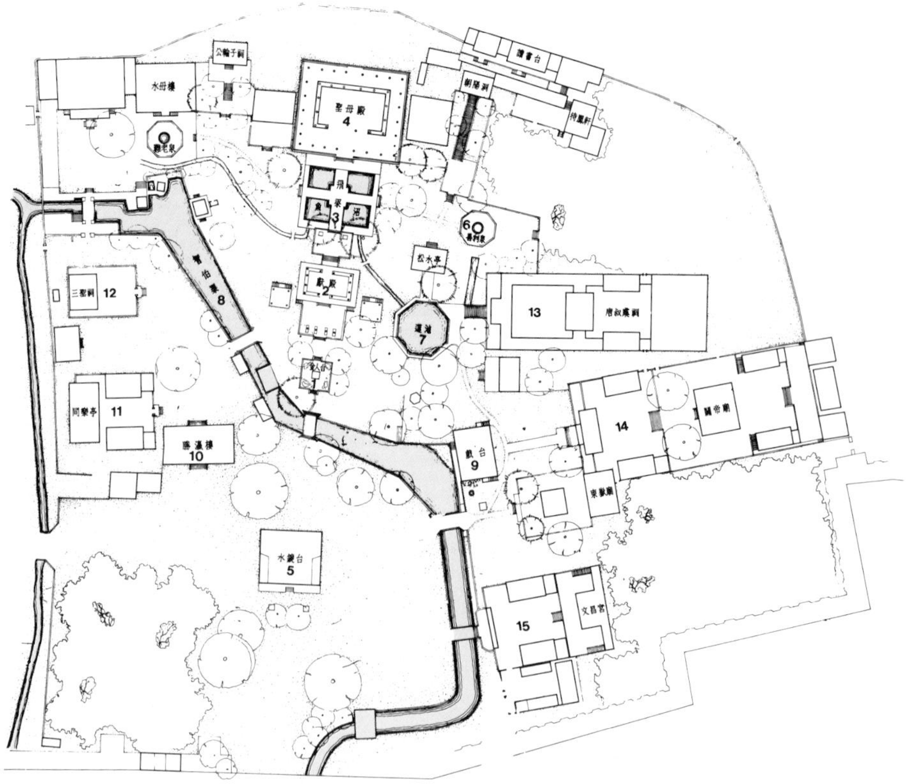

▽ Taiyuan, Shanxi, Jinci, ceremonial hall, bird's-eye view

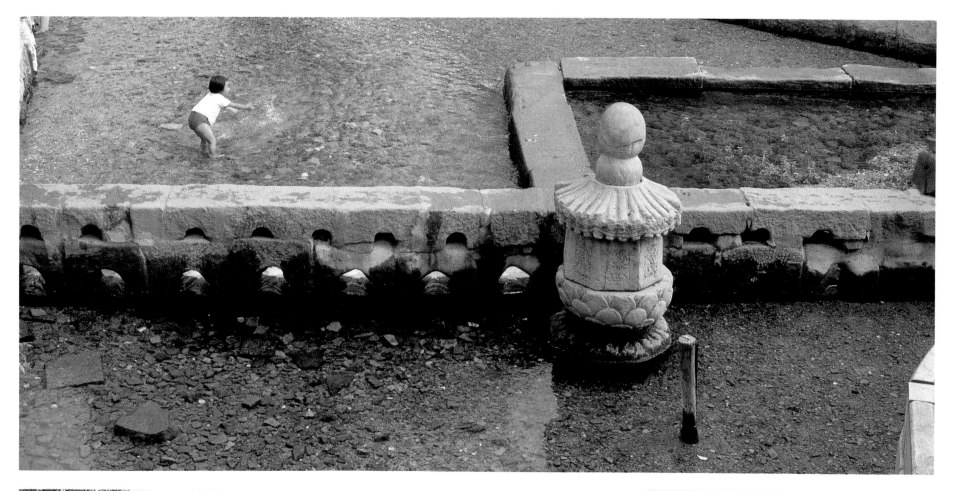

△ Taiyuan, Shanxi, Jinci, ceremonial hall, pool

◁ Taiyuan, Shanxi, Jinci, ceremonial hall, stage

▷ Taiyuan, Shanxi, Jinci, ceremonial hall, hall of sacrifice

▽ Taiyuan, Shanxi, Jinci, ceremonial hall, cross-bridge

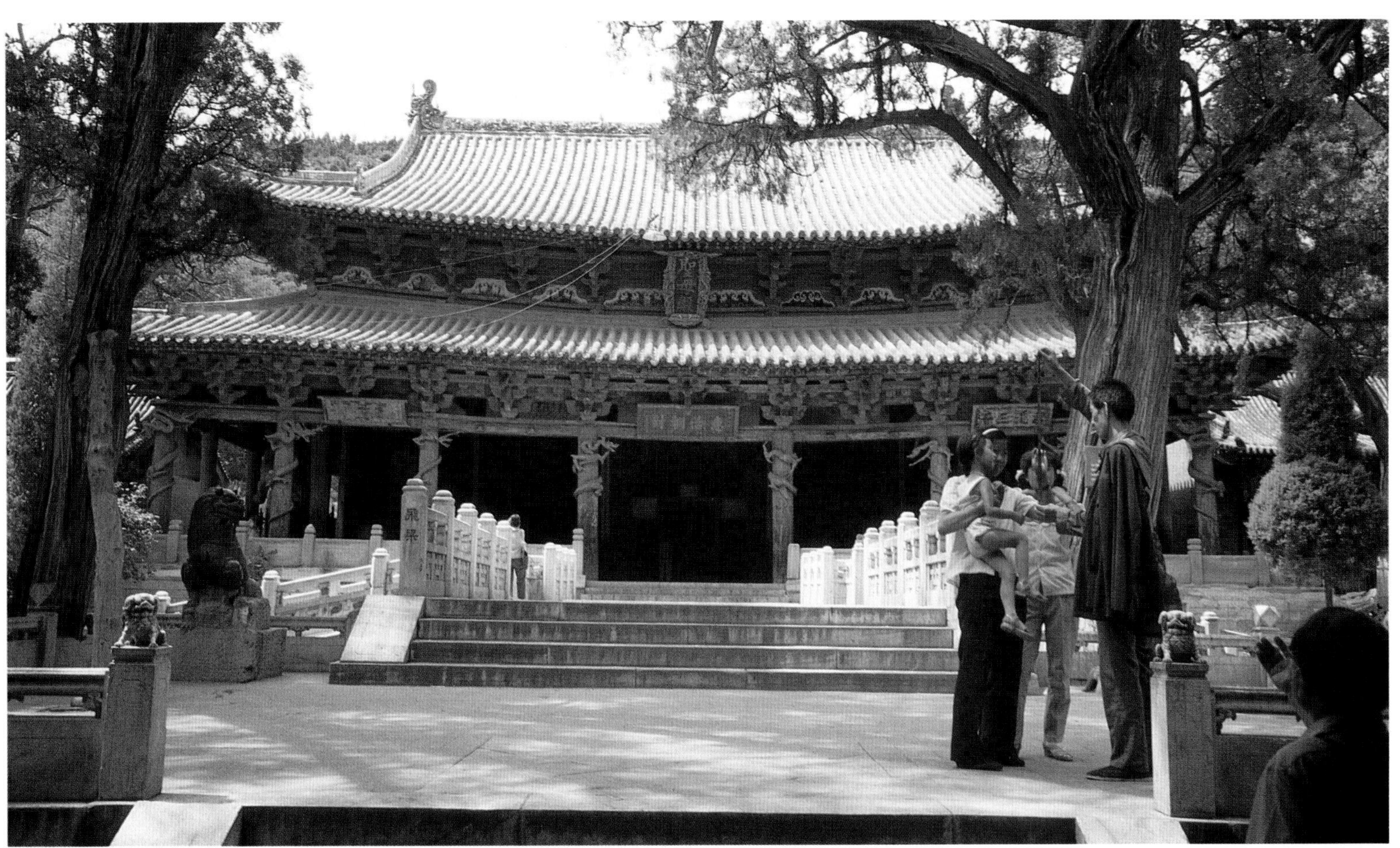

◁ Taiyuan, Shanxi, Jinci, ceremonial hall, Hall of the Sacred Mother

▽ Taiyuan, Shanxi, Jinci, ceremonial hall, cross-bridge, detail

◁ Taiyuan, Shanxi, Jinci, ceremonial hall, portico and guardian

▷ Taiyuan, Shanxi, Jinci, ceremonial hall, eave and coiled dragon column

▽ Taiyuan, Shanxi, Jinci, ceremonial hall, Hall of the Sacred Mother

Key
1 Portico. 2 Guardian statue. 3 Statue of the Sacred Mother. 4 Statues of attendants.

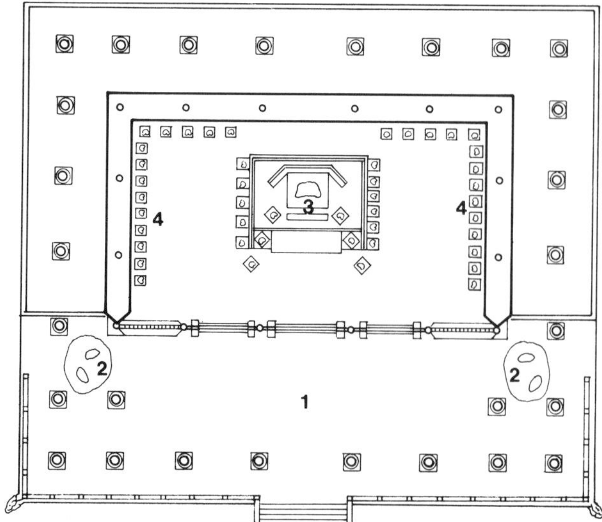

Around the wooden columns are carved coiled, lively, wooden dragons in an open-work style, which is unusual in Chinese architecture. Framed with large beams, there are no columns inside the hall, a statue of the Sacred Mother is seated in the centre and 44 statues of attendants and retinues, all clay moulded in the Song Dynasty, flank both sides. This famous group of graceful statues, each one having a different facial expression and costume, gives a picture of court life in that period.

In between the main hall and Hall of Sacrificial Offerings is a pond, over which is Feiliang (Flying Bridge) in the form of a cross with the intersection raised a little higher thus attaining a graceful curve. This Flying Bridge is supported by wooden beams and brackets on top of 34 stone pillars standing in the fish pond. The bridge and the main hall are believed to have been built at the same time. The form of the bridge, although recorded in history books and paintings, is the only real example in China.

To the east of the main hall is the Dongguan Ting Pavilion (East Spring Pavilion). All the pillars are inclined to the centre and the roof is held up by rafters and brackets only.

Kong Miao (The Confucius Temple)
Qufu, Shang Dong Province

Since Wudi's period of the Han Dynasty, many Confucian Temples have been built. The largest among them is the one developed from the foundation of his birth place and home at Qufu. It covers approximately ten hectares (25 acres) with 620 rooms and was planned according to the axis and courtyard principle. The main hall was built in the Qing Dynasty; it has nine bays and a double half-hip roof of yellow glazed tiles. The peristyle in the front has ten big limestone columns carved with coiled dragons and cloud designs. Yellow tile, dragon and cloud designs were symbols of imperial buildings. Since Confucius was respected as a sage and a king, this temple was allowed to use these symbols.

The pavilion at the centre of the inner court is called Xingtan (The Apricot Platform, 1504 A.D.), built at a place where there was an apricot tree. Confucius supposedly gave lectures to his disciples under this tree.

△ Taiyuan, Shanxi, Jinci, East Spring Pavilion, roof construction

◁ Taiyuan, Shanxi, Jinci, East Spring Pavilion

△ Taiyuan, Shanxi, Jinci, ceremonial hall, Statue of the Sacred Mother

▷ Qufu, Shangdong, Confucius Temple, the Apricot Pavilion, Ming Dynasty, 1504

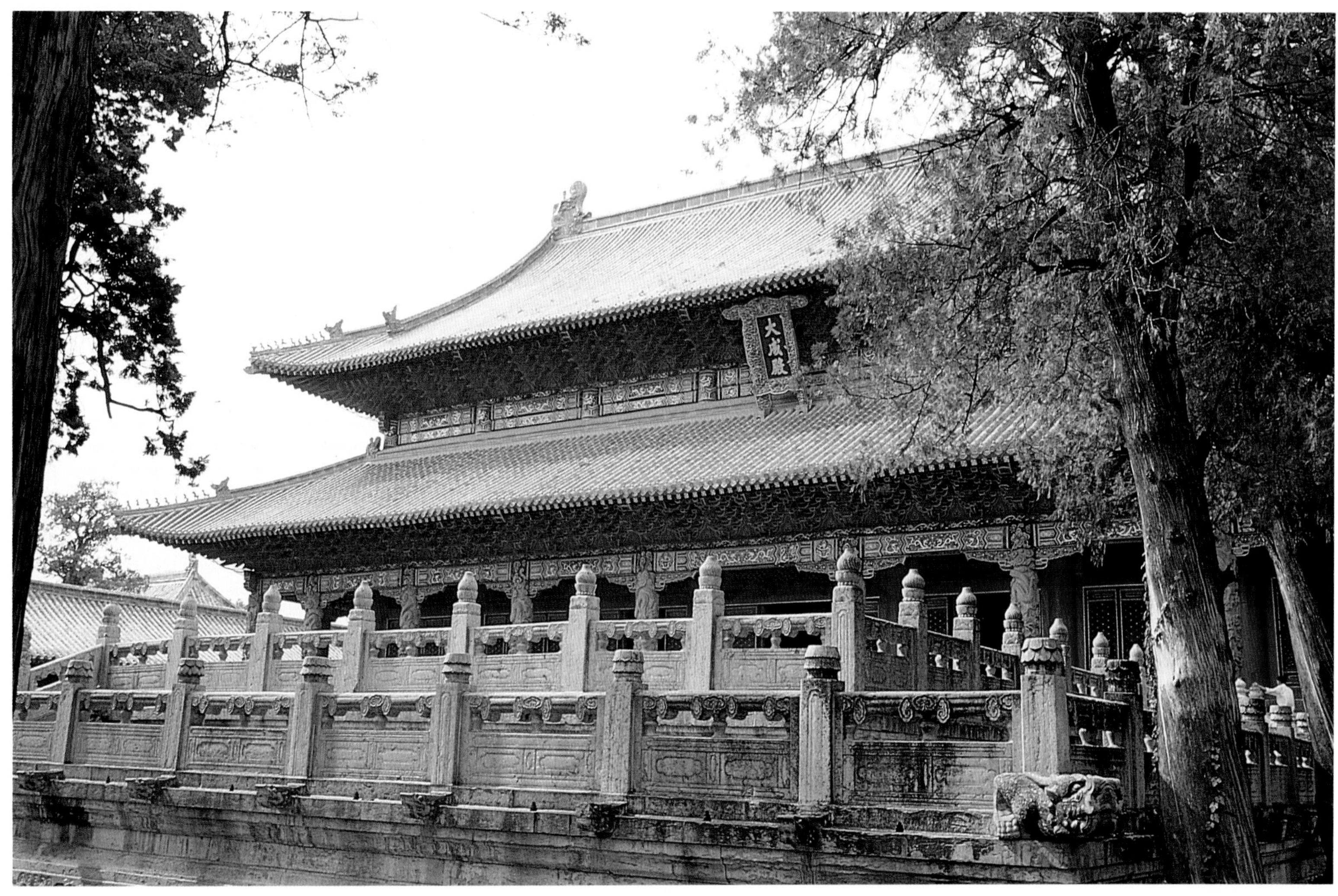

◁ Qufu, Shangdong, Confucius Temple, the main hall, Qing Dynasty, 1730

▽ Qufu, Shangdong, Confucius Temple, the main hall, dragon columns

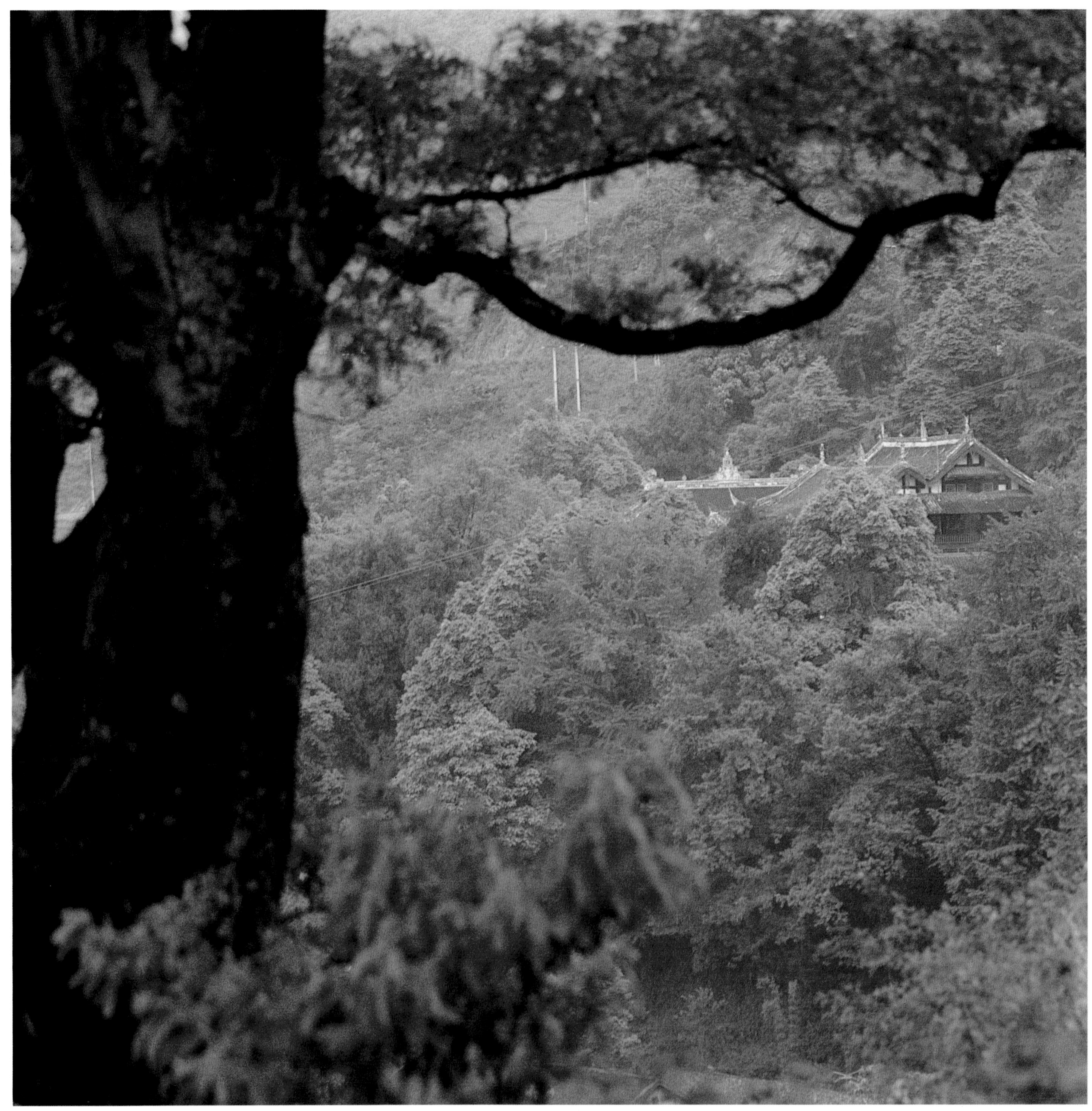

◁ Guan Xian, Sichuan
Erwang Temple

◁ Guan Xian, Sichuan,
Erwang Temple, roof design

PEIFANG, CEREMONIAL ARCH
Peifang was used widely in China to commemorate a man of merit, or a deed. Architecturally, it defines and gives identity to a place. In Anhui Province, many stone arches of this kind were built. One of them is located in Xixian, which is placd at the intersection of the main crossroads. Four arches are placed at right angles to each other forming a small square space in the centre. It is the only one of its kind. The beams were exquisitely carved. Another group of arches was formed by nine arches placed successively along an approach to an important building. This grouping is also unique in China.

▷ Guan Xian, Sichuan,
Chenghuang Miao

Erwang Miao (Temple of Two Kings)
Guanxian, Sichuan Province
This temple was built to commemorate Libing and his son for their irrigation work of harnessing water around the 3rd century B.C. Set on a tree covered hillside, the roof form is of particular interest; instead of using a big roof, several small roofs of different form were used to make it look smaller and more delicate. Black, symbolizing water, was used extensively in this building group.

Chenghuang Miao, Temple of Chenghuang,
Guanxian, Sichuan
Chenghuang is a demigod of Daoism, who supposedly reigned over a city. Since the side halls were built on a steep site along a steep staircase, the roof was designed to progress from bottom to top thus creating a dynamic effect.

▷ Xixian, Xu Guo Fang Gateway, Ming Dynasty, 1527-1596

▷ Xixian, Xu Guo Fang Gateway, Ming Dynasty, 1527-1596

▽ Suzhou, Jiangsu, Gui Youguang Ceremonial Hall

▽ Chengdu, Sichuan, Wuhou Hall, doorway

△ Xixian, Xu Guo Fang Gateway, Ming Dynasty, 1527-1596

◁ Tangyue, Anhui, nine archways

CHAPTER VIII

PALACES AND IMPERIAL GARDENS

◁ Beijing, Forbidden City, Meridian Gateway, eave and details

MY LAST BOOK *BEIJING: THE CORNUCOPIA OF CLASSIcal Chinese Architecture* covered most of the buildings featured in this chapter. Readers who are interested in Beijing and its palaces can find more information in that book.

In the history of world architecture, politics and religion are always the main forces developing grand architecture. China is no exception. After the latter part of the Shang Dynasty, emperors learned that magnificent palace buildings could be used as a means of suppressing slaves and a number of palaces were built to serve this political purpose. During and after the Western Zhou Dynasty and until the Spring and Autumn Periods, emperors built many cities with the palaces as the centre of the city. In those days, simple wooden frame palaces were built on top of high rammed earth podiums and after many years of improvement, the original simple wooden frame method became the main construction system in China. After Qin Shi Huang Di annihilated the other six kingdoms and united China, a great country with centralized power was established. He built the big and magnificent A Fang Gong Palace, which provided buildings for public services and luxurious court life. In the following West Han Dynasty, palaces were also built on high podiums, but the high podium had ceased to be used after the Han moved the capital to Luoyang to the east. The Han Dynasty palaces always occupied the centre of a capital city, their axes coinciding with the axes of the city. Their central location and huge form symbolized the emperor's domination of the whole city, the whole country, the people and the wish to compel the people to be subservient to him.

Many palaces and royal gardens have been recorded in history, but the best preserved and wholesome is the Purple Forbidden City built on the foundation of the Ming Dynasty, the Yi He Yuan (Summer Palace) in Beijing, and the Summer Mountain Resort in Chengde.

THE PURPLE FORBIDDEN CITY, BEIJING

The Purple Forbidden City was the palace of the Ming and Qing emperors. The third emperor Zhu Di moved his capital from Nanjing to Beijing in 1403, and from 1407 he had under his command some 200,000-300,000 workers and artisans and took 14 years to build this the largest and most magnificent palace in the world.

The Ming and Qing palace was divided into an Outer and Inner Court, entirely enclosed by thick, rusty red colour brick walls. The Outer Court was the place of administration and the edict of orders. The main buildings are the Taihe Dian (Hall of Supreme Harmony), the Zhong He Dian (Hall of Perfect Harmony), and the Bao He Dian (Hall for the Preservation of Harmony), and are usually referred to as the Three Great Halls. The Inner Court also has three main halls, the Qian Qing Gong (the Palace of Heavenly Purity), Jiao Tai Dian (Hall of Union) and Kumning Gong (Palace of Eternal Tranquility), and these were the dwellings of the emperors and empresses. Behind the Three Inner Halls is the Imperial Garden or the Qianlong Garden. There are minor halls and side halls at both sides of the Three Inner Halls, and they were the residences of attendants, eunuchs and guards. The planning of the whole ensemble was a forced analogy of the *Kao Gong Ji* of the *Zhou Ritual* and traditional rites. For instance, the Taimiao (Temple of Imperial Ancestors) was placed at the east and the Altar of Society to the west of Tianan Men as an interpretation of the rule 'with the Ancestral Hall at left and the Altar of Society at the right'. The Three Great Halls was an interpretation of the rule 'Three Great Courts'. From Daqing Men to Taihe Men was an analogy of the 'Rule of Five Gates', and the Three Great Halls and the Three Inner Halls were an interpretation of 'the court in the front and dwellings behind'.[2] This planning fully expressed the patriarchal clan system and social hierarchy of the feudal society.

However, the general plan of the Ming and Qing Dynasties palace ensembles was a continuation of palace development of the dynasties before them. From Daqing Men Gate to Prospect Hill is a straight line and the main axis, and all the important buildings were built on this axis, strictly maintaining an axial, symmetrical plan. There are eight big courtyards and eleven large buildings between the Wu Men (Meridian Gateway) and Shenwu Men (Gateway of Divine Military Genius) which form an architectural sequence in hierarchial order.

Chinese palaces are different from their European counterparts, such as Versailles in France, Buckingham Palace in England, or other palaces where all court activities are confined to a single building. In China a palace is in effect a group of buildings, with each activity taking place under a separate roof; the halls, temples, studies, residential halls, etc. stand

◁ Beijing, Forbidden City, Meridian Gateway, Ming Dynasty, 1407-1421

▽ Beijing, Forbidden City, Meridian Gateway, and the Golden Stream

apart with passages, lanes and covered verandahs connecting them. As one walks through the complex, one goes from hall to hall and from court to court. The architectural sequence changes continually, matched by changing views, and the aesthetic quality of the layout can be appreciated only if one follows the sequence as planned.

Wu Men, or the Meridian Gateway, is the main entrance to the Forbidden City and is crowned with five pavilions, from which it derived the name Wu Feng Lou, or the Gateway of Five Phoenixes. Wu Men is horseshoe-shaped in plan, with the entrance in the middle of the horseshoe. The south facade measures 92 metres, with massive walls enclosing a vast paved yard on three sides. The massive, powerful gateway was not only a gateway to the palace, but was also used to issue royal edicts, conduct formal audiences and execute captured rebels. The overall effect is oppressive since even today, while standing in front of this gateway, one cannot help but be awed by the power of this imposing monumental building and experience a fearful feeling. Could this be the effect the original designers wanted to achieve?

By going through the arched opening of Wu Men and climbing the ramp to the platform above, the big court, the bow-shaped Jinshui He (Golden Stream River) and the big Taihe Men Gate are overlooked.

◁ Beijing, Forbidden City, Meridian Gateway, and the Five Dragon Bridges

▷ Beijing, Forbidden City, Taihe Men

◁ Beijing, Forbidden City, Taihe Dian

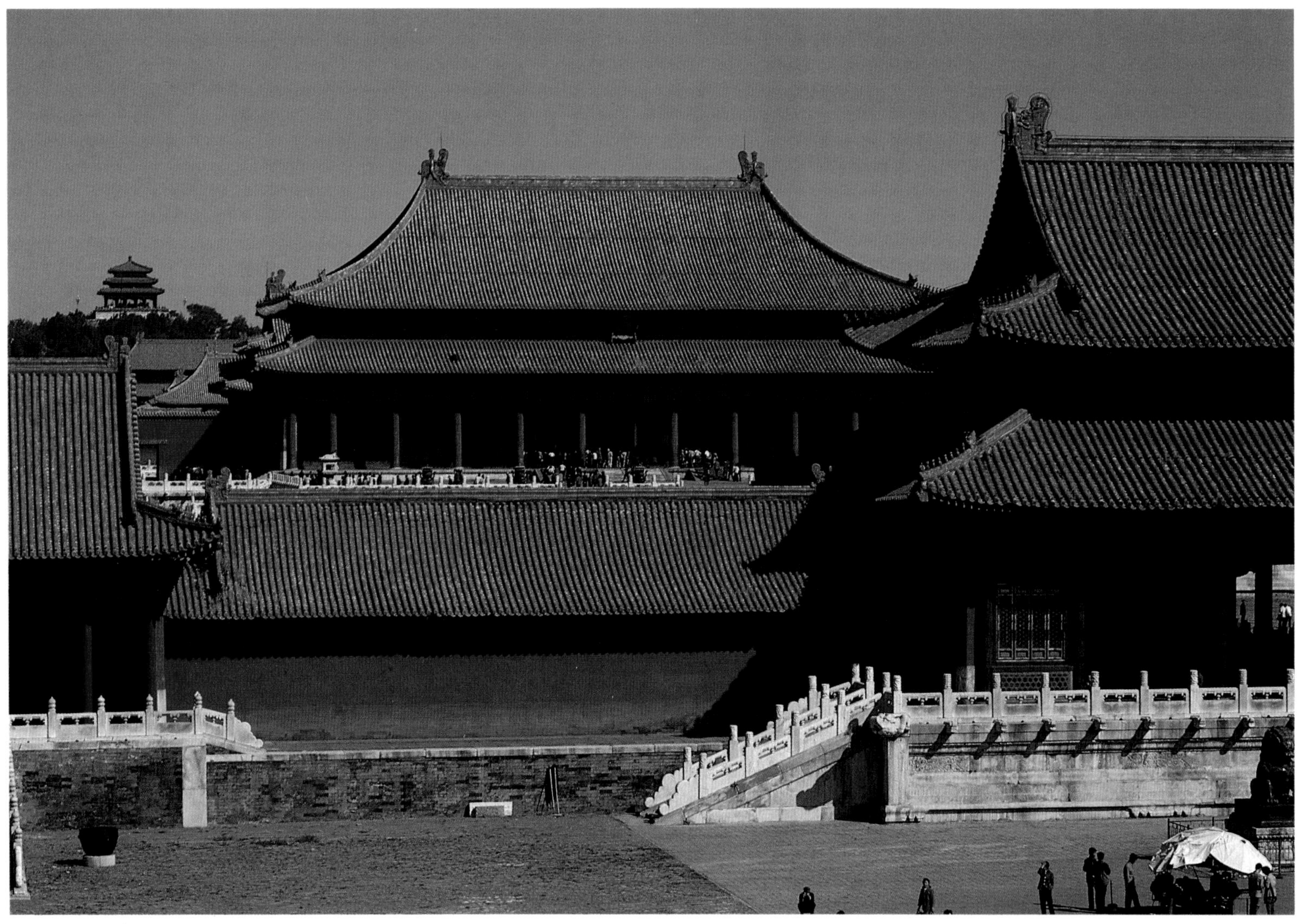

◁ Beijing, Forbidden City, Meridian Gateway, and Taihe Dian

Curiously enough, the meandering stream in this courtyard of formal layout has a Baroque appearance. The white marble balustrades on both banks of the stream with their reflections in the water, and the graceful curve of the stream convey a dynamic and rhythmic feeling to visitors. Five arched bridges, symbolic of the Five Virtues (benevolence, righteousness, rite, wisdom and honesty) are built across the stream, their proximity to each other and centralized position strongly emphasize the main axis of the total complex and make the visitor conscious of the importance of the Three Great Halls. The courtyard in front of Wu Men serves as an introduction to the palace. The bridges continually guide visitors forward but the movement is temporarily arrested at the transitional space at Taihe Men.

Taihe Men, the gateway to the Throne Hall, Taihe Dian, of the palace, stands on a marble platform flanked by a pair of exquisitely carved bronze lions. Lion sculptures were used exclusively in front of important buildings. These guardians of the gateway symbolize strength and authority. Taihe Men is a building with a double-hip roof supported by giant vermilion columns and decorated beams above. Through the door frame, the magnificent imposing Taihe Dian and the big courtyard in front of it attract everyone. Taihe Dian, the most important building in the Forbidden City, is classical Chinese architecture at its best. Together with the two secondary halls behind it, standing on a three-tiered marble platform seven metres in height, are the functional and aesthetic climaxes of the architectural sequence. Its spectacular double-eaved roof of bright yellow tiles is the glory of the Ming and Qing Dynasties. It shines brilliantly under the azure northern sun and above the warm grey paving bricks. The slightly curved roof forms, the horizontal eaves and the shadows they create, together with the horizontal tiers of the platform, express the reposing, solemn nature of the architecture. Here, one can see the difference between the Chinese and Western architectural concepts. In the West, verticality was used to symbolize uprightness, monumentality, and reaching to the sky. Conversely, in China horizontality was used to express sedateness, repose and harmony. The big horizontal roof form was used to represent sky, and the Son of Heaven. As if it envelopes everybody and everything on earth, it is the aegis of all living beings.

The big hall and the big courtyard in front were used to celebrate the birthday of the emperor, the Chinese New Year, and edict of important orders and other important ceremonies. During these occasions, the emperor and ministers stayed inside the hall, while others stood attentively under the big platform in the courtyard. It would not be difficult to visualise why the ancient designer laid out a big space like this to comply with the functional requirements of the ritual.

Taihe Dian not only has a double-eave hip roof, but at each end of the main ridge are 3.4 metres end decorations of dragon design facing each other. The end of the hip ridge has a set of eleven mythological figures. Each circular tile end terminates with a dragon design. The end of the pan tile is of crescent moon shape. Together they protect the rafter underneath from rain water and decorate the roof. The big roof and overhanging eaves are supported by big red wooden columns, of which the central bay is the widest with a span of 8.44 metres. Doors of wood are always in

◁ Beijing, Forbidden City, Taihe Dian, eave design

▽ Beijing, Forbidden City, Baohe Dian, throne

▷ Beijing, Forbidden City, coffered ceiling

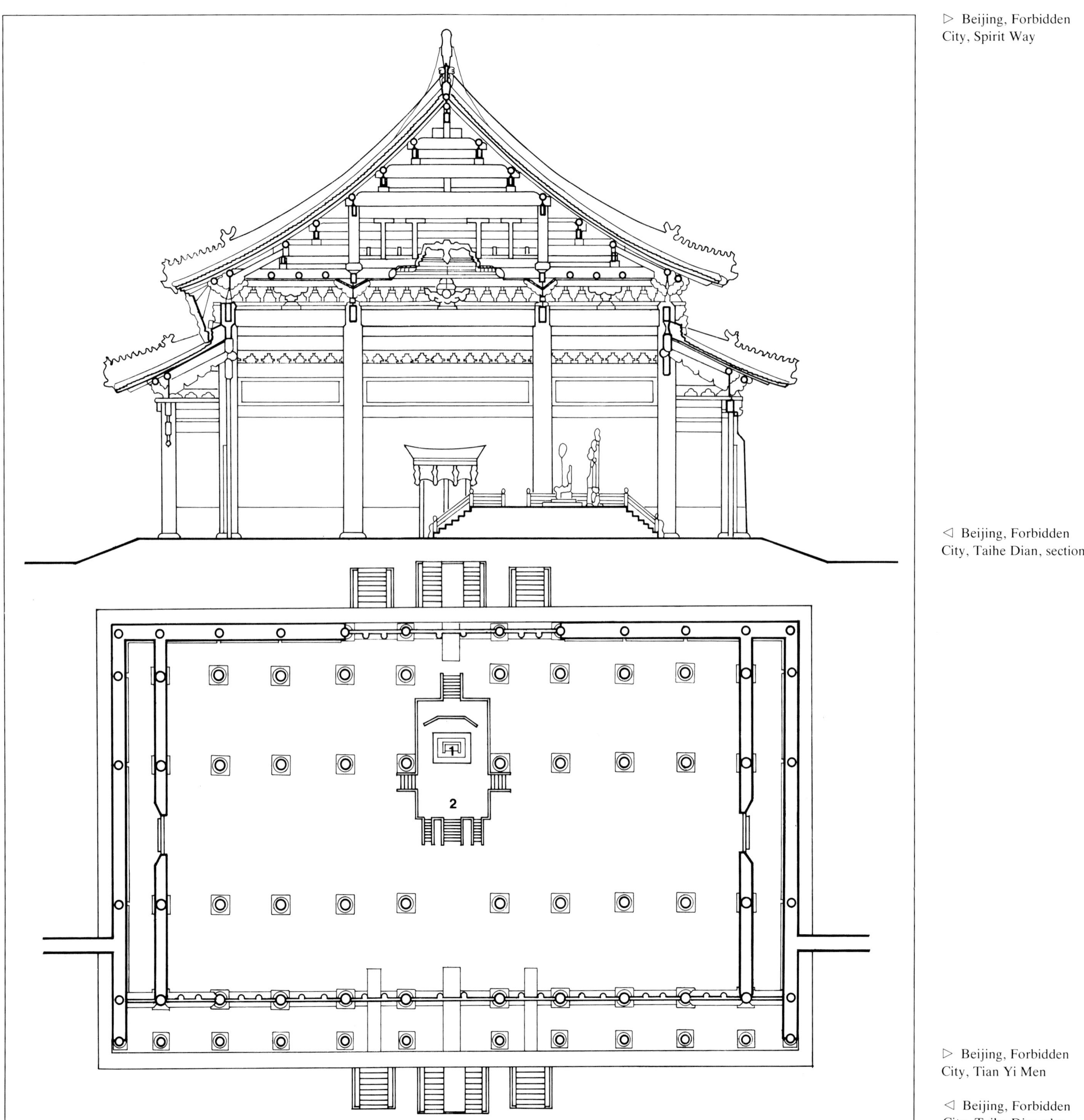

▷ Beijing, Forbidden City, Spirit Way

◁ Beijing, Forbidden City, Taihe Dian, section

▷ Beijing, Forbidden City, Tian Yi Men

◁ Beijing, Forbidden City, Taihe Dian plan

pairs or multiples of two. They are painted in red and gold, with lattice work above and solid panels of dragon designs below, and contrast admirably with the plain plaster walls on both sides. The overhanging eaves are supported by rafters on dougongs and painted with plant designs.

The interior of the hall is luxurious and grand. In the centre is a big gilded throne on top of a platform 1.8 metres high, and behind is an intricately carved wooden throne. Surrounding the throne are eight big columns decorated with entwined gilded dragons, twisting and writhing upwards to the large coffered ceiling. In the centre of the ceiling are two such dragons and between them a big celestial pearl. The peripheral area is painted blue and green so that the gold ceiling stands out clearly in the middle. The platform of the throne, the eight big columns and the coffered ceiling above form an interior vertical space, and in the centre was the emperor, or the Son of Heaven.

Behind Taihe Dian is the Zhong He Dian and Baohe Dian, inside of which are a throne and a desk. From Taihe Dian, just as in a typical house complex, one cannot see the buildings and courts behind. The hall is always in the middle of a courtyard or between two courts. One has to move from court to court, and from hall to hall, in order to experience the sequence. Coming out of the entrance of Taihe Dian and walking around it, one can see the Zhong He Dian from one side in perspective rather than the facade, the three-dimensional building standing in space. To go forward in this way, to appreciate the building and courts one after the other, the space seems without an end.

After Baohe Dian, there is a flight of steps leading to the emperor's private chambers. The steps are bisected by a wide ramp of marble named Bi Shi or 'spirit way', ornamented with dragon carvings. Only the emperor could use the 'spirit way' over which he was carried in a sedan chair. His porters, being lesser mortals, used the steps on either side, as did everyone else. The 'spirit way' is 16.57 metres long, 3.07 metres wide, 1.7 metres thick and weighs about 250 tons. The stone was quarried from a site 100 miles away and moved to this place in the winter when the road was frozen so that it was easy to slide on the ice.

In the Three Inner Halls, the largest is the Qian Qing Gong. It was built in 1797 and was used as the emperor's office. The hall also has a double-eave hip-roof but has only one tier of podium. From the Three Great Halls, a raised path leads to this hall.

Behind the Three Inner Halls is the Imperial Garden, built by Emperor Qianlong, which forms the northern part of the Forbidden City. The arched entrance, Tian Yi Men (One Sky Gateway) which leads to the garden, is of warm, grey brick polished and made in

◁ Beijing, Forbidden City, Tian Yi Men, lion sculpture

▷ Beijing, Forbidden City, Yangxing Den

◁ Beijing, Forbidden City, Yangxing Dian, gateway

△ Beijing, Forbidden City, Yangxing Dian,

▷ Beijing, Forbidden City, corner pavilion

a special way. It goes very well with the white marble platform and the glazed tile roof. At each side of the arch is a Chi Ling, a mythological animal resembling a lion. To one side of the garden and on top of a false hill is Yang Xing Zhai, the study of Prince Guang Xu.

Yang Xin Dian or 'Hall for the Culture of the Mind' is located to the west of the main axis. It was built in the Ming Dynasty in 1723 and served as the office of ministers. The interior was exquisitely executed and it was here that Dowager Cixi once held court. During occasions such as these she would sit behind a curtain so the male ministers could not see her, a rite practised in ancient China.

BI SHU SHAN ZHUANG (THE SUMMER MOUNTAIN RESORT) CHENGDE, HEBEI

Emperor Kang Xi of the Qing Dynasty chose the beautiful scenic mountain plateau of Chengde to build a summer resort palace outside Beijing. Each year, a big hunting party was held. The construction work started in 1703 and was completed in 1708. It covers an area of 56 hectares (140 acres) and the length of the wall is around 19 kilometres (12 miles). The entire resort is in a thickly wooded, serene, hilly place with small lakes and little creeks. It is cool and dry in the summer, which makes an ideal summer place.

The Summer Resort was planned as a courtyard house of the northern style. A series of halls and courtyards were placed along the axis. If compared to the Purple Forbidden City, one can see that it is less adorned and fits more into the natural landscape.

Wu Men or the Meridian Gateway is the main entrance to the palace. A magnificent tablet with four big characters, Bi Shu Shan Zhuang, was hung on top of the doorway. The words were of Kang Xi's calligra-

▷ Chengde, Hebei, Summer Imperial Resort, plan 1703-1708

Key

1 Imperial Summer Resort. 2 Palace. 3 Imperial Garden. Yanyu Lou. 4 Wenjin Ge. 5 Puning Si. 6 Xumifoshou. 7 Putuozhongcheng Si. 8 Pule Si. 9 Anyuan Si. 10 Furen Si. 11 Chengde City.

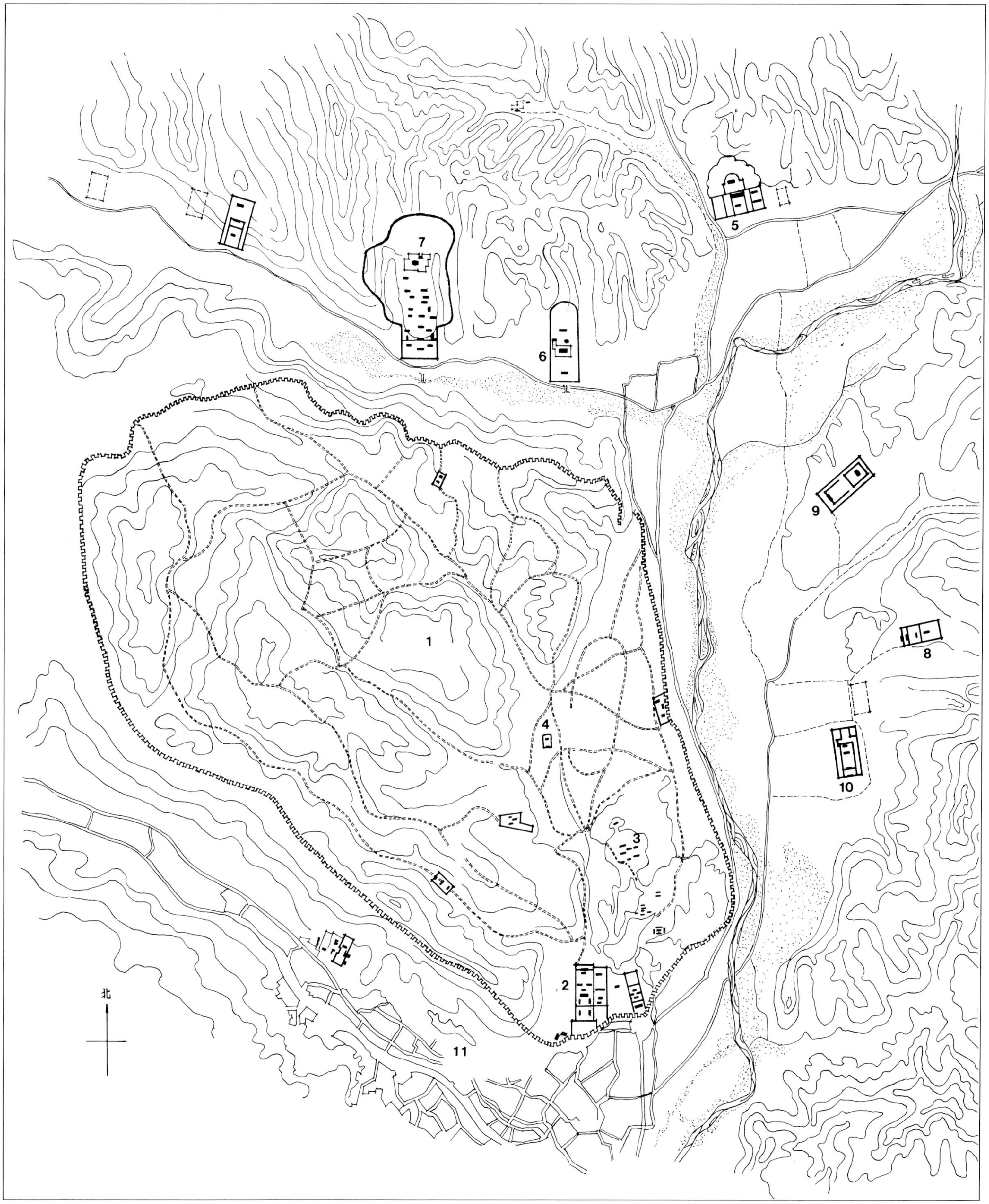

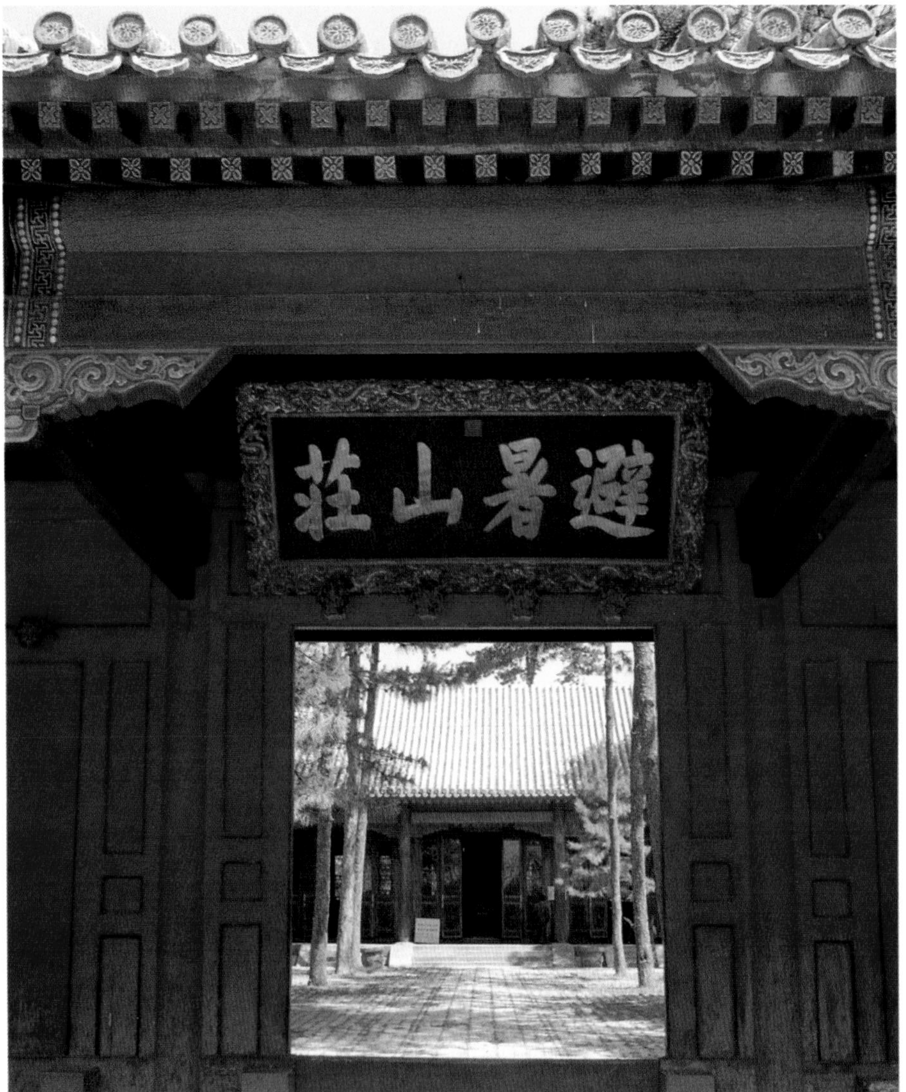

▷ Chengde, Hebei, Summer Imperial Resort, main entrance

▽ Chengde, Hebei, Summer Imperial Resort, eave and column detail

phy. Through the door frame, one catches a glimpse of the main courtyard and the main hall, the Dan Bo Jing Cheng Dian or (Hall of Serenity and Sincerity). There the emperors watched archery, wrestling contests and celebrated important occasions. The hall is seven bays in width, with a depth of three bays. It has a half-hip roof, surrounded by covered verandahs and side halls. Since all the woodwork of this hall is made of a special kind of cedar called Nanmu, it is commonly called the Nanmu Dian. The whole building was not painted except for a thin red line along the eave. It gives a quiet elegant character, and conforms with the idea of Kang Xi: not to waste on carved beams and red sashes, but to fit into the simple beauty of the creeks and woods. Nanmu in the summer generates a particular fragrance which gives the place a special atmosphere.

Inside and at the centre of this hall is a black throne with a padded yellow brocade cushion, and a carved wooden screen encloses the space behind the throne. The coffered ceiling is also exquisitely carved; inside each square is the word 'shou' (longevity), and at each corner of the square is a bat design. Bat in Chinese sounds 'Fo', similar to happiness, so it was used as a symbol of happiness. The last of the halls is called Yun Shan Shen Di Lou or the Pavilion of Cloud Hill. On the second floor and looking towards the north, a panoramic view of the entire lake and mountain can be seen.

As in the Forbidden City, behind the palace is the imperial garden. There are lakes and causeways with buildings dotted here and there. The Wen Jin Ge Library used books of traditional binding to decorate the beams. The causeways were connected with small bridges of different designs. Here the verdant wood, clear ripples, pink and white lotus and green reeds are among the pavilions, halls, and wharves, There is a hall which imitated the Yan Yu Lou (Hall of Misty Rains) of Jia Xing Zhejiang Province and was built on a small isle. The Spring Causeway of Hangzhou Zhejiang was also copied so that this place was made both picturesque and charming.

During the heyday of this resort, there were the 36 Sceneries of Kang Xi, and after this Qianlong added another 36 Sceneries. Most of them, however, were demolished through mishaps and battles. It is lucky that the uniquely styled palace was well preserved. Here we can see even the emperors and empresses, the members of the royal family who, though accustomed to the luxurious life of the palaces, wanted to escape, whenever possible, to a simpler, humane place seeing a natural environment for their abode and retreat. Perhaps this was why, during the long years, the royal families liked to live in the Summer Resort and the Summer Palace (Yi He Yuan) rather than in the magnificent palace on a grand scale.

△ Chengde, Hebei, Summer Imperial Resort, throne

▷ Chengde, Hebei, Summer Imperial Resort, interior of a residential hall

▽ Chengde, Hebei, Summer Imperial Resort, wooden ceiling

▷ Chengde, Hebei, Summer Imperial Resort, Yun Shan Shen Di Lou

▽ Chengde, Hebei, Summer Imperial Resort, royal chamber

△ Chengde, Hebei, Summer Imperial Resort, Wenjin Ge Library, beam decoration

▷ Chengde, Hebei, Summer Imperial Resort, imperial garden

◁ Chengde, Hebei, Summer Imperial Resort, sacrificial table

IMPERIAL GARDENS

During the long years of Chinese history, although many dynasties changed hands, and new replaced the old, yet each of the emperors built gardens for their pleasure seeking. The gardens remaining in existence today, apart from the above-mentioned Imperial Garden in the Mountain Resort and the Purple Forbidden City, are the Three Seas, Yi He Yuan, and Yuan Ming Yuan in Beijing.

Yuan Ming Yuan, the largest in Beijing, is called the Garden of Gardens and was almost totally destroyed by fire and looting in 1860.

The Golden Water Stream forms three lakes: Beihai (the North Sea), Zhong Hai (the Middle Sea) and Nan Hai (the South Sea). As Zhong Hai and Nan Hai are the seat of the central government of the People's Republic of China, it is not open to the public every day. Now only the North Sea Park is a public park. The climax of the park is obviously the Qiong Hua Dao (Hortensia Island) and the white stupa crowing this hilly and wooded island.

Many small gardens inside this park were divided off and each is enclosed by walls. The Jing Xin Zhai (Den of Quiet Heart) garden at the north bank of the park is a small, quiet place. It takes advantage of the natural landscape, to which garden architecture was added. A delicate arched bridge of white marble with a graceful curve was placed across the stream leading to a water pavilion. Another pavilion crowns a higher place, making it a very pleasant vantage point.

However, the Yi He Yuan or the Garden of Cultured Peace is the place admired by all. Yi He Yuan was called the Qing Yi Yuan (Garden of Clear Ripples) and was also badly damaged in 1860. In 1888, to celebrate the sixtieth birthday of the Dowager Cixi, it was rebuilt and renamed. The restored garden retains the pattern of the original and is now the best preserved in Beijing.

Yi He Yuan comprises a hilly northern section which forms the main part of the garden and a southern section of lakes, islands and causeways. In addition, at the northeastern corner is the small secluded Xie Qu Yuan, or the Garden of Harmonious Interest. Since Yi He Yuan has both hills and water and brilliant building groups, this combination of natural and man-made garden deserves to be called an imperial paradise.

Through the entrance and passing through several courtyards and halls is the famous Long Gallery, 728 metres long with 273 bays, which runs parallel to the hill on the right and the old pines, and the marble balustrades and the edge of the lake on the left. Inside, each beam is decorated with a different landscape painting. Walking along this gallery, one is able to admire the scenery on both sides and the decorations

◁ Chengde, Hebei, Summer Imperial Resort, covered bridge

▷ Beijing, Yuan Ming Yuan, Qing dynasty

◁ Chengde, Hebei, Summer Imperial Resort, Hall of Misty Rain

▷ Beijing, Yuan Ming Yuan, Qing dynasty

▷ Beijing, Beihai, (North Sea Park), Jinxing Den

▽ Beijing, Beihai, (North Sea Park), Jinxing Den, marble bridge

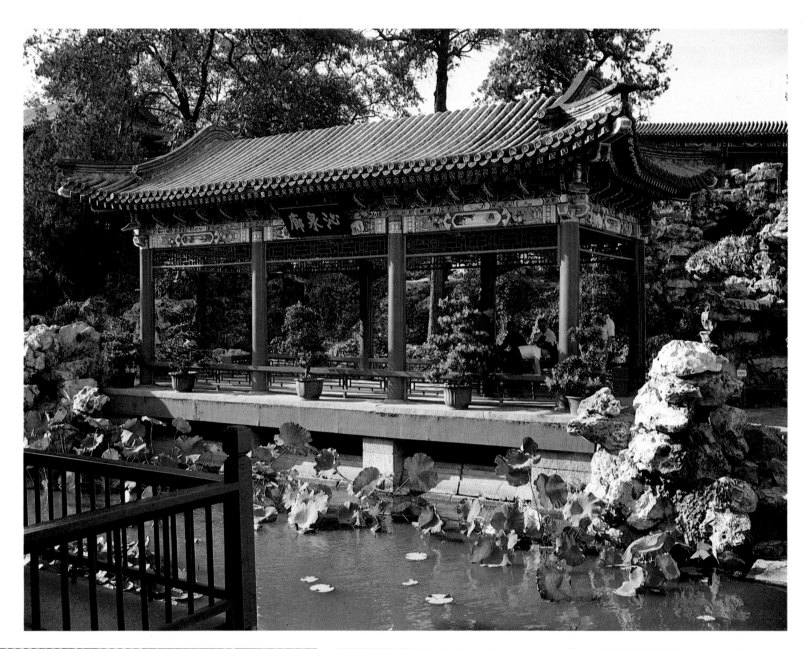

△ Beijing, Yi He Yuan

▷ Beijing, Yi He Yuan, the Long Gallery

◁ Beijing, Beihai, (North Sea Park), Jinxing Den, pavilion

▷ Beijing, Yi He Yuan, big stone staircase

◁ Beijing, Yi He Yuan, temple and Fo Xiang Ge

▷ Beijing, Yi He Yuan, sutra repository

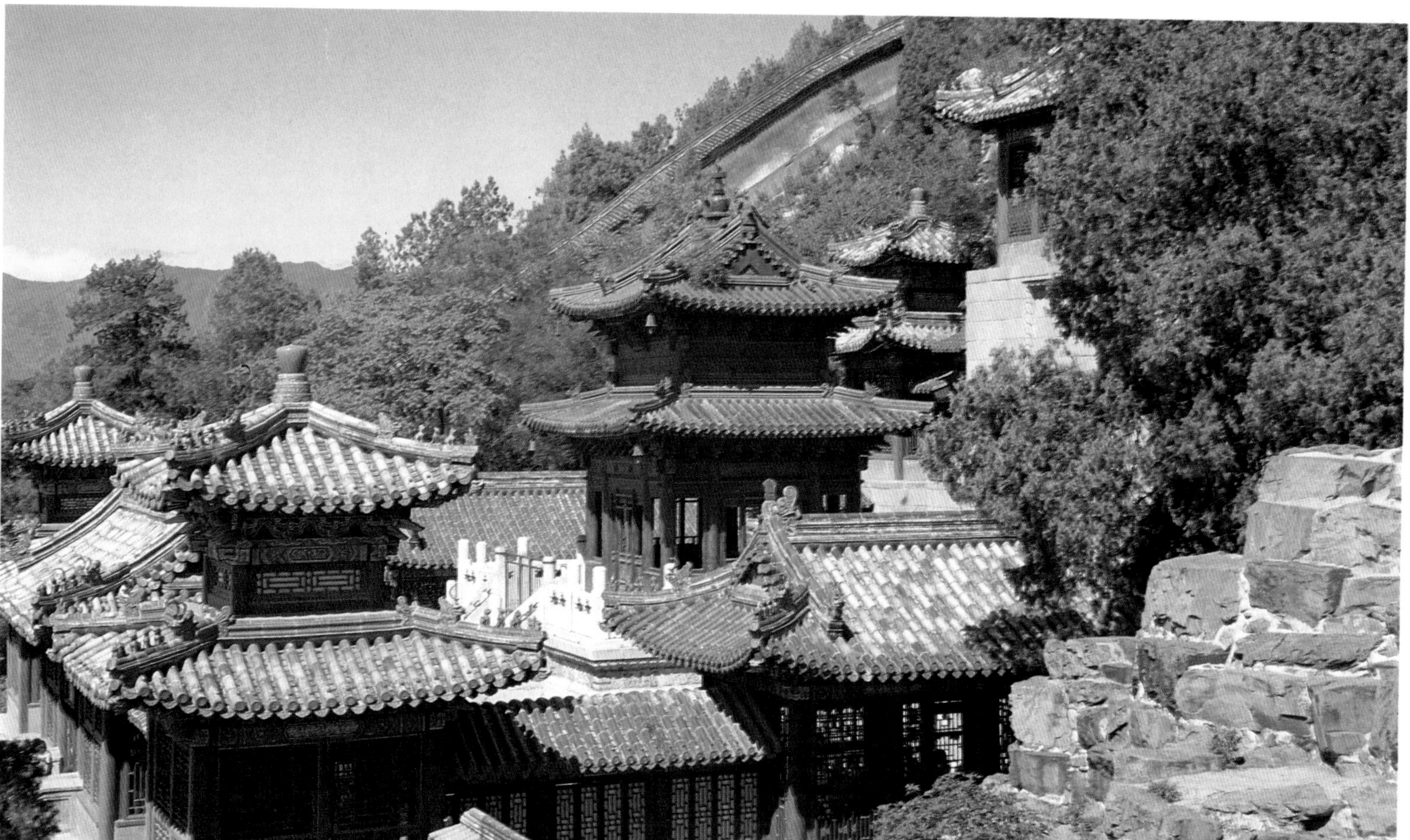

▷ Beijing, Yi He Yuan, courtyard

△ Beijing, Yi He Yuan, Baoyun Ge

△ Beijing, Yi He Yuan, 17 Arch Marble Bridge

on the beams inside. The main attraction of this garden is undoubtedly the magnificent building group on the south slope of the hill. The four-storeyed Fo Xiang Ge (Pavilion of Buddha's Fragrance) and the Lama Temple is the climax and axis of this garden. Together they dominate and thus unite all the big and small buildings around. If we compare this with the private gardens of Jiangsu Province, a totally different design concept can be discovered. The former pursues a grand, brilliant and magnificent air, the latter the poetic and painterly concept of quiet and repose. Different goals produce different results.

To the east of Fo Xiang Ge is a group of green-roofed buildings, the Zhuan Lun Zang, used for the storage of the sutras. At the centre of the group is a large stele topped by four dragons. They are lively and exquisitely carved.

West of Fo Xiang Ge and in line with Zhuan Lun Zang is Baoyun Ge, or the Pavilion of Precious Clouds, which is commonly called the Bronze Pavilion. It extends about six metres in height and is most delicately carved. It is the only building which escaped the big fire of 1860.

From the big platform of Fo Xiang Ge, one can see the Da Xiong Bao Dian, Tian Wang Dian, Gatehouse and Peifang, and to the south is a wide expanse of lake area, the Long Wang miao (Dragon King Temple) with causeways connected by marble bridges at the far

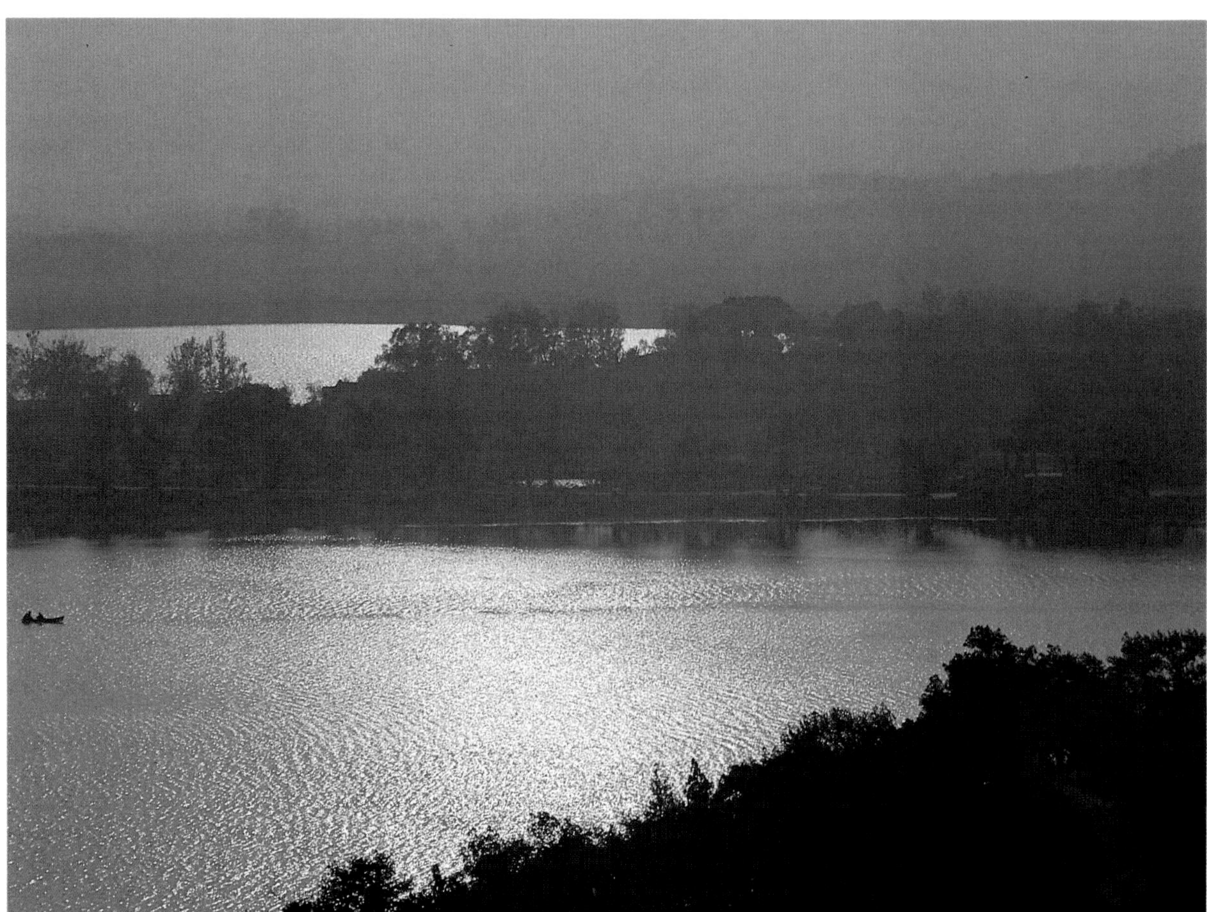

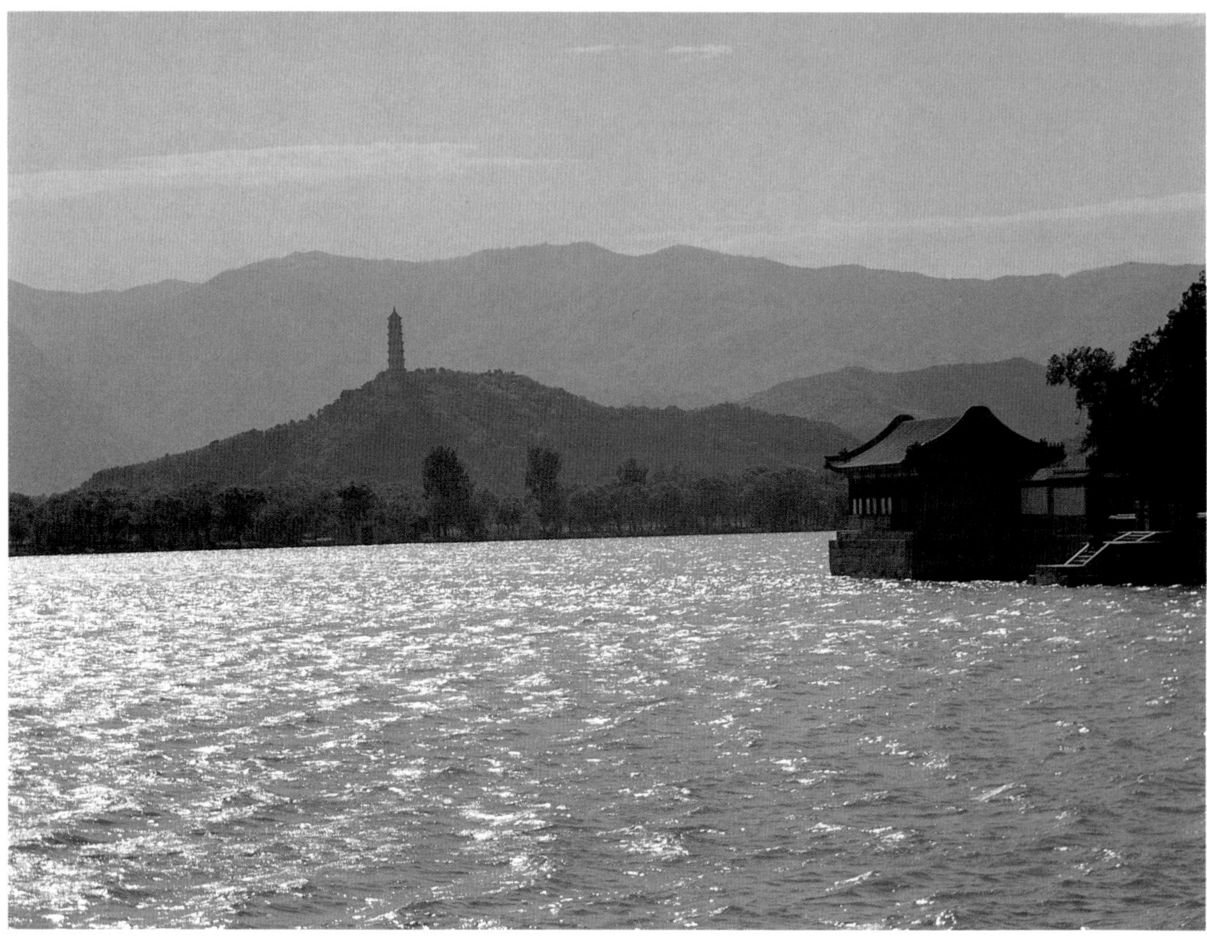

▷ Beijing, Yi He Yuan, stage

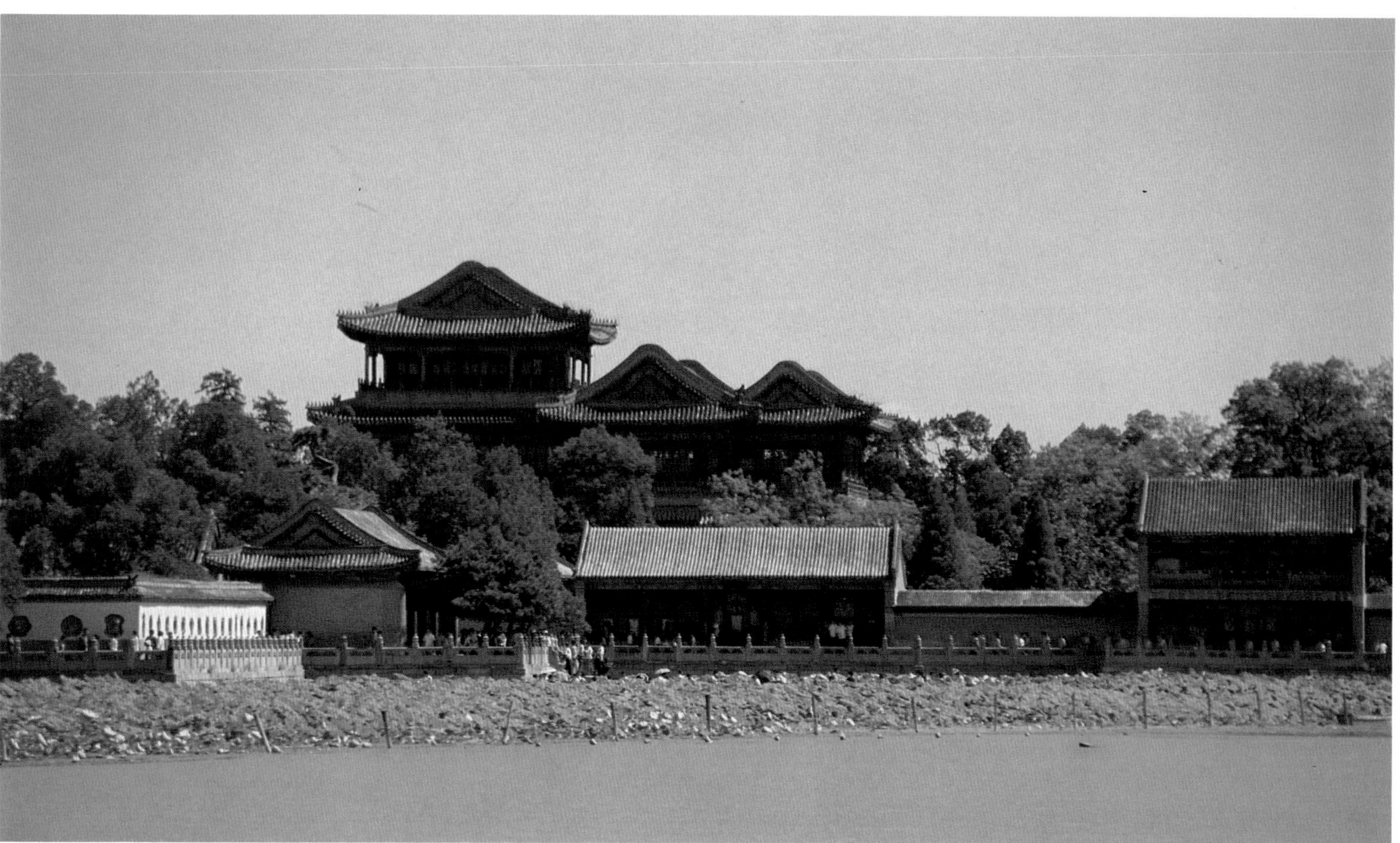

◁ Beijing, Yi He Yuan, Long Wang Miao Island

◁ Beijing, Yi He Yuan, a glazed tile pagoda, borrowed view

▷ Beijing, Yi He Yuan, lake and surrounding buildings

◁ Beijing, Yi He Yuan, Xie Qu Yuan

◁ Beijing, Yi He Yuan, Xie Qu Yuan, verandah

end. The causeways reach to the left and right, as if they were two big arms extending and embracing the water body. The building group of Fo Xiang Ge contrasts with the scenery of the lake, in that one is grand and brilliant, and of ingenious workmanship, whereas the other is quiet and elegant, natural and unadorned. They are contrasting yet blending, a complement to each other. Although the Fo Xiang Ge building group seems a little too crowded, a little too luxurious in relation to Chinese garden design criteria, it can yet be regarded as a beautiful place that makes one enjoy so much and linger on.

In the northeastern corner is Xie Qu Yuan, a garden within a garden. During one of Emperor Qianlong's trips to Wuzi near the Tai Hu Lake, he was charmed by the compactness and elegance of Ji Chang Yuan and on returning to Beijing ordered a similar garden to be built within the Yi He Yuan. It is not a replica but in the same spirit, with a pool in the middle surrounded by pavilions, halls, and verandahs of grey roof tile and green pillars. Waterways are crossed by bridges, and embellished by the ancient pines: a garden of serenity was thus created.

All in all, Yi He Yuan is a masterly combination of the artistry of man and the beauty of nature – a truly fitting setting for the Summer Palace of imperial majesty, deserving to be called a wonderful place for summer, and sublime imperial garden architecture.

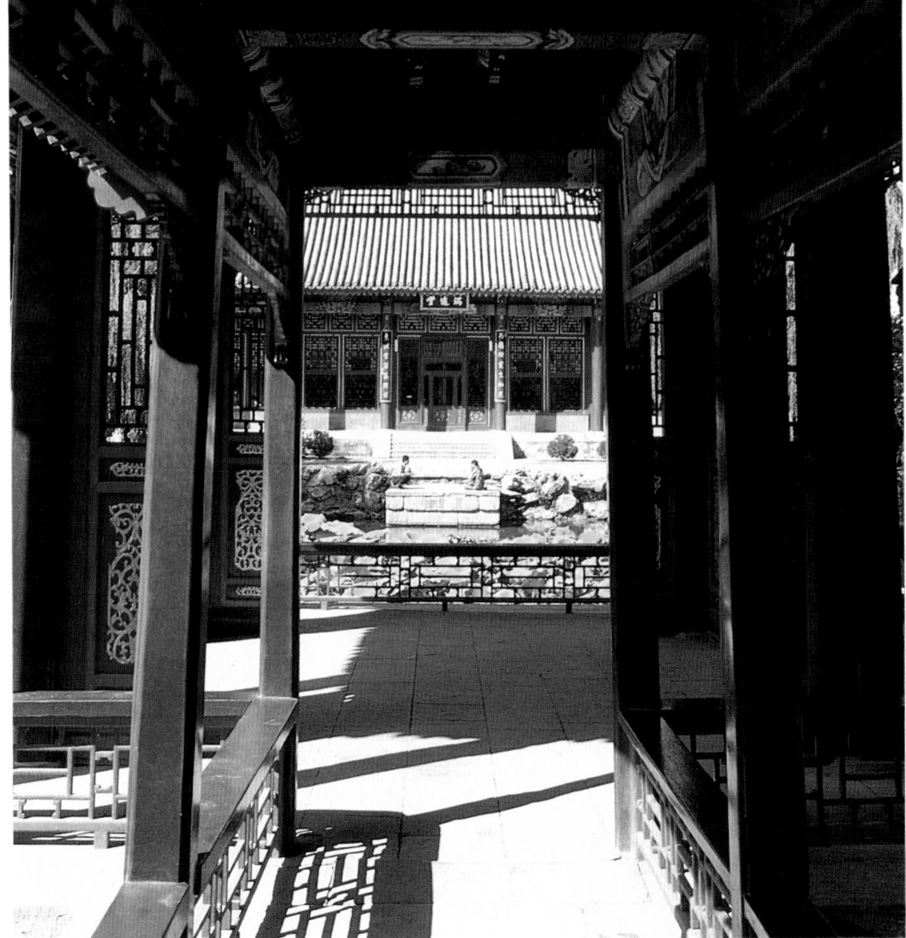

▷ Beijing, Yi He Yuan, Xie Qu Yuan, garden buildings

EPILOGUE

◁ Chengde, Hebei, Xumifoshou, Qing Dynasty, 1780, Sea Elephant

CHINESE ARCHITECTURAL LAYOUT CLOSES AT A BLANK wall; it is a statement terminating the sequence. However, architectural thinking does not conform to these boundaries. This is why I pondered, having completed a typological study of Chinese architecture, whither from here? After a prolonged period of inactivity – a virtual standstill marked by but a few minor modifications – Chinese architecture will again inevitably evolve under the new economic programme and a new architecture be created based on both old and new cultural foundations.

This book is a result of many years of study. It was not my purpose to write a history of Chinese architecture or theoretically set out rules and orders. Rather, I wanted to journey from the originating principles, using them as inspiration to seek the direction in which Chinese architecture may develop in the future. My discussion closes at the end of the 19th century, a time when European and American architecture was undergoing radical changes. In China, although there had been a great deal of building activity, architectural thinking was unsettled. This state of affairs was due partly to the disrupting influence of foreign architectural philosophies. This uncertainty is present in China where there still seems to be a lack of a national architecture as unique as our ancestors had created. This lack of development has, paradoxically, been both helped and hindered by China's 2000 years of relative isolation. It is true that one of the most distinct features of Chinese architecture is its continuity, a continuity that has insured that many fine traditions, styles and principles governing the design of buildings have been preserved and are now considered unique. But the corollary to this is that the architecture has not progressed in line with technological and social developments.

An exploration of the basic principles reveals the elements which created this indigenous architecture. Analogous to an archaeological site I see the past as a series of superimposed layers which we must unravel to expose the progression of human cultures, from ancient nomadic days onwards. Buildings and towns identify many patterns of the use of local materials. By taking this into account as well as factors such as geography and climate we may discover how foreign cultures have been adapted and assimilated to the native cultural soil. The creation of a new architecture in keeping with a new societal order necessitates an analysis of the past. For this reason I began with the ancient myths, stories which reveal the aspirations of a community and give a society its vitality, energy and coherence. The new architecture should fuse both the old and new, regional and universal. Here I read past monuments not just for their aesthetic value but for their deeper value of structural meaning. This includes the ancient handling of architectural sequence, human habitations, open spaces, and the secrets of scale in the fabric of cities. What they achieved were lasting and humane values expressed through the medium of architectural space and form. To study history in this way will not, I hope, lead to a regression into sentimental nostalgia. Instead I would ask the ancient master builders how we should build today.

The 19th and 20th centuries were periods of drastic change; from a lingering feudalistic society to a modern industrial culture. Traditional building types could no longer serve an emerging world faced with the challenges of new aims and technologies. Architectural works are crystallisations of current culture and technology, indications of how a sensitive society thinks and dreams. These products of the human hand and mind are part of our cultural heritage. The flourishing of cultural activity provides a golden time for architects, if they have a will to create.

From the Opium War of 1840 onward the Christian missionaries introduced European Baroque architecture and American colonial building types. Pseudo-Gothic cathedrals and colonial-style schools were erected at a time when Chinese cultural philosophy was spiritless. Since the founding of the Ecole de Beaux-Arts in 1806, its Renaissance-formed attitudes influenced many American schools of architecture. Within the walls of the academies efforts were centred on abstract methods of teaching; sites studied were flat and without context. The belief was that the purpose of architecture was to arrive at sets of standardized abstract rules. This attitude greatly influenced architectural activity of those Chinese students who studied in Europe and America.

During the period 1853-1870, in Napoleon III's reign, Baron Haussman replanned Paris. His high aesthetic regard for monumental sequence made Paris a comprehensively planned and regularized capital. This set an example for capital cities, and influenced programmes of urban restructuring in Vienna, Rome, Leningrad, and Daniel Burnham's plan for Chicago.

This harmful tradition was brought to China by the so-called Soviet experts in the 1950s. Many cities like Shanghai and Hangzhou were planned with abstract principles, without paying any attention to context. Fortunately, the Chinese Government never acquired the funding to carry out these gigantic abstract projects and the fabric of the cities was somehow preserved. But in architectural schools, the damage had been done; many students took this as a prototype of city planning.

During this period the Austrian architect and planner Camillo Sitte stressed in *The Art of Building Cities* the balanced physical relationships and maintenance of continuity, and the importance of harmonious relationships between monuments and dwellings. His book was not widely known in China, unlike the work of other Modern Movement architects. Le Corbusier, in *The City of Tomorrow,* called Sitte's concept a 'pack-donkey's way' and his work 'to turn architecture away, in the most absurd fashion, from its proper path'. In his proposal for the Ville Radieuse the geometric plan owes nothing to context and responds to a rational desire to regulate man's habitat.

Like Le Corbusier, Mies van der Rohe's Illinois Institute of Technology campus in Chicago was also imposed upon the fabric of an existing neighbourhood. Nor is Frank Lloyd Wright's Guggenheim Museum related to the neighbouring building; he had no intention to harmonize with the context, but rather to express his ego. These examples indicate that since the Roman Empire, through the Renaissance down to the present, the beginning of every architectural era had this tendency of imposing upon the existing fabric new ideologies, new concepts trying to dominate the old. The International Style aimed at unification across national borders. It is sad to say that most architects in China today are influenced by either the Beaux-Arts or the Modern Movement, or both.

A Chinese architecture will, no doubt, rise phoenix-like out of its own ashes. On the ruins of old foundations a new architecture, which conforms to present societal needs and is rich in the traditions of Chinese architecture and city planning principles, will emerge. The essence of Chinese architecture is *harmony* and *unity*. Until the close of the last century, these had been preserved; new buildings had copied older ones. Those who maintain that economic development is a prerequisite of all developments blamed the stagnation of the economy as the cause of this continuity. True, but if we go deeper we shall find that in the case of the Chinese, the cause of the slow economic development was a fear that it may foster licentiousness and effeminacy. Unlike in the West, the zest for living and exaltation of natural life is nowhere to be found in Chinese history. Here, in the words of Mencius, 'philosophy came to deal with practical problems rather than the more speculative ones. For under the circumstances there was less scope for creative ingenuity than for resolute self-devotion; less for outward actions than for inward feeling; less opportunity for public achievement, more for private reform.'

Mencius, a great follower of Confucius, went even further by stating: 'For the culture of the heart there is nothing better than the diminution of desire.' Here desire means good living: in his teachings it was held as a motto that one had to limit these desires to attain spiritual perfection. So Chinese people were taught the idea of 'plain living and high thinking'. Making oneself comfortable, providing a house with a bathroom, even heating the house during cold weather were considered luxuries. Zhuangzi went further: 'He that makes mechanical devices is guilty of chicanery'. Here more importance is attached to the quality and fullness of the inner life of the spirit than indulging in physical comforts and pleasure. This cultural tradition had a great impact on the Chinese mind, its aesthetic temperament and moral standard, and hence formed its national consciousness and influenced its architecture.

I have stated that traditional Chinese culture was dominated by Confucian philosophy, complemented by Laozi. The former was called Positivism, the latter Negativism. Laozi stressed the cultivation of the true spiritual man, a complete reversal of the existing order and a return to the 'natural state'. Both philosophies emphasize calmness of mind, quietude, and the notion of world order. When Buddhism fused with the two it stated that those who are concerned merely with outward achievements, having no time for the cultivation of the spirit, become, in course of time, soulless mechanisms; mere labouring is useless. In addition to economic stagnation, these teachings, to a great extent, hampered the initiative to create new architecture. Together, Confucius and Laozi had discharged and evoked intense fervour for cultural development, but failed to initiate modern science and technology.

A regard for harmony and unity is generally lacking in contemporary Chinese architectural practice as well as in other parts of the world. Harmony, one of the teachings of Confucius, is that between heaven and man, between man and man, and between man and land. Unity is found in Chinese architecture in the appearances of buildings – in the unity of materials, construction methods, regularity and dominance. To design and build harmonious physical environments will engender harmonious relationships between men. Newly-built environments should conform to the physical and spiritual needs of the people who use them. They should help to create a feeling of belonging, eliminating discord among people, heightening spiritual life and make people proud of the place they live in. Harmony does not seek to transform or to change the appearance but to preserve the original landscape, fabric, and form of the city; it seeks to express a quality of modesty, not arrogance. In a newly-developed area this is easier but a thorough and sympathetic study of the landscape will greatly help. Although parts of the art of Feng Shui are based on superstition, lessons can still be drawn from the parts that deal with landscape and orientation.

As I have mentioned, the protracted nature of the feudalistic society meant that common people had no right to participate in state affairs. This situation was reflected in the layout of the city plan. There was a lack of places for people to communicate and express their political opinions. The open spaces in front of government buildings were usually used to draw attention to the status of power and wealth, never for political gatherings. Chinese cities are usually regularly planned without the high-rise towers of the West.

I have already elaborated that ancient courtyard houses in China have shared spaces for the whole family – the courtyard and garden, the centre of family activities. At present, for reasons of economy and scarcity of land it is not feasible to build low-rise courtyard houses in large cities. Housing planning today still adheres to the parallel block of the so-called barrack-type of the thirties. The space between blocks is usually an elongated area of ground of identical shape and ambiguous function, not suitable for use. An elongated space gives a feeling of circulation and is not a place for pausing. Only a compact space surrounded by houses or other elements like a courtyard could engender a feeling of relaxation, coziness and repose. People will gather here, sit on benches under trees, watch children playing and talk to each other.

There are many places with a particular strong sense of the past existing in Chinese cities, *genius loci*, especially old shopping streets and markets such as these along Qinhui River at Confucius Temple district in the southern part of Nanjing, and the Xuanmiao Guan market square in Suzhou. New developments can and should absorb the lessons of these valuable examples, instead of copying examples from irrelevant architectural magazines of the West or building replicas of old buildings. Architectural works are not simply for the satisfaction of architects but for the people who use them, enjoy them, feel them. Architects, planners and the local people should work together in order to create a place for all. Buildings are expressions of the cultural background that produced them, so that each country's national culture can generally be felt by the form and decoration of the building. Architects of the

◁ Kansu, Jiayu Guan Fortress, watch tower

International Style maintained that modern building materials and construction methods are universal, so the appearances of buildings should also be universal. This statement, however, ignores national culture.

China is a large country of more than fifty national groups. Because of regional and climatic differences, and different levels of cultural developments, the appearance of each national architecture is different. For instance, in the north, because of the colder weather, buildings are naturally heavier, more massive and more elaborate. In the water country along the Yangtze River valley, because of clement weather, buildings are lighter and on a more human scale. In the north-west buildings use arches and vaults to support the roofs, but in the south-west buildings are mainly of wood with wide overhanging eaves.

In the search for inspiration and aesthetic principles to govern the construction of new buildings, whilst paying regard to our heritage, we need to reject glib reproduction and avoid degeneration into a skin-deep image of the grand style of vernacular combined with pastiche. Classical and vernacular architecture is formed gradually over time; any imitation is artificial, and architects should penetrate to the generating principles and foundations of the past, transforming these into forms that conform to a changing society. This architecture fuses the past and present, the regional and the universal. Again, we need to discover the influences from other cultures and find a way to absorb and take advantage of these. Regional architecture is a precious resource; we can now integrate this with new materials and technologies, when we create a new architecture.

In the past, architectural design and construction, mind and action, worked simultaneously. Very often the owner, together with the designer was directly involved with the construction team. For instance, in private-garden architecture the owner, the painter-designer, and craftsmen worked together. This fine tradition is now gone. Probably, the split of mind and labour, thought and action, are the consequence of the social division of labour. The separation continues.

Ancient cities in China were built rapidly and on a big scale. Monumental buildings or environments, however, did not lose their human scale. Taihe Dian or the Lingen Dian in Beijing are buildings of great scale, but they retain an intimate feeling. Cities were also divided into smaller Fengli, the residential streets and dwelling doorways also corresponding to human scale. Walking along such a street, the endless bleak facades of present-day housing blocks were nowhere to be seen. Instead, a feeling of intimacy and neighbourliness is felt.

Architectural appearances of the past cannot and should not be followed without discretion. Cities and buildings of the past rarely conform to contemporary functional needs. Also, unlike politics, architecture cannot undergo a revolution. In 1955, many city walls were demolished in an attempt to break with the past. Continuity and identity have been lost and people do not like this tendency. Yet to gaze at history and vernacular architecture through a romantic mist results in equally romantic assumptions. Both are harmful to the future of Chinese architecture. It is my wish that we should learn the basic principles or roots of the architecture of the past, absorb these and apply them to our changing society. For all of us, it is important to learn from the past in order to best serve the present plan for the future.

NOTES

CHAPTER I
HISTORICAL BACKGROUND

1.
Zhou Gucheng, *Zhongguo Tong Shi*, Shanghai and Wang Guowei, *Ming Tang Qing Dian Tong Kao, Guan Tang Lin Ji.*
2.
Fang Wen Lan, *Zhongguo Tong Shi Jian Bian, Beijing.*
3.
ibid.

CHAPTER II
THE CHARACTER AND MEANING OF CLASSICAL CHINESE ARCHITECTURE

1.
Zhao Zai, *Guo Shi Yuan Jing*, Taiwan, 1979.
2.
Biography of Wangzi.
3.
Zhou Ritual, Kao Gong Ji, The World Publisher.
4.
K.S. Liu, *Prolegomena to a Study of the Development of Chinese Thought*, 1913, Northwestern University (not published).
5.
Zhou Ritual, Jiao Xin, The World Publishers.
6.
ibid.
7.
Shuo Wen.
8.
G.H. Liu, *Beijing: The Cornucopia of Classical Chinese Architecture*, Singapore, 1982.

CHAPTER III
CITY PLANNING PRINCIPLES

1.
Tongji University, *Zhongguo Cheng Shi Jian She Shi*, Beijing, 1982.
2.
Zhou Ritual, Kao Gong Ji.
3.
ibid.
4.
Zhongguo Cheng Shi Jian She Shi, *op. cit.*
5.
Simaqian, *Shiji, Suqin.*
6.
Dumu, *Afanggong Prose*, Guanyi Publisher.
7.
Simaqian, *Qinshihuang.*
8.
Zhou Ritual, Kaogongji.
9.
Zhongguo Cheng Shi Jian She Shi, *op. cit*
10.
Dumu, *Jiangnan Spring.*
11.
Songminqiu, *Changanzhi.*
12.
Yuanhe Qun Xian Tu Zhi.
13.
Huang Wenbi, *Turfan Kao Gu Ji.*
14.
Hanshu, Chaocuo.
15.
Wangqian, *Song Ping Jiang Cheng Fang Kao.*
16.
Hanshu, Chaocuo.

CHAPTER IV
RELIGIOUS BUILDINGS

1.
Fan Ye, *Late Han Record*, Vol. 103, biography of Tao Qian.
2.
Ge Hong, *Zi Yuan (World Garden)*, the word Ta first appeared in this book.
3.
Liu Dengzheng, *Collected Works of Liu Dengzheng*, Vol. 1, Beijing, 1982, p. 4.
4.
Liu Zhiping, *Chinese Building Types and Construction*, Beijing, 1957, p. 42.
5.
ibid., p. 43.
6.
Nagel's Encyclopedia-Guide, China, Geneva, 1980, p. 563.
7.
History of Han, Biography of Xiongnu.
8.
History of Wei, Chronicle, Shi Lao Zhi (Record of Buddhism and Daosim).
9.
J. Prip-Moller, *Chinese Buddhist Monasteries*, Hong Kong, 1967.
10.
Nagel's Encyclopedia-Guide, China, Geneva, 1980, p. 563.
11.
ibid.

12.
Poems on the Landscape of the Imperial Summer Resort, Chengde, 1979, p. 4.
13.
Luchun, *Wenwo*, No. 10-12, Beijing, 1956.
14.
Yang Xuanzhi, *Luoyang Qielan Ji (Record of Luoyang Buddhist Temples).*
15.
Fang Wenlan, *Zhongguo Tong Shi Jian Bien (A General History of China),* revised edition, Vol. II, Beijing, 1965, p. 512.
16.
Yang Xuanzhi, *Luoyang Jialan Ji (Record of Luoyang Buddhist Temples).*
17.
Liu Guanghua, 'Architectural Sequence and Space', *Journal of Nanjing Institute of Technology*, 1980.
18.
ibid.
19.
ibid.

CHAPTER V
HOUSES

1.
Zhang Huiyan, *Imagined House Plan of Zhou Dynasty Officers.*
2.
Wang Guowei, *Guan Tan Lin Ji, Ming Tang Jin Dian Kao (A General Study of School and Imperial Residential Halls).*
3.
Liu Dengzheng, *History of Classical Architecture.*
4.
Wang Guowei, *op. cit.*
5.
Kingshu Liu, *Prolegomena to a Study of the Development of Chinese Thought,* Evanston, Illinois, 1913.
6.
ibid.
7.
Funeral utensil from the Sha River.
8.
History of the Ming Dynasty.
9.
From a Scroll Painting by Zhang Zeduan, *Life along a river in the Qing Ming District.*

CHAPTER VI
PRIVATE GARDENS

1.
Chuin Tung, *Jiangnan Yuan Lin Zhi* (*Record of Gardens South of the Yangtze River*), Beijing, 1963.
2.
Zhu Qiqian, Prelude to the reprint of *Yuanye* (*Landscape Gardening*).
3.
Zhuangzi, Leiyuko, Yanjing, 1947. Translated by K.S. Liu, *Prolegomena to a Study of Chinese Thought*, Evanston, Illinois, 1913.
4.
K.S. Liu, *Prolegomena to a Study of Chinese Thought*, Evanston, 1913.
5.
ibid.
6.
He Qiming, *On Jikang, Da Er Guo Poem* (*A Study of the Seven Sages of the Bamboo Groves*), Commercial Press, 1966.
7.
Zhu Qiqian, *op. cit.*
8.
Wang Xizhi, *Lan Ting Jixu*, (Preface to the Orchid Pavilion Collection), translations from Osvald Siren, *Gardens of China*, New York, 1949.
9.
Tao Yuanming, *The Home Coming*, translation from O. Siren.
10.
Su Dongpo, *Dongpo Zhi Lin.* On the poems of Wang Wei.
11.
Wang Wei, *Overlooked*, from *Quotations by the Tang Poets*, English translation, Hunan, 1983. The poem was translated by Giles.
12.
Bai Juyi, *Caotang Ji* (*Record of the Thatched Hut*), translation from O. Siren. Some of the translations have been changed by me.
13.
Liu Zhongyan, *Gumtang Xiaoqiu Ji* (*Record of a Little Hillock at Gum Pond*).
14.
Wang Yucheng, *Huanggong Zhulou Ji* (*Record of Huanggong Bamboo Pavilion*).
15.
K.S. Liu, *op. cit.*
16.
ibid.
17.
Qianyong, *On Gardens.*
18.
Dorothy Stroud, *Lancelot Brown*, London, 1950, revised edition, 1975.
19.
From Zhang Zhiqian.
20.
ibid.
21.
K.S. Liu, *op. cit.*
22.
Li Bai, *A Reply*, from *Quotations by the Tang Poets*, English translation, Hunan, 1983.
23.
Wangwei, *Where I Was Born, ibid.*
24.
Wangjia, *A Storm, ibid.*
25.
Zhangbi, *To An Absent Fair One, ibid.*
26.
Jicheng, *Yuanye* (*Landscape Gardening*), annotation by Cheng Zhi, Beijing, 1981.
27.
ibid.
28.
ibid.
29.
ibid.
30.
ibid.
31.
ibid.
32.
Shenfu, *Fushen Liu Ji* (*Six Chapters from a Floating Life*), translated by Shirley M. Black, London, 1960.
33.
ibid.
34.
Jicheng, Yuanye, *op, cit,*
35.
Shenfu, *op. cit.*
36.
Chuin Tang, *Soochow Gardens*, Beijing, 1979.
37.
ibid.

CHAPTER VII
FUNERAL AND CEREMONIAL BUILDINGS

1.
Confucius, *Ji Xiao Xin (On Filial Piety).*
2.
Sima Qian, *Shiji (Historical Records).*

CHAPTER VIII
PALACES AND IMPERIAL GARDENS

1.
Zhou Li (*Zhou Ritual*), Kao Gong Ji.
2.
ibid.

GLOSSARY

◁ Datong, Shanxi, Yun Gong Caves, Northern Wei, 460, carved ceiling and wall surfaces

Bi shi, ramp bisecting steps leading to an important building, spirit way.

Cai, the width of the joint of a duo, was used as the module to determine the dimensions of beam, tie beam and columns.

Cha Zhu Zao, in a multistorey building, the upper columns do not rest directly on the one below, but on a duogong above the lower column so the columns are not aligned perpendicularly. Cha means not aligned; Zhu, column; Zao, construction.

Cheng, city wall, city

Chuan dou, connects closely arranged columns lined along the depth of the building by small beams let into the columns to form a framework.

Cuan jian, conical or pyramidal roof.

Dao, way, reason, isle, island.

Dian, important hall.

Duoba, coffered ceiling of octagonal shape.

Duo, wooden block placed on top of column to support upper members.

Duogong, cluster of brackets put together used to support cantilevered structural members above.

Duo kou, kou means mouth, duo kou means mouth of a duo or width of cai.

Fang, boat, a residential block.

Feng Shui, feng means wind, shui means water, an ancient art to determine the orientation of a building.

Fu dian, hip roof.

Ge, pavilion.

Gong, palace, Daoist temple.

Gong, curved bow-shaped cantilevered wooden element placed transversely on duo to support upper member.

Guan, Daoist temple, pass, fortified gateway.

Hui wen, meandering design.

Jian, bay, unit to decide the size of a building.

Juan pen, the pointed ridge of a gable roof is replaced by a rounded curve, called the rolling top roof.

Lan, verandah.

Lan Yuan, courtyard enclosed on all four sides with verandahs.

Lifang, residential block used after N. Wei.

Lou, multistorey building.

Lu ding, flat roof wrapped around with eaves.

Luli, Lu means gate, li means neighbourhood, residential block in Han Dynasty.

Miao, temple.

Ming tang, bright hall, palace or the office of the king.

Peifang, or pailou, ceremonial arch.

Piyong, school.

Qi, breath.

Que, gateway, marked by two posts.

Renzi roof, gable roof.

Ruyi, decoration hanging from the top of a gable end roof, a symbol of happiness.

Sha, the pinnacle of a pagoda.

Sheng, small wooden block placed on top of a gong to support more gongs.

Shi dao, driveway, middle lane in a city used exclusively by the emperor in the Han Dynasty.

Si, temple.

Ta, pagoda.

Tai, platform.

Tai liang, raised beam construction.

Taimiao, ancestral hall.

Taizi, same as tai, a platform.

Tang, hall.

Tian, heaven.

Tiao, or cheng gong, slanting bracket to support eave overhangs.

Ting, pavilion, hall.

Wen, end decoration on the main ridge of a roof, usually in the design of a dragon's head or a fish.

Xian, county.

Xie, den, study.

Xie shan, half-hip roof.

Xuan, hall, study.

Xuan yu, decoration hanging from the top of a gable end roof, sometimes in the form of a fish, see Ruyi.

Yazi, teeth, to place bricks diagonally to form a tooth-like pattern.

Yuan, garden, courtyard.

Zhai, den.

Zhe jiao, the inclination of columns at either end to the centre. Structurally this inward slanting prevents the column from leaning outward.

Zhuang, a pillar usually carved with Buddhist Sutra.

Zhung lun zhang, revolving sutra repository.

Zumizuo, platform of elaborate design, Zumi means the mountain where buddha stayed, zuo means a platform.

SELECTED BIBLIOGRAPHY

◁ Wutai Shan, Shanxi, Buddha's Peak, column base

Chinese

CHINESE ACADEMY OF SCIENCE, Institute of Archaeology, Xian Banpo. Beijing, 1963.

DUNHUANG WEN WO RESEARCH INSTITUTE. *Dunhuang Frescoes of Tang Dynasty*, (Introduction by Chang Shuhong). Beijing, 1959.

FANG, WENLAN. *A Brief General History of China*, revised edition. Beijing, 1965.

FANG, WENLAN. *Modern History of China*, Beijing, 1962.

GUO, BAOJUN. 'Report on the excavation of Yin Shan Xu, 1950'. *Zhong Guo Archaeology Journal*, No. 5, 1951.

HUANG, WENBI. *Archaeology Record of Turfan*. nd.

JIANGSU ARCHITECTURAL SCIENCE RESEARCH INSTITUTE. *A Preliminary Study of the Resource of Islamic Mosque Architecture In China*. Kunming, 1983.

JI,CHENG.*Yuan Ye (Landscape Gardening)*, (Note and Explanation by Cheng Zhi). Beijing, 1981.

LI, DOU . *Record of Pleasure Boat of Yangzhou*. Zhong Hua Book Story, 1960.

LI, GEFEI. *The Celebrated Gardens of Luoyang*. Gu Jin Yi Shi, nd.

LI, JIE. *Building Standard of Song Dynasty*. The Commercial Press, 1920.

LIANG, SICHENG. *Building Regulations of Qing Dynasty*. Beijing, 1981.

LIU, DENGZHENG. *An Outline of the Chinese House*. Beijing, 1957.

—— *Classical Suzhou Gardens*. Beijing, 1978.

—— *Collected Works of Liu Dengzheng*, Vol. I and II. Beijing, 1984.

—— *History of Classical Chinese Architecture*. Beijing, 1980.

LIU, ZHIPING. *Building Types and Construction of Chinese Architecture*, Beijing, 1957.

MENG, YUANLAO. *Dongjin Menghua Lu*. Classic Publisher, 1957.

QIN, LINGYUN. *The Art of Chinese Frescoes*. Beijing, 1960.

RESEARCH INSTITUTE OF CHINESE ARCHITECTURAL HISTORY. *Zhe Jiang Houses*. Beijing, 1981.

RUANYUAN PRINT. *Thirteen Classics*, (with notes). World Book, nd.

SAN, FU HUANG TU. Sibu Congkan, nd.

SHANXI WEN WO WORKS COMMITTEE. *Yungang Cave Temples*. Beijing, 1977.

SHEN, FU. *Six Chapters from a Floating Life*. Beijing, 1980.

SHENXI WEN WO ADMINISTRATIVE COMMITEE. 'A Survey of Tang Dynasty Qian Ling Tomb'. *Wen Wo*, No. 4, 1964, Beijing.

The Twenty-four Histories. Beina Ben, nd.

TIANJIN UNIVERSITY, CHENGDE WENWO BUREAU. *Classical Architecture of Chengde*. Beijing, 1980.

TONGJI UNIVERSITY. *History of the Chinese City*. Beijing, 1982.

TUNG, CHUIN. *Record of Jiangnan Gardens*. Beijing, 1963.

TUNG, CHUIN. *Suzhou Gardens*. Beijing, 1979.

XU, SONG. *Residential Blocks of Two Tang Dynasty Capitals*. Congsu Jichen, nd.

YANG, XUANZHI. *Record of Luoyang Buddhist Temples*. Zhonghua Book Store, 1963.

YAO, CHENGZHU. *Yingzao Fayuan*, (Edited by Zhang Zhigong). Beijing, 1958.

YE, YUHUA. Nanjing Zhang Yuan. *Journal of Nanjing Institute of Technology*, No. 4, 1980.

ZHANG, HUIYEN. *House Plan of a Zhou Dynasty Officer*. Congwen Book Store, nd.

ZHANG, ZHONGYI. *Ming Dynasty Houses of Huizhou*. Beijing, 1957.

ZHENG, ZHENGDUO. *Selective Frescoes of Yongle Gong*. Beijing, 1958.

ZHUO, GUCHENG. *A General History of China*, Vols. I and II. Shanghai, 1957.

English

BLASER, WERNER. *China Court-House*, Birkhauser, 1979.

BOERSCHMANN, VON E. *Bankunst und Landschafe in China*. E. Wasmuth, Berlin, 1926.

—— *Chinesische Architekture*. E. Wasmuth, Berlin, 1925.

BOYD, ANDREW. *Chinese Architecture and Town Planning*. University of Chicago Press, 1962.

CHANG, AMOS I.T.. *The Tao of Architecture*. Princeton University Press, 1956.

DAVIDSON, A.K.. *The Art of Zen Gardens*. J.P. Tarcher, Inc., Los Angeles, 1983.

HARADA, JIRO. *The Lesson of Japanese Architecture*. C.T. Branford, Co., 1954.

KESWICK, MAGGIE. *The Chinese Garden*. Academy Editions, London, and Rizzoli, New York, 1978.

LIU, GUANGHUA. *Beijing: The Cornucopia of Classical Chinese Architecture*. Graham Brash, Singapore, 1982.

LIU, K.S.. *Prolegomena to a Study of the Development of Chinese Thought*, (unpublished). Northwestern University, 1913.

Nagel's Encyclopedia Guide, China, Nagel Publishers, Geneva, 1980.

NEEDHAM, JOSEPH. *Science and Civilization in China*. Cambridge University Press, 1971.

PIRAZZOLI-T'SERSTEVENS, MICHELE. *Living Architecture, Chinese*. Grosset and Dunlap, 1971.

PRIP-MOLLER, JOHANNES. *Chinese Buddhist Monasteries*. Hongkong University Press, 1967.

SICKMAN, LAURENCE; AND SOPER, ALEXANDER. *The Art and Architecture of China*. Penguin Books, Ltd., Baltimore and Harmondsworth, 1971.

SIREN, OSVALD. *Gardens of China*. New York, 1949.

—— *The Imperial Palaces of Peking*. G. Van Oest, Paris, 1926.

SULLIVAN, MICHAEL. *A Short History of Chinese Art*. University Press, 1967.

WELLS, H.G.. *The Outline of History*, Vols. I and II. Garden City Books, 1961.

WILLIAMS, C.A.S.. *Outline of Chinese Symbolism and Art Motives*. Charles E. Tuttle Co., 1974.

INDEX

Numbers in italics refer to illustrations

◁ Dunhuang, Gansu, Mogao Caves, 366, Sleeping Buddha

A

B

D

G

H

I

J

K

L

M

N

P

Z